BIOINFORMATICS ALGORITHMS

BIOINFORMATICS ALGORITHMS

Techniques and Applications

Edited by

Ion I. Măndoiu and Alexander Zelikovsky

WILEY-
INTERSCIENCE
A JOHN WILEY & SONS, INC., PUBLICATION

Published by John Wiley & Sons, Inc., Hoboken, New Jersey
Published simultaneously in Canada

For general information on our other products and services please contact our Customer Care Department within the U. S. at 877-762-2974, outside the U. S. at 317-572-3993 or fax 317-572-4002.

Wiley also publishes its books in a variety of electronic formats. Some content that appears in print, however, may not available in electronic format.

Library of Congress Cataloging-in-Publication Data:
Bioinformatics algorithms : techniques and applications / edited by Ion I. Mandoiu and Alexander Zelikovsky.
p. cm.
ISBN 978-0-470-09773-1 (cloth)
1. Bioinformatics. 2. Algorithms. I. Mandoiu, Ion. II. Zelikovsky, Alexander.
QH324.2B5472 2008
572.80285–dc22

2007034307

Printed in the United States of America
10 9 8 7 6 5 4 3 2 1

CONTENTS

PREFACE

Bioinformatics, broadly defined as the interface between biological and computational sciences, is a rapidly evolving field, driven by advances in high throughput technologies that result in an ever increasing variety and volume of experimental data to be managed, integrated, and analyzed. At the core of many of the recent developments in the field are novel algorithmic techniques that promise to provide the answers to key challenges in postgenomic biomedical sciences, from understanding mechanisms of genome evolution and uncovering the structure of regulatory and protein-interaction networks to determining the genetic basis of disease susceptibility and elucidation of historical patterns of population migration.

This book aims to provide an in-depth survey of the most important developments in bioinformatics algorithms in the postgenomic era. It is neither intended as an introductory text in bioinformatics algorithms nor as a comprehensive review of the many active areas of bioinformatics research—to readers interested in these we recommend the excellent textbook *An Introduction to Bioinformatics Algorithms* by Jones and Pevzner and the *Handbook of Computational Molecular Biology* edited by Srinivas Aluru. Rather, our intention is to make a carefully selected set of advanced algorithmic techniques accessible to a broad readership, including graduate students in bioinformatics and related areas and biomedical professionals who want to expand their repertoire of algorithmic techniques. We hope that our emphasis on both in-depth presentation of theoretical underpinnings and applications to current biomedical problems will best prepare the readers for developing their own extensions to these techniques and for successfully applying them in new contexts.

The book features 21 chapters authored by renowned bioinformatics experts who are active contributors to the respective subjects. The chapters are intended to be largely independent, so that readers do not have to read every chapter nor have to read them in a particular order. The opening chapter is a thought provoking discussion of the role that algorithms should play in 21st century bioinformatics education. The remaining 20 chapters are grouped into the following five parts:

- Part I focuses on algorithmic techniques that find applications to a wide range of bioinformatics problems, including chapters on dynamic programming, graph-theoretical methods, hidden Markov models, sorting the fast Fourier transform, seeding, and phylogenetic networks comparison approximation algorithms.
- Part II is devoted to algorithms and tools for genome and sequence analysis. It includes chapters on formal and approximate models for gene clusters, and on advanced algorithms for multiple and non-overlapping local alignments and genome things, multiplex PCR primer set selection, and sequence and network motif finding.
- Part III concentrates on algorithms for microarray design and data analysis. The first chapter is devoted to algorithms for microarray layout, with next two chapters describing methods for missing value imputation and meta-analysis of gene expression data.
- Part IV explores algorithmic issues arising in analysis of genetic variation across human population. Two chapters are devoted to computational inference of haplotypes from commonly available genotype data, with a third chapter describing optimization techniques for disease association search in epidemiologic case/control genotype data studies.
- Part V gives an overview of algorithmic approaches in structural and systems biology. First two chapters give a formal introduction to topological and structural classification in biochemistry, while the third chapter surveys protein–protein and domain–domain interaction prediction.

We are grateful to all the authors for their excellent contributions, without which this book would not have been possible. We hope that their deep insights and fresh enthusiasm will help attracting new generations of researchers to this dynamic field. We would also like to thank series editors Yi Pan and Albert Y. Zomaya for nurturing this project since its inception, and the editorial staff at Wiley Interscience for their patience and assistance throughout the project. Finally, we wish to thank our friends and families for their continuous support.

ION I. MĂNDOIU AND ALEXANDER ZELIKOVSKY

CONTRIBUTORS

Sudha Balla, Department of Computer Science and Engineering, University of Connecticut, Storrs, Connecticut, USA

Sergey Bereg, Department of Computer Science, University of Texas at Dallas, Dallas, TX, USA

Anne Bergeron, Comparative Genomics Laboratory, Université du Québec à Montréal, Canada

Paola Bonizzoni, Dipartimento di Informatica, Sistemistica e Comunicazione, Università degli Studi di Milano-Bicocca, Milano, Italy

Broňa Brejová, Department of Biological Statistics and Computational Biology, Cornell University, Ithaca, NY, USA

Dumitru Brinza, Department of Computer Science, Georgia State University, Atlanta, GA, USA

Daniel G. Brown, Cheriton School of Computer Science, University of Waterloo, Waterloo, Ontario, Canada

Zhipeng Cai, Department of Computing Science, University of Alberta, Edmonton, Alberta, Canada

Cedric Chauve, Department of Mathematics, Simon Fraser University, Vancouver, Canada

Bhaskar DasGupta, Department of Computer Science, University of Illinois at Chicago, Chicago, IL, USA

Sérgio A. de Carvalho Jr., Technische Fakultät, Bielefeld University, D-33594 Bielefeld, Germany

Jaime Davila, Department of Computer Science and Engineering, University of Connecticut, Storrs, Connecticut, USA

Gianluca Della Vedova, Dipartimento di Statistica, Università degli Studi di Milano-Bicocca, Milano, Italy

Riccardo Dondi, Dipartimento di Scienze dei Linguaggi, della Comunicazione e degli Studi Culturali, Università degli Studi di Bergamo, Bergamo, Italy

Laurent Essioux, Hoffmann-La Roche Ltd, Basel, Switzerland

Bruce Futcher, Department of Molecular Genetics and Microbiology, Stony Brook University, Stony Brook, NY, USA

Yannick Gingras, Comparative Genomics Laboratory, Université du Québec à Montréal, Canada

Daniel Gusfield, Department of Computer Science, University of California, Davis, CA, USA

Robert W. Harrison, Department of Computer Science, Georgia State University, Atlanta, GA, USA

Jingwu He, Department of Computer Science, Georgia State University, Atlanta, GA, USA

Raja Jothi, National Center for Biotechnology Information, National Library of Medicine, National Institutes of Health, Bethesda, MD, USA

Ming-Yang Kao, Department of Electrical Engineering and Computer Science, Northwestern University, Evanston, IL, USA

Gunnar W. Klau, Mathematics in Life Sciences Group, Department of Mathematics and Computer Science, University Berlin, and DFG Research Center MATHEON "Mathematics for Key Technologies," Berlin, Germany

Mikko Koivisto, Department of Computer Science and HIIT Basic Research Unit, University of Helsinki, Finland

Kishori M. Konwar, Department of Computer Science and Engineering, University of Connecticut, Storrs, Connecticut, USA

Guohui Lin, Department of Computing Science, University of Alberta, Edmonton, Alberta, Canada

Sebastien Lissarrague, Genset SA, Paris, France

Ion I. Măndoiu, Department of Computer Science and Engineering, University of Connecticut, Storrs, Connecticut, USA

Heikki Mannila, Department of Computer Science and HIIT Basic Research Unit, University of Helsinki, Finland

Giancarlo Mauri, Dipartimento di Informatica, Sistemistica e Comunicazione, Università degli Studi di Milano-Bicocca, Milano, Italy

Steven Hecht Orzack, Fresh Pond Research Institute, Cambridge, MA, USA

Pavel Pevzner, Department of Computer Science and Engineering, University of California, San Diego, CA, USA

Teresa M. Przytycka, National Center for Biotechnology Information, National Library of Medicine, National Institutes of Health, Bethesda, MD, USA

Saumyadipta Pyne, The Broad Institute of MIT and Harvard, Cambridge, MA, USA

Sven Rahmann, Bioinformatics for High-Throughput Technologies, Department of Computer Science 11, Technical University of Dortmund, Dortmund, Germany

Sanguthevar Rajasekaran, Department of Computer Science and Engineering, University of Connecticut, Storrs, Connecticut, USA

Pasi Rastas, Department of Computer Science and HIIT Basic Research Unit, University of Helsinki, Finland

Alexander C. Russell, Department of Computer Science and Engineering, University of Connecticut, Storrs, Connecticut, USA

Yi Shi, Department of Computing Science, University of Alberta, Edmonton, Alberta, Canada

Alexander A. Shvartsman, Department of Computer Science and Engineering, University of Connecticut, Storrs, Connecticut, USA

Steve Skiena, Department of Computer Science, Stony Brook University, Stony Brook, NY, USA

Lakshman Subrahmanyan, University of Massachusetts Medical School, Worcester, MA, USA

Sing-Hoi Sze, Departments of Computer Science and of Biochemistry and Biophysics, Texas A&M University, College Station, Texas, USA

Haixu Tang, School of Informatics and Center for Genomic and Bioinformatics, Indiana University, Bloomington, IN, USA

Esko Ukkonen, Department of Computer Science and HIIT Basic Research Unit, University of Helsinki, Finland

Tomáš Vinař, Department of Biological Statistics and Computational Biology, Cornell University, Ithaca, NY, USA

Patra Volarath, Department of Computer Science, Georgia State University, Atlanta, GA, USA

Hao Wang, Department of Computer Science, Georgia State University, Atlanta, GA, USA

Yuzhen Ye, The Burnham Institute for Medical Research, San Diego, CA, USA

Alexander Zelikovsky, Department of Computer Science, Georgia State University, Atlanta, GA, USA

Elena Zotenko, National Center for Biotechnology Information, National Library of Medicine, National Institutes of Health, Bethesda, MD, USA and Department of Computer Science, University of Maryland, College Park, MD, USA

1

EDUCATING BIOLOGISTS IN THE 21ST CENTURY: BIOINFORMATICS SCIENTISTS VERSUS BIOINFORMATICS TECHNICIANS[1]

PAVEL PEVZNER

Department of Computer Science and Engineering, University of California, San Diego, CA, USA

For many years algorithms were taught exclusively to computer scientists, with relatively few students from other disciplines attending algorithm courses. A biology student in an algorithm class would be a surprising and unlikely (though not entirely unwelcome) guest in the 1990s. Things have changed; some biology students now take some sort of *Algorithms 101*. At the same time, curious computer science students often take *Genetics 101*.

Here comes an important question of how to teach bioinformatics in the 21st century. Will we teach bioinformatics to future biology students as a collection of cookbook-style recipes or as a computational science that first explain ideas and builds on applications afterward? This is particularly important at the time when bioinformatics courses may soon become *required* for all graduate biology students in leading universities. Not to mention that some universities have already started undergraduate bioinformatics programs, and discussions are underway about adding new computational courses to the standard undergraduate biology curriculum—a dramatic paradigm shift in biology education.

[1]Reprinted from *Bioinformatics* 20:2159–2161 (2004) with the permission of Oxford University Press.

Bioinformatics Algorithms: Techniques and Applications, Edited by Ion I. Măndoiu and Alexander Zelikovsky

Since bioinformatics is a computational science, a bioinformatics course should strive to present the principles and the ideas that drive an algorithm's design or explain the crux of a statistical approach, rather than to be a stamp collection of the algorithms and statistical techniques themselves. Many existing bioinformatics books and courses reduce bioinformatics to a compendium of computational protocols without even trying to explain the computational ideas that drove the development of bioinformatics in the past 30 years. Other books (written by computer scientists for computer scientists) try to explain bioinformatics ideas at the level that is well above the computational level of most biologists. These books often fail to connect the computational ideas and applications, thus reducing a biologist's motivation to invest time and effort into such a book. We feel that focusing on ideas has more intellectual value and represents a long-term investment: protocols change quickly, but the computational ideas don't seem to. However, the question of how to deliver these ideas to biologists remains an unsolved educational riddle.

Imagine Alice (a computer scientist), Bob (a biologist), and a chessboard with a lonely king in the lower right corner. Alice and Bob are bored one Sunday afternoon so they play the following game. In each turn, a player may either move a king one square to the left, one square up, or one square "north–west" along the diagonal. Slowly but surely, the king moves toward the upper left corner and the player who places the king to this square wins the game. Alice moves first.

It is not immediately clear what the winning strategy is. Does the first player (or the second) always have an advantage? Bob tries to analyze the game and applies a reductionist approach, and he first tries to find a strategy for the simpler game on a 2×2 board. He quickly sees that the second player (himself, in this case) wins in 2×2 game and decides to write the recipe for the "winning algorithm:"

> If Alice moves the king diagonally, I will move him diagonally and win. If Alice moves the king to the left, I will move him to the left as well. As a result, Alice's only choice will be to move the king up. Afterward, I will move the king up again and will win the game. The case when Alice moves the king up is symmetric.

Inspired by this analysis Bob makes a leap of faith: the second player (i.e., himself) wins in any $n \times n$ game. Of course, every hypothesis must be confirmed by experiment, so Bob plays a few rounds with Alice. He tries to come up with a simple recipe for the 3×3 game, but there are already a large number of different game sequences to consider. There is simply no hope of writing a recipe for the 8×8 game since the number of different strategies Alice can take is enormous.

Meanwhile, Alice does not lose hope of finding a winning strategy for the 3×3 game. Moreover, she understands that recipes written in the cookbook style that Bob uses will not help very much: recipe-style instructions are not a sufficiently expressive language for describing algorithms. Instead, she begins by drawing the following table that is filled by the symbols $\uparrow$, $\leftarrow$, $\nwarrow$, and $*$. The entry in position (i, j) (that is, the ith row and the jth column) describes the move that Alice will make in the $i \times j$ game. A $\leftarrow$ indicates that she should move the king to the left. A $\uparrow$ indicates that she should move the king up. A $\nwarrow$ indicates that she should move the king diagonally, and $*$

indicates that she should not bother playing the game because she will definitely lose against an opponent who has a clue.

	0	1	2	3	4	5	6	7	8
0		←	*	←	*	←	*	←	*
1	↑	↖	↑	↖	↑	↖	↑	↖	↑
2	*	←	*	←	*	←	*	←	*
3	↑	↖	↑	↖	↑	↖	↑	↖	↑
4	*	←	*	←	*	←	*	←	*
5	↑	↖	↑	↖	↑	↖	↑	↖	↑
6	*	←	*	←	*	←	*	←	*
7	↑	↖	↑	↖	↑	↖	↑	↖	↑
8	*	←	*	←	*	←	*	←	*

For example, if she is faced with the 3×3 game, she finds a $\nwarrow$ in the third row and third column, indicating that she should move the king diagonally. This makes Bob take the first move in a 2×2 game, which is marked with a $*$. No matter what he does, Alice wins using instructions in the table.

Impressed by the table, Bob learns how to use it to win the 8×8 game. However, Bob does not know how to construct a similar table for the 20×20 game. The problem is not that Bob is stupid (quite the opposite, a bit later he even figured out how to use the symmetry in this game, thus eliminating the need to memorize Alice's table) but that he has not studied algorithms. Even if Bob figured out the logic behind 20×20 game, a more general $20 \times 20 \times 20$ game on a three-dimensional chessboard would turn into an impossible conundrum for him since he never took *Algorithms 101*.

There are two things Bob could do to remedy this situation. First, he could take a class in algorithms to learn how to solve puzzle-like combinatorial problems. Second, he could memorize a suitably large table that Alice gives him and use that to play the game. Leading questions notwithstanding, what would you do as a biologist?

Of course, the answer we expect to hear is "Why in the world do I care about a game with a lonely king and two nerdy people? I'm interested in biology, and this game has nothing to do with me." This is not actually true: the chess game is, in fact, the ubiquitous *sequence alignment* problem in disguise. Although it is not immediately clear what DNA sequence alignment and our chess game have in common, the computational idea used to solve both problems is the same. The fact that Bob was not able to find the strategy for the game indicates that he does not understand how alignment algorithms work either. He might disagree if he uses alignment algorithms or BLAST on a daily basis, but we argue that since he failed to come up with a strategy, he will also fail when confronted with a new flavor of an alignment problem or a particularly complex bioinformatics analysis. More troubling to Bob, he may find it difficult to compete with the scads of new biologists and computer scientists who think algorithmically about biological problems.

Many biologists are comfortable using algorithms such as BLAST or GenScan without really understanding how the underlying algorithm works. This is not substantially different from a diligent robot following Alice's table, but it does have an important consequence. BLAST solves a particular problem only approximately and it has certain systematic weaknesses (we're not picking on BLAST here). Users that do not know how BLAST works might misapply the algorithm or misinterpret the results it returns (see Iyer et al. Quoderat demonstrandum? The mystery of experimental validation of apparently erroneous computational analyses of protein sequences. *Genome Biol.*, 2001, 2(12):RESEARCH0051). Biologists sometimes use bioinformatics tools simply as computational protocols in quite the same way that an uninformed mathematician might use experimental protocols without any background in biochemistry or molecular biology. In either case, important observations might be missed or incorrect conclusions drawn. Besides, intellectually interesting work can quickly become mere drudgery if one does not really understand it.

Many recent bioinformatics books cater to a protocol-centric pragmatic approach to bioinformatics. They focus on parameter settings, application-specific features, and other details without revealing the *computational ideas* behind the algorithms. This trend often follows the tradition of biology books to present material as a collection of facts and discoveries. In contrast, introductory books in algorithms and mathematics usually focus on ideas rather than on the details of computational recipes. In principle, one can imagine a calculus book teaching physicists and engineers how to take integrals *without* any attempt to explain *what is* integral. Although such a book is not that difficult to write, physicists and engineers somehow escaped this curse, probably because they understand that the recipe-based approach to science is doomed to fail. Biologists are less lucky and many biology departments now offer recipe-based bioinformatics courses without first sending their students to *Algorithms 101* and *Statistics 101*. Some of the students who take these classes get excited about bioinformatics and try to pursue a research career in bioinformatics. Many of them do not understand that, with a few exceptions, such courses prepare *bioinformatics technicians* rather than *bioinformatics scientists*.

Bioinformatics is often defined as "applications of computers in biology." In recent decades, biology has raised fascinating mathematical problems, and reducing bioinformatics to "applications of computers in biology" diminishes the rich intellectual content of bioinformatics. Bioinformatics has become a part of modern biology and often dictates new fashions, enables new approaches, and drives further biological developments. Simply using bioinformatics as a toolkit without understanding the main computational ideas is not very different than using a PCR kit without knowing how PCR works.

Bioinformatics has affected more than just biology: it has also had a profound impact on the computational sciences. Biology has rapidly become a large source for new algorithmic and statistical problems, and has arguably been the target for more algorithms than any of the other fundamental sciences. This link between computer science and biology has important educational implications that change the way we teach computational ideas to biologists, as well as how applied algorithms are taught to computer scientists.

Although modern biologists deal with algorithms on a daily basis, the language they use to describe an algorithm is very different: it is closer to the language used in a cookbook. Accordingly, some bioinformatics books are written in this familiar lingo as an effort to make biologists feel at home with different bioinformatics concepts. Some of such books often look like collections of somewhat involved pumpkin pie recipes that lack logic, clarity, and algorithmic culture. Unfortunately, attempts to present bioinformatics in the cookbook fashion are hindered by the fact that natural languages are not suitable for communicating algorithmic ideas more complex than the simplistic pumpkin pie recipe. We are afraid that biologists who are serious about bioinformatics have no choice but to learn the language of algorithms.

Needless to say, presenting computational ideas to biologists (who typically have limited computational background) is a difficult educational challenge. In fact, the difficulty of this task is one of the reasons why some biology departments have chosen the minimal resistance path of teaching the recipe-style bioinformatics. We argue that the best way to address this challenge is to introduce an additional *required* course *Algorithms and Statistics in Biology* in the undergraduate molecular biology curriculum. We envision it as a problem-driven course with all examples and problems being biology motivated. Computational curriculum of biologists is often limited to a year or less of *Calculus*. This tradition has remained unchanged in the past 30 years and was not affected by the recent computational revolution in biology. We are not picking on *Calculus* here but simply state that today algorithms and statistics play a somehow larger role in the everyday work of molecular biologists. Modern bioinformatics is a blend of algorithms and statistics (BLAST and GenScan are good examples), and it is important that this *Algorithms and Statistics in Biology* course is not reduced to *Algorithms 101* or *Statistics 101*. And, god forbid, it should not be reduced to *stamp collection of bioinformatics tools 101* as it is often done today.

PART I

TECHNIQUES

2

DYNAMIC PROGRAMMING ALGORITHMS FOR BIOLOGICAL SEQUENCE AND STRUCTURE COMPARISON

YUZHEN YE

The Burnham Institute for Medical Research, San Diego, CA, USA

HAIXU TANG

School of Informatics and Center for Genomic and Bioinformatics, Indiana University, Bloomington, IN, USA

2.1 INTRODUCTION

When dynamic programming algorithm was first introduced by Richard Bellman in 1953 to study multistage decision problems, he probably did not anticipate its broad applications in current computer programming. In fact, as Bellman wrote in his entertaining autobiography [9], he decided to use the term "dynamic programming" as "an umbrella" for his mathematical research activities at RAND Corporation to shield his boss, Secretary of Defense Wilson, who "had a pathological fear of the word research." Dynamic programming algorithm provides polynomial time solutions to a class of optimization problems that have an *optimal substructure*, in which the optimal solution of the overall problem can be deduced from the optimal solutions of many *overlapping subproblems* that can be computed independently and *memorized* for repeated use. Because it is one of the early algorithms introduced in bioinformatics and it has been broadly applied since then [61], dynamic programming has become an

Bioinformatics Algorithms: Techniques and Applications, Edited by Ion I. Măndoiu and Alexander Zelikovsky

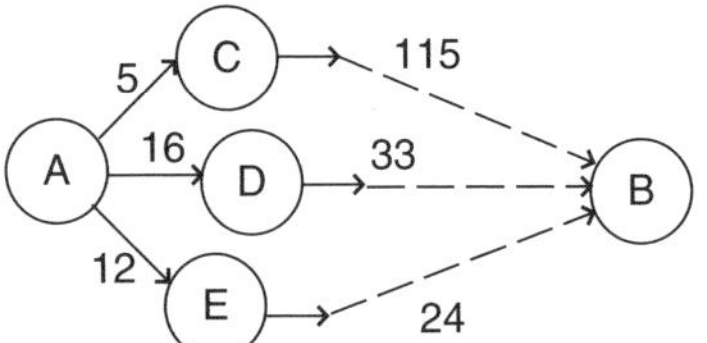

FIGURE 2.1 The dynamic programming algorithm for finding the shortest path between two nodes (e.g., A to B) in a weighted acylic graph.

unavoidable algorithmic topic in any bioinformatics textbook. In this chapter, we will review the classical dynamic programming algorithms used in biomolecular sequence analysis, as well as several recently developed variant algorithms that attempt to address specific issues in this area.

A useful example to illustrate the idea of dynamic programming is the *shortest path problem* in graph theory [19], which is formalized as finding a path between two vertices in a weighted acylic graph such that the sum of the weights of the constituent edges is minimal. Assume that we want to find a shortest path from the source vertex A to the target vertex B (Fig. 2.1). This problem can be divided into subproblems of finding shortest paths from A to all adjacent vertices of A (C, D and E). More importantly, all these subproblems can be solved without depending on each other or vertex B, since there should be no path between A and any vertex of C–E (e.g., C) that passes through B or any other vertex (e.g., D or E) on the acylic graph. Notably, the "acylic" condition is vital for the correctness of this simple solution of the shortest path problem. The vertices and edges in an acylic graph can be sorted in a *partial order* according to their adjacency to the source vertex.

Similar to the shortest path problem, those dynamic programming solvable problems are often associated to the objects with a similar optimal substructure. A typical example of such objects is *strings*, with naturally ordered letters. Hence, many computational problems related to strings can be solved by dynamic programming. Interestingly, the *primary* structures of two most important biomolecules, deoxyribonucleic acids (DNAs) and proteins, are both linear molecules, thus can be represented by plain sequences,[1] although on two different alphabets with limited size (4 nucleotides and 20 amino acids, respectively). Life is simple, in this perspective. Dynamic programming became a natural choice to compare their sequences. Needleman and Wunsch first demonstrated the use of bottom-up dynamic programming to compute an optimal pairwise alignment between two protein sequences [50]. Although this algorithm provides a similar assessment of a pair of sequences, it assumes the similarity between two input sequences is across the entire sequences (called a global alignment algorithm). Smith and Waterman adapted a simple yet important modification to this algorithm to perform local alignments, in which similar parts of input sequences were aligned [63]. The obvious advantage of local alignments in identifying common functional

[1]In bioinformatics, the term *sequence* is used interchangeable with the term *string* that is often used in computer science. From now on, we will mainly use the term *sequence*.

domains or *motifs* has attracted considerable interests and led to the development of several commonly used tools in bioinformatics nowadays, such as FASTA [54] and BLAST [2].

A third class of biomolecules, ribonucleic acids (RNAs), which are also linear, fold into stable secondary structures (i.e., a set of *base pairs* formed by two complementary bases) to perform their biological functions. So they are often represented by sequences of four letters, similar to DNAs, but with annotated *arcs*, where each arc represents a base pair. Interestingly, the base pairs in native secondary structure of an RNA usually do not form pseudoknots, that is, the arcs are not *crossing*. As a result, RNA sequences with annotated arcs can also be sorted into partial ordered *trees* (instead of sequences) [41]. Therefore, many bioinformatics problems related to RNAs, for example, RNA secondary structure prediction [67,53], RNA structure comparison [41], and RNA consensus folding [60], can be addressed by dynamic program algorithms. Unlike RNAs, the native three-dimensional (3D) structures of proteins are difficult to be predicted from their primary sequences and are determined mainly by experimental methods, for example crystallography and nuclear magnetic resonance (NMR). It has been observed that proteins sharing similar 3D structures may have unrelated primary sequences [37]. With more and more protein structures being solved experimentally,[2] there is a need to automatically identify proteins with similar structure but lacking obvious sequence similarity [38]. Although it is not straightforward to represent the protein 3D structures as partially ordered sequences, several commonly used methods for protein structure comparison are also based on dynamic programming algorithms.

2.2 SEQUENCE ALIGNMENT: GLOBAL, LOCAL, AND BEYOND

The study of algorithms for the sequence alignment problem can be traced back to the introduction of the measure of *edit distance* between two strings by Levenshtein [45]. After 40 years of algorithm and software development, sequence alignment is still an active research area, and many problems remain unsolved, especially those related to the alignment of very long genomic sequences [8, 48]. Indeed sequence alignment represents a collection of distinct computational problems, for example, *global alignment*, *local alignment*, and *multiple alignment*, even though their classical solutions all employ dynamic programming algorithms.

2.2.1 Global Sequence Alignment

Given two strings, $V = v_1...v_m$ and $W = w_1...w_n$, a pairwise global alignment is to insert *gaps* (denoted by "-") into each sequence and shift the characters accordingly so that the resulting strings are of the same length l, and form a $2 \times l$ table

[2]Up to date, in the main protein structure repository, Protein Data Bank (http://www.rcsb.org/pdb) [68], there are about 36,000 known protein structures.

(Fig. 2.2 b). Each column may consist of two *aligned* characters, v_i and w_j ($1 \leq i \leq m$, $1 \leq j \leq n$), which is called a *match* (if $v_i = w_j$) or a *mismatch* (otherwise), or one character and one gap, which is called an *indel* (insertion or deletion). A global alignment can be evaluated by the sum of the scores of all columns, which are defined by a similarity matrix between any pair of characters (4 nucleotides for DNAs or 20 amino acids for proteins) for matches and mismatches, and a *gap penalty* function. A simple scoring function for the global alignment of two DNA sequences rewards each match by score +1, and penalizes each mismatch by score $-\mu$ and each indel by score $-\sigma$. The alignment of two protein sequences usually involves more complicated scoring schemes reflecting models of protein evolution, for example, PAM [21] and BLOSUM [33].

It is useful to map the global alignment problem, that is, to find the global alignment with the highest score for two given sequences, onto an *alignment graph* (Fig. 2.2 a). Given two sequences V and W, the alignment graph is a directed acylic graph G on $(n + 1) \times (m + 1)$ nodes, each labeled with a pair of positions (i, j) ($(0 \leq i \leq m$, $0 \leq j \leq n)$), with three types of weighted edges: horizontal edges from (i, j) to $(i + 1, j)$ with weight $\delta(v(i + 1), -)$, vertical edges from (i, j) to $(i, j + 1)$ with weight $\delta(-, w(j + 1))$, and diagonal edges from (i, j) to $(i + 1, j + 1)$ with weight $\delta(v(i + 1), w(j + 1))$, where $\delta(v_i, -)$ and $\delta(-, w_j)$ represent the penalty score for indels, and $\delta(v_i, w_j)$ represents similarity scores for match/mismatches. Any global alignment between V and W corresponds to a path in the alignment graph from node $(0, 0)$ to node (m, n), and the alignment score is equal to the total weight of the path. Therefore, the global alignment problem can be transformed into the problem of finding the longest path between two nodes in the alignment graph, thus can be solved by a dynamic programming algorithm. To compute the optimal alignment score $S(i, j)$ between two subsequences $V = v_1 ... v_i$ and $W = w_1 ... w_j$, that is, the total weight of the longest path from $(0, 0)$ to node (i, j), one can use the following

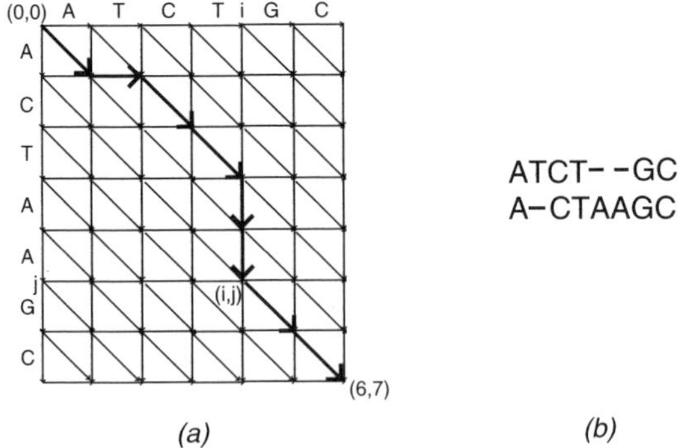

FIGURE 2.2 The alignment graph for the alignment of two DNA sequences, ACCTGC and ACTAAGC. The optimal global alignment (*b*) can be represented as a path in the alignment graph from (0,0) to (6,7) (highlighted in bold).

recurrence:

$$S(i, j) = \max \begin{cases} S(i-1, j-1) + \delta(v_i, w_j) \\ S(i-1, j) + \delta(v_i, -) \\ S(i, j-1) + \delta(-, w_j) \end{cases} \tag{2.1}$$

2.2.2 Fast Global Sequence Alignment

The rigorous global alignment algorithm described above requires both time and space in proportional to the number of edges in the alignment graph, which is the product of two input sequence lengths. Exact algorithms using linear space were devised later, utilizing the *divide-and-conquer* strategy [35, 49]. These alignment algorithms work well for aligning protein sequences, which are not longer than a few thousands amino acid residues. However, the availability of the whole genomes of human and other model organisms poses new challenges for sequence comparison. To improve the speed of dynamic programming algorithms, heuristic strategies are required, such as the commonly used *chaining* method, which was first laid out by Miller and colleagues [15] and later adopted by many newly developed genome global alignment programs [42, 39, 10, 22, 12, 17]. In general, the chaining method consists of three steps (Fig. 2.3a): (1) identify the putative *anchors*, that is, pairs of short similar segments, from the input sequences; (2) build an optimal chain of nonoverlapping anchors from the whole set of putative anchors; and (3) compute the optimal global alignment within the regions constrained by the chained anchors. Given two sequences V and W, an anchor is defined as two subsequences, $v(i, k) = v_i...v_{i+k-1}$ and $w(j, l) = w_j...w_{j+l-1}$, which are similar to each other, for example, with a similarity score $S(i, k; j, l)$ above a threshold. Anchors can be defined in different ways, depending on the fast algorithm used for searching them. For instances, the exact word matching (i.e., $k = l$) is often used since they can be rapidly identified by the hashing technique [19]. Instead of the words with fixed length, maximal exact matches (MEMs) that combine adjacent word matchings are often used to reduce the total number of putative anchors. The remaining anchors are, however, usually still too many to be used for constructing the global alignment. A chaining procedure, first proposed by Wilbur and Lipman [70] and later implemented in FASTA programs [54], is often used to select a nonoverlapping chain of anchors with the highest total similarity score. The original Wilber–Lipman algorithm runs in $O(M^2)$ time, where $M \leq nm$ is the total number of anchors. An improved sparse dynamic programming algorithm [26] can reduce the complexity to $O(MlogM)$. The selected chain of anchors may be used to define a constrained region (Fig. 2.3a) in which an optimal alignment path is constructed. This procedure runs much faster than the regular dynamic programming applied on the entire alignment graph [15]. An interesting extension of the chaining strategy in genome alignment is the *glocal* alignment approach [13]. It extends the definition of putative anchors from the matchings of the words in the same DNA strands to the words from opposite DNA strands, and allowing the swapping of anchors in the chaining step. The resulting alignment can be used to determine putative rearrangement events (Fig. 2.3b).

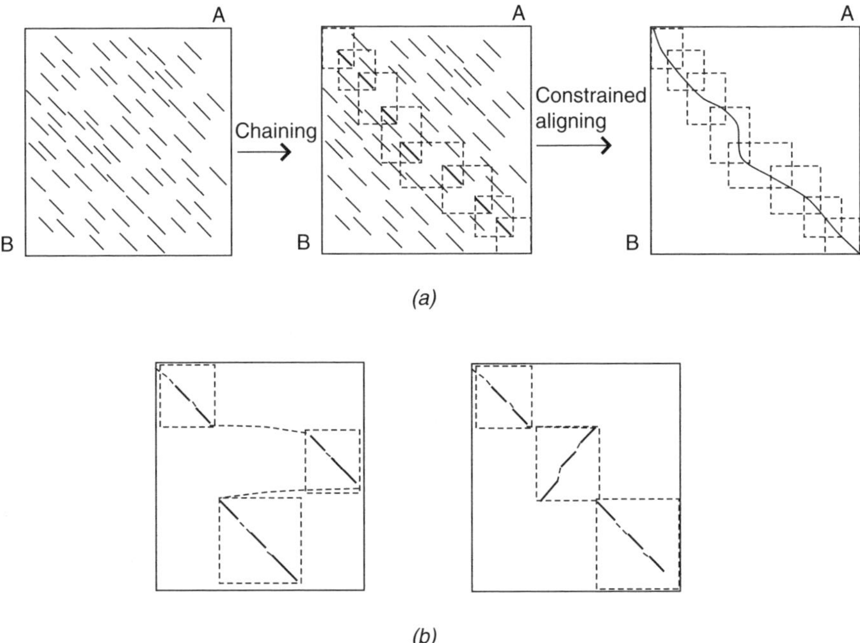

FIGURE 2.3 Fast global sequence alignment. (*a*) The chaining strategy is often adopted for fast aligning two long genomic sequences, which identifies a set of word matching anchors between two sequences, and then selects a nonoverlapping chain of anchors (highlighted in bold). The selected anchors can then be used to define a small constrained region in the alignment graph in which the optimal global alignment is computed. (*b*) Global alignment generalizes the chaining procedure to handle rearrangements between two input genomes, for example, translocations (left) and inversions (right).

Several heuristic methods further speed up the global alignment algorithm, most of which aim at identifying high quality anchors. Maximal unique matches (MUMs) are a special set of word matchings in which two words are unique in each input sequence. Selecting an optimal chain of MUMs can be done in $O(M \log M)$ time by using an extension of the *longest increasing subsequence* algorithm [22]. The other methods for filtering anchors include eliminating isolated anchors that are not close to another anchor within certain distance [23] or examining the word similarity after ungapped extension of the exact matchings [17]. Instead of exact word matching, matching of nonconsecutive positions (*patterns*) can also be used to define anchors with good quality [46].

2.2.3 Local Sequence Alignment

When comparing two biological sequences, their similarity is often not present over the whole sequences. Given two sequences V and W, the local sequence alignment problem aims at finding two subsequences of V and W, respectively, with the highest alignment score. This problem is equivalent to finding the longest path between two arbitrary nodes in the alignment graph. The Smith–Waterman algorithm for local alignment problem adopts a slight different dynamic programming recurrence from the global alignment algorithm,

$$S(i, j) = \max \begin{cases} 0 \\ S(i-1, j-1) + \delta(v_i, w_j) \\ S(i-1, j) + \delta(v_i, -) \\ S(i, j-1) + \delta(-, w_j) \end{cases} \tag{2.2}$$

and the largest score $S(i, j)$ defines the optimal local alignment score, rather than $S(m, n)$ for global alignment [63].

Similar to the global alignment, the rigorous local alignment algorithm runs in quadratic time and needs to be speeded up by heuristic methods in some practices. Various anchoring techniques, as described above, are commonly applied to speed up the local alignment as well. The most successful method, BLAST [2, 3], which filters exact word matchings with ungapped extension, has revolutionized the bioinformatics applications in molecular biology.

2.2.4 Multiple Sequence Alignment

The multiple sequence alignment problem is a natural extension of the pairwise (global and local) alignment algorithms. However, the exact algorithms for this problem are not feasible when the number of sequences to align is large [66]. So heuristic methods for suboptimal multiple alignments are seeked. The most commonly used strategy for multiple alignment is the *progressive* alignment strategy [27], which can lead to a performance guaranteed approximation [32]. Several recently developed programs for multiple genome alignment follow the same approach [12, 11]. On the contrary, some programs for multiple protein alignment [23, 51] are designed based on the strategy of searching for the multiple alignment most consist with the pairwise alignments between all pairs of sequences. Depending on the choice of the target function measuring the consistency, dynamic programming [64] or probabilistic algorithms [23] can be used to solve this optimization problem.

2.2.5 Variants of Sequence Alignment Algorithm: Beyond Linear Sequences

As protein sequences are linear sequences of 20 amino acids and DNAs are linear sequences of 4 nucleotides, classical sequence alignment algorithms use single residues as the basic comparison unit, and position-wise scoring functions (e.g., PAM250 for amino acids) as their similarity measures. As a result, protein/nucleic acid sequence alignment can be solved by dynamic programming that assumes the independence between positions. However, in reality, dependences between residue positions are often observed. For example, a segment of residues in a protein together determines the local structure they form, such as a helix, a strand, or a loop. And the local and global interactions among residues determine the global structure of a protein. By considering the independence of residues, we will be able to generate alignments that are of better quality, and conduct similarity searching with higher sensitivity. Variants of sequence alignment algorithms were developed to account for independence of residues and address different issues. One pioneer work along this direction is the spliced sequence alignment algorithm, which attempts to address eukaryotic gene recognition by assembling different putative exons (i.e, exons are independent units). More recent developments include segment alignment in which local structure segments are used as basic units for protein comparison, partial order alignment that emphasizes not only commonality but also dissimilarity of protein sequences, and RNA alignment that uses the information of secondary structures of RNA. Figure 2.4 shows the commonality and differences of these different algorithms.

2.2.5.1 Spliced Alignment Eukaryotic genes are mosaic structures of exons and introns. Hence, it is a challenge to derive gene structures (i.e., the boundaries of exons and introns) from genomic sequences. One approach that has been developed to predict gene structures is spliced sequence alignment [30]. This method essentially uses related proteins to derive the correct exon–intron structure of a genomic sequence. It starts with the identification of candidate blocks in a given genomic sequences that contains all putative (true or false) exons by selecting all blocks between potential splicing acceptor and donor sites (i.e., between AG and GU dinucleotides). Then, instead of finding the actual exons, the spliced sequence alignment algorithm explores all possible assemblies of blocks to find an assembly with the highest similarity score to a known target protein. This problem is formulated as finding the best path in a weighted graph, in which vertices represent the candidate blocks, edges represent the potential junctions between these blocks, and the path weight is defined as the weight of the optimal alignment between the target protein sequence and the concatenated blocks in the path (see Fig. 2.4a). Using this formulation, the gene recognition (i.e, exon assembly problem) can be solved by a dynamic programming process in polynominal time.

Briefly, the inputs for the original spliced alignment algorithm are a genomic sequence of length n ($G = g_1 ... g_n$), and a target protein sequence of length m ($T = t_1 .. t_m$). Let $\mathfrak{B} = \{B_1, ... B_b\}$ be a set of candidate blocks (exons), $B_k = g_f .. g_i .. g_l$ be a block including position i (first $(k) = f$, last $(k) = l$, $f \leq i \leq l$). $B_1 < B_2$ if B_1 ends before B_2 starts (last (B_1) <first (B_2)). A sequence $\Gamma = (B_1, .., B_p)$ is a *chain* if $B_1 < B_2 .. < B_p$, and the concatenation of strings from the chain Γ by $\Gamma^* = B_1 * B_2 ... * B_p$. Given two strings G and T, $s(G, T)$ denotes the score of the optimal alignment between G and T, which can be found as

$$\max_k S(\text{ last } (k), m, k) \tag{2.3}$$

where

$$S(i, j, k) = \max_{\textit{all chains } \Gamma \textit{ containing block } B_k} s(\Gamma^*(i), T(j)) \tag{2.4}$$

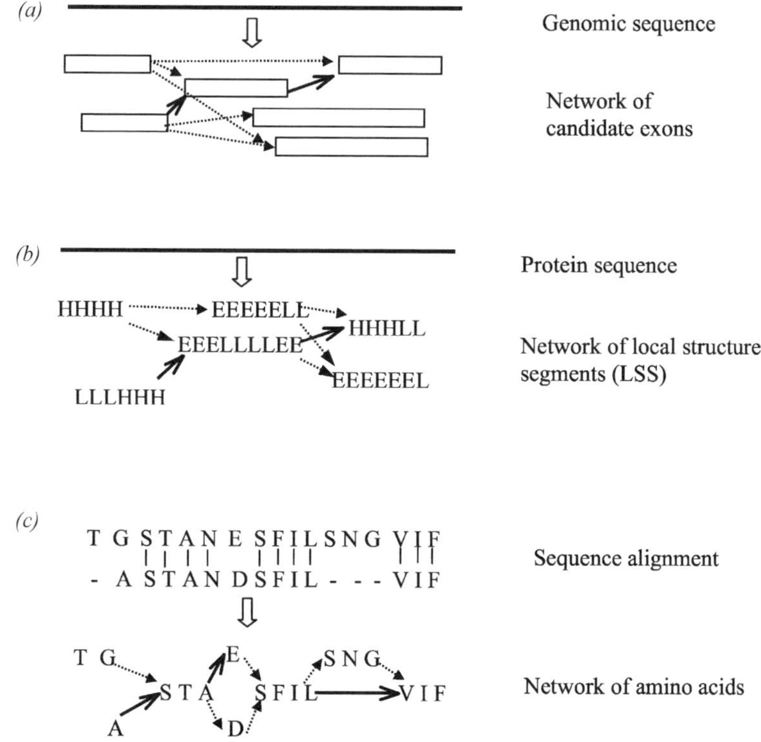

FIGURE 2.4 Various algorithms adopt the similar network matching approach, including the spliced alignment for gene recognition (a), the segment alignment for pairwise protein sequence alignment (b), and partial order alignment for multiple protein sequence alignments (c). In the network matching method, the optimal chain (or path) of the candidates (exons in spliced alignment, local structure segments in segment alignment, and alignment blocks in partial order alignment, respectively) is seeked in a predefined directed acylic graph (network).

The three-dimensional table $S(i, j, k)$ $(1 \leq i \leq n, 1 \leq j \leq m, and 1 \leq k \leq b)$ can be computed recursively by dynamic programming as

$$S(i, j, k) = \max \begin{cases} S(i-1, j-1, k) + \Delta_{g_i, t_j} & \text{if } i \neq first(k) \\ S(i-1, j, k) + \Delta_{indel} & \text{if } i \neq first(k) \\ \max_{l \in \mathfrak{B}(first(k))} S(last(l), j-1, l) + \Delta_{g_i, t_j} & \text{if } i = first(k) \\ \max_{l \in \mathfrak{B}(first(k))} S(last(l), j, l) + \Delta_{indel} & \text{if } i = first(k) \\ S(i, j-1, k) + \Delta_{indel} & \end{cases} \tag{2.5}$$

where Δ_{indel} is the gap penalty, Δ_{g_i, t_j} is the mismatch score, and $\mathfrak{B}(i) = \{k : last(k) < i\}$ is the set of blocks ending before position i in G.

This algorithm can be extended to the alignment of two genomic sequences for gene recognition by finding two chains of blocks of candidate exons, each from one genomic sequence, with the highest pairwise similarity [52].

2.2.5.2 ***Segmental Alignment*** The similar idea as spliced alignment is adopted in the segment alignment (SEA) approach for pairwise protein sequence alignment incorporating local structure information [74]. It is known that secondary or local structure information can help to improve the quality of protein sequence alignment, especially in the cases of comparing distantly homologous or analogous proteins, and to enhance the capability of recognizing of distant homologs. In a secondary structure alignment (SSA) approach, proteins are represented as strings of Q3 symbols (a for α-helix, b for β-strand, and c for coil) of predicted secondary structure [4, 71]. The SSA algorithm is based on an alignment of two sequences of secondary structure symbols, which is mathematically equivalent to the comparison of amino acid sequences and can be solved by regular pairwise sequence alignment algorithm. However, in such approaches, the currently unavoidable mistakes in secondary structure prediction will be propagated into the step of protein comparison and make it even more difficult. Segment alignment algorithm was developed to address this problem by incorporating potential local structure segments and then finding the optimal collection of nonoverlapping segments by matching two networks of local structure segments, deduced from two given proteins.

As the name says, the comparisons in the segment alignment algorithm are not done on individual amino acids, but on predicted (or real) structure segments corresponding to minimal structural units that are often reproduced in various, even nonhomologous proteins ((see Fig. 2.4 b). Given a protein sequence, its local structure segments can be predicted by different local structure prediction methods, for example, the one based on the I-site library of sequence–structure motifs [14], or the one based on profile–profile alignment [55]. All these approaches identify locally similar segments of several consecutive residues from a database of known structures. Once the local structures are predicted for a protein sequence, the protein is then represented as a collection of predicted overlapping local structure segments (LSSs). Afterwards, the task of SEA is to find a chain of LSSs from each protein (represented as a network) optimally matching each other. Similar to the spliced sequence alignment, the segment alignment problem is formulated as a network alignment problem and can be solved by dynamic programming in polynomial time. In SEA, the LSS representation of protein complements the uncertainties of the local structures, caused by either the variance of the structural context or the drawbacks of the prediction methods, by exploiting all potential local structures to make the best use of this information in protein comparison; and SEA not only reports the alignment of two proteins, but also simultaneously confirmed the local structure of each protein based on the collection of matched LSSs.

2.2.5.3 ***Partial Order Alignment*** As compared with the conventional reduced representation of multiple sequence alignments as a linear consensus or profile in row-and-column format, Lee and colleagues first proposed a graph representation of multiple sequence alignment (MSA) (see Fig. 2.4 c) to avoid the loss of (individual) sequence information and gap scoring artifacts [44]. And such graphs themselves can be aligned directly by pairwise dynamic programming, eliminating the need to reduce the MSA to a consensus (profile). In constructing partial order-MSA (PO-MSA), the amino acids that are matched in the alignment are merged into a single node, and the mismatched positions are kept as separate nodes. In short, the PO-MSA is a compact graph representation of MSA with minimum number of nodes and edges, while it keeps all the information of a typical MSA in row-and-column format. The term "partial order" was used because in PO-MSA, the graph obeyed only the linear ordering in the regions of nodes with single outgoing edges. Based on this PO-MSA representation, Lee et al. developed partial order alignment (POA) method, which guarantees that the optimal alignment of each new sequence versus each sequence in the MSA is considered. Also the algorithm has improved speed (linear to the number of sequences) over existing MSA algorithms, enabling construction of massive and complex alignments.

The development of POA is also significant in a way that this algorithm introduces a new edit operator, homologous recombination, into the framework of sequence alignment (it happens naturally in aligning two graphs; e.g., part of a sequence S1 is aligned to sequence S2 and then the next part of S1 can be aligned to sequence S3 instead of S2 as long as the order of the amino acid positions is obeyed). So when it is applied to align protein sequences, it may reveal the multidomain structure of the input sequences if there is any. It can also be applied to align ESTs to detect alternative mRNA forms.

2.3 DYNAMIC PROGRAMMING ALGORITHM FOR RNA SEQUENCE ANALYSIS

RNAs usually function as single strand molecules. The nucleotides of a single RNA secondary molecule can pair with each other (through hydrogen bonds) and form a stable *secondary structure* (Fig. 2.5). The stable secondary structure of an RNA

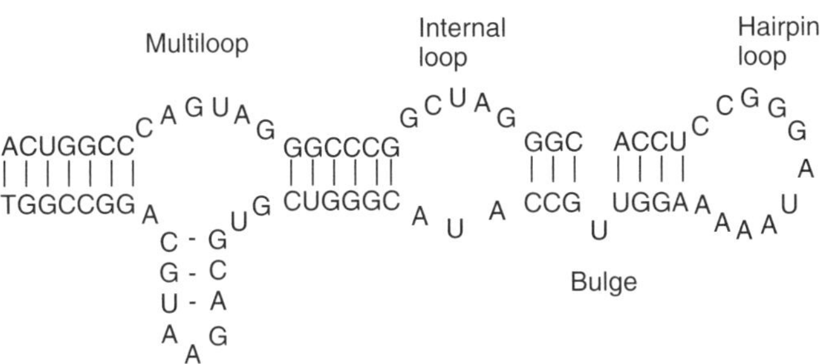

FIGURE 2.5 A schematic illustration of an RNA secondary structure and its loop components.

molecule is often assumed to be the one with the lowest free energy, and the computational problem of finding this stable structure from a given RNA sequence is called the problem of RNA secondary structure prediction. RNA secondary structures can be represented by a set of *arcs* (base pairs) in an RNA sequence. In real RNA structure, these base pairs rarely cross each other and form *pseudoknots*. Hence, for the algorithmic simplicity, the secondary structures with only noncrossing (also called *nested*) arcs are considered.

Since the base pairs are important to stabilize the structure of an RNA, it is often observed that in homologous RNA sequences, two paired bases may both mutate into other bases but maintaining the base pair (referred to as the *compensating mutations*, e. g., a G–C pair may mutate to a A–T pair). Therefore, when comparing two RNA sequences, it is important to take into consideration their secondary structures. Dynamic programming solutions are known to the problem of comparing two RNA sequences with annotated noncrossing *arcs* (base pairs).

2.3.1 RNA Secondary Structure Prediction

The simplest yet popular formulation of RNA secondary structure prediction is to determine the noncrossing structure with the maximum number of base–pairs [67,53]. Consider a given RNA sequence $R = r_1 ... r_n$. The maximum number of nested base pairs that can be formed by the subsequence $r_i ... r_j$, denoted as $S(i, j)$, can be computed recursively:

$$S(i, j) = \max \begin{cases} S(i+1, j-1) + 1 & \text{if } i \text{ is paired with } j \\ S(i+1, j) & \text{if } i \text{ is unpaired} \\ S(i, j-1) & \text{if } j \text{ is unpaired} \\ \max_{i<k<j}(S(i, k) + S(k+1, j) & \text{if } i, j \text{ pair with middle bases} \end{cases} \tag{2.6}$$

This recursion can run efficiently in $O(n^3)$ time, with initiation of $S(i, i) = S(i, i-1) = 0$. With a sophisticated data structure, it is recently shown that the algorithm can speed up to nearly quadratic time for average RNA sequences [69]. In practice, more complex scoring schemes than the simple base pair maximization are adopted. These schemes are based on the thermodynamic model that computes the overall free energy of RNA folding by a sum of energy components for different RNA secondary elements (i.e., stacks and loops). Generalized dynamic programming algorithms have been developed accordingly to optimize these complex target-scoring functions. Nonetheless, the general idea of the algorithm remains the same [47].

The dynamic programming algorithm described above cannot handle pseudoknots, because crossing base pairs are not considered in any of the four conditions in the recursion equation 2.6. Complex dynamic programming algorithms are needed for RNA secondary structure prediction that allows certain type of pseudoknots [57, 1]. But their running time is $O(n^6)$, thus inefficient to be used in practice. To search for pseudoknotted RNA structure, efficient heuristic approaches have to be used [56].

Even the exact algorithms for the RNA secondary structure prediction sometimes make wrong predictions for two reasons. First, the thermodynamic model used for the prediction may be incomplete. For example, the dependence between the secondary structure elements is neglected but may be strong in specific cases. Second, some RNA sequences may have more than one stable structure, and their functional structures are determined by not only their sequences, but also the environment (e.g., their interactions with other RNA molecules [34]). Two approaches have been proposed to overcome these limitations. One approach is to predict all *suboptimal* structures, that is, those with low free energy, but not the lowest free energy. This approach was first proposed by Zuker [75] and was implemented in MFOLD, which can report a collection of possible but not all suboptimal structures [76]. An efficient dynamic programming algorithm to compute k suboptimal structures has been proposed recently, running in time $O(n^4)$ [18]. The other approach attempts to use evolutionary conservation of structures among homologous RNA sequences as the basis for structure prediction. If the similarity between these sequences are appropriate, one can first align them using a multiple sequence alignment algorithm and then deduce their common structure by seeking the highest possible number of compensating mutations. A similar dynamic programming algorithm as in equation 2.6 can be used for the second step, in which the columns in the multiple alignment are treated as the bases in the single sequences, and in the scoring function the number of base pairs is replaced by a measure of compensating mutations between two columns (e.g., the *mutual information content*) [16,36].

Multiple homologous RNA sequences are useful for deducing their common secondary structures. However, aligning multiple RNA sequences so as to preserve their conserved structures is not easy, because there may exist many compensating mutations that decrease their overall sequence similarity. Sankoff first proposed an approach to simultaneously aligning RNA sequences and figuring out their common structures [60]. However, the complexity of this dynamic programming algorithm is $O(n^6)$, where n is the length of RNA sequences. The complexity can be reduced to $O(n^4)$, but only for RNA structures without multiloop (Fig. 2.3) [42]. A recent developed method attempted to solve the same problem based on a dynamic programming algorithm that finds the structurally conserved anchors first [6]. This algorithm considers the RNA secondary structures as a collection of stacks (instead of individual base pairs), thus reduces the computational complexity to $O(k^4)$, where k is the number of predicted putative stacks.

2.3.2 Alignment of RNA Sequences with Known Secondary Structures

Since the secondary structures are preserved among RNA sequences with similar function, it is important to incorporate them when comparing RNA sequences. The RNA secondary structure can be represented as a collection of arcs (base pairs), and based on the knowledge of their configurations, they fall into three classes: *crossing* (i.e., structure known with pseudoknots), *nested* (i.e., structure known without pseudoknots), and *plain* (i.e., structure unknown) [41]. As result, there are six different computational problems that can be formulated for a pairwise comparison of RNA sequences:

- Align(crossing, crossing), for aligning two RNA sequences both with pseudoknotted structures;
- Align(crossing, nested), for aligning one RNA sequence with pseudoknotted structures and another RNA sequence without pseudoknotted structure;
- Align(crossing, plain), for aligning one RNA sequence with pseudoknotted structures and another RNA sequence without known structure;
- Align(nested, nested), for aligning two RNA sequences both without pseudoknotted structures;
- Align(nested, plain), for aligning one RNA sequence with known nonpseudoknotted structures and another RNA sequence without known structure;
- Align(plain, plain), for aligning two RNA sequences without known structures.

Note that the last problem Align(plain,plain) is the same as the pairwise sequence alignment problem. The problems Align(nested, nested) and Align(nested, plain) can be solved by exact dynamic programming algorithms [20, 5], whereas the other problems related to pseudoknotted structures can be solved efficiently only when specific types of pseudoknots are considered [43, 24].

2.4 DYNAMIC PROGRAMMING ALGORITHMS FOR PROTEIN STRUCTURE COMPARISON

Proteins fold into three-dimensional structures, and protein structures are more conserved than protein sequences. So given a protein structure (solved by X ray or NMR techniques), it is of great interests to search for geometrically similar proteins through protein structure comparsion, especially for the cases where the similarity at sequence level is too low to be detected by any sequence-based similarity search program. Generally speaking, protein structure comparison (alignment) is to find the largest structural similarity between two structures (e.g, Fig. 2.6a). It is more difficult than protein sequence comparison, because very often the structural similarity is a global measurement (for examples, RMSD, the root mean squared distance of the $C\alpha$ atoms over all aligned positions) that often cannot be calculated as the sum of pairwise similarity by a dynamic programming procedure. So, for protein structure comparison, either we can use the global measurement of structural similarity and then apply some heuristics methods to find the best structural similarity, or we can carefully design a scoring function that reflects the global structural similarity to a large extent and then apply a dynamic programming algorithm to find alignment with the highest score. Quite a few successful programs belonging to the first type have been developed, but here we focus on the second type of approaches, in which dynamic programming algorithms can be applied to find the solution.

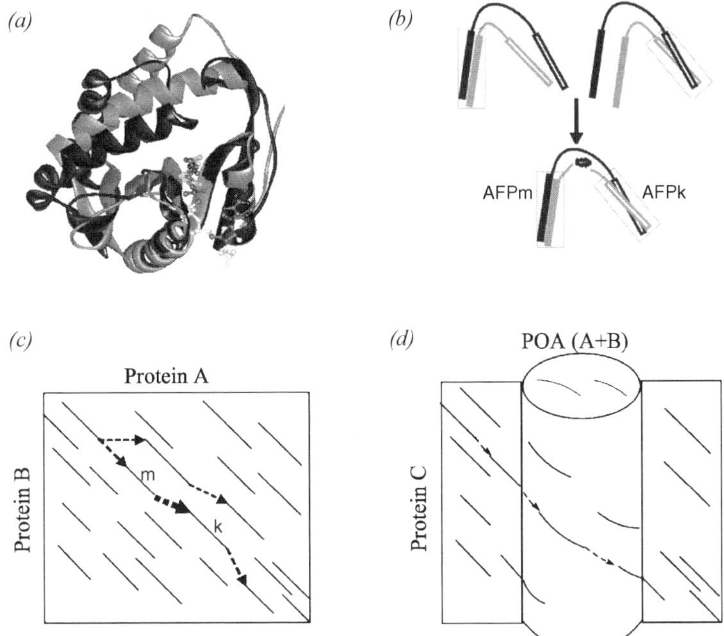

FIGURE 2.6 Structure alignment. (*a*) An example of structure alignment; (*b*) Definition of aligned fragment pair (AFP); (*c*) Pairwise structure alignment by chaining aligned fragment pairs; (*d*) Multiple structure alignment by partial order alignment.

2.4.1 Structure-Based Sequence Alignment

A simple strategy for protein structure comparison is to represent a protein structure as a sequence of characters (1D representation) that describe the structural environment of a residue in a protein (called 3D environment). Then protein structure comparison can be essentially transformed as a general sequence alignment problem, and conventional dynamic programming algorithms for sequence alignment can be used directly for solving these problems, just with different sets of characters and with a different scoring function. This type of structure alignment could be as fast as sequence alignment. Though they may not be as accurate as those methods that consider real 3D structural information, but at least can serve as a quick filter to speed up the structural similarity search, which is often much more time consuming. Main development along this direction includes to find a better 1D representation of 3D structures so that spatial information can be retained as much as possible.

2.4.2 Comparison of Distance Matrix: Double Dynamic Programming

Double dynamic programming algorithm was one of the early programs for structure comparison [65]. It was named because dynamic programming procedure is applied at two different levels: at a low level to get the best score (describing the similarity of spatial environment of residues i and j, measured by a simple distance or more complex function) by assuming residues i in protein A is equivalent to residue j in protein B; and at a high level to get the best alignment out of all the possible (i, j) pairs between protein A and B. Essentially, the low level dynamic programming procedure is to prepare the positional pairwise scoring matrix for the high level dynamic programming.

2.4.3 Segment Chaining Algorithm for Protein Structure Alignment

Given two protein structures, denote a match of two fragments, one from each protein as an aligned fragment pair (AFP), the starting positions of an AFP k in the two proteins as $b^1(k)$ and $b^2(k)$, and its ending positions in the two proteins as $e^1(k)$ and $e^2(k)$, respectively. Each AFP describes one way of superimposing one protein on the other (see Fig. 2.6 b). We call two consecutive AFPs *compatible* if they result in the same (or very similar) superposition of the proteins.

Two programs, FlexProt [62] and FATCAT [72], use the formulation of structure alignment as finding a chain of AFP (consequently the alignment is order dependent, see Fig.2.6c), and adopt dynamic programming algorithm to find the optimal. Both programs allow the structural flexibility (e.g, hinge movement) in structure comparison. FlexProt first searches for the largest set of congruent AFPs in a graph, in which AFPs are represented as vertices and edges and are connected between consecutive vertices with weight that rewards long matching fragments while penalizes interfragment gaps and discrepancies in the relative number of gaps in both proteins. FlexProt then looks for a subset of the AFPs that describes a possible alignment of two structures with flexibility by clustering consecutive AFPs that have a similar 3D transformation. In contrast, FATCAT searches for the best chain of AFPs considering the gaps and twists (structural changes) between consecutive AFPs, each with its own score penalty (equation 2.7); therefore, the minimization algorithm compares on-the-fly solutions involving twists and simple extensions and in this way it performs the alignment and structural flexibility detection simultaneously. A dynamic programming algorithm is used in the chaining process. Denote $S(k)$ as the best score ending at AFP k, calculated as the following

$$S(k) = a(k) + \max_{e^1(m)<b^1(k) \text{ and } e^2(m)<b^2(k)} (S(m) + C(m \to k), 0) \qquad (2.7)$$

where $S(k)$ is the score of AFP k itself (determined by its RMSD and length). $C(m \to k)$ is the score of introducing a connection between AFP m and AFP k (determined by the similarity of their 3D transformations, the mismatched regions, and the gaps created by the connection of these two AFPs).

2.4.4 Partial Order Structural Alignment

Partial order structural alignment [73] is the first algorithm that can perform and visualize multiple alignments of protein structures, simultaneously accounting for their conformational flexibility. It combines the partial order alignment representation and the flexible structure alignment FATCAT. Similar to the partial order sequence alignment, POSA identifies structural regions that are conserved only in a subset of input structures and allows internal rearrangements in protein structures. POSA shows its advantages in cases in which structural flexibilities exist and provides new insights by visualizing the mosaic nature of multiple structural alignments. POSA adopts a progressive strategy to build a multiple structure alignment given a set of input structures in the order provided by a guide tree. So each step involves a pairwise alignment of two partial order alignments (or single structures), using the same formulation of AFP chaining for structure alignment as described above, but in a high dimensional space (see Fig. 2.6d).

2.5 SUMMARY

As one of the most commonly used algorithms in bioinformatics, dynamic programming has been applied to many research topics. Its recent applications have shifted from the classical topics as the comparison of linear sequences to the analysis of nonlinear representations of biomolecules. It should be stressed that although dynamic programming is guaranteed to report an optimal solution, this solution may not be biologically the meaningful one. The biological solution depends not only on the algorithm, but also on how correctly the formulation of the computational problem reflects the reality of the biological systems.

REFERENCES

1. Akutsu T. Dynamic programming algorithm for RNA secondary structure prediction with pseudoknots. *Disc Appl Math* 2000;104:45.
2. Altschul SF, Gish W, Miller W, Myers EW, Lipman DJ. Basic local alignment search tool. *J Mol Biol* 1990;215:3.
3. Altschul SF, Madden TL, Schoffer AA, et al., Gapped BLAST and PSI BLAST: a new generation of protein database search programs. *Nucleic Acids Res* 1997;25:3389.
4. Aurora R, Rose GD. Seeking an ancient enzyme in *Methanococcus jannaschii* using ORF, a program based on predicted secondary structure comparisons. *Proc Natl Acad Sci USA* 1998;95:2818.
5. Bafna V, Muthukrishnan S, Ravi R. Computing similarity between RNA strings. *Proceeding of the 6th Annual Symposium on Combinatorial Pattern Matching (CPM'95)*; **LNCS 937** 1995.p1.
6. Bafna V, Tang H, Zhang S. Consensus folding of unaligned RNA sequences revisited. *J Comp Biol* 2006;13:2.
7. Baker D, Sali A. Protein structure prediction and structural genomics. *Science* 2001;294:93.
8. Batzoglou S. The many faces of sequence alignment. *Brief Bioinfo* 2005;6:6.
9. Bellman R. *Eye of the Hurrican*. Singapore: World Scientific Publishing Company; 1984.
10. Bray N, Dubchak I, Pachter L. AVID: a global alignment program. *Genome Res* 2003;13:97.

11. Bray N, Pachter L. L. MAVID: constrained ancestral alignment of multiple sequences. *Genome Res* 2004;13:693.
12. Brudno M, Do CB, Cooper GM, Kim MF, Davydov E. NISC Comparative Sequencing Program, Green ED, Sidow A, Batzoglou S. LAGAN and Multi-LAGAN: efficient tools for large-scale multiple alignment of genomic DNA. *Genome Res* 2003;13:721–731.
13. Brudno M, Malde S, Poliakov A, Do CB, Couronne O, Dubchak I, Batzoglou S. Glocal alignment: finding rearrangements during alignment. *Bioinformatics* 2003;19:i54.
14. Bystroff C, Baker D. Prediction of local structure in proteins using a library of sequence-structure motifs. *J Mol Biol* 1998;281:565.
15. Chao KM, Hardison RC, Miller W. Constrained sequence alignment. *Bull Math Biol* 1993;55:503.
16. Chiu DK, Kolodziejczak T. Inferring consensus structure from nucleic acid sequences. *Comput Appl Biosci* 1991;7:347.
17. Choi j, Cho H, Kim S. GAME: a simple and efficient whole genome alignment method using maximal exact match filtering. *Comp Biol Chem* 2005;29:244.
18. Clote P. An efficient algorithm to compute the landscape of locally optimal RNA secondary structures with respect to the NussinovâŁ"Jacobson energy model. *J Comp Biol* 2005;12:83.
19. Cormen TH, Leiserson CE, Rivest RL, Stein C. *Introduction to Algorithms. 2nd ed.* Cambridge, MA: MIT Press; 2001.
20. Corpet F, Michot B. RNAlign program: alignment of RNA sequences using both primary and secondary structures. *Comput Appl Biosci* 1994;10:389.
21. Dayhoff MA, Schwartz RM, Orcutt BC. A model of evolutionary change in proteins. *Atlas of Protein Sequence and Structure*. Chapter 5, 1978. p345.
22. Delcher AL, Kasif S, Fleischman RD, Peterson J, White O, Salzberg SL. Alignment of whole genomes. *Nucleic Acid Res* 1999;27(11):2369–2376.
23. Do CB, Brudno M, Batzoglou S. ProbCons: probabilistic consistencybased multiple alignment of amino acid sequences. *Genome Res* 2005;15:330.
24. Dost B, Han B, Zhang S, Bafna V. Structural alignment of pseudoknotted RNA. *10th Annual International Conference of Research in Computational Molecular Biology (RECOMB'06)*; **LNCS 3909;** 2006.p143.
25. Eddy SR. How do RNA folding algorithms work?. *Nat Biotechnol* 2004;22:1457.
26. Eppstein D, Galil Z, Giancarlo R, Italiano GF. Sparse dynamic programming I: linear cost functions. *J. ACM* 1992;39:519.
27. Feng D, Doolittle R. Progressive sequence alignment as a prerequisite to correct phylogenetic trees. *J Mol Evol* 1987;25:351.
28. Fischer D, Eisenberg D. Protein fold recognition using sequence-derived predictions. *Protein Sci* 1996;5:947.
29. Friedberg I, Harder T, Kolodny R, Sitbon E, Li Z, Godzik A. Using an alignment of fragment strings for comparing protein structures. *Bioinformatics* 2007;23(2):e219-e224.
30. Gelfand MS, Mironov AA, Pevzner PA. Gene recognition via spliced sequence alignment. *Proc Natl Acad Sci USA* 1996;93:9061.
31. Gorodkin J, Heyer LJ, Stormo GD. Finding the most significant common stem-loop motifs in unaligned RNA sequences. *Nucleic Acids Res* 1997;25:3724.

32. Gusfield D. Efficient methods for multiple sequence alignment with guaranteed error bounds. *Bull Math Biol* 1993;55:141.
33. Henikoff S, Henikoff JG. Amino acid substitution matrices from protein blocks. *Proc Natl Acad Sci USA* 1992;89:10915.
34. Herschlag D. RNA chaperones and the RNA folding problem. *J Biol Chem* 1995;270:20781.
35. Hirschberg DS. A linear space algorithm for computing maximal common subsequences. *Commun ACM* 1975;18:341.
36. Hofacker IL, Fekete M, Stadler PF. Secondary structure prediction for aligned RNA sequences. *J Mol Biol* 2002;319:1059.
37. Holm L, Sander C. Globin fold in a bacterial toxin. *Nature* 1993;361.
38. Holm L, Sander C. Searching protein structure databases has come of age. *Proteins* 1994;19:165.
39. Jareborg N, Birney NE, Durbin R. Comparative analysis of non-coding regions of 77 orthologous mouse and human gene pairs. *Genome Res*1999;10:950.
40. Jennings AJ, Edge CM, Sternberg MJ. An approach to improving multiple alignments of protein sequences using predicted secondary structure. *Protein Eng* 2001;14:227.
41. Jiang T, Lin G, Ma B, Zhang K. A general edit distance between RNA structures. *J Comput Biol* 2002;9:371.
42. Kent WJ, Zahler AM. Conservation, regulation, synteny and introns in a large-scale *C. Bbriggsae-C. elegans* genomic alignment. *Genome Res* 2000;10:1115.
43. Klein R, Eddy S. Rsearch: finding homologs of single structured RNA sequences. *BMC Bioinfor* 2003;4:44.
44. Lee C, Grasso C, Sharlow MF. Multiple sequence alignment using partial order graphs. *Bioinformatics* 2002;18:452.
45. Levenshtein VI. Binary codes capable of correcting deletions, insertions, and reversals. *Cybernetics Control Theory* 1966;10:707.
46. Ma B, Tromp J, Li M. PatternHunter: faster and more sensitive homology search. *Bioinformatics* 2002;18:440.
47. Mathews DH. Revolutions in RNA secondary structure prediction. *J Mol Biol* 2006;359:526.
48. Miller W. Comparison of genomic sequences: solved and unsolved problems. *Bioinformatics* 2000;17:391.
49. Myers EW, Miller W. Optimal alignments in linear space. *Comput Appl Biosci* 1988;4:11.
50. Needleman SB, Wunsch CD. A general method applicable to the search for similarity in the amino acid sequence of two proteins. *J Mol Biol.* 1970;48:443.
51. Notredame C, Higgins DG, Heringa J. T-Coffee: a novel method for fast and accurate multiple sequence alignment. *J Mol Biol* 2000;302:205.
52. Novichkov PS, Gelfand MS, Mironov AA. Gene recognition in eukaryotic DNA by comparison of genomic sequences. *Bioinformatics* 2001:17:1011.
53. Nussinov R, Jacobson AB, A.B. Fast algorithm for predicting the secondary structure of single-stranded RNA. *Proc Natl Acad Sci USA* 1990;77:6309.
54. Pearson WR, Lipman DJ. Improved tools for biological sequence comparison. *Proc Natl Acad Sci USA* 1988;85:8.

55. Plewczynski D, Rychlewski L, Ye Y, Jaroszewski L, Godzik A. Integrated web service for improving alignment quality based on segments comparison. *BMC Bioinfor* 2004;5:98.
56. Reeder J, Hochsmann M, Rehmsmeier M, Voss B, Giegerich R. Beyond Mfold: recent advances in RNA bioinformatics. *J Biotechnol* 2006;124:41.
57. Rivas E, Eddy SR. A dynamic programming algorithm for RNA structure prediction including pseudoknots. *J Mol Biol* 1999;285:2053.
58. Rychlewski L, Godzik A. Secondary structure prediction using segment similarity. *Protein Eng* 1997;10:1143.
59. Rychlewski L, Jaroszewski L, Li W, Godzik A. Comparison of sequence profiles. Strategies for structural predictions using sequence information. *Protein Sci* 2000;9:232.
60. Sankoff D. Simultaneous solution of the RNA folding, alignment and protosequence problems. *SIAM J Appl Math* 1985;45:810.
61. Sankoff D. The early introduction of dynamic programming into computational biology. *Bioinformatics* 2000;16:41.
62. Shatsky M, Nussinov R, Wolfson HJ. Flexible protein alignment and hinge detection. *Proteins* 2002;48:242.
63. Smith TF, Waterman MS. Identification of common molecular subsequences. *J Mol Biol* 1980;147:195.
64. Sze SH, Lu Y, Yang Q. A polynomial time solvable formulation of multiple sequence alignment. *J Comp Biol* 2006;13:309.
65. Taylor WR, Orengo CA. Protein structure alignment. *J Mol Biol* 1989;208:1.
66. Wang L. Jiang T. On the complexity of multiple sequence alignment. *J Comput Biol* 1994;1:337.
67. Waterman MS, Secondary structure of single stranded nucleic acids. *Adv Math* **Suppl Stud** 1978;I:167.
68. Westbrook J, Feng Z, Jain S, Bhat TN, Thanki N, Ravichandran V, Gilliland GL, Bluhm W, Weissig H, Greer DS, Bourne PE, Berman HM. The Protein Data Bank: unifying the archive. *Nucleic Acids Res* 2002;30:245.
69. Wexler Y, Zilberstein CB, M. Ziv-Ukelson: A Study of accessible motifs and RNA folding complexity. *10th Annual International Conference of Research in Computational Molecular Biology (RECOMB'06)*; **LNCS 3909** 2006.p473.
70. Wilbur WJ, Lipman DJ. Rapid similarity searches of nucleic acid and protein data banks. *Proc Natl Acad Sci USA* 1983;80:726.
71. Xu H, Aurora R, Rose GD, White RH. Identifying two ancient enzymes in archaea using predicted secondary structure alignment. *Nat Struct Biol* 1999;6:750.
72. Ye Y, Godzik A. Flexible structure alignment by chaining aligned fragment pairs allowing twists. *Bioinformatics* 2003;19:ii246.
73. Ye Y, GodzikA. Multiple flexible structure alignment using partial order graphs. *Bioinformatics* 2005;21:2362.
74. Ye Y, Jaroszewski L, Li W, Godzik A. A segment alignment approach to protein comparison. *Bioinformatics* 2003;19:742.
75. Zuker M. On finding all suboptimal foldings of a RNA molecule. *Science* 1989;244:48.
76. Zuker M. Mfold web server for nucleic acid folding and hybridization prediction. *Nucleic Acids Res* 2003;31:3406.

3

GRAPH THEORETICAL APPROACHES TO DELINEATE DYNAMICS OF BIOLOGICAL PROCESSES

TERESA M. PRZYTYCKA

National Center for Biotechnology Information, National Library of Medicine, National Institutes of Health, Bethesda, MD, USA

ELENA ZOTENKO

National Center for Biotechnology Information, National Library of Medicine, National Institutes of Health, Bethesda, MD, USA, and Department of Computer Science, University of Maryland, College Park, MD, USA

3.1 INTRODUCTION

Graphs are used in Computational Biology to model the relationships between biological entities. For example, experimentally determined protein interactions are commonly represented by a graph, the so-called *protein interaction network*, where proteins are nodes and every pair of interacting proteins is connected by an edge. Even though such a representation may not capture all the complexity of protein interactions in underlying biological processes, the study of the topological properties of these networks has become an important tool in searching for general principles that govern the organization of molecular networks. For example, it was observed that in protein interaction networks some types of small-size subnetworks are much more abundant than would be expected by chance [54]. The discovery of these overrepresented subnetworks or *network motifs* has led to investigation of their

Bioinformatics Algorithms: Techniques and Applications, Edited by Ion I. Măndoiu and Alexander Zelikovsky

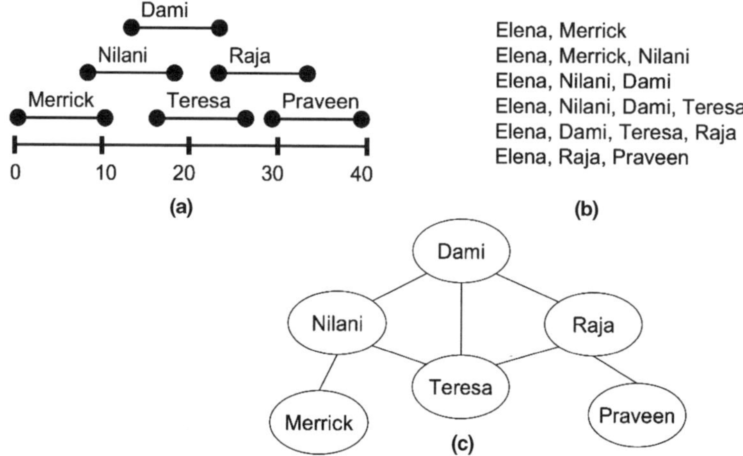

FIGURE 3.1 Elena's story. (**a**) The order in which Elena's friends, Merrick, Nilani, Dami, Teresa, Raja, and Praveen, join the walk. Each friend is represented by an interval showing his/her stretch of the walk. (**b**) Julian's pictures. There are six pictures showing the participants when each friend joins the walk. (**c**) The supporters overlap graph: Elena's friends are nodes and there is an edge between two friends if they were walking together.

information processing properties [65] and network evolution mechanisms that could account for their emergence [53]. Usage of graph theoretical tools is not limited to the study of protein interaction networks, graphs are also used to model metabolic networks (processes), gene coexpression, gene coregulation, phylogenies, and so on.

In general, graphs are not required to have any type of regularity. This makes them very flexible combinatorial objects, which are able to represent complex and diverse relationships. In practice, however, graphs that model real world phenomena often belong to families of graphs with a special structure, which can be exploited to gain an insight into the phenomenon that generated the graph. To clarify this statement, we start with a following toy example taken from everyday life.

Example Elena decided to walk 40 miles to raise funds for an important cause. Her friends provide her with support by walking along her, but each of them walks only for 10 miles (see Fig. 3.1a). Her husband, Julian, volunteers to document the event and takes a group picture every time a new supporter joins Elena (see Fig. 3.1b). After the event is completed Julian handles Elena a box with photographs. Elena notices that the pictures are not ordered and then she learns that Julian lost somewhere the film. Can she reconstruct the order her supporters joined the walk without the film, that is, can she use the information in Fig. 3.1b to tell that her friends joined the walk in the following order (Merrick, Nilani, Dami, Teresa, Raja, and Praveen)? If Julian had lost the film before developing it (so Elena does not have her precious pictures) but her supporters remember their walking partners. However, they do not remember the order in which these partners joined. Would she still be able to reconstruct the history of events? Interestingly, if except for the very beginning and very end, she never walked alone and remembers a person who supported her first, she can reconstruct this order: in the first case she would be able to recover the order completely; in the second case she still would be able to reconstruct the order except for the relative placement of Dami and Teresa; she would not be able to tell whether Dami joined the walk before Teresa or the other way around.

In the example above, Elena exploits the special structure of the supporters overlap graph in Fig. 3.1c to understand the "real world phenomenon," the participation of her friends in the fund raising event in Fig. 3.1a. The graph in Fig. 3.1c is an *interval graph*, meaning that there is a set of intervals on a real line such that vertices of the graph are in one-to-one correspondence with the intervals in the set and there is an edge between a pair of vertices if and only if the corresponding intervals intersect; the set of intervals is called an *interval representation* of the graph. Interval graphs are a special case of *intersection graphs*, graphs whose vertices are in one-to-one correspondence with a family of sets such that there is an edge between a pair of vertices if and only if the corresponding pair of sets have a nonempty intersection. Coming back to our example, the supporters overlap graph in Fig. 3.1c is an interval graph with one possible interval representation shown in Fig. 3.1a. Given the graph in Fig. 3.1c, Elena won't be able to reconstruct the history of events up to the smallest detail, such as Merrick joined the walk 8 miles before Nilani, but she would be able to tell that all possible valid (Merrick is the first to join the walk and everybody walks for exactly 10 miles) interval representations of this graph result in the same order (up to relative placement of Dami and Teresa) of her friends joining the walk.

In this chapter, we will demonstrate how graph theoretical tools are used in Computational Biology to elucidate the dynamics of biological processes. In particular, we will show applications of the well-studied graph family known as *chordal graphs*. Chordal graphs are exactly these graphs that are intersection graphs of subtrees of a tree, and therefore they include interval graphs that can be seen as intersection graphs of subtrees of a path (a degenerate tree). We start with a background information on graph theoretical tools used to deal with chordal graphs (see Section 3.2). We then proceed to show how these tools are applied to two problems in Computational Biology: phylogenetic tree reconstruction (see Section 3.3) and formation of multiprotein complexes (see Section 3.4). In both applications, structure of a certain graph is exploited (in a manner similar to the toy example above) to elucidate the dynamic behavior of the underlying biological process. In the first application, we are interested in the dynamics of evolution, that is, the order in which the taxa evolved from a common ancestor. In the second application, we are interested in the dynamics of multiprotein complex formation during a biological process, such as cell signaling, that is, how multiprotein complexes are formed during the process and the order in which proteins join these complexes.

3.2 GRAPH THEORY BACKGROUND

The purpose of this section is to provide the reader with an overview of relevant graph theoretic results for chordal, interval, and cograph graph families. We state here results that are used in the biological applications of these graph families discussed in latter sections. For a thorough treatment of chordal graphs and interval graphs, we refer the reader to now a classical book by Golumbic [36]; other excellent references are a recent book on intersection graph theory by McKee and McMorris [51], a chapter "An introduction to chordal graphs and clique trees" by Blair and Peyton in [33], and a set of lecture notes by Shamir [64]. For an overview of structural and algorithmic properties of cographs, we refer the reader to the paper by Corneil et al. [19]; modular decomposition is surveyed in a paper by Mohring and Radermacher[55], a nice overview can also be found in a chapter "Decompositions and forcing relations in graphs and other combinatorial structures" by McConnel in [37].

We assume that all graphs are undirected and connected. We denote by $G = (V, E)$ a graph with a set of vertices V and a set of edges E. Given a graph $G = (V, E)$, a subgraph $G' = (V', E')$ is an *induced subgraph* of G if V' is a subset of V and E' contains all the edges of the original graph whose both end points are in V'; we may also say that G' is a subgraph of G *induced* by V'. For a vertex $v \in V$, we use $\mathcal{N}(v)$ to denote the set of v's neighbors in G, that is, $\mathcal{N}(v) = \{u \mid (v, u) \in E\}$. We use "$-$" to denote set difference operation such that for two sets X and Y the set $X - Y$ contains elements that are in X but not in Y.

3.2.1 Chordal Graphs

In a cycle, a *chord* is an edge that connects two nonconsecutive vertices of the cycle. For example, a cycle $\{a, b, c, d\}$ in Fig. 3.2a has a chord (b, d). A *chordal graph* is a graph that does not contain chordless cycles of length greater than three; other names given to graphs having this property are *rigid circuit graphs* and *triangulated graphs*. Chordality is a *hereditary graph property*, meaning that any induced subgraph of a chordal graph is chordal.

In a graph, an ordering of vertices $\{v_1, \ldots, v_n\}$ is a *perfect elimination ordering* (PEO) if and only if for every position i, the subgraph induced by the neighbors of v_i that appear later on in the ordering is complete, that is, the subgraph induced by $\mathcal{N}(v_i) \cap \{v_{i+1}, \ldots, v_n\}$ is complete. For example, in the graph of Fig. 3.2a, the ordering $\{a, b, c, e, f, d\}$ is a PEO while the ordering $\{a, b, c, d, e, f\}$ is not. It was shown by Fulkerson and Gross [26] that only chordal graphs can have a PEO.

Theorem 3.1 *[26] A graph is chordal if and only if there exists a perfect elimination ordering of its vertices.*

This alternative characterization of chordal graphs is used by two linear time chordal graph recognition algorithms [60,67]. Given a graph, both algorithms produce an ordering of its vertices, which is a PEO if and only if the input graph is chordal. Therefore, to determine whether the input graph is chordal it suffices to check that the ordering output by the algorithm is a PEO. The earliest algorithm, due to Rose and

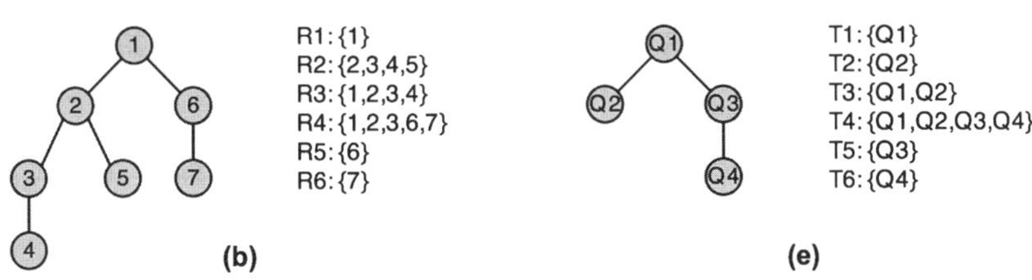

FIGURE 3.2 (**a**) A chordal graph $G = (V, E)$. (**b**) A tree representation of G: the tree is on the left and the family of subtrees is on the right. (**c**) There are four maximal cliques in the graph, Q_1, Q_2, Q_3, and Q_4. (**d**) The clique graph of G. The clique graph is the intersection graph of $\{Q_1, Q_2, Q_3, Q_4\}$. (**e**) A clique tree representation of G: the clique tree is on the left and the family of subtrees is on the right. It should be noted that a clique tree is a valid tree representation of a chordal graph. Indeed, every vertex in the graph corresponds to a subtree of the clique tree and two vertices are adjacent if and only if their corresponding subtrees intersect.

Tarjan [60], uses a *Lexicographic Breadth-First Search*(LexBFS), a modified version of the widely known *Breadth First Search* [17] algorithm, to order the vertices of the graph.

A *maximal clique* in a graph is a subset of vertices that form a maximal complete subgraph. Given a graph G, we will use $\mathcal{Q}(G)$ to denote the set of all maximal cliques in G and $K(G)$ to denote the *clique graph* of G, where vertices of $K(G)$ are maximal cliques in G, and there is an edge between a pair of vertices (maximal cliques) if their intersection is not empty. As an illustration consider the graph in Fig. 3.2a. This graph has four maximal cliques, which are shown in Fig. 3.2c. The clique graph $K(G)$ is shown in Fig. 3.2d; it has four vertices Q_1, Q_2, Q_3, and Q_4 and is complete as every pair of vertices (maximal cliques) has a nonempty intersection. (In this case, all maximal cliques contain vertex $d \in V$ of the original graph G.)

Even though computing all maximal cliques of a general graph is a difficult problem [28], all maximal cliques of a chordal graph can be computed efficiently. Moreover, the number of maximal cliques in a chordal graph is at most $|V|$. (For details please refer to Section 4.2.1 in the chapter by Blair and Peyton [33].)

Let $\mathcal{F} = \{R_1, \ldots, R_n\}$ be a family of subsets. The *intersection graph of* $\mathcal{F}$ is a graph $G = (V, E)$ where $V = \mathcal{F}$ and $E = \{(R_i, R_j) \mid R_i \cap R_j \neq \emptyset\}$, that is, the vertices of the graph are the subsets in $\mathcal{F}$, and there is an edge between two vertices (subsets) if their intersection is not empty. It can be shown that every graph is isomorphic to the intersection graph of some family of subsets; the family of subsets can be thought as an alternative representation of the graph and is called an *intersection representation* of the graph. A variety of well-known graph classes can be characterized by putting restrictions on intersection representations of graphs in the class. For example, an *interval graph* is isomorphic to the intersection graph of a family of closed intervals on the real line and a *chordal graph* is isomorphic to the intersection graph of a family of subtrees of a tree.

Even though the study of chordal graphs goes back to 1958, the characterization in terms of allowable intersection representations was given only in the 70's [13,31,69]. In particular, it was established that a graph is chordal if and only if it is isomorphic to the intersection graph of a family of subtrees of a tree; the tree and the family of subtrees are called a *tree representation* of the chordal graph. Figure 3.2b shows a tree representation of a chordal graph in Fig. 3.2a. Moreover, it was shown that every chordal graph $G = (V, E)$ has a special tree representation, the so-called *clique tree representation*, in which the tree is a spanning tree of $K(G)$ and the family of subtrees $\mathcal{F} = \{T_v \mid v \in V\}$ is defined by setting each T_v to the set of maximal cliques that contain v. For example, Fig. 3.2e shows a clique tree representation for a chordal graph in Fig. 3.2a. This is summarized in the following theorem.

Theorem 3.2 *[13,31,69] Let $G = (V, E)$ be a graph. The following statements are equivalent*

1. *G is a chordal graph.*
2. *G is isomorphic to the intersection graph of a family of subtrees of a tree.*
3. *There exists a spanning tree of the clique graph $K(G)$ such that for every $v \in V$ the subgraph of this tree induced by the set of maximal cliques containing v, $\{Q \mid Q \in \mathcal{Q}(G)$, and $v \in Q\}$, is connected.*

Given a chordal graph, all possible clique tree representations can be efficiently computed. One approach [7] is based on the fact that clique trees are exactly maximum weight spanning trees of the clique graph $K(G)$, where the weight function on the edges of $K(G)$ is defined as the amount of overlap between two maximal cliques, that is, $w(Q', Q'') = |Q' \cap Q''|$. Thus, in order to compute all possible clique tree representations of a chordal graph, one simply needs to compute all maximum weight spanning trees of the clique graph $K(G)$, for example, by using an algorithm from [32]. Another approach [40] builds on a connection between the edges of a clique tree of a chordal graph and the set of minimal vertex separators in the graph.

Given a graph $G = (V, E)$ not necessarily chordal, one is often interested in finding a set of edges E' such that addition of E' to the graph makes it chordal; the set of edges that does the job is called a *triangulation* of G. As a complete graph is chordal by definition, any graph can be trivially triangulated by setting E' to be the set of all the nonedges in the graph, $E' = (V \times V) - E$. One may further ask for a triangulation that possesses additional properties. A *minimal triangulation* of a graph is a triangulation that is not properly contained in any other triangulation. A minimal triangulation can be found efficiently [60] using a variant of the LexBFS algorithm for recognition of chordal graphs. A *minimum triangulation* of a graph is the triangulation with the smallest number of edges. Even though finding a minimum triangulation of a graph is a difficult problem [72], there are *fixed-parameter tractable* solutions [14,46]. For example, an algorithm in [14] takes $(|V| + |E|)O(4^k/(k+1)^{3/2})$ to find a minimum triangulation of $G = (V, E)$ when G has a triangulation whose size does not exceed k. Therefore, if the size of minimum triangulation is small, it can be found efficiently.

3.2.2 Interval Graphs

An *interval graph* is any graph that is isomorphic to the intersection graph of a family of intervals on a real line; the family of intervals is called an *interval representation* or sometimes an *interval realizer* of the graph. Not every graph has an interval representation; consider, for example, a chordless cycle of length four. The "invention" of interval graphs is commonly attributed to the Hungarian mathematician Gyorgy Hajos who in 1957 posed the problem of characterizing this family of graphs. Interval graphs also appear in the work of the American biologists Seymour Benzer [6] who used them to support his hypothesis that genetic material is organized into a structure having linear topology.

The first linear time algorithm for recognizing interval graphs is due to Booth and Leuker [11]. In their paper, the authors show how to test whether a family of subsets of some ground set U has a *consecutive ones* property, meaning that the members of the family can be linearly ordered in such a way that for every element in U the subsets containing it are consecutive in the linear order. Therefore, according to the theorem below, an interval graph is recognized by testing whether the set of its maximal cliques has a consecutive ones property.

Theorem 3.3 *[34] A graph is an interval graph if and only if its maximal cliques can be ordered in a linear fashion such that for every vertex in the graph the set of maximal cliques that contain it is consecutive.*

The above characterization implies that interval graphs are chordal. Indeed, if maximal cliques of a chordal graph can be arranged in a tree then maximal cliques of an interval graph can be arranged on a path. Therefore, interval graphs are exactly these chordal graphs that have a clique tree representation, which is a path.

In a graph $G = (V, E)$, an ordering of vertices $\{v_1, \ldots, v_n\}$ is an *interval ordering* (I-ordering) if and only if for every pair of positions $i < j$ the following holds: if $(v_i, v_j) \in E$ then $(v_i, v_k) \in E$ for every $i < k < j$. Recently, another linear time algorithm for recognition of interval graphs was proposed [18], which utilizes the fact that only interval graphs can have an I-ordering. The main idea is to use a multisweep

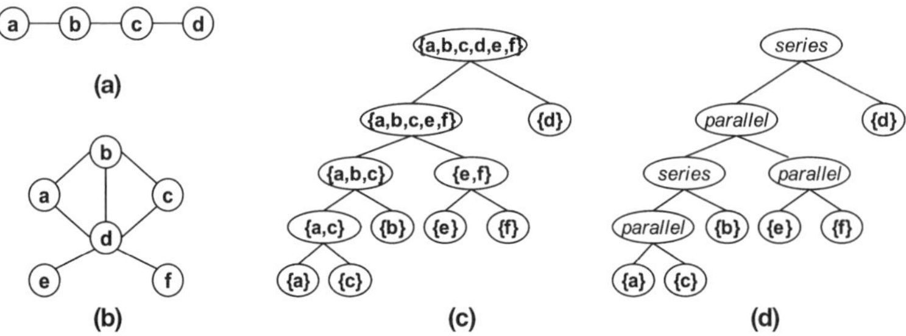

FIGURE 3.3 (**a**) A prime graph. (**b**) A nonprime graph. (**c**) The modular decomposition tree of the graph in (**b**). (**d**) The modular decomposition tree can be used to derive a Boolean expression for the maximal cliques in a graph. The Boolean expression is constructed by moving along the tree from the leaves to the root, replacing each "series" node with an $\wedge$ operator and each "parallel" node with an $\vee$ operator. The Boolean expression for the cograph in (**b**) is $(((a \vee c) \wedge b) \vee e \vee f) \wedge d$.

LexBFS algorithm to produce an ordering of the vertices of a graph, which is an I-ordering if and only if the input graph is an interval graph.

3.2.3 Modular Decomposition and Cographs

A *module* in a graph $G = (V, E)$ is a set of vertices, X, that have exactly the same set of neighbors in $V - X$, that is, for every pair of vertices u and v in X the following holds $\mathcal{N}(u) \cap (V - X) = \mathcal{N}(v) \cap (V - X)$. For any vertex v, the set $\{v\}$ trivially satisfies the requirement for being a module and so does the set of all vertices in the graph, V; these sets are called *trivial modules*.

A graph that only has trivial modules is *prime*; for example, the graph in Fig. 3.3a is prime, while the graph in Fig. 3.3b is not. A nonprime graph will have other modules in addition to the trivial modules. Two modules in a graph *overlap* if they share vertices but neither module properly contains the other. A module is *strong* if it does not overlap any other module in the graph and *weak* otherwise; by definition trivial modules are strong modules.

The strong modules in a graph $G = (V, E)$ can be organized into a hierarchical structure where every module is attached to the smallest module that contains it. It can be argued that this construction results in a unique tree, the *modular decomposition tree* of the graph, with the trivial modules of the form $\{v\}$ being the leaves of the tree, the module V being the root, and all other strong modules being the internal nodes. The modular decomposition tree of the graph in Fig. 3.3b is shown in Fig. 3.3c. This graph has 11 modules, all of which are strong.

Even though weak modules of a graph do not directly appear in the modular decomposition tree, it can be shown that every weak module is a union of strong modules that are directly attached to the same internal node in the modular decomposition tree. When this happens the internal node is labeled as *degenerate*; internal nodes that are not degenerate are labeled as *prime*. Furthermore, the union of any subset of children of a degenerate node is a module (necessarily weak). Therefore, the modular decomposition tree captures all modules in the graph: the strong modules are the nodes of the tree and the weak modules are the unions of children of degenerate internal nodes.

Let X be a module in a graph $G = (V, E)$ represented by an internal node of the modular decomposition tree and let $\mathcal{C}$ be the set of modules that correspond to its children. A *quotient graph* associated with X is obtained by contracting every module in $\mathcal{C}$ into one node in the subgraph of G induced by X, G_X. For any pair of modules Y and Y' in $\mathcal{C}$, either all edges $Y \times Y'$ belong to E or none does ($(Y \times Y') \cap E = \emptyset$). Therefore, the quotient graph associated with X completely specifies the edges of G_X that are not within one module in $\mathcal{C}$. Moreover, it can be shown that the quotient graph associated with a module that corresponds to a degenerate node is either a complete graph or a complement of a complete graph. If we label degenerate nodes as *series* whenever the corresponding quotient graph is complete and *parallel* otherwise, and record the structure of quotient graphs associated with prime nodes, then the modular decomposition tree together with this additional information completely specifies the structure of the graph.

A *complement reducible graph* (a cograph) can be recursively defined in the following manner: (i) a single vertex graph is a cograph; (ii) if $G_1, \ldots, G_k$ are cographs then so is their union $G_1 \cup G_2 \cdots \cup G_k$; (iii) if G is a cograph then so is its complement $\bar{G}$; A pair of nodes, u and v, in a graph are *siblings* if they have exactly the same set of neighbors, that is, $\mathcal{N}(u) - \{v\} = \mathcal{N}(v) - \{u\}$. If the nodes of the pair are connected by an edge, we call them *strong siblings* and *weak siblings* otherwise. The following theorem summarizes some of the structural properties of cographs given in the paper by Corneil et al. [19].

Theorem 3.4 *Let $G = (V, E)$ be a graph. The following statements are equivalent.*

- *G is a cograph.*
- *Every nontrivial induced subgraph of G has a pair of siblings.*
- *G does not contain an induced subgraph isomorphic to a path of length four (P_4).*

Cographs are exactly graphs with the modular decomposition tree without prime modules. Therefore, the modular decomposition tree of a cograph with the "series"/"parallel" labeling of nodes provides an alternative representation of the graph. This representation is closely related to the *cotree* representation for cographs [19]. In particular, the modular decomposition tree can be used to generate a Boolean expression describing all the maximal cliques in a cograph and obtain efficient algorithms for other otherwise difficult combinatorial problems [19]. The Boolean expression is constructed by moving along the tree from the leaves to the root, replacing each "series" node with an $\wedge$ operator and every "parallel" node with an $\vee$ operator. For example, Fig. 3.3d shows how to obtain the Boolean expression for the graph in Fig. 3.3b. For a cograph, the modular decomposition tree can be constructed in linear time [20].

3.3 RECONSTRUCTING PHYLOGENIES

Consider a set of taxa, where each taxon is represented by a vector of attributes, the so-called *characters*. We assume that every character can take one of a finite number of states and the set of taxa evolved from a common ancestor through changes of states of the corresponding characters. For example, the set of taxa can be described by columns in multiple sequence alignment of protein sequences. In this case, each column in the alignment is a character that can assume one of twenty possible states. Parsimony methods seek a phylogenetic tree that explains the observed characters with the minimum number of character changes along the branches of the tree.

In our working example for this section, the set of taxa includes eight species shown in Fig. 3.4a; each species is described by two binary characters. As there

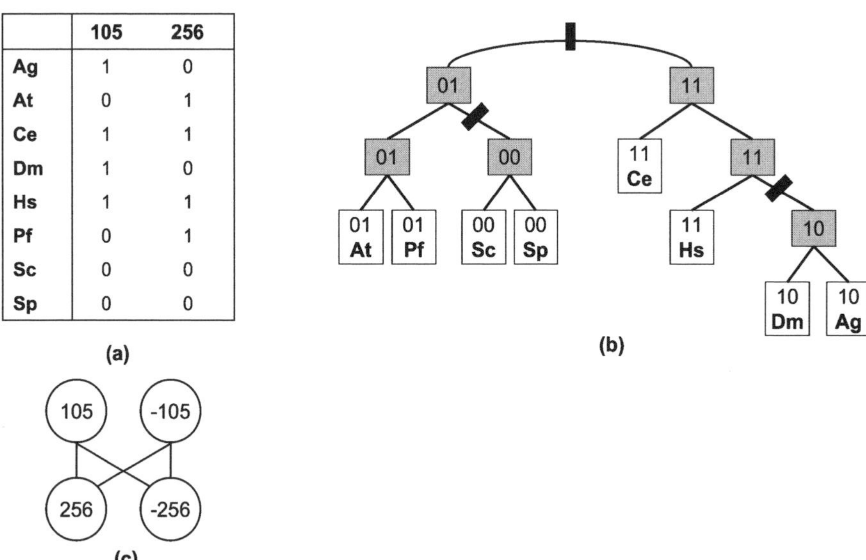

	105	256
Ag	1	0
At	0	1
Ce	1	1
Dm	1	0
Hs	1	1
Pf	0	1
Sc	0	0
Sp	0	0

FIGURE 3.4 A set of eight species: *Anopheles gambiae* (Ag), *Arabidopsis thaliana* (At), *Caenorhabditis elegans* (Ce), *Drosophila melanogaster* (Dm), *Homo sapiens* (Hm), *Plasmodium falciparum* (Pf), *Saccharomyces cerevisiae* (Ag), and *Saccharomyces pombe* (Sp). (**a**) The species are described by binary characters that correspond to the presence (value of 1) or absence (value of 0) of introns. This is truncated data limited to just two introns (105 and 256) out of about 7236 from the study of Rogozin et al. [59]. (**b**) A phylogenetic tree: the leaves are the species in the set and are labeled with the input character states; the internal nodes are ancestral species and are labeled with the inferred character states. This particular tree requires three character changes , which are marked with solid bars on the corresponding edges.(**c**) The character overlap graph. There are four vertices, one vertex per character state, 105 (state "1" of the character "intron 105"), −105 (state "0" of the character "intron 105"), 256 (state "1" of the character "intron 256"), and −256 (state "0" of the character "intron 256"). Two vertices are connected by an edge if corresponding character states are observed together in some taxon. The edge (105, −256), for example, is due to species Ag and Dm.

are $(2n-5)!/(2^{n-3}(n-3)!)$ unrooted binary trees on n labeled vertices [15], there are $11!/(2^5 5!) = 10,395$ possible phylogenetic trees for the set of species in our example. One such tree is shown in Fig. 3.4b. Once the tree topology is fixed, an optimal assignment/assignments of the character states to the internal nodes can be efficiently computed [25]; the assignment of characters in Fig. 3.4b is optimal for this tree topology and requires three character changes.

We call a phylogenetic tree a *perfect phylogeny* if every character state arose only once during evolution or in other words the subgraph of the tree induced by the nodes having this character state is connected. The phylogenetic tree in Fig. 3.4b is not a perfect phylogeny as the character state 0 for the character "intron 256" arose twice, once in the part of the tree defined by Sc and Sp, and another time in the part of the tree defined by Dm and Ag. Given a phylogenetic tree, the number of changes due to a specific character is bounded from below by the number of states this character assumes minus one. It is easy to see that the lower bound is achieved only when each character state induces a connected subgraph of the tree; in the phylogenetic tree of Fig. 3.4b the character "intron 105" achieves the lower bound, while the character "intron 256" does not. Therefore, a perfect phylogeny is the best tree in a sense that it achieves this lower bound for every character. A perfect phylogeny often does not exist and we start this section with an example of how Chordal Graph Theory can be used to address the `Character Compatibility Problem`: Given a set of taxa, does there exist a perfect phylogeny for the set?

When a set of taxa admits a perfect phylogeny, we say that the characters describing the set are *fully compatible* or just *compatible*. The compatibility criteria is quite restrictive, in the case of intron data, for example, it means that for every intron the transition from "0" state to "1" state occurred only once during evolution. We conclude this section by showing how Chordal Graph Theory can be used to relax the compatibility criteria in a meaningful way when taxa are described by a set of binary characters.

3.3.1 A Perfect Phylogeny and Triangulating Vertex-Colored Graphs

From the set of input taxa we can construct a *partition intersection graph* in the following manner: (i) introduce a vertex for every character state; (ii) put an edge between two vertices if the corresponding character states are observed in one or more taxa together. In our working example, the partition intersection graph will have four vertices, 105 (state "1" of the character "intron 105"), −105 (state "0" of the character "intron 105"), 256 (state "1" of the character "intron 256"), and −256 (state "0" of the character "intron 256") (see Fig. 3.4c). The name "partition intersection graph" is due to the fact that each character state corresponds to a subset of taxa, the taxa that have this character state, and the subsets of character states of a character partition the set of taxa under consideration.

There is an important connection between partition intersection graphs and the `Character Compatibility Problem`. Indeed, if a set of taxa admits a perfect phylogeny then there exists a phylogenetic tree, where for each character state the tree vertices having this state form a subtree. As there is an edge in the partition intersection graph between every pair of character states whose subtrees intersect in the leaves of the phylogenetic tree, this graph is either chordal or can be triangulated without introducing edges between vertices that correspond to the states of the same character. (Additional edges may be necessary to account for subtree intersection, which occurs only at internal nodes of the phylogenetic tree.) The partition intersection graphs were used by Buneman [13] (in his paper the author refers to these graphs as *attribute overlap graphs*) to show that the `Character Compatibility Problem` reduces in polynomial time to the `Triangulating Vertex Colored Graph Problem`. In the latter problem, we are given a graph $G(V, E)$ and a proper coloring of its vertices, $c : V \rightarrow Z$. A vertex coloring is proper if there does not exist an edge in G whose end points are assigned the same color by the coloring. We want to determine if there exists a chordal graph $\hat{G}(V, \hat{E})$ such that $E \subset \hat{E}$ and $\hat{G}$ is properly colored by c, that is, no edges between vertices of the same color were introduced in the process of triangulating G. If such chordal graph exists, we say that G can be c-triangulated.

Theorem 3.5 *[13] A set of taxa has a perfect phylogeny if and only if the corresponding partition intersection graph can be c-triangulated, where vertex coloring function c assigns the same color to the character states of the same character and different colors to the character states of different characters.*

Kannan and Warnow [44] showed the polynomial time reduction in the opposite direction: from the `Triangulating Vertex Colored Graph Problem` to the `Character Compatibility Problem`, thus, establishing that the two problems are equivalent. This result was later used by Bodlaender et al. [9] to show that the `Character Compatibility Problem` is NP-complete. Even though the `Character Compatibility Problem` is hard in general, there are efficient algorithms when one or more of the problem's natural parameters are fixed: n the number of taxonomic units, k the number of characters, and r the maximum number of states per character. Later on, we will see how to apply the Buneman's theorem to derive a polynomial time solution for two characters $k = 2$. For three characters there is a series of algorithms that run in linear time [10,42,44]. For arbitrary fixed k there is an $O(r^{k+1}k^{k+1} + nk^2)$ algorithm due to McMorris et al. [52]. When the number of character states is bounded, the problem can also be solved efficiently. There is a simple linear time algorithm to test if any number of binary characters is compatible due to Gusfield [39]. For four-state characters there is an $O(n^2k)$ algorithm due to Kannan and Warnow [45]. For arbitrary fixed r there is an $O(2^{3r}(nk^3 + k^4))$ algorithm due to Agarwala and Fernandez-Baca [2].

The Buneman's theorem can be used to readily derive a well-known test for checking whether a pair of binary characters is compatible. The test is attributed to Wilson [70]; it says that a pair of binary characters is compatible if and only if there does not exist a set of four taxa having all possible character states, 00, 01, 10, and 11. The same test can be derived through application of the Buneman's theorem. According to the theorem, a pair of binary characters, is compatible if and only if the corresponding partition intersection can be c-triangulated. As there are only two binary characters, the partition intersection graph is bipartite and each set of the bipartition contains two vertices (see, for example, Fig. 3.4c). Such a graph is either acyclic and therefore can be trivially c-triangulated, or it contains a square and therefore does not have a c-triangulation as any attempt to eliminate the square would add an edge between two vertices of the same color. The square in the partition intersection graph corresponds to the presence of the four taxa with all possible combinations of character values: 00, 01, 10, and 11, where 00, for example, means that both characters have state "0." The compatibility test can be extended to a pair of characters with more than two states ($r > 2$). In this case, the partition intersection graph would still be bipartite and the number of vertices in each bipartition is r. It can be easily shown that this graph can be c-triangulated if and only if it is acyclic. Therefore, testing compatibility of two characters reduces to testing whether the partition intersection graph is acyclic, which can be done efficiently, for example, using any of the graph search algorithms such as BFS or DFS [17].

3.3.2 Character Stability

Assume that we are dealing with a set of characters that are difficult to gain but relatively easy to lose. A classic example of such characters are introns [23]. Introns are noncoding DNA sequences that interrupt the flow of a gene coding sequences in eukaryotic genes. They are remarkably conserved between some lineages (e.g., between Arabidopsis and Human), but they are lost at a significant rate in other organisms (e.g., Worm) [59]. Parsimony methods applied to introns produced an incorrect tree [59] indicating that the data contains misleading characters. One way of eliminating such misleading characters is to restrict attention to a maximum set of compatible characters. However, under the condition that the characters are hard to gain but are frequently lost, a large enough set of compatible characters may not exist. To address this problem, Przytycka [57] proposed a new consistency criterion called *stability criterion*.

The definition of the stability criterion is phrased as a property of a graph closely related to the partition intersection graph and called a *character overlap graph*. A character overlap graph for a set of taxa is a graph $G = (V, E)$, where V is a set of characters, and $(u, v) \in E$ if there exists a taxon T in the set such that both u and v are present in T. Note that the character overlap graph is simply a subgraph of the partition intersection graph for a set of binary characters that is induced by the set of characters in state "1."

To motivate the concept of stability, consider a set of characters A, B, C, D, and a set of four taxa described respectively by character pairs: (A, B), (B, C), (C, D), and (D, A). That is the first taxon has characters A and B in state "1" (and the rest in state "0"), second B and C in state "1," and so on. In such a case, the corresponding character overlap graph is simply a square (see Fig. 3.5a). There are two possible topologies for the evolutionary tree for this set of taxa as illustrated in Fig. 3.5b–c. The number of character changes implied by each topology is the same. However, in the first case, characters, B and D, have to change their state twice (and at least three

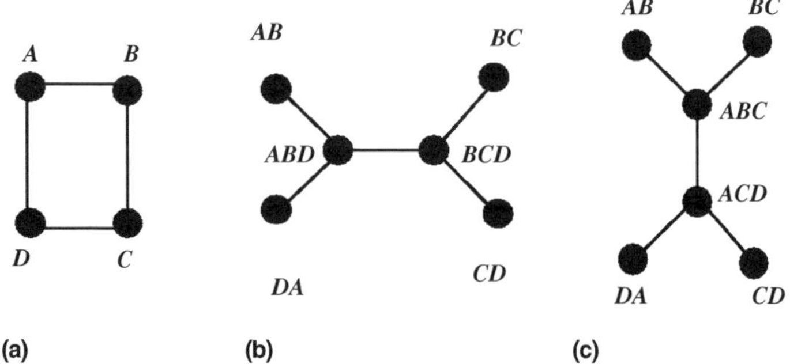

FIGURE 3.5 The two possible (up to symmetry) topologies for an evolutionary tree for four taxa containing characters respectively: (A, B), (B, C), (C, D), and (D, A). In each case, one pair of characters has to change state twice and the selection of such pair determines the topology of the tree.

of these character changes have to be deletions) while in the second case, characters, C and A, have to change their state twice. If we knew which pair is more preserved in a given lineage relative to the other pair, we would be able to select the more likely topology. Similar situation occurs when we consider a larger cycle. This motivates the following concept of stability.

We say that a character is *stable* if it does not belong to a chordless cycle in the character overlap graph. Otherwise, we say that the stability of the character is *challenged* and *number of challenges* is equal to the number of chordless cycles to which the character belongs. Note that the stability criterion can also identify characters that are preferentially conserved in one lineage but lost in many other lineages, as stability of such characters is likely to be challenged by other characters. Directly from the property of stability, we observe that the set of characters is stable only if the corresponding character overlap graph is chordal. In particular, it can be easily shown that a set of characters such that each character is gained at most once and lost at most once (called in [57] *persistent characters*) is stable [57]. Note that even the persistency criterion is significantly less stringent than the compatibility criterion discussed before as it allows for two changes of a character state.

Unfortunately, the problem of finding the minimum number of nodes whose removal leaves a graph chordal is NP-complete [48]. To go around this problem, [57] use a simple heuristic. Namely, rather than considering all chordless cycles, they considered only squares. The squares were then eliminated by a greedy algorithm that iteratively removed characters belonging to the largest number of squares. After all squares are removed, they applied the Dollo parsimony (the maximum parsimony model that does not allow for multiple insertions of the same character) to construct the evolutionary tree based on the remaining characters.

The utility of a variant of this approach has been demonstrated by using it to construct the evolutionary tree from intron data compiled by Rogozin et al. [59]. This data contains information about introns found in conserved (and orthologous) genes of eight fully sequenced organisms: *Arabidopsis thaliana* (At), *Homo sapiens* (Hs),

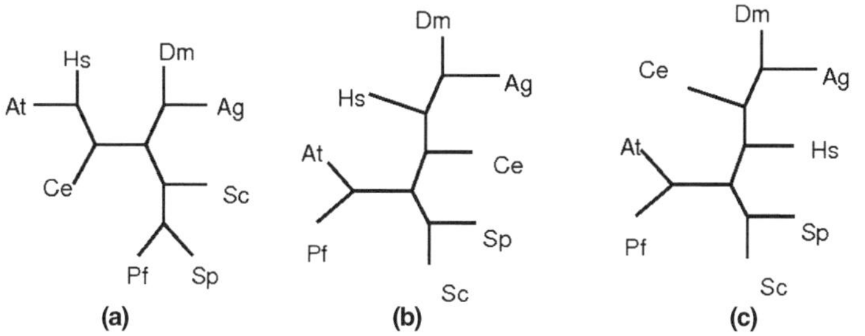

FIGURE 3.6 Three tree topologies for organisms: *Arabidopsis thaliana* (At), *Homo sapiens* (Hs), *C. elegans* (Ce), *Drosophila melanogaster* (Dm), *Anopheles gambaie* (Ag), *Saccharomyces cerevisiae* (Sc), *Schizosaccharomyces pombe* (Sp), and *Plasmodium falciparum* (Pf). (**a**) The incorrect Dollo parsimony tree computed from intron data. (**b**) The tree consistent with Coelomata hypothesis. This is also exactly the tree obtained after applying the squares removal procedure. (**c**) The tree consistent with Ecdysozoa hypothesis.

C.elegans (Ce), *Drosophila melanogaster* (Dm), *Anopheles gambaie* (Ag), *Saccharomyces cerevisiae* (Sc), *Schizosaccharomyces pombe* (Sp), and *Plasmodium falciparum* (Pf). Introns are identified by their starting position with respect to the coding sequence. The data contains 7236 introns; however, most of these introns are observed in one organism only and thus are not informative. After eliminating these single-organism entries, 1790 introns were left. Define *intron pattern* to be a 0/1 vector of length eight that defines, for a given intron, which species have that intron and which do not. Note that with eight species there are $2^8 - 9$ different intron patterns (the subtraction corresponds to the assumption that each intron of interest must be in at least two species). Thus, some patterns are represented multiple times. The patterns that appear significantly more often than is expected by chance are considered to be more informative. Let n_i be the number of times pattern i is observed in the intron data, and r_i expected number of occurrences of the pattern by chance. Define $p_i = n_i/r_i$ to be the significance of the intron pattern i. Let S_i be the number of squares, in which an intron with pattern i is involved. In this setting, the greedy square removal algorithm was set to remove iteratively intron patterns that maximize the value S_i/p_i. This provides a trade-off between maximizing the number of removed squares and minimizing the significance of the removed intron patterns. The resulting evolutionary tree was consistent with the Coelomata hypothesis ([1,8,16,71]). In contrast, the compatibility criterion failed to produce a meaningful tree in this case. The counterpart to the Coleometa hypothesis is the Ecdysozoa hypothesis ([3,35,49,56,61]) (see Fig. 3.6).

3.4 FORMATION OF MULTIPROTEIN COMPLEXES

The complexity in biological systems arises not only from various individual protein molecules but also from their organization into systems with numerous interacting partners. In fact, most cellular processes are carried out by *multiprotein complexes*, groups of proteins that bind together to perform a specific task. Some proteins form stable complexes, such as the ribosomal complex that consists of more than 80 proteins and four RNA molecules, while other proteins form transient associations and are part of several complexes at different stages of a cellular process. A better understanding of this higher order organization of proteins into overlapping complexes is an important step toward unveiling functional and evolutionary mechanisms behind biological networks.

Data on protein interactions are collected from the study of individual systems, and more recently through high-throughput experiments. There are many types of protein interactions, but in our quest to understand the dynamics of multiprotein complex formation, we are mostly interested in physical protein interactions and interactions through being a member of the same protein complex, which we briefly review here.

There is a physical interaction between a pair of proteins if they come into a close contact or bind each other. High-throughput discovery of physical protein interactions is based on an experimental technique called *yeast two hybrid* (Y2H) [24]. To determine whether a pair of proteins, A and B, are able to physically interact, A is fused to a DNA binding domain and B is fused to a transcription activation domain. Physical interaction between A and B brings the DNA-binding domain and the transcription activation domain in proximity, which activates the transcription of the corresponding gene called a *reporter gene*. The expression level of the reporter gene is monitored and serves as a measure of physical interaction between proteins A and B. This technique was applied on a genome-wide scale to map physical protein interaction maps for several model organisms, most notably *Saccharomyces cerevisiae* [43,68].

A pair of proteins may not physically interact but may still be members of the same protein complex. High-throughput discovery of this type of protein interaction is based on an experimental technique called *tandem affinity purification followed by mass spectrometry* (TAP/MS) [58]. In the TAP/MS approach, a protein of interest, which is called a *bait*, is tagged and used as a "hook" to pull out proteins that form a complex with it. These proteins are then identified by mass spectrometry techniques. The TAP/MS approach was used not only to map the interactome of *Saccharomyces cerevisiae* [29,30,41,47] but also to study protein complexes involved in different signaling pathways [12].

Protein interactions are routinely represented by a graph, a *protein interaction network*, with vertices being the proteins and edges being the interactions. These graphs offer a static view of protein interactions in the cell, even though some proteins change their interacting partners and participate in different protein complexes. Can the topology of inherently static protein interaction network be used to elucidate the temporal order of dynamic multiprotein complex formation? In this section, we review two such attempts: Farach-Colton et al. [22] used interval graphs to study the way in which various proteins join the ribosome maturation pathway, Zotenko et al. [73] used chordal graph and cographs to study the order in which various complexes are formed during cell signaling and other cellular processes.

3.4.1 Ribosomal Assembly

Ribosomes are massive molecular machines that are the major players in protein synthesis, they use a messenger RNA template to produce a polypeptide chain of newly created protein molecule. In eukaryotic cells, ribosomes consists of two subunits, the so-called 40S (small) and 60S (large) particles, which together account for four ribosomal RNAs and around 80 ribosomal proteins. Recent proteomic studies in *Saccharomyces cerevisiae* have identified around 200 auxiliary proteins that are involved in the assembly of ribosomal subunits but are not part of mature ribosomes. The ribosome synthesis is believed to proceed in an orderly pathway, the *ribosome assembly pathway*, and even though the main players of the pathway are known, little is known about the order in which these proteins join the pathway. For a minireview see [21].

Farach-Colton and colleagues [22] proposed an interval model to represent the assembly pathway of the 60S ribosomal particle. In this model, an auxiliary protein "enters" the pathway at some point and "leaves" the pathway at a latter point to never enter the pathway again. The model further assumes that a protein participates in the pathway through binding to other proteins currently in the pathway, therefore, the assembly line can be thought of as an evolution of one protein complex to which proteins bind as they enter the pathway and from which proteins dissociate as they leave the pathway. Under this model, the protein interaction network that spans the auxiliary proteins involved in the pathway should be an interval graph: each auxiliary protein is an interval and two proteins interact if and only if their intervals overlap. Therefore, the protein interaction network can be used to reconstruct the order in which the auxiliary proteins join the pathway.

Unfortunately, even if the proposed model captures correctly the ribosome assembly mechanism, experimental errors, and incompleteness of protein interaction data may make the protein interaction network loose its interval graph property. To overcome this problem, the authors use a variant of the multisweep LexBFS algorithm [18] to produce an ordering of vertices in the protein interaction network. The algorithm uses several iterations/sweeps of the LexBFS algorithm, where the first LexBFS sweep starts from an arbitrary vertex of the graph and every subsequent LexBFS sweep uses the orderings produced by the previous iterations to choose the start vertex and break ties. If the network is an interval graph, then the ordering produced by the algorithm is an I-ordering. If, on the contrary, the network is not an interval graph then the ordering as a whole won't be an I-ordering but it will induce an I-ordering on the vertices of some interval subgraph of the network; which subgraph would be correctly ordered depends on the order, in which the vertices of the network are encountered by the algorithm. Thus, the authors suggest that computing an I-ordering of vertices of the graph is a reasonable step toward reconstruction, the order in which the auxiliary proteins join the pathway.

The authors tested their approach on the protein interaction network spanning 96 auxiliary proteins involved in the assembly of the 60S particle. As part of the interaction data comes from TAP/MS experiments, it captures only interaction between the 25 bait proteins and other auxiliary proteins in a 96×25 protein interaction matrix. The rows/columns of the matrix were randomly permuted and supplied as an input to the multisweep LexBFS algorithm. The experiment was performed 5000 times and the rank of each protein in each of the 5000 orderings was recorded. Even though the input graph is not an interval graph only two different orderings emerged, which are denoted by $\mathcal{O}_1$ and $\mathcal{O}_2$. If an ordering of vertices is close to an I-ordering, then the absolute difference in rank between any pair of adjacent vertices cannot be arbitrarily large. Therefore, the authors establish significance of the two discovered orderings by the average difference in rank over two sets of protein interactions: a set of protein interactions comprising the network and thus seen by the algorithm, and a set of protein interactions not seen by the algorithm. The authors found that for both seen and unseen interactions, the average difference for the $\mathcal{O}_1$ and $\mathcal{O}_2$ is significantly lower than average differences obtained with: (i) orderings produced by randomly permuting the proteins; (ii) orderings computed by the algorithm on random graph having the same degree distribution as the original input graph.

3.4.2 Multiprotein Complex Formation During Cell Signaling

In order to adapt to their environment, cells have to detect and respond to a vast variety of external stimuli. The detection and translation of these stimuli to a specific cellular response is achieved through a mechanism called *signal transduction pathway* or *signaling pathway*. The general principles of signal propagation through a pathway are common to almost all signaling pathways. First, an extracellular stimulus, usually a chemical ligand, binds to a membrane bound receptor protein. The energy from this interaction changes the state of the receptor protein, thus activating it. The active receptor is able to pass the signal to the *effector system* that generates the cell's response. A variety of proteins, the so-called *signaling proteins*, carry information between the receptor protein and the effector system. *Protein kinases*, for example, are special enzymes that add a phosphate group to certain residues of certain proteins through a process called *phosphorylation*, thus, activating or suppressing the protein's ability to interact with other proteins.

The pattern of protein interaction during cell signaling is an excellent example of transient protein interactions and dynamic complex formation. For example, consider a sequence of events in one of the best-studied signaling pathways, the mating pheromone signaling pathway in *Saccharomyces cerevisiae* (for more information see a review by Bardwell [4]). There are two mating types of yeast cells. When a yeast cell is stimulated by a pheromone secreted by a cell of an opposite mating type, it undergoes a series of physiological changes in preparation for mating, which include significant changes in gene expression of about 200 genes, oriented growth toward the partner, and changes in the cell cycle. Signal propagation through the pathway is achieved through interaction of some 20 proteins, a schematic representation of the pathway and description of corresponding protein interactions are given in Fig. 3.7.

Research efforts required to obtain the amount of detailed knowledge about a signaling pathway as is currently available for the mating pheromone pathway is enormous. Can the readily available high-throughput experimental data on protein

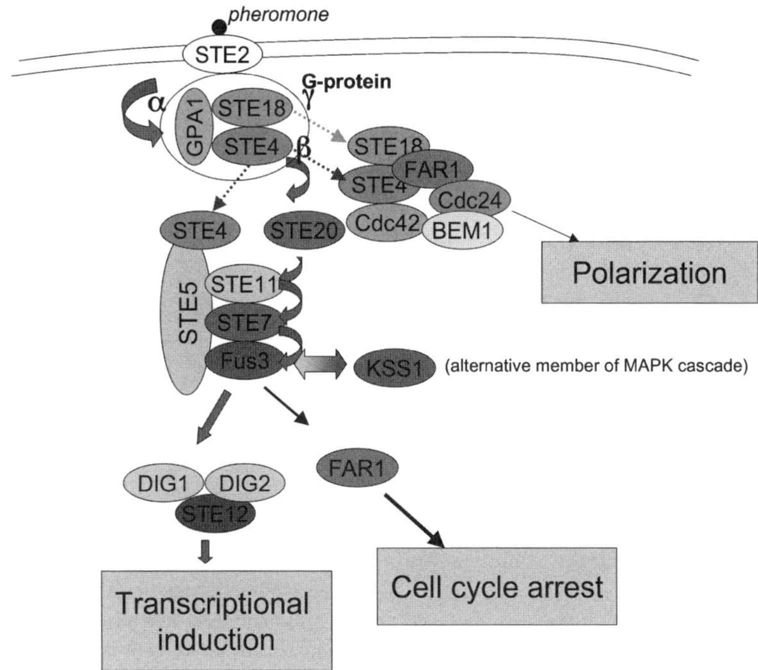

FIGURE 3.7 A schematic representation of the key components of the pheromone signaling pathway assembled from information in [4,38,50]. A pheromone peptide binds a G-protein coupled receptor or GPCR (STE2/STE3). Activated receptor binds and activates a trimeric G-protein: G_α subunit (GPA1), G_β subunit (STE4), and G_γ subunit (STE18). The flow of information then proceeds via a three-tiered mitogen-activated protein kinase (MAPK) cascade and results in activation of STE12 transcription factor and subsequent upregulation of about 200 genes. The MAPK cascade also activates FAR1 protein, which is hypothesized to trigger a G_1 cell cycle arrest through an interaction with CDC28, a master regulator of the cell cycle. The MAPK cascade consists of three protein kinases STE11, STE7, and either FUS3 or KSS1, which activate each other sequentially through phosphorylation. Thus, STE11 activates STE7, which in turn activates either FUS3 or KSS1. The phosphorylation process is enhanced through a presence of a scaffold protein STE5, which binds and thus colocalizes all three components of the MAPK cascade. Activated FUS3 and KSS1 proteins in turn bind their substrates, DIG1/DIG2/STE12 complex and FAR1 protein. Another branch of the pathway, which includes proteins STE4, STE18, FAR1, CDC24, CDC42, and BEM1 is responsible for triggering a "polarized growth toward the mating partner" or polarization response.

interactions be used to elucidate some information about the pathway, such as the order of complex formation during signal propagation? In a recent work Zotenko et al. [73] have proposed a graph-theoretic method, Complex Overlap Decomposition (COD), that tries to recover the order of protein complex formation from the topology of protein interaction network that spans the pathway components. (The pathway components can be obtained from literature. Alternatively, putative pathway

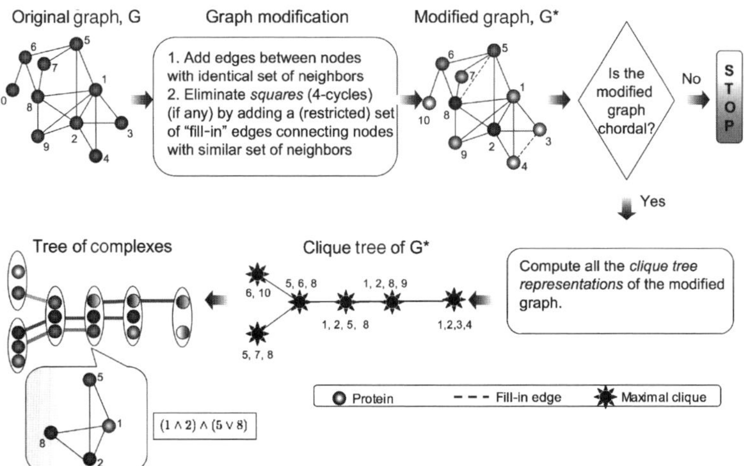

FIGURE 3.8 An illustration of the Complex Overlap Decomposition (COD) method. An edge, (3, 4), connecting a pair of weak siblings is added to the graph. A fill-in edge between proteins 5 and 8 is added to eliminate all five 4-cycles in the graph: {5, 6, 8, 7}, {1, 5, 7, 8}, {2, 5, 7, 8}, {1, 5, 6, 8}, and {2, 5, 6, 8}. If the modified graph is chordal, all clique tree representations are computed and each such representation is extended into a *Tree of Complexes* representation of the original graph. The Tree of Complexes is constructed by projecting each maximal clique in the modified graph, G^*, to a functional group in the original graph G. For example, a four node maximal clique, {1, 2, 5, 8}, in G^* is projected to a four node functional group in G, by removing a fill-in edge (5, 8). Each functional group is represented by a Boolean expression, such as $(1 \wedge 2) \wedge (5 \vee 8)$, which means that the functional group contains two variants of a complex, {1, 2, 5} and {1, 2, 8}. This figure is reproduced from [73].

components can be automatically extracted from genome-wide protein interaction networks by computational methods [63,66].)

The main idea behind the COD method, which is depicted in Fig. 3.8, is to provide a representation of the protein interaction network that is analogous to a clique tree representation for chordal graphs, but in which nodes are cographs (representing functional groups) rather than maximal cliques (representing protein complexes). A *functional group* is either a protein complex (maximal clique in the protein interaction network) or a set of alternative variants of such complex. Such a representation accounts for two phenomena that are clearly illustrated in the pheromone signaling pathway described above: (i) the dynamic complex formation does not always follow a linear pathway but rather has a tree structure, where various branches correspond to the activation of different response systems; (ii) there may be several variants of a protein complex, such as MAPK complex centered at the scaffold protein, which may include either $KSS1$ or $FUS3$ proteins but not both. It should be noted that cographs and their modular decomposition were previously used by Gagneur et al. to expose the hierarchical organization of protein complexes [27].

If a set of functional groups in a network were known then each functional group could be turned into a clique through addition of missing edges and clique tree construction algorithm could be applied to the modified network. As the functional groups are not known in advance, the authors propose a heuristic for their automatic delineation, where a set of edges is added to the network so that the maximal cliques in the modified network correspond to putative functional groups.

The COD method's edge addition strategy and its biological motivation builds on a functional interpretation of weak siblings in the network. Recall that a pair of nodes in a graph are weak siblings if they are not adjacent to each other but are adjacent to exactly the same set of nodes. In terms of protein interaction networks, weak siblings are proteins that interact with the same set of proteins but do not interact with each other. In particular, proteins that can substitute for each other in a protein interaction network may have this property. Similarly, weak siblings may correspond to a pair of proteins that belong to the same protein complex but are not connected by an edge due to missing data or an experimental error. Therefore, the heuristic first connects every pair of weak siblings by an edge. If the modified graph is not chordal an additional set of edges that connect pairs of proteins close to being weak siblings is added; each such edge is a diagonal in one or more *squares*, chordless cycles of length four, in the graph. The heuristic finds a minimum cost set of diagonals that eliminates all the squares in the graph, where the cost of a diagonal is inversely proportional to the amount of overlap between the neighborhoods of its end points.

If the modification step succeeds, that is, the modified graph is chordal, all the clique tree representations of the modified graph are constructed and then extended to the *Tree of Complexes representations* of the original graph. The COD algorithm keeps track of all the edge additions and uses this information to delineate functional groups by projecting each maximal clique onto the original network and removing all introduced edges contained in the clique. For example, in the modified graph of Fig. 3.8, a maximal clique with four nodes, $\{1, 2, 5, 8\}$, is projected to a functional group by removing an edge connecting proteins 5 and 8. This functional group contains two variants of a protein complex, $\{1, 2, 5\}$ and $\{1, 2, 8\}$, which are compactly represented by the Boolean expression $(1 \wedge 2) \wedge (5 \vee 8)$. If, on the contrary, the modified graph is not chordal, the COD method stops without producing the representation.

The authors demonstrated the effectiveness of their approach by decomposing protein interaction networks for two signaling pathways: the mating pheromone signaling pathway and the NF-kB signaling pathway. Here, we apply the COD method to the pheromone signaling pathway, where the pathway components were taken from [4] (Table 1) and protein interactions that span the pathway components from the DIP database [62] (version 01/16/2006; core set of interactions). The network is shown in Fig. 3.9a. Since proteins STE2/STE3 are disconnected from the rest of the components, we have removed them from the network in our analysis. The COD method adds three diagonals to eliminate eleven squares in the network: (STE4,BEM1), (FUS3, KSS1), and (GPA1, STE5), which results in

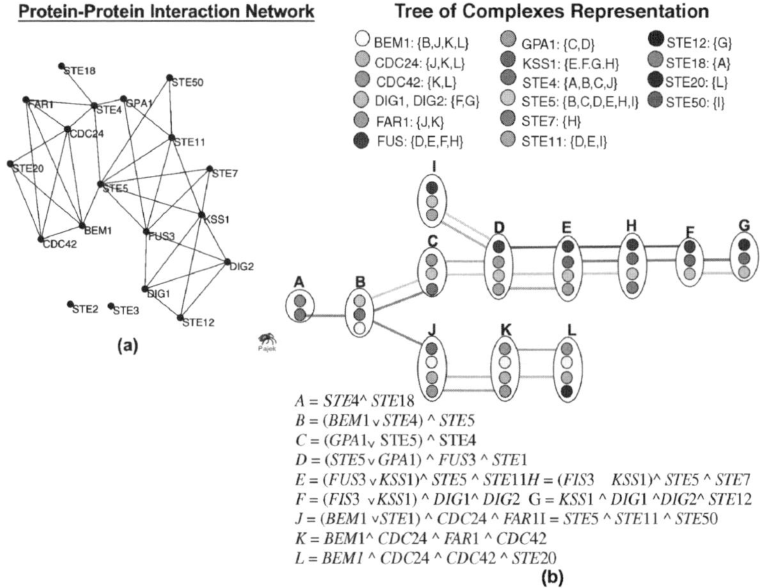

FIGURE 3.9 The mating pheromone signaling pathway. (**a**) The protein interaction network for the components of the pathway. The network was drawn with Pajek [5]. (**b**) One of the twelve possible Tree of Complexes representations for the network.The activation of the pathway corresponds to node A in the tree that contains the G_β (STE4) protein. From node A, the Tree of Complexes splits into two branches. One branch roughly corresponds to the MAPK cascade activated response, while another branch roughly corresponds to the polarization response. The MAPK cascade branch spans four nodes in the tree: I, D, E, and H. The activation of transcription factor complex by $FUS3$ and $KSS1$ is in nodes F and G. The polarization branch spans nodes J, K, and L.

twelve functional groups listed in Fig. 3.9 along with the corresponding Boolean expressions. There are twelve Tree of Complexes representations for this protein interaction network one of which is shown in Fig. 3.9b. All the representations agree on the interconnection pattern between functional groups, $B - E$, H, and $J - L$. The difference between various tree variants comes from how functional groups A, $F - G$, and I are connected to the rest of the tree: (i) functional group A can be attached either through (A, C), or (A, B), or (A, J); (ii) functional group I through (I, E), or (I, D); (iii) functional group F through (F, E) or (F, H).

Compare the representation in Fig. 3.9b to the schematic representation of the pheromone signaling pathway shown in Fig. 3.7. Using only protein interaction information, the COD method was able to recover two branches of the pathway, the MAPK cascade branch and the polarization branch. The MAPK cascade branch spans four nodes in the tree: I, D, E, and H. The polarization branch spans nodes J, K, and L.

ACKNOWLEDGMENTS

This work was supported by the Intramural Research Program of the NIH, National Library of Medicine.

REFERENCES

1. Adoutte A, Balavoine G, Lartillot N, Lespinet O, Prud'homme B, de Rosa R. The new animal phylogeny: reliability and implications. *Proc Nat Acad Sci USA* 2000;97:4453–4456.
2. Agarwala R, Fernandez-Baca D. A polynomial time algorithm for the perfect phylogeny problem when the number of character states is fixed. *SIAM J Comput* 1994;23:1216–1224.
3. Aguinaldo AM, Turbeville JM, Linford LS, Rivera MC, Garey JR, Raff RA, Lake JA. Evidence for a clade of nematodes, arthropods and other moulting animals. *Nature* 1997;387:489–493.
4. Bardwell L. A walk-through of the yeast mating pheromone response pathway. *Peptides* 2005;26:339–350.
5. Batagelj V, Mrvar A. Pajek—Program for large network analysis. *Connections* 1998; 2:47–57.
6. Benzer S. On the topology of genetic fine structure. *Proc Nat Acad Sci USA* 1959;45: 1607–1620.
7. Bernstein PA, Goodman N. Power of natural semijoins. *SIAM J Comput* 1981;10:751–771.
8. Blair JE, Ikeo K, Gojobori T, Hedges SB. The evolutionary position of nematodes. *BMC Evol Biol* 2002;2:7.
9. Bodlaender H, Fellows M, Warnow TJ. Two strikes against perferct phylogeny. *ICALP*; 1992.
10. Bodlaender H, Kloks T. A simple linear time algorithm for triangulating three-colored graphs. *J Algorithms* 1993;15:160–172.
11. Booth KS, Lueker GS. Testing for consecutive ones property, interval graphs, and graph planarity using PQ-Tree algorithms. *J Comput Syst Sci* 1976;13:335–379.
12. Bouwmeester T, Bauch A, Ruffner H, Angrand PO, Bergamini G, Croughton K, Cruciat C, Eberhard D, Gagneur J, Ghidelli S. A physical and functional map of the human TNF-alpha/NF-kappaB signal transduction pathway. *Nat Cell Biol* 2004;6:97–105.
13. Buneman P. A characterization of rigid circuit graphs. *Discrete Math* 1974;9:202–215.
14. Cai L. Fixed-parameter tractability of graph modification problems for hereditary properties. *Inf Process Lett* 1996;58:171–176.
15. Cavalli-Sforza LL, Edwards AWF. Phylogenetic analysis. Models and Estimation Procedures. *Evolution* 1967;21:550–570.
16. Ciccarelli FD, Doerks T, von Mering C, Creevey CJ, Snel B, Bork P. Toward automatic reconstruction of a highly resolved tree of life. *Science*, 2006;311:1283–1287.

17. Cormen TH, Leiserson CE, Rivest RL, Stein C. *Introduction to algorithms*. 2nd ed. The MIT Press; 2001.
18. Corneil DG, Olariu S, Stewart L. The ultimate interval graph recognition algorithm? *Proceedings of the 9th ACM-SIAM Simposium on Discrete Algorithms (SODA)*; 1998.
19. Corneil DG, Perl Y, Stewart L. Complement reducible graphs. *Discrete Appl Math* 1981;3:163–174.
20. Corneil DG, Perl Y, Stewart LK. A linear time recognition algorithm for cographs. *SIAM J Comput* 1985;14:926–934.
21. Dlakic M. The ribosomal subunit assembly line. *Genome Biol* 2005;6:234.
22. Farach-Colton M, Huang Y, Woolford JLL. Discovering temporal relations in molecular pathways using protein–protein interactions. *Proceedings of the 8th Annual International Conference on Research in Computational Molecular Biology*; San Diego. California: USA; 2004. pp.150–156.
23. Felsenstein J. *Inferring phylogenies*. Sinauer Associates; 2004.
24. Fields S, Song O. A novel genetic system to detect protein–protein interactions. *Nature* 1989;340:245–246.
25. Fitch WM. Toward defining the course of evolution: Minimum change for a specified tree topology. *Syst Zool* 1971;20:406–416.
26. Fulkerson DR, Gross OA. Incidence matrices and interval graphs. *Pacific J Math* 1965;15:835–855.
27. Gagneur J, Krause R, Bouwmeester T, Casari G. Modular decomposition of protein interaction networks. *Genome Biol* 2004;5:R57.
28. Garey MR, Johnson DS. *Computers and intractability: A guide to the theory of NP-completeness*. W.H. Freeman and Company; 1979.
29. AC Gavin, et al. Proteome survey reveals modularity of the yeast cell machinery. *Nature* 2006;440:631–636.
30. Gavin AC, Bosche M, Krause R, Grandi P, Marzioch M, Bauer A, Schultz J, Rick JM, Michon AM, Cruciat CM. Functional organization of the yeast proteome by systematic analysis of protein complexes. *Nature* 2002;415:141–147.
31. Gavril F. The intersection graphs of subtrees in trees are exactly the chordal graphs. *J Comb Theory B* 1974;16:47–56.
32. Gavril F. Generating the maximum spanning trees of a weighted graph. *J Algorithm* 1987;8:592–597.
33. George A, Gilbert JR, Liu JWH, editors. *Graph theory and sparse matrix computations*, chapter 1. Springer: New York; 1993.
34. Gilmore PC, Hoffman AJ. A characterization of comparability graphs and of interval graphs. *Canad J Math* 1964;16:539–548.
35. Giribet G, Distel DL, Polz M, Sterrer W, Wheeler WC. Triploblastic relationships with emphasis on the acoelomates and the position of Gnathostomulida, Cycliophora, Plathelminthes, and Chaetognatha: A combined approach of 18S rDNA sequences and morphology. *Syst Biol* 2000;49(3):539–562.
36. Golumbic MC. *Algorithmic Graph Theory and Perfect Graphs*, Vol. 57 of *Annals of Discrete Mathematics*. 2nd ed. Elsevier, 2004.

37. Golumbic MC, Hartman IB-A, editors. *Graph Theory, Combinatorics and Algorithms: Interdisciplinary Applications*, Chapter 4, Springer; 2005; pp. 63–105.

38. Gruhler A, Olsen JV, Mohammed S, Mortensen P, Faergeman NJ, Mann M, Jensen ON. Quantitative phosphoproteomics applied to the yeast pheromone signaling pathway. *Mol Cell Proteomics* 2005;4(3):310–327.

39. Gusfield D. Efficient algorithms for inferring evolutionary trees. *Networks* 1991;21:19–28.

40. Ho C, Lee RCT. Counting clique trees and computing perfect elimination schemes in parallel. *Inform Proc Lett* 1989;31:61–68.

41. Ho Y, Gruhler A, Heilbut A, Bader GD, Moore L, Adams SL, Millar A, Taylor P, Bennett K, Boutilier K. Systematic identification of protein complexes in saccharomyces cerevisiae by mass spectrometry. *Nature* 2002;415:180–183.

42. Idury R, Schaffer A. Triangulating three-colored graphs in linear time and linear space. *SIAM J Discrete Math* 1993;6:289–294.

43. Ito T, Chiba T, Ozawa R, Yoshida M, Hattori M, Sakaki Y. A comprehensive two-hybrid analysis to explore the yeast protein interactome. *Proc Nat Acad Sci USA* 2001;98:4569–4574.

44. Kannan S, Warnow TJ. Triangulating three-colored graphs. *SIAM J Discrete Math* 1992;5:249–258.

45. Kannan S, Warnow TJ. Inferring evolutionary history from DNA sequences. *SIAM J Comput* 1994;23:713–737.

46. Kaplan H, Shamir R, Tarjan RE. Tractability of parameterized completion problems on chordal, strongly chordal, and proper interval graphs. *SIAM J Comput* 1999;28:1906–1922.

47. Krogan NJ et al. Global landscape of protein complexes in the yeast Saccharomyces cerevisiae. *Nature* 2006;440(7084):637–643.

48. Lewis JM, Yannakakis M. The node-deletion problem for hereditary properties is NP-complete. *J Comput Syst Sci* 1980;20:219–230.

49. Mallatt J, Winchell CJ. Testing the new animal phylogeny: first use of combined large-subunit and small-subunit rRNA gene sequences to classify the protostomes. *Mol Biol Evol* 2002;19:289–301.

50. Matheos D, Metodiev M, Muller E, Stone D, Rose MD. Pheromoneinduced polarization is dependent on the Fus3p MAPK acting through the formin Bni1p. *J Cell Biol* 2004;165(1):99–109.

51. McKee TA, McMorris FR. Topics in intersection graph theory. *SIAM Monographs on Discrete Mathematics and Applications. SIAM*; 1999.

52. McMorris FR, Warnow TJ, Wimer T. Triangulating vertex-colored graphs. *SIAM J Dis Math* 1994;7:196–306.

53. Middendorf M, Ziv E, Wiggins CH. Inferring network mechanisms: The Drosophila melanogaster protein interaction network. *Proc Nat Acad Sci USA* 2005;102:3192–3197.

54. Milo R, Shen-Orr S, Itzkovitz S, Kashtan N, Chklovskii D, Alon U. Network motifs: Simple building blocks of complex networks. *Science* 2002;298:824–827.

55. Mohring RH, Radermacher FJ. Substitution decomposition for discrete structures and connections with combinatorial optimization. *Ann Discrete Math* 1984;19:257–356.

56. Peterson KJ, Eernisse DJ. Animal phylogeny and the ancestry of bilaterians: Inferences from morphology and 18S rDNA gene sequences. *Evol Dev* 2001;3(3):170–205.
57. Przytycka TM. An important connection between network motifs and parsimony models. *RECOMB*; 2006.
58. Rigaut G, Shevchenko A, Rutz B, Wilm M, Mann M, Séraphin B. A generic protein purification method for protein complex characterization and proteome exploration. *Nat Biotechnol* 1999;17(10):1030–1032.
59. Rogozin IB, Wolf YI, Sorokin AV, Mirkin BG, Koonin EV. Remarkable interkingdom conservation of intron positions and massive, lineage-specific intron loss and gain in eukaryotic evolution. *Curr Biol* 2003;13:1512–1517.
60. Rose DJ, Tarjan RE. Algorithmic aspects of vertex elimination. *SIAM J Appl Math* 1978;34:176–197.
61. Roy SW, Gilbert W. Resolution of a deep animal divergence by the pattern of intron conservation. *Proc Nat Acad Sci USA* 2005;102(12):4403–4408.
62. Salwinski L, Miller CS, Smith AJ, Pettit FK, Bowie JU, Eisenberg D. The Database of Interacting Proteins: the 2004 update. *Nucl Acid Res* 2004;32:D449–D451.
63. Scott J, Ideker T, Karp RM, Sharan R. Efficient algorithms for detecting signaling pathways in protein interaction networks. *J Comput Biol* 2006;13(2):133–144.
64. Shamir R. Advanced topics in graph theory. Technical report, Tel-Aviv University; 1994.
65. Shen-Orr S, Milo R, Mangan S, Alon U. Network motifs in the transcriptional regulation network of escherichia coli. *Nat Genet* 2002;31.
66. Steffen M, Petti A, Aach J, D'haeseleer P, Church G. Automated modelling of signal transduction networks. *BMC Bioinformatics* 2002;3:34.
67. Tarjan RE, Yannakakis M. Simple linear-time algorithms to test chordality of graphs, test acyclicity of hypergraphs, and selectively reduce acyclic hypergraphs. *SIAM J Comput* 1984;13(3):566–579.
68. Uetz P, Giot L, Cagney G, Mansfield TA, Judson RS, Knight JR, Lockshon D, Narayan V, Srinivasan M, Pochart P. A comprehensive analysis of protein–protein interactions in Saccharomyces cerevisiae. *Nature* 2000;403:623–627.
69. Walter JR. *Representation of rigid circuit graphs*. Ph.D. thesis, Wayne State University; 1972.
70. Wilson EO. A consistency test for phylogenies based on contemporaneous species. *Syst Zool* 1965;14:214–220.
71. Wolf YI, Rogozin IB, Koonin EV. Coelomata and not Ecdysozoa: Evidence from genome-wide phylogenetic analysis. *Genome Res* 2004;14:29–36.
72. Yannakakis M. Computing the minimum fill-in is NP-complete. *SIAM J Algebraic Discrete Method* 1981;2:77–79.
73. Zotenko E, Guimarães KS, Jothi R, Przytycka TM. Decomposition of overlapping protein complexes: A graph theoretical method for analyzing static and dynamic protein associations. *Algorithms Mol Biol* 2006;1(1):7.

4

ADVANCES IN HIDDEN MARKOV MODELS FOR SEQUENCE ANNOTATION

BROŇA BREJOVÁ

Department of Biological Statistics and Computational Biology, Cornell University, Ithaca, NY, USA

DANIEL G. BROWN

Cheriton School of Computer Science, University of Waterloo, Waterloo, Ontario, Canada

TOMÁŠ VINAŘ

Department of Biological Statistics and Computational Biology, Cornell University, Ithaca, NY, USA

4.1 INTRODUCTION

One of the most basic tasks of bioinformatics is to identify features in a biological sequence. Whether these features are the binding sites of a protein, the regions of a DNA sequence that are most subjected to selective pressures, or coding sequences found in an expressed sequence tag, this phase is fundamental to the process of sequence analysis.

While a variety of computational tools that people have been needing to perform this task have been used over the course of the time, the currently dominant tool in biological sequence annotation is the hidden Markov model (HMM). HMMs have been used in so many contexts over the course of the last 15 years that they almost

Bioinformatics Algorithms: Techniques and Applications, Edited by Ion I. Măndoiu and Alexander Zelikovsky

require no introduction. They are used in computational gene finders to predict the structure of genes in newly sequenced genomes. They are used in protein sequence analysis to identify substructural elements. They are used to discover regulatory sequences in DNA to identify ancestry patterns in pedigrees, and truly for almost any feature detection problem in biological sequences.

As such, it may seem that their use is so routinized that there is nothing more to learn about them: that 15 years of their use in biological sequence analysis mined the field for all of its interesting problems many years ago. Fortunately, this is anything but the case. As the fields of genomics and proteomics advance, a variety of new challenges have come to fore in the algorithmic analysis of HMMs. For example, if we have a large amount of training data and can train an HMM to closely model the many complex features of the data, will that necessarily improve the quality of our predictions on new data? How can we properly model the distributions of the lengths of complex sequence features in HMMs? How can we incorporate evolutionary conservation information into the creation of HMMs that properly model DNA sequences and into the algorithms for their analysis?

This chapter considers the use of HMMs in sequence analysis, starting from the simplest cases (simple HMMs, with simple structures, simple training algorithms, and simple decoding procedures) and moving to situations of great complexity, incorporating very recent ideas from machine learning theory. We present the basic algorithms and their extensions, and give suggestions of directions where future research can be most useful. Throughout, we make reference to the important applications in which these algorithms are used and to why the field has experienced continuous advancement over the last many years.

4.2 HIDDEN MARKOV MODELS FOR SEQUENCE ANNOTATION

In this section, we illustrate the use of HMMs for biological sequence annotation. We will focus on the simplification of one of the most prominent uses of HMMs in sequence annotation: the problem of gene finding. Assume we are given a section of a DNA sequence containing a single protein-coding gene, and our goal is to locate the regions of this sequence that code for a protein. In eukaryotes, such regions may be interrupted by noncoding segments called *introns*. Therefore, our task is to label each nucleotide of the DNA sequence with one of the three labels, indicating whether the nucleotide comes from a coding region, an intron, or an intergenic region (see Fig. 4.1).

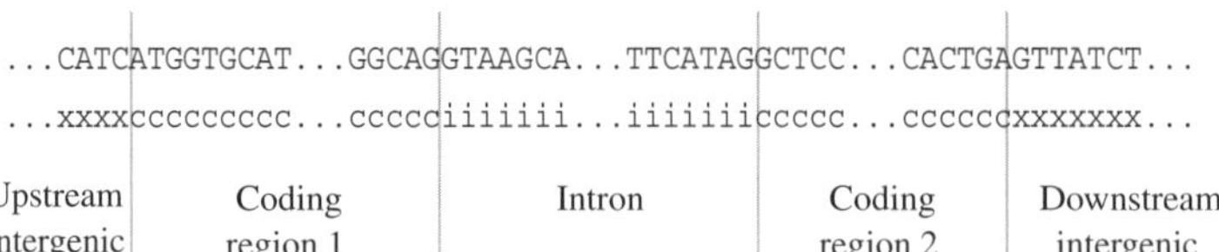

FIGURE 4.1 In gene finding, the goal is to label each nucleotide of a given DNA sequence as coding (c), intron (i), or intergenic (x).

More generally, the problem of labeling every symbol of a biological sequence with its functional category is the *sequence annotation problem*, and such a sequence of labels is an *annotation* of a sequence.

For our gene finding problem, we use our knowledge of gene structure and a collection of training data to design an HMM that characterizes typical DNA sequences and their gene annotations. Then we use this model to find the highest probability annotations for novel, unannotated DNA sequences.

4.2.1 Hidden Markov Models

An HMM is a generative probabilistic model for modeling sequence data that come from a finite alphabet. An HMM consists of a finite set of states and three sets of parameters called the initial, emission, and transition probabilities. The initial probability s_k is defined for each state k of the model. The transition probability $a_{k,\ell}$ is defined for each pair of states (k, ℓ), and the emission probability $e_{k,b}$ is defined for each state k and each symbol b of the output alphabet. The initial probabilities form a probability distribution, as do the transition probabilities $a_{k,\ell}$ at each state k and the emission probabilities $e_{k,b}$ for each k.

An HMM generates a sequence step by step, one symbol in each step. First, a start state is randomly generated according to the initial probabilities. Then, in each step, the model randomly generates one symbol and moves to a new state. Both the new symbol and the next state depend only on the current state. If the current state is k, the symbol b will be generated with probability $e_{k,b}$, and the next state will be ℓ with probability $a_{k,\ell}$.

In n steps, the HMM generates a sequence $X = x_1, \ldots, x_n$ and traverses a sequence of states (or *state path*) $H = h_1, \ldots, h_n$. For a fixed length n, the HMM defines a probability distribution over all possible sequences X and all possible state paths H; in particular, the probability that the model will traverse the state path H and generate the sequence X is the following product of the model parameters:

$$\Pr(H, X) = s_{h_1} \left(\prod_{i=1}^{n-1} e_{h_i,x_i} a_{h_i,h_{i+1}} \right) e_{h_n,x_n}. \tag{4.1}$$

4.2.2 Choosing the Topology and the Parameters of an HMM

To approach our gene finding problem, we will first build an HMM that models DNA sequences and their corresponding genes. Our model will have four states: one state representing the intergenic region upstream of the gene, one representing coding regions of the gene, one representing introns, and one representing the region downstream of the gene. Each state will emit symbols over the alphabet {A,C,G,T}. In this way, the sequence generated by the HMM will represent a DNA sequence, with the corresponding state path identifying its correct annotation.

Transitions between some pairs of states should never occur. There will be no transitions between introns and intergenic regions, nor between the two states representing

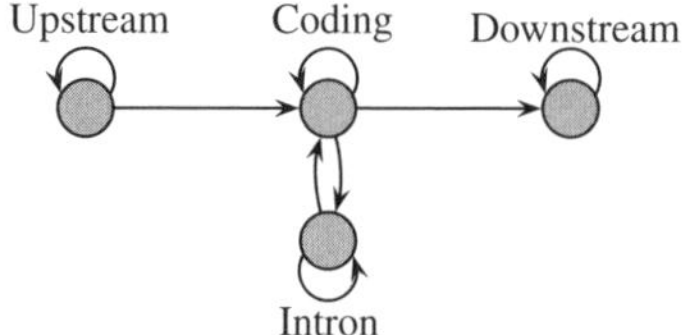

FIGURE 4.2 Topology of a simplified HMM for gene finding.

upstream and downstream intergenic regions. To visualize the structure of the HMM (also called its *topology*), we use a directed graph, where vertices correspond to the states and edges to nonzero probability transitions (see Fig. 4.2).

Next, we determine the emission and transition probabilities for each state, using a *training set* T containing sequences with known annotation. Because we have designated each state in our model to represent a region of a particular function, we can use these annotations to determine the proper state path H_i for each of the sequences X_i in the training set T. We would like our generative model to generate sequences whose distributions and annotations are similar to those observed in the training set T. Formally, using the *maximum likelihood estimation* principle, we want to set the emission and transition probabilities to maximize the likelihood of the training data: that is, to maximize $\prod_i \Pr(H_i, X_i)$ over all possible parameters for the model. To maximize this probability it is sufficient to count the frequency of using each transition in the training set to estimate the transition probabilities and the frequency of emission of each symbol in each state to estimate the emission probabilities. In other contexts, this training process can be quite a bit more complicated; for example, when the training set T is unannotated or when a given sequence and a annotation could correspond to multiple-paths in the HMM; we discuss this scenario in Section 4.6.

However, in our simple case, we have created a probabilistic model of sequences and their annotations. In the next section, we show how to use this probabilistic model to annotate a novel DNA sequence.

4.2.3 HMM Decoding: The Viterbi Algorithm

Once the HMM topology is set and its parameters trained, we can use it to find genes in a newly unlabeled DNA sequence X. In other words, we seek an appropriate state path H^* that best explains how the model could have produced X; this process is called *HMM decoding*.

The simplest measure of "best" is to find the path that has the maximum probability in the HMM, given the sequence X. Recall that the model gives the joint probabilities $\Pr(H, X)$ for all sequence/annotation pairs, and as such, it also gives the posterior probability $\Pr(H|X) = \Pr(H, X)/\Pr(X)$, for every possible state path H through the model, conditioned on the sequence X. We will seek the path with maximum posterior probability. Given that the denominator $\Pr(X)$ is constant in the conditional probability formula for a given sequence X, maximizing the posterior probability is equivalent to finding the state path H^* that maximizes the joint probability $\Pr(H^*, X)$.

The most probable state path can be found in time linear in the sequence length by the Viterbi algorithm [30,76]. This simple dynamic programming algorithm computes the optimal paths for all prefixes of X; when we move from the i-length prefix to the $(i+1)$-length prefix, we need only add one edge to one of the precomputed optimal paths for the i-length prefix.

For every position i in the sequence and every state k, the algorithm finds the most probable state path $h_1, \ldots, h_i$ to generate the first i symbols of X, provided that $h_i = k$. The value $V[i, k]$ stores the joint probability $\Pr(h_1, \ldots, h_i, x_1, \ldots, x_i)$ of this optimal state path. Again, if $h_1, \ldots, h_i$ is the most probable state path generating $x_1, \ldots, x_i$ that ends in state h_i, then $h_1, \ldots, h_{i-1}$ must be the most probable state path generating $x_1, \ldots, x_{i-1}$ and ending in state h_{i-1}. To compute $V[i, k]$, we consider all possible states as candidates for the second-to-last state, h_{i-1} and select the one that leads to the most probable state path, as expressed in the following recurrence:

$$V[i,k] = \begin{cases} s_k \cdot e_{k,x_1}, & \text{if } i = 1 \\ \max_\ell V[i-1,\ell] \cdot a_{\ell,k} \cdot e_{k,x_i}, & \text{otherwise.} \end{cases} \tag{4.2}$$

The probability $\Pr(H^*, X)$ is then the maximum over all states k of $V[n, k]$, and the most probable state path H^* can be traced back through the dynamic programming table by standard techniques. The running time of the algorithm is $O(nm^2)$, where n is the length of the sequence and m is the number of states in the HMM.

4.2.4 More Complex HMMs

We have demonstrated the basic techniques needed to use HMMs for sequence annotation. However, the models actually used in practice are more complex than the one shown in Fig. 4.2. We rarely have only one state for each feature in the HMM, and it is quite possible that we need to incorporate more positional dependencies into the probabilities of the HMM. We will explain this in the context of our gene-finding example.

First, note that coding regions are composed of codons that each encode one amino acid. Therefore, it is advisable to model coding regions by a three-state cycle rather than a single state to properly keep this structure. Codons can be interrupted by an intron, so we use multiple copies of the intron submodel, a technique that originated in finite state machines to enforce that the next coding region after the intron starts at the proper codon position. Boundaries of coding regions are marked by special sequence signals that require additional states in the model. Finally, DNA sequence usually contains multiple genes on both strands. Figure 4.3 shows an HMM topology that encodes all of these additional constraints.

In addition, as noted, we may want to incorporate positional dependencies into the HMM. This is most often done by allowing higher order states. In a state of order o, the probability of generating the character b is a function of the o previously generated characters (all states in a standard HMM are of order zero). The emission table has the form $e_{k,b_1,\ldots,b_o,b}$, where $\sum_b e_{k,b_1,\ldots,b_o,b} = 1$ for a fixed state k and characters

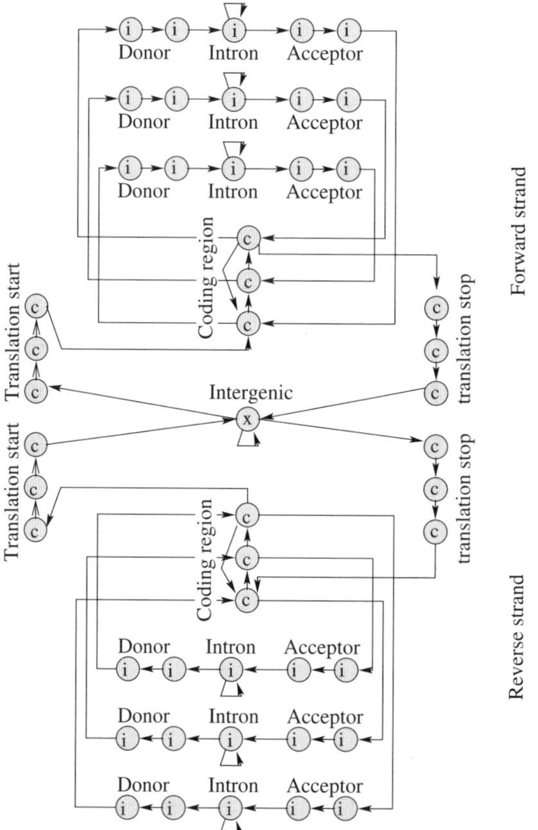

FIGURE 4.3 Topology of a simple HMM gene finder. The acceptor and donor regions correspond to the signals at the ends and beginnings of introns.

$b_1, \ldots, b_o$. In an HMM with all states of order o, Formula (4.1) generalizes as follows (we ignore the special case of the first o characters):

$$\Pr(H, X) = s_{h_1} \left(\prod_{i=1}^{n-1} e_{h_i, x_{i-o}, \ldots, x_i} a_{h_i h_{i+1}} \right) e_{h_n, x_{n-o}, \ldots, x_n}. \tag{4.3}$$

The Viterbi algorithm for finding the most probable state path can be adapted easily to handle higher order states with the same running time. Similarly, training the parameters of higher order HMMs by maximum likelihood is straightforward using procedures analogous to those shown in Section 4.2.2. HMMs for gene finding typically use states of order between two and five.

4.2.5 More Examples of Biological Sequence Annotation with HMMs

The use of HMMs in sequence annotation is not only limited to gene finding, but they have also been used in a host of applications across the field.

One of the first applications of HMMs in bioinformatics was to segment DNA sequences into regions with similar GC content levels [20]. Similarly, we can partition the sequence to homogeneous regions based on other criteria, for example, the degree of sequence conservation in multiple species [69].

In DNA sequences, eukaryote and prokaryote gene finding is the dominant HMM application. In eukaryotic organisms the difficulty in the problem stems from the presence of introns and the often small, and highly variable, proportion of protein coding sequence in the genome [15,41,70]. The existence of alternative splicing also complicates the field, as individual positions of a sequence may be found in both intron and exon depending on the transcript, though recent work [3,17] has moved in this direction. Gene finding in prokaryotes and viruses needs to handle overlapping genes and the problem of insufficient training data in newly sequenced genomes [46,51]. HMMs can also be used for other tasks related to gene finding, such as promoter detection [57].

Proteins are generally hard to analyze from sequence only since their function is largely determined by their fold. Amino acids that are distant in the sequence may interact once the protein is folded because they are physically close. However, HMMs can successfully be applied to recognize aspects of protein function that are governed by motifs located in contiguous stretches of the sequence.

One such example is transmembrane protein topology prediction. Transmembrane proteins are partially embedded inside the cellular membrane. The topology of such a protein identifies the regions that are found in transmembrane helices (parts traversing the membrane), cytoplasmic loops (parts inside the cell), and noncytoplasmic loops (parts extending outside the cell).

Figure 4.4 shows an overview of a simple HMM that could be used for predicting these topologies. The HMM topology enforces the simple physical constraint that cytoplasmic loops must be separated from noncytoplasmic loops by transmembrane helices. Krogh et al. [44] and Tusnády and Simon [73] used similar HMMs in their topology prediction tools. A special class of transmembrane proteins, β-barrel proteins, is also successfully modeled by HMMs [26,49]. More generally, we can try to predict the secondary structure of arbitrary proteins, labeling each amino acid as a part of an α-helix, β-sheet, or loop [6,16,33].

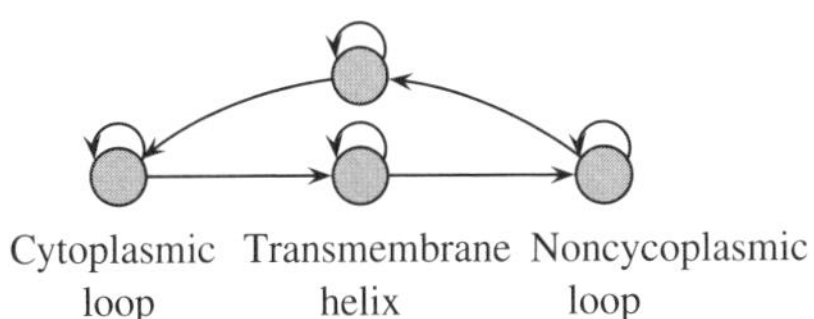

FIGURE 4.4 Simplified topology of an HMM for transmembrane topology prediction.

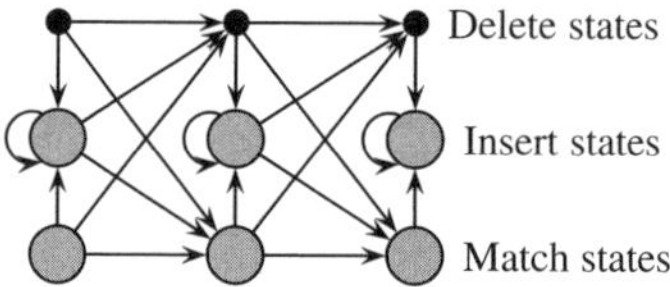

FIGURE 4.5 A section of a profile HMM with three match states. Delete states are silent; that is, they do not emit any characters.

HMMs are closely related to the problem of aligning two DNA or protein sequences. In Section 4.5 we discuss pair HMMs, which provide a probabilistic framework for scoring pairwise alignments.

In protein sequence analysis, HMMs are often used to align the residues of a newly sequenced protein to a model of a family of homologous proteins. This is most typically done using a prominent class of hidden Markov models called profile HMMs [43]. A profile HMM has a regular structure consisting of a match state for every conserved column of the multiple alignment and insert and delete states that model insertions and deletions in the alignment, as shown in Fig. 4.5. Thanks to their regular structure, they can be created automatically and stored in a database, such as Pfam [29]. Computing the maximum probability path in a profile HMM is equivalent to optimizing a very simple form of multiple alignment.

We can also create a handcrafted topology for recognizing a particular signal, protein family, or fold. Examples include models to identify signal peptides [56], and for discovering coiled-coil proteins [23] and glycolipid-anchored membrane proteins [32].

Schultz et al. [64] use profile HMMs to detect recombination in HIV strains. They build a profile HMM for each known subtype, adding transitions with a low probability between states corresponding to the profiles of different subtypes. In their formulation, the annotation of a given query sequence identifies which parts belong to which subtype.

Another interesting recent use of HMMs that incorporates recombination is due to Rastas et al. [62], who use an HMM to assist them in haplotype inference and in discovering recombination points in genotype data. From genotype data, they train a hidden model to represent approximations of ancestral haplotypes and allow transitions between these due to recombinations over the course of evolutionary time scales. Given a genotype, which is the conflation of two haplotypes and each representing a path through the network, they compute the maximum probability pair of paths that can give rise to that genotype. The sequences from these two paths are then the inferred haplotypes.

Finally, we note that although the focus of this chapter is biological sequence annotation, hidden Markov models are used for similar tasks in other domains. Speech recognition was one of the first HMM application areas [61]. In natural language processing, HMMs were applied to several tasks, for example, tagging the words with their parts of speech [19], segmentation of text to topics [79], and extraction of information [66]. They can also be applied to areas as diverse as music composer recognition [60] and fire detection [54].

4.3 ALTERNATIVES TO VITERBI DECODING

The Viterbi decoding algorithm is widely used because of its simplicity and efficiency. It is not the only appropriate decoding algorithm for all HMM applications. This section presents several alternative decoding contexts and appropriate algorithms for them.

4.3.1 Maximizing the Number of Correctly Explained States: Posterior Decoding

Posterior decoding focuses on individual positions in the sequence and tries to maximize the probability that they are properly explained. This is in contrast to Viterbi decoding, which computes the globally optimal state path. The simplest posterior decoding question is what state most likely generated symbol i in the HMM output?

The most probable path is not necessarily helpful in answering this question. Many different state paths in the HMM can generate the same sequence s, and in position i, it is possible that many of them will agree on the same state. To compute the posterior probability $P(h_i = k \mid X)$ of state k at position i, conditioned on the entire sequence X, we add the probabilities of all paths using state k at position i. The posterior probability can be decomposed as follows:

$$\Pr(h_i = k \mid X) = \sum_{\ell} \frac{F_i(k, X) \cdot a_{k,\ell} \cdot B_{i+1}(\ell, X)}{\Pr(X)}, \tag{4.4}$$

where $F_i(k, X) = \Pr(h_i = k, x_1, \ldots, x_i)$, and the probability of generating the first i symbols of X and ending in the state k, is called the *forward probability* of state k at position i, and $B_{i+1}(\ell, X) = \Pr(h_{i+1} = \ell, x_{i+1}, \ldots, x_n)$, the probability of starting in state ℓ and generating the rest of the sequence, $x_{i+1}, \ldots, x_n$, is called the *backward probability* of state ℓ at position $i + 1$. The forward probabilities for a given sequence X and a given hidden Markov model can be computed in $O(nm^2)$ time using the standard forward algorithm [8]; the backward probabilities can be computed by the backward algorithm in the same running time.

Using Formula (4.4) and the results of the forward and backward algorithms, we can compute the posterior probabilities of all states at all positions of the sequence X in $O(nm^2)$ time. Note that the posterior probability of the whole sequence $\Pr(X)$, which is the denominator in Formula 4.4, is also obtained as a side product of the forward algorithm: it is $\sum_\ell F_n(\ell, X)$.

We can use the posterior probabilities in a number of ways. A human user can simply examine them to look for interesting features; [44] display a plot of the posterior probabilities of individual states along with the most probable annotation. The plot highlights the parts of the annotation that are most certain and the other hypotheses that might be reasonably likely. We can also compute the posterior probability of an entire candidate sequence feature, such as an exon, by summing the probabilities of all paths sharing that feature in a specific location of the sequence. Genscan [15] provides a list of the most probable alternative exons, including the ones not found on the most probable path. These exons can then be tested experimentally or used as an input for further processing. Larsen and Krogh [46] go one step further and compute the statistical significance of discovered genes, computing the expected number of genes with a given score that would occur in a random sequence of certain length.

We can also decode sequences using posterior probabilities. In *posterior decoding*, we choose the highest posterior probability state at each position of the sequence: $h_i^* = \arg\max_k \Pr(h_i = k \mid X)$. This approach maximizes the expected number of positions in the decoding that have the right state. By contrast, Viterbi decoding maximizes the probability of the entire state path, even though this path may have exceedingly low probability. It may be the case that the posterior decoding has better overall quality.

Still, the posterior decoding can be a composition of unrelated high probability paths. This can reach a point of ridiculousness: two adjacent states in the posterior annotation may not even be connected by an edge in the HMM. The probability of such a sequence of states being the source of the query sequence is zero: it is inconsistent with the basic assumptions encoded in the model topology.

Different authors have addressed this concern through adding a postprocessing step where we attempt to maximize a different objective function. After computing all posterior state probabilities, using the forward–backward algorithm, we restrict the choice to the paths that use only transitions present in the HMM topology. Kill et al. [37] find the path that maximizes the sum of the posterior state probabilities, trying to maximize the number of correctly predicted states. This is done by straightforward dynamic programming, similar to the Viterbi algorithm, in time $O(nm^2)$. Using a similar method, Furiselli et al. [26] maximize the product of posterior probabilities in the postprocessing step.

4.3.2 Maximizing the Annotation Probability: The Multiple Path Problem

Each state in an HMM used to annotate sequences is labeled with the feature to which it corresponds. In gene finding, we label states as coming from exons, introns, and so on. Each state path naturally corresponds to a sequence of labels or an *annotation*. This annotation encapsulates the semantic meaning given to the sequence by the HMM path.

This mapping between state paths and annotations is not always one to one: several state paths may correspond to the same annotation. Such paths provide “alternative origins” of the sequence but have the same semantic meaning. Thus, if we seek the most probable meaning, or annotation, for the sequence, we should add probabilities of all of these state paths.

We will describe an HMM that has multiple state paths with the same annotation as having the *multiple-path problem*. Figure 4.6a shows a simplified HMM for gene finding with its state labels depicted by the state colors. If the start state of the HMM is fixed, this HMM does not have the multiple-path problem, even though multiple

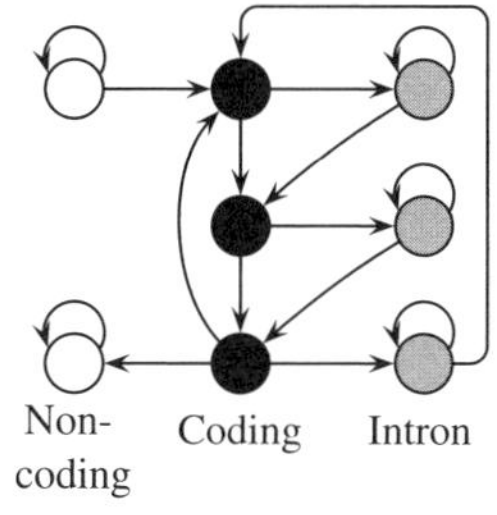

(a) Without multiple-path problem

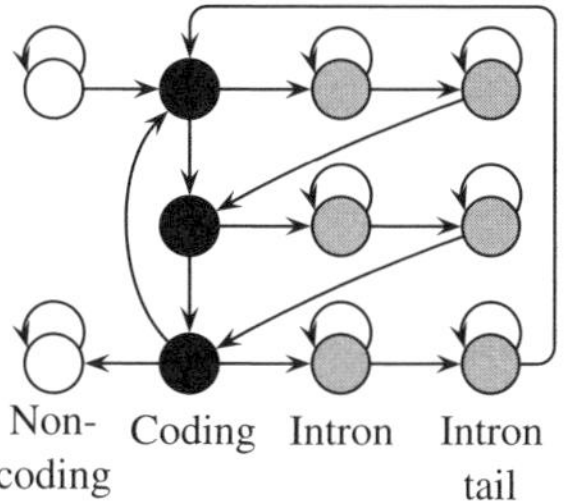

(b) With multiple-path problem

FIGURE 4.6 Simple models of exon/intron structure.

states share the same color. Given an annotation, we can identify the single state that corresponds to each black and gray position.

However, if we move to a slightly more complex model, things quickly change. The model in Fig. 4.6a embodies the assumption that the nucleotide composition of introns is homogeneous. However, vertebrate intronic sequences contain a variable-length tail that is rich in nucleotides C and T [15]. To incorporate this information, we can include a second intron state representing such a tail, as shown in Fig. 4.6b, where the new state has substantially different emission probabilities from the first one. This change creates the multiple-path problem because there are always several high-probability alternatives for the transfer from the "intron" state to the "tail" state. The probabilities of all of these paths may be quite low, and Viterbi decoding may thus lead us to a completely different gene structure that results from fewer paths.

Even though the model in Fig. 4.6b is a more truthful representation of real sequences than the one in Fig. 4.6a, it may provide worse results when used with the Viterbi algorithm [13]. This paradoxical conclusion results because we will be biased toward annotations with fewer uses of the intron module, since each use of that module tends to greatly drop path probabilities.

In practice, gene finders often solve this problem by fixing the number of nucleotides in the pyrimidine-rich intron tail [12,15,70]. The resulting model does not have the multiple-path problem and can be decoded by the Viterbi algorithm.

Sometimes, though, the multiple-path problem is not easily removed. In these cases, we would like to compute the most probable annotation directly. Unfortunately, this is not feasible for all model topologies. Brejova et al. [13] constructed an HMM with 34 states for which it is NP-hard to compute the most probable annotation. As such, we are not likely to find an efficient algorithm to find the most probable annotation.

We can respond to this negative conclusion by resorting to heuristic algorithms, not guaranteed to find the most probable annotation, that perform better than the Viterbi algorithm. A popular example is the N-best algorithm [65], which was shown to give good results in several biological applications [41,44]. We can also use posterior decoding, as in Section 4.3.1, and thereby join together all of the many paths that go through all states with the same label. Still, this approach will be prey to all of the other limitations of the posterior decoding technique.

However, we can characterize special classes of HMMs for which the most probable annotation can be computed efficiently. For example, for HMMs that do not have the multiple-path problem, we can find the most probable annotation by the Viterbi algorithm in $O(nm^2)$ time. Vinar [75] has shown a hierarchy of algorithms that can decode increasingly wider classes of HMMs but at a cost of increasing running time $O(n^{d+1}m^{d+2})$ for a parameter d. In the rest of this section, we describe the most practical of these algorithms that runs in $O(n^2m^3)$ time.

This running time is feasible for analyzing protein or mRNA sequences that are much shorter than genomic DNA. This algorithm can find the most probable labeling for a wide class of models with the multiple-path problem, including the gene-finding HMM shown in Fig. 4.6b and models used for predicting the topology of transmembrane proteins and finding coding regions in mRNA sequences. It can also be applied as a heuristic to HMMs outside of its target class, much as the N-best algorithm can.

The main observation is that many HMMs with the multiple-path problem still have a fair amount of structure in the way that sequence features flow from one to another. Specifically, for these HMMs, while many paths may represent the same annotation, the edges used to transition between the sequence features in the annotation are always the same for all of the paths. We call the edges that transition between states of different labels *critical edges.*

The *extended annotation* of a state path $h_1h_2, \ldots, h_n$ is the pair (L, C), where $L = \lambda_1, \lambda_2, \ldots, \lambda_n$ is the sequence of labels of each state in the path and $C = c_1, c_2, \ldots, c_k$ is the sequence of all critical edges followed on that path. There can be several state paths with the same extended annotation; for example, in Fig. 4.6b, these are the paths that differ only in position of entering the intron tail state; they all follow the same edge from gray to white.

We can extend the Viterbi algorithm to compute the most probable extended annotation. Fortunately, many HMMs (including the one Fig. 4.6b) have one to one correspondence between extended annotations and annotations, and thus can be decoded by this algorithm. We can even test automatically if a given HMM has this property [13], called the *critical edge condition.*

The algorithm again uses dynamic programming, summing all of the paths within every feature, to obtain the maximum probability extended annotation. In the Viterbi algorithm, we compute the values $V[i, k]$, the maximum probability of a state path for the sequence $x_1, \ldots, x_i$ over all paths ending in state k. In the extended Viterbi algorithm, we instead compute $L[i, k]$, the maximum probability of an extended annotation (L, C) of the sequence $x_1, \ldots, x_i$, where the model is in state k at position i; that is, $L[i, k] = \max \Pr(x_1, \ldots, x_i, (L, C), h_i = k)$.

At each step, we examine all possible durations of the last segment with the same label and instead of choosing the single most probable path in that segment with that length, we compute the sum of all possible appropriate-length state paths in this segment. If the segment starts at position j of the sequence, let $P[j, i, k, \ell]$ be this sum; it is the probability of generating the sequence $x_j, \ldots, x_i$, starting in state k and ending in state ℓ, using only states with the same label λ (both states k and ℓ must also have this same label). We get the following recurrence:

$$L[i, k] = \max_{j \leq i} \max_{\ell} \max_{\ell'} L[j-1, \ell'] \cdot a_{\ell',\ell} \cdot P[j, i, \ell, k]. \tag{4.5}$$

We compute the values of L in the order of increasing i. For each i, we compute all relevant values of $P[j, i, k, \ell]$ in order of decreasing j by the following recurrence (this is similar to the standard backward algorithm):

$$P[j, i, k, \ell] = \sum_{\ell' \text{ with label } \lambda} e_{k,x_j} \cdot a_{k,\ell'} \cdot P[\ell', \ell, j+1, i]. \tag{4.6}$$

This algorithm finds the most probable extended annotation in any HMM in $O(n^2m^3)$ time.

4.3.3 Finding Many Paths: Sampling from the Posterior Distribution

Instead of finding the most probable state path, we can also sample a collection of state paths according to the conditional probability distribution $\Pr(H \mid X)$ defined by the HMM. The following algorithm for sampling from HMM was introduced by Zhu et al. [82].

We first precompute all values of $B_i(k, X)$ by the backward algorithm as outlined in Section 4.3.1. In the first step, we randomly choose initial state h_1, where the probability of starting in state k is proportional to $s_k \cdot B_1(k, X)$. After that, in the ith step, we choose the next state h_i with probability proportional to $a_{h_{i-1},h_i} \cdot B_i(h_i, X)$. The probability of choosing path $H = h_1, \ldots, h_n$ by this randomized algorithm is exactly $\Pr(H \mid X)$, so we are sampling from the conditional distribution of state paths, given the output sequence X.

Sampling may be useful if we need to provide several alternative annotations instead of a single prediction. For example, several possible high probability annotations may be needed for the purpose of experimental verification. In gene finding, genes may have several splicing variants; the same DNA sequence is transcribed into multiple proteins using different combinations of splice sites. SLAM [17] and AUGUSTUS [71] use this method to generate multiple gene annotations as potential alternative transcripts. On the contrary, as each of these will likely have extremely low probability, they are likely unreliable as overall predictions for the entire sequence.

4.4 GENERALIZED HIDDEN MARKOV MODELS

The lengths of features found in biological sequences can come from extremely complex distributions. Unfortunately, simple HMMs are not necessarily effective at modeling these distributions. For example, the simplest way to model a region of variable length is with a single HMM state that has a transition to itself (a self-loop),

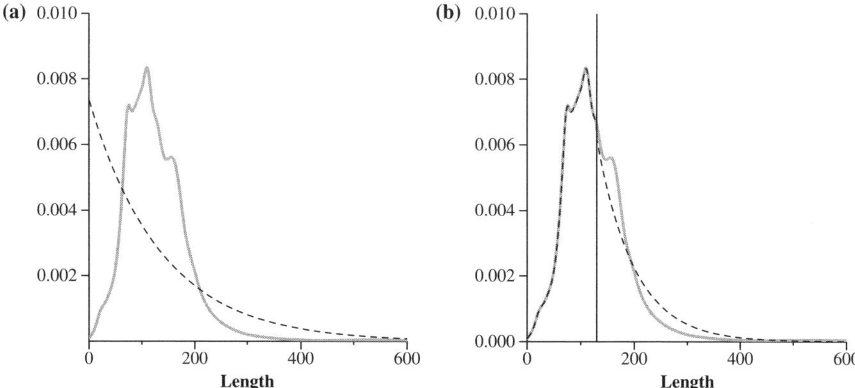

FIGURE 4.7 Length distribution of internal exons on human chromosome 22. (**a**) Best fit by geometric distribution. (**b**) Best fit by geometric-tail distribution with $t = 130$.

with transition probability p. The probability that the HMM stays in such a state for exactly ℓ steps is $(1 - p)p^{\ell-1}$, so the distribution of lengths of regions generated by this state will be geometric. However, length distributions of biological sequence elements are far from geometric. Figure 4.7a shows length distribution of internal exons in human genes and its best approximation by a geometric distribution.

This section shows a variety of methods to address this problem. Some involve changes to the generative behavior to improve the ability to model more complicated distributions. The simplest such approaches can substantially increase the decoding time from $O(nm^2)$ to $O(n^2m^2)$; for long DNA sequences, this order of magnitude change is unacceptable. We thus present methods that compromise between modeling accuracy and decoding time.

4.4.1 Generalized HMMs and Explicit State Duration

In *generalized HMMs*, self-loop transitions are replaced by states generating their state durations explicitly. Upon entering a state, the generative model first chooses the duration d, which is the number of symbols that will be generated in this state. For each state h, the probability distribution δ_h that determines these random variables is explicitly represented in the model. After d symbols are generated in the state, the model follows a transition to a new state.

To compute the most probable state path that generates a particular sequence of symbols, we must modify the Viterbi algorithm. In each step of the dynamic programming, in addition to examining all potential last transitions, we also have to consider all possible durations of the last state. If $V[i, k]$ is again the probability of the most probable path generating the first i symbols $x_1, \ldots, x_i$ and finishing in state k, assuming that in the next step the model will transit out of state k or finish the generation process, the recurrence characterizing the dynamic programming must change as follows:

$$V[i, k] = \max_{1 \le j \le i} [\text{emit}(k, j, i) \cdot \delta_k(i - j + 1) \cdot \max_{\ell} V(j - 1, \ell) \cdot a_{\ell,k}], \tag{4.7}$$

where emit(k, j, i) is the emission probability of generating the sequence of symbols $x_j, \ldots, x_i$ in state k. The straightforward implementation of this dynamic programming gives an $O(n^3m^2)$ running time, where n is the length of the sequence and m is the number of the states, since the computation of emit(v, j, i) takes $O(n)$ time in the worst case. However, it is possible to reduce the running time to $O(n^2m^2)$ using a precomputation that requires $O(nm)$ time, after which it is possible to compute emit(v, j, i) in constant time for any i and j (see [53] for details).

This sort of runtime, which is quadratic in the length of the query sequence, is reasonable for short sequences, such as proteins. It is not feasible for long DNA sequences. Two straightforward solutions to reduce the running time are used in practice.

First, we can place an upper bound of d on the number of characters produced by each state (as in [61]). Then, the running time will be $O(ndm^2)$. In speech recognition applications, it is usually possible to keep the bound d relatively small, as the state durations may be phonemic durations, so this approach yields a reasonable decoding algorithm with practical running time. However, such a bound is often hard to find in biological applications.

Second, we observe that we can stop our dynamic programming search for lengths that may be emitted by the current state whenever emit$(k, j, i) = 0$. For example, this is a common stopping condition for exon states in gene finding: we can stop searching upon reading an in-frame stop codon. Burge and Karlin [15] used this approach in their gene finder Genscan to model exons with generalized states and complex distributions, still achieving reasonable decoding runtimes. Unfortunately, this approach does not extend to intron distributions: there is no common sequence forbidden to them.

4.4.2 Distributions with Geometric Tails

One way of decreasing the running time, even when no upper bound on the length of the state durations is available, is to restrict the family of length distributions allowed in the generalized states. One example of this approach is due to Brejova and Vinar [14], which restricts the family of durations to ones with *geometric tails*. Such distributions are robust enough to characterize the lengths of many important biological elements effectively.

A geometric-tail distribution for the duration of a state is the joining of two distributions: the first part is an arbitrary length distribution, and the second part is a geometric tail. Specifically, there is a parameter t where, for values of i less than or equal to t, the probability $\delta_k(i)$ is explicitly set, while for values of i greater than t, $\delta_k(i) = \delta_k(t) \cdot q_k^{i-t}$. The values of $\delta_k(t)$ and q_k are set to maximize the likelihood of the length distributions of training data, and the explicit probabilities found in $\delta_k(i)$ for $i < t$ are set to match observed values after smoothing.

Such distributions can model the lengths of many functional segments of biological sequences, even with small values of the tail start parameter t. For example, Fig. 4.7b shows the geometric-tail distribution with $t = 130$ that best approximates the length distribution of human internal exons.

[14] emphasize models with small values of the parameter t because they also design an efficient decoding algorithm with $O(nmt + nm^2)$ runtime. The Viterbi algorithm for generalized HMMs in recurrence (4.7) explicitly considers all possible durations of state k. For geometric-tail distributions, we can reduce the running time by distinguishing between two cases: durations less than or equal to t_k and durations longer than t_k.

In particular, let $Q[i, k]$ be the probability of the most probable path generating the first i symbols of the sequence and spending at least last t_k steps in state k. To compute the value of $Q[i, k]$, we consider two cases: either the ith character extends the duration of the state k, which was already at least t_k, or generating the ith character brings the duration of state k to exactly t_k steps. The value of $Q[i, k]$ can then be used in computing $V[i, k]$, instead of checking all durations longer than t:

$$V[i,k] = \max \begin{cases} Q[i,k], & \text{(duration at least } t_k\text{)} \\ \max\limits_{1\le d<t_k} [\text{emit}\,(k, i-d+1, i)\cdot \delta_k(d) \\ \qquad \cdot \max\limits_{\ell} V[i-d,\ell]\cdot a_{\ell,k}] & \text{(duration less than } t_k\text{)}, \end{cases} \tag{4.8}$$

$$Q[i,k] = \max \begin{cases} Q[i-1,k]\cdot q_k \cdot e_{k,x_i} & \text{(duration more than } t_k\text{)} \\ \text{emit}\,(k, i-t_k+1, i)\cdot \delta_k(t_k)\cdot \max\limits_{\ell} V[i-t_k,\ell]\cdot a_{\ell,k} \\ \qquad \text{(duration exactly } t_k\text{)}. \end{cases} \tag{4.9}$$

A straightforward dynamic programming algorithm implemented based on this recurrence would take $O(ntm^2)$ time, which [14] improve to $O(nmt + nm^2)$ by precomputing values of $\max_\ell V[i, \ell] \cdot a(\ell, k)$.

In gene finding, this technique was used in ExonHunter [12,14] to model the length distributions of exons and introns; the gene finder Augustus [70] uses a similar approach shown in Section 4.4.3 to model the length distributions of introns.

The distributions of much longer features can also be modeled in an extension of this approach. The gene finder ExonHunter [12] models the lengths of intergenic features, for which a simple geometric tail distribution would require $t \approx 10^4$, by replacing a single-state model of intergenic region with a two-state model that allows one to approximate this distribution. The first state generates symbols in blocks of length $\sqrt{t}$, where the number of blocks is determined by a geometric-tail distribution and tail begins at $\sqrt{t}$. The second state generates only up to $\sqrt{t}$ symbols, with uniform length distribution. This method replaces the original length distribution with a step-function approximation, where the steps happen at intervals of $\sqrt{t}$, as shown in Fig. 4.8. The model that represents this distribution can be decoded in

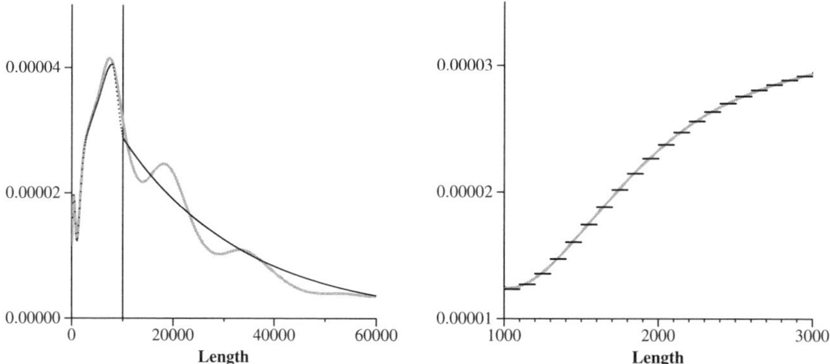

FIGURE 4.8 Step-function approximation of intergenic length distribution in human chromosome 22. The right plot shows detail of the step-function character of the distribution.

$O(nm\sqrt{t} + nm^2)$ time, which is practical even for the large values of t needed to model intergenic regions.

4.4.3 Gadgets of States

An alternative way of avoiding the geometric length distributions for individual states in hidden Markov models is to model a single sequence element by multiple states instead of a single state. Durbin et al. [25] (recently also reexamined by Johnson [35]) discuss several ways to model nongeometric length distributions by replacing a single state with a group of states that shares the same set of emission probabilities. Transitions are added inside this group so that the probability of staying within the group for ℓ steps is close to the probability that the modeled feature has length ℓ.

Consider the gadget in Fig. 4.9a. The leftmost transition is the sole entry point to the submodel, and the rightmost transition is the exit. If the gadget consists of n states, the probability of generating a feature of length $\ell > n$ is $f(\ell) = \binom{\ell-1}{n-1} p^{\ell-n}(1-p)^n$, which can be used to model a wide variety of gamma distributions (see Fig. 4.9b). One example of this approach is found in [46], who used three copies of their codon model, each with its own self-loop, to model the length distribution of genes in bacteria.

The geometric-tail distributions with parameter t discussed in the previous sections can be generated by a gadget of t states, shown in Fig. 4.10; for $i < t$, the probability of generating a feature with length i is $\prod_{j<i}(1 - p_j)p_i$, while if $i \geq t$, then $\delta_k(i) = \prod_{j=1\ldots t-1}(1 - p_j)q^{i-t-1}(1 - q)$.

Such a construction was used by Nielsen and Krogh [56] for protein modeling and by Stanke and Waack [70] in gene finding. The modified Viterbi algorithm for geometric-tail distributions shown in the previous section is essentially equivalent to running the classical Viterbi algorithm on such an HMM, though it is more memory efficient, since the Viterbi probabilities $V[i, k]$ are not stored for the extra states within the gadget.

In general, one can use any topology of states in a gadget; distributions that can be represented in such a way are called *phase-type distributions*, and they play an

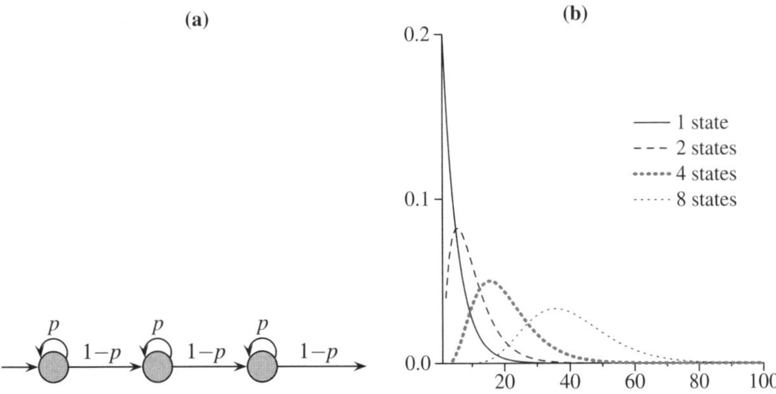

FIGURE 4.9 (**a**) A gadget of states generating nongeometric length distributions; (**b**) depending on the number of states and probability p, different distributions from a subclass of the discrete gamma distributions $\Gamma(p\ell, 1)$ can be generated.

important role in queuing and systems theory (see [21] for a recent overview). This approach of using phase-type distributions suggests what appears to be an ideal framework for modeling general length distributions in HMMs: fix the number of states in each gadget depending on the desired running time, and then find the best approximation of the length distribution observed in training data. With increasing size of the gadget, we can approximate any desired length distribution arbitrarily well [5].

Unfortunately, most gadgets, such as the one shown in Fig. 4.9a, introduce the multiple-path problem discussed in Section 4.3.2, so Viterbi decoding is inappropriate for them. Indeed, Vinar [75] showed that the result of decoding the HMM with a gadget shown in Fig. 4.9a with Viterbi decoding is equivalent to the result of decoding an HMM where the same feature has essentially a geometric length distribution.

This unhappy result leaves us with two options: compute the most probable labeling by the extended Viterbi algorithm from Section 4.3.2 or use other decoding strategy, such as posterior decoding. Note that since the extended Viterbi runs in quadratic time in the length of the sequence, the former strategy is no better than using arbitrary length distributions and the algorithm from Section 4.4.1.

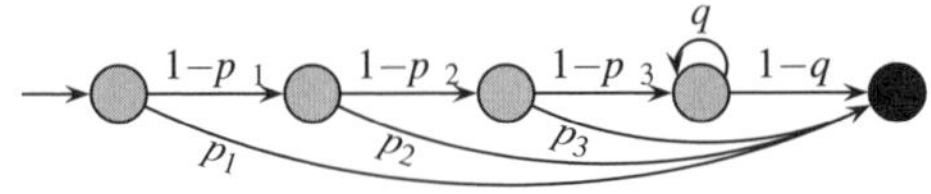

FIGURE 4.10 A gadget of states generating a geometric-tail length distribution with $t = 4$. The black circle represents the first state of the next submodel of the HMM.

4.5 HMMS WITH MULTIPLE OUTPUTS OR EXTERNAL INFLUENCES

In the previous sections, we have considered HMMs that modeled a single DNA or protein sequence and its annotation. This approach, however, is not appropriate to the more contemporary domain in which we may have much external information that is helpful in annotating a sequence accurately. In this section, we consider a variety of ways in which HMMs can incorporate such external evidence. Many of these change the structure of the output of the HMM, while others influence the decoding algorithms.

Perhaps the most readily available source of information is predicted evolutionary homology. A large number of DNA and protein sequences are publicly available in databases such as GenBank [9]. For a given sequence of interest, we may find its likely homologs in a database and exploit typical patterns of evolution to improve the annotation. Functionally important regions usually evolve much more slowly and are well conserved even between relatively distant species; on the contrary, random mutations often accumulate more quickly in regions with fewer functional constraints [68]. Another source of evidence is the results of biological experiments aimed at elucidating sequence features and their function. For example, in gene finding, EST sequencing and tiling array experiments may confirm that certain regions of the genome are exons.

An example of additional information in gene finding is illustrated in Fig. 4.11. The figure shows significant alignments of a distantly related genome, known proteins, and expressed sequence tags to a genomic region containing the human URO-D gene. In this case, the additional evidence provides a human observer enough information to have a very good idea about the structure of the gene. The process of incorporating such information into the automatic annotation that results from decoding an HMM, on the contrary, is not necessarily nearly as simple: we must design systems that are efficient to decode and efficiently trained, and that are able to accommodate errors and imprecisions in the external sources of information.

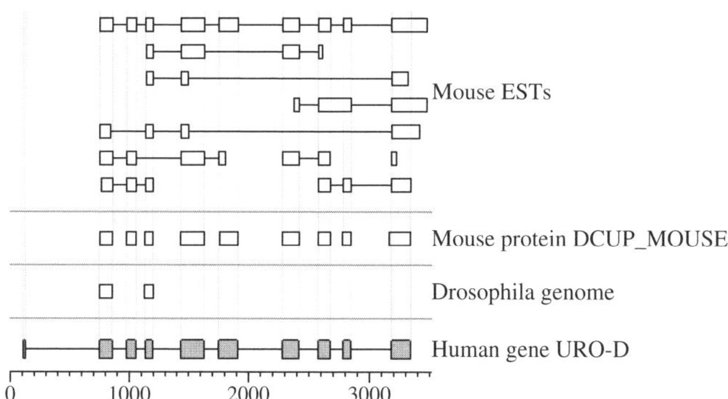

FIGURE 4.11 Evidence supporting annotation of human URO-D gene. Significant alignments from fruit fly genome, known mouse proteins, and mouse ESTs are represented as boxes.

4.5.1 HMMs with Multiple Outputs

One way of incorporating additional evidence into HMMs is to represent each source of evidence as a new *informant* sequence. We can then extend the HMM to generate the informant sequences as part of its output, alongside with the original query sequence whose annotation we seek.

These extensions are perhaps most easily described in the framework of Bayesian networks. A Bayesian network is a generative probabilistic model whose output is N variables. The dependencies among these variables are shown by representing the variables as the vertices of a directed acyclic graph. We generate values for the variables in topological order so that the values of all of the variables that are the predecessors of a variable are determined before its value. To be more specific, consider a variable X, with parents $X_1, \ldots, X_k$. The parameters of the Bayesian network specify the conditional probability $\Pr(X = x \mid X_1 = x_1, \ldots, X_k = x_k)$ for all combinations of the values $x, x_1, \ldots, x_k$. Once the values of the parent variables are fixed, we can generate the value of X from this conditional distribution.

HMMs easily fit into this Bayesian network framework: an HMM that generates a sequence of a fixed length n can be represented as a Bayesian network with $2n$ variables: for each emitted symbol, we have one variable representing the symbol itself and one variable representing the hidden state emitting the symbol (see Fig. 4.12). We can also represent higher order states by including additional edges between the observed variables as demonstrated in the figure.

One approach to incorporating external evidence into the HMM is to represent the evidence sources by informant sequences, which also depend on the hidden states of the network. We translate each external source into a sequence of n symbols from a finite alphabet, where each symbol in the informant sequence must correspond to one symbol of the query sequence. For example, we can encode a genome-to-genome alignment as a sequence of n symbols from the alphabet $\{0, 1, \ldots\}$ by characterizing each base of the query DNA sequence as "aligned with match" (symbol "1"), "aligned with mismatch" (symbol "0"), or "unaligned" (symbol "."); this is the encoding scheme used in the gene finder TwinScan [39].

We can represent this approach by adding a variable for each informant sequence at each sequence position to our Bayesian network. If we have $k - 1$ external

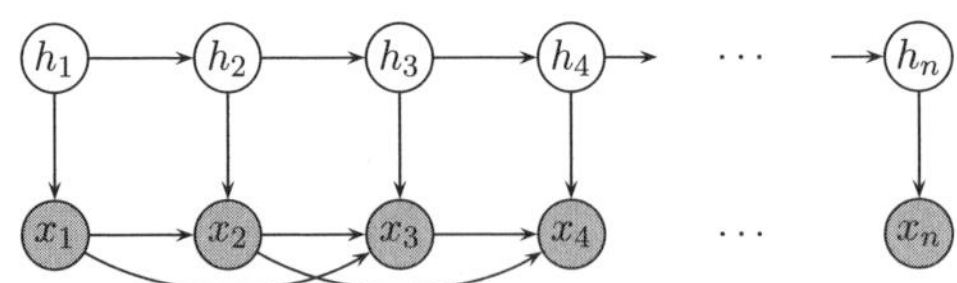

FIGURE 4.12 A hidden Markov model with second-order states, represented as a Bayesian network. The top row of variables represents the state path $h_1, \ldots, h_n$ through the HMM. The bottom row represents the emitted DNA sequence $x_1, \ldots, x_n$. The conditional probabilities of the Bayesian network are defined by the initial, transition, and emission probabilities of the HMM: $\Pr(h_1) = s_{h_1}$, $\Pr(h_i | h_{i-1}) = a_{h_i,h_{i-1}}$, and $\Pr(x_i | h_i, x_{i-1}, x_{i-2}) = e_{h_i,x_{i-2},x_{i-1},x_i}$. The observed variables, which indicate the DNA sequence, are shaded in the figure.

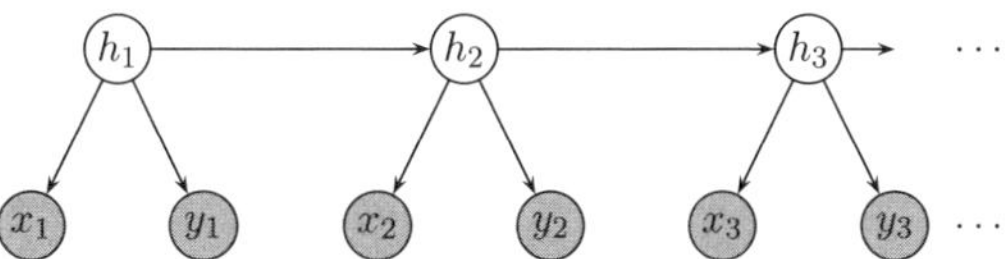

FIGURE 4.13 A representation of the generative probabilistic model of the TwinScan gene finder [39] as a Bayesian network. The h_i variables each represent one state of the HMM; variable x_i represents one nucleotide of the query DNA sequence, and y_i represents the conservation between this nucleotide and some other genome over a special alphabet with symbols for matched, mismatched, and unaligned positions. (TwinScan actually uses emission tables of order 5, which can be depicted by adding additional edges, as shown in Fig. 4.12.)

information sources, the network will have $n(k + 1)$ variables: n state variables, n variables for the query sequence, and n variables for each of the $k - 1$ informant sequences. The simplest way to add these new variables is to make the symbols of all k sequences conditionally independent given the state at each position. Figure 4.13 shows such a model for $k = 2$. Korf et al. [39] used this approach to incorporate genome-to-genome alignments into gene finding. Pavlovic et al. [58] transformed the outputs of a collection of gene-finding programs into informant sequences and used this same sort of approach to join their predictions into a single prediction; their system does not even involve the query DNA sequence as one of the network's outputs.

Training and decoding of these extended HMMs is analogous to regular HMMs: maximum likelihood parameters can be obtained by simple frequency counting from annotated sequences, and we can straightforwardly modify the Viterbi algorithm (and other decoding algorithms) to account for the multiple emission probabilities in each step. The main limiting factor of these models is not their algorithms but is the assumption of conditional independence between individual output sequences, which is clearly violated in most applications.

Instead, when the evidence consists of multiple alignment of sequences known to have evolved from a common ancestor, we can use *phylogenetic HMMs*, a model design that reflects known evolutionary relationships between these sequences. In particular, we can arrange the Bayesian network so that the topology of the network is identical to the phylogenetic tree representing the evolutionary history of the sequences, as in Fig. 4.14, which shows a model of a human query sequence and additional sequences from mouse, rat, and chicken. In this Bayesian network, we can partition all sequence variables into two sets at every position i: the set of observed variables O_i, corresponding to the sequences in the leaves of the phylogenetic tree, and the set of unobserved variables U_i, corresponding to the unknown ancestral sequences.

The unobserved variables complicate both training and decoding. To train the model, we must use the EM algorithm instead of simple frequency counting [24]. For decoding, at each position i and for each state h_i, we need to compute the likelihood of the corresponding tree submodel $\Pr(O_i \mid h_i)$. This probability can be computed from the probability distribution $\Pr(O_i, U_i \mid h_i)$ defined by the phylogenetic tree model by

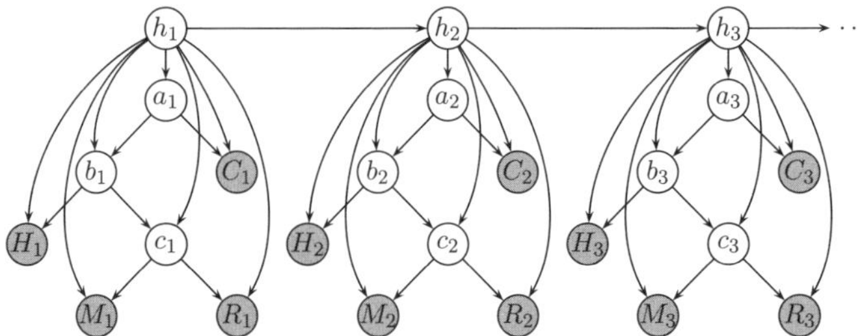

FIGURE 4.14 A simple phylogenetic hidden Markov model depicted as a Bayesian network. Each variable h_i represents one state of the HMM, the variables H_i, M_i, R_i, C_i each represent single positions of human, mouse, rat, and chicken from one column of a multiple genome alignment, and the variables a_i, b_i, c_i represent the unknown ancestral sequences. Observed variables are shaded. For example, the value of H_i depends on its ancestor b_i and on the HMM state h_i. The state determines mutation rate, since mutations occur more frequently in noncoding regions.

marginalizing unobserved variables:

$$\Pr(O_i \mid h_i) = \sum_{U_i} \Pr(O_i, U_i \mid h_i). \tag{4.10}$$

The number of terms in this sum is exponential in the number of unobserved variables. However, since the generative model has a tree structure, we can compute this sum in time linear in the number of all variables by using Felsenstein's peeling algorithm [27], which performs dynamic programming by starting at the leaves and proceeding to the root of the tree.

We can introduce higher order states for the observed variables, as described at the beginning of this section. However, introducing higher order states for the unobserved variables is more complicated: it requires substantial modification of the decoding algorithm [69], and the running time becomes exponential in the order of the states.

Another modification of phylogenetic HMMs [34] involves rooting the phylogenetic tree in the query sequence rather than in the common ancestor (see Fig. 4.15). The advantage of this approach is that the resulting probability distribution can be

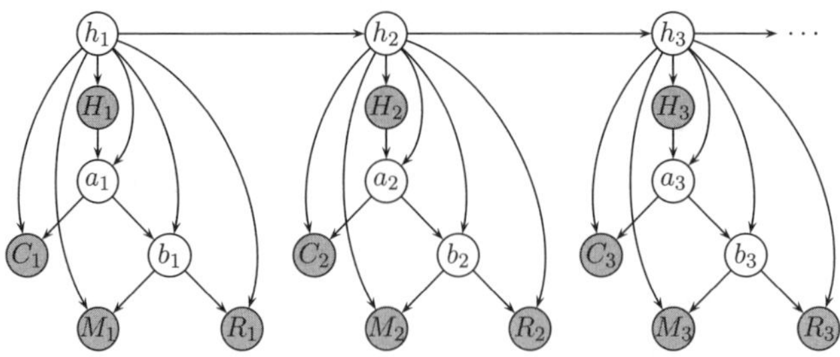

FIGURE 4.15 Modified phylogenetic hidden Markov model, with query sequence positioned at the root of the phylogenetic tree.

decomposed into a product of two terms: the probability that the HMM generates the query sequence and that the contribution from the variables introduced by the other sequences. The emission and transition probabilities of HMM states can be trained and tuned separately as in a single-sequence gene finder, and the parameters required for including additional evidence can be trained afterward.

An important issue is the parametrization of random variables associated with the query and informant sequences. In phylogenetic HMMs, most variables have two parents: the state variable and the parent in the phylogenetic tree. Thus if the alphabet size is σ, the number of states is m, and the number of sequences is N, we must train $\Theta(Nm\sigma^2)$ parameters. We can reduce this number by employing a nucleotide substitution model based on a standard continuous Markov chain model of evolution. For example, the simplest Jukes–Cantor model [36], which assumes a uniform rate for all single-point mutations, requires only a single parameter per sequence and state. In more complex models of evolution, such as the general reversible model of Rodriguez et al. [63], the substitution rate matrix (requiring $\Theta(\sigma^2)$ parameters for each state) is shared among all branches of the phylogenetic tree, and one parameter corresponding to the branch length of an edge in the phylogenetic tree needs to be trained for each sequence and state. Using such a model of evolution will reduce the number of parameters to $\Theta(Nm + m\sigma^2)$, thus substantial savings even for moderate number of species.

Phylogenetic HMMs were first introduced in evolution studies [28,80]. [33] were the first to apply them for sequence annotation in the problem of secondary structure prediction. As genomes of multiple organisms have become available, phylogenetic HMMs have been applied to genomic sequences for tasks such as gene finding [34,50,59,67] and identifying conserved elements in genomes [68]. Phylogenetic HMMs are also useful for finding overlapping genes in compact viral genomes [51].

The accuracy of HMM when used to analyze protein sequences can also be improved by using multiple sequence alignments of several proteins that are known to be homologous with a query sequence. However, we typically do not know the phylogenetic tree representing the evolution of these proteins. Instead, researchers have developed variants of HMMs that emit a profile specifying the relative frequency of each amino acid at each position of the sequence. Unlike phylogenetic HMMs, these models do not capture the strong correlation between closely related sequences but only summarize the features of the many rows of the alignment. However, they require far simpler parameter estimation. HMMs emitting profiles were used to predict secondary structure of proteins by [16], topology of β-barrel membrane proteins by [49], and topology of helical transmembrane proteins by [74].

4.5.2 Positional Score Modification

We can incorporate external evidence into an HMM using other methods besides Bayesian network approaches. In an HMM, the joint probability $\Pr(H, X)$ of sequence X and state path H is computed as a product of emission and transition probabilities (see Eq. 4.1). The methods presented in this section place additional factors into this product, while keeping the decoding algorithm viable.

All possible annotations of a particular sequence are represented as different state paths through the HMM. Consider a piece of additional evidence E. It can be seen as a probabilistic hypothesis about the true annotation, whose validity depends on whether E comes from a believable source: if the origin of the evidence is trustworthy (with some probability P_E), then only paths from some set H_E should be considered. On the contrary, with probability $1 - P_E$, the evidence is untrustworthy and we should disregard it.

For example, in transmembrane topology prediction, we may see a motif that suggests that the ith amino acid in the query sequence is found inside the cytoplasm. Then the set H_E consists of all paths through the HMM that mark the ith amino acid as being from a cytoplasmic loop, and the probability $(1 - P_E)$ is the probability that the match is not a real functional occurrence of this motif, and we should disregard the evidence entirely.

When given such an evidence, we recognize two events: E_+ (the evidence is correct), and E_- (the evidence is wrong). We can write as follows:

$$\Pr(H, X \mid E) = P_E \cdot \Pr(H, X \mid E_+) + (1 - P_E) \cdot \Pr(H, X \mid E_-)\,. \tag{4.11}$$

Note that $\Pr(H, X \mid E_+) = 0$ for paths H not found in H_E; if the evidence is correct, it is specifically eliminating certain paths from being possible. If the evidence is wrong, it should have no effect on predictions, and therefore we say $\Pr(H, X \mid E_-) = \Pr(H, X)$. If we already know that $H \in H_E$, additional evidence does not give us any new information, and addition of such evidence should not change relative probabilities of paths; consequently, we can say $\Pr(H \mid H_E, X) = \Pr(H \mid E_+, X)$. Finally, we assume (obviously unrealistically) that the probability of the sequence should be independent of the event E_+, and we can say $\Pr(X) = \Pr(X \mid E_+)$.

Using these assumptions, we obtain after simple manipulation the following updated probability distribution over all possible annotations:

$$\Pr(H, X \mid E) = \begin{cases} (1 - P_E) \cdot \Pr(H, X), & \text{if } H \notin H_E \\ \left(1 - P_E + \frac{P_E}{\Pr(H_E \mid X)}\right) \cdot \Pr(H, X), & \text{if } H \in H_E. \end{cases} \tag{4.12}$$

Intuitively, the probabilities of all paths that agree with the evidence are multiplied by a factor greater than one, and probabilities of all paths that do not agree with the evidence are multiplied by a factor smaller than one. The relative probability of paths within each category remains unchanged.

The computational complexity of decoding under this new probabilistic model depends on the form of the set H_E of paths that are consistent with evidence. If H_E contains all the paths that annotate a point in the sequence with a particular label or with any label from a set of labels, we can slightly modify the Viterbi algorithm to compute the most probable state path. The quantity $\Pr(H_E \mid X)$ needed for the bonus factor can be obtained by the forward–backward algorithm.

This method was first derived and used in a gene finding program GenomeScan [81] to incorporate protein homology into gene finding. The same method was also used to improve prediction of transmembrane protein topology by Xu et al. [77]. In their case, the evidence was composed of motif hits that indicate strong preference for cytoplasmic or noncytoplasmic loops at certain sites in the sequence.

A disadvantage of the GenomeScan approach is that it is unclear how to integrate multiple pieces of additional evidence (such as multiple protein hits or multiple motifs), particularly if they are not independent. In an attempt to solve this problem, the next method incorporates evidence in the form of additional multiplicative terms at each position of the sequence. An important difference is that given a particular alignment, GenomeScan method alters the probability at one position only, while in what follows we boost the probability independently at each position covered by the alignment.

Assuming independence between the sequence X and all additional evidence E, we can use Bayes' rule to obtain

$$\Pr(H \mid X, E) \propto \Pr(H \mid X) \cdot \frac{\Pr(H \mid E)}{\Pr(H)}. \tag{4.13}$$

Though this independence assumption is not true in practice, we can often limit dependencies by avoiding using the same features of the sequence in both the HMM and the additional evidence. For example, in gene finding, the HMM mostly models short windows of the sequence (signals, local coding potential, etc.), while the additional evidence may represent database searches, such as alignments to EST or protein sequences.

Whether we can develop an efficient decoding algorithm depends mostly on the family of probability distributions that we use to represent the contribution of the additional evidence $\Pr(H \mid E)/\Pr(H)$. In the simplest case, we assume positional independence for both the posterior probability conditioned on the evidence $\Pr(H \mid E) = \prod_{i=1}^{n} \Pr(h_i \mid E)$ and the prior probability $\Pr(H) = \prod_{i=1}^{n} \Pr(h_i)$. To partially compensate for the positional independence assumption, we can add a scaling factor $\alpha < 1$ as follows:

$$\Pr(H \mid X, E) \propto \Pr(H \mid X) \cdot \left(\frac{\Pr(H \mid E)}{\Pr(H)}\right)^{\alpha}. \tag{4.14}$$

In this particular scenario, we can easily modify the Viterbi algorithm to find the most probable annotation H given both sequence X and evidence E are in time linear in the length of the sequence.

For a single source of evidence, we can directly estimate the posterior probabilities $\Pr(h_i \mid E)$ from a training dataset. However, multiple sources of evidence would typically present many combinations of local information, requiring exponential number of parameters to train. Brejova et al. [12] developed a method for expressing and combining information from several sources of additional evidence using partial probabilistic statements to express the implications of the evidence and the quadratic programming to combine all the statements concerning a particular position in the sequence into a posterior distribution $\Pr(h_i \mid E)$.

In the context of gene finding, the method of multiplying $\Pr(H, X)$ by additional factors was successfully used to incorporate a variety of sources of information (such as genome, EST, and protein alignments) into a single model; two examples are HMMGene [42] and ExonHunter [12].

[72] designed a method that tries to overcome the positional independence assumptions. Let us assume that the evidence E is expressed as a set of "hints": intervals in the query sequence. In the simplest case, each hint supports a single state of the generalized HMM (more complex variations are possible). We say that a given state path is *compatible* with hint (i, j) if the part of the query sequence $x_i, \ldots, x_j$ is all generated in the state supported by the interval. Otherwise, we say that the state path is *incompatible*. For example, in gene finding, we can represent EST alignments as a set of intervals, each supporting an exon state in the HMM.

Each hint is assigned a position in the sequence at its right end. Only a single hint e_i is allowed to end at each position i. Also, if there is no hint ending at position i, we will say $e_i = \pitchfork$, corresponding to a vacuous hint. We will create a model that will generate not only the sequence X but also the sequence of hints as follows:

$$\Pr(H, X, e_1, \ldots, e_n) = \Pr(H, X) \cdot \prod_{i=1}^{n} \Pr(e_i \mid H, X) . \tag{4.15}$$

The probability $\Pr(e_i \mid H, X)$ is either $q^{\pitchfork}$ if the hint at position i is $\pitchfork$, q^+ if the hint is compatible with H, or q^- if the hint is incompatible with H. These parameters are trained by frequency counting on the training data. Note that this model is not truly a generative model for hints, since we do not generate the left ends of the hints, yet we use them to determine compatibility or incompatibility of each state path. The Viterbi algorithm can be again easily modified to accommodate these interval hints, and if $q^+ > q^-$, it asymptotically takes no longer than the underlying decoding of the generalized HMM.

The interval hints were used in the gene finder AUGUSTUS+ [72]. They enforce better consistency of final predictions with the evidence, since the bonus factor q^+ is not awarded for state paths that match an interval only partially.

4.5.3 Pair Hidden Markov Models

In the previous sections, we have reviewed several methods that break the problem of sequence annotation into two steps. First, a general search tool is used to identify local alignments between the query sequence and a sequence database. Next, this information is incorporated using some HMM-based method. The main disadvantage of the two-step approach is that the initial general-purpose alignment algorithm does not take into account the structure of the annotation problem.

For example, in gene finding, alignments of a protein or EST with the query DNA may extend beyond exon boundaries to surrounding introns, and alignments of two homologous genes may have misaligned splice sites. Such mistakes are propagated to the second stage and may affect the accuracy of gene finding.

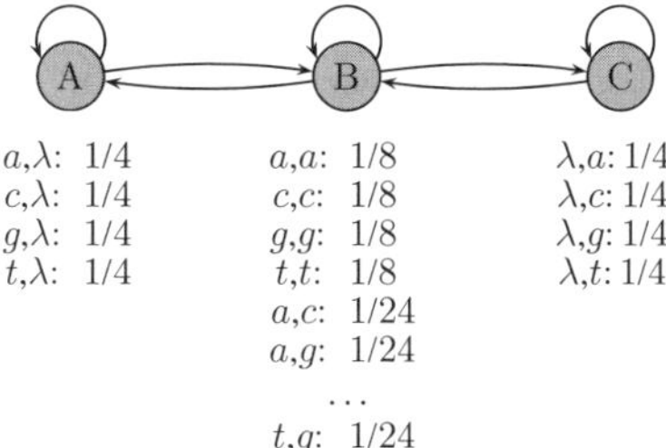

FIGURE 4.16 A simple pair HMM. The symbol λ in the emission probability tables represents empty string. State B generates the ungapped portion of the alignment. State A generates characters only in the first sequence, and state C generates characters only in the second sequence. The alignment gaps induced by states A and C have geometrically distributed lengths.

This problem can be avoided by simultaneously annotating and aligning two sequences in a single step. This process can be modeled by a *pair HMM*. Pair HMMs are HMMs that generate two sequences at the same time, but where a state of a model can generate a character in one sequence or both sequences. Pairs of characters generated in the same step correspond to homologous positions from the two sequences. If only one character is generated in a given step, it corresponds to a sequence position in that sequence with no homolog in the other sequence due to an insertion or deletion. Simple pair HMMs, such as the one in Fig. 4.16, can be used to represent a traditional global alignment of two sequences [25], with a natural relationship between the logarithm of the probability of a path in the HMM and the score of an alignment according to traditional schema. More complex pair HMMs can represent pairwise alignments that incorporate more flexibility in the models of the lengths and conservation levels of different parts of the alignment.

Pair HMMs differ in an essential way from the multiple output HMMs introduced in Section 4.5.1: they have an alignment of the output sequences fixed and in each step generate a character in each output sequence. If the alignment contains a gap, they generate a special character, for example, a dash. On the contrary, the output sequences of pair HMMs do not identify the pairs of characters emitted in the same step; when we decode a pair HMM, the goal is to *discover* such homologies.

The program SLAM [2], predicts genes simultaneously in two homologous genomic sequences, under the assumption that they have the same exon structure. Their pair HMM has separate states for exons, introns, signals, and intergenic regions, as in HMMs for gene finding. Each state not only can emits pairs of sequences with conservation patterns typical for the sequence feature represented by the state but can also allow for insertions or deletions, where a position in one sequence is not matched to the other. DoubleScan [52], is similar, but can also predict genes with different exon–intron structure. GeneWise, by [10], uses pair HMMs to align a protein sequence to a genomic sequence. The noncoding states emit characters only in the genomic sequence, while coding states emit a triplet of nucleotides in the genomic sequence and a single amino acid in the protein sequence.

The main disadvantage of pair HMMs is their high running time. Given two sequences generated by a pair HMM, we do not know which pairs of characters from these two sequences were generated at the same time; indeed, this is what decoding is to discover. The modified Viterbi algorithm that finds the most probable alignment of two sequences, and their annotations, is equivalent to an extension of classic global alignment algorithms, and as for those algorithms, its runtime is proportional to the product of the sequence lengths. Although such a running time is infeasible in many situations, different heuristics can be used to make the pair HMM approach more practical [2,52]. This approach is also hard to extend to multiple sources of information because its running time grows exponentially with the number of sequences, again as is true for classical algorithms for multiple alignment.

4.6 TRAINING THE PARAMETERS OF AN HMM

In the previous sections, we considered the simplest scenario of HMM parameter estimation: maximum likelihood training in an HMM without the multiple paths problem on a completely annotated training set. This method is applied if we can determine the target state path for each sequence in the training set. In this case, it is sufficient to count the frequency of each transition and emission to estimate the model parameters that maximize the likelihood of the training data. Unfortunately, HMM training is not always so simple.

In this section, we explore several other scenarios for HMM training. First, when only unannotated or partially annotated sequences are available, we need to use unsupervised or semisupervised training to estimate the parameters of the model. Second, often a single parameter set does not capture properties of all query sequences well, and we may want to adapt the parameter set to the query sequence before making a prediction. Finally, we may choose to use different optimization criteria instead of maximum likelihood principle.

4.6.1 Unsupervised and Semisupervised Training

Supervised learning can be applied only when the annotation is known for each sequence in the training set, and there is a one to one correspondence between such an annotation and the state paths in the HMM. If this is not the case, we need to apply more complex methods for training. The task is, as in the supervised case, to find the parameters of the HMM with a given topology that maximize the likelihood of the training set.

There is no general exact algorithm known for solving this unsupervised training problem efficiently; some modifications have even been shown to be NP-hard [1,31]. The method most commonly used, the Baum–Welch algorithm [7], is an iterative heuristic and can be considered a special case of the general EM algorithm for learning maximum likelihood models from incomplete data [24].

The Baum–Welch algorithm starts from an initial set of model parameters θ_0. In each iteration, it changes the parameters as follows:

1. Calculate the expected number of times each transition and emission is used to generate the training set T in an HMM whose parameters are θ_k.
2. Use the frequencies obtained in step 1 to reestimate the parameters of the model, resulting in a new set of parameters θ_{k+1}.

The first step of the algorithm can be viewed as creating a new *annotated* training set $T^{(k)}$, where for each *unannotated* sequence $X \in T$, we add every possible pair (X, H) of the sequence X and any state path, weighted by the conditional probability $\Pr(H \mid X, \theta_k)$ of the path H in the model with parameters θ_k, given the sequence X. The second step then estimates new parameters θ_{k+1}, as in the supervised scenario, based on the new training set $T^{(k)}$. The Baum–Welch algorithm achieves the same result in $O(nm^2)$ time per iteration using the forward and backward algorithms to avoid explicitly creating this exponentially large training set. Details can be found, for example, in [25, Chapter 3.3].

Baum [7] has shown that the likelihood of the training set improves (or stays the same) in each iteration of this algorithm. However, this does not guarantee that the Baum–Welch algorithm reaches optimal model parameters: it may instead reach a local maximum or a saddle point in the parameter space [24].

A modification of the Baum–Welch algorithm, called *Viterbi training*, is also often used in practice. In the first step of the algorithm, instead of considering all possible paths through the model, we only consider the most probable path. However, this algorithm is not guaranteed to increase the likelihood of the observed data in each step [25, Chapter 3.3].

The Baum–Welch algorithm can also be used in the semisupervised scenario. For example, Krogh et al. [44] train a transmembrane topology predictor on a dataset where the exact boundaries of transmembrane helices are not known. Therefore, they allow the boundary to occur anywhere within a short window of the sequence. We can modify step 1 of the algorithm to include only paths that agree with such partial annotations.

4.6.2 Adjusting Models to Query Sequences

Supervised and semisupervised training assume that the training and testing sets contain samples independently generated from the same underlying distribution of sequences and their annotations. In some situations, such an assumption is not appropriate.

For example, Tusnády and Simon [73] argue that the amino acid composition of transmembrane helices cannot be adequately described by the same set of emission probabilities for all transmembrane proteins. Instead, they propose to segment a given protein so that the difference in distribution between helix and nonhelix regions is maximized. This is essentially achieved by optimizing the HMM emission probabilities with respect to the query sequence using unsupervised training. We can train the parameters not only on the single query sequence but also on its homologs, assuming that they represent independent samples generated by the same HMM. In this way, we can use the information from homologous sequences without constructing multiple sequence alignment and without assuming that the annotation is the same in all sequences. Tusnády and Simon [73] use emission parameters estimated on an annotated training set as pseudocounts in each step of the Baum–Welch algorithm.

Chatterji and Pachter [18] use a similar approach to find genes in multiple homologous genomic regions by biasing parameters of a typical HMM gene finder to match specifically the genes on the input. The parameters of the model and gene predictions are iteratively improved by Gibbs sampling. Thus, after each iteration, gene predictions in all input sequences will tend to be more similar to each other, and the parameters of the model will fit the input sequences more closely.

We may also need to adjust parameters of a gene finder when applying it to a newly sequenced genome. In such a case, we rarely have sufficiently large training set of manually annotated sequences. One approach is to identify easy to find genes, such as those with a strong protein match in a database, and train the HMM using those genes [46]. Korf [40] has considered adjusting parameters trained on a different species by Viterbi training on the new species. Lomsadze et al. [48] have shown that a careful procedure can obtain parameters of a eukaryotic gene finder on a new species in a completely unsupervised fashion, starting with a very simple set of manually created parameters.

4.6.3 Beyond Maximum Likelihood

So far, we have considered algorithms that trained HMM parameters by maximizing the likelihood of the training set. A common criticism of the maximum likelihood (ML) approach in the machine learning literature is that it maximizes the wrong objective (see, for example, [41]). Our goal in decoding is to retrieve the annotation H that maximizes $\Pr(H|X)$, where the sequence X is fixed. Therefore, instead of maximizing the joint probability $\Pr(H, X)$ of the training sequences, this perspective argues that we should concentrate on maximizing the conditional probability $\Pr(H|X)$, since the sequence X is fixed in the decoding phase, and it does not matter whether its probability is low or high. This optimization criterion is known as *conditional maximum likelihood* (CML).

In the context of hidden Markov models, CML was used in applications in bioinformatics [41] and natural language processing [38]. Even if the sequences are annotated, there is no known closed formula or EM algorithm that would estimate the parameters of the model to optimize the conditional maximum likelihood. Instead, numerical gradient descent methods are used to achieve local maximum. In these studies, slight [38] to significant [41] improvement was observed compared to models trained by ML.

A theoretical analysis is available in the context of the simpler data classification problem, where a similar dichotomy occurs between the naive Bayes classifier (which is equivalent to ML) and logistic regression (equivalent to CML). In this context, Ng and Jordan [55] have shown that even though using CML gives asymptotically lower error, ML requires significantly fewer training samples to converge to the best model: it requires only a logarithmic number of samples with respect to the number of parameters compared to the linear number of samples required for convergence in CML. Thus ML training is appropriate if only a small number of samples are available, while it is better to use CML when the training set is large. It is not known whether these results extend to the case of more complex models, such as HMMs, where we are doing more than merely classifying a sample into categories. We may also ask (and no known answer exists to this question) whether the better response to an increase in training data is to switch from ML to CML, or to switch to a more accurate model of reality that requires a larger number of parameters.

One major disadvantage of HMMs optimized for CML is that it is hard to interpret their emission and transition probabilities. The generative process associated with the HMM no longer generates sequences that look like sequences from the training set. The probabilities no longer represent frequencies observed directly in the sequence, which makes it hard to incorporate prior knowledge about the problem into the probabilistic model by applying restrictions on parameters of the model or by creating a custom model topology.

For example, the HMM modeling the topology of transmembrane proteins in Fig. 4.4 has two states representing transmembrane helices. It may be reasonable to assume that since the sequences corresponding to these two states serve the same function (membrane transition) that in an ML model both states should share the same emission probabilities. On the basis of this assumption, we can reduce the number of parameters (and thus the number of sequences required for training) by *tying* those parameters together, forcing them to be the same. On the contrary, since in CML method the emission probabilities are set to maximize the conditional probability of the annotation given the sequence, rather than the likelihood of the sequence, it is not clear that the emission probabilities in these two states should be similar, even if the sequences attributed to these states are similar.

Conditional random fields [45] further continue in the direction of CML training, abandoning the probabilistic interpretation of emission and transition probabilities and replacing them with undirected potentials that do not need to be normalized to 1. They were applied in bioinformatics for recognizing protein structure motifs [47] and for finding genes [22].

Some recent extensions abolish the probabilistic interpretation of HMMs altogether. Instead, they consider the following problem directly: set the parameters of the model (without normalization restrictions) so that the model discriminates well between correct and incorrect annotations. These models, such as hidden Markov support vector machines [4] and convex hidden Markov models [78], are inspired by maximum margin training and kernel methods in support vector machines [11], which are very successful methods for the classification problem.

4.7 CONCLUSION

On our tour through HMMs and their use in biological sequence annotation, we have seen both the most traditional HMM algorithms and their most exotic extensions. We have seen extensions to the decoding algorithms to handle many cases where multiple different paths through the HMM correspond to the same semantic meaning and algorithms to handle generalized HMMs, in which the lengths of features may come from complex, nongeometric distributions. We have seen many ways in which HMMs can operate on multiple sequences, and in all these cases we have argued why these extensions are useful in modeling and annotating biological sequences.

Many of these extensions rely upon the conceptual simplicity of the basic HMM framework: unlike the parameters of a neural network or of a support vector machine, the parameters of a hidden Markov model trained for maximum likelihood are extremely simple to understand. Even for their more complex extensions (such as phylogenetic HMMs or pair HMMs), one can quickly determine the semantic meaning of the parameters and imagine ways to make them estimated more accurately, or to change the topology of the HMM to more closely model reality (though, of course, our discussion of the multiple-path problem in Section 4.3.2 shows that this may not be entirely wise). Even the more complex decoding approaches to handle external information, such as those of Section 4.5.2, can be seen as a way of mathematically encoding sensible intuitive concepts.

Perhaps the most important question for the future of HMMs, then, is whether increasingly sophisticated HMM modeling, training, and decoding procedures can continue to maintain this conceptual simplicity while still allowing the use of ever more and more complex forms of sequence data. Can we incorporate a useful understanding of the three-dimensional geometry of molecules into HMM analysis? Can we usefully train HMMs to understand the evolutionary relationships among thousands of sequences? Can we annotate features and subfeatures of biological sequences that are allowed to overlap each other in complex ways, and where a feature is not simply a contiguous segment of DNA? These questions, and numerous others, will be the subject of the research of the next many years in HMM analysis.

ACKNOWLEDGMENTS

The work of all three authors has been supported by the Natural Sciences and Engineering Research Council of Canada. We are grateful to many colleagues for interesting discussions over the last several years, including Ming Li, Burkhard Morgenstern, Dale Schuurmans, Gregory Kucherov, Ian Korf, and Dan Gusfield.

REFERENCES

1. Abe N, Warmuth MK. On the computational complexity of approximating distributions by probabilistic automata. *Machine Learning* 1992;9(2–3):205–260.
2. Alexandersson M, Cawley S, Pachter L. SLAM: cross-species gene finding and alignment with a generalized pair hidden Markov model. *Genome Res* 2003;13(3):496–502.
3. Allen JE, Salzberg SL. A phylogenetic generalized hidden Markov model for predicting alternatively spliced exons. *Algor Mol Biol* 2006;1(1):14.

4. Altun Y, Tsochantaridis I, Hofmann T. Hidden Markov support vector machines. *ICML 2003: 20th International Conference on Machine Learning*. AAAI Press; 2003. pp. 3–10.
5. Asmussen S, Nerman O, Olsson M. Fitting phase-type distributions via the EM algorithm. *Scan J Stat* 1996;23(4):419–441.
6. Aydin Z, Altunbasak Y, Borodovsky M. Protein secondary structure prediction for a single-sequence using hidden semi-Markov models. *BMC Bioinformatics* 2006;7:178.
7. Baum LE. An inequality and associated maximization technique in statistical estimation for probabilistic functions of Markov processes. *Inequalities III, Proceeding of the Third Symposium*. New York: Academic Press; 1972. pp. 1–8.
8. Baum LE, Eagon JA. An inequality with applications to statistical estimation for probabilistic functions of Markov processes and to a model for ecology. *Bull Am Mathe Soc* 1967;73:360–363.
9. Benson DA, Karsch-Mizrachi I, Lipman DJ, Ostell J, Rapp BA, Wheeler DL. GenBank. *Nucleic Acids Res* 2000;28(1):15–18.
10. Birney E, Clamp M, Durbin R. GeneWise and Genomewise. *Genome Res* 2004; 14(5):988–995.
11. Boser BE, Guyon IM, Vapnik VN. A training algorithm for optimal margin classifiers. *COLT 1992: 5th Annual Workshop on Computational Learning Theory*. ACM Press;1992. pp. 144–152.
12. Brejová B, Brown DG, Li M, Vinař T. Exonhunter: A comprehensive approach to gene finding. *Bioinformatics* 2005;21(S1):i57–i65.
13. Brejová B, Brown DG, Vinař T. The most probable labeling problem in HMMs and its applications to bio informatics. *WABI 2004: Algorithms in Bioinformatics*, Vol. 3240 of *Lecture Notes in Bioinformatics*. Bergen, Norway: Springer; 2004. pp. 426–437.
14. Brejová B, Vinař T. A better method for length distribution modeling in HMMs and its application to gene finding. *CPM 2002: Combinatorial Pattern Matching, 13th Annual Symposium*, Vol. 2373 of *Lecture Notes in Computer Science*. Fukuoka, Japan: Springer; 2002. pp. 190–202.
15. Burge C, Karlin S. Prediction of complete gene structures in human genomic DNA. *J Mol Biol* 1997;268(1):78–94.
16. Bystroff C, Thorsson V, Baker D. HMMSTR: a hidden Markov model for local sequence-structure correlations in proteins. *J Mol Biol*. 2000;301(1):173–180.
17. Cawley SL, Pachter L. HMM sampling and applications to gene finding and alternative splicing. *Bioinformatics* 2003;19(S2):II36–II41.
18. Chatterji S, Pachter L. Large multiple organism gene finding by collapsed Gibbs sampling. *J Comput Biol* 2005;12(6):599–608.
19. Church KW. A stochastic parts program and noun phrase parser for unrestricted text. *Proceedings of the 2nd conference on Applied natural language processing*, Morristown, NJ, USA: 1988; pp.136–143. Association for Computational Linguistics.
20. Churchill GA. Stochastic models for heterogeneous DNA sequences. *Bull Math Biol* 1989;51(1):79–94.
21. Commault C, Mocanu S. Phase-type distributions and representations: some resuts and open problems for system theory. *Int J Control* 2003;76(6):566–580.
22. Culotta A, Kulp D, McCallum A. Gene prediction with conditional random fields. Technical Report UM-CS-2005-028, University of Massachusetts, Amherst, 2005.

23. Delorenzi M, Speed T. An HMM model for coiled-coil domains and a comparison with PSSM-based predictions. *Bioinformatics* 2002;18(4):617–625.

24. Dempster AP, Laird NM, Rubin DB. Maximum likelihood from incomplete data via the EM algorithm. *J R Stat Soc Ser B* 1977;39(1):1–38.

25. Durbin R, Eddy S, Krogh A, Mitchison G. *Biological sequence analysis: Probabilistic models of proteins and nucleic acids*. Cambridge University Press; 1998.

26. Furiselli P, Martelli PL, Casadio R. A new decoding algorithm for hidden Markov models improves the prediction of the topology of all-beta membrane proteins. *BMC Bioinformatics* 2005;6(S4):S12.

27. Felsenstein J. Evolutionary trees from DNA sequences: a maximum likelihood approach. *J Mol Evol* 1981;17(6):368–376.

28. Felsenstein J, Churchill GA. A hidden Markov model approach to variation among sites in rate of evolution. *Mol Biol Evol* 1996;13(1):93–104.

29. Finn RD, Mistry J, Schuster-Bockler B, Griffiths-Jones S, Hollich V, Lassmann T, Moxon S, Marshall M, Khanna A, Durbin R, Eddy SR, Sonnhammer EL, Bateman A. Pfam: clans, web tools and services. *Nucleic Acid Res* 2006;34(Database issue):D247–D251.

30. Forney GD. The Viterbi algorithm. *Proc IEEE* 1973;61:268–278.

31. Gillman D, Sipser M. Inference and minimization of hidden Markov chains. *COLT 1994: Proceedings of the 7th Annual Conference on Computational Learning Theory*. ACM Press; 1994. pp. 147–158.

32. Gilson PR, Nebl T, Vukcevic D, Moritz RL, Sargeant T, Speed TP, Schofield L, Crabb BS. Identification and stoichiometry of glycosylphosphatidylinositol-anchored membrane proteins of the human malaria parasite Plasmodium falciparum. *Mol Cell Proteomics* 2006;5(7):1286–1289.

33. Goldman N, Thorne JL, Jones DT. Using evolutionary trees in protein secondary structure prediction and other comparative sequence analyses. *J Mol Biol* 1996; 263(2):196–208.

34. Gross SS, Brent MR. Using multiple alignments to improve gene prediction. *RECOMB 2005: Proceedings of the 9th Annual International Conference on Research in Computational Molecular Biology*, Vol. 3500 of *Lecture Notes in Computer Science*. Springer; 2005. pp. 374–388.

35. Johnson MT. Capacity and complexity of HMM duration modeling techniques. *IEEE Signal Proc Let* 2005;12(5):407–410.

36. Jukes TH, Cantor C. *Evolution of protein molecules*. Academic Press; 1969. pp. 21–132.

37. Käll L, Krogh A, Sonnhammer ELL. An HMM posterior decoder for sequence feature prediction that includes homology information. *Bioinformatics* 2005; 21(S1):i251–i257.

38. Klein D, Manning CD. Conditional structure versus conditional estimation in NLP models. *EMNLP 2002: Conference on Empirical Methods in Natural Language Processing*: Association for Computational Linguistics; 2002. pp. 9–16.

39. Korf I, Flicek P, Duan D, Brent MR. Integrating genomic homology into gene structure prediction. *Bioinformatics* 2001;17(S1):S140–S148. ISMB.

40. Korf I. Gene finding in novel genomes. *BMC Bioinformatics* 2004;5:59.

41. Krogh A. Two methods for improving performance of an HMM and their application for gene finding. In *ISMB 1997: Proceedings of the 5th International Conference on Intelligent Systems for Molecular Biology*. 1997; pp.179–186.

42. Krogh A. Using database matches with for HMMGene for automated gene detection in Drosophila. *Genome Res* 2000;10(4):523–528.
43. Krogh A, Brown M, Mian IS, Sjolander K, Haussler D. Hidden Markov models in computational biology. applications to protein modeling. *J Mol Biol* 1994;235(5):1501–1501.
44. Krogh A, Larsson B, von Heijne G, Sonnhammer EL. Predicting transmembrane protein topology with a hidden Markov model: application to complete genomes. *J Mol Biol* 2001;305(3):567–570.
45. Lafferty J, McCallum A, Pereira F. Conditional random fields: Probabilistic models for segmenting and labeling sequence data. In *ICML 2001: 18th International Conference on Machine Learning*. Morgan Kaufmann, San Francisco, CA: 2001. pp. 282–289.
46. Larsen TS, Krogh A. EasyGene–a prokaryotic gene finder that ranks ORFs by statistical significance. *BMC Bioinformatics* 2003;4:21.
47. Liu Y, Carbonell J, Weigele P, Gopalakrishnan V. Protein fold recognition using segmentation conditional random fields (SCRFs). *J Comput Biol* 2006;13(2):394–406.
48. Lomsadze A, Ter-Hovhannisyan V, Chernoff YO, Borodovsky M. Gene identification in novel eukaryotic genomes by self-training algorithm. *Nucleic Acid Res* 2005;33(20):6494–6496.
49. Martelli PL, Fariselli P, Krogh A, Casadio R. A sequence-profile-based HMM for predicting and discriminating beta barrel membrane proteins. *Bioinformatics* 2002;18(S1): S46–S53.
50. McAuliffe JD, Pachter L, Jordan MI. Multiple-sequence functional annotation and the generalized hidden Markov phylogeny. *Bioinformatics* 2004;20(12):1850–1850.
51. McCauley S, Hein J. Using hidden Markov models and observed evolution to annotate viral genomes. *Bioinformatics*. 2006;22(11):1308–1316.
52. Meyer IM, Durbin R. Comparative ab initio prediction of gene structures using pair HMMs. *Bioinformatics* 2002;18(10):1309–1318.
53. Mitchell C, Harper M, Jamieson L. On the complexity of explicit duration HMMs. *IEEE Trans Speech Audio Process*, 1995;3(3):213–217.
54. Müller HC. New approach to fire detection algorithms based on the hidden Markov model. *AUBE 2001: 12th International Conference on Automatic Fire Detection*. National Institute of Standards and Technology, 2001. pp. 129–138.
55. Ng AY, Jordan MI. On discriminative vs. generative classifiers: A comparison of logistic regression and naive Bayes. In *NIPS 2002: Advances in Neural Information Processing Systems* MIT Press; 2002. pp. 841–848.
56. Nielsen H, Krogh A. Prediction of signal peptides and signal anchors by a hidden Markov model. In *ISMB 1998: Proceedings of the 6th International Conference on Intelligent Systems for Molecular Biology*. AAAI Press; 1998.pp.122–130.
57. Ohler U, Niemann H, Rubin GM. Joint modeling of DNA sequence and physical properties to improve eukaryotic promoter recognition. *Bioinformatics* 2001;17(S1):S199–S206.
58. Pavlović V, Garg A, Kasif S. A Bayesian framework for combining gene predictions. *Bioinformatics* 2002;18(1):19–27.
59. Pedersen JS, Hein J. Gene finding with a hidden Markov model of genome structure and evolution. *Bioinformatics* 2003;19(2):219–227.

60. Pollastri E, Simoncelli G. Classification of melodies by composer with hidden Markov models. *WEDELMUSIC 2001: The 1st International Conference on WEB Delivering of Music*. IEEE Computer Society; 2001. pp. 88–95.

61. Rabiner LR. A tutorial on hidden Markov models and selected applications in speech recognition. *Proc IEEE* 1989;77(2):257–285.

62. Rastas P, Koivisto M, Mannila H, Ukkonen E. A hidden Markov technique for haplotype reconstruction. *WABI 2005: Algorithms in Bioinformatics*, Vol. 3692 of *Lecture Notes in Computer Science*. Springer; 2005. pp. 140–151.

63. Rodriguez F, Oliver JL, Marin A, Medina JR. The general stochastic model of nucleotide substitution. *J Theor Biol* 1990;142(4):485–501.

64. Schultz A, Zhang M, Leitner T, Kuiken C, Korber B, Morgenstern B, Stanke M. A jumping profile hidden Markov model and applications to recombination sites in HIV and HCV genomes. *BMC Bioinformatics* 2006;7:265.

65. Schwartz R, Chow YL. The *N*-best algorithms: an efficient and exact procedure for finding the *N* most likely sentence hypotheses. *ICASSP 1990: Acoustics, Speech, and Signal Processing*. pages 81–84, vol. 1, 1990.

66. Seymore K, McCallum A, Rosenfeld R. Learning hidden Markov model structure for information extraction. *AAAI'99 Workshop on Machine Learning for Information Extraction*. 1999.

67. Siepel A, Haussler D. Computational identification of evolutionarily conserved exons. *RECOMB 2004: Proceedings of the 8th Annual International Conference on Research in Computational Molecular Biology*. ACM Press; 2004. pp. 177–186.

68. Siepel A, Bejerano G, Pedersen JS, Hinrichs AS, Hou M, Rosenbloom K, Clawson H, Spieth J, Hillier LW, Richards S, Weinstock GM, Wilson RK, Gibbs RA, Kent WJ, Miller W, Haussler D. Evolutionarily conserved elements in vertebrate, insect, worm, and yeast genomes. *Genome Res* 2005;15(8):1034–1040.

69. Siepel A, Haussler D. Combining phylogenetic and hidden Markov models in biosequence analysis. In *RECOMB '03: Proceedings of the 7th Annual International Conference on Research in Computational Molecular Biology* New York, NY, USA: ACM Press; 2003. pp. 277–286.

70. Stanke M, Waack S. Gene prediction with a hidden Markov model and a new intron submodel. *Bioinformatics* 2003;19(S2):II215–II225.

71. Stanke M, Keller O, Gunduz I, Hayes A, Waack S, Morgenstern B.AUGUSTUS: ab initio prediction of alternative transcripts. *Nucleic Acids Res* 2006;34(W):W435–W439.

72. Stanke M, Schoffmann O, Morgenstern B, Waack S. Gene prediction in eukaryotes with a generalized hidden Markov model that uses hints from external sources. *BMC Bioinformatics* 2006;7:62.

73. Tusnády GE, Simon I. Principles governing amino acid composition of integral membrane proteins: application to topology prediction. *J Mol Biol* 1998;283(2):489–506.

74. Viklund H, Elofsson A. Best alpha-helical transmembrane protein topology predictions are achieved using hidden Markov models and evolutionary information. *Protein Sci* 2004;13(7):1908–1917.

75. Vinař T. *Enhancements to Hidden Markov Models for Gene Finding and Other Biological Applications*. PhD thesis, University of Waterloo, October 2005.

76. Viterbi AJ. Error bounds for convolutional codes and an asymtotically optimum decoding algorithm. *IEEE Trans Inform Theory* 1967;IT13:260–267.

77. Xu EW, Kearney P, Brown DG. The use of functional domains to improve transmembrane protein topology prediction. *J Bioinform Comput Biol* 2006;4(1):109–113.
78. Xu L, Wilkinson D, Southey F, Schuurmans D. Discriminative unsupervised learning of structured predictors. *ICML 2006: International Conference on Machine Learning*. 2006.
79. Yamron JP, Carp I, Gillick L, Lowe S, van Mulbregt P. A hidden Markov model approach to text segmentation and event tracking. *ICASSP 1998: IEEE International Conference on Acoustics, Speech, and Signal Processing*. 1998. pp. 333–336.
80. Yang Z. A space-time process model for the evolution of DNA sequences. *Genetics* 1995; 139(2):993–1005.
81. Yeh RF, Lim LP, Burge CB. Computational inference of homologous gene structures in the human genome. *Genome Res* 2001;11(5):803–806.
82. Zhu J, Liu JS, Lawrence CE. Bayesian adaptive sequence alignment algorithms. *Bioinformatics* 1998;14(1):25–39.

5

SORTING- AND FFT-BASED TECHNIQUES IN THE DISCOVERY OF BIOPATTERNS

SUDHA BALLA, SANGUTHEVAR RAJASEKARAN, AND JAIME DAVILA

Department of Computer Science and Engineering, University of Connecticut, Storrs, Connecticut, USA

5.1 INTRODUCTION

Molecular Biologists have witnessed an astronomical growth of biosequence data (DNA, RNA, and protein sequences) due to efforts of several sequencing projects over the past decade. Understanding the information contained in such data is vital to decipher gene function, causes of disease in humans, and rational drug design. A fundamental technique adopted by molecular biologists to extract such meaningful information is identifying common *patterns* or *motifs* among biosequences. Discovering motifs in a set of unaligned DNA sequences could aid in locating biologically functional regions such as promoters, transcription factor binding sites, splice sites. Ungapped regions in the multiple alignment of a set of protein sequences could help classifying proteins of unknown function into known protein families. Identifying unique regions in the messenger RNA (mRNA) of genes could aid in the design of gene-specific short-interference RNAs (siRNAs), thus, reducing the risk of off-target gene silencing in gene-based therapy for certain neurological disorders and cancers. The huge volume of biosequence data available calls for novel computational techniques to discover motifs in a given set of sequences, say DNA, RNA, or proteins.

Bioinformatics Algorithms: Techniques and Applications, Edited by Ion I. Măndoiu and Alexander Zelikovsky

Therefore, several variants of the motif discovery problem could be identified in the computational literature; many of them have been proved to be NP-hard. The numerous algorithms proposed for such variants adopt fundamental concepts and salient data structures of computer science to identify the desired motifs. Dynamic programming algorithms have been proposed for alignment of the input sequences to identify ungapped segments of biological importance. Algorithms that represent the patterns of the input as graphs and trees to discover common motifs have been proposed. Data structures such as suffix trees and suffix arrays (refer [34]) have been proved to be powerful to solve complex string problems efficiently in linear time. In this chapter, we would discuss novel algorithms, which adopt strategies significantly different from those adopted by several known algorithms, to address a few salient problems in the domain of molecular biology that require discovering motifs in a set of biosequences. These algorithms employ basic sorting techniques and simple data structures such as arrays and linked lists and have been proved to perform better in practice than many of the known algorithms when applied to synthetic and real biological datasets.

Measuring similarities among biological sequences has numerous applications. For instance, functionalities of newly sequenced genes can be inferred. Similarity measurements can also help in identifying motifs. In this chapter, we also consider FFT-based efficient algorithms for measuring similarities.

The rest of this chapter is organized as follows: Section 2 describes how sorting can be used as a technique to identify biopatterns (or motifs) in a given set of DNA, RNA, or protein sequences. In Section 3, we discuss some classic motif discovery problems, a brief account of the algorithms proposed for the same in the literature and algorithms that are based on sorting for these problems. Section 4 is devoted to a discussion on FFT-based similarity algorithms. Section 5, concludes the chapter.

5.2 SORTING AND BIOPATTERN DISCOVERY

The basic idea is to create a collection of all the l-mers (where the length of the desired motif is l) that represent the "motif space" from the input sequences, sort the collection lexicographically and scan through the sorted collection to identify the motifs of interest. In the following section, we explain in detail how the elements of the collection are generated from the input for each of the problems that we discuss.

There are many ways to sort such a collection. For instance, it can be sorted using any comparison-based algorithm such as quick sort, merge sort. But, if we have additional information about the elements in the collection, radix sort could be employed. For a detailed discussion on sorting algorithms refer [37] and [19]. We know that DNA and RNA sequences are from a fixed alphabet of size 4 and protein sequences are from an alphabet of size 20. In our problems, if we represent every l-mer in the collection as an integer value, we know that the values of elements in the collection lie strictly in the range $[0, |\Sigma|^l]$, that is, every element in the collection can be thought of as a $(\log_2|\Sigma|)l$-bit binary number, where Σ is the alphabet of the input sequences. Radix sort sorts the elements with respect to some number of bits at a time starting from the Least Significant Bits (LSBs). For example, these elements can be sorted with respect to w bits at a time, where w is the word length of the computer. In this case, the elements in the collection can be sorted in $(\log_2|\Sigma|)(l/w)$ phases where each phase takes linear time.

For DNA sequences, the alphabet $\Sigma = \{a, c, t, g\}$. In this alphabet g is the complement of c and a is the complement of t. We map the elements of Σ into integers as follows: $a = 0, c = 1, t = 2$, and $g = 3$. Thus, we need two bits to represent each member of Σ and a $2l$-bit number can represent an l-mer.

5.3 MOTIF DISCOVERY AND RELATED PROBLEMS

In this section, we will discuss a few salient problems in molecular biology that require discovery of biopatterns in a set of DNA, RNA, or protein sequences. We will deal with a classic motif discovery problem, called the Planted (l, d)-motif problem, in detail. We will discuss algorithms to discover motifs based on edit distances. We will also look at three problems that are very closely related to motif discovery, called the Primer Selection Problem, the problem of discovering patterns that participate in a phenomenon called RNA Interference (RNAi) in the cells of organisms and the Specific Selection of siRNA Patterns in entire genomic data. For each of these problems, we give a brief account of the algorithms that have been proposed in the literature followed by a discussion on algorithms that employ sorting techniques to identify the patterns of interest.

5.3.1 Planted (l, d)-Motif Problem

The Planted (l, d)-motif Problem is a classic problem of motif discovery in molecular biology with application in identifying transcription factors and their binding sites for a set of coregulated genes, promoters, splicing sites, and so on. Tompa [62] studied the problem of identifying very short motifs of length about 5–7 with 0, 1, or 2 substitutions, to address the ribosome binding site problem and proposed an exact algorithm for the same. When concluding the paper, he had posed the question of devising algorithms to accommodate longer patterns with proportionately more substitutions allowed. Pevzner and Sze [48] addressed this question by devising two novel algorithms that effectively identified motifs of length 15 with 4 substitutions. They formally formulated the problem as the Planted (l, d)-motif problem, which had also been considered by Sagot [57] as follows.

5.3.1.1 Planted (l, d)-Motif Problem (PMP) Input are t nucleotide sequences of length n each and integers l and d. The problem is to identify a motif M of length l, given that each input sequence contains a variant of M, the variants being at a hamming distance of at most d from M.

But there are algorithms earlier to Tompa's work that have been proposed in the literature to identify motifs in a set of DNA sequences that could be binding sites for regulatory elements. Lawrence and Reilly [42] proposed an algorithm based on

Expectation Maximization (EM) to identify such motifs. Bailey and Elkan's [4] contribution, algorithm MEME, was an extension of Lawrence and Reilly's work to discover multiple occurrences of a motif in a set of sequences and also to discover multiple planted motifs for a given input. Lawrence et al. [41] presented an algorithm based on Gibbs Sampling, called the GibbsDNA. Hertz and Stormo [35] devised a greedy algorithm CONSENSUS to identify functional relationships by aligning DNA, RNA or protein sequences. They used a log-likelihood scoring scheme to arrive at the information content of an alignment and the algorithm picked those alignments with highest information content. CONSENSUS successfully identified 19 of 24 sites of the DNA binding protein CRP-transcription factor in 18 DNA sequences of *E. coli*, each about 105 nt in length.

The "challenge problem" addressed by Pevzner and Sze was the (15, 4) instance of PMP stated above in $t = 20$ sequences each of length $n = 600$. Algorithm WINNOWER attempts to identify large cliques in a multipartite graph G, constructed with the patterns of length l in the input sequences as its vertices. Two vertices u and v in G are connected by an edge iff u and v belong to two different sequences of the input and their hamming distance, that is, the number of substitutions needed to convert u to v and vice versa, $d(u, v) \leq 2d$. Algorithm WINNOWER treats all edges of G equally and does not distinguish edges that correspond to high and low similarities. Algorithm SP-STAR attempts to overcome this drawback by using a sum-of-pairs scoring function and a local improvement strategy to identify the best occurrences of the motif in the input set.

Buhler and Tompa [12] showed that there are instances of PMP that are more challenging than the (15, 4) instance and devised an algorithm called PROJECTION to solve such instances. They concluded that WINNOWER and SP-STAR failed to solve the (14, 4), (16, 5), and (18, 6)-motif problems for the same values of t and n as above, while their algorithm PROJECTION succeeded in doing so. Algorithm PROJECTION uses the principle of random projections to arrive at better seeds of the input for an EM algorithm. It uses a hash function $h(x)$ constructed using k of the l positions chosen at random, and hashes all substrings of length l of the input sequences into buckets based on their value w.r.t. the k positions. It is based on an intuition that if $k < (l - d)$ a number of the t variants of M would hash into the same bucket. A probability weight matrix arrived from the substrings hashed on to highly enriched buckets is used as the initial seed to the EM algorithm. The work presented a probabilistic analysis of PMP to arrive at the difficult instances of PMP, such as the (9, 2), (11, 3), (13, 4), (15, 5), (17, 6)-motif problems and stated that these problems are inherently unsolvable by PROJECTION as the number of spurious hits (patterns that appear by random chance) for these instances is more than one (Table 2 of [12]).

Algorithms MULTIPROFILER [38], PatternBranching, and ProfileBranching [49] also address PMP and were shown to perform well in practice for several instances on the problem on random and real biological data.

All the algorithms discussed above employ local search techniques and may not output the desired planted motif always. We refer to such algorithms as *approximate algorithms*. The performance of such approximate algorithms is measured using a factor called the *performance coefficient* in the literature. Let K be the number

TABLE 5.1 Performance of Approximate Algorithms on (15, 4) Instance of PMP

Algorithm	Year	ρ
GibbsDNA	1993	0.12
MEME	1995	0.10
CONSENSUS	1999	0.07
WINNOWER	2000	0.92
PROJECTION	2001	0.93
PatternBranching and ProfileBranching	2003	$\approx$ 1.00 and 0.57

of actual residue positions (tl) of the input that correspond to the variants of motif M. Let P be the number of such residue positions predicted by an algorithm. *Performance Coefficient* (ρ) is defined as the ratio $(K \cap P)/(K \cup P)$. Algorithms that always output the correct answer are referred to as *exact algorithms*. While for approximate algorithms $0 < \rho < 1$, for exact algorithms $\rho = 1$. Table 5.1 gives the performance of several algorithms discussed above on the (15,4) instance of PMP. There are several exact algorithms in the literature proposed for PMP in [10,11,32,57,58,60,62,63]. Such algorithms are *exhaustive enumeration algorithms* and as aptly stated in [12], they become impractical for the challenging instances of PMP. A salient exact algorithm called MITRA was proposed by Eskin and Pevzner [28] that adopts a mismatch tree data structure to represent the pattern space and performs a depth first search on the mismatch tree to identify the planted motif for a given input. MITRA was shown to be successful in identifying monads (simple planted motifs) and dyads (complex planted motifs that appear in pairs separated by a varying gap length in each input sequence) in synthetic and real biological data. The voting algorithm [18] adopts hashing techniques to identify planted motifs.

There have also been contributions to PMP by researchers who have addressed closely related problems in [9,10] (Substring Parsimony Problem), [33] (Closest String Problem), [29] (Common Approximate Substring Problem), and [43] (Consensus Patterns Problem).

For PMP, exact algorithms that adopt sorting techniques were first presented in [51]. The runtime of the basic algorithm Planted Motif Search (PMS) is $O(tnl^d|\Sigma|^d(l/w))$, where w is the word length of the computer. Like most of the algorithms in the literature, the sorting approach is based on exploring the neighborhood of input patterns, exploiting the fact that the motif M is an element in the d-neighborhood of at least one substring of length l in every input sequence. The basic algorithm for PMP, Algorithm PMS is as follows:

Algorithm PMS {

1. Generate all possible l-mers from out of each of the t input sequences. Let C_i be the collection of l-mers from out of S_i for $1 \leq i \leq t$.
2. For all $1 \leq i \leq t$ and for all $u \in C_i$, generate all l-mers v,

such that u and v are at a hamming distance of at most d.
Let the collection of l-mers corresponding to C_i be C'_i, for $1 \leq i \leq t$.
The total number of patterns in any C'_i is $O(nl^d|\Sigma|^d)$.

3. Sort all the l-mers lexicographically in every C'_i, $1 \leq i \leq t$.
   Let L_i be the sorted list corresponding to C'_i.
4. Merge all the L_is ($1 \leq i \leq t$).
   Output the generated (in step 2) l-mer that occurs in all the L_is.

}

We know that there are $(n - l + 1)$ substrings of length l in each of the t input sequences, and the number of elements in the d-neighborhood of a string of length l is $\sum_{i=0}^{d} {}^{l}C_i|\Sigma|^i$. If $d < (l/2)$, then, the total number of elements in the collection is $O(tnl^d|\Sigma|^d)$. Each element in the collection is represented as $(2l/w)$ computer words and hence the following theorem holds.

Theorem 5.1 *PMP can be solved by PMS in time $O(tnl^d|\Sigma|^d(l/w))$, where w is the word length of the computer. The space complexity of PMS is $O(tnl^d|\Sigma|^d(l/w))$.*

Algorithm PMS generates the neighborhood of l-mers of all the input sequences at the same time. But we know that a variant of the motif M appears in every input sequence and hence will be contained in the collection of elements that represent the neighborhood of l-mers from one input sequence. Therefore, PMS could be modified into a memory efficient version described as follows.

Algorithm PMS1 {

Generate all possible l-mers from out of the first input sequence S_1.
Let C_1 be the collection of these l-mers. For all $u \in C_1$, generate all l-mers v such that u and v are at a hamming distance of at most d.
Sort the collection of these l-mers and let L be the sorted collection.
for $i := 2$ to t do {

1. Generate all possible l-mers from out of the input sequence S_i.
   Let C_i be the collection of these l-mers.
2. For all $u \in C_i$, generate all l-mers v such that u and v are at a hamming distance of at most d.

Let the collection of these l-mers be C_i'.
3. Sort all the l-mers in C_i'. Let L_i be the sorted list.
4. Merge L_i and L and keep the intersection in L, i.e., $L := L \cap L_i$.
}
L now has the motif(s) of interest, output L.
}

Note that the space complexity of PMS1 improves by a factor of t as it retains the neighborhood of only one sequence at every stage of processing. Hence, we get the following theorem.

Theorem 5.2 *PMP can be solved by PMS1 in time $O(tnl^d|\Sigma|^d(l/w))$, where w is the word length of the computer. The space complexity of PMS1 is $O(nl^d|\Sigma|^d(l/w))$.*

If motif M occurs in every input sequence, then every substring of M also occurs in every input sequence. In particular, there are at least $(l - k + 1)$ k-mers (for $d < k \leq l$) such that each one of them occurs in every input sequence at a hamming distance of at most d. Let K be the collection of k-mers that represent the $(l - k + 1)$ substrings of M. Also, in every input sequence S_i, there will be $(l - k + 1)$ consecutive positions at which there would be occurrences of the elements of K such that an l-mer could be formed by putting together the k-mers of these positions.

An improved algorithm, algorithm PMS2, is presented in [51] that exploits the above fact to discover planted motifs in two phases. In the first phase, all $(d + c)$-mers (for some appropriate value c) that occur in each of the input sequences at a hamming distance of at most d are identified (all valid $M_{(d+c)}$ for the input set). Potential l-mers are formed from the strategy explained above from the $(d + c)$-mers. In the second phase, each l-mer M' of the first phase is checked to see if it is a valid planted motif for the input.

For instances with l from 9 to 20, algorithm PMS1 took about 1 or 2 s when $d = 2$ and around 20 s when $d = 3$. Algorithm PMS2 found the planted motif in about 220 seconds for instances with l from 13 to 20 and $d = 4$. These results show better performance when compared to the two different versions of MITRA reported in [28], namely, MITRA-Count and MITRA-Graph. For the (11, 2) instance, MITRA-Count and MITRA-Graph take 1 min each. For the (12, 3) instance, MITRA-Count and MITRA-Graph take 1 min and 4 min, respectively. For the (14, 4) instance, MITRA-Count takes 4 min and MITRA-Graph takes 10 min. Also, the PMS algorithms solve the challenge instances (9, 2), (11, 3), and (13, 4) in time 1.43 s, 19.84 s, and 228.94 s, respectively, which were deemed difficult in [12] owing to the number of spurious solutions possible being greater than one.

Buhler and Tompa [12] examined orthologous sequences from a several organisms taken upstream of the following types of genes: preproinsulin, dihydrofolate reductase (DHFR), metallothioneins, and c-fos, to identify known transcriptional regulatory elements (data due to Blanchette [10]). On these datasets, the PMS algorithms found the published motifs similar to the ones reported in [12].

Space efficient exact algorithms PMSi and PMSP that adopt better pruning techniques while searching the motif space have been proposed in [20] and have solved the (15, 5) and (17, 6) instances of PMP in 35 minutes and 12 h, respectively. These algorithms explore the d-neighborhood of substrings of length l (say u) from the first sequence, one at a time, to check for the planted motif, considering only a subset of substrings from other sequences that would qualify to be a variant w.r.t. u, that is, those substrings at a hamming distance of at most $2d$ from u. Furthermore, improvements on these algorithms is included in [21] , obtaining a significantly faster algorithm called PMSprune, which handles harder instances reducing the running time.

5.3.2 Discovering Edit Distance-based Motifs

The discussion in the previous section considers only point mutations as events of divergence, but evolutionarily speaking, there are insertions and deletions of residues that occur to cause such divergence in biosequences. Therefore, researchers have considered to employ the Levenshtein distance (or edit distance) instead of hamming distance to extract common motifs in a set of sequences. Rocke and Tompa [55] present an algorithm based on the Gibbs Sampling approach of Lawrence et al. [41] that adopts a relative entropy scoring function to identify best scoring motif occurrences, taking into account gaps in the occurrences. Sagot [57] proposed algorithms that adopt suffix tree data structure to discover common motifs in a set of biosequences based on hamming distance and also extended them to the edit distance-based model. The problem of discovering motifs based on edit distance is formally stated as follows.

Given n sequences $S_1, S_2, \ldots, S_n$, each of average length m from a fixed alphabet Σ, and integers l, d, and q, find all the patterns of length l in the input, with occurrences in at least q of the n sequences, each such occurrence being at an *edit distance* of at most d from the patterns themselves.

The suffix tree algorithm given by Sagot [57] has a runtime of $O(n^2 m l^d |\Sigma|^d)$ and a space requirement of $O(n^2 m/w)$, where w is the word length of the computer. An algorithm with an expected runtime of $O(nm + d(nm)^{(1+pow(\epsilon))} \log nm)$ where $\epsilon = d/l$ and $pow(\epsilon)$ is an increasing concave function was proposed by Adebiyi and Kaufmann [1]. The value of $pow(\epsilon)$ is roughly 0.9 for protein and DNA sequences.

A sorting-based algorithm Deterministic Motif Search (DMS) that has the same runtime complexity as Sagot's algorithm was proposed by Rajasekaran et al. in [52]. Algorithm DMS generates the neighborhood of every substring of length l in the input, the elements being at an *edit distance* of at most d from the substrings themselves. Call this collection A. Note that the elements in A will have lengths in the range $[(l-d), (l+d)]$. The number of elements in A is $O(nml^d|\Sigma|^d)$. A collection B consisting of all substrings of the input with lengths in the range $[(l-d), (l+d)]$ is also generated, duplicates within the same sequences removed. Clearly, the size of

B is $O(nmd)$. Collections A and B are sorted and merged. Let the merged collection be C. Collection C is then scanned to identify those elements of A that have occurred in collection B from at least q distinct sequences of the input. The significance of algorithm DMS lies in the fact that it uses simple radix sorting techniques and arrays as underlying data structure to identify the desired patterns with a potential to perform better in practice than the suffix tree-based approach. A survey on motif search algorithms is [50].

5.3.3 Primer Selection Problem

An experimental method in molecular biology, Polymerase Chain Reaction (PCR), is performed in the laboratories to create multiple copies of a DNA sequence. This process, called *amplification*, requires a pair of short single-stranded synthetic DNA strings, typically 15 to 20 nucleotides long that exactly match the beginning and end of the DNA fragment to be amplified, called *forward* and *reverse* primers. Multiplex PCR (MP-PCR) is a variant of PCR, which enables simultaneous amplification of multiple DNA fragments of interest in one reaction by using a mixture of multiple primers [15]. The presence of multiple primers in MP-PCR can lead to severe problems, such as unintended amplification products caused by mispriming or lack of amplification due to primer cross hybridization. To minimize these problems, it is critical to minimize the number of primers involved in a single MP-PCR reaction, particularly, when the number of DNA sequences to be amplified is large. This can be achieved by selecting primers that would simultaneously act as forward and/or reverse primers for several of the DNA sequences in the input set. The problem of minimizing the number of primers is called the Primer Selection Problem (PSP) and has been well studied, for example, in [24–26, 47].

Pearson et al. [47] proved that PSP is NP-Complete by a reduction from the minimum set cover problem, and gave an exact algorithm based on the branch-and-bound technique and a greedy heuristic guaranteeing a logarithmic approximation factor. Doi and Imai [24] considered biological constraints such as the GC-content, complementarity of the primers and the length of amplification in their approximation algorithm. In [25], the authors analyzed a more rigorous version of the primer selection problem by considering primer orientation and the length constraint on the amplified product. Konwar et al. [39] address MP-PCR primer design with amplification length constraints using a *potential greedy* technique.

An advanced technique of designing primers with multiple bases in each position of the primer [40] led to a higher degree of primer reuse in MP-PCR. Such primers are called *Degenerate Primers* and require no involved methods than those required to synthesize regular primers. The advent of this technique shifted the focus to the problem of selecting degenerate primers for a given set of DNA sequences, called the Degenerate Primer Design Problem (DPDP). The *degeneracy* of a degenerate primer p_d is the product of the number of bases in each position of the primer, that is, $\prod_{i=1}^{l} p_d[i]$, where l is the length of p_d. It can also be viewed as the number of distinct nondegenerate primers that could be formed out of it. For example, if the degenerate primer is $p_d = \mathrm{A\{CT\}GC\{ACG\}T\{GA\}}$, it has degeneracy 12; the distinct nondegenerate primers represented in p_d are ACGCATG, ACGCATA, ACGCCTG, ACGCCTA, ACGCGTG, ACGCGTA, ATGCATG, ATGCATA, ATGCCTG, ATGCCTA, ATGCGTG, and ATGCGTA. p_d is said to *cover* a given DNA sequence s iff s contains at least one of the nondegenerate primers of p_d as its substring. Linhart and Shamir formulated many variants of DPDP in [45] and proved them to be NP-hard. One such variant, called the Maximum Coverage Degenerate Primer Design Problem (MC-DPDP), emerges when a bound is imposed on the degeneracy of the primers designed, as highly degenerate primers may give excessive mispriming. The goal is then shifted to design a minimum number of degenerate primers for the given set of sequences such that each degenerate primer has a degeneracy of at most the bound specified and covers as many input sequences as possible. A number of algorithms have been proposed for MC-DPDP, defined as follows.

Given n DNA sequences of length m nucleotides each, primer length l and degeneracy threshold d, find a set of degenerate primers of maximum coverage, each of length l and degeneracy at most d, that collectively cover all the input sequences.

Rose et al. [56] proposed an algorithm called *CODEHOP* that designs hybrid primers with nondegenerate consensus clamp at the $5'$ region and a degenerate $3'$ core region. In Wei, Kuhn, and Narasimhan's [64] work, algorithm *DePiCt* that has a similar flavor, designs primers of low degeneracy and high coverage for a given set of aligned amino acid sequences based on hierarchical clustering. In an effort to identify genes belonging to the same family, Fuchs et al. [31] devised a two phase algorithm called *DEFOG*. In its first phase, *DEFOG* introduces degeneracy into a set of nondegenerate primer candidates selected due to their best entropy score. Linhart and Shamir [46] proposed an algorithm called *HYDEN* for the first phase of *DEFOG* and reported good practical performance in experiments on synthetic and real biological data. Souvenir et al. [59] proposed the *MIPS* algorithm for a variation of MC-DPDP, discussed in their paper as the Partial Threshold Multiple Degenerate Primer Design (PT-MDPD), that uses an iterative beam search technique to design its degenerate primers. Experimental results for varying number of input sequences and different target degeneracy, the sequences being uniformly distributed i.i.d. sequences of equal length, were reported in [59]. It was shown that MIPS always produced a smaller number of primers than HYDEN. For a survey of algorithms on Primer Selection, see [5].

MIPS starts with a set of primers (called *2 primers*) that cover two sequences from an input of n sequences, adopting a FASTA lookup table to identify those substrings of length l that match in at least six consecutive positions. It extends the coverage of the primers in the candidate set by one additional sequence, introducing degeneracy in the primers if necessary, retains a subset of these primers of lowest degeneracy (the number determined by an input parameter called *beam size b*) for the next iterative step until none of the primers can be extended further without crossing the target degeneracy d. At this point, the primer with the lowest degeneracy is selected and the sequences that it covers are removed from the input set and the procedure is repeated until all the sequences are covered.

MIPS has an overall time complexity of $O(bn^3mp)$, where b is the beam size, n is the number of sequences, m is the sequence length, l is the primer length, and p is the cardinality of the final set of selected degenerate primers. The number of iterations MIPS takes to identify an *n-primer*, that is, a primer that covers all the n input sequences, is $O(n)$. This is because in the kth step of the iteration, it generates candidate primers for the $(k+1)$th step such that their degeneracy either increases or remains the same while their coverage increases by exactly one more sequence. Thus, even in the simplest case of a string of length l appearing as a substring in all the input sequences, MIPS would perform n iterations to identify the nondegenerate *n-primer*.

An algorithm called DPS has been given in [8]. DPS has been shown to have a better runtime than that of MIPS in the worst case. It employs sorting techniques and a new strategy of ranking the primers in every iteration as defined below.

Let the *coverage efficiency* $e(P)$ of a degenerate primer P be the ratio of the number $(c(P))$ of sequences it amplifies or covers to its degeneracy $(d(P))$, that is, $e(P) = c(P)/d(P)$.

Candidate primers are kept in a priority queue. Let $P1$ and $P2$ be two degenerate primers in the priority queue of candidate primers and let $e(P1) > e(P2)$, then the priority of $P1$ is higher than that of $P2$. If $e(P1) = e(P2)$, then the primers are ranked in the nondecreasing order of their degeneracy.

Similar to MIPS, at any time the algorithm DPS keeps a collection of b *best primers*. In a given iteration, these b primers are *merged* with every l-mer in the input sequences that are yet to be covered. Each such merged l-mer is a potential primer. Thus, a collection of at most bmn candidate primers is examined in any iteration. There could be duplicates in this collection. This collection is sorted to identify duplicates. The coverage lists of duplicates are merged. As a result, for each candidate in the collection of unique candidates, its *coverage efficiency* is computed. Based on the coverage efficiency, the best b primers are picked for the next iteration.

Now, let us look into the number of iterations algorithm DPS will perform to design 1 primer of degeneracy at most d. As the algorithm identifies unique primer candidates in each iteration, the candidates generated for the next iteration will always have a degeneracy strictly greater than the degeneracy of the candidate in the current iteration. For a degeneracy of d, the number of positions that can be degenerate in any primer strictly lies in the range, $[\lceil \log_{|\Sigma|} d \rceil : \lfloor \log_2 d \rfloor]$. If we consider the number of symbols that could be added to a nondegenerate primer to create a degenerate primer of degeneracy at most d, strictly the range is $[\lfloor \log_2 d \rfloor : (|\Sigma| - 1) * \lceil \log_{|\Sigma|} d \rceil]$. Thus, the number of iterative steps algorithm DPS can perform to identify a single primer P of the output is $O(|\Sigma| \log_{|\Sigma|} d)$. Thus, the overall time complexity of algorithm DPS is $O(|\Sigma| \log_{|\Sigma|} dbn^2mp)$.

[45] introduced another variant of DPDP called the Minimum Degeneracy Degenerate Primer Design with Errors Problem (MD-DPDEP). Here, the goal is to identify one degenerate primer of minimum degeneracy to cover all the input sequences. A special case of MD-DPDEP, called Minimum Degeneracy Degenerate Primer Design Problem (MD-DPDP) is discussed in [46]. Apart from proving its NP-hardness, little focus has been given to MD-DPDEP in the literature.

Let $S = \{S_1, S_2, \ldots, S_n\}$ be the set of input DNA sequences and $|S_i| = m$, $1 \leq i \leq n$. Let $l, l \ll m$ be the length of the degenerate primer p_d designed for the input set. Consider any input string S_i. Let $S_i[j, \ldots, (j+l-1)]$ denote the substring of length l starting at position j of S_i. Let $\text{dist}(p_d, S_i[j, \ldots, (j+l-1)])$ denote the hamming distance between p_d and $S_i[j, \ldots, (j+l-1)]$. As discussed earlier, we say that p_d *covers* S_i iff for some j of S_i, $\text{dist}(p_d, S_i[j, \ldots, (j+l-1)]) = 0$. Generally, a small number of mismatches or *errors* are allowed between $S_i[j, \ldots, (j+l-1)]$ and p_d, which will not hinder the proper binding of the primer to the string during MP-PCR experiments. Let e, $0 \leq e \leq l$, be the number of mismatches allowed, (i.e.) p_d *covers* S_i iff for some j of S_i, $\text{dist}(p_d, S_i[j, \ldots, (j+l-1)]) \leq e$. The MD-DPDEP is defined as follows. MD-DPDP is a special case of MD-DPDEP where $e = 0$.

Given the set S of n input DNA sequences and integers l and e, MD-DPDEP is to find a single degenerate primer p_d of length l and minimum degeneracy, say d, that covers all the input strings of S such that for some j of S_i, $\text{dist}(p_d, S_i[j, \ldots, (j+l-1)]) \leq e$ for each input sequence S_i, $1 \leq i \leq n$.

In [7], algorithm MinDPS is proposed for MD-DPDEP. It designs p_d consisting of two parts, the nondegenerate part α and the degenerate part β, similar to algorithm *CODEHOP*. MinDPS consists of two phases, Phase I designing α adopting algorithm PMS1, and Phase II designing β of p_d adopting algorithm DPS. Based on the probabilistic analysis of [12], MinDPS arrives at the expected length of α, such that there exists a planted $(|\alpha|, e)$-motif for the input sequences. In Phase I, it finds a set of $(|\alpha|, e)$-motifs for the input sequences using algorithm PMS1.

Let M be a $(|\alpha|, e)$-motif for the input set. Let $S_i[j_i, \ldots, (j_i + |\alpha| - 1)]$, $1 \leq i \leq n$, be the variants of M in the input sequences. Let the hamming distance $\text{dist}(\alpha, S_i[j_i, \ldots, (j_i + |\alpha| - 1)]) = e'_i$. If $e''_i = e - e'_i$, then, $\text{dist}(\beta, S_i[(j_i + |\alpha|), \ldots, (j_i + |\alpha| + |\beta| - 1)]) \leq e''_i$. Let N_i denote the set of strings of length $|\beta|$, such that for each element $\nu \in N_i$, $\text{dist}(\nu, S_i[(j_i + |\alpha|), \ldots, (j_i + |\alpha| + |\beta| - 1)]) \leq e''_i$. If there are more than one variant of M in a given input sequence S_i, all such variants are considered to construct the elements of N_i. Phase II of MinDPS constructs a degenerate primer β of length $(l - |\alpha|)$ considering the elements of the sets N_i, $1 \leq i \leq n$ as candidates from each sequence of the input. Algorithm *DPS* is employed to design β.

Algorithm MinDPS is reported to perform well in practice, achieving primers with degeneracy around 200-fold less than the expected degeneracy on real biological datasets when $e = 3$.

5.3.4 Discovering Endogenous RNAi Patterns in Genomes

RNA Interference or RNAi ([30]) is a phenomenon that inhibits the expression of target genes by the introduction of double-stranded RNA (dsRNA) molecules into the cells of organisms. RNAi has become a widely adopted technique in laboratories to study pathways and determine gene functions in various species. Recent studies show that it could be adopted as a therapy to treat diseases like cancers and genetic disorders in which the mutant gene responsible for the initiation and progression of such disorders is targeted and suppressed [13]. The dsRNA molecules, either synthetic (*in vitro*) or those synthesized *in vivo* as a hairpin loop, are cut into fragments

21–23 nt long (short-interference RNA or siRNA) by a Dicer enzyme present in the cell. These siRNAs associate themselves to RNA Induced Silencing Complex (RISC) and eventually become single stranded. Then, the RISC identifies the substring of the target mRNA that is *antisense* to one of the two strands of the siRNA attached to it, binds to the mRNA and cleaves it into two near the center of the siRNA strand. The cell identifies the split mRNA as unwanted material and destroys it. Thus, the protein that would be translated from the mRNA will not be produced and the silencing of the gene responsible for the production of the protein is achieved. This process is called *RNAi by degradation*. *RNAi by inhibition* is another process where micro RNAs (miRNA) approximately 22 nt long bind to sites within the $3'$ Untranslated Region (UTR) of the target mRNA and prevent its translation into the corresponding protein ([44]). For a detailed treatment of RNAi please refer to [2]. In *RNAi by inhibition*, perfect matching between the miRNA and the mRNA target site is not necessary but for *RNAi by degradation*, an exact matching is necessary between the siRNA strand and the substring of the target mRNA.

In [36], the problem of detecting endogenous dsRNA control elements and their corresponding mRNA target for *RNAi by degradation* in genome sequences is discussed. In this case, the dsRNA control element is a Stem-Loop-Stem (hpRNA) structure formed *in vivo* by the occurrence of two substrings 20–25 nt long, complementary to one another within a small distance along the genome sequence and a third occurrence, which is part of the target gene, that is either one of the above two occurrences that is anywhere in the genome. The first phase is of detecting all such triple repeats in a genome sequence and an algorithm based on a suffix tree data structure is given to detect triplets of at least 20 nt length in [36]. Formally, the problem is described as follows.

5.3.4.1 The Triple Repeat Identification Problem (TRIP) Input are a sequence $S = s_1, s_2, \ldots, s_n$ from an alphabet Σ, and integers l and d. For each element of Σ, a member of this alphabet is defined to be its complement. If L is an l-mer of S, let L^{rc} stand for the reverse complement of L. The goal is to output every l-mer, L, of S if L^{rc} occurs within a distance d of L in S, and either L or L^{rc} occurs one more time in S.

In [36], the authors report a memory requirement of 12 GB for a genome (*C. elegans*) of size 100 Mb and the time required is mentioned as 4 h on a single processor. Such large memory requirements are due to building a suffix tree for the entire genome sequence and its reverse complement. Also, paging could become a very serious issue if the entire suffix tree does not reside in the main memory.

In [6], two algorithms are proposed, *CaTScan1* and *CaTScan2* (for Control And Target Scan), that adopt sorting techniques to identify the triplets. Implementation results of both the algorithms show better performance in practice in space as well as time when compared to the suffix tree algorithm.

Algorithm *CaTScan1* adopts the radix sorting approach as follows. Let C be a collection of elements of the form $e = (p, o, v)$, holding the positional (p), orientational (o), and value (v) information of l-mers in S. For every l-mer l_i starting at position

i, $1 \leq i \leq (n-l+1)$, in S, $e_i^f = (p_i^f, o_i^f, v_i^f)$, and $e_i^{rc} = (p_i^{rc}, o_i^{rc}, v_i^{rc})$ are the two elements representing itself and its reverse complement respectively in C, such that, $p_i^f = p_i^{rc} = i, o_i^f = 0, o_i^{rc} = 1, v_i^f = 2l$-bit number of l_i, and $v_i^{rc} = 2l$-bit number of l_i^{rc}. Elements of C are sorted with respect to the integer values of their corresponding l-mers using radix sort. A scan of the sorted collection C will be sufficient to identify the desired triplets and output them.

For very large genomes, the memory required by *CaTScan1* could become a bottleneck as it involves holding the values of each v_i^f and v_i^{rc}, two $2l$-bit integers in memory in addition to position i and its two orientations 0 and 1. In an effort to further reduce the memory requirement of *CaTScan1*, algorithm *CaTScan2* employs a combination of MSBs first and LSBs first integer sorting. Let k be any integer, $1 \leq k \leq l$. In the first phase, the l-mers and their corresponding reverse complements of S are partitioned into 4^k parts (as $|\Sigma| = 4$), with respect to the value of the first k symbols. In particular, two l-mers will be in the same part if their first k symbols are the same. Let $A[1 : 4^k]$ be an array of linked lists. For each position i in S, let v_i^f be the $2k$-bit integer value of $s_i, s_{i+1}, \ldots, s_{i+k-1}$ and v_i^{rc}, the value of the reverse complement. The tuple $(i, 0)$ is added to the list $A[v_i^f]$ and $(i, 1)$ to the list $A[v_i^{rc}]$. Now, there are at most 4^k *independent* sorting subproblems (one for each list of the array A). Each list of A is processed independently, sorted w.r.t. the last $(l-k)$ symbols of the corresponding l-mers using LSBs first sorting.

The advantage of the first phase is very clear. There are nearly $2n$ l-mers and their reverse complements in S. Assume that each symbol of S is picked uniformly randomly from the alphabet Σ. Also assume that the l-mers are independent (which is clearly false since the l-mers could be overlapping). An analysis making this assumption has been proved to hold well in practice (as in [12]). Then, the expected size of each list of A is $2n/4^k$. Using Chernoff bounds [17], we can show that the size of each list is no more than $(1+\epsilon)2n/4^k$ with high probability, for any fixed $\epsilon > 0$. If cln is the amount of memory employed by algorithm *CaTScan1*, then with *CaTScan2*, the space occupied by A is no more than $16n$ (considering that each i is a 32-bit integer; there are n positions on S, and $2n$ entries in the linked lists of A; each entry in the linked list is an i and a reference to the next element in the list, thus, requiring $4 * 2n * 2 = 16n$ bytes of space). The space used to process each list of A is no more than $cl(1+\epsilon)2n/4^k$ with high probability and can be reused for the different lists of A. As a result, the memory used by the new algorithm is $16n + cl(1+\epsilon)2n/4^k$ with high probability (where the probability is over the space of all possible inputs). An example value for k is 6. Also, the memory requirement of *CaTScan2* is further reduced (to nearly $8n + cl(1+\epsilon)2n/4^k$) by realizing the lists of A as an array of 4^k arrays whose initial size is calculated by an additional prescan of the sequence S.

When run on a PowerEdge 2600 Linux server with 4 GB of RAM and dual 2.8 GHz Intel Xeon CPUs, employing only one of these CPUs to process the *C. elegans* genome to identify triplets of length 21 nt, *CaTScan1* takes about 8 min and no more than 2.5 GB of memory, while *CaTScan2* takes about 11 min and no more than

1 GB of memory, achieving a speedup of 30 and 23, respectively, while reducing the memory requirement by a factor of 4.8 and 12, respectively, over the suffix tree approach.

5.3.5 Specific Selection of siRNA Patterns in Complete mRNA Data

The Specific Selection Problem arises from the need to design siRNA that aims at gene silencing [27]. These short sequences target specific mRNA and cause the degradation of such mRNA, inhibiting the synthesis of the protein generated by it. These sequences are usually of small length, usually consisting of between 20 and 25 nucleotides. However, a length of 21 is used in practice and usually two of the nucleotides are predetermined, so the problem becomes one of designing sequences of length 19.

An important criterion in the design of the siRNA is that the sequence should minimize the risk of off-target gene silencing caused by hybridization with the wrong mRNA. This hybridization may occur because the number of mismatches between the sequence and an unrelated sequence may be too small or because they share a long enough subsequence. Formally, the problem can be described as follows.

5.3.5.1 The Specific Selection Problem Input are a collection of strings $\mathcal{S} = \{s_1, \ldots, s_n\}$ from an alphabet Σ, and integers l and d. We are interested in finding a collection of l-mers $\mathcal{X} = \{x_1, \ldots, x_n\}$ where for all $i = 1, \ldots, n$, x_i appears in s_i and it does not appear in x_j for $j \neq i$ with less than a distance of d.

It is clear that this problem can be solved in $O(N^2)$ time, where $N := \sum_{i=1}^{n} |s_i|$. However, such an approach becomes impractical when we are dealing with complete mRNA data where N could be of the order of 10^8.

In [66], this problem was studied under the name of *unique oligo* problem, and in [61], a more general problem is considered under the name of *probe design* problem, imposing more conditions on the designed l-mers, which include homogeneity—which is measured by the melting temperature of the probe and the CG content—and sensitivity—which is calculated using the free energy of the probe. Their solution strategy is based on determining whether for each candidate l-mer it appears with up to d mistakes in the other sequences by making use of a precalculated index for small q-mers or seeds, and then extending contigous hits of q-mers with few mismatches. The running time of these approaches depends critically on the values of q and the number of mismatches which are used, which in turn depends heavily on the combination of values of l and d.

In [65], this problem was considered in the context of designing an siRNA that would target a particular mRNA sequence. It is pointed out that in cases such as the ones that arise from designing siRNA where $N \sim 10^8$, $19 \leq l \leq 23$, and $d = 3, 4$ the previous strategy is computationally very intensive, hence, the occurrences of an l-mer in a sequence with up to d mistakes is calculated by making use of overlapping—instead of contiguous—q-mers or seeds allowing a few mismatches, and it is shown that this approach outperforms the previous methods by orders of magnitude. In particular it is claimed that for $l = 19$, $d = 3$, and $N = 5 \times 10^7$, the number of occurrences of an l-mer with up to d mismatches in a database of size N can be calculated in nearly 10^{-2} s on a Xeon CPU with a clock rate of 3.2 GHz and 2 GB of main memory. This would imply that if we want to solve the (l, d) specific selection problem in this case, we would take close to 6 days of calculation.

In [22], the algorithm *SOS* (for Specific Off-target Selection) is proposed, adopting sorting techniques to identify specific l-mers. The algorithm is shown to be practical when processing the complete mRNA of Human and Drosophila, running in less than 4 h and outperforming previous approaches.

The algorithm SOS can be described as follows:

Algorithm SOS {
  Let X be a collection of (x, i) such that x is an l-mer of s_i.
  for all $(j_1, \ldots, j_d)$ with $1 \leq j_1 < \cdots < j_d \leq l$ do {
  1. Sort the collection of $X = \{(x, i)\}$ according to the values
     of positions $\{1, \ldots, n\} \setminus \{j_1, \ldots, j_d\}$ using radix-sort.
  2. Scan the sorted collection, marking consecutive l-mers that agree on the
     set of positions $\{1, \ldots, n\} \setminus \{j_1, \ldots, j_d\}$ and appear at different s_i.
  }
  Output the unmarked l-mers.
}

It is clear then that Algorithm SOS can be implemented in $O(N(l/w)(\binom{l}{d}))$ time and $O(N \log |\Sigma|(l/w))$ memory, where w is the word size of the computer. One big advantage of Algorithm SOS is the fact that for a fixed value of l and d, the algorithm is linear in N, making it practical for high values of N. However, it is sensitive on the parameter l and particularly sensitive on parameter d, making it practical for values of $d \leq 5$. Notice furthermore, that we can decrease the memory used by the algorithm SOS to $O(N)$ by storing the l-mers in collection X by their position numbers.

This algorithm was implemented in C was run on a Power Edge 2600 Linux Server with 4GB of RAM and dual Xeon 2.8 Ghz CPU's—only one that was used. In processing the Human mRNA data, we used close to 1.5 Gb of RAM and in the case of the Drosophila we used close to 700 Mb of RAM, due to the fact that we store the l-mers as 64 bit numbers. In the particular case of the Human mRNA with $l = 19$ and $d = 3$, SOS took 3 h and 22 min, outperforming the results in [65] by almost two orders of magnitude.

5.4 FFT-BASED ALGORITHMS FOR SIMILARITY MEASUREMENT

Measuring similarities among biological sequences has numerous applications. For instance, functionalities of newly sequenced genes can be inferred. Similarities can be defined in a number of ways. The edit distance can serve as a measure of similarity. (The edit distance refers to the minimum number of deletions, insertions, or replacements needed to transform one sequence into the other.) Another measure of similarity employs a matrix M that assigns a score for every pair of bases. Given two sequences, A and B, for each possible alignment between the two, we compute the total score and pick the alignment with the maximum score.

Both global and local similarities could be of interest depending on the context. Global similarity captures the similarity between the two entire sequences. Local similarity refers to the similarity between a subsequence of one sequence and a subsequence of the other sequence. Often, local similarities could give biologically more meaningful information than global similarities.

Given two sequences, BLAST identifies all the *maximal segment pairs* in them. BLAST is a widely employed local similarity software [3]. If A and B are any two sequences, BLAST identifies all the pairs (A', B') where A' is a subsequence of A, B' is a subsequence of B, both A' and B' are of the same length, the similarity score between A' and B' is at least S (for some specified S), and these two subsequences are maximal, i.e., they can neither be expanded nor shrunk to increase the similarity score. Any such pair is called a Maximal Segment Pair (MSP). Any similarity score matrix such as PAM [23] can be used by BLAST in computing scores between two subsequences. Other local alignment algorithms can be found, for example, in [54].

5.4.1 A Simple Algorithm

Global similarity between two sequences of length n each can be computed as follows. We align the two sequences in each possible way and compute a score for each alignment. For each alignment, the score can be computed in $O(n)$ time. Since there are $\Theta(n)$ possible alignments, this simple algorithm runs in time $O(n^2)$.

Let $A = a_0, a_1, \ldots, a_{n-1}$ and $B = b_0, b_1, \ldots, b_{n-1}$ be two given sequences. There are $2n - 1$ possible alignments between A and B. In alignment 0, a_0 overlaps with b_{n-1}; In alignment 1, a_0 overlaps with b_{n-2} and a_1 aligns with b_{n-1}; and so on. Let $c_i = \sum_{k=0}^{i} a_{i-k} b_{n-k-1}$ for $0 \leq i \leq (n-1)$ and $c_{n+j} = \sum_{k=j}^{n-1} a_k b_{k-j}$ for $1 \leq j \leq (n-1)$.

Note that c_j computes something corresponding to alignment j (for $0 \leq j \leq (2n-1)$). In particular, c_j computes the sum of products of matching elements in alignment j. Given A and B, the problem of computing c_j for $0 \leq j \leq (2n-1)$ is known as the *convolution problem*. The c_j values are known as convolution coefficients. The convolution problem can be solved in $O(n \log n)$ time using FFT algorithms (see, for example, [37]).

Theorem 5.3 *The convolution of two given sequences of length n each can be computed in $O(n \log n)$ time.*

Global similarities for all possible alignments of two given sequences $a_0, a_1, \ldots, a_{n-1}$ and $b_0, b_1, \ldots, b_{n-1}$ from an alphabet Σ can be computed by performing $|\Sigma|^2$ convolution operations. Since each convolution takes $O(n \log n)$ time, the total time needed is $O\left(|\Sigma|^2 n \log n\right)$. More details on this algorithm follow.

Let $\Sigma = \{\sigma_1, \sigma_2, \ldots, \sigma_k\}$. Define the binary sequence $A^{\sigma_\ell} = a_0^{\sigma_\ell}, a_1^{\sigma_\ell}, \ldots, a_{n-1}^{\sigma_\ell}$, where $a_j^{\sigma_\ell} = 1$ if $a_j = \sigma_\ell$ and $a_j^{\sigma_\ell} = 0$ otherwise (for $1 \leq \ell \leq k$ and $0 \leq j \leq n-1$). Similarly, define $B^{\sigma_m} = b_0^{\sigma_m}, b_1^{\sigma_m}, \ldots, b_{n-1}^{\sigma_m}$, where $b_j^{\sigma_m} = 1$ if $b_j = \sigma_m$ and $b_j^{\sigma_m} = 0$

otherwise (for $1 \leq m \leq k$ and $0 \leq j \leq n-1$). The basic idea behind the algorithm is to compute the convolution of A^{σ_ℓ} and B^{σ_m} (for $1 \leq \ell \leq k$ and $1 \leq m \leq k$) and from all of these convolution results compute the similarity scores for each possible alignment of A and B.

If s_i is the score corresponding to the ith alignment of A and B (for $0 \leq i \leq (2n-1)$), then s_i is given by $\sum_{\ell=1}^{k} \sum_{m=1}^{k} c_i^{\sigma_\ell,\sigma_m} M(\sigma_\ell, \sigma_m)$, where $M(\sigma_\ell, \sigma_m)$ is the score of aligning σ_ℓ with σ_m. Here, $c_i^{\sigma_\ell,\sigma_m}$ is the ith convolution coefficient (corresponding to the ith alignment) of A^{σ_ℓ} and B^{σ_m}.

Since $k^2 (= |\Sigma|^2)$ convolutions are involved, the total runtime of the above algorithm is $O\left(|\Sigma|^2 n \log n\right)$, yielding the following.

Theorem 5.4 *If A and B are two given sequences of length n each, we can compute the global similarity scores between them for each possible alignment in $O\left(|\Sigma|^2 n \log n\right)$ time.*

Example 1 Let $\Sigma = \{g, c, t, a\}$, $A = a, t, c, t, g, t, a, a, c, t, g, t$, and $B = \{g, g, a, t, a, c, g, t, c, c, g, a\}$. Then, $A^c = 0, 0, 1, 0, 0, 0, 0, 0, 1, 0, 0, 0$, and $B^t = 0, 0, 0, 1, 0, 0, 0, 1, 0, 0, 0, 0$. When A^c and B^t are convolved, the convolution coefficients give us information about the global similarities between A^c and B^t. In particular, for each possible alignment between A^c and B^t, we get to know the number of matches such that a c in the sequence A pairs with a t in B corresponding to this alignment.

Some clever encodings [16] can be used to reduce the number of FFT computations involved in the above algorithm (though the asymptotic runtime will remain the same).

5.4.2 Faster Algorithms

In this section, we describe two algorithms of Rajasekaran, Jin, and Spouge [53] whose runtimes are better than that of the previous algorithm (c.f. Theorem 5.4). Let $A = a_0, a_1, \ldots, a_{n-1}$ and $B = b_0, b_1, \ldots, b_{n-1}$ be the two given input sequences and let $\Sigma = \{\sigma_1, \sigma_2, \ldots, \sigma_k\}$. We perform k different computations, one for each member of Σ. The computation corresponding to σ_q (for $1 \leq q \leq k$) proceeds as follows. Form the binary sequence $A^{\sigma_q} = a_0^{\sigma_q}, a_1^{\sigma_q}, \ldots, a_{n-1}^{\sigma_q}$, where $a_i^{\sigma_q} = 1$ if $a_i = \sigma_q$ and $a_i^{\sigma_q} = 0$ otherwise (for $0 \leq i \leq (n-1)$). Define a sequence $B^{\sigma_q} = M(\sigma_q, b_0), M(\sigma_q, b_1), \ldots, M(\sigma_q, b_{n-1})$, where $M(\sigma_q, b_j)$ is the score for matching σ_q with b_j (for $0 \leq j \leq (n-1)$).

Now, we compute the global similarity scores between A^{σ_q} and B^{σ_q} for each possible alignment between the two. This can be done using a convolution operation in $O(n \log n)$ time (c.f. Theorem 5.3). Let $s_i^{\sigma_q}$ be the similarity score corresponding to alignment i, for $0 \leq i \leq (2n-1)$.

We repeat the above computation for each σ_q in Σ. Then, the global similarity score between A and B with respect to alignment i is computed as $s_i = \sum_{q=1}^{k} s_i^{\sigma_q}$ (for $0 \leq i \leq (2n-1)$). The total runtime of the above algorithm is $O(|\Sigma| n \log n)$. Thus, we get the following.

Theorem 5.5 *The global similarities between two given sequences of length n each, for all possible alignments, can be computed in* $O(|\Sigma| n \log n)$ *time.*

A slightly different algorithm can also be devised for the similarities problem. The idea is to perform only one convolution operation that can give us all the results corresponding to the $|\Sigma|$ operations done above. This is done constructing two sequences of length $|\Sigma|n$ each and computing the similarities between them using a convolution operation.

To be more specific, let $A = a_0, a_1, \ldots, a_{n-1}$ and $B = b_0, b_1, \ldots, b_{n-1}$ be the two given input sequences with $\Sigma = \{\sigma_1, \sigma_2, \ldots, \sigma_k\}$.

A' and B' are the two sequences we will construct with $|A'| = |B'| = |\Sigma|n$. For every element of A there will be k binary entries in A' and for every element of B there will be k entries in B'. In particular, a_i will be represented in A' as $a_i^{\sigma_1}, a_i^{\sigma_2}, \ldots, a_i^{\sigma_k}$ where $a_i^{\sigma_q} = 1$ if $a_i = \sigma_q$ and $a_i^{\sigma_q} = 0$ otherwise (for $1 \leq q \leq k$).

Consider the example of $\Sigma = \{g, c, t, a\}$, $A = c, t, a, a$, and $B = g, g, t, c$. In this case $A' = 0, 1, 0, 0,\ 0, 0, 1, 0,\ 0, 0, 0, 1,\ 0, 0, 0, 1$.

The elements in B' corresponding to b_j are: $M(\sigma_1, b_j), M(\sigma_2, b_j), \ldots, M(\sigma_k, b_j)$ (for $0 \leq j \leq (n-1)$). Here, $M(\sigma_q, b_j)$ is the score for matching σ_q in A with b_j in B (for $1 \leq q \leq k$ and $0 \leq j \leq (n-1)$).

In the above example, $B' = M(g, g), M(c, g), M(t, g), M(a, g), M(g, g), M(c, g), M(t, g), M(a, g),\quad M(g, t), M(c, t), M(t, t), M(a, t),\quad M(g, c), M(c, c), M(t, c), M(a, c)$.

We compute the global similarities between A' and B' for all possible alignments. This involves the convolution of two sequences of length kn each. The time needed is $O(kn \log(kn))$. Clearly, the similarities of interest will be given by these convolution coefficients (though some of the coefficients are not of interest to us). We obtain the following.

Theorem 5.6 *The global similarities between two sequences of length n each from an alphabet* Σ *can be computed in time* $O(|\Sigma| n \log(|\Sigma| n))$.

5.5 SUMMARY

In this chapter, we discussed in detail how sorting-based techniques could be applied to discover motifs in a set of biosequences. We also looked at some problems related to motif discovery, in which such techniques could be employed to obtain better performance in time and space compared to existing algorithms in the literature. A related problem of similarity measurement has also been discussed. FFT-based algorithms for similarity measurement have been explored. We hope that through this discussion, we could impress upon our readers the power and utility of basic techniques such as sorting and FFT in solving several challenging problems in computational biology.

ACKNOWLEDGMENTS

This work has been supported in part by the NSF Grant ITR-0326155 and a UTC endowment.

REFERENCES

1. Adebiyi EF, Kaufmann M. Extracting common motifs under the Levenshtein measure: Theory and experimentation. *Proceeding of the Workshop on Algorithms for Bioinformatics (WABI). LNCS Vol. 2452*. Springer-Verlag. 2002. pp. 140–156.
2. Agrawal N, Dasaradhi PVN, Mohmmed A, Malhotra P, Bhatnagar RK, Mukherjee SK. RNA interference: biology, mechanism, and applications. Microbiol Mol Biol Rev 2003;657–685.
3. Altschul SF, Gish W, Miller W, Myers EW, Lipman DJ. Basic Local Alignment Search Tool. *J Mol Biol* 1990;215:403–410.
4. Bailey TL, Elkan C. Fitting a mixture model by expectation maximization to discover motifs in biopolymers. *Proceedings of the Second International Conference on Intelligent Systems for Molecular Biology*; 1994. pp. 28–36.
5. Balla S, Davila J, Rajasekaran S. Approximation Algorithms for the Primer Selection, Planted Motif Search, and Related Problems. In: Gonzalez TE, editor. *Approximation Algorithms and Metaheuristics*; CRC Press; 2006. pp. 75–1.
6. Balla S, Rajasekaran S. Space and Time Efficient Algorithms for Discovering RNAi Patterns in Genome Data. *3rd International Symposium on Bioinformatics Research and Applications (ISBRA 2007), LNBI Vol. 4463*; 2007. pp. 260–269.
7. Balla S, Rajasekaran S. An Efficient Algorithm for Minimum Degeneracy Primer Selection. *IEEE Trans Nanobiosci Special Issue Comput Nanobiosci* 2007;1(6):12–17.
8. Balla S, Rajasekaran S, Mandoiu II. Efficient algorithms for degenerate primer search. *Int J Foundation Comput Sci (IJFCS)*, 2007;18(4):899–910.
9. Blanchette M. Algorithms for phylogenetic footprinting. *Proceedings of the Fifth Annual International Conference on Computational Molecular Biology*; 2001.
10. Blanchette M, Schwikowski B, Tompa M. An exact algorithm to identify motifs in orthologous sequences from multiple species. *Proceedings of the Eighth International Conference on Intelligent Systems for Molecular Biology*; 2000. pp. 37–45.
11. Brazma A, Jonassen I, Vilo J, Ukkonen E. Predicting gene regulatory elements in silico on a genomic scale. *Genome Res* 1998;15:1202–1215.
12. Buhler J, Tompa M. Finding motifs using random projections. *Proceedings of the Fifth Annual International Conference on Computational Molecular Biology (RECOMB)*; 2001.
13. Caplen NJ, Mousses S. Short Interfering RNA (siRNA)-Mediated RNA Interference (RNAi) in Human Cells. *Ann N Y Acad Sci* 2003;1002:56–62.
14. Chalk AM, Wahlestedt C, Sonnhammer ELL. Improved and automated prediction of effective siRNA. *Biochem Biophys Res Commun* 2004;319:264–274.
15. Chamberlain JS, Gibbs RA, Rainer JE, Nguyen PN, Casey CT. Deletion screening of the Duchenne muscular dystrophy locus via multiplex DNA amplification. *Nucleic Acids Res* 1988;16:11141–11156.

16. Cheever EA, Overton GC, Searls D. Fast Fourier Transform-Based Correlation of DNA Sequences Using Complex Plane Encoding. *CABIOS*; 1991;7(2):143–154.
17. Chernoff H. A measure of asymptotic efficiency for tests of a hypothesis based on the sum of observations. *Ann Math Statistic* 1952;493–507.
18. Chin FYL, Leung HCM. Voting algorithms for discovering long motifs. *Proceedings of the Third Asia Pacific Bioinformatics Conference (APBC)*; 2005. pp. 261–271.
19. Cormen TH, Leiserson CE, Rivest RL, Stein C. Introduction to Algorithms; MIT Press; 2001.
20. Davila J, Balla S, Rajasekaran S. Space and time efficient algorithms for planted motif search. *Proceedings of the 6th International Conference on Computational Science (ICCS 2006)/ 2nd International Workshop on Bioinformatics Research and Applications (IWBRA 2006) LNCS Vol. 3992*; 2006. pp. 822–829.
21. Davila J, Balla S, Rajasekaran S. Fast and Practical Algorithms for Planted (l, d) Motif Search. *IEEE Trans Comput Biol Bioinformatics (TCBB)*, 2007. Forthcoming.
22. Davila J, Balla S, Rajasekaran S. Fast Algorithms for Selecting Specific siRNA in Complete mRNA Data. *7th International Workshop on Algorithms in Bioinformatics (WABI)*; 2007;4645:302–309.
23. Dayhoff MO, Schwartz RM, Orcutt BC. A Model of Evolutionary Change in Proteins. In: Dayhoff MO, editor. *Atlas of Protein Sequence and Structure Vol. 5(3)*. National Biomedical Research Foundation; 1978. pp. 345–352.
24. Doi K, Imai H. Greedy algorithms for finding a small set of primers satisfying cover length resolution conditions in PCR experiments. *Proceedings of the 8th Workshop on Genome Informatics (GIW)*; 1997. pp. 43–52.
25. Doi K, Imai H. A Greedy algorithm for minimizing the number of primers in Multiple PCR Experiments. *Genome Informatics* 1999. pp. 73–82.
26. Doi K, Imai H: Complexity properties of the primer selection problem for PCR Experiments. *Proceedings of the 5th Japan-Korea Joint Workshop on Algorithms and Computation*; 2000. pp. 152–159.
27. Elbashir S, Harboth J, Lendeckel W, Yalcin A, Weber K, Tuschtl T. Duplexes of 21-nucleotide RNAs mediate RNA interference in cultured mammalian cells. *Nature*; 2001;411:494–498.
28. Eskin E, Pevzner PA. Finding composite regulatory patterns in DNA sequences. *Bioinformatics* 2002;S1:354–363.
29. Evans PA, Smith AD, Wareham HT. On the complexity of finding common approximate substrings. *Theor Comput Sci* 2003;306:407–430.
30. Fire A, Xu S, Montgomery MK, Kostas SA, Driver SE, Mello CC. Potent and specific genetic interference by double-stranded RNA in Caenorhabditis elegans. *Nature*; 1998;391:806–811.
31. Fuchs T, Malecova B, Linhart C, Sharan R, Khen M, Herwig R, Shmulevich D, Elkon R, Steinfath M, O'Brien JK, Radelof U, Lehrach H, Lancet D, Shamir R. DEFOG: A practical scheme for deciphering families of genes. *Genomics*; 2002;80(3):1–8.
32. Galas DJ, Eggert M, Waterman MS. Rigorous pattern-recognition methods for DNA sequences: analysis of promoter sequences from *Escherichia coli*. *J Mol Biol* 1985;186(1):117–128.
33. Gramm J, Niedermeier R, Rossmanith P. Fixed-parameter algorithms for Closest String and Related Problems. *Algorithmica* 2003;37:25–42.

34. Gusfield D. *Algorithms on Strings, Trees and Sequences*. Cambridge University Press; 1997.
35. Hertz G, Stormo G. Identifying DNA and protein patterns with statistically significant alignments of multiple sequences. *Bioinformatics* 1999;15:563–577.
36. Horesh Y, Amir A, Michaeli S, Unger R. A rapid method for detection of putative RNAi target genes in genomic data. *Bioinformatics* 2003;19(2):ii73–ii80.
37. Horowitz E, Sahni S, Rajasekaran S. *Computer Algorithms*. W.H. Freeman Press; 1998.
38. Keich U, Pevzner PA. Finding motifs in the Twilight Zone. *Bioinformatics* 2002; 18:1374–1381.
39. Konwar KM, Mandoiu II, Russell AC, Shvartsman AA. Improved algorithms for multiplex PCR primer set selection with amplification length constraints. *Proceedings of the 3rd Asia Pacific Bioinformatics Conference (APBC)*; 2005. pp. 41–50.
40. Kwok S, Chang SY, Sninsky JJ, Wang A. A guide to the design and use of mismatched and degenerate primers. *PCR Meth Appl* 1994;3:S39–S47.
41. Lawrence CE, Altschul SF, Boguski MS, Liu JS, Neuwald AF, Wootton JC. Detecting subtle sequence signals: a Gibbs sampling strategy for multiple alignment. *Science*; 1993;262:208–214.
42. Lawrence CE, Reilly AA. An Expectation Maximization (EM) algorithm for the identification and characterization of common sites in unaligned bipolymer sequences. Proteins 1990;7:41–51.
43. Li M, Ma B, Wang L. Finding similar regions in many sequences. *J Comput Syst Sci* 2002;65:73–96.
44. Lim LP, Lau NC, Weinstein EG, Abdelhakim A, Yekta S, Rhoades MW, Burge CB, Bartel DP. The microRNAs of Caenorhabditis elegans. *Genes Develop* Vol. 17;2003. pp. 991–1008.
45. Linhart C, Shamir R. The degenerate primer design problem – Theory and Applications. *J Comput Biol* 2005;12(4); pp. 431–456.
46. Linhart C, Shamir R. The degenerate primer design problem. *Bioinformatics*; 2002;18(1); pp. S172–S180.
47. Pearson WR, Robins G, Wrege DE, Zhang T. On the primer selection problem in polymerase chain reaction experiments. *Discrete Appl Math* Vol. 71;1996. pp. 231–246.
48. Pevzner PA, Sze S-H. Combinatorial approaches to finding subtle signals in DNA sequences. *Proceedings of the Eighth International Conference on Intelligent Systems in Molecular Biology*; 2000. pp. 269–278.
49. Price A, Ramabhadran S, Pevzner PA. Finding subtle motifs by branching from sample strings. *Bioinformatics* 2003. 1(1); pp. 1–7.
50. Rajasekaran S. Algorithms for Motif Search. In Handbook of Computational Molecular Biology Aluru S, editor. Chapman & Hall/CRC; 2006. pp. 37-1–37-21.
51. Rajasekaran S, Balla S, Huang C-H. Exact Algorithms for Planted Motif Problems. *J Comput Biol* 2005. 12(8); pp. 1117–1128.
52. Rajasekaran S, Balla S, Huang C-H, Thapar V, Gryk M, Maciejewski M, Schiller M. High-performance Exact Algorithms for Motif Search. *J Clin Monit Comput* 2005. Springer. 19(4-5). pp. 319–328.

53. Rajasekaran S, Jin X, Spouge JL. The Efficient Computation of Position-Specific Match Scores with the Fast Fourier Transform. *J Comput Biol* 2002. 9(1); pp. 23–33.

54. Rajasekaran S, Nick H, Pardalos PM, Sahni S, Shaw G. Efficient Algorithms for Local Alignment Search. *J Comb Optim* 2001;5(1):117–124.

55. Rocke E, Tompa M. An algorithm for finding novel gapped motifs in DNA sequences. *Proceedings of the 2nd International Conference on Computational Molecular Biology*; 1998. pp. 228–233.

56. Rose TM, Schultz ER, Henikoff JG, Pietrokovski S, McCallum CM, Henikoff S. Consensus-degenerate Hybrid Oligonucleotide Primers for amplification of distantly related sequences. *Nucl Acid Res* 1998;26(7):1628–1635.

57. Sagot MF. Spelling approximate repeated or common motifs using a suffix tree. LNCS Vol. 1380. Springer-Verlag; 1998. pp. 111–127.

58. Sinha S, Tompa M. A statistical method for finding transcription factor binding sites. *Proceedings of the Eighth International Conference on Intelligent Systems for Molecular Biology*; 2000. pp. 344–354.

59. Souvenir R, Buhler J, Stormo G, Zhang W. Selecting Degenerate Multiplex PCR Primers. *Proceedings of the 3rd International Workshop on Algorithms in Bioinformatics (WABI)*; 2003. pp. 512–526.

60. Staden R. Methods for discovering novel motifs in nucleic acid sequences. *Comput Appl Biosci* 1989. 5(4); pp. 293–298.

61. Sung WK, Lee WH. Fast and Accurate Probe Selection Algorithm for Large Genomes. *Proceedings of the 2003 IEEE Bioinformatics Conference (CSB)*; 2003. pp. 65–74.

62. Tompa M. An exact method for finding short motifs in sequences, with application to the ribosome binding site problem. *Proceedings of the 7th International Conference on Intelligent Systems for Molecular Biology (ISMB)*; 1999. pp. 262–271.

63. van Helden J, Andre B, Collado-Vides J. Extracting regulatory sites from the upstream region of yeast genes by computational analysis of oligonucleotide frequencies. *J Mol Biol* 1998;281(5):827–842.

64. Wei X, Kuhn DN, Narasimhan G. Degenerate Primer Design via Clustering. *Proceedings of the 2003 IEEE Bioinformatics Conference (CSB)*; 2003. pp. 75–83.

65. Yamada T, Morishita S. Accelerated off-target search algorithm for siRNA. *Bioinformatics*; 2005;21(8):1316–1324.

66. Zheng J, Close TJ, Jiang T, Lonardi S. Efficient selection of unique and popular oligos for large EST databases. *Bioinformatics*; 2004;20(13):2101–2112.

6

A SURVEY OF SEEDING FOR SEQUENCE ALIGNMENT

DANIEL G. BROWN

Cheriton School of Computer Science, University of Waterloo, Waterloo, Ontario, Canada

We survey recent work in the seeding of alignments, particularly the follow-ups from the 2002 work of Ma, Tromp, and Li that brought the concept of spaced seeds into the bioinformatics literature [25]. Our focus is on the extensions of this work to increasingly complicated models of alignments, coming up to the most recent efforts in this area.

6.1 INTRODUCTION

Sequence alignment is one of the basic tasks of bioinformatics. The basic use of alignment is to attempt to identify regions of sequences that are *homologous*, that is, which share a common evolutionary origin. In practice, of course, this is not really possible; the algorithms used in sequence alignment do not identify sequences with common origin, but only sequences that have surprisingly strong similarity, according to a scoring function. This similarity may arise due to chance, due to convergent evolution, or due to any of a variety of other origins. However, the standard claim made of sequence alignment algorithms is that if two sequences have an extremely strong match that is highly improbable for unrelated random sequences, it is probably the case that those sequences are, in fact homologous.

As such, the process of finding local alignments among a set of long sequences consists largely of two phases: first, one runs a combinatorial algorithm that creates

Bioinformatics Algorithms: Techniques and Applications, Edited by Ion I. Măndoiu and Alexander Zelikovsky

the alignments and then one performs statistical tests to identify which alignments are "surprisingly strong," for a variety of definitions of this threshold. Descriptions of what makes a homology "surprisingly strong" are beyond the scope of this survey; here, we will focus instead on the first phase: identifying the alignments themselves. In fact, we will focus the majority of our attention on only one part of this phase, which is the process of finding "seeds" for local alignments. Despite the seeming smallness of this focus, however, there is a host of beautiful mathematics and algorithmic ideas hiding inside it. Moreover, this single part of the alignment process turns out to control both the runtime of heuristic alignment algorithms and their usefulness, as it is largely responsible for the algorithms' sensitivity and specificity.

This area has had an amazing renaissance since 2000. Spurred on by advances in the technology of genome sequencing (which were creating enormous corpora of DNA sequence needing analysis), sequence alignment technology simply had to become substantially more speedy, or it was going to become a limiting factor in analysis. Still, one probably would not have expected that the technology developed would be as mathematically lovely as what has happened, nor that the wealth of research that would develop in this area would be as large or as deep as it has been.

We will begin with a formal description of alignments, to get a proper mathematical description of the domain, and a brief review of the standard results in this area. Then, in Section 6.3, we will describe how to estimate the usefulness of simple approaches to alignment seeding. In Section 6.4, we will present the first of several recent advances in this area, due to Ma, Tromp, and Li [25], which gives a quite novel way of understanding the problem of alignment seeding. We will present the mathematical algorithms, as well, that allow one to compute sensitivity and specificity of such approaches. In Section 6.5, we will discuss a variety of extensions to this idea, due to a host of different authors, all of which build upon the basic ideas. In Section 6.4.5, we will focus on a particularly useful trick, where one seeds alignments off of a match to any of a potentially large number of patterns. In Section 6.6, we will mention some theoretical developments in this domain.

6.2 ALIGNMENTS

A sequence alignment is a way of representing the relationship between two biological sequences. In a very important sense, a sequence alignment is a hypothesis: it hypothesizes that specific positions of two biological sequences share a common ancestry. It can also be seen as a combinatorial object as well, and this perspective can be exceedingly useful. Here, we will give a formal definition of sequences and sequence alignments, and briefly discuss how they are produced. As this is largely standard material, the reader is referred to standard textbooks [12,15] for more detail.

6.2.1 Formal Definitions

A biological sequence $S = s_1, \ldots, s_n$ is a sequence of symbols over a finite alphabet Σ. Common examples of Σ include the DNA alphabet $\{A, C, G, T\}$, or the 20-letter alphabet of symbols that represent the amino acids found in proteins. More esoteric alphabets include the IUPAC alphabet that allows a position in a sequence to be any nonempty subset of the DNA alphabet. This 15-letter alphabet conveniently allows for uncertainty in a position of a sequence, particularly in inferred ancestral sequence; we will use it when discussing multiple alignments in Section 6.4.5.

The length of biological sequences can be extremely large; the human genome, for example, is approximately 3×10^9 letters long. Moreover, the sequence S might not be a single sequence, but the concatenation of a collection of sequences; for example, one might use all of the sequences of GenBank as the sequence S, which is in the order of 10^{11} in length.

A global alignment A between two sequences $S = s_1, \ldots, s_n$ and $T = t_1, \ldots t_m$, over the same alphabet Σ, is a pair of sequences S' and T', both of the same length, which result from inserting zero or more special gap characters, indicated by the symbol $-$ (not found in Σ), before the first character of either S or T, and after each symbol of S and symbol of T. The ith column of A consists of the ith symbols of S' and of T'. If this consists of two symbols s_j and t_k, we say that they are aligned to each other, while if it consists of a character from S, s_j, and the special gap character $(-)$, we say that s_i is aligned to a gap (and correspondingly if a gap is aligned to t_k). By convention, we will never choose to align a gap character $(-)$ to another gap character: each column of the alignment will include at least one character from S or from T.

In addition to global alignments, local alignments are important; these consist of global alignments (as defined before) of consecutive substrings of S with consecutive substrings of T. Whether one is computing local or global alignments tends to be application dependent: if we are aligning short regions that are known to be completely homologous in S and T, global alignment is appropriate, as it allows us to potentially identify the exact evolutionary homology between two sequences. Meanwhile, if two sequences include long stretches of homologous and nonhomologous regions, a collection of local alignments may be a better representation of the evolutionary relationship.

Considering global alignments, the length (number of columns) of alignments is always between $\max(n, m)$ and $n + m$, inclusive. With this in mind, we can easily count all possible alignments.

Theorem 6.1 *The number of distinct alignments of two sequences S and T that are n and m symbols long, respectively, and where S is at least as long as T, equals:* $\sum_{i=n,\ldots,n+m} \binom{i}{n} \cdot \binom{n}{i-m}$.

Proof. This is easily shown by noting that the number of columns in an alignment must be between n and $n + m$, and that for a given number of columns i, we must pick which $i - n$ columns are the gap symbol in S', and then which $i - m$ columns are the gaps in T', noting that they must be among the n columns where we did not place a gap in S'. ■

This number, of course, grows exponentially fast as a function of n and m, so we cannot simply explore all possible alignments of reasonably long sequences (let alone those of million-symbol or billion-symbol sequences). Instead, one must develop algorithms to cleverly find correct alignments.

However, a preliminary step in the process is more philosophical: one must give a way of preferring one of this large combinatorial set of alignments over another! Scoring of alignments is itself a rich and beautiful topic, which we discuss in a broader context in Section 6.5.3.1.

6.2.2 Meanings and Algorithms for Alignment

For now, though, we note that this process derives from an even more important task: identifying the meaning of an alignment. We will say that if s_j is aligned to t_k in an alignment that this represents the hypothesis that these positions of the sequence are homologous: they derive from a common ancestral symbol (which may or may not be equal to s_j or t_k, regardless of whether these symbols are themselves the same character). If the positions s_j to $s_{j'}$ are aligned to gap positions in T', then we say that these columns of the alignment result from one or more insertion events adding symbols to the sequence S since the common ancestor that it shared with T, or deletion events removing characters from T, or both. Again, the ancestral or inserted symbols need not exactly match the symbols in S; subsequent mutations may have changed them. And, finally, gaps in S' aligned to symbols in T correspond in this interpretation to insertions into T or deletions from S.

With this understanding of the meaning of an alignment A of S and T, there are still an infinite number of different explanations that can be given for how we get from a common ancestor to S and T, given an alignment A. Still, with a probabilistic model of evolution, we can assign a probability to each of these. Satisfyingly, as we shall see in Section 6.5.3.1, we can easily represent the probability of the highest likelihood such explanation with the score of an alignment, using a simple scoring function. We give a scoring matrix $M[a, b]$, for all a and b in Σ, which gives the score of aligning the symbol a in S to the symbol b in T, and add these values from M up for all columns where there are no gaps. Typically, $M[a, a]$ is positive, while the score for aligning different symbols may be positive or negative. For gaps, we traditionally use "affine" penalties, where the score of a string of k gap symbols in S' or T' flanked by symbols from Σ on both sides is of the form $o + (k - 1)e$, for (typically negative) constants o and e, called the "gap open" and "gap extension" penalties, respectively.

Now, with this scoring approach in mind, and with a match scoring matrix M and the constants o and e known, we can declare one alignment to be the best of all of the numerous possible alignments of S and T. (It is interesting that over the wide range of all possible choices of M, o, and e, there are typically only a very small number of optimal alignments [31].)

For simple alignment-scoring models, the optimal global alignment of S and T is easily computed by classical dynamic programming models, in $\Theta(nm)$ time. The key observation is that if a region of an optimal alignment starts and ends with matching symbols (not a gap), then the region must be an optimal alignment of the subintervals of S and T. (This is not quite true for regions that are flanked by gaps, as we need to keep track of whether a gap is being opened, at cost o, or extended, at cost e; however, the addition to the accounting is quite small, and results in only a doubling of the overall runtime [33].)

As such, in $\Theta(nm)$ time, we can compute the optimal global or local alignment of S and T, assuming we know the parameters of the alignment process; additionally, we can even use recent mathematical technology of Pachter and Sturmfels [31] to find the range of parameter space over which that alignment is optimal.

However, there is a serious problem: the $\Theta(nm)$ runtime is still unacceptable if the values of n and m are large, such as if they are both on the order of billions. One must compromise something: either one must develop a faster algorithm or one must reduce one's requirements, and not demand optimal alignments. Typically, for local alignment, practitioners reduce their requirements and run heuristic algorithms that are not guaranteed to always find the optimal alignments.

Heuristic sequence alignment has a fairly wide history, but the most important place in this history probably comes when this area was joined by several people who were familiar with ideas from string indexing. In particular, the simple idea of hash tables and other such structures has been extremely useful here.

Consider the idea of local alignment: while one can compute in $\Theta(nm)$ time the optimal alignment between an interval in S and an interval of T, this may be of no interest at all! Suppose that S and T are unrelated: then, the best local alignment is no better than no alignment! As such, we can easily imagine a slight variation on the traditional local alignment problem: find the optimal local alignment of S and T that is above a certain threshold of score, or that satisfies some other easily tested minimum standard, or fail if no such alignment exists. This problem, we shall see, can be solved in much less time than the classical algorithms for the traditional sequence alignment will give. Or, we can solve a much less well-posed problem: given S and T, efficiently find many or most alignments between them that satisfy a threshold. This is much more vague of a problem, yet still it is the underlying problem behind classic sequence alignment programs like BLASTP and BLASTN [2] .

6.3 TRADITIONAL APPROACHES TO HEURISTIC ALIGNMENT

With the vague problem from the previous section (find many high scoring alignments between S and T) in mind, we now will describe the way in which traditional programs have solved this problem. In particular, we will focus on how BLASTN and BLASTP, and programs of their ilk, have solved this problem, before moving on to more contemporary solutions in Sections 6.4 and 6.5.

6.3.1 Indexing and Heuristic Methods

The trick is quite simple: we find all alignments between S and T that share a highly conserved "core." In the case of BLASTN, this is a region of 10 or 11 consecutive symbols that are identical in both S and T (and that are not highly repetitive). In the case of BLASTP, this is a Three or Four letter interval of S and of T where the score of the ungapped alignment between those symbols is above some minimum threshold score (such as +11 or +13). Focusing solely on BLASTN, such intervals, or "seeds," can easily be found by indexing the k-letter subsequences of S: we produce a trie structure of all k-letter subsequences of S (for $k = 11$, for example), and then traverse through the trie, following the links corresponding to the sequence T, thus finding the places in S where each k-letter subsequence of T is matched (if it is matched at all).

From each of these initial seeds, then, we can start to build actual local alignments: we align the intervals to the left and to the right of each seed. If the intervals on both sides of the seed are not closely aligning, we can quickly assert that the exact match of k symbols occurred by chance, while if they do form a good alignment, we can build the local alignment in its totality, by building a global alignment in both directions until it has a low score (or a region that does not allign well).

We see, then, that heuristic local alignment seems to consist of three phases: indexing one or more of the sequences, using the index to identify possible alignment seeds, and then building local alignments from the seeds. How does the timing of these three phases balance out?

The first phase, typically, requires linear time: most indexing structures allow us to build an index of a sequence S in $O(n)$ time, or at most $O(kn)$ time, where the word size in the index is k. Similarly, the second phase requires linear time to traverse through T, though if there are r seeds found between S and T, we clearly need $\Theta(r)$ time and space to store them all. So the overall work of the first two phases is $\Theta(n + m + r)$. The third phase, however, is much harder to predict: if each of the r seeds is a good one, it may take extensive time to build the local alignments around each.

Still, in practice, most seeds turn out to be of low usefulness, and are discarded. If our procedure consists of attempting to build an ungapped (or nearly ungapped) short alignment around each alignment seed, and then throwing out the seed as unuseful if it quickly seems not to be extending to a good alignment, we can assume that the algorithm is expected to take $O(1)$ time for each bad seed. Assuming that bad seeds profoundly dominate good seeds, then, the final phase of the algorithm will take $O(r)$ time overall, giving an overall runtime of $O(n + m + r)$. Since we need $O(n + m)$ time just to read in the sequences, this may be a huge improvement over the $O(nm)$ runtime from the traditional sequence alignment approach. Similarly, if an index for S already exists, and we read in a new sequence T, the runtime to find seeds and build alignments will be $O(m + r)$, again assuming the overall alignment time is $O(r)$.

6.3.2 How Many Alignments are Found?

But what of r? How large is it? And how many good alignments that we might want to be finding are not found with our approach to heuristic alignment search?

In order to answer these questions, we need some models of what related and unrelated sequences actually look like, to see if truly homologous sequences will satisfy the seeding requirements, and to see how often unrelated sequences will.

The simplest probabilistic model of unrelated sequences is to imagine S and T as random noise; for the case of nucleotide sequences, where $\Sigma = \{A, C, G, T\}$, this corresponds to choosing uniformly over all 4^n and 4^m possible sequences. In two such random noise sequences, a k-letter sequence of one sequence matches a k-letter sequence of the other with probability 4^{-k}. As such, if we assume that unrelated seeds dominate related seeds, then the expected value of r is $(n-k+1)(m-k+1)4^{-k}$, and thus the overall expected runtime for a heuristic aligner of the type we have been describing is $O(n+m+nm4^{-k})$.

In this very abstracted model, then, the runtime roughly quadruples (because the number of false hits quadruples) every time we reduce k by 1, thereby reducing the stringency of the seeding requirement. However, each time we do this, the probability of finding a seed in a true alignment goes up: more true alignments will thus be discovered. Can we characterize the tradeoff?

For this, we will need models of true alignments as well. For now, we note that a seed of the sort we need can only occur in ungapped regions of alignments. If we model the positions of such ungapped alignments as independent of each other, and as being matching characters with probability p and mismatching with probability $1-p$, and we fix a length a for the ungapped regions, we can easily compute the probability that such an alignment includes a k-letter long exact match.

Theorem 6.2 *The probability that an a-letter ungapped alignment, in which positions have probability p of being matching and $1-p$ of being mismatched, includes k consecutive matching symbols can be computed in $O(ak)$ time.*

Proof. We will demonstrate this by dynamic programming: let $P(i, j)$ be the probability that an alignment of length i that is forced to start with j matching symbols, but for which the $i-j$ subsequent symbols are unfixed, has a region of length k with matching symbols. We seek $P(a, 0)$.

Clearly, $P(i, j) = 0$ if i is less than k, as the alignment is too short. And, if $i \geq k$ and $j = k$, then $P(i, j) = 1$. We need only to consider what happens for $i \geq k$ and $j < k$. In this case, position $j+1$ of the alignment is a match with probability p, and a mismatch with probability $1-p$. If it is a mismatch, then any region of k consecutive symbols must occur after the first $j+1$ symbols. As such, $P(i, j) = p \cdot P(i, j+1) + (1-p) \cdot P(i-(j+1), 0)$. We can easily compute each value of P in constant time, and the overall value of $P(a, 0)$ can be found in $O(ak)$ time, as desired. ∎

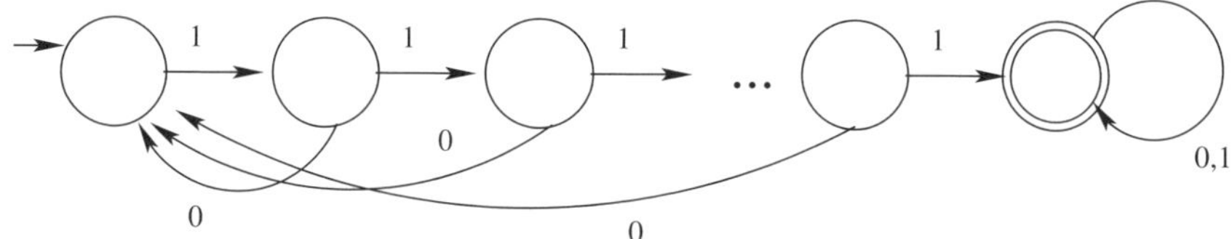

FIGURE 6.1 The simplest automaton that accepts all binary strings corresponding to alignments with k consecutive matches in them. The automaton has a total of $k+1$ states.

In the interest of having consistent terminology, we will call the fraction of alignments that have a seed, according to our model, the "sensitivity" of that approach, and the fraction of random, unrelated positions with a seed, we will call the seed approach's "false positive rate."

6.3.2.1 A Different Perspective We can see a remarkably different perspective on this process if we instead consider the alignment as being represented by a binary sequence $A = a_1, \ldots, a_a$, where $a_i = 1$ if position i of the ungapped alignment is of matching sequences and $a_i = 0$ otherwise. In this formulation, there is a match to the seeding requirement exactly when A is in the regular language represented by the regular expression $(0+1)^*1^k(0+1)^*$. The smallest deterministic finite automaton for this language is shown in Fig. 6.1. We can compute, for each i in the range from 0 to a, the probability that after reading in i random characters, the automaton is in state j of the automaton; then, if we are interested in sensitivity, the question we are seeking to answer is whether after a symbols are read, the automaton is in its accept state. The two approaches are equivalent (and give comparable algorithms), but we will often use the automaton representation in what follows.

It is, for example, very convenient when we consider BLASTP's seeding approach. Recall that in BLASTP, we will find a seed between two sequences when they share a region of length k, where k is 3 or 4, for which the total score of their short ungapped region crosses a threshold. We can treat the alignment sequence A as a sequence of scores over a discrete set F of possibilities, each with an attached probability; let us treat this set F as the alphabet for the sequence A. With this in mind, we then identify a regular expression that defines all possible score substrings of length k over the set F that cross the threshold. Then, we can compute a deterministic finite automaton for the language of all strings over F that include a substring satisfying the regular expression, and compute the probability of ending a string in the accept state.

To be more formal, let D be such a finite automaton with q states, $d_1, \ldots, d_q$, where d_q is the accept state and d_1 is the start state; suppose that $\delta_j(f)$ be the label of the state that the automaton transitions to from state d_j upon reading the symbol f. Let $A = a_1, \ldots, a_a$ be an a-letter-long random string of symbols over the alphabet F, where the probability that $a_i = f$ is p_f, and all positions of A are independent. Let

$P[i, j]$ be the probability that the automaton is in state d_j after reading in i symbols of A. If we have computed $P[i-1, j]$ for all states d_j, then we can compute the values of $P[i, j]$ by starting them all at zero and adding $P[i-1, j]p_f$ to $P[i, \delta_j(f)]$ for all choices of j and f. In this manner, we can work our way to longer and longer strings, and, in $O(|F|qa)$ time, we can compute the value of $P(a, q)$, which is what we desired. (For that matter, it is worth noting that if one thinks of the transitions in the automaton as being akin to traversing the states of a Markov chain, we are simply computing the a power of the transition matrix of the Markov chain; we can use successive doubling approaches to reduce the dependency of the runtime of this check to be logarithmic, not linear, in a.)

6.3.2.2 Which Seeding Approach to Use? With the traditional BLASTN algorithm, then, there is only one parameter that is k, the seed size. Increasing it will reduce runtime, by reducing the number of seeds found, and at the same time will reduce the number of true alignments found; reducing k will increase both runtime (by increasing the number of false seeds found) and the sensitivity.

Yet, this turns out to be an unhappy bargain. The traditional approach to nucleotide alignment is to set $k = 11$, which places a false positive hit roughly every 4^{11} cells, if the DNA is totally random noise. Yet if we are assuming that ungapped regions of alignments are 64 positions long and 70% conserved (that is, every position has probability 0.7 of being a match and 0.3 of being a mismatch), the algorithm described in the previous section finds that the probability of an alignment having a hit is just 0.30. Meanwhile, BLASTN has traditionally been very slow, and certainly would not scale comfortably to large-scale alignments of many genomes.

One faster way is to change the seeding requirement; instead of requiring one 11-letter exact match, we can require two nine-letter exact matches between S and T, separated by the same amount in both sequences. This is the approach used in Version 2 of BLAST [3]. Interestingly, we can estimate the sensitivity of the approach in a way analogous to that presented in Section 6.3.2.1. If we again look at the binary sequence A that represents the alignments we can represent the ungapped alignments that are hit as the regular language represented by the expression $(0+1)^*1^k(0+1)^*1^k(0+1)^*$. All we need to do is produce a deterministic automaton for this language (the smallest such automaton is in Fig. 6.2), and again apply the algorithm of Section 6.3.2.1 to it, to ask what the probability is that after a symbols are read, we are in the accept state of the automaton. We can similarly compute the probability that two hits are found in a short range of unrelated sequences, though there is some awkwardness here, in that we need to estimate this probability by putting an upper limit on how far the two matches are from each other.

The two-hit approach to seeding does often give robust improvements in sensitivity and false positive rates. Still, there is substantial overhead in placing two matching hits together, which may not be properly accounted for in this estimate.

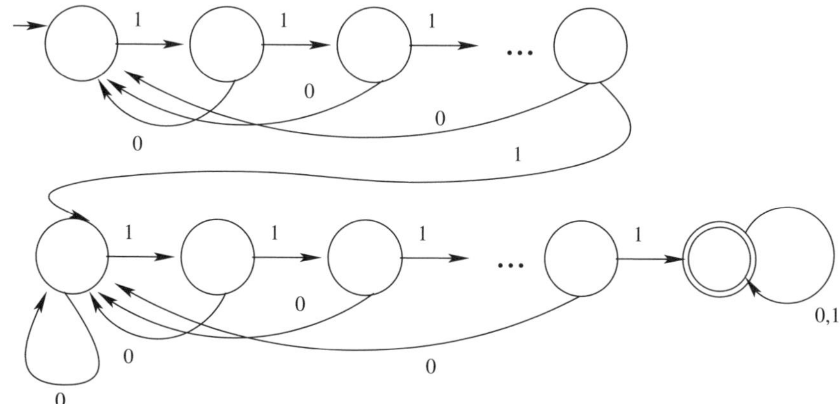

FIGURE 6.2 A simple automaton that accepts all binary strings that have two nonoverlapping hits to a k-continuous match pattern. The automaton has $2k + 1$ states, and accepts the regular language $(0 + 1)^*1^k(0 + 1)^*1^k(0 + 1)^*$.

6.4 MORE CONTEMPORARY SEEDING APPROACHES

We focused in the previous section on the sensitivity of a seeding approach and the false positive rate. However, the other great advantage of BLAST-style seeding is the simple way in which we find the seed matches for alignments. At its simplest, we can think of this as a hash table of the k-symbol substrings of S being used to find exact matches to k-symbol substrings of T. The ease of lookup is the key feature here; it is trivial to find all matches for a position of T in S. But, if all we are doing is building hash tables, they need not be of consecutive substrings of S, but could be of more complex patterns, such as of nonconsecutive positions.

This idea seems trivial, but is actually extremely useful. We will characterize such a nonconsecutive pattern by a sequence Q, of length ℓ, of zeros and ones: ones will indicate positions in the seed pattern where there must be a match between S and T in order to create a hit, and zeros will indicate "don't care" positions. To be formal, we will call such a sequence $Q = q_1, \ldots, q_\ell$ a "spaced seed pattern"; its number of ones is its "weight," w. The alignment sequence A hits the seed pattern Q if and only if there exists a position i such that in all positions j, where $q_j = 1$, $a_{j+i-1} = 1$.

It is a triviality to find all spaced seed hits between S and T for a given Q: we first produce a hash table of the ℓ-symbol substrings of S, projected onto the w positions of Q that have value 1. Then in the second phase, we compare them against the ℓ-symbol substrings of T, again projected onto the w positions of Q with value 1. Exact matches will give rise to seed hits. With the hits, we can proceed to the third phase of extension and alignment building. The overall runtime may go up by a modest factor, as we can no longer build a trie of k-letter substrings of S, but need a hash table, but nonetheless, the overall runtime is still only slightly worsened.

But why would anyone make this change? Is there an advantage to be borne by switching to this approach for seeding? In fact, there is an enormous improvement in sensitivity: for the simple Bernoulli model of alignments with $a = 64$ and $p = 0.7$, the best seed of weight 11 is 50% more sensitive than the BLAST consecutive pattern, which is equivalent to the seed $Q = (1, 1, 1, 1, 1, 1, 1, 1, 1, 1, 1)$.

6.4.1 Why are Spaced Seeds Better?

This surprising result arises because of an unexpected advantage: the hits to spaced seeds are more independent than hits to unspaced seeds. As such, even though the expected number of hits in an alignment of a given length and strength is similar for spaced and for unspaced seeds, in the spaced seed, the expected number of hits, given that there is at least one hit, is substantially greater.

If X is the random variable that is the number of hits in a random alignment, it is sufficient to find at least one hit: then we will find the alignment. Thus, the sensitivity is $\Pr[X \geq 1]$. Meanwhile, $E[X]$ is the expected number of hits, and $E[X|X \geq 1]$ is the expected number of hits, assuming that the number of hits is at least 1. A simple identity shows that $E[X] = E[X|X \geq 1] \cdot \Pr[X \geq 1]$, so $\Pr[X \geq 1] = E[X]/E[X|X \geq 1]$. If we hold the numerator of the fraction roughly constant, and drop the denominator, then the sensitivity will rise.

That does not explain, however, why the expected value of X, given that X is at least 1, is smaller for spaced seeds. (Nor, for that matter, does it explain why $E[X]$ stays roughly constant.) Let us answer the second question first: for any position i of A, if there are enough positions that follow position i to allow for a hit to the seed (spaced or unspaced), then the probability of a hit occurring in the model where all sites in A are independent and equal to 1 with probability p is p^w, where w is the seed weight. In an alignment of length a, then, the expected number of hits is $(a - \ell + 1)p^w$. If ℓ is small in comparison to a, then, this is roughly constant for all spaced seed patterns.

Why is $E[X|X \geq 1]$ smaller for spaced seeds? Consider the unspaced seed of length w, and suppose there is a hit at site i. Then, the probability of a hit at site $i + 1$ is p; the first $w - 1$ needed matches for the hit already exist. As such, if there is one hit, there is likely to be more than one hit, and the subsequent hits are wasted. Meanwhile, if we consider the spaced seed 101001, and move forward one position from a hit, *none* of the needed matches for the next match are already included, so the probability of an immediately neighbouring hit is just p^3, which is much smaller. (Of course, if we move one position further to the right, one of the needed matches is present, but the overall probabilities give substantially lower conditional expectation to the spaced seed.)

This, then, is the essential property: a good spaced seed has very little internal periodicity, and as such, hits to spaced seeds tend to be more independent. The real benefit, though, is that we can also compute the theoretical sensitivity of a seeding approach, and use it to pick the best seed pattern for a particular task.

6.4.2 Computing the Sensitivity of Spaced Seeds

With the automaton-based approach described in Section 6.3.2.1, computing the sensitivity of a spaced seed Q is no more complicated than for a consecutive seed: we identify a finite automaton that accepts the language of all strings that include a match to Q, and then compute the probability that a random string (according to a fixed probability distribution) of length a is a member of Q using the same algorithm in Section 6.3.2.1. For example, for the seed 10011, there is a hit in any alignment A that is a member of the language represented by the regular expression $(0+1)^*1(0+1)(0+1)11(0+1)^*$. The smallest automaton for this language is found in Fig. 6.3.

In general, for a seed of weight w and length ℓ, this automaton will have $O(\ell 2^{\ell-w})$ states, and then we can simply apply the same algorithm as before, which will give us the sensitivity of the spaced seed in $O(\ell a 2^{\ell-w})$ time. A variety of other exponential-time algorithms exist for this operation, coming from a variety of different perspectives, with the first due to Keich et al. [17]; still, the important feature to note is that they all require time exponential in the number of "don't-care" positions in the seed. Also, recall the important fact that these slow algorithms are computing the theoretical sensitivity of a spaced seeding approach, not actually being used to align sequences; there, the runtime is, again, the index-building time plus the seed-finding time plus the alignment-building time.

There are an exponential number of spaced seeds of a given maximum length ℓ that have $\ell - w$ don't-care positions, so we see a very slow procedure will be necessary to find the optimal seed pattern for a single probabilistic model of alignment. Still, this procedure, conceivably, would only be done once, and then the optimal seed pattern found will be used for a large number of alignments, so the overall cost is still moderate.

Some complexity results exist that show that computing the optimal spaced seed for a given probabilistic model of alignments is NP-hard, though for Bernoulli models, there is a strong connection to combinatorial design problems of finding patterns with

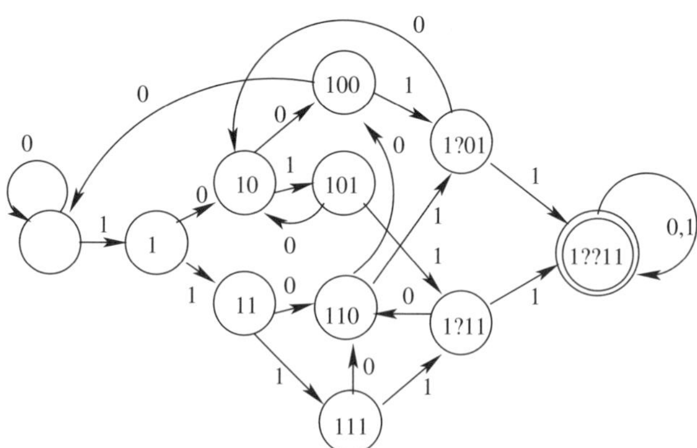

FIGURE 6.3 A simple automaton that accepts all binary strings that have a hit to the spaced seed 10011. This automaton accepts the language $(0+1)^*1(0+1)(0+1)11(0+1)^*$.

low autocorrelation. In some very nice work, Buhler et al. [9] give a connection to spectral graph theory, showing the importance of the eigenvalues of the transition matrix of the Markov chain that describes transitions in the automaton that we have described. There are also some theoretical results that document that any spaced seed will, in fact, have its first hit start at a position whose expected distance from the start of the alignment is shorter than that for an unspaced seed, which gives some theoretical justification to the use of them (though, of course, the true test is in the usefulness of these models). See Section 6.6 for more details on this fascinating work.

6.4.3 Spaced Seeds in Practice

Spaced seeds were initially described [25] in context of the PatternHunter sequence alignment package. The idea is similar to a few earlier ideas in the pattern-matching literature, though the PatternHunter authors were unfamiliar with this work [22]. One advantage of the spaced-seeds approach is that it is possible to optimize the seed to a specific domain; most previous work had been theoretical and had not considered the question of choosing a pattern that maximized sensitivity. For example, Buhler [8] had used locality-sensitive hashing to find matches between long intervals of two alignments, but his approach chose a large number of random seed patterns, not a pattern specifically chosen for its quality.

A program that uses similar approaches to PatternHunter is YASS [29,30], due to Kucherov and Noé. Their approach also allows for multihit models, as for BLAST version 2, described above, where there is a mismatch in the lengths of the regions between the hits; this allows one to model short gaps. YASS also includes several extensions to spaced seeds, some of which are described in Section 6.5. Spaced seeds have also been used by Brown and Hudek in their multiple DNA alignment software, as a way of finding good anchors for multiple alignments [7,16]. There, the seeds are used to anchor multiple alignments; further detail is in Section 6.4.5

6.4.4 More Complicated Alignment Models

The independent Bernoulli model of DNA sequence alignments in the previous section is clearly unrealistic; in practice, DNA sequence alignments have internal variation, positional dependence, and of course, they also have gaps. In this section, we continue using spaced seeds as our framework for alignment seed generation, but we consider their sensitivity to more realistic alignment models.

A first observation, made by both Buhler et al. [9] and Brejová et al. [4], concerns the structure of alignments of coding sequences. Both groups made the observation that the redundancy of the genetic code makes modeling alignments of coding sequences with independent Bernoulli variables silly: as is well known, the third position of codons are subject to substantially less evolutionary pressure than the other two positions. In fact, this observation had been used by Kent in his program WABA [19], which had implicitly used the seed model 110110110..., though without the language or structure of spaced seeds.

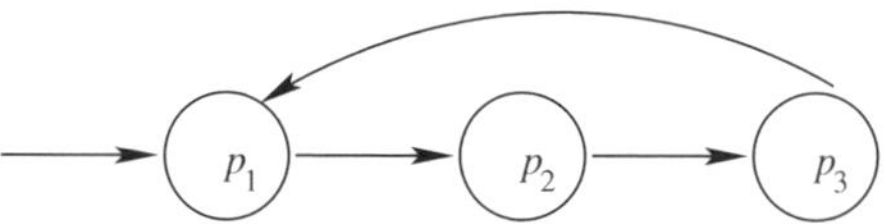

FIGURE 6.4 A hidden Markov model for three-periodic sequences. This HMM emits binary sequences where the probability that position i in the sequence is a one equals $p_{i \bmod 3}$. Each state is labeled with its probability of emitting a one.

How can we incorporate this dissimilarity into the spaced seed framework we have developed? The approach of Brejová et al. [4] is to model the binary alignment sequence A, which represents whether positions are matches or mismatches, as the emissions from a hidden Markov model. A simple HMM for three-periodic sequences, where each position of a codon has a specified probability of being a match, but all positions are independent, is shown in Fig. 6.4; we can also very easily create an HMM that models sequences with dependencies within codons (which has seven degrees of freedom, since we emit one of the eight choices of binary sequences of length three), or even an HMM with various levels of conservation inside an alignment. Brejová et al. [4] represented coding alignments with a model with four levels of similarity, using Baum–Welch [12] training to set the parameters of each of the four submodels.

Joining such an HMM into the automaton-based framework we have described before to compute seed sensitivity turns out to be quite straightforward. Suppose that the automaton D, with the q states $d_1, \ldots, d_q$, accepts the language of binary strings that correspond to alignments that satisfy a seeding requirement that we wish to analyze, and suppose that the hidden Markov model H, with η states, describes the sequences that corresponds to our probabilistic model of a particular type of alignment. What we are seeking is that if we read in a string from H into the automaton D, of length ℓ, we will wind up in the accept state of D at the end. Before, we were computing the probability that after reading i symbols, the automaton was in each state; now, we need to compute the probability of being in a particular state in *both* the automaton and the HMM.

Specifically, let $P[i, j, k]$ be the probability that after i symbols of A have been read, the automaton D is in state d_j, and the hidden Markov model is in state h_k. If we know all of the values of $P[i-1, j, k]$, we can compute them for moving forward one symbol: if the probability that state h_k emits symbol a is $E_k(a)$, and the probability that from state h_k we transition to state $h_{k'}$ is $T_k(k')$, then we need to add $p[i-1, j, k]E_k(a)T_k(k')$ to $p[i, \delta_j(a), k']$ (and do so for all choices of j, k, a, and k'). The overall runtime to compute the values of $P[\ell, \ldots]$ is $O(\ell q|\Sigma|\eta^2)$. In fact, if the HMM includes only t nonzero probability transitions, not η^2, then the runtime is $O(\ell q|\Sigma|t)$.

What we find when we use this approach is that seeds that are aware of the three-periodic structure of alignments, and that optimize the sensitivity for these models, dramatically outperform seeds that are optimal for nonaware models. Table 6.1, from Brejová et al. [4], shows that the optimal seed for the Bernouill model, PH-OPT, is in the middle of the pack among the possible seeds with length at most 18 and weight

TABLE 6.1 Ranks of Seeds Under Different Probabilistic Models. The Table Shows the Rank of Each of the Chosen Seeds in a Testing Set of True Alignments as well as Under Each of the Considered Probabilistic Models. The Seed DATA-OPT is the One that Performs Best, but its Sensitivity is very Close to that of HMM-OPT, Which has the Best Sensitivity According to a Hidden Markov Model of Coding Alignments. The WABA Seed is Designed to be a Good Spaced Seed, Yet is Reasonably Effective. The Seed PH-OPT Optimizes the Bernoulli Model of Alignments, but is Quite Poor in this Domain, While the BLAST Seed is Truly Awful. The Seed WORST is the Worst According to Both the HMM and the Real Data

	Testing Data		Rank Under a Model		
Seed	Rank	Sens	HMM	Bernoulli	Name
11011011000011011	1	0.855	2	9746	DATA-OPT
11011000011011011	2	0.851	1	9746	HMM-OPT
11011011011011	22	0.814	17	24187	WABA
111001001001010111	11258	0.585	10427	1	PH-OPT
1111111111	24270	0.451	24285	24310	BLAST
10101010101010111	24310	0.386	24310	24306	WORST

10, while the optimal seeds are very much aware of the three-periodicity of codon alignments, such as the seed 11011000011011011.

Note again that the switch here has no effect on the overall runtime: the runtime results largely from false positives, which are comparably frequent for both spaced seed approaches (and, indeed, for unspaced seeds). The advantage comes in that we are modeling the difference between homologous sequences and nonhomologous sequences more accurately.

6.4.5 Multiple Seeds

In our formulation so far, we have not changed the actual algorithm for local alignment much from the traditional one: we still build an index (albeit of spaced patterns) of one string, we still search the other string to find matches against the index, and then we build alignments out of the discovered matches.

A remarkable opportunity of the spaced seeds approach, though, is to change this theme. Instead of a single seed pattern, we attempt to find matches to a collection of seed patterns, chosen not to have much overlap in the alignments that they match. Clever choice of such patterns can allow us to match an increasing fraction of true alignments, while having minimal effect on the runtime (and the false-positive rate). The initial suggestion of this multiple-seed approach is to be found in the original Ma et al. [25] paper that proposed spaced seeds, yet they offered no sort of optimization.

In their work on vector seeds, discussed in Section 6.5, Brejová et al. [5] discuss the use of greedy algorithms for this domain. More interesting optimization algorithms for this problem were proposed essentially simultaneously and independently by Sun and Buhler [34], who used hill climbing, and by Xu et al. [36,37], who used integer programming techniques. The multiple seed approach is also implemented in the second version of PatternHunter [23].

To be specific, the idea is to first build a set of g indexes of the string S, each of which corresponds to a different spaced seed pattern, and then search the string T against *each* of the indexes, extending all pairs from S and T that match in any of the indexes. We note that the runtime now must be seen to increase: it is no longer $O(n + m + f)$, where f is the number of hits found, but rather $O(gn + gm + f)$: we need to build g indexes, and we need compare T against each of them. Memory issues may begin to be significant as well: storing multiple indexes can be quite expensive, and we might run into paging issues. Still, it is immediately clear that this is potentially useful: if we have two different seed patterns Q_1 and Q_2, which have corresponding regular expressions q_1 and q_2, the regular language $(0 + 1)^*(q_1 + q_2)(0 + 1)^*$ consists of all alignment patterns that can be detected in this approach. It is thus clear how to extend our previous algorithms for computing seed sensitivity to this domain. The result of wisely choosing two seeds is striking: Xu et al. [36,37] show that using three seeds of the same weight gives sensitivity comparable to that of using one seed with the weight lowered by one. The difference is that the false positive rate is only three-fourths as high. Similar results are shown by Brejová et al. [5] for the vector seed model described in Section 6.5: multiple vector seeds strictly dominate the false-positive performance of a single seed with comparable sensitivity.

This can be continued in a remarkably effective direction: we can achieve 100% sensitivity without requiring quadratic runtime! To be specific, suppose that we want to find all ungapped alignments of length 25 that include at most five mismatches in them. We can find the smallest set of seeds $Q_1, \ldots, Q_\chi$ of a fixed weight such that the union of the languages corresponding to each of the Q_i includes all alignment strings of length 25 with at least 20 ones: if we use the corresponding set of seed patterns to build a collection of hash tables, then with those seeds, we can find all desired alignments. The number of false positives will still not be extremely large, as there are only a constant number of hash tables. In this manner, we can discover all alignments of the desired type, in an overall runtime that is vastly smaller than might be predicted. Some interesting theorems toward this direction are shown by Kucherov et al. [21], and preliminary results of the use of this idea appear in Xu et al. [37].

To actually find these optimal sets of seeds, however, is not easy: it is NP-hard [36,37], in fact. However, a good set of seeds can be found either by using the obvious greedy algorithm (choose the best seed, then add the seed that most increases its sensitivity, and so on) [34] or by using integer programming [36,37].

We will briefly describe the integer programming approach described by Xu et al. [36,37]. We collect all of the possible alignment patterns (or a large subset of them) of a particular length and with fewer than a set bound of mismatches in them; let this set be $\mathcal{A} = \{A_1, \ldots, A_n\}$. Then let $\mathcal{Q} = \{Q_1, \ldots, Q_m\}$ be a set of seeds, and let H_i be the set of all of the A_j that are matched by seed Q_j. We can now cast the question of finding the optimal set of seeds as an instance of MAXIMUM-COVER: we want to choose the set of k seeds such that the union of their corresponding H_i sets is as large as possible.

As an integer program, this is easily cast: let $y_i = 1$ if we choose to include seed Q_i and zero otherwise, and let $x_j = 1$ if one of our chosen seeds matches alignment pattern A_j. Then we want to maximize $\sum_j x_j$ subject to the requirements that $x_j \leq \sum_{i:A_j \in H_i} y_i$ and $\sum_i y_i = k$. The first requirement maintains the requirement that we only count alignments that are actually hit, while the second forces us to use only k seeds.

While this can easily be shown to be NP-hard, as we can encode any SET-COVER instance in this manner, in practice, such integer programs easily solve using standard solvers, and easily identify a good set of relatively nonredundant seeds for homology search.

6.5 MORE COMPLICATED SEED DESCRIPTIONS

A different generalization of spaced seeds is required in order to make them useful for protein alignment, as positions do not simply match or not match in such domains. The broadest generalization of this form is called "vector seeds", is due to Brejová et al. [5], and has also been applied to nucleotide alignments as well. However, the vector seed model is largely theoretical; more practical descriptions of how to make variations on it practical as a way of aligning sequences have been developed by Kisman et al. [20], by Brown and Hudek (for multiple DNA alignment) [7,16], and by Sun and Buhler [35], for DNA alignments that incorporate different penalties for different sorts of mismatches. Cs̈urös and Ma [10,11] have approximated vector seeds using multipass filters and what they call "daughter seeds."

In order to work our way into this domain, we will begin with a presentation of the simpler results in this domain for DNA alignment, which also gives context for why this approach arose. Then, we will present the application to protein alignment, and some extensions.

6.5.1 Why Extend Spaced Seeds?

Contemporaneously with the development of spaced seeds, Jim Kent developed his extremely widely used alignment program BLAT [18], the BLAST-like Alignment Tool. BLAT is similar to BLAST, yet it includes an extension to the seeding ideas that is very helpful. Instead of requiring k consecutive positions that *exactly* match, BLAT allows one or two of the k positions to include a mismatch.

In effect, this is equivalent to the union of a collection of spaced seeds. For example, if we allow one mismatch in k positions, this is equivalent to the k spaced seeds $1^{k-1}0$, $1^{k-2}01$, $1^{k-3}011$, and so on. And, if we allow two mismatches in k positions, this is equivalent to the $k(k-1)/2$ seeds of length k with weight $k-2$. (We note that Kent's idea slightly preceded the spaced seed idea of Ma, Tromp, and Li, let alone the idea of using multiple seeds.)

One can implement BLAT-style seeding in a variety of ways, but perhaps the simplest is to still build a single hash table structure of all of the k-letter substrings of S, and then for each k-letter substring of T, look up all $3k+1$ strings that differ from that substring in at most one position (or all $(9k(k-1)/2)+3k+1$ strings that differ in at most two positions, if that is the seeding requirement). This will find all of the desired matches between S and T.

What is the consequence of this strategy? The memory usage is clearly much lower than for the multiple seeds approach: we only build a single hash table. However, the hash table is queried many more times for each substring of T; instead of looking into the table a couple of times, we look into it potentially dozens or hundreds of times. The consequence of this is that if the hash table is largely empty, our runtime will now be dominated by lookups that are largely empty. If, instead, most substrings from T have enough matches in S that most hash table cells examined are populated, then the majority of runtime will continue to be dominated by the extension phase applied after we have a large number of seeds.

To see this in its most extreme form, consider again the question in the last section, about guaranteeing 100% sensitivity for ungapped alignments with length 25 and at most five mismatches. Essentially tautologically, we can do this by using the BLAT approach, where there is a hit exactly when there is a seed of length 25, and we can allow at most five mismatches. We could build a hash tabel of 25-letter substrings of S, and search for all nearby strings to substrings of T in it. However, for every substring of T, there are $\sum_{i=0...5}\binom{25}{i}\cdot 3^i = 14,000,116$ hash table entries we would have to examine, which is of course silly, particularly as unless our input data is of the length approximately $4^{25}\approx 10^{15}$, the vast majority of these would be empty. (Of course, we would have no false positives, either.)

As such, the BLAT search approach only really works when the number of possible hash table entries is comparable to the length of the string S or smaller; otherwise, we are dominated by misses in the table lookup phase. Still, for modest lengths of seeds, there is a huge increase in sensitivity over the BLAST approach.

Why does this advantage exist? For a different reason than for spaced seeds, actually. For BLAT-style seeds, the advantage is that at a given expected number of hits per true alignment, the false positive rate is substantially smaller for seeds that allow one or two internal mismatches than for BLASTN-style unspaced seeds. For example, if the true alignments have probability $p=0.7$ of a match, and the null model is of random DNA, so there, $p=1/4$, then the probability of a hit to the 11-letter unspaced seed at a single place is $0.7^{11}\approx 0.02$, while the probability of a false positive in random noise is $0.26^{11}\approx 2.4\times 10^{-7}$. For the BLAT seed that requires 13 matches in 14 consecutive positions, the probability of a true hit at a site is approximately 3.4%, while the probability of a false hit drops to 1.53×10^{-7}. As such, we will have higher sensitivity at lower false positive rates. In fact, the overall effect is comparable to that of a single well-chosen spaced seed.

6.5.2 Vector Seeds

However, as with unspaced seeds, the BLAT hits cluster. Brejová et al. [5] proposed resolving this by a generalization of all of the seeding approaches we have seen, called "vector seeds." Vector seeds are described by a seed pattern vector of integers, v of length ℓ and a threshold T; there is a hit between the vector seed $Q = (v, T)$ and an alignment sequence A when there exists a position i such that $v \cdot (a_i, \ldots, a_{i+\ell-1}) \geq T$. For example, the BLASTN approach is equivalent to the vector seed $(\overbrace{(1, \ldots, 1)}^{k}, k)$, while the BLAT approach is equivalent to $(\overbrace{(1, \ldots, 1)}^{k}, k-1)$ or $(\overbrace{(1, \ldots, 1)}^{k}, k-1)$. A spaced seed v with weight w is equivalent to the vector seed (v, w). And, we can generalize this: if we are willing to allow two mismatches, then the vector seed $(v, w-2)$ allows this many mismatches.

Vector seeds are more general: the vector seed $((1, 2, 0, 1, 2, 0, 1, 2), 8)$ can be useful for coding sequence alignments, as it allows a single mismatch, but only in the first position of a triplet (second positions mutate less often than first positions). They are not universally general, of course, but they do allow for substantial improvements over the sensitivity and false positive rates of a single vector seed.

We note that for both BLAT and vector seed approaches, it is still straightforward to estimate the sensitivity of a seed to a particular alignment model; again, one creates a DFA that accepts the language of strings that include a hit, and again, one computes the probability that the DFA accepts a string of a given length.

What is the relative advantage of multiple seeds versus the vector seed approach for DNA alignment? For simple DNA alignment scoring approaches, where positions either count as matches or mismatches, the primary advantage is that one need only build one hash table, rather than many. Aside from that, there is really no advantage; the vector seed idea is largely a handy generalization, not a useful way of actually discovering alignments. After all, even vector seed hits will cluster more than well-chosen spaced seed hits, and a single vector seed does represent many different spaced seeds.

Still, the idea has been productive; Csürös and Ma [10] have explored an approach that approaches the simplicity of the one hash table vector seed through "daughter" seeds, where they essentially implement a multipass filter as their way of identifying hits. In subsequent work [11], they extend this to still more complicated models for seeding that are also extremely efficient.

6.5.3 More Complicated Alignments

Vector seeds, and their analogs, do shine, though, in the case of more complicated scoring schema. We first explain how they can be made useful for DNA alignment, and then extend to protein alignment. We first give a quick review of how scoring schema work for alignment.

6.5.3.1 Alignment Scoring For DNA alignment, it has been traditional to score all matches with the same positive score, and all mismatches with the same negative score. This is, however, not appropriate for protein alignments, where sequences that are very closely related may have had many minor modifications in them that have had minimal effect on their biochemistry. For example, substitutions of valine, leucine, and isoleucine for each other tend to be moderate in their effects, while changing valine to tryptophan might be very important.

The way this is taken into account is to make the score of aligning two symbols reflect the extent to which those symbols often occur homologously in real sequences. In particular, we can imagine a model that creates ungapped alignments of two sequences, where p_{ij} is the probability of seeing symbol i in S aligned with symbol j from T. Our null model will assume that the sequences are unrelated, so $q_i q_j$ is the probability of seeing symbol i randomly in S and symbol j in T. The amount by which p_{ij} is bigger than $q_i q_j$ indicates the strength of the extent to which the p model of related sequences is preferred over the q model of unrelated sequences; as such, if $\log(p_{ij}/q_i q_j) > 0$, we have evidence of the sequences being related. In practice, such log-odds ratio values are the typical form of the scores used in sequence alignment software, and if we work from the initial scoring matrix, we can compute the probabilities of the p_{ij} and q_j values.

Further, we can use these values to estimate the score of an ungapped alignment of a given length that is presumed to come from a particular model; as such, we can compute the probability that at a given position in an alignment, the pair of aligned symbols has a given score, so we can give the distribution of scores in true and unrelated alignments. This will be essential as we compute the sensitivity of alignment seeding approaches.

6.5.3.2 Complicated DNA Scoring Many researchers have built DNA alignment systems that include more complex scoring schemes; perhaps the most significant is BLASTZ [32]. All of them give less negative scores to transitions, where two aligned symbols are not the same, but either are both purines (A and G) or both pyrimidines (C and T), than to transversions, where the matched symbols are one purine and one pyrimidine. Transition mutations are more common to be retained, and as such, they are more common in true homologies. However, this gives rise to a question: how to seed local alignments?

Vector seeds offer an obvious answer: if, for the purpose of the seeding phase, we see an alignment as being a string over a three-symbol alphabet corresponding to matches, transitions and transversions, where matches score $+2$, transitions score $+1$ and transversions score 0, then we might seek a hit to a vector seed where the vector has k ones, and the threshold is $2k - 1$ or $2k - 2$; this would allow at most one transition, with the threshold $2k - 1$, or at most two transitions or one transversion, with the threshold $2k - 2$. (To allow only transitions, we can instead score transversions with the score $-\infty$.) These approaches are used in the seeding in both BLASTZ and in the very interesting alignment program YASS [29,30]. Sun and Buhler [35] also give an approach that picks many such seeds to maximize overall performance, where the false positive rate is estimated using a hidden Markov model trained on real data.

6.5.3.3 Protein Alignments Vector seeds were originally created for use with protein alignments [5], but they actually are not immediately useful for this purpose. The reason is that it is actually rarer that protein alignments cluster as many hits together: while after a BLASTN hit, another BLASTN hit is very likely, this is less true for protein alignments, as highly conserved regions of proteins tend to be much shorter in practice.

As such, the expansion in seed length required for a vector seed like ((1, 0, 0, 1, 1), 13), as compared to the traditional BLASTP seeding approach, which is essentially the vector seed ((1, 1, 1), 13), is harmful enough that it is not always better to switch to using a single vector seed for protein alignment.

However, in follow-up work [6], Brown examined the effect of using multiple vector seeds for protein alignment, particularly in concert with a system of filtration that threw out hits with no high scoring region around the hit. This approach has been quite successful, and resulted in a fivefold reduction in false positive rates at the same level of sensitivity as for BLASTP. The optimization is slightly different than the multiple spaced seed optimization of Xu et al. [36,37], because the sensitivity of protein alignment must be extremely high, almost 100%, due to the constraints of the field. As such, the optimization done in his paper [6] focuses on computing the minimum false positive rate needed to ensure 100% sensitivity to a set of test alignments.

A somewhat similar approach was derived by Kisman et al. [20] in the protein alignment package tPatternHunter; they allow hits to a collection of possible seed patterns, with an extra immediate filtration step to throw out bad hits. Again, the reported speed is substantially improved over BLASTP.

6.5.3.4 Seeding Multiple Alignments Another use for more complicated seeding models has been in the seeding of global multiple alignments. Brown and Hudek [7,16] used an extension to vector seeds in finding the anchor points upon which they hung their heuristic multiple alignments. Their progressive alignment system works by attempting to find surprisingly strong matches between inferred ancestral sequences at internal nodes of a guide phylogenetic tree.

What is different between this application and previous uses for vector seeds is that Brown and Hudek allow uncertainty in the estimation of the positions of the ancestral sequence: they allow the use of the full 15-letter IUPAC DNA alphabet that includes ambiguous symbols. As such, they build a theoretical log-odds scoring system for this more complicated scenario, and then pick, at each internal node of the guide tree, a seeding pattern and threshold that will minimize the amount of alignment error induced by the anchoring process.

Their seeding approach is a two-pass filter that slightly extends vector seeds. An ungapped alignment seed consists of a binary vector and threshold (v, T), where each position of a seed match, even the ones where $v_i = 0$ must have a nonnegative score, and the total score of the positions with value $v_i = 1$ is at least T. This approach was more successful at both avoiding hit clustering and in avoiding false positive rates than the simpler vector seed approach.

6.5.3.5 Seeding Alignments with Gaps Continuing our tour through alignment models, we note that none of the alignments we have discussed have allowed for gaps to be present in seeds, but only mismatches. Generally, this limitation has not been especially serious: strong alignments of homologous protein or DNA sequences usually do have reasonably long, highly conserved, ungapped stretches in them.

However, two different systems have arisen which do not require the seeding of an alignment to be found in an ungapped region. The first of these is YASS [29,30], which is a DNA sequence alignment program. It uses spaced seeds and some extensions to them, but allows one to set a seeding requirement that requires multiple hits, yet still allows for the region between the gaps to be unequal in length in S and in T. This implicitly allows for the existence of small gaps in the alignment that includes S and T. The mathematics used to estimate the sensitivity of YASS is based on a simple model of evolution where after every position of aligned sequence, there is a possibility of a position that is a gap from either sequence. As a general rule, this approach has the potential to increase sensitivity quite a bit, but may also be costly due to false positives rising; allowing many positions for the two seed matches to occur can be quite costly. Still, YASS is comparable in speed and effectiveness to PatternHunter [29,30].

A much more recent paper uses the possibility of gaps in a domain where allowing for their existence is essential: tandem repeat finding. Tandem repeats are often quite short, and the matches between them can be interspersed with many small gaps, as they are highly prone to insertion and deletion mutations. As such, if one is searching for them, even a spaced seed will not be effective; one would need a very short pattern to avoid having it be disrupted by a gap. Mak et al. [27] use an approach that allows the seed pattern to include positions that can represent zero or one symbols from each of S and T, thus allowing for very short gaps to exist in the seed region. This, combined with the now straightforward extension of "don't care" positions, as in spaced seeds, gives a nice improvement in sensitivity of a seeding approach for such alignments, again at minimal cost in false positives. This clear advantage is particularly nice in this case, as the false positive rates tolerated are substantially higher than for typical DNA alignment, because consumers expect tandem repeat finders to be very sensitive.

Computing the sensitivity in these models requires small changes to the model that is generating the alignment, but can still be done using essentially the same dynamic programming calculation described in Section 6.3.2.1; Mak and her co-authors describe it by reference to the Aho–Corasick automaton [1] for the set of patterns their seed models will match, but the technique is equivalent.

6.6 SOME THEORETICAL ISSUES IN ALIGNMENT SEEDING

In Section 6.4.1, we have given somewhat informal arguments for why alignments are better seeded with spaced seeds and their extensions than with the unspaced seeds that preceded them. We will conclude this review with some comments about the theoretical status of such questions.

6.6.1 Algorithmic and Complexity Questions

Early questions in this area consisted mostly of development of reasonably efficient dynamic programming algorithms to compute the sensitivity of a particular seeding approach to the Bernoulli model of DNA alignments; Keich et al. [17] gave the first such algorithm, and then it was expanded and slightly varied to include all of the various extensions discussed in this chapter. There were still questions that existed at that time, though, about other complexity issues in spaced seeds, many of which have been since resolved.

The simplest such question is whether computing the optimal single seed of a given weight and length for a given alignment model is NP-hard. The answer is yes, if we are allowed to make the alignment model extremely perverse: we can encode the clauses of a SAT instance in the set of possible alignments we may need to discover, and then allow the seed to encode the truth assignment. If the instance is satisfiable, there exists a seed with 100% sensitivity, while if not, there is no such seed. See Li et al. [23] for more detail.

The same authors also discussed whether multiple seed selection is NP-hard; here, they show that the problem of computing the sensitivity of a nonconstant-sized set of seeds is NP-hard, even for the simple Bernoulli model of alignments, if the set of possible seeds is given. This is done by showing that if we could compute the sensitivity of a particular set of seeds, we could solve a 3-SET-COVER instance. They finally show, by a simple reduction, that computing the optimal seed set for a particular set of alignments is equivalent to MAXIMUM-COVERAGE, and is hence also NP-hard.

More recently, Li et al. [24] have extended this by showing that computing the probability of a single seed having a hit to the uniform Bernoulli model is also NP-hard. This is done by an exceedingly detailed counting argument, where they again show that computing the sensitivity of a single seed to the Bernoulli model is equivalent to solving 3-SET-COVER.

Similar work by Nicolas and Rivals [28] show that identifying whether a seed misses any ungapped alignments of a given length with a fixed number of mismatches is also NP-hard. Their work starts from the EXACT-3-SET-COVER problem, but again does very delicate counting to identify which strings are missed. They also prove some nonapproximability results about estimating the sensitivity of multiple seeds.

Finally, we note that computing the optimal single seed for the Bernoulli model should not be NP-hard, as the set of optimal seeds for different lengths ℓ and a constant weight w is sparse, and if a sparse set is NP-hard, then $P = NP$ [26].

6.6.2 Combinatorial Questions

But there is another obvious set of questions. Fundamentally, why is a spaced seed better, past the heuristic observation about seed hits not clumping as much? Much of the work that seeks to resolve this question has relied on work from the early 1980s of Guibas and Odlyzko [14], who were studying patterns in binary strings. The connection between this theory and questions about spaced seeds has been extremely fruitful.

Buhler et al. [9] gave a partial answer to this, by studying the spectral structure of the transition matrix of the Markov chain that describes the behavior of the automaton we have been discussing throughout this chapter. Using this approach, they show that the asymptotic spacing of spaced seed hits is preferable to that of unspaced seed hits.

This approach was very recently extended by Li et al. [24], giving tighter bounds on the asymptotic bounds given by the spectral results. In fact, their results also show that one can estimate the sensitivity of a spaced seed for regions of arbitrary length very accurately, in time not dependent on the length of the homology region. (The proofs are not found in the conference version of their paper.)

Analogously, Li et al. [23] used a martingale argument to show that the expected position of the first hit, in an infinite-length alignment, to a spaced seed comes before the first hit to an unspaced seed; this suggests that for large alignments, the sensitivity of the spaced seed will again be higher.

6.7 CONCLUSIONS

Alignment seeding has been an extremely active area of research for the past few years: dozens of researchers have worked on this problem, largely due to the excitement caused by the original PatternHunter paper of Ma, Tromp, and Li [25]. In many ways, the area seems to have achieved a new level of mathematical maturity that was previously lacking: an extensive amount of combinatorial and probabilistic analysis has been joined into the field, along with much algorithm and complexity research.

What may be the next focus is research into the other two phases of the alignment process: the indexing phase at the beginning of the process, which is highly memory constrained, and the alignment phase at the end, which is of course the current time bottleneck. Another focus may be on using multiple scoring functions for heuristic alignment; the recent work of Pachter and Sturmfels [31] on parameter estimation, and of Fernández-Baca and Venkatachalam on parametric alignment [13], for example, may point the way in this direction.

Still, looking back at the past 6 years, it is not exaggeration to say that sequence alignment has had a surprising renaissance. We can hope that subsequent periods are comparably fruitful for it and for other domains of bioinformatics.

REFERENCES

1. Aho AV, Corasick MJ. Efficient string matching: an aid to bibliographic search. *Commun ACM* 1975;18(6):333–340.
2. Altschul SF, Gish W, Miller W, Myers EW, Lipman DJ. Basic local alignment search tool. *J Mol Biol* 1990;215(3):403–410.
3. Altschul SF, Madden TL, Schaffer AA, Zhang J, Zhang Z, Miller W, Lipman DJ. Gapped BLAST and PSI-BLAST: a new generation of protein database search programs. *Nucl Acid Res* 1997;25(17):3389–3392.
4. Brejová B, Brown DG, Vinař T. Optimal spaced seeds for homologous coding regions. *J Bioinformatics Comput Biol* 2004;1(4):595–610. Early version appeared in CPM 2003.
5. Brejová B, Brown DG, Vinař T. Vector seeds: an extension to spaced seeds. *J Comput Syst Sci* 2005;70(3):364–380. Early version appeared in WABI 2003.

6. Brown DG. Optimizing multiple seed for protein homology search. *IEEE/ACM T Comput Biol Bioinform* 2005;2(1):29–38. Early version appeared in WABI 2004.
7. Brown DG, Hudek AK. New algorithms for multiple DNA sequence alignment. *Proceedings of WABI 2004*; 2004; pp. 314–325.
8. Buhler J. Efficient large-scale sequence comparison by locality-sensitive hashing. *Bioinformatics* 2001;17:419–428.
9. Buhler J, Keich U, Sun Y. Designing seeds for similarity search in genomic DNA. *J Comput Syst Sci* 2005;70:342–363. Early version appeared in RECOMB 2003.
10. Csürös M, Ma B. Rapid homology search with two-stage extension and daughter seeds. *Proceedings of COCOON 2005*; 2005; pp. 104–114.
11. Csürös M, Ma B. Rapid homology search with neighbor seeds. *Algorithmica* 2006. Forthcoming.
12. Durbin R, Eddy S, Krogh A, Mitchison G. *Biological Sequence Analysis: Probabilistic Models of Proteins and Nucleic acids*. Cambridge University Press, 1998.
13. Fernández-Baca D, Venkatachalam B. Parametric analysis for ungapped Markov models of evolution. *Proceedings of CPM 2005*; 2005; pp. 394–405.
14. Guibas LJ, Odlyzko AM. String overlaps, pattern matching and nontransitive games. *J Comb Theor A* 1981;30:183–208.
15. Gusfield D. *Algorithms on Strings, Trees, and Sequences: Computer Science and Computational Biology*. Cambridge University Press, 1997.
16. Hudek AK, Brown DG. Ancestral sequence alignment under optimal conditions. *BMC Bioinform* 2005;6:273.
17. Keich U, Li M, Ma B, Tromp J. On spaced seeds for similarity search. *Discrete Appl Math* 2004;138(3):253–263.
18. Kent WJ. BLAT–the BLAST-like alignment tool. *Genome Res* 2002;12(4):656–664.
19. Kent WJ, Zahler AM. Conservation, regulation, synteny, and introns in a large-scale *C. briggsae – C. elegans* genomic alignment. *Genome Res* 2000;10(8):1115–1125.
20. Kisman D, Li M, Ma B, Wang L. tPatternHunter: gapped, fast and sensitive translated homology search. *Bioinformatics* 2005;21(4):542–544.
21. Kucherov G, Noé L, Roytberg M. Multiseed lossless filtration. *IEEE/ACM T Comput Biol Bioinformatic* 2005;2(1):51–61. Preliminary version appeared in CPM 2004.
22. Li M. Personal communication, 2006.
23. Li M, Ma B, Kisman D, Tromp J. PatternHunter II: Highly sensitive and fast homology search. *J Bioinformatics Comput Biol* 2004;2(3):417–439. Early version in GIW 2003.
24. Li M, Ma B, Zhang L. Superiority and complexity of the spaced seeds. *Proceedings of SODA 2006*; 2006; pp. 444–453.
25. Ma B, Tromp J, Li M. PatternHunter: faster and more sensitive homology search. *Bioinformatics* 2002;18(3):440–445.
26. Mahaney SR. Sparse complete sets for NP: solution of a conjecture of Berman and Hartmanis. *J Comput Sys Sciences* 1982;25:130–143.
27. Mak D, Gelfand Y, Benson G. Indel seeds for homology search. *Bioinformatics* 2006; 22:e341–e349. Proceedings of ISMB 2006.
28. Nicolas F, Rivals E. Hardness of optimal spaced seed design. *Proceedings of CPM 2005* 2005; pp. 144–155.

29. Noé L, Kucherov G. Improved hit criteria for DNA local alignment. *BMC Bioinform* 2004;5(149).
30. Noé L, Kucherov G. YASS: enhancing the sensitivity of DNA similarity search. *Nucl Acid Res* 2005;33 (web-server issue):W540–W543.
31. Pachter L, Sturmfels B. Parametric inference for biological sequence analysis. *P Nat Acad Scie* 2004;101:16138–16143.
32. Schwartz S, Kent WJ, Smit A, Zhang Z, Baertsch R, Hardison RC, Haussler D, Miller W. Human-mouse alignments with BLASTZ. *Genome Res* 2003;13:103–107.
33. Smith TF, Waterman MS. Identification of common molecular subsequences. *J Mol Biol* 1981;147:195–197.
34. Sun Y, Buhler J. Designing multiple simultaneous seeds for DNA similarity search. *J Comput Biol* 2005;12:847–861. Preliminary version appeared in RECOMB 2004.
35. Sun Y, Buhler J. Choosing the best heuristic for seeded alignment of DNA sequences. *BMC Bioinform* 2006;7:133.
36. Xu J, Brown D, Li M, Ma B. Optimizing multiple spaced seeds for homology search. *Proceedings of CPM 2004*; 2004; pp. 47–58.
37. Xu J, Brown D, Li M, Ma B. Optimizing multiple spaced seeds for homology search. *J Comput Biol* 2006; Forthcoming.

7

THE COMPARISON OF PHYLOGENETIC NETWORKS: ALGORITHMS AND COMPLEXITY

Paola Bonizzoni

Dipartimento di Informatica, Sistemistica e Comunicazione, Università degli Studi di Milano-Bicocca, Milano, Italy

Gianluca Della Vedova

Dipartimento di Statistica, Università degli Studi di Milano-Bicocca, Milano, Italy

Riccardo Dondi

Dipartimento di Scienze dei Linguaggi, della Comunicazione e degli Studi Culturali, Università degli Studi di Bergamo, Bergamo, Italy

Giancarlo Mauri

Dipartimento di Informatica, Sistemistica e Comunicazione, Università degli Studi di Milano-Bicocca, Milano, Italy

7.1 INTRODUCTION

Studying the evolutionary histories of extant species and their ancestors has been one of the fundamental tasks of biology since Darwin's work, where the idea of evolutionary tree (or phylogeny) has been introduced. A phylogeny is a rooted tree whose leaves are labeled by the extant species and where each internal node is a (hypothetical) common ancestor of its descendent leaves. For the last 150 years, biologists have

Bioinformatics Algorithms: Techniques and Applications, Edited by Ion I. Măndoiu and Alexander Zelikovsky

struggled to compile phylogenies by using the scarce information available, such as phenotypes and a few genetic data, with the ultimate goal of building the "tree of life," where the evolutionary history of all species on earth is represented.

In the last two decades, terrific advances in both Biotechnology and Bioinformatics have led to a huge increase in the number of phylogenies that are available for interested scholars. More precisely, biotechnology advances allow to obtain genetic sequences from various species, making feasible to compare separately different genes of the same set of species to obtain a phylogeny with a stronger evidence. Moreover the number of efficient computational methods in phylogenetics has tremendously increased, in turn leading to the availability of an even larger number of phylogenies.

Unfortunately, the underlying problems under the most widely accepted models, such as maximum parsimony or maximum likelihood, are NP-hard and therefore unlikely to have an efficient exact algorithmic solution. The main consequence is that the number of possible solutions taken into account during the execution of an algorithm, usually increases exponentially with the number of investigated taxa, hence even the most impressive algorithmic solution can assume unpractical time requirements for very large instances, even though it is currently tractable dealing with fairly large datasets (i.e., a few hundreds of taxa).

Evolutionary trees are a suitable mean for representing histories where the only interesting event is speciation, that is, a genetic mutation appears in some individuals of a species giving rise to a new subspecies. But the actual biological representation of evolutionary histories is even more complex, as recent findings have shown that an evolutionary tree is not always adequate, due to some kinds of biological events such as gene duplications, where a single gene mutates into two distinct copies afterward evolving separately, or lateral gene transfer, where some genetic material is inherited by an unrelated species. In these cases a more involved representation, such as an evolutionary network, is needed.

These facts result in the broad problem of comparing phylogenies (or evolutionary networks) to combine them into a single representation (i.e., an evolutionary tree or network). The main goal of the present review is to give a unified description of some fundamental computational approaches to face comparison of general phylogenetic representations, with an emphasis on combinatorial properties, models, and methods. We analyze how these methods have been implemented by efficient computational procedures.

The general problem will be classified into three related subproblems, each with its own motivations and results: (i) computing a common subtree (or subnetwork), (ii) computing a supertree (or supernetwork), (iii) reconciling trees.

The problem of computing a common subtree (also known as *consensus tree*) of a set of trees over the same set of taxa arises from the aforementioned fact according to which phylogenetic trees are usually constructed by using data obtained from different sources, such as molecular and morphological data. Therefore, there are strong motivations for extracting from those phylogenetic trees a strongly supported phylogeny.

The problem of computing a supertree finds its main motivation in the daunting task of computing the "tree of life." Since the set of known species is too large for any known phylogeny reconstructing algorithm, a sound approach is to construct some phylogenies on overlapping sets of taxa, and then to combine them into a unique phylogeny summarizing all information contained in the original phylogenies.

The two problems are easily generalized to networks and share two common computational issues: (i) finding some suitable criteria to amalgamate or combine the input phylogenetic networks into a single representation, (ii) designing some efficient polynomial-time algorithms to compute the desired output data.

A first step in facing these issues has been the introduction of some basic mathematical tools to compare the branching structures of the phylogenies of interest. These tools are efficiently computable functions (mappings) relating nodes of two compatible trees or networks. As all the interesting instances are those where the input trees are not the same and the goal is to determine a unique phylogeny agreeing on all input data, edges or taxa must be removed to guarantee the removal of branching differences among phylogenies; this leads to the introduction of optimization criteria. The most commonly used criterion is the one of maximizing the number of taxa inducing a common phylogeny, which can be found (by means of the chosen mapping) in all input data.

The most investigated mapping in phylogenetic comparison is *homeomorphism*. A homeomorphism between two trees specifies an isomorphism of trees under contraction of degree-2 nodes (each internal node x with only one child is deleted and the two edges previously incident on x are merged into a new edge). In consensus tree methods, this notion leads to the maximum agreement subtree (MAST) problem. It consists of finding a phylogenetic tree with the largest set of taxa for which a homeomorphic copy is included in all input trees.

The MAST is applied to compare different types of phylogenetic data. Mainly, it is a first basic approach in finding a consensus among gene trees, when reconciling different gene trees to a species tree.

More generally, it is practically used to obtain the largest intersection of a set of phylogenies inferred from different datasets. This largest intersection is used to measure the similarity of different estimated histories or to identify species that are implied in horizontal gene transfer.

The refinement mapping has been introduced as a less restrictive mapping to compare general trees. Indeed, while homeomorphic trees are obtained by contracting nodes with only one child, trees obtained through refinement, that is, *comparable trees*, differ only by the contraction of a set of edges (endpoints of an edge are merged together). This notion is crucial in the recent methods of amalgamating phylogenies over overlapping sets of taxa, or supertree methods. Indeed, in most cases the input phylogenies have different sets of taxa, and thus the primary goal is to compute a supertree T including all input taxa and displaying all input trees, that is, the subtree of T over the set of taxa of each input tree T_i is a refinement of T_i.

The third and final subproblem examined in this review arises in comparative phylogenetics and is the reconciliation (or inference) of *species tree* from *gene trees*.

A gene tree is obtained by analyzing the evolutionary history of a specific gene, present in all species under investigation, where different copies of a gene may be present in the species studied, resulting in two or more leaves in the tree sharing a common label. Instead a species tree is a phylogenetic tree representing the evolutionary history of a set of species, therefore, each label can be associated to at most one leaf of a species tree.

Different studies have shown that the species and gene evolutions do not necessarily agree, and that similarly the evolutionary histories of two different genes for a given set of species do not necessarily agree. Thus the problem is twofold: a species tree and a gene tree might not agree, and two gene trees over the same set of species might be different. This divergence between gene trees is due to biological events that affect the evolution of a gene. Indeed events such as *duplication* of a gene, *loss* of a gene, and *lateral gene transfer* (or horizontal gene transfer) are involved in genes evolution. On the contrary, species trees represent the evolution history of a set of species only in term of *speciation*.

Just as for the above mentioned comparison problems, a basic task in reconciliation of gene trees is to infer a single tree from trees over the same sets of taxa, but in this case, the single tree must be inferred with respect to mappings that preserve the set of taxa and minimize the differences between gene trees due to the specific evolutionary events. Moreover, the comparison of gene trees with a putative species tree is also relevant to infer a scenario of evolutionary events.

In this review, we present several approaches dealing with the problem of comparing gene trees in order to infer a species tree. It must be observed that this framework takes into account events that give rise to nontree structures, such as lateral gene transfers and hybridizations. Indeed, these events are represented by edges that connect nodes on different branches of a tree. Phylogenetic networks appear to be a natural mathematical structure that allows to handle such situations and are therefore central in our treatment of the subject.

This review is structured as follows: first we will introduce the basic definitions that will be used throughout the paper, then we will devote one section to each class of problems studied, beginning with the problem of computing a common subtree, going on with the problem of computing a supertree, and concluding with the problem of reconciling a set of gene trees with a species tree.

7.2 BASIC DEFINITIONS

Let Λ be a finite set of labels, representing the set of extant species (taxa) under investigation. A *rooted network N over Λ* or simply *network*, is a directed connected graph $N = (V, E)$ containing a unique vertex with no incoming edges, called *root* of N and denoted by $r(N)$ and a labeling function from the set $L(N)$ (or simply L whenever the network is clear from the context) of all vertices with no outgoing edges, called leaves of N, to the set of labels Λ is defined. The root of N represents the common ancestor of all taxa.

A *phylogenetic network* N is a network over Λ in which each internal node, that is, distinct from the leaves, has outdegree at least 2. Given a phylogenetic network N, then $\Lambda(N)$ denotes the set of all labels associated to leaves of N.

The undirected version N_u of a phylogenetic network N, obtained by removing the direction of all edges in N, might clearly contain some cycles: in fact N_u contains a cycle if and only if N is not a phylogenetic tree. Indeed *phylogenetic trees* are a special case of phylogenetic networks, more precisely they consist of all phylogenetic networks N such that N_u is acyclic. Consequently, all properties of networks also hold for trees. In particular, phylogenetic trees whose leaves are in bijection with the set of labels, are called *uniquely labeled*. Moreover, the undirected version N_u of a phylogenetic network N may be unrooted if no vertex is distinguished as the root of N.

Given a rooted network N and a node v of N, we denote by $N(v)$ the *complete subgraph* of N rooted at v consisting of v and all of its descendants. Then $L(v)$ is the set of leaves of such a subgraph.

The branching structure of a network represents the evolutionary relationships among the ancestor species. Notice that two or more leaves may share a common label. Also when a network is acyclic, it is possible to topologically sort the vertices so that a vertex always appears after all its ancestors, allowing for the definition of *children* and *parent* of any given vertex, as usual for trees.

Given a phylogenetic network N, its internal nodes can be classified according to their indegree: the vertices with indegree one are called *regular*, while vertices with indegree at least 2 are called *hybridization* nodes. Clearly a phylogenetic tree does not contain hybridization nodes.

Given a node x of a network N, the *cluster* of x, denoted by $\mathcal{C}(\mathrm{x})$, is the set of labels of all the descendants of x in N. An important property of uniquely labeled phylogenetic trees is that a tree of this type is completely specified by its set of clusters (or clades).

A collection $\mathcal{C}$ of subsets of a set Λ of labels is a *cluster system over* Λ if Λ and all of its singletons are elements of $\mathcal{C}$; $\mathcal{C}$ is *treelike* if no two of its sets overlap, that is for each $C_1, C_2 \in \mathcal{C}$, $C_1 \cap C_2 \in \{C_1, C_2, \emptyset\}$. By the above definition, it is immediate to verify that a uniquely labeled phylogenetic tree over the set Λ of leaves is equivalent to a treelike cluster system over Λ. Let $\mathcal{C}(\mathrm{T})$ denote the set of clusters of all nodes of T.

Some classes of phylogenetic trees are of particular interest since they can be used to represent specific situations. A special type of phylogenetic tree is the *gene tree*, which represents the evolutionary histories of different genes and is a rooted directed binary tree, leaf-labeled by the set Λ, where an element of Λ can be used to label more than one leaf. Indeed, multiple occurrences of the same label in a gene tree are related to different biological events such as gene duplications. Similarly, a *species tree* is a rooted binary trees whose leaves are uniquely labeled by the set Λ.

When dealing with rooted networks, a fundamental notion is that of *least common ancestor* of a set of nodes. Let A be a subset of the nodes of a phylogenetic network N, then a *least common ancestor* (or shortly lca) of A in N is a node x of N from which all nodes in A can be reached and closest to set A (i.e., the sum of the lengths of every path from x to a node in A is minimum). It is immediate to notice that such a node always exists, since all nodes of N can be reached from the root of N. Moreover, the least common ancestor of a set A of nodes is unique in phylogenetic trees.

In the following, given a network N, by $V(N)$ we denote the set of vertices of N, by $A(N)$ the set of directed edges or arcs of N and by $E(N)$ the undirected edges (or simply edges) underlying the set $A(N)$. Observe that when dealing with phylogenetic trees there exists a unique orientation of the tree induced by the root, that is, arcs are directed from the root toward the leaves.

7.2.1 Network Mappings and Display

In this section, we introduce some basic mappings between vertices of two given networks. These mappings are used in the next sections to compare a collection of phylogenetic networks by identifying a branching structure representing their common history. We assume that all mappings map a leaf l_1 to another leaf l_2 only if l_1 and l_2 have the same label.

Two networks N_1, N_2 are *isomorphic* if there exists a bijection or isomorphism ϕ from $V(N_1)$ to $V(N_2)$ preserving leaf labels such that $(\phi(v_1), \phi(v_2)) \in A(N_2)$ if and only if $(v_1, v_2) \in A(N_1)$. A network N_1 is *homeomorphic* to N_2 if there exists an *homeomorphism* ϕ from $V(N_1)$ to $V(N_2)$, that is, a surjection such that $(\phi(v_1), \phi(v_2)) \in A(N_2)$ if and only if there exists a path from v_1 to v_2 in $A(N_1)$ consisting of nodes with both indegree and outdegree 1.

The notion of homeomorphic network can be alternatively defined by means of the *vertex contraction* operation that is applied to a node v of indegree and outdegree 1: it consists of creating an arc connecting the vertex parent of v to the child of v and removing v and all arcs incident on it. Thus, a network N_1 is homeomorphic to N_2 whenever N_2 is isomorphic to the network obtained from N_1 after contracting all nodes of indegree and outdegree 1. Similarly, the *arc contraction* operation consists of removing an arc and merging its incident vertices. This operation is used to define another mapping between two networks.

A network N_1 is a *refinement* of N_2 if there exists a surjection ϕ from $V(N_1)$ to $V(N_2)$, such that $(\phi(v_1), \phi(v_2)) \in A(N_2)$ if and only if v_1 is connected to v_2 after a sequence of some arc contractions applied to network N_1. Observing the type of mappings we have defined above, assume that two networks related by the mapping are all leaf-labeled by the same set Λ. Whenever networks to be compared are over different, but overlapping, set of leaves, then the notion of network displaying another network as defined below, has a crucial role.

Let L be a subset of the leaves of N. Then, the *restriction* of N to L, denoted by $N|L$, consists of the network obtained from N by retaining only nodes along with their incident arcs that are in a path from a leaf in L to the least common ancestor of L in N. We also say that $N|L$ is the subgraph induced by L. The *topological restriction* of N to L, denoted by $N|_tL$, consists of the network obtained from $N|L$ by applying all possible vertex contractions. Since in uniquely leaf-labeled networks the leaves can be identified by the set of their labels, the notion of restriction and topological restriction are simply given w.r.t. to a set Λ of leaf labels.

A network N_1 *displays* N_2 if all leaves of N_2 are also leaves of N_1 and the topological restriction of N_1 to the leaves of N_2 is a refinement of N_2. Informally, network

N_1 displays N_2 if all information represented by the branching in N_2 is contained in N_1.

Observe that when mappings are applied to trees T_1 and T_2 over the same set of leaf labels, they induce fundamental relationships between clusters of the two trees. Indeed, notice that T_1 is homeomorphic to T_2 iff $\mathcal{C}(T_1) = \mathcal{C}(T_2)$, while T_1 displays T_2 if and only if $\mathcal{C}(T_1) \supseteq \mathcal{C}(T_2)$.

Some mappings defined on pairs of trees are also characterized in terms of triples of leaves, as a phylogenetic tree can be described by listing the set of triples of leaves and their induced branchings. More precisely let T be a phylogenetic tree, and let a, b, c be three of its leaves. Then, the tree $T|_t\{a, b, c\}$ assumes one of four possible configurations. Three of these configurations are binary trees and are called *rooted triples*: they are denoted as $(ab|c)$ if a and b are at distance 2 from the root while c is at distance 1, $(ac|b)$ if a and c are at distance 2 from the root while b is at distance 1, $(bc|a)$ if b and c are at distance 2 from the root while a is at distance 1. A last configuration, denoted $(a|b|c)$, occurs if a, b, and c are all at distance 1 from the root and is called a *fan*. We will denote by $t(T)$ and $f(T)$, respectively, the set of rooted triples and the set of fans of the tree T. A well-known characterization of homeomorphism and refinement states that

Lemma 7.1 *A tree T is homeomorphic to T' iff all rooted triples and fans of T and T' are isomorphic, that is, $f(T) = f(T')$ and $t(T) = t(T')$. A tree T is a refinement of tree T' iff rooted triples of T refine fans of T', that is, $t(T') \subseteq t(T)$ and for each $(a|b|c) \in f(T') - f(T)$ one of $(ab|c)$, $(ac|b)$, $(bc|a)$ is in $t(T)$.*

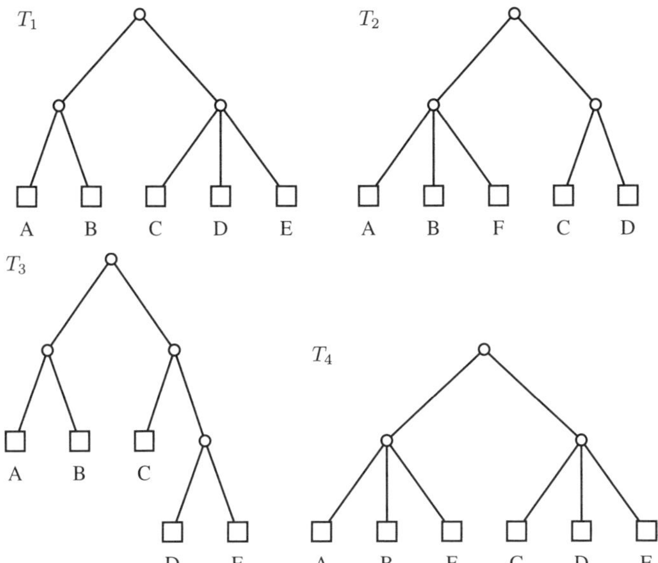

FIGURE 7.1 Examples of phylogenetic trees.

If tree T is a refinement of tree T', then T is called *compatible* to T'. Observe that if there exists a triple a, b, c such that $T|_t\{a, b, c\}$ and $T'|_t\{a, b, c\}$ induce different rooted triples, then T and T' are not homeomorphic and they are in *hard conflict* on the triple a, b, c. Similarly, if given a triple a, b, c, $T|_t\{a, b, c\}$ is a rooted triple while $T'|_t\{a, b, c\}$ is a fan, then T cannot be homeomorphic to T' (and vice versa) and trees T and T' are in *soft conflict* on the triple a, b, c.

In Fig. 7.1, some examples of phylogenetic trees are represented (note that the orientation of edges is not represented as implicitly given by the root). Please notice that T_4 displays T_1 and T_2, while also T_3 displays T_1, but not T_2. In the next two sections, we will assume that all phylogenetic trees are uniquely labeled, if not differently specified.

7.3 SUBTREES AND SUBNETWORKS

In this section, we will deal with trees or networks that are uniquely leaf-labeled by the same set of species or taxa. The methods used to compare such kinds of networks remove as fewer leaves as possible inducing branching differences in the networks so that the result is a *consensus subnetwork* or *subtree*. A classical criterion used to infer a consensus subtree consists of finding a largest set of taxa (leaves) that induces an agreement subtree that can be retrieved in all input trees according to some specific notions of mappings, as introduced in Section 7.2.1. The choice of different mappings leads to the definition of different comparison problems on unrooted and rooted phylogenetic trees. The foremost example of mapping is homeomorphism, which leads to the MAST problem, initially proposed by Finden and Gordon [17]. Note that this criterion is weaker than isomorphism among trees while it is more restrictive of the refinement mapping. This last notion leads to a variant of the maximum agreement subtree that is of particular interest in comparing nonbinary input trees: the maximum compatible tree (MCT) problem, that was initially proposed by Hamel and Steel in [25] to specifically compare nonbinary trees over a common subset of leaves. Indeed, in an evolutionary tree, a node with more than two descendants usually represents an incomplete resolution of the grouping of its descendants. In this situation, the compatible subtree of two input trees is able to group sets of taxa with a least common ancestor that can have many children in one input trees and only a few in the other tree.

Clearly, the maximum compatibility criterion on a set of trees produces a subset of taxa that is at least as large as the set of taxa of a maximum agreement subtree, as it is a weaker criterion than homeomorphism. Notice that over binary trees the two criteria produce the same tree. Recently, those notions on trees have been extended to obtain phylogenetic subnetworks (Fig. 7.2).

7.3.1 Subtrees

Let us now give more formal definitions of the problems studied. The notions of homeomorphism and isomorphism applied to a collection $\mathcal{T} = \{T_1, \ldots, T_n\}$ of phylogenetic trees lead to the following notions of consensus subtree. An *agreement*

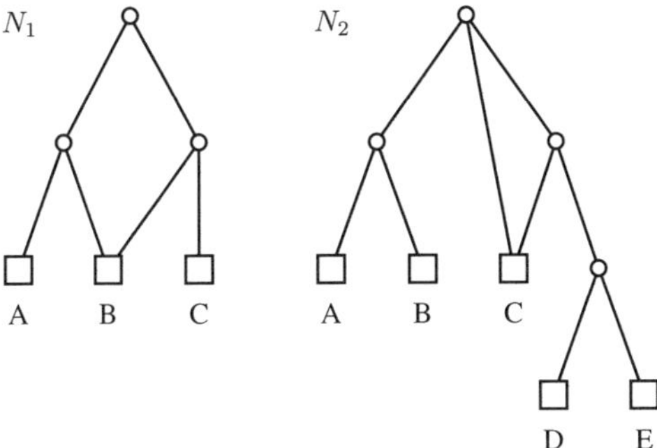

FIGURE 7.2 Examples of phylogenetic networks.

homeomorphic subtree (respectively, *agreement isomorphic subtree*, *compatible subtree*) of $\mathcal{T}$ is a phylogenetic tree T such that each tree $T_i|L(T)$ is homeomorphic (respectively isomorphic, compatible) to T. Clearly, the above different notions lead to the general comparison Problem 7.1, where σ-subtree stands for one of agreement homeomorphic, agreement isomorphic, or compatible subtree.

PROBLEM 7.1 Maximum Consensus σ-Subtree

Input: a set $\mathcal{T} = \{T_1, \ldots, T_k\}$ of phylogenetic trees.
Output: a σ-subtree of $\mathcal{T}$ with the largest set of leaves, or maximum σ-subtree.

The three main variants of Problem 7.1, for σ equal to agreement homeomorphic, agreement isomorphic, or compatible, are called respectively *Maximum Agreement Homeomorphic Subtree* problem (MAST), *Maximum Agreement Isomorphic Subtree* (MIT), and *Maximum Compatible Subtree* (MCT). Observe that the problem MCT over binary trees is equivalent to the MAST problem.

Variants of the MAST, MIT, and MCT problems are naturally obtained by changing the parameter used in the objective function. Instead of using the size of the leaf set to find an agreement subtree, the whole size of the solution tree could be maximized in an optimal solution.

7.3.2 Computational Complexity and Algorithmic Solutions

The degree of the input trees is a key parameter for determining whether MAST and MIT are easy or hard to solve; in fact both have polynomial-time algorithms when at least one of the input trees has bounded degree [2], while both are NP-hard for three unbounded-degree trees.

Algorithms for computing a MAST over two rooted or unrooted binary trees have been extensively studied. We list some of the most interesting results that appeared in the literature for the MAST problem, starting with instances of two trees on n leaves each. MAST can be solved in $O(n \log n)$ time for two (rooted and unrooted) binary trees [9], in $O(d^{0.5} n \log n(2n/d))$ time for two trees of maximum degree d [30], and $O(n^{1.5})$ time for two generic trees [29]. For k trees, the most efficient algorithm is a $O(n^d + kn^3)$ time algorithm [14] when one tree has maximum degree d. Given p the smallest number of leaves whose removal leads to the existence of an agreement subtree, a $O(\min(3^p kn, c^p + kn^3))$ time algorithm for general trees has been proposed in [5] (where $c \approx 2.311$). This result improves over the previously known $O(3^p kn \log n)$ time algorithm [13], which established that MAST is fixed-parameter tractable in p.

The computational complexity of MCT problem is quite different; in fact, it is NP-hard just on two trees one of which is of unbounded degree [26]. Moreover, it has a $O(2^{2kd} n^k)$ time algorithm for trees of maximum degree d [19]. Similarly as MAST, the problem on general trees can be solved in $O(\min(3^p kn, c^p + kn^3))$ time, given p is the smallest number of leaves whose removal leads to the existence of an agreement subtree [5] (where $c \approx 2.311$).

7.3.3 Dynamic Programming Algorithms

We will now concentrate on an exact algorithm for solving MAST on two input trees. A main technique used in several algorithms for the MAST problem as well as in its restrictions is dynamic programming (DP). An earlier DP algorithm for two trees has been proposed in [37] and has been later extended to MCT on two trees and on k rooted trees of bounded degree d to achieve the result in [19] listed previously.

Let us describe the basic idea of the DP algorithm of [37] on two d-bounded-degree input trees T, T' having the same set L of leaves. Recall that given a node v, $T(v)$ is the complete subtree of T with root v. Then, let us denote by mast(x, y) the optimum over the trees $T(x)$ and $T'(y)$, where x and y are two nodes of T and T', respectively. Clearly, the value of the solution for T, T' is given by mast$(r(T), r(T'))$. As usual for a DP algorithm, the main step consists in defining the value of mast(x, y) recursively. First notice that if x and y are both leaves, then mast$(x, y) = 1$ if and only if x and y have the same label, otherwise mast$(x, y) = 0$. Similarly if x is a leaf, but y is not, then mast$(x, y) = 1$ if and only if x has the same label as one of the leaves of $T'(y)$. A symmetric property holds for the case that only y is a leaf.

Let us now assume that neither x nor y is a leaf. As a consequence, two main distinct cases must be considered. Let L' be the subset of L that is the leaf set of a maximum agreement subtree of $T(x)$ and $T'(y)$. The first case holds when the least common ancestor of L' in $T(x)$ and $T'(y)$ is the root of each tree $T(x)$ and $T'(y)$, respectively. Then, observe that $L' = L_1 \cup L_2 \cdots \cup L_{\mathrm{m}}$, where sets L_i, L_j are pairwise disjoint and each set L_{i} is the leaf set of a maximum agreement subtree of trees $T(x_{\mathrm{l}})$, $T'(y_{\mathrm{k}})$, for x_{l} and y_{k} children of x and y, respectively. Notice that the size of L_{i} is given by mast(x_{l}, y_k). Since sets L_i, L_j are pairwise disjoint, it follows that the cardinality of L' is obtained by summing mast(x_{i_h}, y_{j_h}), for each pair (x_{i_h}, y_{j_h}) in a set $\{(x_{i_1}, y_{j_1}), \ldots, (x_{i_m}, y_{j_m})\}$, where all $x_{i_1}, \ldots, x_{i_m}$ are distinct children of x, $y_{\mathrm{j}_1}, \ldots, y_{\mathrm{j}_\mathrm{m}}$ are distinct children of y and m is the minimum of the numbers of children of x and y. Let us define a *pairing* of x and y as a set of m disjoint pairs each one made of a child of x and a child of y. Then mast(x, y) is equal to the maximum cost of a possible pairing. This value corresponds to the maximum weight matching in a bipartite undirected graph G_{xy} where the vertices are the children of x and y, and each edge (x_i, y_j) has weight equal to mast(x_i, y_j). For our purposes, maximal weighted matching in bipartite graphs can be computed in $O(m\sqrt{n}\ \log n)$ time [18].

A different situation holds if only a descendant of node x or of node y is the least common ancestor in T and T' of the leaf set of an optimal solution. In this case, given x_i a child of x and y_j a child of y, it holds that mast$(x, y) = \max_{i,j}\{\text{mast}(x_i, y), \text{mast}(x, y_i), \text{mast}(x_i, y_j)\}$. Clearly, we are unable to know which of the two cases discussed above holds, therefore we must choose the maximum over all possibilities.

The basic implementation of the above equations leads to a quadratic time algorithm [37], which has been subsequently improved to $O(n \log n)$ time in [28] by using sparse dynamic programming based on the proof that the number of interesting pairs of nodes x, y for which mast(x, y) must be computed to get the optimal solution is at most $O(n \log n)$. The further efficiency achieved by the algorithm of [29] for two trees of bounded degree d is based on an improved technique to compute the maximum weight matchings of bipartite graphs satisfying certain structural properties.

An $O(n^d + kn^3)$ time algorithm improving a previous result in [2] has been given in [14] by cleverly extending the DP algorithm discussed above. In this case, the coefficient of the recurrence equation has a k-tuple of parameters consisting of one node from each input tree, and instead of a pairing it is necessary to construct a k-*pairing* that is defined as a set of disjoint k-tuples, where each k-tuple contains exactly one child of each node currently considered.

Let $T_1, \ldots, T_k$ be a collection of k input trees all with leaf set L and where some tree has maximum degree d. The basic idea in [14] is to find recursively a k-tuple $\bar{v} = (v_1, \ldots, v_k)$, where each v_i consists of the root of the subtree $T_i|L'$ such that L' is the leaf set of a maximum agreement subtree.

A fast recurrence for computing mast$(\bar{v})$ is obtained by defining a linear ordering $>$ among k-tuples representing roots of agreement subtrees of the input trees such that $>$ is of size $O(n^3)$ and can be computed in $O(kn^3)$. The linear order obeys the following properties proved in [14]: (i) $\bar{v} > \bar{w}$ iff each element w_i is a child of v_i in some agreement tree, (ii) there are $O(n)$ active directions, where an *active direction for* $(\bar{v}, \bar{w})$ is defined as $\bar{d} = \{d_1, \ldots, d_k\}$ such that $\bar{v} > \bar{w}$ and w_i is a d_i child of v_i.

Given a vertex $\bar{v}$ of the linear ordering, mast$(\bar{v})$ is computed by finding a k-pairing for $\bar{v}$, consisting of a set $\{\bar{d}_1, \ldots, \bar{d}_l\}$ such that $\bar{d}_i$ is an active direction for $(\bar{v}, \bar{w}_i)$ and mast$(\bar{w}_1) + \ldots +$ mast$(\bar{w}_l)$ is of maximum value. Due to the degree bound, it must be that $l \leq d$. Computing an optimal k-pairing can be done by constructing the vertex-weighted *compatibility graph* $G(\bar{v})$ with vertices the active directions from $\bar{v}$ and edges the pairs $(\bar{d}_i, \bar{d}_j)$ where $\bar{d}_i$ and $\bar{d}_j$ differ in all coordinates. Each vertex $\bar{d}$ is weighted by the value $\max\{\text{mast}(\bar{w}) : \bar{d} \text{ active direction for the pair } (\bar{v}, \bar{w})\}$. Consequently, it can be easily proved that an optimal k-pairing for $\bar{v}$ corresponds to a maximum weighted clique of graph $G(\bar{v})$. The computation of such clique requires

$O(n^d)$ time. Based on the above steps the optimum for all input trees is computed via DP as the maximum value mast($\bar{v}$) over all k-tuples in the linear ordering.

7.3.4 Fixed-Parameter and Approximation Algorithms

Since in practice the input trees usually agree on the majority of the leaves, it is relevant to study the approximation of the complementary versions of MAST and MCT (called, respectively, CMAST and CMCT), where we want to minimize the number p of leaves that must be removed in order to obtain an homeomorphic (or compatible) subtree. The parameter p is used to design fixed-parameter algorithms for CMAST and CMIT [5]. The algorithms rely on two well-known characterizations of homeomorphism and refinement based on rooted triples stated in Lemma 7.1. By this result, the homeomorphism or refinement among two trees is simply tested by verifying that no conflicting triples exist between the two trees. Precisely, given trees T and T', T is homeomorphic to T' if the trees are not in hard or soft conflicts on all triples. However, a soft conflict among two homeomorphic trees T and T' does not forbid the existence of a tree compatible with both trees T, T'. Indeed, the following result relates MAST and MCT problems over a collection $\mathcal{T}$ of trees to conflicting triples.

Observation 7.1 *Let $\mathcal{T}$ be a collection of trees over the same leaf set L and let $L' \subseteq L$. Then T is an agreement (or compatible) subtree of $\mathcal{T}$ with leaf set L' iff no triple of elements in L' is a hard or soft conflict (or hard conflict) in $\mathcal{T}$.*

Observation 7.1 leads to a reduction from MAST and MCT problems to the 3-Hitting Set problem. More precisely, we consider parametric versions of MAST and MCT consisting in finding an agreement and compatible subtree of a set $\mathcal{T}$ of trees [5] having at least $n - p$ leaves, for a fixed value p. The instance of 3-Hitting Set problem is a collection of triples of elements over the universe U and a parameter p. The problem asks for a *hitting set* (i.e., a subset H of U intersecting each triple in the collection) of size at most p, if such set exists. Clearly, in the reduction of parametric MAST and MCT, the input collection of 3-Hitting Set consists of all conflicting triples over the leaf set of the input trees. The hitting set H to be computed is the set of leaves that must be removed to get the agreement and compatible subtree.

The above reduction leads to algorithms solving CMAST and CMCT. Indeed, it is possible to compute triples in a tree over n leaves in $O(n^3)$. Thus, knowing the set X of triples on which k trees are in conflict requires $O(kn^3)$ time. The set X and the parameter p constitute the instance of the 3-Hitting Set problem, which can be solved in $O(2.27^p + kn^3)$ time [13], using the fixed-parameter algorithm in [32].

An alternative algorithm for CMAST and CMCT has been recently given in [5] based on two linear-time procedures: (P1) a linear-time algorithm to test whether two rooted trees are isomorphic (or compatible), or otherwise identify a triple of leaves on which they disagree, or are *a conflict* and (P2) a linear-time algorithm that on two input trees returns a tree T minimally refining them if such a tree exists, or otherwise returns a conflict. The algorithm works in two steps on input, a collection $\mathcal{T}$ of trees and a parameter p:

1. it uses the procedure P1 or P2 to test whether the collection $\mathcal{T}$ consists of all isomorphic or comparable trees, otherwise it finds a triple a, b, c on which two trees in $\mathcal{T}$ have a conflict,
2. alternatively, for each label l in $\{a, b, c\}$, recursively the algorithm looks for a subtree without conflicts in the new input consisting of the collection $\mathcal{T}$ of trees topologically restricted to $L - \{l\}$ and parameter $p - 1$.

The above algorithm can be implemented to run in $O(3^p kn)$ time. By combining the two strategies in [5] the fixed-parameter $O(\min\{3^p kn, 2.27^p + kn^3\})$ time complexity of CMAST and CMCT stated before has been proved.

The reduction to 3-Hitting Set leads also to an interesting approximation algorithm for CMAST. Starting from [2] several papers propose 3-approximation algorithms; most recently a linear time (i.e., $O(kn)$ time) 3-approximation algorithm has been proposed for CMAST on k (rooted and unrooted) trees on n taxa [4]. In the same paper, an $O(kn + n^2)$ time 3-approximation algorithm has been proposed also for CMCT.

The simplest 3-approximation algorithm basically consists of the reduction to 3-Hitting Set, which can be computed in $O(kn^3)$ time as seen before. Successively given $ct(L)$ the set of all conflicting triples, the algorithm iteratively chooses an arbitrary triple $\{a, b, c\} \in ct(L)$ and removes from $ct(L)$ all triples intersecting $\{a, b, c\}$ while adding a, b, c to the hitting set H (which is initially empty). Let X be the set of triples chosen by the algorithm, the 3-factor approximation follows from the fact that $|H| = 3|X|$, while the optimal solution of CMAST has at least $|X|$ elements. Indeed, all triples in X are disjoint which implies that at least one element of each triple in X must be in the hitting set.

The complement versions are hard to approximate, more precisely CMAST is APX-hard (i.e., it cannot be approximated arbitrarily well by a polynomial-time algorithm) on three input trees, while CMCT is APX-hard even on two trees [4]. On the other hand, the original problems MAST, MIT, and MCT are even harder to approximate, as they are as hard as Max Clique, that is, no polynomial-time algorithm can compute an approximate solution within a factor $n^{1-\epsilon}$ unless $NP = P$ [4,7]. Moreover, MAST and MIT cannot be approximated with any constant ratio even on instances of three trees [7,26].

7.3.5 Subnetworks

The MAST problem can be generalized to phylogenetic networks that are not trees but such that their leaves are in bijection with the set L of leaf labels. Indeed, given two networks N_1 and N_2, an *agreement homeomorphic network* of N_1 and N_2 is a network N such that for a given leaf subset $L' \subseteq L$ every restriction $N_i|L$, for $i \in \{1, 2\}$, is homeomorphic to N.

The NP-hardness results of the MAST problem clearly extends also to phylogenetic networks, while some polynomial-time algorithms have been given for the case of two input networks [8].

7.3.6 Open Problems

Variants of the MAST, MIT and MCT problems are naturally obtained by changing the parameter used in the objective function. Indeed, the whole size of the solution tree could be maximized in an optimal agreement subtree, instead of the size of the leaf set. In this case, optimization criteria based either on edges or clusters could be used to find an optimal consensus subtree. Few papers have investigated this direction and thus we do not know whether these criteria could produce consensus trees retaining as many leaves as in the MAST or MCT solutions. In particular, it could be interesting to define mappings between a pair of trees based on clusters or edges that allow to find an agreement subtree retaining all leaves. This question is partially addressed in the next two sections.

Another research direction that has been deeply explored regards the application of the maximum agreement subtree as a measure of similarity to compare networks or trees that are not necessarily uniquely leaf-labeled. Examples of such an application come from gene tree inference and several other areas of computational biology where it is required to compare unrestricted labeled trees. Algorithms for computing MAST for unrestricted labeled trees are given in [30].

Restricted versions of the MAST problem obtained by assuming a leaf ordering of the input trees [12] have been recently investigated. More precisely, in the *ordered maximum homeomorphic* (OMAST) problem the input trees are *ordered* trees, that is rooted trees where the left to right order of the children of each node is relevant, while in the *uniformly ordered MAST* (UOMAST) problem the input trees are *leaf ordered* trees, that is, trees having the same leaf label ordering. The leaf-labeled ordered variants of MAST problem on k trees with n leaves can be solved in $O(kn^3)$ time for UOMAST and $O(n^3 min\{nk, n + n \log^{k-1} n\})$ for OMAST [12].

7.4 SUPERTREES AND SUPERNETWORKS

The goal of this section is to give an overview of computational methods for comparing phylogenetic networks that infer a supernetwork merging the information of a collection of input networks. We focus on methods for comparing arbitrary and usually large structures, hence we do not study problems where the input structures have fixed size, such as quartet-based methods for reconstructing phylogenies (we refer the interested reader to [16] for a complete description of quartet-based methods), even though those problems have been deeply investigated in the literature. Moreover, we deal only with methods that do not use additional information besides the branching structure of the networks to infer a supernetwork.

We first deal with supertree methods that applied in comparing phylogenetic trees. As observed in the introduction, in contrast to consensus tree methods introduced in the previous section, the supertree approaches are specifically designed to merge a collection of input trees over different sets of leaves, even though sometimes they can also be used to compare identically leaf-labeled trees.

By using tree mappings introduced in Section 7.2.1, we can define methods for supertree inference that are based on the idea of retaining a largest set of taxa obtained by removing those taxa that induce conflicts among all trees or contradictory rooted triples. These methods naturally lead to extend to the case of a supertree the notions of agreement and compatible subtree discussed in the previous section.

A complementary approach to compute a supertree requires that all taxa appearing in at least one input tree must necessarily appear also in the output supertree, where all information encoded in the input trees must be present. Also for this approach, the notion of tree mapping (especially of tree refinement) is central for formally defining the idea of information preservation.

7.4.1 Models and Problems

The simplest and more general problem that arises in supertree inference is the construction of a compatible supertree.

PROBLEM 7.2 Compatible Supertree

Input: a set $\mathcal{T} = \{T_1, \ldots, T_k\}$ of phylogenetic trees.
Output: a tree T displaying all trees in $\mathcal{T}$.

This formulation has the drawback that such a supertree is not guaranteed to exist, even though the problem seems quite easy to solve, as we are looking for a tree T whose set of clusters contains those of the input trees. Moreover, such a supertree exists if and only if no two input clusters (possibly in different trees) are overlapping. Please notice that the problem is much harder on unrooted trees than on rooted trees; in fact, computing (if it exists) a compatible unrooted supertree displaying all input trees not only is NP-hard [35] but also cannot be solved by any generic algorithm (without time constraints!) invariant with respect to permutations of leaves' labels [36].

By requiring that clusters of the supertree displaying all trees preserve some strict relationships between clusters of the input trees, we obtain a variant of the Compatible supertree problem that is related to the agreement subtree method.

PROBLEM 7.3 Total Agreement Supertree

Input: a set $\mathcal{T} = \{T_1, \ldots, T_k\}$ of phylogenetic trees, with T_i leaf-labeled over $\Lambda(T_i)$.
Output: a phylogenetic tree T leaf-labeled over $S = \cup_{i \le k} \Lambda(T_i)$ such that each tree $T|\Lambda(T_i)$ is homeomorphic to T_i.

Observe that in the total agreement supertree problem, the computed tree T is such that $\mathcal{C}(T|\Lambda(T_i)) = \mathcal{C}(T_i)$ while given the output tree T' of the Compatible supertree problem, it holds that $\mathcal{C}(T_i)$ is included in $\mathcal{C}(T'|\Lambda(T_i))$.

Again, the total agreement supertree problem might not have a solution, thus we consider an optimization version of the above mentioned problem obtained by relaxing the constraint of retaining in the supertree all leaves of the input trees and requiring to construct an agreement supertree with as many leaves as possible. Such optimization criterion leads to problems that are strongly related to MAST, MIT and MCT.

Indeed, applying network mappings to an instance consisting of a collection $\mathcal{T} = \{T_1, \ldots, T_k\}$ of phylogenetic trees lead to the following notions of supertree of $\mathcal{T}$ over a set S of leaves such that $S \subseteq \cup_{i \leq k} \Lambda(T_i)$.

An *agreement homeomorphic* (resp. *agreement isomorphic*) supertree of $\mathcal{T}$ over S is a phylogenetic tree T such that for each tree T_i, $T|\Lambda(T_i)$ is homeomorphic to the topological restriction of T_i to S (resp. for each T_i, $T|\Lambda(T_i)$ is isomorphic to $T|S$). A *compatible supertree* of $\mathcal{T}$ over S is a phylogenetic tree T such that for each tree T_i, $T|_t\Lambda(T_i)$ is a refinement of the topological restriction of T_i to S. As in Section 7.3, we use the notion of σ-supertree to denote either agreement homeomorphic, or agreement isomorphic, or compatible supertree. The following general problem is then defined, leading to three different variants that we group under the name of *consensus supertree* problems (please notice that those problems must not be confused with computing the strict consensus tree).

PROBLEM 7.4 Maximum Consensus σ-Supertree

Input: a set $\mathcal{T} = \{T_1, \ldots, T_k\}$ of leaf-labeled phylogenetic trees, where each T_i is labeled over $\Lambda(T_i)$.
Output: a leaf-labeled phylogenetic σ-supertree T of $\mathcal{T}$ over a set $S \subseteq \cup_{i \leq k} \Lambda(T_i)$ such that T has the largest set of leaves.

Then the *Maximum Agreement Homeomorphic Supertree* (MASP), the *Maximum Agreement Isomorphic Supertree* (MISP), and the *Maximum Compatible Supertree* (MCSP) problems are three variants of Problem 7.4 where the σ-supertree is, respectively, an agreement homeomorphic, an isomorphic, or a compatible supertree.

Since the most common application of supertree methods is to amalgamate the results of various studies and to construct the *tree of life*, obtaining a result that excludes some of the species studied is not acceptable. Therefore, the main application of Problem 7.4 is to measure the similarity among the input trees. Thus, we need to find some generalizations of Problem 7.2 guaranteeing that all input species are in the resulting supertree. The problems introduced in the following of the current section have only appeared in the literature in their decision version (i.e., construct such a tree if it exists), while we give the optimization versions in order to overcome the fact that, among all possible solutions, some are more interesting.

PROBLEM 7.5 Most Compatible Supertree

Input: a set $\mathcal{T} = \{T_1, \ldots, T_k\}$ of phylogenetic trees, with T_i leaf-labeled over $\Lambda(T_i)$.
Output: a tree T displaying the trees $\{T_1, \ldots, T_k\}$,

Goal: to minimize the sum over all T_i of the number of edges where each pair $T_i, T|_t\Lambda(T_i)$ differs.

A different formulation with an important biological motivation is called NESTEDSUPERTREE [10], where nested taxa are allowed in the input data. The notion of nested taxon allows to represent the fact that some information is known about the taxonomy of some species. This results in some internal nodes being labeled (besides all leaves), and that such labels must be taken into account when computing the supertree.

PROBLEM 7.6 Most Compatible NestedSupertree

Input: a set $\mathcal{T} = \{T_1, \ldots, T_k\}$ of phylogenetic trees, where all leaves and possibly some internal nodes of T_i are labeled over $\Lambda(T_i)$.
Output: a tree T displaying the trees $\{T_1, \ldots, T_k\}$,
Goal: to minimize the sum over all T_i of the number of edges where each pair $T_i, T|_t\Lambda(T_i)$ differs.

In Section 7.2, we have introduced the fact that a tree T_1 displays another tree T_2 (over the same label set as T_1) if and only if the clusters of T_1 include those of T_2. Such property can be generalized to a class of networks, called *regular* networks [3], therefore, such class is a natural candidate for generalizing the supertree problems. Notice that the property does not hold for generic networks.

Definition 7.1 A network N is regular if and only if for each pair v_1, v_2 of vertices of N the following conditions hold: (i) the sets $\mathcal{C}(v_1)$ and $\mathcal{C}(v_2)$ are different, (ii) $\mathcal{C}(v_1) \subset \mathcal{C}(v_2)$ implies that there exists a path from v_1 to v_2, and (iii) if there exist two distinct (directed) paths from v_1 to v_2, both contain at least two arcs.

PROBLEM 7.7 Minimum Compatible Regular Supernetwork

Input: a set $\mathcal{N} = \{N_1, \ldots, N_k\}$ of networks.
Output: a regular network N minimizing the number of nontree arcs and displaying all networks in $\mathcal{N}$

The most natural problem modeling regular network comparison is that of computing a minimum-size (i.e., minimum number of arcs) regular network displaying a set of input networks. The criterion of minimizing the number of arcs in N is due to the fact that adding hybridization arcs (i.e., arcs inducing a cycle in the undirected version of N) allows N to display more networks, and at the same time it makes N less likely to represent an evolutionary history which is usually "treelike." Two versions of Problem 7.7 are possible, depending on the fact that introducing new species is allowed or forbidden. Those two versions, albeit apparently similar, can lead to hugely different solutions. Given a set $\mathcal{N}$ of regular networks, $h(\mathcal{N})$ and $h^+(\mathcal{N})$ denote the optima of Problem 7.7 where the creation of additional species is, respectively, forbidden or allowed. In [3] it is shown that it is possible to construct a set $\mathcal{N}$, consisting of two phylogenies, for which $h^+(\mathcal{N}) = 1$, but $h(\mathcal{N})$ is arbitrarily large.

7.4.2 Algorithms

Among all possible algorithms, we are interested in those satisfying three fundamental properties: (i) being polynomial-time computable, (ii) computing a supertree displaying all (not necessarily proper) subtrees shared by all input trees, (iii) being invariant w.r.t. instance isomorphisms. The first polynomial-time algorithm for solving Problem 7.2 with all the above properties appeared in the celebrated paper [1] and is called the BUILD algorithm. Such algorithm is guaranteed to compute a supertree displaying all input trees, provided that such a supertree exists. The drawback of this approach is that nothing is computed if such a supertree does not exist.

Clearly, we are interested in finding a suitable supertree (or a supernetwork) that displays all input trees. A brief description of BUILD will help in gaining some insights in the problem. At each step BUILD computes an undirected graph G whose vertices are the species in the input trees and two species are adjacent if and only if they are clustered together in some proper cluster of an input tree (i.e., for at least one input tree the least common ancestor of those two species is not the root). The algorithm computes the connected components $C_1, \ldots, C_p$ of G, makes each such C_i one of the clusters of the supertree, then recurses over the new set of trees obtained by the topological restriction of each input tree on the sets $C_1, \ldots, C_p$, provided that $p > 1$. If, at any point, $p = 1$ and G contains more than two vertices, the algorithm halts without computing any supertree. In fact, it is immediate to notice that in such case no supertree can display all input trees, as all edges of G represent a pair of species that must be included in some proper cluster of the supertree. On the contrary, the main contribution of [1] is the proof that such procedure successfully computes the desired supertree, that is, all graphs considered during the execution of the algorithm G are not connected.

Since failures of BUILD correspond to graphs G that are connected, a natural approach for constructing a supertree (or a supernetwork) is therefore to remove some edges of G whenever G is connected, so that the resulting graph is disconnected and the idea of BUILD can be applied: the MINCUT approach, introduced by [34], exploits exactly this idea. In that paper, a nontrivial weighting scheme is employed and a minimum-weight cut of a closely related graph is computed. Then, the algorithm recurses on all connected components. The algorithm uses an associated graph $G/E^{\max}$, computed from G by first weighting all edges (x, y) with the number of input trees where x and y are in the same proper cluster, and then merging all nodes that are connected by an edge whose weight is equal to the number of input trees. The minimum cut is computed on $G/E^{\max}$ and the recursive steps are on the connected components of this new graph.

The rationale for dealing with $G/E^{\max}$ is that edges with weight equal to the number of input trees corresponds to proper clusters that are confirmed by all input trees, therefore, merging nodes connected by such edges enforces the goal of guaranteeing that clusters of all input trees must also be in the result.

There is an important drawback of MINCUT pointed out by [33]: a branching appearing in an input tree and not contradicted by any input trees might not be in the computed supertree as it can be in a minimum cut. In [33], a modified version of MINCUT is presented for overcoming such difficulty. The algorithm removes from $G/E^{\max}$ all contradicted edges, hence ensuring that all uncontradicted edges are not present in a minimum cut. Nonetheless some difficulties are still present; for example, the removal of all contradicted edges might be too harsh, as it does not allow to discriminate among all possible cuts that are preserving all uncontradicted edges.

A different extension of BUILD, due to Daniel and Semple [10] and called NESTEDSUPERTREE, has been designed to solve Problem 7.6, that is, when nested taxa are allowed in the input data (i.e., some internal nodes can be labeled). NESTEDSUPERTREE is a polynomial-time algorithm that computes a supertree displaying all input trees (if such a supertree exists), moreover, it removes some (but not all) conflicts among input trees (from this point of view it is also an improvement of MINCUT). The first kind of unremoved conflict is the pairwise inconsistency that happens when there are two nodes a and b both appearing in two input trees, and a is a proper descendant of b in exactly one such tree. If the input trees have no pairwise inconsistencies, the algorithm creates new labels for all previously unlabeled internal nodes, then it constructs a mixed (i.e., containing both directed arcs and undirected edges) graph—called descendancy graph—whose vertices are the labels of the input trees and all rooted triples $(ab|c)$ that are not contradicted by any input tree. The arcs of the descendancy graph are the pairs of labels (a, b) where b is an ancestor of a in some input tree, moreover, for each rooted triple $ab|c$ there are two outgoing arcs $((ab|c), a)$ and $((ab|c), b)$. Undirected edges of the descendancy graph are the (unordered) pairs of labels (a, b) where a and b are not comparable (i.e., the associated clusters are disjoint) in some input tree. The algorithm looks for a directed cycle in the descendancy graph D; if such a cycle exists the computation finishes with an ancestor–descendant contradiction without computing any tree.

If D is acyclic, then NESTEDSUPERTREE is guaranteed to compute a supertree with a recursive procedure. Initially, it computes a set S_0 containing a set of labels in D that have neither incoming arcs nor incident edges (this case corresponds to unconflicting input trees). If no such label exists, then S_0 is posed equal to any nonempty set of labels with no incoming arcs (this case corresponds to some conflicts in the input trees, the arbitrary choice of S_0 represents how the conflicts are resolved). Then S_0 is made the root of the computed tree and its elements are removed from D; the algorithm also removes all rooted triples $ab|c$ where c and ab are not in the same strongly connected component of D. Finally, all strongly connected components of D are added to the set of clusters of the output tree and the procedure recurses on all such strongly connected components.

Now, we can survey some known results related to the MASP and MCSP problems. Observe that agreement and compatible subtree and supertree problems share the same optimal solutions whenever the collection of input trees are over the same leaf-labeled set. Given T_1, T_2 two trees with n leaves, a simple procedure working in $O(n)$ time, can be used to extend an optimal solution of MAST and MCT over $L(T_1) \cap L(T_2)$ to an optimal solution of MASP and MCSP, respectively, over the two trees as proved in [5,27].

On the negative side, we notice that increasing the number of input trees quickly leads to hard problems. In fact some recent results on MASP have been given in [27], showing that, differently from MAST, the problem is NP-hard on just three bounded-degree trees or on an unrestricted number of rooted triples. Moreover the optimization versions of both MASP and MCSP, where we want to minimize the number of leaves to remove in order to obtain a feasible solution, cannot have a constant approximation factor unless P = NP, and are $W[2]$-hard (i.e., no efficient fixed-parameter algorithm is possible).

7.4.3 Open Problems

The optimization criterion of Problems 7.5 and 7.6 is inspired by parsimony, but it would be interesting to investigate if a different criterion, such as computing the supertree with fewest edges, would be more biologically meaningful.

Another research direction is that of improving the algorithms MinCut and its variant of [33]. In fact, it is reasonable that the difference (or the ratio) between the number of input trees where an edge e is present and the number of input trees where e is contradicted should be a key parameter for determining whether e must be retained in the output solution or not. It would be interesting to design and analyze some algorithms with a more refined criterion for choosing the edges to cut.

Also, NestedSupertree could be extended with a more refined algorithm for selecting the set S_0, which is currently any set of labels with no incoming arcs or incident edges. It would be interesting to find an optimization criterion leading to a more biologically meaningful supertree without making the overall algorithm unfeasible.

7.5 RECONCILIATION OF GENE TREES AND SPECIES TREES

Until now, we have considered the possibility of representing the evolution of a set of species by means of a uniquely leaf-labeled phylogenetic tree or network; in this section we will consider a different scenario, where we are given the information concerning the evolution of a set of homologous genes in different species. Different evolutionary trees can be built to represent the evolutionary histories of different genes in the studied set of species. Each tree representing the evolution of a gene is a *gene tree*. Similarly, the evolution of a set of species is usually represented using a *species tree*. Many studies have shown that the evolution of the species and the evolution of the genes might not agree. Thus a species tree and a gene tree can be different, moreover, gene trees that represent the evolution of different genes can be different. This divergence between genes evolution is due to some biological events such as *duplication* of a gene, the *loss* of a gene, and *lateral* (or *horizontal*) *gene transfer* (in Fig. 7.3, the tree T_G presents a gene duplication in the topmost node labeled BD). On the contrary, species trees represent the evolutionary history of a set of species only in terms of *speciation*. The inference of a species tree from a collection of divergent gene trees is a fundamental issue in phylogenetics and strongly motivates the design

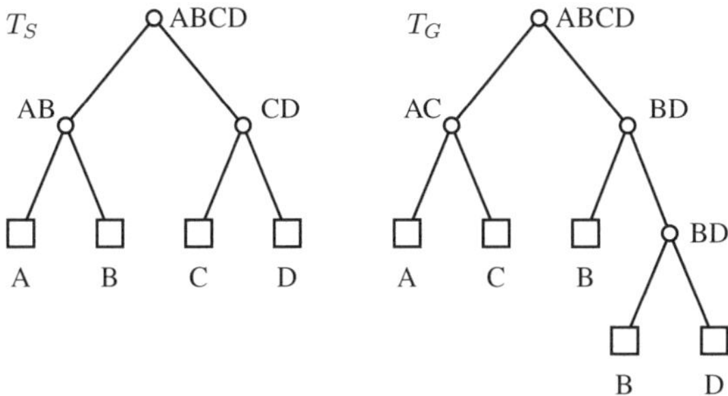

FIGURE 7.3 A species tree T_S and a gene tree T_G. Each node is associated with a cluster.

of combinatorial models to compare gene trees and to reconcile them into a species tree.

Preliminary definitions on species and gene trees have been given in Section 7.2, while we introduce here the basic mappings used to compare a gene tree and a species tree. First, given a set S of taxa, a species tree T_S, and a gene tree T_G are two leaf-labeled rooted binary trees, where each leaf is labeled by a taxon in S. A species tree has the additional restriction that no two leaves share a common label. An example of species tree and gene tree is given in Fig. 7.3.

Notice that for a species tree, a cluster identifies unambiguously a node of the tree. Given a gene tree T_G and a species tree T_S, the trees T_G and T_S are called *comparable* iff $\Lambda(T_G) \subseteq \Lambda(T_S)$, in which case we can define a mapping $\lambda_{T_G,T_S} : V(T_G) \rightarrow V(T_S)$ associating each vertex of T_G with a vertex of T_S. The mapping usually adopted when comparing a gene tree and a species tree is the *least common ancestor mapping*, in short *lca*. We recall that the *lca* mapping associates with each node g of T_G the node s of T_S such that $\mathcal{C}(s)$ is the smallest cluster of T_S containing $\mathcal{C}(g)$. Observe that a leaf with label x of T_G is mapped by *lca* mapping in the unique leaf of T_S having label x. In what follows we assume that, unless otherwise stated, λ_{T_G,T_S} is the *lca* mapping. In the following, given two nodes x, y, by $x \subset y$ we denote that y is an ancestor of x. Moreover, given a tree T and a node v of T, let us recall that $T(v)$ denotes the complete subtree of T rooted in v.

7.5.1 Evolutionary Events

In gene trees and species trees comparison (Fig. 7.4), *speciation* is by far the most common evolutionary event and is considered the "normal" event, while other events can be considered "special." Indeed, speciation is represented in a species tree as a node evolving in its two children, modeling the fact that along the evolutionary process two different species were generated from a single species. Usually, the models we will introduce follow the parsimonious principle of minimizing the number of "special" events. The models mainly differ in the set of possible special events. The first of such "special" events is gene *duplication*. In this case, the portion of DNA encoding a given gene appears twice in a certain species, and those two copies of the gene evolve independently from that point. This fact is modeled by the following definition.

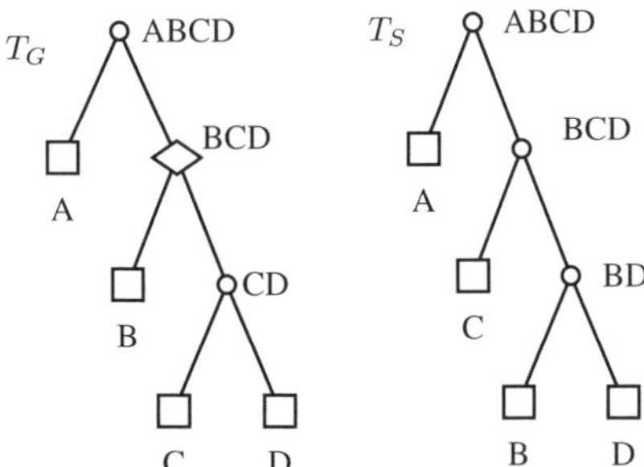

FIGURE 7.4 A duplication in node BCD of gene tree T_G.

Definition 7.2 (Duplication). Let T_G be a gene tree and let T_S be a species tree comparable with T_G. Let g be an internal node of T_G, then a duplication happens in g if $\lambda_{T_G,T_S}(f(g)) = \lambda_{T_G,T_S}(g)$ for some children $f(g)$ of g in T_G.

Given a gene tree T_G and a species tree T_S which are comparable, a measure of the similarity of the two trees is the *duplication cost*, denoted by $\text{dup}(T_G, T_S)$, and defined as the number of nodes of T_G where a duplication occurs. Furthermore, duplications can be efficiently computed, as the following property shows a recurrence that can be easily translated into a DP algorithm.

Proposition 7.1 *Let r_g be the root of the gene tree T_G, let $c_l(r_g)$, $c_r(r_g)$ be the children of r_g. If a duplication occurs in r_g then $dup(T_G, T_S) = 1 + dup(T_G(c_l(r_g)), T_S) + dup(T_G(c_r(r_g)), T_S)$.*

Another event that can occur during the evolution is the *loss* of a gene in some species. The number of gene losses can be computed from the *lca* mapping λ_{T_G,T_S}. Assume that $T'_S = T_S|_t\Lambda(T_G)$. Given the *lca* mapping λ_{T_G,T'_S} from T_G to T'_S, let g, g' be two nodes of T'_S such that $C(g) \subseteq C(g')$, then we denote by $d(g, g')$ the number of nodes in T_S on the path from $\lambda_{T_G,T'_S}(g')$ to $\lambda_{T_G,T'_S}(g)$. The number of losses associated with T_G is the sum over all nodes g of T_G of the value l_g associated with node g and defined as follows:

$$l_g = \begin{cases} 0 & \text{if } \lambda_{T_G,T'_S}(g) = \lambda_{T_G,T'_S}(c_r(g)) = \lambda_{T_G,T'_S}(c_l(g)) \\ d(c_l(g), g) + 1 & \text{if } \lambda_{T_G,T'_S}(c_l(g)) \subset \lambda_{T_G,T'_S}(g) \text{ and} \\ & \lambda_{T_G,T'_S}(g) = \lambda_{T_G,T'_S}(c_r(g)) \\ d(c_l(g), g) + d(c_r(g), g) & \text{if } \lambda_{T_G,T'_S}(c_l(g)) \subset \lambda_{T_G,T'_S}(g) \text{ and} \\ & \lambda_{T_G,T'_S}(c_r(g)) \subset \lambda_{T_G,T'_S}(g); \end{cases}$$

Given a gene tree T_G and a species tree T_S, which are comparable, another measure of the similarity of the two trees is the *mutation cost*, denoted by $l(T_G, T_S)$ and defined as follows: $l(T_G, T_S) = \text{dup}(T_G, T_S) + \sum_{g \in T_G} l_g$.

The last evolutionary event that is considered during gene evolution is *lateral gene transfer* or horizontal gene transfer. During a lateral gene transfer event, some genetic

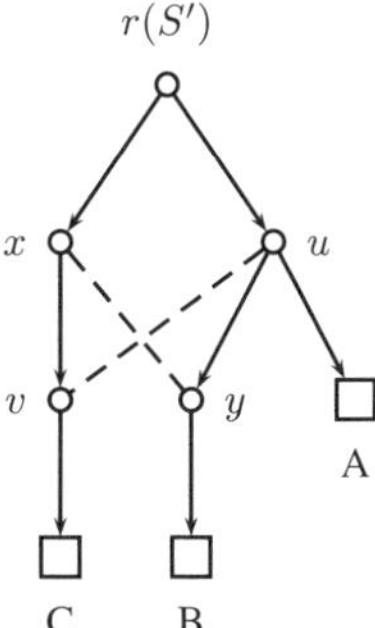

FIGURE 7.5 A mixed graph corresponding to a scheme violating Condition 1 of Definition 7.3 (edges are dashed).

material is transferred from a taxon t_1 to another taxon t_2, which is not a descendant of t_1. When a later transfer occurs during the evolution of a gene along an arc (u, v) of the gene tree T_G, then the evolution occurs not only along an arc (x, y) of the species tree T_S but also along another arc (x', y') of T_S. This situation is described in T_S by means of the *subdivision* operation of an arc $e = (x, y)$ in T_S consisting of removing edge e, which is replaced by a path made of two new edges $(x, s(e))$ and $(s(e), y)$.

A single lateral transfer is modeled by the subdivision of a pair of arcs (a, a'), called *lateral pair* and by the addition of a new arc, called *transfer arc* for the lateral pair, that is either $(s(a), s(a'))$ or $(s(a'), s(a))$, depending on the direction of the transfer.

The occurrence of lateral transfers in a species tree T_S implies adding a set of transfer arcs A' to a tree T'_S obtained by subdivisions. Mainly, we have two different representations: the mixed graph and the union graph induced by T'_S and A', which are both graphs with vertex set $V(T'_S)$. The *union graph* induced by T'_S and A' and denoted as $T'_S \cup A'$ has arcs of T'_S and of A'. The *mixed graph* induced by T'_S and A', denoted by $T'_S \cup E(A')$, has arcs of T'_S and edges obtained by removing the direction of the arcs in A'.

Definition 7.3 Let T_G be a gene tree and T_S be a species tree, then a *lateral transfer scheme for T_S* is a pair (T'_S, A'), where T'_S is obtained by subdivisions of lateral pairs P in T_S and A' is a set of transfer arcs for P such that

1. the mixed graph $T'_S \cup E(A')$ does not contain a directed mixed cycle;
2. for each arc (u, v) in A', vertex u has indegree 1 and outdegree 2 in $T'_S \cup A'$, vertex v in A' has indegree 2 and outdegree 1 in $T'_S \cup A'$.

Observe that condition 1 of Definition 7.3 forbids cycles in the mixed graph $T'_S \cup E(A')$. Indeed there is a mixed cycle in Fig. 7.5. The lateral transfer from x to y would imply that there is a point in time where the two species x and y coexisted. Similarly, the lateral transfer from u to v would imply that there is a point in time where the two species u and v coexisted. However, since y exists after u, it follows that no such point in evolution can exist.

Informally, the pair (T'_S, A') represents the evolutionary histories of the taxa in $L(T_S)$ using speciation and lateral gene transfers that are represented by the set A' (see Fig. 7.5). In order to model the evolution represented by a gene tree T_G, we have to define a *scenario* that defines the mapping from T_G to the species tree T_S showing at which point of evolution lateral gene transfers occurred. A fundamental parameter associated with a scenario is the *α-activity* of a gene. Informally, the activity level of a gene tree is the number of copies of the gene that exist in the genome of a taxon at a certain point of evolution.

Definition 7.4 Let T_G be a gene tree and T_S a species tree, a *lateral transfer scenario* [24] for T_S and T_G is a triple (T'_S, A', h), where (T'_S, A') is a lateral transfer scheme for T_S and $h : V(T'_S) \to 2^{V(T_G)}$ is a function such that

1. $r(T_G) \in h(r(T'_S))$ and the subtree of T_G induced by $h(r(T'_S))$ is connected;
2. if v_1 and v_2 are distinct children of v_0 in T_G, with $v_1, v_2 \notin h(r(T'_S))$, then there exists a node x_0 of T'_S with children x_1 and x_2 in $T'_S \cup A'$ s.t. (a) $v_i \in h(x_i)$ with $i \in \{0, 1, 2\}$, (b) x_i is a vertex such that the set $\{v \in h(x_i)\}$ is maximal;
3. if v_1 and v_2 are children of v_0 in T_G, $v_1 \in h(r(T'_S))$ and $v_2 \notin h(r(T'_S))$, then there exists a child x of $r(T'_S)$ s.t. $v_2 \in h(x)$;
4. for each $v \in V(T_G)$, the inverse image of v through h induces a directed path in T'_S;
5. for each $x \in V(T_S) \setminus \{r(T'_S)\}$, no two members of $h(x)$ are one the ancestor of the other one;
6. $h(l) = \{l\}$ for each $l \in L(T_S)$.

The requirements of Definition 7.4 guarantee that h is leaf-preserving and maps the root of T_S to the root of T_G (Fig. 7.6). The combination of conditions $2-4$ ensures that T_G appears in T_S and arcs direction in T_G and T_S is the same. Conditions 2 and 5 forbid both outgoing arcs from a vertex in a gene tree to correspond to lateral gene transfers. Condition 6 establishes leaf to leaf association between T_G and T_S.

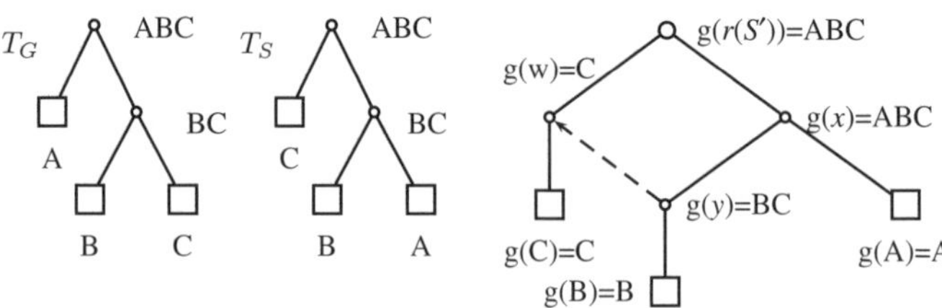

FIGURE 7.6 A gene tree T_G, a species tree T_S, a lateral transfer scheme, and a possible 1-activity scenario (the arc representing a lateral transfer is dashed).

A lateral transfer scenario (or scenario) is *α-active* iff $\max_{x \in T'_S}\{|h(x)|\} \leq \alpha$. The *cost* of a scenario (T'_S, A', h) w.r.t. T_G is expressed by the formula $\sum_{(x,y)\in A'} |\{(u, v) \in E(T_G) : u \in h(x), v \in h(y)\}| + |V(T_G[h(r(T'_S))]) \setminus L(T_G[h(r(T'_S))])|$, where by $T_G[V']$ we denote the forest of subtrees that have nodes in V', with $V' \subseteq V(T_G)$. Hence, the first part of the cost of a α-active lateral transfer scenario is the number of arcs of T_G that are related by the function h to the arcs in A', while the second part is the number of internal nodes of T_G that are associated by h with the root of T'_S.

The model described above has been extended [24] in order to handle both lateral transfers and duplications. Such extension is obtained by adding to the scenario a set $D \subseteq V(T_G)$ (representing the set of duplications) and to condition 2 of Definition 7.4 the requirement that $x_1 = x_2$ if and only if $v_0 \in D$, thus forbidding duplications to lateral gene transfer.

A different model for comparing a gene tree and a species tree, is called *reconciled tree*. More precisely, given a gene tree and species tree, a minimum reconciled tree of T_G and T_S is a rooted full binary tree of minimum size that satisfies three fundamental properties.

Definition 7.5 A *minimum reconciled tree* [31] $R(T_G, T_S)$ of a gene tree T_G and a species tree T_S, is a smallest tree satisfying the following properties:

1. a subtree of $R(T_G, T_S)$ is homeomorphic to T_G,
2. $\mathcal{C}(R(T_G, T_S)) = \mathcal{C}(T_S)$,
3. for every internal node x of $R(T_G, T_S)$ either $\mathcal{C}(c_l(x)) \cap \mathcal{C}(c_r(x)) = \emptyset$ or $\mathcal{C}(c_l(x)) = \mathcal{C}(c_r(x)) = \mathcal{C}(x)$.

Given a gene tree T_G and a species tree T_S, a reconciled tree $R(T_G, T_S)$ is used to represent and identify evolutionary events (Fig. 7.7). More precisely, a duplication occurs in a node x of $R(T_G, T_S)$ if and only if $\mathcal{C}(c_l(x)) = \mathcal{C}(c_r(x)) = \mathcal{C}(x)$. Let R' be subtree of $R(T_G, T_S)$ homeomorphic to T_G . A loss occurs in a node x of R' if at least one of $c_l(x)$ and $c_r(x)$ is not in R'.

7.5.2 Combinatorial Problems

In the previous section, we have introduced the evolutionary events that are commonly considered in phylogenetic comparison of gene trees and species trees. In what follows we consider two of the most relevant classes of combinatorial problems that have been studied in this field.

In the first type of problem, we are given a set of (possibly contradictory) gene trees and we want to compute a species tree that better represents the evolutionary histories of the given gene trees. The assumption behind this approach is that the correct species tree is the one that minimizes the differences with the given gene trees. In what follows we will refer to this kind of problems as *agreement problems*.

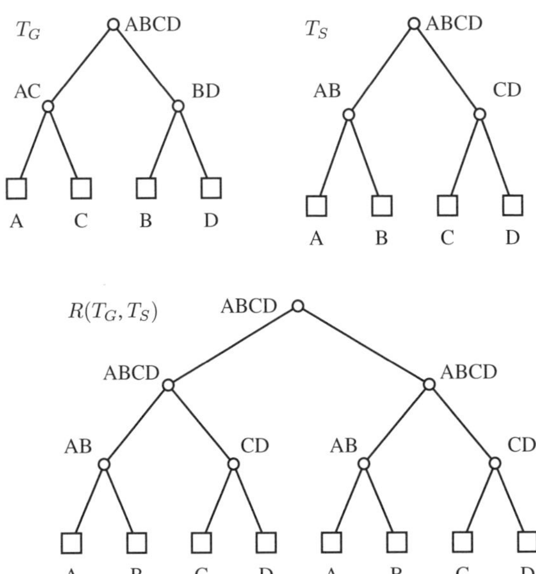

FIGURE 7.7 A gene tree T_G, a species tree T_S, and a reconciled tree $R(T_G, T_S)$. Note that $\mathcal{C}(R(T_G, T_S) = \{ABCD, AB, CD, A, B, C, D\}$ the set of clusters of T_S; the subtree of $R(T_G, T_S)$ homeomorphic to T_G consists of the root, both children of the root (each with cluster $ABCD$), the left leaves with labels A and C, the right leaves with labels B and D; a duplication occurs in the root, since the root has cluster $ABCD$ and its two children have both cluster $ABCD$; four losses occurred in the two nodes with clusters AB and in the two nodes with clusters CD.

In the second problem, we are given a gene tree and a species tree and we want to compare the two trees in order to explain the differences between them by identifying which evolutionary events occurred during the evolution of the gene in that set of species. The assumption behind this approach is that the gene tree and the species tree considered are correct. In what follows, we will refer to this kind of problems as *events inference problems*.

7.5.2.1 Agreement Problems Informally, the instance of an agreement problem is a collection of gene trees $T_{G_1}, \ldots, T_{G_k}$ and the solution is a species tree having minimum distance from the trees in the collection. Different definitions of an agreement problem can be introduced on the basis of the distinct measures of similarity between a gene tree and a species tree discussed in Section 7.5.1.

The first problem we introduce regards the reconstruction, based on the duplication cost, of a species tree from a collection of gene trees.

PROBLEM 7.8 Optimal Species Tree Reconstruction with Duplication Cost

Input: gene trees $T_{G_1}, T_{G_2}, \ldots, T_{G_k}$.

Output: a species tree T_S such that the duplication cost $\sum_{i=1}^{k} \text{dup}(T_{G_i}, T_S)$ is minimum.

The problem is known to be NP-hard [31] and W[1]-hard if parameterized by the number of trees [15]. However, it is known to have fixed-parameter algorithms. More precisely, [38] proposed a fixed-parameter $O(4^d n^3 k^2)$ time algorithm when the parameter d is the number of duplications. This algorithm is based on a property of bipartitions of $\Lambda(T_S)$. Observe that the set of clusters of a species tree are a treelike cluster system for $\Lambda(T_S)$, hence each internal node x of T_S produces a bipartition $(\Lambda_{x_1}, \Lambda_{x_2})$ of a subset Λ_x of $\Lambda(T_S)$, where each Λ_{x_i} is the cluster associated to a children of x.

Given a bipartition (Λ_1, Λ_2) of Λ_{T_S}, the number of duplications induced by such a bipartition can be easily computed, hence the algorithm first builds all bipartitions of $\Lambda(T_S)$ inducing no more than d duplications. Then, for each bipartition (Λ_1, Λ_2), it computes recursively the bipartitions of Λ_1 and of Λ_2, so that the clusters obtained induce at most d duplications. The procedure stops when either we find a treelike cluster system (the species tree) that induces at most d duplications or there is no such cluster system. Finally, the algorithm computes such solutions using a search tree whose height is at most d.

Another main agreement problem is obtained by using the mutation cost that is computed by combining three such events: speciation, duplication, and loss.

PROBLEM 7.9 Optimal Species Tree Reconstruction with Mutation Cost

Input: gene trees $T_{G_1}, T_{G_2}, \ldots, T_{G_k}$.
Output: a species tree T_S minimizing the mutation cost $\sum_{i=1}^{k} l(T_{G_i}, T_S)$.

The problem is known to be NP-hard [31] and admits a dynamic programming algorithm for a restriction called width-k version [22].

7.5.2.2 Event Inference Problems In this section, we will deal with event inference problems. Informally, the instance of this kind of problem is a collection of gene trees (eventually consisting of exactly one gene tree) and a species tree; the solution is a description (usually given by a tree) of the special evolutionary events that explain the differences between the gene trees and the species tree. In [31], the problem of computing all loss events is investigated. Consider a duplication d_u in a node u of T_G. A node v of T_S can be classified as follows:

- *mixed* in d_u if $\mathcal{C}(v) \cap \mathcal{C}(c(u)) \neq \emptyset$ for every child $c(u)$ of u;
- *speciated* in d_u if $(v) \cap \mathcal{C}(c_l(u)) \neq \emptyset$, but $\mathcal{C}(v) \cap \mathcal{C}(c_r(u)) = \emptyset$ or vice versa, for $c_l(u)$ and $c_r(u)$ the two children of u;
- *gapped* in d_u if $\mathcal{C}(v) \cap \mathcal{C}(c(u)) = \emptyset$ for every child $c(u)$ of u.

We say that a *loss event* occurs at a maximal node $v \in T_S$ so that v is a descendant of $lca(u)$ in T_S and is speciated or gapped in d_u. Informally, this fact is equivalent to computing the root r_d of the minimal subtree in T_S, such that all the loss events associated with d_u are contained in the subtree of T_S rooted in r_d. In particular, a unique loss event occurs in a node on the path from $\text{lca}(u)$ to any leaf in T_S. Next we state formally the problem of computing all loss events.

PROBLEM 7.10 Loss Events Computation Problem

Input: a gene tree T_G and a species tree T_S, such that $\Lambda(T_G) = \Lambda(T_S)$.
Output: for each duplication d that occurs at a node $g \in T_G$, the (unique) subtree $T_S(\text{lca}^{-1}(g))$ of T_S with all the loss events as its leaves.

Observe that a tree that is a solution of the previous problem, does not necessarily have leaves with labels in $\Lambda(T_S)$. Indeed the leaves of such a tree can be labeled by clusters of T_S. In [31], a linear time algorithm to compute all loss events is proposed. Next, we define formally the problem concerning the construction of reconciled trees.

PROBLEM 7.11 Minimum Reconciliation Gene-Species Tree

Input: a gene trees T_G and a species tree T_S.
Output: computing a minimum reconciled tree $R(T_G, T_S)$.

The Minimum Reconciliation Gene-Species Tree problem has a polynomial-time dynamic programming algorithm relying on the following recursive definition [6].

Two basic operations on trees allow to construct a minimum reconciled tree. Given two trees T_1 and T_2, the *composition* of the trees, denoted by $T_1 \triangle T_2$, is a tree obtained connecting a new node r to $r(T_1)$ and $r(T_2)$. The node r is the root of the tree $T_1 \triangle T_2$. The *replacement* of T_1 with T_2, denoted by $T_1(t \rightarrow T_2)$ is the tree obtained by replacing in T_1 the subtree rooted at t with T_2.

Definition 7.6 Let T_G, T_S be, respectively, a gene tree and a species tree. Let G_l and G_r (S_l and S_r, respectively) the subtrees of T_G (of T_S) rooted in the children $c_l(r(T_G))$ and $c_r(r(T_G))$ of $r(T_G)$ (respectively, $c_l(r(T_S))$ and $c_r(r(T_S))$ of $r(T_S)$.)

Then $R(T_G, T_S)$ is equal to T_G if T_G and T_S are both single nodes, in which case they are simultaneously roots and leaves, otherwise $R(T_G, T_S)$ is equal to

1. $T_S(\text{lca}(c_l(r(T_S))) \rightarrow R(T_G, S_l)))$ if $\text{lca}(r(T_G)) \subseteq c_l(r(T_S))$.
2. $R(G_l, S_l) \triangle R(G_r, S_r)$, if $\text{lca}(r(T_G)) = r(T_S)$, $\text{lca}(c_l(r(T_G)))$ and $\text{lca}(c_r(r(T_G)))$ are mapped to $s_1 \subseteq c_l(r(T_S))$ and $s_2 \subseteq c_r(r(T_S))$, respectively.
3. $R(G_l, T_S) \triangle R(G_r, T_S)$, if $\text{lca}(r(T_G)) = r(T_S)$, and at least one of $\text{lca}(c_l(r(T_G)))$ and $\text{lca}(c_r(r(T_G)))$ is equal to $r(T_S)$.

In [6], it is shown that Definition 7.6 computes a tree that satisfies the properties for the reconciled tree and such a tree has also minimum size. Furthermore, given a gene tree T_G and a species tree T_S, there exists a unique minimum reconciled tree for T_G and T_S [6], which is also the tree inducing the minimum number of duplications and losses [21]. Next, we introduce the main problem for the lateral gene transfer model.

PROBLEM 7.12 **α-Active Lateral Gene Transfer Problem**

Input: gene tree T_G and species tree T_S.
Output: find a minimum cost α-active lateral transfer scenario for T_S and T_G.

The restriction of α-active Lateral Gene Transfer Problem where $\alpha = 1$ is APX-hard [11,23], while it has a $O(2^{4T}|S|^2)$ fixed-parameter algorithm [23], where the parameter T is the cost of the scenario. For arbitrary α there is an $O(4^{\alpha}(4T(\alpha + T))^T|L|^2)$ time algorithm [23].

The extension of the problem that considers both duplications and lateral gene transfers is known to be NP-hard [24] and admits a fixed-parameter tractable algorithm [24] that computes the minimum number of duplications and lateral transfers.

7.5.3 Open Problems

A deep understanding of the approximation complexity of the agreement problems is still needed. More precisely, the only known result is the 2-factor approximation algorithm for the variant of Optimal Species Tree Reconstruction with Duplication Cost (see Problem 7.8) in which the duplication cost is slightly modified to obtain a metric d [31]. In this variant, all gene trees are uniquely labeled. Moreover, given a gene tree T_G and a species tree T_S, the *symmetric duplication cost* between T_G and T_S is defined as $d(T_G, T_S) = \frac{1}{2}(\mathrm{dup}(T_S, T_G) + \mathrm{dup}(T_G, T_S))$. The new version of the problem remains NP-hard while admitting a 2-approximation algorithm [31].

An interesting open problem on species trees and gene trees is the computational complexity of reconstructing a species tree from a set of gene trees over instances consisting of a constant number of gene trees or even of two gene trees only.

An extension of the reconciliation approach (see Definition 7.5 and Problem 7.11) is proposed in [20] by introducing a notion of extended reconciled tree allowing the identification of lateral gene transfers, in addition to duplication and losses. A notion of scenario is also introduced to identify lateral transfers. A dynamic programming algorithm to compute a scenario inducing a minimum reconciliation cost is given [20]. Also notice that no approximation algorithms are known for the event inference problems presented in this section.

REFERENCES

1. Aho AV, Sagiv Y, Szymanski TG, Ullman JD. Inferring a tree from lowest common ancestors with an application to the optimization of relational expressions. *SIAM J Comput* 1981;10(3):405–421.
2. Amir A, Keselman D. Maximum agreement subtree in a set of evolutionary trees: Metrics and efficient algorithms. *SIAM J Comput* 1997;26(6):1656–1669.
3. Baroni M, Semple C, Steel M. A framework for representing reticulate evolution. *Ann Comb* 2004;8(4):391–408.
4. Berry V, Guillemot S, Nicolas F, Paul C. On the approximation of computing evolutionary trees. *Proceedings of the 11th Annual International Computing and Combinatorics Conference (COCOON)*; 2005. pp.115–125.
5. Berry V, Nicolas F. Improved parameterized complexity of the maximum agreement subtree and maximum compatible tree problems. *IEEE Trans Comput Biol Bioinformatics* 2006;3(3):289–302.
6. Bonizzoni P, Della Vedova G, Dondi R. Reconciling a gene tree to a species tree under the duplication cost model. *Theor Comput Sci* 2005;347(1–2):36–53.
7. Bonizzoni P, Della Vedova G, Mauri G. Approximating the maximum isomorphic agreement subtree is hard. *Int J Found Comput Sci* 2000;11(4):579–590.
8. Choy C, Jansson J, Sadakane K, Sung W-K. Computing the maximum agreement of phylogenetic networks. *Theor Comput Sci* 2005;335(1):93–107.
9. Cole R, Farach-Colton M, Hariharan R, Przytycka T, Thorup M. An $O(n \log n)$ algorithm for the maximum agreement subtree problem for binary trees. *SIAM J Comput* 2000;30(5).
10. Daniel P, Semple C. A class of general supertree methods for nested taxa. *SIAM J Discrete Math* 2005;19(2):463–480.
11. DasGupta B, Ferrarini S, Gopalakrishnan U, Paryani NR. Inapproximability results for the lateral gene transfer problem. *J Comb Optim* 2006;11(4):387–405.
12. Dessmark A, Jansson J, Lingas A, Lundell E-M. Polynomial-time algorithms for the ordered maximum agreement subtree problem. *Proceedings of the 15th Symposium on Combinatorial Pattern Matching (CPM)*; 2004. pp. 220–229.
13. Downey R, Fellows M. *Parametrized Complexity*. Springer Verlag, 1998.
14. Farach-Colton M, Przytycka TM, Thorup M. On the agreement of many trees. *Inf Proces Lett* 1995;55(6):297–301.
15. Fellows M, Hallett M, Stege U. Analogs and duals of the MAST problem for sequences and trees. *J Algorithm* 2003;49:192–216.
16. Felsenstein J. *Inferring Phylogenies*. Sinauer Associates, 2003.
17. Finden C, Gordon A. Obtaining common pruned trees. *J Classifi* 1985;2:255–276.
18. Gabow HN, Tarjan RE. Faster scaling algorithms for network problems. *SIAM J Comput* 1989;18(5):1013–1036.
19. Ganapathysaravanabavan G, Warnow T. Finding a maximum compatible tree for a bounded number of trees with bounded degree is solvable in polynomial time. *Proceedings of the 3rd International Workshop Algorithms in Bioinformatics (WABI)*; 2001. pp.156–163.
20. Gòrecki P. Reconciliation problems for duplication, loss and horizontal gene transfer. *Proceedings of the of 8th Annual International Conference on Computational Molecular Biology (RECOMB2004)*; 2004. pp. 316–325.

21. Gòrecki P, Tiuryn J. On the structure of reconciliations. *Proceedings of the RECOMB Satellite Workshop on Comparative Genomics RG 2004*. of *LNCS*, Vol. 3388. 2004. pp. 42–54.
22. Hallett M, Lagergren J. New algorithms for the duplication-loss model. *Proceedings of 4th Annual International Conference on Computational Molecular Biology (RECOMB2000)*; 2000. pp. 138–146.
23. Hallett M, Lagergren J. Efficient algorithms for lateral gene transfer problems. *Proceedings of 5th Annual International Conference on Computational Molecular Biology (RECOMB2001)*; 2001. pp. 149–156.
24. Hallett M, Lagergren J, Tofigh A. Simultaneous identification of duplications and lateral transfers. *Proceedings of the 8th Annual International Conference on Computational Molecular Biology (RECOMB2004)*; 2004. pp. 347–356.
25. Hamel A, Steel MA. Finding a common compatible tree is NP-hard for sequences and trees. *App Math Lett* 1996;9(2):55–60.
26. Hein J, Jiang T, Wang L, Zhang K. On the complexity of comparing evolutionary trees. *Discrete Appl Math* 1996;71:153–169.
27. Jansson J, Ng JH-K, Sadakane K, Sung W-K. Rooted maximum agreement supertrees. *Proceedings of the 6th Latin American Theoretical Informatics Symposium (LATIN)*; 2004. pp. 499–508.
28. Kao -Y, Lam TW, Przytycka TM, SungW-K, Ting H-F. General techniques for comparing unrooted evolutionary trees. *Proceedings of the 29th Symposium Theory of Computing (STOC)*; 1997. pp. 54–65.
29. Kao M-Y, Lam TW, Sung W-K, Ting H-F. A decomposition theorem for maximum weight bipartite matchings with applications to evolutionary trees. *Proceedings of the 7th European Symposium on Algorithms (ESA)*; 1999. pp. 438–449.
30. Kao M-Y, Lam TW, Sung W-K, Ting H-F. An even faster and more unifying algorithm for comparing trees via unbalanced bipartite matchings. *J Algorithm* 2001;40(2):212–233.
31. Ma B, Li M, Zhang L. From gene trees to species trees. *SIAM J Comput* 2000;30(3): 729–752.
32. Niedermeier R, Rossmanith P. An efficient fixed-parameter algorithm for 3-hitting set. *J Discrete Algorithm* 2003;1(1):89–102.
33. Page RDM. Modified mincut supertrees. *Proceedings of the 2nd International Workshop Algorithms in Bioinformatics (WABI)*; 2002. pp. 537–552.
34. Semple C, Steel M. A supertree method for rooted trees. *Discrete App Math* 2000; 105(1–3):147–158.
35. Steel M. The complexity of reconstructing trees from qualitative characters and subtree. *J Classif* 1992;9:91–116.
36. Steel M, Böcker S, Dress A. Simple but fundamental limits for supertree and consensus tree methods. *Syst Biol* 2000;49(2):363–368.
37. Steel M, Warnow T. Kaikoura tree theorems: Computing the maximum agreement subtree. *Inf Process Lett* 1993;48(2):77–82.
38. Stege U. Gene trees and species trees: The gene-duplication problem in fixed-parameter tractable. *Proceedings of the 6th International Workshop on Algorithms and Data Structures (WADS99)*, Vol. 1663 of *LNCS*; 1999. pp. 288–293.

PART II

GENOME AND SEQUENCE ANALYSIS

8

FORMAL MODELS OF GENE CLUSTERS

ANNE BERGERON

Comparative Genomics Laboratory, Université du Québec à Montréal, Canada

CEDRIC CHAUVE

Department of Mathematics, Simon Fraser University, Vancouver, Canada

YANNICK GINGRAS

Comparative Genomics Laboratory, Université du Québec à Montréal, Canada

8.1 INTRODUCTION

Genomes evolve through small-scale events, such as point mutations in the DNA sequence, and large-scale events, known as *rearrangements*, that reorganize the genetic material along chromosomes [23,39,48]. Such rearrangements not only can involve very few genes, such as the mutation/loss of genes due to the accumulation of point mutations, and tandem duplications or short reversals, but can also be at a much higher scale, such as large reversals or even whole-genome duplications. It results from these evolutionary events that, when comparing two or more genomes in terms of their gene orders, that is, the order of genetic markers along their chromosomes, it is very unlikely that these gene orders are identical, even for very close species; see, for example, recent works on primates [43] or on different strains of a same bacterial organism [35]. However, gene orders are not random, and the comparison of gene orders of related species shows genome segments that exhibit homogeneous gene content, with sometimes similar gene order. These groups of segments are

Bioinformatics Algorithms: Techniques and Applications, Edited by Ion I. Măndoiu and Alexander Zelikovsky

usually called *conserved gene clusters* or gene clusters, the notion of conserved being implicit.

Conserved gene clusters can be the result of several biological mechanisms, but basically they could be defined as "genomic regions that share a common ancestor" [28]. For example, they can result from functional pressure that requires that a group of genes stays close along the genomes. The most widely studied example of such groups of genes are operons in prokaryotic genomes, which are transcribed in a single messenger RNA and need to have their genes located contiguously in the genome [35,36,52]; it has also been suggested that being part of a given biochemical network [45] or coexpression [42] could be correlated with belonging to a same gene cluster. Segments of genomes with homogeneous gene content can also result very mechanically from the evolutionary proximity between the genomes: there was not enough time from the speciation event leading to observed genomes to break such groups of genes. This phenomenon can add noise in the detection of functional gene clusters, but it is worth noting that the resulting clusters carry an important information for computing evolution scenarios [6,7], reconstructing ancestral genomes [9], or identifying positional and ancestral homologs [12,17].

The detection of conserved gene clusters is a challenge for both the biological and mathematical communities, with applications in comparative genomics, annotation of genomes, and phylogenomics. There are essentially two families of methods for detecting conserved gene clusters. The first approach attacks this problem on very pragmatic grounds, primarily based on the detection of short conserved genomic segments, such as consecutive gene pairs that are easy to detect. This collection of conserved segments is then processed, in general using a heuristic, to obtain a set of gene clusters. See [37] for a survey on this topic. However, these methods lack a formal definition of the notion of gene cluster in terms of genomic segments and sets of genes involved in clusters. This can produce incoherent results as clustering short conserved segments can form genomic segments that have very different gene content but are grouped in a same cluster [47].

In this chapter, we survey a different approach in the detection of gene clusters that has been developed in the last fews years by various groups of researchers for gene order analysis. This approach relies on (1) formal definitions of what is a set of genomic segments that defines a conserved gene cluster and (2) algorithms that search and compare genomes of a dataset to detect all the sets of genomic segments that satisfy a given definition. Starting with conserved adjacencies and common intervals, we will work through several variants that allow for duplications and missing genes. We will also show that most variants are necessary, in the sense that they try to capture a biological reality that does not care about formal models. We will also see that the algorithmic challenges in detecting gene clusters are nontrivial. Depending on the model, efficient solutions can be easy to obtain, can require a lot of ingenuity, or sometimes do not even exist.

8.2 GENOME PLASTICITY

8.2.1 Genome Representations

The genetic information of species is stored in molecules called *chromosomes* that consist of two complementary strands of DNA. Each DNA strand is a string of basic units, the nucleotides, that have two extremities called the 5′ and 3′ extremities. Consecutive nucleotides are connected by joining the 3′ extremity of one to the 5′ extremity of the other. Figure 8.1 illustrates a small segment of chromosome: note that the 5′ and 3′ extremities of the two strands of DNA are in opposite directions. Nucleotides on a strand come in four different types, cytosine, guanine, adenine, and thymine, abbreviated, by the letters C, G, A, and T respectively. The nucleotides on the complementary strand are uniquely determined by the Watson–Crick complement relation in which C is always paired with G, and A is always paired with T.

From an information processing perspective, the knowledge of only one strand is sufficient to recover the whole molecule. However, the information contained on a strand is decoded in a sequential way going from the 5′ extremity to the 3′ extremity, allowing both strands to carry biologically meaningful information. It is thus customary to represent the information present on a chromosome by identifying a substring of one strand of a chromosome and specifying in which *orientation* it must be read, positive or negative. These substrings can correspond to any type of features found on a chromosome: genes, domains, operons, synteny blocks, banding patterns, among others. We will refer collectively to such features as "genes," using a more detailed terminology when necessary. We will also assume that genes are nonoverlapping substrings of chromosomes. This is not always the case, especially for small organisms such as viruses that have to compress their genetic information in very short chromosomes, but this assumption constitutes a reasonable compromise. A chromosome, or part of it, can thus be represented by a string such as

$$(a \quad b \quad -c \quad d \quad -e \quad f),$$

in which letters stand for genes and a negative sign signals a negative orientation.

The comparison of gene content and order between two species also relies in a fundamental way on our ability to tell when two genes are the "same" or not. This is not a trivial task, and numerous approaches have been tried since the discovery of the first rearranged chromosomes. In [22], Dobzhansky and Sturtevant divided the genome of fruit flies into 100 arbitrary sections that were called "genes" and that were recognizable under the microscope by their banding patterns. Two genes from different genomes were "equal" if they shared the same pattern.

FIGURE 8.1 The double strand structure of chromosomes.

When the term gene is taken in its modern sense of a sequence of nucleotides that is transcribed into RNA, most of the techniques of identification of similar genes rely on sequence alignments [44], either of the nucleotide sequences themselves, or the corresponding amino acid sequences if the RNA molecules are translated into proteins. This produces reliable results, especially for slow evolving genes such as those found in animal mitochondria [14], for example.

In some recent studies, such as [16], based on very large synteny blocks, equivalent segments of chromosomes are detected using small anchors whose order and orientation are conserved between species. This approach allows to ignore rearrangements whose size fall below a fixed threshold.

Whatever the approach used to define equal genes, comparing gene orders ultimately boils down to comparing strings of signed letters. For a fixed set $\mathcal{S}$ of genes, when strings representing two genomes contain exactly one occurrence of each gene in $\mathcal{S}$, in either orientation, we refer to these strings as *permutations*. For example, the following strings

$$G_1 = (a \quad b \quad -c \quad d \quad -e \quad f) \text{ and } G_2 = (-a \quad d \quad -e \quad b \quad -c \quad f)$$

are permutations of the set of genes $\{a, b, c, d, e, f\}$. The strings

$$G_3 = (a \quad b \quad -c \quad a \quad d \quad -e \quad f) \text{ and } G_4 = (-a \quad d \quad -e \quad -c \quad f)$$

are not permutations since gene a is duplicated in genome G_3, and gene b is missing in genome G_4.

The choice of representing genomes by permutations or strings with duplicated genes has implications on both the biological and computational sides of genome analysis. Indeed, as we will see later, the computational complexity of handling strings with duplicated genes is higher than for permutations. At the same time, from a biological point of view, it is a strong hypothesis to assume that a gene is present in a single copy in a set of genomes. Thus, aside from a few exceptions, such as animal mitochondrial genomes that have few duplicated genes, representing a set of genomes by a set of permutations often implies a nontrivial preliminary analysis that clears ambiguities due to duplicated genes; examples of such “preprocessing” can be found in the alignment process used to define synteny blocks [16] or in the process of ortholog assignments [5,24].

8.2.2 Genome Rearrangements

The goal of this section is to give the reader some intuitions about the nature and extent of genome rearrangements that happened during evolution.

8.2.2.1 Rearrangements That Preserve Gene Content These type of rearrangements can be described as the result of a series of cut and join operations performed on the chromosomes of a genome. Breaking and repairing chromosomes into new configurations can affect gene order and gene orientation. While the

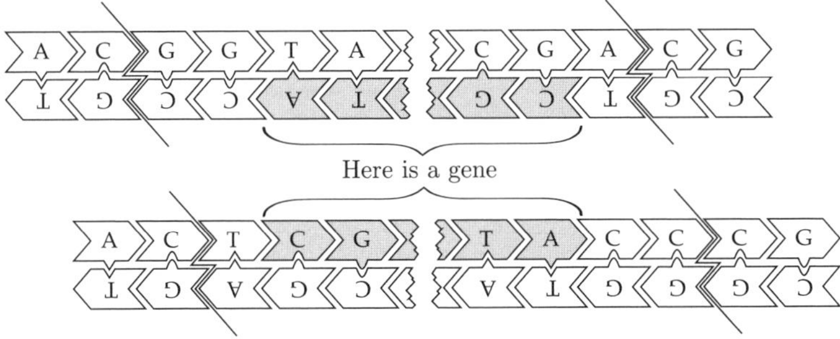

FIGURE 8.2 An inversion changes the orientation of the genes of the inverted segment.

first modification is easy to understand, the change in gene orientation deserves a little more attention since it is a consequence of the double strand structure of the chromosomes.

The upper part of Fig. 8.2 shows a chromosome that is broken at two places. The segment in the middle can either be correctly repaired or repaired in the wrong direction, as shown in the lower part of Fig. 8.2. However, since a 3′ extremity can only be reconnected to a 5′ extremity, this results in the exchange of strands. Genomic features that are on one of the strands of the inverted segment thus change their orientation, but are otherwise intact.

In one of the first papers on genome rearrangements [22], Dobzhansky and Sturtevant observed *inversions* of large segments of chromosomes in closely related species of *Drosophila* (see Fig. 8.3). When comparing more distant species, hundreds of small and large inversions can be detected [16].

Closely related to inversions are *translocations* between chromosomes. This happens when two different chromosomes exchange parts of their genetic material. Even in relatively close species, translocations can be extensive. For example, a comparison

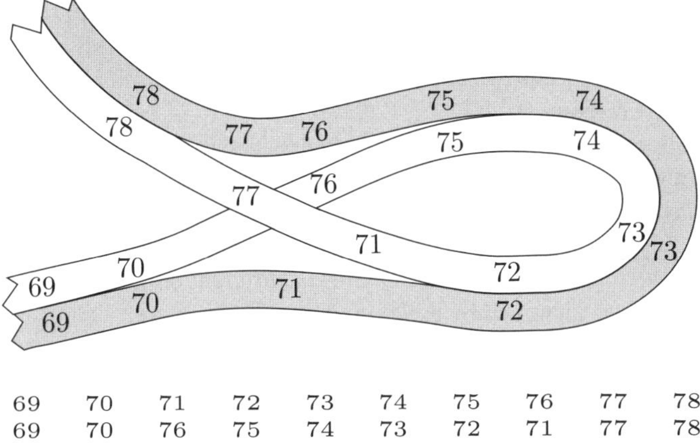

FIGURE 8.3 Fragment of the dataset constructed in 1938 by Dobzhansky and Sturtevant to compare whole genomes.

TABLE 8.1 Number of Occurrences of Four Domains in Two Species of α-Proteobacteria

PFAM family	*Agrobacterium tumefaciens*	*Rhizobium meliloti*
ABC_tran PF00005	497	262
BPD_transp1 PF00528	420	189
HTH_1 PF000126	149	95
LysR_substrate PF03466	148	89

between human and concolor gibbon chromosomes reveals that at least 31 translocations are necessary to explain the observed rearrangements [31]. *Fusions* and *fissions* of chromosomes are the special cases of translocations that modify the total number of chromosomes of an organism. A striking example of this type of rearrangement is given by the human chromosome 2, which is the result of a fusion of two smaller chromosomes found in most great apes [30].

A last rearrangement operation that does not change gene content is the *transposition*, in which a genomic segment is displaced within a chromosome but keeps its original orientation. Animal mitochondrial genomes, for example, provide numerous examples of transposed elements [49].

8.2.2.2 Rearrangements That Modify Gene Content

Gene content is modified by three main processes: duplications, losses, and exchanges of genetic material with close or symbiotic species.

Duplications can affect whole genomes: the bread wheat (*Triticum aestivum*) has 21 pairs of chromosomes that can be grouped into seven groups of triplicated chromosomes. This organization is quite recent, and the triplicated chromosomes retain a high similarity [41]. More ancient duplications are more difficult to establish, since many genes are lost or change function. For example, evidence of an ancient whole-genome duplication was discovered in yeasts [51]. Having access to extra genetic material meant that the evolving yeasts could "experiment" with part of their genetic material while retaining vital functions: as a result, modern yeasts with duplicated genomes are adapted to many different environments, but different species can have very different gene content.

On a smaller genomic scale, duplications are extensive. Most sequenced genomes contain segments that are similar at the nucleotide level, but at different places along the same chromosome or even on different chromosomes. Domains, genes, or even groups of genes can be present in several hundred copies in a genome. Table 8.1 gives examples of the number of occurrences of four different domains in two species of α-proteobacteria, as identified by the Pfam database [3].

8.3 BASIC CONCEPTS

Before introducing formally the notion of gene cluster, we give an intuitive definition. Basically, a gene cluster is a *set of genes* that, for biological reasons, has been kept "more or less together," or in other words, *in a same segment* in different genomes. There are several biological reasons that can prevent a set of genes to be dispersed by the rearrangements that occur during the evolution: co-transcription as operons, for example [36,52], co-regulation as part of a biochemical network [45], or evolutionary proximity.

From the combinatorial point of view, it is important to note the very different nature of the two notions used to define a cluster, that is, sets—with no order between the genes in a given set—and genome segments that are strings of genes and thus totally ordered. The key point in a formal definition of a gene cluster is then the relationship between the set of genes and the genome segments that define the cluster. We discuss this approach in the next section.

8.3.1 Highlighting Sets of Genes

In order to formalize the notion of sets of genes that are "more or less together" in different genomes, we must first look at the problem in a more general context: How do sets of letters behave in strings or permutations? For example, *highlighting* the set of letters {e, g, n} in the sentence

"rearrangements of genomes involve genes and chromosomes"

reveals groups that, at least in the case of the substrings "gene" and "gen", share a common—semantic—function. On the other hand, highlighting the set of letters {a, c, v} in the same sentence

"rearrangements of genomes involve genes and chromosomes"

does not seem to produce any interesting result.

These examples illustrate a major pitfall that one has to face in defining clusters as sets of genes: there is an exponential number of sets of genes. As we will see it with max-gap clusters in strings, for example, this can result in models that define an exponential number of gene clusters, ruling out any hope of a polynomial time detection of all gene clusters in such models. However, depending on both the combinatorial nature of the considered data (strings or permutations) and the definition of genome segments that define clusters, it is possible to define gene cluster models that are tractable.

A second question is what is an *occurrence* of a gene cluster. In our example, it seems reasonable to consider the substrings "nge", "gene", and "gen" as occurrences of the set {e, g, n}, but given the proximity of the substrings "nge" and "en" in the word "rearrangement"—they are separated by a single letter, it might be interesting to join them together in a single occurrence by bridging the *gap* of one letter. This would reduce the number of occurrences of the cluster defined by the set {e, g, n} to two "gene" and "ngemen", and this last occurrence being a nonexact occurrence due to the letter "m". Such a decision to accept an outsider in an occurrence of a cluster may also be wise from a biological point of view since genes can be gained or lost, or can change function, which translates, in terms of strings, as gaps or as missing genes.

This example illustrates the importance of the definition of the genome segments that define a cluster. In this chapter, we take the point of view to consider the intruder genes in occurrences of clusters under the point of view of the gaps they create, which has been followed in most recent approaches.[1] We thus have the following definition:

Definition 8.1 Given a set of genes S and a chromosome C represented by the string $g_1 g_2 \ldots g_k$, an *occurrence* of the set S is a substring $g_i \ldots g_j$ such that

(1) Both g_i and g_j belong to the set of genes S.
(2) The set of genes S is contained in the multiset $\{g_i \ldots g_j\}$.
(3) If a substring of $g_i \ldots g_j$ contains no gene of S, then its length must be smaller or equal to δ, a fixed integer that represents the maximal allowed *gap* size.
(4) The flanking substrings $g_{i-1-\delta} \ldots g_{i-1}$ and $g_{j+1} \ldots g_{j+1+\delta}$ contain no gene in S. (Extremities of chromosomes are padded with characters not in S as necessary.)

When $\delta = 0$, we usually refer to occurrences as "without gaps."

With a gap size $\delta = 0$, the three occurrences of the set {e, g, n} in the sentence "rearrangements of genomes involve genes and chromosomes" are the substrings "nge," "gene," and "gen"; with a gap size $\delta = 1$, there are again three occurrences, but the first occurrence is now the substring "ngemen,"

The next basic concept is illustrated by the following example. When the set of letters {m, o, s} is highlighted in the sentence

"rearrangements of genomes involve genes and chromosomes,"

the two occurrences of the set with gap size $\delta = 1$ are the substrings "omes" and "omosome." The presence of the letter "e" in both occurrences suggests that a more meaningful set of genes to consider could be the set {e, m, o, s}. The relationship between these two sets is captured by the following definition.

Definition 8.2 Given a set of genes S and genomes represented by a set of strings $\mathcal{G}$, a set of genes T is an *extension* of the set S if

(1) $S \subset T$
(2) Each occurrence of S in $\mathcal{G}$ is a substring of an occurrence of T.

In the example sentence, with $\delta = 1$, the two occurrences of the set {e, m, o, s} are "enomes" and "omosomes," and both of which contain an occurrence of {m, o, s} as a substring. Since {m, o, s} has only two occurrences, {e, m, o, s} is an extension

[1]Note however that a different point of view was taken in [19].

of {m, o, s}. On the other hand, the set {e, g, n, m} is not an extension of the set {e, g, n} since there is one occurrence of {e, g, n}, namely the occurrence within the word "gene" that is not a substring of an occurrence of {e, g, n, m}.

The point of view of this chapter will be purely combinatorial. Once gene clusters are identified, it is necessary to distinguish clusters whose existence could be merely due to random factors from those whose existence rests on other causes. These aspects are studied, for example, in [29].

8.3.2 An Elementary Model: Conserved Segments

Various formal models for gene clusters are obtained by imposing requirements on the subsets of genes that are allowable, on the types of strings that are considered, and on the number and nature of the occurrences.

Perhaps the simplest model is when we assume that genomes are permutations of each other and require occurrences of clusters to be equal. Because strings represent DNA molecules, the notion of equality must be adapted to capture the fact that an inverted string is the "same" as the original. Two strings $g_1 g_2 \ldots g_k$ and $h_1 h_2 \ldots h_k$ are *equal* if either (1) for all i, $g_i = h_i$, or (2) for all i, $g_i = -h_{k-i+1}$. We have

Definition 8.3 Let $\mathcal{G}$ be a set of signed permutations on the set of genes $\mathcal{S}$. A subset of $\mathcal{S}$ is a *conserved segment* if it has an occurrence in each permutation of $\mathcal{G}$, without gaps, and all occurrences are equal.

Conserved segments capture the notion of sets of genes that occur in the same order and same orientation in different genomes. For example, consider the following permutations:

$$G_1 = (a \quad b \quad -c \quad d \quad -e \quad f) \text{ and } G_2 = (-a \quad d \quad -e \quad f \quad c \quad -b).$$

Apart from the trivial conserved segments formed by singletons, the sets $\{b, c\}$, $\{d, e\}$, $\{e, f\}$, $\{d, e, f\}$ are all conserved segments. We are usually interested in *maximal* conserved segments, that is, conserved segments without extension. In this example, these are $\{a\}$, $\{b, c\}$, and $\{d, e, f\}$. In each permutation, the boundaries between two occurrences of maximal conserved segments are called *breakpoints*. For example, the breakpoints of G_1 with respect to G_2 are

$$G_1 = (a \parallel b \quad -c \parallel d \quad -e \quad f).$$

Maximal conserved segments form a partition of the set $\mathcal{S}$ and appear as consecutive elements in each permutation of $\mathcal{G}$, which are very desirable properties from a computational point of view. Identifying them can be done in $\mathcal{O}(Kn)$ time complexity, where K is the number of permutations in $\mathcal{G}$, and n the number of genes in $\mathcal{S}$. The computation involves the following steps:

(1) Choose an arbitrary ordering I of the set of genes $\mathcal{S}$.

(2) For each permutation in $\mathcal{G}$, construct a table indexed by I, which gives the position and the sign of the corresponding gene.
(3) Choose one permutation G in $\mathcal{G}$ and test, for each consecutive pair of genes $g_i g_{i+1}$ of G, whether it is a conserved segment. If it is not, mark a breakpoint between g_i and g_{i+1}.

When using very large datasets, it is a current practice to consider conserved segments as a single "gene," since there are no rearrangements within these segments. This is especially true when comparing close species, which often share very long conserved segments. For example, in the following three permutations, each integer represents a large conserved block in the chromosomes X of the human, mouse, and rat; reverse orientation is indicated by overlined integers. This dataset is adapted from [16].

$$
\begin{aligned}
\text{Human} &= (1\ 2\ 3\ 4\ 5\ 6\ 7\ 8\ 9\ 10\ 11\ 12\ 13\ 14\ 15\ 16)\\
\text{Mouse} &= (\overline{6}\ \overline{5}\ 4\ 13\ 14\ \overline{15}\ 16\ 1\ \overline{3}\ 9\ \overline{10}\ 11\ 12\ \overline{7}\ 8\ \overline{2})\\
\text{Rat} &= (\overline{13}\ \overline{4}\ 5\ \overline{6}\ \overline{12}\ \overline{8}\ \overline{7}\ 2\ 1\ \overline{3}\ 9\ 10\ 11\ 14\ \overline{15}\ 16)
\end{aligned}
$$

By construction, this set of permutations does not have any conserved segment. However, the comparison of these permutations two by two reveals conserved segments for each pair of species. For example, rat and mouse share the segment $\{4, 5, 13\}$, rat and human share $\{5, 7\}$, and mouse and human share $\{5, 6\}$.

This type of analysis was used, for example, in phylogenetic studies and for the reconstruction of ancestral genomes [11]. For larger sets of permutations, it is possible to relax the definition of conserved segments and ask for occurrences in at least J permutations in the set $\mathcal{G}$, but not necessarily in all. This is done at the cost of added algorithmic complexity.

Most properties of conserved segments do not hold anymore when the chromosomes contain duplicated genes. Indeed, the definition of conserved segment can be extended to strings, but they do not form a partition of the set $\mathcal{S}$ of genes, neither do they define clear breakpoint regions (see [13] for an example of using conserved segments to define breakpoints in a set of strings). We observe a similar phenomenon with the various gene cluster models in the next section.

8.4 MODELS OF GENE CLUSTERS

8.4.1 Common Intervals in Permutations

The notion of common intervals is a first generalization of conserved segments in which we relax the conditions that genes appear in the same order or the same orientation. It was first introduced by Uno and Yagiura [50] in the case of two permutations, and various efficient algorithms have since been developed for K permutations. Since orientation is not necessarily conserved, in this section we ignore the signs of genes.

Definition 8.4 Let $\mathcal{G}$ be a set of permutations on the set of genes $\mathcal{S}$. A subset of $\mathcal{S}$ is a *common interval* if it has an occurrence in each permutation of $\mathcal{G}$, without gaps.

Intuitively, a common interval is a set whose elements are consecutive in both permutations, thus intervals in both permutations. Note that singletons are always common intervals and are sometimes referred to as *trivial* common intervals. Consider the following two permutations:

$$G_1 = (\ 1\ \ 2\ \ 3\ \ 4\ \ 5\ \ 6\ \ 7\ \ 8\ \ 9\ \ 10\ \ 11\ )$$
$$G_2 = (\ \underline{\underline{\underline{\underline{4\ \ \underline{\underline{2\ \ \underline{1}\ \ 3}}}\ \ \underline{\underline{\underline{7\ \ 8}\ \ \underline{6\ \ 5}}}}}\ \ \underline{11\ \ \underline{9\ \ 10}}}\ ).$$

The common intervals of G_1 and G_2, except for the singletons, are underlined in the second permutation. When, as it is the case in this example, one of the permutation is the identity permutation, all common intervals are sets of consecutive integers since their occurrence in the identity permutation is an interval.

Underlining the same common intervals in the identity permutation highlights some of the properties of common intervals of permutations:

$$G_2 = (\ 4\ \ 2\ \ 1\ \ 3\ \ 7\ \ 8\ \ 6\ \ 5\ \ 11\ \ 9\ \ 10\ )$$
$$G_1 = (\ 1\ \ 2\ \ 3\ \ 4\ \ 5\ \ 6\ \ 7\ \ 8\ \ 9\ \ 10\ \ 11\ ).$$

For example, if two common intervals have a nontrivial intersection, such as $\{1, 2, 3, 4, 5, 6, 7, 8\}$ and $\{5, 6, 7, 8, 9, 10, 11\}$, then the intersection of these common intervals is also a common interval, since it is an interval in both permutations. More formally we have

Definition 8.5 Two sets S and T *overlap* if

(1) their intersection is nonempty, and
(2) neither S is contained in T, nor T is contained in S.

Proposition 8.1 *Let S and T be two overlapping common intervals of a set of permutations $\mathcal{G}$, then $S \cap T$, $S \cup T$, $S \setminus T$, and $T \setminus S$ are all common intervals of the set $\mathcal{G}$.*

The number of common intervals of a set of permutations on n elements is $\mathcal{O}(n^2)$. This bound is achieved, for example, when one compares two equal permutations: each interval is then a common interval and there are $(n + 1)(n/2)$ of them. On the other hand, from a biological perspective, a huge number of common intervals merely reflect that parts of genomes under study are very similar. This fact has hindered the use of common intervals in comparative genomics because most of common intervals in "real" genomes are very repetitive. For example, the following permutations

$$\begin{array}{lcccccccccccccc} G_3 & = & (& 1 & 2 & 3 & 4 & 5 & 6 & 7 & 8 & 9 & 10 & 11 &) \\ G_4 & = & (& 4 & 2 & 3 & 1 & 11 & 10 & 9 & 8 & 7 & 6 & 5 &) \end{array}$$

have 26 nontrivial common intervals, but most of them seems to be related, such as $\{5, 6\}$, $\{6, 7\}$, and $\{5, 6, 7\}$. A significant advance has been made in recent years to formally distinguish interesting common intervals from less interesting ones [33]. It is the identification of *strong* common intervals.

Definition 8.6 Let $\mathcal{G}$ be a set of permutations. A *strong* common interval is a common interval of $\mathcal{G}$ that does not overlap any other common intervals of $\mathcal{G}$.

For example, permutations G_3 and G_4 have only four strong common intervals that are underlined in G_4, and these illustrate very nicely the respective structures of the two permutations:

$$\begin{array}{lcccccccccccccc} G_3 & = & (& 1 & 2 & 3 & 4 & 5 & 6 & 7 & 8 & 9 & 10 & 11 &) \\ G_4 & = & (& 4 & 2 & 3 & 1 & 11 & 10 & 9 & 8 & 7 & 6 & 5 &). \end{array}$$

Strong intervals have very rich and deep combinatorial properties [10], as well as they capture relevant biological relations [7,33]. One of their most attractive features, from both point of views, is that there are few of them, and these few can be used to generate all common intervals. The proof of the following proposition is worth reading, since it introduces a basic construction.

Proposition 8.2 *Let $\mathcal{G}$ be a set of permutations on n elements. The number of strong common intervals of $\mathcal{G}$ is in $\mathcal{O}(n)$.*

Proof. Two strong common intervals are either disjoint, or one is contained in the other. All singletons and the set $\{1, 2, \ldots, n\}$ are strong common intervals. Consider the tree in which each strong common interval is the child of the smallest strong common interval that properly contains it. Each node of this tree has thus at least two children, its root is the set $\{1, 2, \ldots, n\}$ and its leaves are the singletons. Therefore, the total number of its internal nodes is less than n. ■

It is thus possible to report and display the strong common intervals as a tree using the inclusion relation. For example, the tree in Fig. 8.4 corresponds to the strong common intervals of G_3 and G_4.

Such trees are examples of a general structure, known as PQ-trees [15], that was developed to represent sets of permutations. These are ordered trees whose nodes are classified as either P-nodes or Q-nodes. In the tree of strong common intervals of a set of permutations $\mathcal{G}$, if the leaves are ordered according to one of the permutations in $\mathcal{G}$, then for each node N exactly one of the following is true:

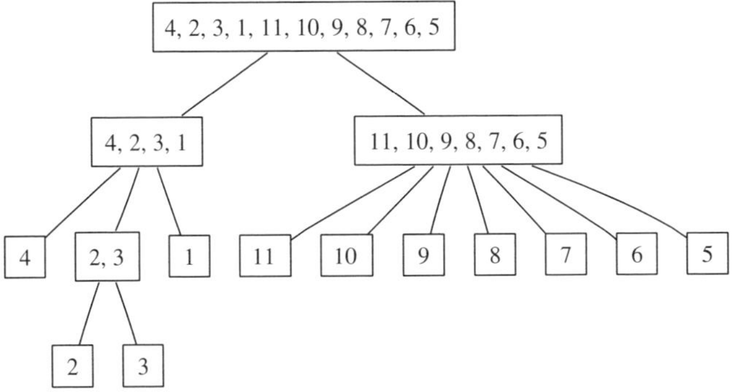

FIGURE 8.4 The tree of strong common intervals of the permutations G_3 and G_4. Leaves are ordered according to G_4.

(1) [Q-nodes] Any union of consecutive children of N is a common interval of $\mathcal{G}$.

(2) [P-nodes] No union of consecutive children of N is a common interval of $\mathcal{G}$, except the union of all its children—in this case the union equals N itself.

In PQ-trees, the P-nodes are traditionally depicted as roundish boxes and the Q-nodes as rectangular boxes. The tree of Fig. 8.4 has only Q-nodes. A more general example is given by the tree of Fig. 8.5, which represents the strong common intervals of the permutations:

$$G_5 = (\ 1\ \ 2\ \ 3\ \ 4\ \ 5\ \ 6\ \ 7\ \ 8\ \ 9\ \ 10\ \ 11\ )$$
$$G_6 = (\ 1\ \ 4\ \ 2\ \ 5\ \ 3\ \ 11\ \ 10\ \ 8\ \ 9\ \ 7\ \ 6\ ).$$

In Fig. 8.5, the node corresponding to the strong common interval $\{4, 2, 3, 5\}$ is a P-node, since no union of consecutive children is a common interval. This representation of strong common intervals allows them to serve as a basis for generating all common intervals of a set of permutations. We have

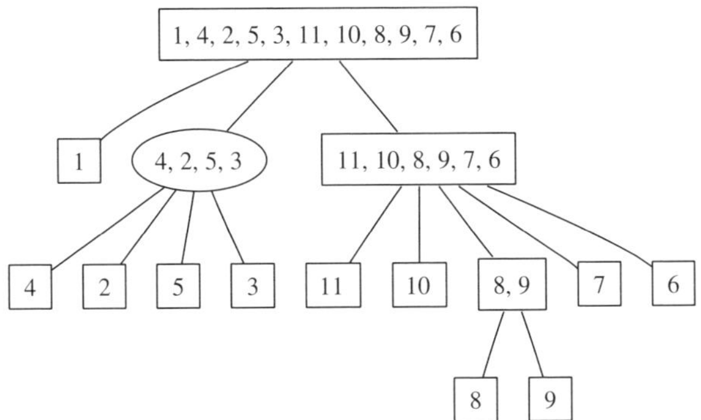

FIGURE 8.5 The tree of strong common intervals of the permutations G_5 and G_6. Leaves are ordered according to G_6.

Proposition 8.3 *[10] Let T be the PQ-tree of the strong common intervals of a set $\mathcal{G}$ of permutations, ordered according to one of the permutations in $\mathcal{G}$. A set S is a common interval of $\mathcal{G}$ if and only if it is the union of consecutive nodes of children of a Q-node or the union of all children of a P-node.*

8.4.1.1 Computing Common Intervals and Strong Intervals The algorithmic history of efficient computation of common and strong intervals has an interesting twist. From the start, Uno and Yagiura [50] proposed an algorithm to compute the common intervals of two permutations whose theoretical running time was $\mathcal{O}(n + N)$, where n is the number of elements of the permutation, and N is the number of common intervals of the two permutations. Such an algorithm can be considered as optimal since it runs in time proportional to the sum of the size of the input and the size of the output. However, the authors acknowledged that their algorithm was "quite complicated" and that, in practice, simpler $\mathcal{O}(n^2)$ algorithms run faster on randomly generated permutations.

Building on Uno and Yagiura's work, Heber and Stoye [27] proposed an algorithm to generate all common intervals of a set of K permutations in time proportional to $Kn + N$, based on Uno and Yagiura analysis. They achieved the extension to K permutations by considering the set of *irreducible* common intervals that are common intervals and that are *not* the union of two overlapping common intervals. As for the strong intervals, the irreducible common intervals also form a basis of size $\mathcal{O}(n)$ that generates the common intervals by unions of overlapping irreducible intervals.

The drawback of these algorithms is that they use complex data structures that are difficult to implement. A simpler way to generate the common intervals is to compute a basis that generates intervals using intersections instead of unions.

Definition 8.7 Let $\mathcal{G}$ be a set of K permutations on n elements that contains the identity permutation. A *generator* for the common intervals of $\mathcal{G}$ is a pair (R, L) of vectors of size n such that

(1) $R[i] \geq i$ and $L[j] \leq j$ for all $i, j \in \{1, 2, \ldots, n\}$,
(2) $(i, \ldots, j)$ is a common interval of $\mathcal{G}$ if and only if $(i, \ldots, j) = (i, \ldots, R[i]) \cap (L[j], \ldots, j)$.

It is not immediate that such generators even exist, but it turns out that they are far from unique, and some of them can be computed using elementary data structures such as stacks and arrays [10]. The algorithms are easy to implement, and the theoretical complexity is $\mathcal{O}(Kn + N)$. The strong common intervals can also be computed in $\mathcal{O}(Kn)$.

8.4.1.2 The Use of Common Intervals in Comparative Genomics Datasets based on permutations that use real "genes" are not frequent in comparative genomics since real genes are often found in several copies within the genome of an organism. In order to obtain permutations, it is possible to eliminate all duplicates, or even better,

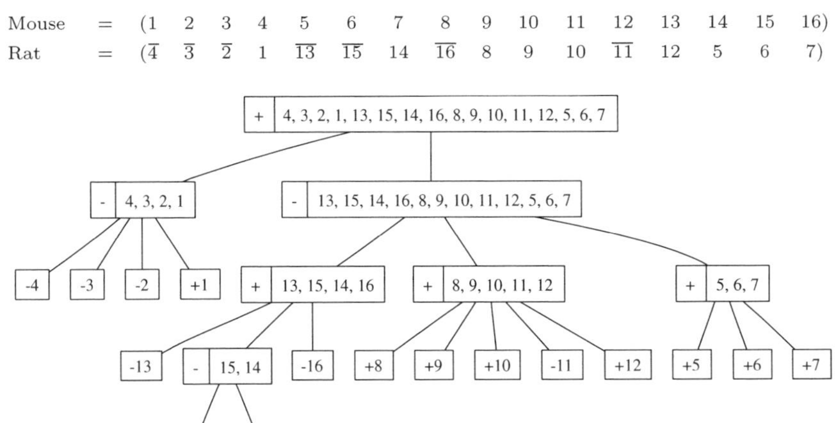

FIGURE 8.6 Comparing the rat and mouse X chromosomes.

to retain only one copy [38]. However, in some small chromosomes, such as animal mitochondrion genomes, genes are not often duplicated, and it is possible to extract permutations from the gene order without sacrificing too much information. In [1], for example, common intervals are used to define a distance between plant chloroplast genomes.

On the other hand, datasets that are constructed using large synteny blocks, such as in [16], naturally yield permutations. In this context, common intervals and strong common intervals have been used, for example, for the evaluation of proposed evolution scenarios between species [6] or for the construction of evolution scenarios [7]. In these applications, the impact of rearrangement operations on the structure of common intervals is taken into account to propose a rearrangement scenario between two genomes.

For example, Fig. 8.6 represents the strong common intervals of two signed permutations representing conserved block in the chromosomes X of the rat and the mouse. Each strong interval is marked by either a "+" or a "−" sign, using the sign of the element of the permutation for the leaves and the fact that the numbers are increasing or decreasing for the other nodes. Inverting all strong intervals that have a sign different from their parent yields a scenario that conserves, for each intermediate scenario, all common intervals of the two permutations.

8.4.2 Max-gap Clusters in Permutations

The first formal model of gene clusters in permutations that allows gaps was introduced in [8] under the name of *gene teams*. Even if the range of its applications is limited, it remains the only model whose formal properties can be fully analyzed, as in [28] where they are called *max-gap clusters*, whose output size is reasonable, and for which efficient algorithms exist.

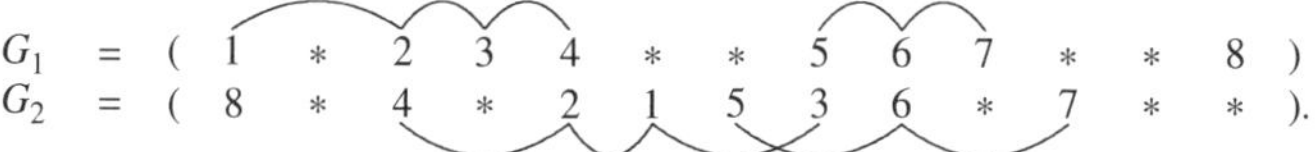

FIGURE 8.7 Gene teams of G_1 and G_2 with gap size $\delta = 1$.

Definition 8.8 Let $\mathcal{G}$ be a set of strings on the set of genes $\mathcal{S} \cup \{*\}$ such that each string is a permutation of $\mathcal{S}$ when the symbols $\{*\}$ are removed. Let $\delta \geq 0$ be a fixed integer. A subset of $\mathcal{S}$ is a *gene team* if it has an occurrence with maximum gap size δ in each permutation of $\mathcal{G}$ and has no extension.

Consider, for example, the two following strings:

$$G_1 = (\ 1 * 2\ 3\ 4 * * 5\ 6\ 7 * * 8\ )$$
$$G_2 = (\ 8 * 4 * 2\ 1\ 5\ 3\ 6 * 7 * *\ ).$$

The gene teams of G_1 and G_2 with gap size $\delta = 1$ are $\{1, 2, 3, 4\}$, $\{5, 6, 7\}$, and $\{8\}$. It is important to note that occurrences of teams can overlap; Fig. 8.7 illustrates this fact by joining the various members of a team with arcs. Even though occurrences of gene teams can overlap, they always form a partition of the set of genes $\mathcal{S}$. This is a consequence of the following proposition.

Proposition 8.4 *Let S and T be two gene teams of the set of strings $\mathcal{G}$. If $S \cap T \neq \emptyset$, then $S = T$.*

Proof. Consider a substring $g_i \dots g_j$ in one of the strings G of $\mathcal{G}$ that contains all genes of $S \cup T$, and such that both g_i and g_j are in $S \cup T$. We first show that each substring of $g_i \dots g_j$ of length greater than δ contains at least a gene from $S \cup T$, implying that $g_i \dots g_j$ is an occurrence of $S \cup T$. In order to prove this, suppose that a substring $g_k \dots g_{k+\delta}$ contains no gene in $S \cup T$, and both flanking genes are in $S \cup T$. Then these genes cannot be both in S, or both in T, since S or T would not have an occurrence in the string G. Therefore, one is an element of S and the other of T, and the occurrences of S and T in this string are on different sides of the substring $g_k \dots g_{k+\delta}$, implying that $S \cap T = \emptyset$. Now, since the string G was arbitrary, we have shown that $S \cup T$ is an extension of both S and T, which is ruled out by definition, thus $S = T$. ■

The first consequence of Proposition 8.4 is that the number of gene teams is $\mathcal{O}(n)$, where n is the number of elements of $\mathcal{S}$. This will be our last model with such a desirable property. Proposition 8.4 also allows the computation of gene teams through partition refinement techniques. The best complexity achieved up to now is $\mathcal{O}(Kn \log^2(n))$ [4], where K is the number of strings in $\mathcal{G}$.

8.4.3 Common Intervals in Strings

In the previous section, we generalized the notion of common intervals in permutations by allowing gaps in occurrences of a set of genes defining a cluster. We now describe another natural extension of common intervals in permutations, which is the notion of common intervals in strings.

Definition 8.9 Let $\mathcal{G}$ be a set of strings on the set of genes $\mathcal{S}$. A subset of $\mathcal{S}$ is a *common interval* if it has an occurrence in each string of $\mathcal{G}$, without gaps.

The above definition is identical to the definition of common intervals in permutations (Defination 8.4) except for one word "strings" instead of "permutations," and this model is used to analyze genomes with many duplicates. This representation is particularly adapted to the study of genomes at the level of "genes" and "domains" under the classical biological definition of these two words.

For example, in

$$G_1 = (f \;\; e \;\; c \;\; e \;\; b \;\; e \;\; d) \text{ and } G_2 = (a \;\; b \;\; b \;\; e \;\; c \;\; b \;\; c \;\; d \;\; b \;\; e \;\; c),$$

the set $\{b, e\}$ is a common interval that has one occurrence in G_1, $(e \;\; b \;\; e)$ and two occurrences in G_2, $(b \;\; b \;\; e)$ and $(b \;\; e)$. The other common intervals are $\{b\}$, $\{c\}$, $\{e\}$, $\{c, e\}$, $\{b, c, e\}$, and $\{b, c, d, e\}$.

8.4.3.1 Properties of Common Intervals in Strings. A major difference with common intervals of permutations, due to the possible repetition of genes in strings, is that a common interval S of the strings $\mathcal{G}$ can have two or more occurrences in a genome that do not overlap due to the point 3 of Definition 8.1. Hence, using common intervals of sequences allows to detect gene clusters that have been rearranged by duplication events, either internal duplications resulting in several copies of a gene of the cluster, or large-scale duplications resulting in several copies of the whole clusters; this is an important strength of this model.

The first question raised by the definition of gene clusters as common intervals in strings is the computational cost of such a higher biological accuracy. It happens that this model is very tractable and, in fact, only slightly more costly to handle than common intervals of permutations. Indeed, since every occurrence of a common interval is without gap, every substring of a genome of $\mathcal{G}$ can be occurrence of at most one gene cluster, which immediately leads to the following proposition.

Proposition 8.5 *Let N be the sum of the lengths of the strings in $\mathcal{G}$. The number of common intervals in $\mathcal{G}$ and the number of occurrences of all common intervals in $\mathcal{G}$ are in $\mathcal{O}(N^2)$.*

Hence the maximum number of common intervals is quadratic in the size of the genomes in both cases, permutations and strings, which is a direct consequence of considering occurrences without gaps. However, an important difference with permutations relies on the internal structure of the set of common intervals in strings. In permutations, the existence of linear space basis of the set of common intervals, irreducible intervals, and strong intervals is central in the linear time and space complexity of algorithms. Currently, no such basis has been found for common intervals in strings (see [33] for an attempt to use *PQ*-trees with strings, which is applicable when very few duplicated genes exist).

8.4.3.2 Detecting Common Intervals in Strings. Because of the lack of internal structure, the algorithms used to detect the set of common intervals in a set of strings $\mathcal{G}$ and the occurrences of each common interval are very different in nature than the algorithms used for detecting common intervals in permutations and are much less elegant. They rely on the enumeration of the *fingerprints* of $\mathcal{G}$.

Given a substring $g_i \ldots g_j$ of a string of $\mathcal{G}$, its *fingerprint* is the subset of $\mathcal{S}$, the gene alphabet, containing the genes appearing in $g_i \ldots g_j$. For example, the fingerprint of $(b \;\; b \;\; e \;\; c \;\; b \;\; c)$ is $\{b, c, e\}$. The *fingerprint* of $\mathcal{G}$ is the set of all the fingerprints of all substrings of $\mathcal{G}$. It follows immediately that a common interval of $\mathcal{G}$ is a fingerprint of $\mathcal{G}$ that appears in each string of $\mathcal{G}$, which implies that computing the common intervals of $\mathcal{G}$ reduces to the appropriate filtering of the set of fingerprints of $\mathcal{G}$.

Detecting the set of fingerprints of a set of strings was first considered by Amir et al. in [2]. The key of their algorithm is an efficient encoding scheme for fingerprints that associates, to each fingerprint, a unique name computed from the elements of $\mathcal{S}$ it contains. Their encoding is efficient in the sense that, if two fingerprints differ only by one element, computing the name of the second one from the first one requires a limited complexity ($\mathcal{O}(\log(n))$), where n is the number of elements of $\mathcal{S}$. This property allows to compute the number of different fingerprints by using a sliding window on the considered string of total length N in time $\mathcal{O}(nN\log(n)\log(N))$. Two recent papers used the same principle but improved the fingerprint naming technique introduced by Amir et al. to compute the set of fingerprints of $\mathcal{G}$ in time $\mathcal{O}(nN\log(n))$ (see [21]) and $\mathcal{O}((occ + N)\log(n))$ respectively, where occ is the total number of occurrences of the fingerprints of $\mathcal{G}$ (see [32]). Another family of algorithms, initiated by Didier [20] and improved in [40] and [21], allows to compute the fingerprints of $\mathcal{G}$ in time $\mathcal{O}(N^2)$, and note that the property to be independent from the number of genes is important as in most comparative genomics applications, n is in $\mathcal{O}(N)$. These two families of algorithms offer, as far as we know, the only nontrivial ways to compute the set of common intervals of a set of strings.

8.4.3.3 Using Common Intervals in Strings. Common intervals of strings have been used in two problems: detection of conserved gene clusters, which was the initial goal they were designed for, and assignment of positional homologs. We conclude this section by describing briefly these applications, which will allow us to outline the advantages and shortcomings of this formal model.

Detection of Conserved Gene Clusters. The algorithm of Schmidt and Stoye, described in [40] and adapted to compute intervals that are common to a subset of the strings in $\mathcal{G}$, is the basis of the algorithm used in the software GECKO [25]. However, GECKO brings additional important features that address weaknesses of the common interval model.

A first improvement of the basic common interval model relies on the ability of GECKO to avoid displaying clusters that have an extension (see Definition 8.2). This is an important practical feature, as it reduces significantly the size of the output. A second improvement addresses the main problem of common intervals as models of gene clusters: it is very unlikely that a cluster keeps the same gene content in all the genomes of a dataset, especially if they span a large evolutionary spectrum. In such a case, these clusters cannot be detected by common intervals. To solve this problem, GECKO uses a heuristic postprocessing that agglomerates common intervals in groups such that all common intervals in a given group share at least a minimum fraction—a user-defined parameter—of their genes with a particular common interval of this group. This way of grouping common intervals, in order to define less strict clusters, is inspired from the heuristic methods used to compute gene clusters, and it adds flexibility. The price to pay is more noisy output, since a given common interval can belong to several groups.

Inferring Positional Homologs. When genomes contain duplicated genes, a major question is to elucidate the evolutionary relationships between the several copies of a given gene that form a family of homologous genes. Several kinds of relationships have been defined, and the most commonly considered being the notions of *orthologs* and *paralogs* that are defined in terms of the evolutionary history of gene families. This problem has attracted a lot of attention since such knowledge has been shown to be helpful in understanding the function of the genes of a gene family. Recently, several other notions of homology have been defined in terms of gene order, such as *positional homologs* [18] and *ancestral homologs* [38], that are used to propose interesting putative pairs of orthologs. In the gene order approaches, these homologs are deduced from a pairing between the genes of two compared genomes that define a signed permutation and that optimize a given combinatorial criterion, for example, a genetic distance [24] or the number of common intervals in the resulting permutation [17].

In [12], it was shown that using directly common intervals in strings as anchors of a global matching, in a way that is similar to methods for whole-genome alignments, offers an interesting alternative to the parsimonious approach to infer positional homologs from gene orders and performs at least as well as methods based on more complicated combinatorial objects, such as the breakpoint graph in [24].

8.4.4 Max-Gap Clusters in Strings

Max-gap clusters in strings are the most general formal model of gene clusters: gaps are allowed, duplications and missing genes are taken care of, and there is no requirement that a cluster be present in all species under study. Unfortunately, there is little hope that the automatic detection of these types of clusters will be computationally feasible for large datasets.

Definition 8.10 Let $\mathcal{G}$ be a set of strings on the set of genes $\mathcal{S}$, and $\delta \geq 0$ a fixed integer. A subset of $\mathcal{S}$ is a *max-gap cluster* if it has an occurrence with maximum gap size δ in at least one string of $\mathcal{G}$ and has no extension.

Each type of cluster that we examined in the preceding sections provides examples of max-gap clusters, but the general notion indeed seems to be truly adapted for certain type of biological data. For example, in the genome of *Nostoc* sp. *PCC 7120*, we have the following five occurrences with gap size $\delta = 1$ of a set of three domains:

$$CABC, \quad CA * ABCC, \quad ABCC, \quad A * ABC * CB, \quad A * BCCABC,$$

where stars "$*$" stand in for domains not in the set $\{A, B, C\}$. These five patterns are among the dozens of variations on the associations of these three domains that are actually found in bacteria. Thus, there is clearly a need to be able to consider models that allow for gaps and duplicate genes. However, as we will see in the next paragraphs, known bounds for the size of the output—that is, the number of max-gap clusters in a given set of strings $\mathcal{G}$—are currently exponential in the number of genes in $\mathcal{S}$. This implies that the running time of algorithms that detect max-gap clusters can be unreasonably long.

8.4.4.1 ***Algorithmic Complexity*** Clearly, testing for all possible subsets as candidate max-gap clusters is out of the question for any realistic set of genes. Some reasonable hypothesis, such as limiting the size of the gap, and considering sets that have at least one occurrence in the genomes under study are helpful and allow the computation of max-gap clusters for interesting sets of genomes with thousands of genes [34]. For the comparison of exactly two genomes, and with the additional hypothesis that a cluster must have an occurrence in both genomes, He and Goldwasser [26] describe a polynomial algorithm to compute them.

However, even with a gap size equal to 1, there can be an exponential number of subsets that have at least one occurrence and possibly no extension, as the following example shows. Consider a genome segment of the form

$$ag_1 \dots g_n z$$

in which all the genes are different. We will compute T_n, the number of subsets of $\{a, g_1, \dots, g_n, z\}$ that contain genes a and z and that have an occurrence with maximum gap size of 1 in the segment.

For $n = 0$, the number of such subsets is 1, and for $n = 1$, there are two of them: $\{a, z\}$ and $\{a, g_1, z\}$. Suppose now that $n \geq 2$. A subset that has an occurrence in the segment, and contains both a and z, either

(1) contains both g_{n-1} and g_n or
(2) contains g_{n-1} but not g_n or
(3) contains g_n but not g_{n-1}.

Clearly, the three cases are disjoint. In the first case, removing genes g_{n-1} and g_n from the subset yields a subset that has an occurrence in the segment $ag_1 \dots g_{n-2}z$. Conversely, adding genes g_{n-1} and g_n to such a subset yields a subset that has an occurrence in the segment $ag_1 \dots g_{n-1}g_nz$. Thus, the number of subsets covered by case (1) is T_{n-2}.

The two remaining cases are treated together. Consider the T_{n-1} subsets that have an occurrence in $ag_1 \ldots g_{n-1}z$. All subsets that contain gene g_{n-1} also have occurrences with gap size 1 in $ag_1 \ldots g_{n-1}g_n z$ by skipping gene g_n, and all those that do not contain gene g_{n-1} can be extended to occurrences in $ag_1 \ldots g_{n-1}g_n z$ by adding gene g_n, since they must contain gene g_{n-2}. The inverse bijection is obtained by removing gene g_n from all subsets covered by case (3). Thus, the total number of subsets covered by case (2) and (3) is T_{n-1}, yielding the recurrence equation

$$T_n = T_{n-1} + T_{n-2},$$

with initial conditions $T_0 = 1$ and $T_1 = 2$.

This equation has, unfortunately, a well-known solution that grows exponentially with n. Its closed form is

$$T_n = \frac{(1+\sqrt{5})^{n+2} - (1-\sqrt{5})^{n+2}}{2^{n+2}\sqrt{5}},$$

and the sequence $\{T_n\}$ is known as the *Fibonacci* sequence. As a measure of its growth, we have, for example, $T_{10} = 144$ and $T_{20} = 17711$, and $T_{30} = 2178309$.

8.4.4.2 The Combinatorial Beauty of Nature In the preceding section, we proved that the theoretical number of max-gap clusters could be exponential with respect to the number of genes. How do real genomes behave? It seems that, at least at certain levels of complexity, nature does experiment in a combinatorial way.

The STRING database [46] predicts functional associations between genes or domains in prokaryotic genomes, based on the identification of genomic segments where they appear close together. Using STRING, we looked at occurrences of subsets of the following five domains: (A) COG2202—PAS/PAC domain, (B) COG0642—Signal transduction histidine kinase, (C) COG0784—CheY-like receiver, (D) COG2203—GAF domain, and (E) COG2200—EAL domain.

The first of these five domains, COG2202, was chosen among the few dozens that have many duplicates in bacterial genomes. The next four are the best scoring for functional association with COG2202, as predicted by STRING. This choice is somewhat arbitrary, and other sets of domains were also shown to exhibit the same combinatorial behavior.

If we exclude trivial subsets consisting of one element, there are 26 possible subsets of the set $\{A, B, C, D, E\}$. Of these, we found that 19 had at least one occurrence with $\delta = 2$ among 11 different genomes. Table 8.2 gives examples of occurrences for each of the 19 subsets. It illustrates in a striking way why the general model of max-gap clusters must eventually be replaced by heuristics in some applications. With more and more organisms to compare, it is tempting to predict that all the "not found" lines in Table 8.2 will eventually be filled up.

TABLE 8.2 Occurrences of Various Subsets of Domains in Prokaryotic Genomes. Stars "$*$" Stand in for Domains Not in the Set $\{A, B, C, D, E\}$.

Subset	Occurrence	Species
$\{A, B\}$	$ABAB$	*Nostoc sp. PCC 7120*
$\{A, C\}$	AC	*Leptospira interrogans*
$\{A, D\}$	$A * ADA$	*Methanosarcina acetivorans*
$\{A, E\}$	AE	*Escherischia coli*
$\{B, C\}$	$BC * *C$	*Xanthomonas campestris*
$\{B, D\}$	DB	*Leptospira interrogans*
$\{B, E\}$	(not found)	
$\{C, D\}$	$CC * D * *C$	*Nostoc sp. PCC 7120*
$\{C, E\}$	$E * *C$	*Bacillus halodurans*
$\{D, E\}$	$E * D$	*Xanthomonas axohopodis*
$\{A, B, C\}$	CAB	*Xanthomonas campestris*
$\{A, B, D\}$	$ADADB$	*Methanosarcina acetivorans*
$\{A, B, E\}$	$B * A * E$	*Pseudomonas aeruginosa*
$\{A, C, D\}$	$ADA * C$	*Sinorhizobium meliloti*
$\{A, C, E\}$	$AC * E$	*Agrobacterium tumafaciens*
$\{A, D, E\}$	(not found)	
$\{B, C, D\}$	$DBCB$	*Nostoc sp. PCC 7120*
$\{B, D, E\}$	(not found)	
$\{B, C, E\}$	$C * EBB * C$	*Xylella fastidiosa*
$\{C, D, E\}$	(not found)	
$\{A, B, C, D\}$	$DAD * CAB$	*Nostoc sp. PCC 7120*
$\{A, B, C, E\}$	$CE * ABC$	*Pseudomonas aeruginosa*
$\{A, B, D, E\}$	(not found)	
$\{A, C, D, E\}$	(not found)	
$\{B, C, D, E\}$	(not found)	
$\{A, B, C, D, E\}$	$ADABCECB$	*Nostoc sp. PCC 7120*

8.5 CONCLUSION

We described in this chapter a hierarchy of formal models that have been defined to detect conserved gene clusters. One of the important points that we can outline is the strong link between the biological complexity that these models try to capture and their computational complexity. It appears very clearly that the limiting factors are the presence of duplicated genes (i.e. strings versus permutations) and the existence of clusters whose occurrences do not have the same gene content: indeed, the detection of common intervals in strings and max-gap clusters in permutations is very tractable. It then remains open to define general models of gene clusters that consider both nonexact occurrences and strings and that are tractable.

The first way to attack this problem could be to try to extend the notion of common intervals, that is, the only known tractable model handling strings to define a model with nonexact occurrences but without using the notion of gap, as it was shown that even the shortest possible gap of 1 can lead to an exponential number of clusters. The first attempt was done in [19], with a model of *common intervals with errors* that adds flexibility by bounding a number of genes of an occurrence of a cluster that do not belong to the cluster. However, even in this model the number of generated clusters can be exponential.

Another possibility would be to rely on combinatorial properties of gene clusters in order to refine gene cluster models and then reduce the number of produced clusters by eliminating nonsignificant clusters. For example, one of the reasons for the definition of common intervals with errors is that it ensures a minimum *density* [28] of each occurrence, roughly defined as the ratio between genes belonging to the cluster and the intruders. Other properties of gene clusters that are worth to be investigated are also described in [28].

Finally, it would be very natural to include the phylogenetic information, when available, in the definition of gene cluster models. This approach has been shown to be very interesting in a heuristic approach and in a probabilistic framework [53], but it is not obvious how it would fit in the purely combinatorial framework we described in this chapter.

ACKNOWLEDGMENTS

The different models described in this chapter were developed by a strongly interacting community of researchers. The authors wish to acknowledge that the connected component of the transitive closure of the collaboration relation, as defined by the bibliography of this chapter, and that contains the three authors also contains 29 other persons. This means that formal definitions of gene clusters is a collective endeavor, and we thank them all.

REFERENCES

1. Adam Z, Turmel M, Lemieux C, Sankoff D. Common intervals and symmetric difference in a model-free phylogenomics, with an application to streptophyte evolution. *J Comput Biol* 2007;14(4):436–45.
2. Amir A, Apostolico A, Landau GM, Satta, G. Efficient text fingerprinting via Parikh mapping. *J Disc Algorithms* 2003;1(5–6):409–421.
3. Bateman A, Coin L, Durbin R, Finn RD, Hollich V, Griffiths-Jones S, Khanna A, Marshall M, Moxon S, Sonnhammer EL, Studholme DJ, Yeats C, Eddy SR. The Pfam protein families database. *Nucl Acids Res* 2004;32:D138–D141.
4. Béal MP, Bergeron A, Corteel S, Raffinot M. An algorithmic view of gene teams. *Theoret Comput Sci* 2004;320(2-3): 395-418.
5. Belda E, Moya A, Silva FJ. Genome rearrangement distances and gene order phylogeny in γ-proteobacteria. *Mol Biol Evol* 2005;22(6):1456–1467.
6. Bérard S, Bergeron A, Chauve C. Conserved structures in evolution scenarios. *Lecture Notes in Bioinformatics, Vol. 3388.* Springer; 2005. pp. 1–15.
7. Bérard S, Bergeron A, Chauve C, Paul C. Perfect sorting by reversals is not always difficult. *IEEE/ACM Trans Comput Biol Bioinform* 2007;4(1):4–16.

8. Bergeron A, Corteel S, Raffinot M. The algorithmic of gene teams. *Lecture Notes in Computer Science, Vol. 2452*. Springer; 2002. pp. 464–476.
9. Bergeron A, Blanchette M, Chateau A, Chauve C. Reconstructing ancestral gene orders using conserved intervals. *Lecture Notes in Bioinformatics, Vol. 3240*. Springer; 2004. pp. 14–25.
10. Bergeron A, Chauve C, de Montgolfier F, Raffinot M. Computing common intervals of K permutations, with applications to modular decomposition of graphs. *Lecture Notes in Computer Science, Vol. 3669*. Springer. pp. 779–790.
11. Blanchette M, Kunisawa T, Sankoff D. Gene order breakpoint evidence in animal mitochondrial phylogeny, *J Mol Evol* 1999;49:193–203.
12. Blin G, Chateau A, Chauve C, Gingras Y. Inferring positional homologs with common intervals of sequences. *Lecture Notes in Bioinformatics, Vol. 4205*. Springer; 2006. pp. 24–38.
13. Blin G, Chauve C, Fertin G. Gene order and phylogenetic reconstruction: application to γ-Proteobacteria. *Lecture Notes in Bioinformatics, Vol. 3678*. Springer; 2005. pp. 11–20.
14. Boore JL. Animal mitochondrial genomes. *Nucl Acids Rese* 1999;27(8):1767–1780.
15. Booth KS, Lueker GS. Testing for the consecutive ones property, interval graphs, and graph planarity using PQ-tree algorithms. *J Comput System Sci* 1976;13(3):335–379.
16. Bourque G, Pevzner PA, Tesler G. Reconstructing the genomic architecture of ancestral mammals: Lessons from human, mouse, and rat genomes. *Genome Research* 2004;14(4):507–516.
17. Bourque G, Yacef Y, El-Mabrouk N. Maximizing synteny blocks to identify ancestral homologs. *Lecture Notes in Bioinformatics, Vol. 3678*. Springer; 2005. pp. 21–34.
18. Burgetz IJ, Shariff S, Pang A, Tillier ERM. Positional homology in bacterial genomes. *Evol Bioinformatics Online* 2006;2:42–55.
19. Chauve C, Diekmann Y, Heber S, Mixtacki J, Rahmann S, Stoye J. On common intervals with errors. Report 2006-02, Technische Fakultät der Universität Bielefeld, Abteilung Informationstechnik, 2006.
20. Didier G. Common intervals of two sequences. *Lecture Notes in Bioinformatics, Vol. 2812*. Springer; 2003. pp. 17–24.
21. Didier G, Schmidt T, Stoye J, Tsur D. Character sets of strings. *J Disc Algorithms* 2007;5(2):330–340.
22. Dobzhansky T, Sturtevant AT. Inversions in the Chromosomes of *Drosophila pseudoobscura*. *Genetics* 1938;23:28–64.
23. Eichler EE, Sankoff D. Structural dynamics of eukaryotic chromosome evolution. *Science* 2003;301(5634):793–797.
24. Fu Z, Chen X, Vcici V, Nan P, Zhong Y, Jiang T. A parsimony approach to genome-wide ortholog assignment. *Lecture Notes in Bioinformatics, Vol. 3909*. Springer; 2006. pp. 578–594.
25. Gecko. *Gene Clusters Identification in Prokaryotes*. Software available on the website `http://bibiserv.techfak.uni-bielefeld.de/gecko`.
26. He X, Goldwasser MH. Identifying conserved gene clusters in the presence of homology families. *J Comput Biol* 2005;12(6):638–656.
27. Heber S, Stoye J. Finding all common intervals of k permutations. *Lecture Notes in Computer Science, Vol. 2089*. Springer; 2001. pp. 207–218.

28. Hoberman R, Durand D. The incompatible desiderata of gene cluster properties. *Lecture Notes in Bioinformatics, Vol. 3678*. Springer; 2005. pp. 73–87.
29. Hoberman R, Sankoff D, Durand D. The statistical analysis of spatially clustered genes under the maximum gap criterion. *J Comput Biol* 2005;12(8):1081–1100.
30. Ijdo JW, Baldini A, Ward DC, Reeders ST, Wells RA. Origin of human chromosome 2: An ancestral telomere-telomere fusion. *Proc Nat Acad Sci USA* 1991;88:9051-9055.
31. Koehler U, Bigoni F, Wienberg J, Stanyon R. Genomic reorganization in the concolor gibbon (Hylobates concolor) revealed by chromosome painting. *Genomics* 1995;20;30(2):287–92.
32. Kolpakov R, Raffinot M. New algorithms for text fingerprinting. *Lecture Notes in Computer Science, Vol. 4009*. Springer; 2006. pp. 342–353.
33. Landau GM, Parida L, Weimann O. Gene proximity analysis across whole genomes via PQ trees. *J Comput Biol* 2005;12(10):1289–1306.
34. Pasek S, Bergeron A, Risler JL, Louis A, Ollivier E, Raffinot M. Identification of genomic features using microsyntenies of domains: domain teams. *Genome Research* 2005; 15(6):867–74.
35. Price MN, Arkin AP, Alm EJ. The life-cycle of operons. *PLoS Genetics* 2006;2(6):e96.
36. Rogozin IB, et al.: Connected gene neighborhoods in prokaryotic genomes. *Nucl Acids Res* 2002; 30(10):2212–2223.
37. Rogozin IB, Makarova KS, Wolf YI, Koonin EV. Computational approaches for the analysis of gene neighborhoods in prokaryotic genomes. *Brief Bioinform* 5(2):131–149.
38. Sankoff D. Genome rearrangement with gene families. *Bioinformatics* 1999;15(11): 909–917.
39. Sankoff D. Rearrangements and chromosomal evolution. *Curr Opin Genet Dev* 2003;13(6):583–587.
40. Schmidt T, Stoye J. Quadratic time algorithms for finding common intervals in two and more sequences. *Lecture Notes in Computer Science, Vol. 3109*. Springer; 2004. pp. 347–358.
41. Sears ER. Nullisomic-tetrasomic combinations in wheat. In: Riley R, Lewis KR, editors *Chromosome Manipulation and Plant Genetics*. Edinburg: Oliver and Boyd; 1966. pp. 29–45.
42. Semon M, Duret L. Evolutionary origin and maintenance of coexpressed gene clusters in mammals. *Mol Biol Evol* 2006;23(9):1715–1723.
43. She X, et al. A preliminary comparative analysis of primate segmental duplications shows elevated substitution rates and a great-ape expansion of intrachromosomal duplications. *Genome Research* 2006;16(5):576–583.
44. Smith TF, Waterman MS. Identification of common molecular subsequences. *J Mol Biol* 1981;147:195–197.
45. Snel B, Bork P, Hyunen MA. The identification of functional modules from the genomic association of genes. *Proc Nat Acad Sci USA* 2002;99:5890–5895.
46. Snel B, Lehmann G, Bork P, Hyunen MA. STRING: a web-server to retrieve and display the repeatedly occurring neighbourhood of a gene. *Nucl Acids Res* 2000;28(18):3442–3444.
47. St-Onge K, Bergeron A, Chauve C. Fast Identification of gene clusters in prokaryotic genomes. Texts in Algorithms, Vol 5. College Publications; 2005.

48. Tamames J. Evolution of gene order conservation in prokaryotes. *Genome Biol* 2001;2(6):RESEARCH0020.
49. Thao ML, Baumann L, Baumann P. Organization of the mitochondrial genomes of whiteflies, aphids, and psyllids (Hemiptera, Sternorrhyncha). *BMC Evol Biol* 2004;4:25.
50. Uno T, Yagiura M. Fast algorithms to enumerate all common intervals of two permutations. *Algorithmica* 2000;26(2):290–309.
51. Wolfe KH, Shields DC. Molecular evidence for an ancient duplication of the entire yeast genome. *Nature* 1997;387:708–713.
52. Xie G, Keyhani NO, Bonner CA, Jensen RA. Ancient origin of the tryptophan operon and the dynamics of evolutionary change. *Microbiol Mol Biol Rev* 2003;67(3):303–342.
53. Zheng Y, Anton BP, Robert RJ, Kasif S. Phylogenetic detection of conserved gene clusters in microbial genomes. *BMC Bioinformatics* 2005;6:243.

9

INTEGER LINEAR PROGRAMMING TECHNIQUES FOR DISCOVERING APPROXIMATE GENE CLUSTERS

SVEN RAHMANN

Bioinformatics for High-Throughput Technologies, Department of Computer Science 11, Technical University of Dortmund, Dortmund, Germany

GUNNAR W. KLAU

Mathematics in Life Sciences Group, Department of Mathematics and Computer Science, Free University Berlin, and DFG Research Center MATHEON *"Mathematics for Key Technologies," Berlin, Germany*

9.1 INTRODUCTION

The chapter by Bergeron et al. in this volume introduces the concept of conserved gene clusters among several related organisms and motivates their study. We do not repeat the contents here; instead we assume that the reader is familiar with that chapter. It presents four principal combinatorial models for gene clusters, along with their algorithms: common intervals ("exact" gene clusters) versus max-gap clusters (a particular kind of "approximate" gene clusters) in permutations (assuming the same gene content in each genome, disallowing gene duplications) versus sequences (or strings, where different gene contents and duplicated or removed genes are allowed). The authors note that defining a general gene cluster model beyond max-gap clusters in strings that captures biological reality well is not an easy task. Even if we

Bioinformatics Algorithms: Techniques and Applications, Edited by Ion I. Măndoiu and Alexander Zelikovsky

succeeded, discovering all gene clusters according to the model definition might be a computationally hard problem.

The present chapter takes a practical approach to these fundamental issues. Instead of arguing for or against one particular model, we present a class of models for approximate gene clusters that can be written as integer linear programs (ILPs) and include well-known variations, for example, common intervals, r-windows, and max-gap clusters or gene teams. While the ILP formulation does not necessarily lead to efficient algorithms, it provides a general framework to study different models and is competitive in practice for those cases where efficient algorithms are known. We show that it allows a nonheuristic study of large approximate clusters across several prokaryotic genomes.

Different ways to model gene clusters are discussed in the previous chapter; alternatives have also been surveyed by [6]. Difficulties in finding a universally accepted model include the following.

1. The problem has been attacked from two sides. One philosophy is to specify an algorithm and constructively define the algorithm's results as conserved gene clusters. The drawbacks of this approach are that it is unclear how such an algorithm maps to the biological reality, and that statistical analysis of the results becomes difficult. The other philosophy is to provide a formal specification of what constitutes a gene cluster (modeling step), and then design an algorithm that finds all clusters that satisfy the specification (solving step).
2. It is not easy to formally specify what we are looking for. Should we choose a narrow definition at the risk of missing biologically interesting gene sets, or a wide definition and browse through many biologically uninteresting sets?

We believe that it is preferable to use separate modeling and solving steps. This allows us to first focus on tuning the model for biological relevance, and only then worry about efficient algorithms. Therefore, we propose a framework for defining the *approximate gene cluster discovery problem* (AGCDP), as defined in Section 9.2.5, as well as many variants, as an integer linear program (ILP; see [11], for a general introduction). We shall not be concerned with efficiently solving the ILPs that we define; for computational experiments, we have used the commercial solver CPLEX [7] that works reasonably well in practice.

Our goal is to make as few restrictions in the model as possible. In particular, we assume that genes are represented by integers in such a way that paralogous and orthologous genes receive the same number. Genomes therefore are sequences of (unsigned) integers, not necessarily permutations. Homology detection is a delicate procedure, so we must assume that our representation contains errors. As a consequence, we need an error-tolerant formalization of the cluster concept.

For certain special cases of the ILP formulations, special-purpose algorithms exist. Using them would solve the corresponding problem more efficiently than using a general ILP solver. However, a general framework has the advantage that the objective functions and constraints can be easily modified without designing and implementing a new algorithm. The ILP formulation thus allows to test quickly whether a model makes sense from a biological point of view. Incidentally, it also performs well in practice on the known easy formulations. Existing definitions that can be modeled in our framework include common intervals in permutations [5], common intervals in arbitrary sequences [10], gene teams or max-gap clusters [1,8], and r-windows [3], for example.

This chapter is structured as follows. Section 9.2 provides our basic model of gene clusters; and Section 9.3 shows how to formulate the resulting discovery problem as an ILP. Several variations and extensions of the basic model are presented together with the necessary ILP modifications in Section 9.4, demonstrating the flexibility of the approach. We present computational results in Section 9.5, and a concluding discussion in Section 9.6. This chapter is based on and extends our WABI paper [9], where the ILP formulation was first published. Code and datasets for our computational experiments can be found at `http://ls11-www.cs.unidortmund.de/people/rahmann/research`.

9.2 BASIC PROBLEM SPECIFICATION

9.2.1 Genes and Gene Sets

Genes are represented by positive integers. If the same integer occurs more than once in the same genome, the genes are paralogs of each other. If the same integer occurs in different genomes, the genes may be orthologs or paralogs. There is also a *special gene* denoted by **0** that represents a different gene at every occurrence, and whose purpose is to model any gene for which no homolog exists in the dataset. The *gene universe* or *gene pool* is denoted by $\mathcal{U} := \{\mathbf{0}, 1, \ldots, N\}$ for some integer $N \geq 1$. We are looking for a subset of the gene pool without the special gene, that is, $X \subset \mathcal{U}$ with $\mathbf{0} \notin X$, called the *reference gene set*, whose genes occur in close proximity in each genome.

9.2.2 Genomes

A genome is modeled as a sequence of genes; we do not consider intergenic distances. We emphasize that a genome need not be a permutation of the gene pool; each gene (family) can occur zero times, once, or more than once in each genome. Restricting genomes to permutations allows remarkably efficient algorithms (e.g., [1,5]), but restricts the model too much for most biological applications.

To specify the basic problem, we assume that genomes consist of a single linear chromosome. The cases of several chromosomes and of a circular chromosome are discussed in Section 9.4.2. We consider m genomes; the length of the ith genome is n_i: $g^i = (g^i_1, \ldots, g^i_{n_i})$, $i = 1, \ldots, m$. In the basic model, we look for an approximate occurrence of X in every genome; in Section 9.4, we describe how to relax this objective.

9.2.3 Genomic Intervals and Their Gene Contents

A *linear interval* in a genome $g = (g_1, \ldots, g_n)$ is an index set J, which is either the empty interval $J = \emptyset$, or $J = \{j, j+1, \ldots, k\}$, written as $J = [j : k]$, with

$1 \leq j \leq k \leq n$. The *gene content* of $J = [j : k]$ in g is the set $G_J := \{g_j, \ldots, g_k\}$. Note that G_J is a set, and neither a sequence nor a multiset (a variant using multisets is discussed in Section 9.4). The *length* of $J = [j : k]$ is $|J| = k - j + 1$. The gene content of $J = \emptyset$ is $G_\emptyset = \emptyset$, and its length is $|J| = |\emptyset| = 0$.

9.2.4 Objective

The goal is to find a gene set $X \subset \mathcal{U}$ without the special gene ($0 \notin X$), and a linear interval J_i for each genome $i \in \{1, \ldots, m\}$, such that, informally, X is roughly equal to $G^i_{J_i}$ for all i, where $G^i_{J_i}$ denotes the gene content of J_i in the ith genome.

The agreement of X and the gene content $G^i_{J_i}$ is measured by the number $|G^i_{J_i} \setminus X|$ of genes additionally found in the interval although they are not part of X ("additional genes") and by the number $|X \setminus G^i_{J_i}|$ of X genes not found in the interval ("missing genes").

Since gene clusters of different sizes behave differently, it makes sense to parameterize the problem by specifying the size of the reference gene set $|X|$ by enforcing $|X| = D$ or $|X| \geq D$, for a fixed size D, or a range $D^- \leq |X| \leq D^+$, for a given interval $[D^-, D^+]$.

9.2.5 Finding an Optimal Gene Cluster

There are several ways to cast the above criteria into an optimization problem: We can let them contribute to the objective function, or select thresholds and use them as hard constraints, or both. We start with a formulation with as few hard constraints as possible. The first goal is to find an optimal gene cluster (in terms of the cost function defined below).

Basic Approximate Gene Cluster Discovery Problem (Basic AGCDP)

Given

- the gene pool $\mathcal{U} = \{0, 1, \ldots, N\}$,
- m genomes $(g^i)_{i=1,\ldots,m}$, where $g^i = (g^i_1, \ldots, g^i_{n_i})$,
- a size range $[D^-, D^+]$ for the reference gene set (possibly $D^- = D^+ =: D$),
- integer weights $w^- \geq 0$ and $w^+ \geq 0$ that specify the respective cost for each missed and additional gene in an interval,

find $X \subset \mathcal{U}$ with $0 \notin X$ and $D^- \leq |X| \leq D^+$, and a linear interval J_i for each genome in order to minimize

$$c := c(X, (J_i)) = \sum_{i=1}^{m} \left[w^- \cdot |X \setminus G^i_{J_i}| + w^+ \cdot |G^i_{J_i} \setminus X| \right].$$

In Section 9.3 we show how to write this problem as an ILP; the complexity is discussed in Section 9.6. In practice, distinct clusters X with the same optimal cost c^* or cost close to c^* may exist, and it is not sufficient to find a single arbitrary optimal one.

9.2.6 Finding All Interesting Gene Clusters

Once we know the optimal cost c^*, we introduce a constraint

$$c(X, (J_i)) \leq (1 + \gamma) \cdot c^*$$

with a tolerance parameter $\gamma > 0$, and then enumerate the feasible points (X, J, c) with this additional constraint. The set of feasible points may be redundant in the sense that several solutions lead to similar X, or to different intervals J_i, with the same gene content, etc. Therefore, we are mainly interested in sufficiently distinct X. After finding one reference gene set X^*, we can force a distinct solution by adding a new constraint $|X \Delta X^*| \geq T$ for a positive threshold T. Here Δ denotes symmetric set difference.

As noted above, the problem is formulated with specific bounds for the reference set size: $|X| \in [D^-, D^+]$ or $|X| = D$. This is useful if we already have an idea of the gene cluster size that we want to discover. Otherwise, we can solve the problem for several values of D. For technical reasons, further discussed below, it is not recommended to choose a large range $[D^-, D^+]$.

9.2.7 Discussion of the Modeling Approach

The formulation of the approximate gene cluster discovery problem as a minimization problem differs from the existing combinatorial formulations. They state that a gene set X, together with its locations (J_i), is an approximate gene cluster if certain conditions are satisfied, but do not take into account how close they are to being violated. This can lead to an exponentially large solution size in terms of the error tolerance parameter [2], producing many similar solutions. The approach taken here is different. We do not give a closed definition of the set of all approximate gene clusters, but only of the *best* clusters in terms of the objective function. In this way, we always obtain a solution unless we constrain the objective function. Also, we have formulated the problem for each gene set size $|X|$ separately to better cope with relative errors $c(X)/|X|$, which otherwise would prohibit a linear programming formulation (see the next section). Our way to obtain all "interesting" gene clusters is then iterative: to discover each new X, the constraint that X has to be sufficiently different from all previously discovered clusters is added to the problem formulation. This may not be the most elegant solution (especially if ties have to be broken arbitrarily), but in practice it effectively reduces output size (see Section 9.5.2). We will come back to this discussion in Section 9.6.

9.3 INTEGER LINEAR PROGRAMMING FORMULATION

To cast the basic AGCDP into an ILP framework, we need to represent the reference gene set X, the intervals J_i, and the gene contents $G^i_{J_i}$, as well as several auxiliary variables. Table 9.1 gives an overview.

9.3.1 Modeling the Reference Gene Set X

We model X as a binary vector $x = (x_0, \ldots, x_N) \in \{0, 1\}^{N+1}$, where we set $x_q = 1$ if and only if $q \in X$. We demand

$$x_0 = 0 \quad \text{and} \quad D^- \leq \sum_q x_q \leq D^+ .$$

9.3.2 Modeling the Intervals J_i

To model the selected interval J_i in genome i, we use binary indicator vectors $z^i = (z^i_j)_{j=1,\ldots,n_i}$. A linear interval in genome i is characterized by the fact that the ones in z^i occur consecutively. We enforce this property by introducing auxiliary binary vectors ${}^+z^i = ({}^+z^i_1, \ldots, {}^+z^i_{n_i})$ and ${}^-z^i = ({}^-z^i_1, \ldots, {}^-z^i_{n_i})$ that model increments and decrements, respectively, in z^i.

We thus set $z^i_1 = {}^+z^i_1 - {}^-z^i_1$, and for $2 \leq j \leq n_i$: $z^i_j = z^i_{j-1} + {}^+z^i_j - {}^-z^i_j$. We forbid a simultaneous increment and decrement at each position: ${}^+z^i_j + {}^-z^i_j \leq 1$ for all $j = 1, \ldots, n_i$; and we allow at most one increment and decrement: $\sum_{j=1}^{n_i} {}^+z^i_j \leq 1$ and $\sum_{j=1}^{n_i} {}^-z^i_j \leq 1$.

Recall that all the three vectors z^i, ${}^+z^i$, and ${}^-z^i$ are elements of $\{0, 1\}^{n_i}$. It is easy to see that each linear interval can be written in a unique way with this parameterization: For the empty interval, use zero vectors for ${}^+z$ and ${}^-z$. For the interval $[j : k]$ with $1 \leq j \leq k < n_i$, set ${}^+z^i_j = 1$ and ${}^-z^i_{k+1} = 1$. If $k = n_i$, then ${}^-z$ is the zero vector.

TABLE 9.1 Overview of Variables and Expressions Representing Objects and Quantities in the Basic ILP Formulation. All Variables are Binary

Main Objects	ILP Variables (Binary)
Reference gene set X	$x = (x_q)_{q=0,\ldots,N}$
Interval J_i in ith genome	$z^i = (z^i_j)_{j=1,\ldots,n_i}, i = 1, \ldots, m$
Gene content $G^i_{J_i}$ of J_i in g^i	$\chi^i = (\chi^i_q)_{q=0,\ldots,N}, i = 1, \ldots, m$
Auxiliary Objects	**ILP Variables (Binary)**
Increments in z^i	${}^+z^i = ({}^+z^i_j)_{j=1,\ldots,n_i}, i = 1, \ldots, m$
Decrements in z^i	${}^-z^i = ({}^-z^i_j)_{j=1,\ldots,n_i}, i = 1, \ldots, m$
Intersection $X \cap G^i_{J_i}$	$\iota^i = (\iota^i_q)_{q=0,\ldots,N}, i = 1, \ldots, m$
Target Quantities	**ILP Expression**
$\#\{$Missing genes in $g^i\}$: $\lvert X \setminus G^i_{J_i} \rvert$	$\sum_{q=0}^{N} x_q - \iota^i_q$
$\#\{$Additional genes in $g^i\}$: $\lvert G^i_{J_i} \setminus X \rvert$	$\sum_{q=0}^{N} \chi^i_q - \iota^i_q$

An Alternative We present an alternative way to model the intervals J_i on each genome $i \in [1, \ldots, m]$, which has been brought to our attention by Marcus Oswald (Heidelberg). This formulation works without the auxiliary vectors ${}^{+}z^i$ and ${}^{-}z^i$ and characterizes feasible interval vectors z^i by means of the following class of inequalities:

$$z^i_{j_1} - z^i_{j_2} + z^i_{j_3} \mp \cdots - z^i_{j_{2k}} + z^i_{j_{2k+1}} \leq 1 \tag{9.1}$$

for $1 \leq j_1 < j_2 < \cdots < j_{2k+1} \leq n_i$, where k is any natural number.

It can be shown that this class contains only the nontrivial facet-defining inequalities of the polyhedron P_{interval} that correspond to the convex hull of incidence vectors of feasible intervals in the linear case. Furthermore, violated inequalities of this class can be separated in linear time. In other words, due to a fundamental result in polyhedral theory [4], the following procedure leads to a polynomial time algorithm for optimizing a linear function over the set of feasible intervals: (i) Start with only the trivial inequalities and optimize, (ii) check whether the optimal, possibly fractional, solution *violates* an inequality 9.1, that is, whether an inequality of this class exists that cuts off the current solution but no feasible integral solution. This problem is referred to as the *separation problem* and can be solved in linear time for this special case. If the answer is negative, the current solution corresponds to an optimal interval; it must be integral because (9.1) and the trivial inequalities define the facets of P_{interval}. Otherwise, add the violated inequality and repeat step (ii). Of course, the additional variables and constraints in our formulation for the optimal gene cluster problem complicate the solution process.

9.3.3 Modeling the Intervals' Gene Contents $G^i_{J_i}$

The gene content $G^i_{J_i}$ in genome i is modeled by another indicator vector $\chi^i = (\chi^i_q)_{q=0,\ldots,N}$: If some position j is covered by the chosen interval J_i, the corresponding gene must be included in the gene content; thus $\chi^i_{g^i_j} \geq z^i_j$ for all $j = 1, \ldots, n_i$ (recall that g^i_j is constant). On the other hand, if some gene $q \in \{1, \ldots, N\}$ is not covered by J_i, it must not be included: $\chi^i_q \leq \sum_{j:g^i_j=q} z^i_j$ for all $q \in \{0, \ldots, N\}$. For each genome i, the above two families of inequalities map the selected intervals exactly to the selected gene contents. Note that if gene q never appears in genome i, the sum inequality yields $\chi^i_q = 0$, as desired.

9.3.4 Modeling the Target Function

To model the target function, we need the intersection between X and the selected gene content $G^i_{J_i}$ in the ith genome. We define another family of indicator vectors for $i = 1, \ldots, m$: $\iota^i = (\iota^i_q)_{q=0,\ldots,N}$ that we force to model the set intersection $X \cap G^i_{J_i}$ via the inequalities $\iota^i_q \leq x_q$, $\iota^i_q \leq \chi^i_q$, and $\iota^i_q \geq x_q + \chi^i_q - 1$. Then the terms of the target function are

$$|X \setminus G^i_{J_i}| = \sum_{q=0}^{N} (x_q - \iota^i_q); \qquad |G^i_{J_i} \setminus X| = \sum_{q=0}^{N} (\chi^i_q - \iota^i_q).$$

9.3.5 Basic ILP Formulation: Theorem

Figure 9.1 presents the whole basic formulation at a glance. After the above discussion, we may state: The ILP in Fig. 9.1 correctly represents the basic AGCDP from Section 9.2.5.

Given integers $N \geq 1, m \geq 2, (n_i)_{i=1,\ldots,m}$ with $n_i \geq 1, (g^i_j)_{i=1,\ldots,m;\, j=1,\ldots,n_i}$ from $\{\mathbf{0}, 1, \ldots, N\}, 1 \leq D^- \leq D^+ \leq N, w \geq 0$ and $w \geq 0$,

$$\min \sum_{i=1}^{m} \left[w^- \cdot \sum_{q=0}^{N} (x_q - \iota^i_q) + w^+ \cdot \sum_{q=0}^{M} (\chi^i_q - \iota^i_q) \right] \quad \text{subject to}$$

$$\begin{aligned}
x_q &\in \{0, 1\} && (q = 0, 1, \ldots, N) \\
x_0 &= 0 && \\
\textstyle\sum_{q=0}^{N} x_q &\geq D^- && \\
\textstyle\sum_{q=0}^{N} x_q &\leq D^+ &&
\end{aligned}$$

$$\begin{aligned}
z^i_j,\ z^i_j,\ z^i_j &\in \{0, 1\} && (i = 1, \ldots, m,\ ,\ j = 1, \ldots, n_i) \\
z^i_1 &= z^i_1 - z^i_1 && (i = 1, \ldots, m) \\
z^i_j &= z^i_{j-1} + z^i_j - z^i_j && (i = 1, \ldots, m,\ j = 2, \ldots, n_i) \\
z^i_j + z^i_j &\leq 1 && (i = 1, \ldots, m,\ j = 1, \ldots, n_i) \\
\textstyle\sum_{j=1}^{n_i} z^i_j &\leq 1 && (i = 1, \ldots, m) \\
\textstyle\sum_{j=1}^{n_i} z^i_j &\leq 1 && (i = 1, \ldots, m)
\end{aligned}$$

$$\begin{aligned}
\chi^i_q &\in \{0, 1\} && (i = 1, \ldots, m,\ q = 0, 1, \ldots, N) \\
\chi^i_{g^i_j} &\geq z^i_j && (i = 1, \ldots, m,\ j = 1, \ldots, n_i) \\
\chi^i_q &\leq \textstyle\sum_{j: g^i_j = q} z^i_j && (i = 1, \ldots, m,\ q = 0, 1, \ldots, N)
\end{aligned}$$

$$\begin{aligned}
\iota^i_q &\in \{0, 1\} && (i = 1, \ldots, m,\ q = 0, 1, \ldots, N) \\
\iota^i_q &\leq x_q && (i = 1, \ldots, m,\ q = 0, 1, \ldots, N) \\
\iota^i_q &\leq \chi^i_q && (i = 1, \ldots, m,\ q = 0, 1, \ldots, N) \\
\iota^i_q &\geq x_q + \chi^i_q - 1 && (i = 1, \ldots, m,\ q = 0, 1, \ldots, N)
\end{aligned}$$

FIGURE 9.1 ILP formulation for the basic AGCDP; see Table 9.1 for variables.

9.4 EXTENSIONS AND VARIATIONS

This section presents extensions and variations of the basic AGCDP, together with the necessary changes to the ILP formulation, and demonstrates the versatility of the ILP approach for gene cluster discovery.

9.4.1 Constraining and Varying the Objective Function

The basic ILP in Fig. 9.1 always has a feasible solution; an upper bound of the cost is easily obtained by taking any set of size D^- for X, empty intervals in all genomes, and paying the cost of $m \cdot D^- \cdot w^-$ for missing all genes in X. In many applications, it makes no sense to consider intervals in which more than a fraction δ^- of the reference genes X are missing or which contain more than a fraction δ^+ of additional genes. Therefore, we could restrict the search space by enforcing $\sum_{q=0}^{N} (x_q - \iota_q^i) \leq \lfloor \delta^- \cdot D^+ \rfloor$ and $\sum_{q=0}^{N} (\chi_q^i - \iota_q^i) \leq \lfloor \delta^+ \cdot D^+ \rfloor$. This may, of course, lead to an empty feasible set.

Instead of paying separately for missed and additional genes, we may argue that we should view occurrences of both errors as substitutions to the maximum possible extent. Assuming equal weights $w^- = w^+ = 1$ leads to a cost contribution of $\max \{|X \setminus G_{J_i}^i|, |G_{J_i}^i \setminus X|\}$ instead of the sum for the ith genome; see also [2]. More generally, we may replace the original objective function by

$$\min \sum_{i=1}^{m} \max \left\{ w^- \cdot \sum_{q=0}^{N} (x_q - \iota_q^i),\ w^+ \cdot \sum_{q=0}^{M} (\chi_q^i - \iota_q^i) \right\}$$

by introducing new variables $c_i^- := w^- \cdot \sum_{q=0}^{N} (x_q - \iota_q^i)$ and $c_i^+ := w^+ \cdot \sum_{q=0}^{N} (\chi_q^i - \iota_q^i)$. We let $c_i = \max \{c_i^-, c_i^+\}$ by introducing inequalities $c_i \geq c_i^-$ and $c_i \geq c_i^+$ for $i = 1, \ldots, m$ and writing the objective function as

$$\min \sum_{i=1}^{m} c_i,$$

which fixes c_i at the maximum of c_i^- and c_i^+, and not at a larger value.

9.4.2 A Single Circular Chromosome or Multiple Linear Chromosomes

Bacterial genomes usually consist of a single circular chromosome, that is, any circular permutation of $g = (g_1, \ldots, g_n)$ in fact represents the same genome, and the start and end points are arbitrary. Therefore, we need to allow intervals that "wrap around." Extending the definition of a linear interval from Section 9.2, we say that an *interval* is either a linear interval or a wrapping interval.

A *wrapping interval* in $g = (g_1, \ldots, g_n)$ is a nonempty index set $J := [j \mid k] := \{j, j+1, \ldots, n, 1, \ldots, k\}$, with $1 \leq j, k \leq n$ and $j > k + 1$.

The *gene content* of a wrapping interval is $G_J \equiv G_{[j|k]} := \{g_j, \ldots, g_n, g_1, \ldots, g_k\}$, and its *length* is $|J| = n - j + 1 + k$. We specifically disallow $j = k + 1$ because this would induce the whole genome, for which we already have the linear interval $[1 : n]$.

As an example, in a genome of length 3, there are seven linear intervals: ($\emptyset$, $[1 : 1]$, $[2 : 2]$, $[3 : 3]$, $[1 : 2]$, $[2 : 3]$, $[1 : 3]$), and a single wrapping interval: $[3 \mid 1]$.

For a wrapping interval in g^i, the ones in the indicator vector z^i occur in two distinct blocks with the first block starting at position $j = 1$, and the second block ending at position n_i. Therefore, there are two points j with ${}^+z^i_j = 1$, but only if $j = 1$ is one of them. To allow arbitrary intervals (empty, linear, or wrapping), all we need to do is to change the sum constraint for ${}^+z^i$ from Fig. 9.1 into $\sum_{j=2}^{n_i} {}^+z^i_j \leq 1$ $(i = 1, \ldots, m)$.

We may also allow multiple linear chromosomes: we extend the gene universe by another special number -1 and concatenate the chromosomes of the ith genome into a single vector g^i as before, representing chromosome borders by -1. We constrain the interval selection variables z^i_j wherever $g^i_j = -1$ to be $z^i_j = 0$; this ensures that the interval J_i does not extend over a chromosome border.

9.4.3 Genome Selection (Quorum Parameter)

So far we have requested that X occurs in every input genome, or incurred a possibly severe cost of at most $w^- \cdot |X|$ if no gene of X appears in the genome. When we look for approximate gene clusters in a large set of genomes, and only require that the cluster occurs in some of them, it is desirable to relax this penalty.

We extend the formulation with an index set $I \subset \{1, \ldots, m\}$, and refer to the genomes indexed by I as the *selected genomes*; these are treated as before, that is, missing and additional genes in the selected intervals are penalized by w^- and w^+, respectively. For nonselected genomes, we force that J_i is the empty interval, but we only incur a flat penalty $\rho \geq 0$ that should be chosen substantially smaller than $w^- \cdot D^-$. We also specify a *quorum*, that is, a minimal number $\mu \leq m$ of genomes to be selected, by demanding $|I| \geq \mu$. The cost function becomes

$$c := c(X, I, (J_i)) = \sum_{i \in I} \left[w^- \cdot |X \setminus G^i_{J_i}| + w^+ \cdot |G^i_{J_i} \setminus X| \right] + (m - |I|) \cdot \rho.$$

For the ILP, we model I as another binary vector $y = (y_1, \ldots, y_m) \in \{0, 1\}^m$ with $y_i = 1$ if and only if $i \in I$. We have the constraint $\sum_{i=1}^m y_i \geq \mu$. To enforce $J_i = \emptyset$ for $i \notin I$, we use the inequalities $z^i_j \leq y_i$ for all $i = 1, \ldots, m$, $j = 1, \ldots, n_i$.

It remains to properly rewrite the target function. The obvious approach to

$$\min \sum_{i=1}^{m} \left[y_i \cdot \left(w^- \cdot \sum_{q=0}^{N} (x_q - \iota^i_q) + w^+ \cdot \sum_{q=0}^{M} (\chi^i_q - \iota^i_q) \right) + (1 - y_i) \cdot \rho \right]$$

does not work because this function is nonlinear in the variables because of the products $y_i \cdot x_q$.

However, a simple solution is available when X is constrained to be of fixed size $D^- = D^+ = D$: If $y_i = 0$, then z^i, χ^i, and ι^i are the zero vector and under the old cost function, we would pay $D \cdot w^-$. Now we only pay ρ; therefore we can write the objective function as

$$\min \quad \sum_{i=1}^{m} \left[w^- \cdot \sum_{q=0}^{N} (x_q - \iota_q^i) + w^+ \cdot \sum_{q=0}^{M} (\chi_q^i - \iota_q^i) + (1 - y_i) \cdot (\rho - Dw^-) \right].$$

If $D^- < D^+$, the above approach does not work, unless we change the flat penalty from ρ into $\rho + |X| - D^-$, which may put larger X at a disadvantage. In that case we can use the same formulation as above with D replaced by D^-.

For the general case of $D^- < D^+$ and a true flat penalty ρ, we can use a so-called big-M approach: We write the objective function as

$$c = \rho \cdot \sum_{i=1}^{m} (1 - y_i) + \sum_{i=1}^{m} L_i,$$

where the L_i are new auxiliary variables, which we will force to take values

$$L_i = \begin{cases} \sum_{q=0}^{N} \left(w^- \cdot (x_q - \iota_q^i) + w^+ \cdot (\chi_q^i - \iota_q^i) \right) =: \ell_i & \text{if } y_i = 1, \\ 0 & \text{if } y_i = 0. \end{cases}$$

We achieve this via inequalities $L_i \geq 0$ and $L_i \geq \ell_i - M \cdot (1 - y_i)$ for all $i = 1, \ldots, m$ and a constant M larger than any possible value of ℓ_i. If $y_i = 1$, the inequality becomes $L_i \geq \ell_i$; and since the objective function c is to be minimized, this will lead to $L_i = \ell_i$. If $y_i = 0$, it becomes $L_i \geq -M'$ for some $M' \geq 0$ and is dominated by the nonnegativity constraint $L_i \geq 0$. Often, however, such a big-M approach causes problems for the ILP solver, as it easily leads to weak LP relaxations [11].

9.4.4 Gene Multisets

Instead of modeling X and the neighborhoods G_j^i as gene sets, we may model them as *multisets* and interpret the objective function for multisets, for example, $|[1, 3, 3] \setminus [1, 2, 3]| = |[3]| = 1$ and $|[1, 2, 3] \setminus [1, 3, 3]| = |[2]| = 1$, whereas previously $|\{1, 3, 3\} \setminus \{1, 2, 3\}| = |\emptyset| = 0$ and $|\{1, 2, 3\} \setminus \{1, 3, 3\}| = |\{2\}| = 1$. Several changes need to be made as follows.

- All of x, χ^i, and ι^i become nonnegative integer vectors.
- The gene contents χ^i are defined as multiplicities: $\chi_q^i = \sum_{j:g_j^i = q} z_j^i$ for all $q = 0, \ldots, N$, $i = 1, \ldots, m$.
- The intersection vectors $\iota^i = (\iota_q^i)$ are replaced by minima: $\iota_q^i := \min\{x_q, \chi_q^i\}$. This is achieved by inequalities $\iota_q^i \leq x_q$ and $\iota_q^i \leq \chi_q^i$ for all i and q. The structure

of the target function ensures that indeed the minimum of x_q and χ_q^i and not a smaller value will be taken.

9.4.5 Using a Reference Genome

Even in the basic AGCDP, there is a lot of freedom because the reference gene set X need not occur exactly in any of the genomes. In some cases, however, a reference genome may be known and available. This makes the problem much easier, and an ILP formulation would not be required, and the solver could be easily replaced by simpler specialized algorithms. It is reassuring, however, that a reference genome can be easily integrated into the formulation: Without loss of generality, let g^1 be the reference genome. We force $x_q = \chi_q^1 = \iota_q^1$ for $q = 0, \ldots, N$, and possibly $y_1 = 1$, if we are using genome selection.

9.4.6 Modeling Common Intervals, Max-Gap Clusters, and *r*-Windows

By specifying appropriate target functions and constraints, the ILP approach can be used to model existing definitions of gene clusters. For those mentioned here, efficient algorithms exist, and we certainly cannot beat them. It is still convenient that we can treat them in the ILP framework, too.

To model exact common intervals in the sense of [10], we restrict the cost function to take the value zero (i.e., we allow no additional and no missing genes), and set $w^- = w^+ = 1$. Additionally, we can apply genome selection with $\rho = 0$ and a reasonably large value for μ. From the result, we only use the reference set X and disregard the intervals.

The specification of max-gap clusters or gene teams [1] is a generalization of common intervals; and demands that between adjacent genes from the reference set X, there are at most δ genes not from X. For $\delta = 0$, we obtain again common intervals. For $\delta > 0$, the max-gap condition states that in each subinterval of J_i of length $\delta + 1$, we need at least one X-gene. For each $i = 1, \ldots, m$ and each $j = 1, \ldots, n_i - \delta$ we have that if $z_j^i + \cdots + z_{j+\delta}^i = \delta + 1$, then $\iota_{g_j}^i + \iota_{g_{j+1}}^i + \cdots + \iota_{g_{j+\delta}}^i \geq 1$ must hold. Each implication can be written as an inequality

$$\iota_{g_{j+1}}^i + \cdots + \iota_{g_{j+\delta}}^i \geq z_j^i + \cdots + z_{j+\delta}^i - (\delta + 1) + 1 \quad (i = 1, \ldots, m;\ j = 1, \ldots, n_i - \delta).$$

We use $w^- = 1$ and $w^+ = 0$ and constrain the target function to zero. To find maximal max-gap clusters, that is, those not contained in a larger one, we enumerate all max-gap clusters of each size D and subsequently filter out those contained in larger ones.

An r-window cluster for two genomes is defined as a pair of intervals of length r that share at least D genes [3]. To find them, we demand $|X| = D$, set $w^- = 1$, $w^+ = 0$, constrain the target function to zero, and demand that $\sum_{j=1}^{n_i} z_j^i = r$ for each $i = 1, \ldots, m$.

9.5 COMPUTATIONAL RESULTS

We have implemented a C++ software tool that reads in a set of genomes, solves one of the integer linear programming formulations presented in Sections 9.3 and 9.4 using the CPLEX optimization library [7], and outputs the list of optimal and close to optimal gene clusters. All experiments were performed on an AMD 2.2 GHz Opteron 64 bit processor with 8 GB of main memory using CPLEX 9.03.

9.5.1 Hidden Clusters in Artificial Data

We generate artificial problem instances for benchmarking as follows: We randomly generate six genomes of roughly 1000 genes each ($N = 2000$) with 5% of **0**-genes. For each $D \in \{5, 10, 15, 20, 25\}$, we generate a cluster and hide a perturbed permutation of it in five randomly selected genomes, taking care that the different clusters do not overlap.

Using $w^- = 2$, $w^+ = 1$ and the appropriate value of D, we solve the ILP first with genome selection, setting $\rho = 2D/5$. We retrieve all the five clusters in 29 min, 45 min, 8 min, 113 s, and 14 s, respectively.

Without genome selection, running times are much faster, but we can run into problems because of the high penalty for the genome in which the cluster is missing: We retrieve the clusters of sizes 5, 10, 15, and 25 in 17 min, 7 min, 163 s, and 4 s, respectively. For $D = 20$, we obtain a different cluster than the hidden one that obtains a better target function value without genome selection.

While the running times vary with each instance, the times shown here are representative. This experiment indicates the importance, but also the high complexity of genome selection.

9.5.2 Comparison of Two Organisms

The genomes of *C. glutamicum* and *M. tuberculosis* consist of 3057 and 3991 annotated genes, respectively. The annotated gene set is available at `http://ls11-www.cs.unidortmund.de/people/rahmann/research`. We compute the optimal objective function value $c^*(D)$ for each cluster size $D \in [5,500]$ for the basic formulation with $w^- = w^+ = 1$ (total CPU time: almost 25 days, on average 1:15 h per instance). Figure 9.2 shows the running time per instance as well as the optimal normalized costs $c^*(D)/D$. Local minima correspond to large approximate clusters with comparatively few errors. As Fig. 9.3 illustrates for $D = 51$, the ILP formulation discovers clusters that cannot be detected by any method that does not consider approximate clusters. The largest exact cluster has size 11.

In a next step, we enumerate all fundamentally different close-to-optimal solutions for the local minima of Fig. 9.2, using the approach described in Section 9.3. We set the suboptimality parameter γ to 0.2. Interestingly, there are not too many different clusters with solution values within 20% of the optimum, as shown in Table 9.2. The solution lists might be an interesting starting point for further biological investigations. Figure 9.4 shows the output of our software for $D = 61$.

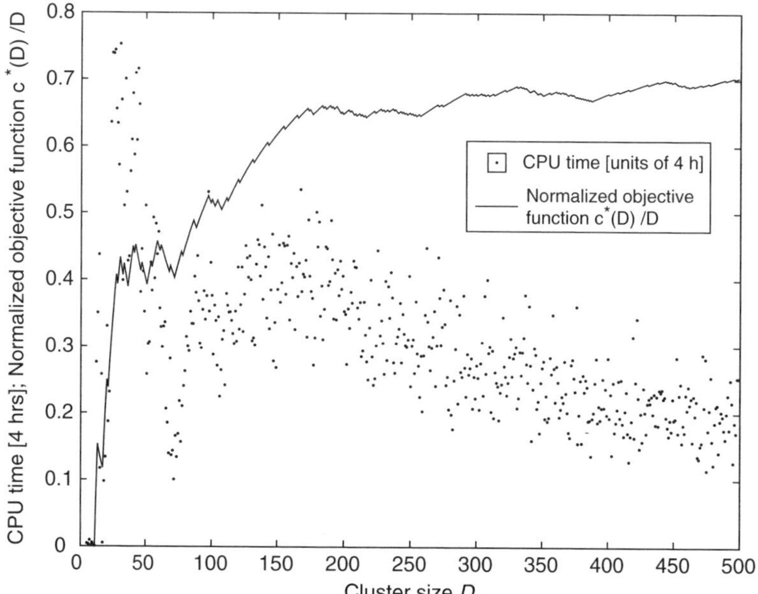

FIGURE 9.2 Comparison of *C. glutamicum* and *M. tuberculosis*: For each cluster size $D \in [5,500]$, the running time in units of 4 h, and the normalized optimal value of the objective function is shown. Note the local minima in the objective function, for example, at $D = 51$. The apparent correlation between objective function and running time indicates that good approximate clusters are easier to compute than bad clusters.

9.5.3 A 28-Cluster in a 20-Genome Set

We attempt to find a large approximate gene cluster in several genomes. We thank Thomas Schmidt (Bielefeld) for providing a dataset of the following twenty bacterial genomes (number of genes given in brackets): *B. longum* (1727), *B. subtilis* (4103), *C. diphtheriae* (2272), *C. efficiens* (2942), *C. glutamicum* (3057), *E. coli* K12 (4288), *L. lactis* (2266), *L. xyli* (2030), *M. avium* (4350), *M. leprae* (1605), *M. tuberculosis* (3991), *N. farcinica* (5683), *P. acnes* (2297), *P. aeruginosa* (5566), *P. putida* (5350), *S. avermitilis* (7575), *S. coelicolor* (7768), *S. thermophilum* (3337), *T. whipplei* (808), and *W. succinogenes* (2044).

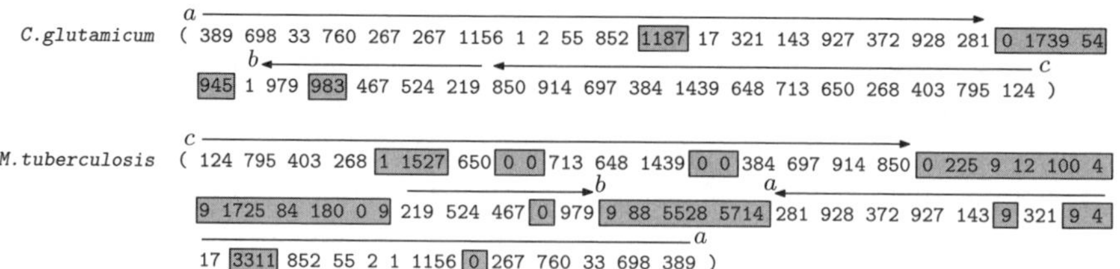

FIGURE 9.3 Visualization of an interesting optimal cluster in *C. glutamicum* and *M. tuberculosis* ($D = 51$). Differing genes are marked in gray. Three conserved regions, *a*, *b*, and *c* occur in the cluster.

TABLE 9.2 Cluster Sizes D and (Sub-)Optimal Solution Values c of Fundamentally Different Solutions with $c \leq 1.2 \cdot c^*$, where c^* is the Corresponding Optimal Value (Marked in Bold Face)

D	c
16	**2**
21	**5**
28	**11**, 12, 12, 12, 13, 13, 13, 13, 13, 13, 13
32	**13**, **13**, **13**, 15, 15, 15, 15
36	**14**
41	**18**, 19, 20, 21, 21, 21
46	**19**, 21
51	**20**, 24
55	**23**
61	**27**, 29, 32
68	**28**
72	**29**
78	**34**, 39
88	**42**, 47
107	**54**, 58

We perform the first analysis step with a fixed reference genome as described in Section 9.4.5, since we can solve the ILP much faster for this variant of the problem: it takes less than 5 min to find an optimal solution. The solution contains four almost empty intervals, namely, of *C. diphtheriae*, *C. efficiens*, *C. glutamicum*, and *N. farcinica*, which we remove from the dataset. For the remaining 16 genomes we use the standard formulation (without reference genome and without genome selection) using $w^- = w^+ = 1$ and $|X| \in [28,50]$. After 11 h of CPU time, we find an optimal approximate gene cluster visualized in Fig. 9.5.

So far we have not made attempts to interpret the cluster from a biological point of view, but we note that the cluster occurs exactly in two genomes: *B. subtilis* and *S. avermitilis*.

9.6 DISCUSSION

The modeling framework for approximate gene clusters discussed in this chapter possesses unique features that are worth discussing in detail.

9.6.1 Objective Function Versus Constraints

In contrast to purely combinatorial definitions, the approach discussed here does not necessarily characterize the set of desired clusters by hard constraints, but can also assign a cost value (the objective function) to each cluster candidate. In fact, we can go to both extremes: in Section 9.4.6, we showed that by using particular weight choices and hard constraints on the objective function and the other quantities, several

```
solution list for instance svndata/CgMt.csd
options:
D- = 61
D+ = 61
w = 1
circular: 0
fixed reference genome: 0
genome selection: 0
plus/minus: 1
gamma = 0.2
@ 4793.47s: { 1 4 9 22 14 17 12 46 1452 124 84 15 88 37 180 219 155 321 143 927 372 928
281 1739 54 945 979 983 467 524 850 914 697 384 1439 648 713 650 268 403 795 221 461 709 888
407 1193 921 458 457 307 229 100 225 1725 1527 2219 297 4047 5528 5714 }
|X| = 61
obj. function value c = 27
  C.glutamicum
  [1561..1603] (43)
  ( 17 321 143 927 372 928 281 0 1739 54 945 1 979 983 467 524 219 850 914 697 384 1439 648
    713 650 268 403 795 124 221 46 461 709 0 888 407 1193 921 458 457 307 155 229 )
  + { 0 },  - { 4 9 12 14 15 22 37 84 88 100 180 225 297 1452 1527 1725 2219 4047 5528 5714 }
  M.tuberculosis
  [1401..1476] (76)
  ( 229 155 307 2219 457 458 921 9 9 1193 407 888 709 461 14 37 297 9 4047 0 9 9 1452 46 15
    22 15 124 795 403 268 1 1527 650 0 0 713 648 1439 0 0 384 697 914 850 0 225 9 12 100 4 9
    1725 84 180 0 9 219 524 467 0 979 9 88 5528 5714 281 928 372 927 143 9 321 9 4 17 )
  + { 0 },  - { 54 221 945 983 1739 }

@ 24638.6s: { 2 1 4 9 55 33 17 12 13 16 124 60 84 88 180 1187 219 1115 5899 2248 2247
1315 1519 5898 389 698 760 267 1156 852 321 143 927 372 928 281 1739 54 945 979 983 467 524
850 914 697 384 1439 648 713 650 268 403 795 100 225 1725 1527 5528 5714 3311 }
|X| = 61
obj. function value c = 29
  C.glutamicum
  [1532..1589] (58)
  ( 16 5899 2248 2247 60 1315 0 0 0 0 0 0 2 0 1519 1115 5898 389 698 33 760 267 267 1156 1 2
    55 852 1187 17 321 143 927 372 928 281 0 1739 54 945 1 979 983 467 524 219 850 914 697
    384 1439 648 713 650 268 403 795 124 )
  + { 0 },  - { 4 9 12 13 84 88 100 180 225 1527 1725 3311 5528 5714 }
  M.tuberculosis
  [1428..1491] (64)
  ( 124 795 403 268 1 1527 650 0 0 713 648 1439 0 0 384 697 914 850 0 225 9 12 100 4 9 1725 84
    180 0 9 219 524 467 0 979 9 88 5528 5714 281 928 372 927 143 9 321 9 4 17 3311 852 55 2 1
    1156 0 267 760 33 698 389 13 9 60 )
  + { 0 },  - { 16 54 945 983 1115 1187 1315 1519 1739 2247 2248 5898 5899 }

@ 47537.5s: { 51 1 8 48 151 9 61 50 53 12 131 34 122 38 40 23 384 89 958 620 642 730 503
1119 138 3613 500 816 1207 2294 1347 1024 1222 721 1616 5888 5887 100 781 1065 1064 450 990
559 158 441 623 725 1030 2847 3563 4507 2691 3562 2213 2693 478 2692 2015 3561 3560 }
|X| = 61
obj. function value c = 32
  C.glutamicum
  [2096..2144] (49)
  ( 38 958 620 642 730 503 1119 53 138 151 53 1 53 53 48 3613 500 816 0 1207 2294 1347 1024 122
    1 1222 8 1 1 721 1616 5888 131 0 5887 100 51 34 40 8 781 1065 1064 450 0 990 559 158 441 )
  + { 0 },  - { 9 12 23 50 61 89 384 478 623 725 1030 2015 2213 2691 2692 2693 2847 3560 3561
                3562 3563 4507 }
  M.tuberculosis
  [2176..2237] (62)
  ( 3563 38 958 620 642 730 503 1119 53 138 151 53 1 53 53 4507 0 0 23 9 48 8 500 816 50 89
    1207 1347 2691 3562 122 1 1222 8 2847 721 1616 2213 1 100 2693 478 725 2692 12 34 2015 8
    384 623 450 1064 1065 781 3561 1030 990 559 158 61 3560 441 )
  + { 0 },  - { 40 51 131 1024 2294 3613 5887 5888 }
```

FIGURE 9.4 Exemplary output of our freely available software: Solution list for $D = 61$, containing all fundamentally different optimal and close-to-optimal solutions.

existing combinatorial models can be reproduced. On the other hand, it is known that the size of the feasible set (gene sets X and their interval locations J_i) in more general combinatorial formulations [2] can be exponential in the error tolerance parameter; yet it can also be empty. Therefore, the value of the objective function (as opposed to

```
approx. cluster  X, |X| = 28: { 76 631 584 541 615 540 597 602 539 538 673 596 537 583 536 319 535 534 533 582 686 595 532 543 439
                                818 531 640 }

B.longum         ( 631 584 541 615 540 597 602 539 538 673 596 ---  ---  ---- ---  ---- ---  537 583 536 319 - 535 534 533 582 686
B.subtilis       ( 631 584 541 615 540 597 602 539 538 673 596 ---  ---  ---- ---  ---- ---  537 583 536 319 - 535 534 533 582 686
E.coli K12       ( 631 584 541 615 540 597 602 539 538 673 596 ---  ---  ---- ---  ---- ---  537 583 536 319 - 535 534 533 582 686
L.lactis         ( 631 584 541 615 540 597 602 539 538 673 596 ---  ---  ---- ---  ---- ---  537 583 536 319 0 535 534 533 582 686
L.xyli           ( 631 584 541 615 540 597 602 539 538 673 596 ---  ---  ---- ---  ---- ---  537 583 536 --- - 535 534 533 582 686
M.avium          ( 631 584 541 615 540 597 602 539 538 673 596 780  202  2084 943  2084 216  537 583 536 319 - 535 534 533 582 686
M.leprae         ( 631 584 541 615 540 597 602 539 538 673 596 ---  ---  ---- ---  ---- ---  537 583 536 319 - 535 534 533 582 686
M.tuberculosis   ( 631 584 541 615 540 597 602 539 538 673 596 780  ---  ---- 943  2084 ---  537 583 536 319 - 535 534 533 582 686
P.acnes          ( 631 584 541 615 540 597 602 539 538 673 596 ---  ---  ---- ---  ---- ---  537 583 536 319 - 535 534 533 582 686
P.aeruginosa     ( 631 584 541 615 540 597 602 539 538 673 596 ---  ---  ---- ---  ---- ---  537 583 536 319 - 535 534 533 582 686
P.putida         ( 631 584 541 615 540 597 602 539 538 673 596 ---  ---  ---- ---  ---- ---  537 583 536 319 - 535 534 533 582 686
S.avermitilis    ( 631 584 541 615 540 597 602 539 538 673 596 ---  ---  ---- ---  ---- ---  537 583 536 319 - 535 534 533 582 686
S.coelicolor     ( 631 584 541 615 540 597 602 539 538 673 596 ---  ---  ---- ---  ---- ---  537 583 536 319 - 535 534 533 582 686
S.thermophilum   ( 631 584 541 615 540 597 602 539 538 673 596 ---  ---  ---- ---  ---- ---  537 583 536 319 - 535 534 533 582 686
T.whipplei       ( 631 584 541 615 540 597 602 539 538 673 596 ---  ---  ---- ---  ---- ---  537 583 536 --- - 535 534 533 582 686
W.succinogenes   ( --- 584 541 615 540 597 602 539 538 --- 596 ---  ---  ---- ---  ---- ---  537 583 536 --- - 535 534 533 582 ---

B.longum           595 ---  ---  --  ---  - - - 532 543 ---  --  --  --  439 818 531 ---  )
B.subtilis         595 ---  ---  --  ---  - - - 532 543 ---  --  --  76  439 818 531 640  )
E.coli K12         595 ---  ---  --  ---  - - - 532 --- ---  --  --  --  --  818 531 640  )
L.lactis           595 ---  ---  --  ---  - - - 532 543 1759 50  89  50  439 818 531 640  )
L.xyli             595 ---  ---  --  ---  - - - 532 543 ---  --  --  76  439 818 531 640  )
M.avium            595 ---  ---  --  ---  - - - --- --- ---  --  --  --  --- --- --- ---  )
M.leprae           595 2709 3573 --  ---  - - - 532 543 ---  --  --  76  --- --- --- ---  )
M.tuberculosis     595 ---  ---  --  ---  - - - --- --- ---  --  --  --  --- --- --- ---  )
P.acnes            595 0    0    43  176  0 1 0 532 543 ---  --  --  76  439 818 531 640  )
P.aeruginosa       595 ---  ---  --  ---  - - - 532 --- ---  --  --  --  --- 818 531 640  )
P.putida           595 ---  ---  --  ---  - - - 532 --- ---  --  --  --  --- 818 531 640  )
S.avermitilis      595 ---  ---  --  ---  - - - 532 543 ---  --  --  76  439 818 531 640  )
S.coelicolor       595 ---  ---  --  ---  - - - 532 543 ---  --  --  76  439 818 531 640  )
S.thermophilum     595 ---  ---  --  ---  - - - 532 543 0    --  --  --  439 818 531 640  )
T.whipplei         595 ---  ---  --  ---  - - - 532 543 185  --  --  --  439 818 531 640  )
W.succinogenes     595 ---  ---  --  ---  - - - 532 --- ---  --  --  76  439 --- 531 640  )
```

FIGURE 9.5 Manually produced alignment of optimal approximative cluster found in 16 bacterial genomes. The intervals found in *E. coli K12*, *L. lactis*, *L. xyli*, *M. avium*, *M. tuberculosis*, *P. aeruginosa*, *P. putida*, and *T. whipplei* have been reversed for the purpose of visualization.

only the fact that it stays below a certain threshold) holds useful information. In the formulation of Sections 9.2.5 and 9.2.6, we have therefore taken the approach to first find the *best* cluster(s) and then enumerate suboptimal ones that are *fundamentally different* from the relatively better ones. This reduces output size without actually missing interesting gene clusters. The best option in practice may well be to minimize the objective function under a hard constraint on its value: if the feasible set is empty, there are no gene clusters of interest.

9.6.2 Complexity Considerations

The complexity of the basic model comes from the fact that we use a reference set X of genes that need not occur exactly in any genome. While we have not attempted to formally prove the corresponding decision problem NP-hard, the difficulties encountered by the ILP solver, and the similarity to the median string problem, provide some evidence. The problem becomes even harder (empirically in terms of CPU time) if genome selection is allowed. The situation changes if we require that X occurs in at least one genome without errors. Then a naive polynomial-time algorithm works as follows:

> Tentatively set X to the gene set of each interval in each genome. For each genome g, except the one where X is taken from, compare X to the character set of each interval J in g, compute the cost according to the number of missing

and additional genes, and pick the interval J_g^* in g with minimum cost c_g^*. Now genome selection can be easily applied: simply remove as many costly genomes as possible without violating the quorum parameter. The total cost of X (without genome selection) is $c(X) = \sum_g c_g^*$. Either report the overall best set X, or report each X, where $c(X)$ remains below a given threshold (of course, this "algorithm" can be drastically optimized for efficiency).

This also shows that the hard part of the general model is discovering the gene sets X; their (optimal) locations within each genome are easy to find.

9.6.3 Perspectives

The ILP formulations open a new perspective to the field of approximate gene cluster discovery, and are usable in practice. The general ILP framework allows to check different gene cluster models for biological relevance before designing optimized algorithms, and to discover optimal medium-sized to large approximate clusters that contain no smaller exact ones if they exist and if the ILP solver can handle the problem.

We believe that the formulations and the solver can be fine-tuned to solve the same instances rather faster, even if the basic AGCDP with or without genome selection is indeed NP-hard. We are experimenting with alternative methods for genome selection and with the alternative formulation of the consecutive-ones property of the interval indicators z_j^i mentioned in Section 9.3.2. Experiments with a branch-and-cut approach based on separating these inequalities have shown that it is currently inferior to the implementation that relies on the formulation with the auxiliary variables. The reasons for this behavior are worth investigating; we hope that we can improve the running time of the method by incorporating knowledge about the polyhedral structure.

A desideratum for the future is to avoid solving the problem for each gene set size D separately. So far this is convenient because it allows simplifications in some formulations, but it seems to slow down the solver drastically. Yet, a fixed $|X| = D$ is also necessary because optimal objective function values for different $|X|$ do not compare well: even "good" clusters of size 30 might have higher cost than "bad" clusters of size 5. Normalizing the cost function by $|X|$ seems a promising idea, as this corresponds to a notion of relative error. Fractional programming techniques could be explored towards this end.

An open problem is statistics (significance computations) for gene clusters from the ILP formulations with different objective functions in the spirit of [3] to better judge whether an observed gene cluster is in fact an interesting discovery.

Naturally, we do not expect a consensus on the "correct" way to model approximate gene clusters soon; however, the methods presented in this chapter are potentially general enough to cover most of the interesting models and provide a good basis to start from while developing efficient specialized algorithms for particular submodels.

ACKNOWLEDGMENTS

We thank Thomas Schmidt for providing datasets, and Jens Stoye, Yoan Diekmann, Julia Mixtacki, and Marcus Oswald for helpful discussions.

REFERENCES

1. Bergeron A, Corteel S, Raffinot M. The algorithmic of gene teams. *Workshop on Algorithms in Bioinformatics (WABI)*, Vol. 2452 of *LNCS*; 2002. pp. 464–476.
2. Chauve C, Diekmann Y, Heber S, Mixtacki J, Rahmann S, Stoye J. On common intervals with errors. Technical Report 2006-02, Universität Bielefeld: Abteilung Informationstechnik, Technische Fakultät; 2006. ISSN 0946–7831.
3. Durand D, Sankoff D. Tests for gene clustering. *J Comput Biol* 2003;10(3-4):453–482.
4. Grötschel M, Lovász L, Schrijver A. The ellipsoid method and its consequences in combinatorial optimization. *Combinatorica* 1981;1:169–197.
5. Heber S, Stoye J. Algorithms for finding gene clusters. In: Gascuel O, Moret B, editors. *Proceedings of the First International Workshop on Algorithms in Bioinformatics, WABI 01, Vol. 2149 of Lecture Notes in Computer Science*. Berlin: Springer Verlag; 2001. pp. 252–263.
6. Hoberman R, Durand D. The incompatible desiderata of gene cluster properties. In: McLysaght A, Huson DH, editors. *Comparative Genomics: RECOMB 2005 International Workshop, Vol. 3678 of LNCS*; 2005. pp. 73–87.
7. ILOG, Inc. CPLEX. `http://www.ilog.com/products/cplex`, 1987–2006.
8. Li Q, Lee BTK, Zhang L. Genome-scale analysis of positional clustering of mouse testis-specific genes. *BMC Genomics* 2005;6(1):7.
9. Rahmann S, Klau GW. Integer linear programs for discovering approximate gene clusters. In: Bucher P, Moret B, editors. *Proceedings of the 6th Workshop on Algorithms in Bioinformatics (WABI), Vol. 4175 of LNBI*; Springer; 2006. pp. 298–309.
10. Schmidt T, Stoye J. Quadratic time algorithms for finding common intervals in two and more sequences. In: Sahinalp SC, Muthukrishnan S, Dogrusoz U, editors. *Proceedings of the 15th Annual Symposium on Combinatorial Pattern Matching, CPM 2004, Vol. 3109 of LNCS*, 2004. pp. 347–358.
11. Wolsey LA. Integer programming. *Wiley Interscience Series in Discrete Mathematics and Optimization*. John Wiley & Sons; 1998.

10

EFFICIENT COMBINATORIAL ALGORITHMS FOR DNA SEQUENCE PROCESSING

Bhaskar DasGupta

Department of Computer Science, University of Illinois at Chicago, Chicago, IL, USA

Ming-Yang Kao

Department of Electrical Engineering and Computer Science, Northwestern University, Evanston, IL, USA

10.1 INTRODUCTION

The modern era of molecular biology began with the discovery of the double helical structure of DNA. Today, sequencing nucleic acids, the determination of genetic information at the most fundamental level, is a major tool of biological research [44]. This revolution in biology has created a huge amount of data at great speed by directly reading DNA sequences. The growth rate of data volume is exponential. For instance, the volume of DNA and protein sequence data is currently doubling every 22 months [32]. One important reason for this exceptional growth rate of biological data is the medical use of such information in the design of diagnostics and therapeutics [22,31]. For example, identification of genetic markers in DNA sequences would provide important informations regarding which portions of the DNA are significant, and would allow the researchers to find many disease genes of interest (by recognizing them from the pattern of inheritance). Naturally, the large amount of available data poses a serious challenge in storing, retrieving and analyzing biological information.

Bioinformatics Algorithms: Techniques and Applications, Edited by Ion I. Măndoiu and Alexander Zelikovsky

A rapidly developing area, *computational biology*, is emerging to meet the rapidly increasing computational need. It consists of many important areas such as information storage, sequence analysis, evolutionary tree construction, protein structure prediction [22,31]. It is playing an important role in some biological research. For example, sequence comparison is one of the most important methodological issues and most active research areas in current *biological sequence analysis*. Without the help of computers, it is almost impossible to compare two or more biological sequences (typically, at least a few hundred character long). Applications of sequence comparison methods can be traced back to the well-known *Human Genome Project* [43], whose objective is to decode this entire DNA sequence and to find the location and ordering of genetic markers along the length of the chromosome. These genetic markers can be used, for example, to trace the inheritance of chromosomes in families and thereby to find the location of disease genes. Genetic markers can be found by finding DNA polymorphisms, that is, locations where two DNA sequences "spell" differently. A key step in finding DNA polymorphisms is the calculation of the *genetic distance*, which is a measure of the correlation (or similarity) between two genomes.

In this chapter, we discuss computational complexities and approximation algorithms for a few DNA sequence analysis problems. We assume that the reader is familiar with the basic concepts of exact and approximation algorithms [20,42], basic computational complexity classes such as P and NP [23,26,36] and basic notions of molecular biology such as DNA sequences [24,45].

10.2 NONOVERLAPPING LOCAL ALIGNMENTS

As we have already seen, a fundamental problem in computational molecular biology is to elucidate similarities between sequences and a cornerstone result in this area is that given two strings of length p and q, there are local alignment algorithms that will score pairs of substrings for "similarity" according to various biologically meaningful scoring functions and we can pull out all "similar" or high scoring substring pairs in time $O(pq + n)$, where n is the output size [45]. Having found the high scoring substring pairs, a global description of the similarity between two sequences is obtained by choosing the disjoint subset of these pairs of highest total score. This problem is in general referred to as the "nonoverlapping local alignment" problem. We also mention a more general "d-dimensional version" of this problem involving $d > 2$ sequences, where we score d substrings, one from each sequence, with a similarity score and the goal is to select a collection of disjoint subsets of these d-tuples of substrings maximizing the total similarity.

A natural geometric interpretation of the problem is via selecting a set of "independent" rectangles in the plane in the following manner [3]. Each output substring pair being represented as a rectangle; Fig. 10.1 shows a pictorial illustration of the relationship of a rectangle to local similarity between two fragments of two sequences. This gives rise to the following combinatorial optimization problem. We are given a set S of n positively weighted axis parallel rectangles. Define two rectangles to be

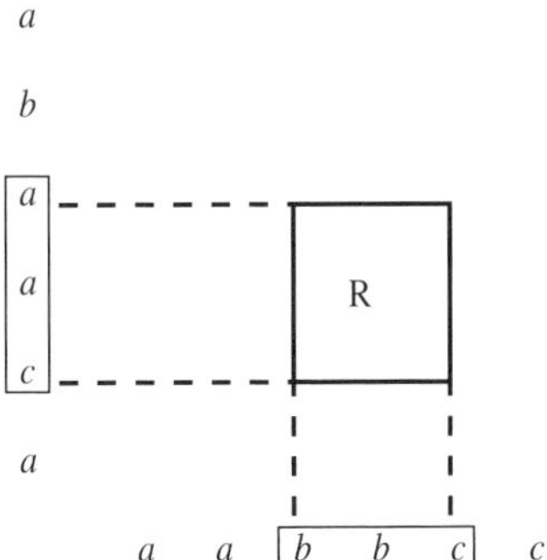

FIGURE 10.1 The rectangle R captures the local similarity (match) between the fragments *aac* and *bbc* of the two sequences; weight of R is the strength of the match.

independent if for each axis, the projection of one rectangle does not overlap that of another. The goal is to select a subset $S' \subseteq S$ of *independent* rectangles from the given set of rectangles of total maximum weight. The *unweighted* version of the problem is the one in which the weights of all rectangles are identical. In the d-dimensional version, we are given a set of positively weighted axis parallel d-dimensional hyper-rectangles[1] such that, for every axis, the projection of a hyper-rectangle on this axis does not enclose that of another. Defining two hyper-rectangles to be independent if for every axis, the projection of one hyper-rectangle does not overlap that of another; the goal is to select a subset of *independent* hyper-rectangles of total maximum weight from the given set of hyper-rectangles.

The nonoverlapping local alignment problem, including its special case as defined by the IR problem described in Section 10.2.2, is known to be NP-complete. The best-known algorithm for the general version of the nonoverlapping local alignment problem is due to [8], who provide a $2d$-approximation for the problem involving d-dimensional hyper-rectangles. In the sequel, we will discuss two important special cases of this problem that are biologically relevant.

10.2.1 The Chaining Problem

The chaining problem is the following special case [24, page 326]. A subset of rectangles is called a *chain* if no horizontal or vertical line intersects more than one rectangle in the subset and if the rectangles in the subset can be ordered such that each rectangle in this order is below and to the right of its predecessor. The goal is to find a chain of maximum total similarity. This problem can be posed as finding the longest path in a directed acyclic graph and thereby admits an optimal solution in $O(n^2)$ time, where n is the number of rectangles. However, using a sparse dynamic programming method, the running time can be further improved to $O(n \log n)$ [27].

[1] A d-dimensional hyper-rectangle is a Cartesian product of d intervals.

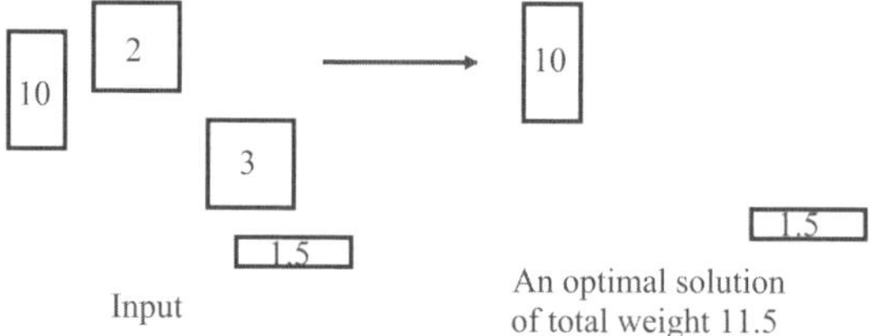

FIGURE 10.2 An illustration of the IR problem.

10.2.2 The Independent Subset of Rectangles (IR) Problem

In this problem, first formulated by [3], for each axis, the projection of a rectangle on this axis does not enclose that of another; this restriction on the input is biologically justified by a preprocessing of the input data (fragment pairs) to eliminate violations of the constraint. See Fig. 10.2 for an pictorial illustration of the problem.

Consider the graph G formed from the given rectangles in which there is a node for every rectangle with its weight being the same as that of the rectangle and two nodes are connected by an edge if and only if their rectangles are *not* independent. It is not difficult to see that G is a five-claw free graph [3] and the IR problem is tantamount to finding a *maximum-weight* independent set in G. Many previous approaches have used this connection of the IR problem to the five-claw free graphs to provide better approximation algorithms by giving improved approximation algorithms for d-claw free graphs. For example, using this approach, Bafna et al. [3] provided a polynomial time approximation algorithm with a performance ratio[2] of $\frac{13}{4}$ for the IR problem and Halldórsson [25] provided a polynomial time approximation algorithm with a performance ratio of $2+\varepsilon$ (for any constant $\varepsilon > 0$) for the unweighted version of the IR problem.[3] The current best approximation algorithm for the IR problem is due to Berman [9] via the same approach that has a performance ratio of $\frac{5}{2}+\varepsilon$ (for any constant $\varepsilon > 0$).

Many of the above mentioned algorithms essentially start with an arbitrary solution and then allows small improvements to enhance the approximation quality of the solution. In contrast, in this section we review the usage of a simple greedy two-phase technique to provide an approximation algorithm for the IR problem with a performance ratio of three that runs in $O(n \log n)$ time [10,15]. The two-phase technique was introduced in its more general version as a multiphase approach in the context of realtime scheduling of jobs with deadline in [11,12]; we review the generic nature of this technique in Section 10.2.2.1. Although this approximation algorithm does not improve the worst-case performance ratios of previously best algorithms, it is simple to implement (involving standard simple data structures such as stacks and binary trees), and runs faster than the algorithms in [3,9,25].

[2]The performance ratio of an approximation algorithm for the IR problem is the ratio of the total weights of rectangles in an optimal solution to that in the solution provided by the approximation algorithm.

[3]For this and other previous approximation algorithms with an ε in the performance ratio, the running time increases with decreasing ε, thereby rendering these algorithms impractical if ε is small. Also, a straightforward implementation of these algorithms will run in at least $\Omega(mn)$ time.

10.2.2.1 The Local-ratio and Multiphase Techniques The multiphase technique was introduced formally in the context of realtime scheduling of jobs by the investigators in [11,12]. Informally and very briefly, this technique works as follows.

(a) We maintain a stack **S** containing objects that are tentatively in the solution. **S** is initially empty before the algorithm starts.
(b) We make $k \geq 1$ *evaluation passes* over the objects. In each evaluation pass
   - we inspect the objects in a specific order that is easy to compute (e.g., rectangles in the plane in the order of their right vertical side),
   - depending on the current content of **S**, the contents of **S** during the previous passes as well as the attributes of the current object, we compute a score for the object,
   - we push the object to **S** if the score is above a certain threshold.
(c) We make one *selection pass* over the objects in **S** in a specific order (typically, by popping the elements of **S**) and select a subset of the objects in **S** that satisfy the feasibility criteria of the optimization problem under consideration.

Closely related to the two-phase version of the multiphase technique, but somewhat of more general nature, is the *local-ratio* technique. This technique was first developed by Bar-Yehuda and Even [7] and later extended by Berman et al. [4] and Bar-Yehuda [6]. The crux of the technique is as follows [5]. Assume that given an n-dimensional vector $\vec{p}$, our goal is to find a n-dimensional *solution* vector $\vec{x}$ that maximizes (respectively, minimizes) the inner product $\vec{p} \cdot \vec{x}$ subject to some set $\mathcal{F}$ of *feasibility constraints* on $\vec{x}$. Assume that we have decomposed the vector $\vec{p}$ to two vectors $\vec{p_1}$ and $\vec{p_2}$ with $\vec{p_1} + \vec{p_2} = \vec{p}$ such that, for some $r \geq 1$ (respectively, $r \leq 1$), we can find a solution vector $\vec{x}$ satisfying $\mathcal{F}$ which r-approximates $\vec{p_1}$ and $\vec{p_2}$, that is, which satisfies both $\vec{p_1} \cdot \vec{x} \geq r \cdot \max_{\vec{y}}\{\vec{p_1} \cdot \vec{y}\}$ and $\vec{p_2} \cdot \vec{x} \geq r \cdot \max_{\vec{y}}\{\vec{p_2} \cdot \vec{y}\}$ (respectively, $\vec{p_1} \cdot \vec{x} \leq r \cdot \min_{\vec{y}}\{\vec{p_1} \cdot \vec{y}\}$ and $\vec{p_2} \cdot \vec{x} \leq r \cdot \min_{\vec{y}}\{\vec{p_2} \cdot \vec{y}\}$). Then, $\vec{x}$ also r-approximates $\vec{p}$. This allows a given problem to be recursively broken down in subproblems from which one can recover a solution to the original problem. The local-ratio approach makes it easier to extend the results to a larger class of problems, while the multiphase approach allows to obtain better approximation ratios in many important special cases.

The multiphase technique was used in the context of job scheduling in [11,12] and in the context of opportunity cost algorithms for combinatorial auctions in [1]. We will discuss the usage of the two-phase version of the multiphase approach in the context of the IR problem [10,15] in the next section. In some cases, it is also possible to explain the multiphase or the local-ratio approach using the primal-dual schema; for example, see [5].

10.2.2.2 Application of the Two-Phase Technique to the IR Problem The following notations and terminologies are used for the rest of this section. An interval $[a, b]$ is the set $[a, b] = \{x \in \mathbf{R} : a \leq x \leq b\}$. A rectangle R is $[a, b] \times [c, d]$ for some two intervals $[a, b]$ and $[c, d]$, where $\times$ denotes the Cartesian product. The weight of a rectangle R is denoted by $w(R)$. We assume that the reader familiar with standard techniques and data structures for the design and analysis of algorithms such as in [20].

Let $R_1, R_2, \ldots, R_n$ be the n input rectangles in our collection, where $R_i = X_i \times Y_i$ for some two intervals $X_i = [d_i, e_i]$ and $Y_i = [f_i, g_i]$. Consider the intervals $X_1, X_2, \ldots, X_n$ formed by projecting the rectangles on one axis and call two intervals X_i and X_j independent if and only if the corresponding rectangles R_i and R_j are independent. The notation $X_i \simeq X_j$ (respectively, $X_i \not\simeq X_j$) is used to denote if two intervals X_i and X_j are independent (respectively, not independent).

To simplify implementation, we first sort the set of numbers $\{d_i, e_i \mid 1 \leq i \leq n\}$ (respectively, the set of numbers $\{f_i, g_i \mid 1 \leq i \leq n\}$) and replace each number in the set by its rank in the sorted list. This does not change any feasible solution to the given problem; however, after this $O(n \log n)$ time preprocessing we can assume that $d_i, e_i, f_i, g_i \in \{1, 2, \ldots, 2n\}$ for all i. This assumption simplifies the design of data structures for the IR problem.

Now, we adopt the two-phase technique on the intervals $X_1, X_2, \ldots, X_n$. The precise algorithm is shown in Fig. 10.3. The solution to the IR problem consists of those rectangles whose projections are returned in the solution at the end of the selection phase.

To show that the algorithm is correct we just need to show that the selected rectangles are mutually independent. This is obviously ensured by the final selection phase. To implement this algorithm, we need to compute TOTAL(X_i) efficiently. Using the fact that the intervals are considered in nondecreasing order of their end points, we

```
(* definitions *)
    a triplet (α, β, γ) is an ordered sequence of three values α, β and γ;
    L is sequence that contains a triplet (w(R_i), d_i, e_i)
        for every R_i = X_i × Y_i with X_i = [d_i, e_i];
        L is sorted so the values of e_i's are in nondecreasing order;
    S is an initially empty stack that stores triplets;
    TOTAL(X_j) returns the sum of v's of those triplets (v, a, b) ∈S
    such that [a, b] ≄ X_j;
(* evaluation phase *)
    for ( each (w(R_i), d_i, e_i) from L )
    {
        v ← w(R_i) − TOTAL([d_i, e_i]);
        if ( v > 0 ) push((v, d_i, e_i),S);
    }
(* selection phase *)
    while ( S is not empty )
    {
        (v, d_i, e_i) ← pop(S);
        if ( [d_i, e_i] ≃ X for every interval X in our solution )
            insert [d_i, e_i] to our solution;
    }
```

FIGURE 10.3 Algorithm TPA-IR: Adoption of the two-phase technique for the IR problem.

can reduce this to the problem of maintaining a data structure $\mathcal{D}$ for a set of points in the plane with coordinates from the set $\{1, 2, \ldots, 2n\}$ such that the following two operations can be performed.

Insert(v, x, y)**:** Insert the point with coordinates (x, y) (with $x, y \in \{1, 2, \ldots, 2n\}$) and value v in $\mathcal{D}$. Moreover, if Insert(v, x, y) precedes Insert(v', x', y'), then $y' \geq y$.

Query(a, b, c)**:** Given a query range (a, b, c) (with $a, b, c \in \{1, 2, \ldots, 2n\} \cup \{-\infty, \infty\}$), find the sum of the values of all points (x, y) in $\mathcal{D}$ with $a \leq x \leq b$ and $y \geq c$.

One can solve this problem in $O(n \log n)$ time and space preprocessing and $O(\log n)$ per query by using an appropriately augmented binary search tree; see [10,15] for details. We can therefore implement the entire algorithm in $O(n \log n)$ time and space.

We now sketch the main points of the proof of the performance ratio of Algorithm TPA-IR as detailed in [10,15]. let B be a solution returned by Algorithm TPA-IR and A be any optimal solution. For a rectangle $R \in A$, let us define the *local conflict number* β_R to be the number of those rectangles in B that were *not* independent of R *and* were examined no earlier than R by the evaluation phase of Algorithm TPA-IR and let $\beta = \max_{R \in A} \beta_R$. First, we show that Algorithm TPA-IR has a performance ratio of β. Next, we can show that the performance ratio of Algorithm TPA-IR is 3 by showing that for the IR problem, $\beta = 3$. First note that $\beta = 3$ is possible; see Fig. 10.4. Now we show that $\beta > 3$ is impossible. Refer to Fig. 10.4. Remember that rectangles in an optimal solution contributing to β must not be independent of our rectangle R and must have their right vertical right on or to the right of the vertical line L. Since rectangles in an optimal solution must be independent of each other, there can be at most one optimal rectangle crossing L (and, thereby conflicting with R in its projections on the x axis). Any other optimal rectangle must lie completely to the right of L and therefore may conflict with R in their projections on the y axis only; hence there can be at most two such rectangles.

10.2.2.3 Further Discussions Algorithm TPA-IR makes a pass on the projections of the rectangles on the x axis in a nondecreasing order of the end points of the projections. Can we improve the performance ratio if we run TPA-IR separately on the projections on the x axis in left-to-right and in right-to-left order of end points and take the better of the two solutions? Or, even further, we may try running Algorithm TPA-IR two more times separately on the projections on the y axis in top-to-bottom and in bottom-to-top order and take the best of the four solutions. It is easy to draw an example that shows that even then the worst-case performance ratio will be 3. We already exploited the planar geometry induced by the rectangles for the IR problem to show that $\beta \leq 3$. Further research may be necessary to see whether we can exploit the geometry of rectangles more to design simple approximation algorithms with performance ratios better than 2.5 in the weighted case or better than 2 in the unweighted case.

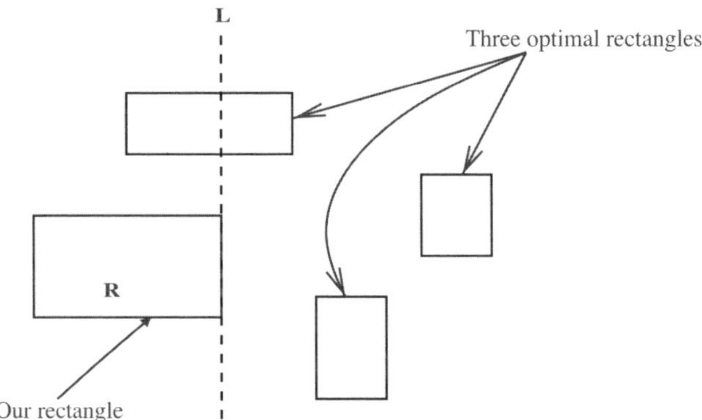

FIGURE 10.4 A tight example for Algorithm TPA-IR showing $\beta = 3$ is possible.

For the d-dimensional version, Algorithm TPA-IR can be applied in an obvious way to this extended version by considering the projections of these hyper-rectangles on a particular axis. It is not difficult to see that $\beta \leq 2d - 1$ for this case [19], thus giving a worst-case performance ratio of $2d - 1$. Whether one can design an algorithm with a performance ratio that increases less drastically (e.g., sublinearly) with d is still open.

10.3 GENOME TILING PROBLEMS

There are currently over 800 complete genome sequences available to the scientific community, representing the three principal domains of life: bacteria, archaea, and eukaryota [35]. Genome sequences vary widely in size and composition. In addition to the thousands of sequences that encode functional proteins and genetic regulatory elements, most eukaryotic genomes also possess a large number of *noncoding* sequences that are replicated in high numbers throughout the genome. These repetitive elements were introduced over evolutionary time and consists of families of transposable elements that can move from one chromosomal location to another, retroviral sequences integrated into the genome via an RNA intermediate, and simple repeat sequences that can originate de novo at any location. Nearly 50% of human genomic DNA is associated with repetitive elements. The presence of repeat sequences can be problematic for both computational and experimental biology research. For example, BLAST searches [2] with queries containing repeats against large sequence databases often result in many spurious subsequence matches, obscuring significant results and wasting computational resources. Although it is now standard practice to screen query sequences for repetitive elements, doing so subdivides the query into a number of smaller sequences that often produce a less specific match than the original. In an experimental context, when genomic sequence is used to investigate the binding of complementary DNA, repetitive elements can generate false positive signals and mask true positives by providing highly redundant DNA binding sites that compete with the meaningful targets of complementary probe sequences.

Genomic DNA can be screened for repeat sequences using specialized programs such as RepeatMasker [39], which performs local subsequence alignments [41] against a database of known repetitive elements [28]. Repeats are then masked within the query sequence, whereby a single nonnucleotide character is substituted for the nucleotides of each repeat instance. This global character replacement preserves the content and relative orientation of the remaining subsequences, which are then interspersed with character blocks representing the repetitive elements identified during the screening process.

Although the screening and/or removal of repeats is generally beneficial, additional problems may arise from the resulting genomic sequence fragmentation. Following repeat sequence identification, the remaining high complexity component (i.e., nonrepetitive DNA) exists as a population of fragments ranging in size from a few nucleotides to several kilobases. For organisms such as *Homo sapiens*, where the genome contains many thousands of repeat elements, the vast majority of these high complexity sequence fragments are below 1 Kb in size. This situation presents a significant impediment to both computational and experimental research. Bioinformatics analyses often benefit from the availability of larger contiguous sequences, typically 1 Kb and larger, for homology searches and gene predictions. Similarly, very small sequences (< 200 bp) are of limited use in many high throughput experimental applications. These constraints provide the basis of the tiling problems formalized in this section.

DNA Microarray Design A principal motivation for looking at the tiling problems considered in this paper is their application to the design of DNA microarrays for efficient genome analysis. The microarrays we consider here are constructed from amplified genomic DNA. Each element consists of a relatively long (typically 300 bp–1.2 Kb) sequence of genomic DNA that is acquired via the *polymerase chain reaction* (PCR) [33] in which a segment of DNA may be selectively amplified using a chemical system that recreates DNA replication *in vitro*. Although the size resolution of these array elements is not as fine as that of high density oligonucleotide systems, PCR-based (or *amplicon*) microarrays provide experimental access to much larger regions of contiguous genomic DNA. The tiling algorithm described here has recently been used to design a microarray of this type to represent the complete sequence of human chromosome 22 [37]. When considering PCR-based microarrays, we are concerned with finding the maximum number of high complexity subsequence fragments given a genomic DNA sequence whose repetitive elements have been identified and masked. A maximal-coverage amplicon array can then be designed by deriving an optimal tile path through the target genomic sequence such that the best set of fragments is selected for PCR amplification. Determining this tile set allows one to achieve optimal coverage of high complexity DNA across the target sequence, while simultaneously maximizing the number of potential subsequences of sufficient size to facilitate large-scale biological research.

10.3.1 Problem Statements

On the basis of the applications discussed in Section 10.3, we now formalize a family of tiling problems. The following notations are used uniformly throughout the rest of the paper:

- $[i, j)$ denotes the set of integers $\{i, i+1, \ldots, j-1\}$;
- $[i, j] = [i, j+1)$;
- $f[i, j)$ and $f[i, j]$ denote the elements of an array f with indices in $[i, j)$ and $[i, j]$, respectively.

Our tiling problems build upon a basic genome tiling algorithm which we call the *GTile problem* and describe as follows. The input consists of an array $c[0, n)$ of real numbers and two integer size parameters ℓ and u. A subarray $B = c[i, j)$ is called a *block* of *length* $j - i$ and *weight* $w(B) = \sum_{k=i}^{j-1} c_k$, the weight of a set of blocks is the sum of their weights and a block is called a *tile* if its length belongs to $[\ell, u]$. Our goal is to find a set of pairwise disjoint tiles with the maximum possible weight. The tiling problems of interest in this paper are variations, restrictions, and generalizations of the GTile problem specified by a certain combinations of the following items.

10.3.1.1 Compressed Versus Uncompressed Input Data This is motivated by a simple binary classification of the high complexity regions of the genome sequence from their low complexity counterparts. Now all entries of $c[0, n)$ is either x or $-x$ for some *fixed* $x > 0$. Hence, the input sequence can be more efficiently represented by simply specifying beginnings and endings of *blocks of identical values*.[4] In other words, we can compress the input sequence $c[0, n)$ to a sequence of integers (indices) $S[0, m+1)$ such that

- $S_0 = 0$, $S_m = n+1$, $S_1 \geq S_0$ and $S_i > S_{i-1}$ for all $i \in [2, m]$;
- each element of $c[S_{2j}, S_{2j+1})$ is x for all $0 \leq j \leq \lfloor m/2 \rfloor$;
- each element of $c[S_{2j-1}, S_{2j})$ is $-x$ for all $0 < j \leq \lfloor (m+1)/2 \rfloor$.

We note that the input size $m+1$ of such a compressed input data is typically *significantly smaller* than n. As a result, we can get significantly faster algorithms if we can design an algorithm for compressed inputs with a running time nearly linear in m. Furthermore, this also allows one to develop efficient hybrid approach to solving the tiling problems: first use a crude binary classification of the regions to quickly obtain an initial set of tiles and then refine the tiles taking into consideration the relative importances of the high complexity elements.

10.3.1.2 Unbounded Versus Bounded Number of Tiles Another important item of interest is when the number of tiles that may be used is at most a given value t, which could be considerably smaller than the number of tiles used by a tiling with no

[4]Notice that a $\{0, 1\}$ classification of the high complexity regions from the low complexity ones is not suitable since then we do not penalize for covering low complexity regions and solving the tiling problem becomes trivial.

restrictions on the number of tiles. This is motivated by the practical consideration that the capacity of a microarray as obtainable by current technology is bounded.

10.3.1.3 Overlapping Versus Nonoverlapping Tiles To enhance searching sequence databases for homology searches to allow for the case when potential matches can be found at tile boundaries, it may be useful to relax the condition of disjointness of tiles by allowing two tiles to share at most p elements for some given (usually small) $p > 0$. However, to ensure that we do not have too many overlaps, we need to *penalize* them by subtracting the weight of each overlapped region from the sum of weights of all tiles, where the *weight* of each overlapped region is the sum of the elements in it. In other words, if $\mathcal{T}$ is the set of tiles and $\mathcal{R}$ is the set of elements of C that belong to more than one tile in $\mathcal{T}$, then the weight is $\sum_{T\in\mathcal{T}} w(T) - \sum_{c_i\in\mathcal{R}} c_i$.

10.3.1.4 One-Dimensional Versus d-Dimensional Generalization of the GTile problem in d-dimensions has applications in database designs and related problems [16,18,29,30,34].[5] In this case, we are given a d-dimensional array $\mathcal{C}$ of size $n_1 \times n_2 \times \cdots \times n_d$ with $2d$ size parameters $\ell_1, \ell_2, \ldots, \ell_d, u_1, u_2, \ldots, u_d$, a tile is a rectangular subarray of $\mathcal{C}$ of size $p_1 \times p_2 \times \cdots \times p_d$ satisfying $\ell_i \le p_i \le u_i$ for all i, the weight of a tile is the sum of all the elements in the tile and our goal is again to find a set of tiles such that the sum of weights of the tiles is maximized.

We examine only those combinations of the above four items that are of importance in our applications simplify exposition, unless otherwise stated explicitly, the GTile problem we consider is *one dimensional* with *uncompressed* inputs, *unbounded* number of tiles and *no overlaps*. In addition to the previously defined notations, unless otherwise stated, we use the following notations and variables with their designated meanings throughout the rest of the paper: $n+1$ is the number of elements of the (uncompressed) one-dimensional input array $c[i, j)$, $n_1 \le n_2 \le \cdots \le n_d$ are the sizes of the dimensions for the d-dimensional input array, $w(\mathcal{T})$ is the weight for a *set* of tiles $\mathcal{T}$, t is the given number of tiles when the number of tiles is bounded and p is the maximum overlap between two tiles in one-dimension. Finally, all logarithms are in base 2 unless stated otherwise explicitly.

10.3.2 Related Work

Tiling an array of numbers in one or more dimensions under various constraints is a very active research area (e.g., see [16–18,29,30,34,40]) and has applications in several areas including database decision support, two-dimensional histogram computation and resource scheduling. Several techniques, such as the slice-and-dice approach [16], the shifting technique [26, Chapter 9] and dynamic programming methods based on binary space partitions [17,29,34] have proven useful for these problems. Our problems are different from the tiling problems in [16,17,29,30,34,40]; in particular, we do not require partitioning of the entire array, the array entries may

[5] For example, in two dimensions with $\ell_1 = \ell_2 = 0$ and $u_1 = u_2 = \infty$ this is precisely the ARRAY-RPACK problem discussed in [29].

TABLE 10.1 [13,14] A Summary of the Results for the Genome Tiling Problems. All the Algorithms are Either New or Direct Improvements of any Previously Known. The Parameter $\varepsilon > 1$ is any Arbitrary *Constant*. A s-Subset is a Subset of s Elements. For the d-dimensional Case, $M = \Pi_{i=1}^{d} n_i(u_i - \ell_i + 1)$, $N = \max_{1 \le i \le d} n_i$ and $\frac{u}{\ell} = \max_i \frac{u_i}{\ell_i}$. For Our Biology Applications $p \le 100 < \ell/2 \ll n, t \simeq n/u + \ell, m \ll n$ and $\ell/u - \ell < 6$. The Column Labeled "Approximation Ratio" Indicates Whether the Algorithm Computes the Optimal Solution Exactly or, for an Approximation Algorithm, the Ratio of the Total Weight of Our Tiling to that of the Optimum

Version of GTile	Time $O()$	Space $O()$	Approximation ratio
Basic	n	n	Exact
Overlap is from a s-subset of $[0, \delta]$, $\delta < \ell/2$	sn	n	Exact
Compressed input	$m\frac{\ell}{u-\ell}$	$m\frac{\ell}{u-\ell}$	Exact
Number of tiles given	$\min\{n \log \frac{n}{\ell}, nt\}$	n	Exact
d-dimensional	$\left(\left(\frac{u}{\ell}\right)\varepsilon\right)^{4\left(\frac{u}{\ell}\right)^2\varepsilon^2} M\varepsilon^2$	M	$\left(1 - \frac{1}{\varepsilon}\right)^d$
d-dimensional, number of tiles given	$tM + dM \log^{\varepsilon} M$ $+dN\frac{\log N}{\log\log N}$	M	$\left(\Pi_{i=1}^{d-1}\left(\lfloor 1 + \log n_i \rfloor\right)\right)^{-1}$
	$M^{(2^{\varepsilon}-1)^{d-1}+1}\,dt$	$M^{(2^{\varepsilon}-1)^{d-1}+1}\,dt$	$\left(\Pi_{i=1}^{d-1}\left(\lfloor 1 + \frac{\log n_i}{\varepsilon} \rfloor\right)\right)^{-1}$

be negative and there are lower and upper bounds on the size of a tile. Other papers that most closely relate to our work are the references [38] and [46]. The authors in [38] provide an $O(n)$ time algorithm to find all *maximal* scoring subsequences of a sequence of length n. In [46] the authors investigate computing maximal scoring subsequences that contain no subsequences with weights below a particular threshold.

TABLE 10.2 [13,14] Summary of Target Chromosome Sequences. The Sequences Increase in Repeat Density with the Complexity of the Genome, Causing a Greater Degree of Fragmentation and Loss of High Complexity Sequence Coverage in the Unprocessed Chromosomes. This Situation Is Especially Problematic in the Higher Eukaryotes Such As Human and Mouse

Chromosome	Nucleotides	Repeat Elements	Repetitive DNA (bp)	% Repeats	High Complexity DNA (bp)
C. elegans chrV	20,916,335	16,575	2,414,183	11.5	18,502,152
A. thaliana chrI	30,074,119	14,490	3,557,144	11.8	26,516,975
D. melanogaster chr3	51,243,003	27,259	3,106,633	6	48,136,370
M. musculus chr1	196,842,934	288,551	90,532,869	46	106,310,065
H. sapiens chr1	246,874,334	308,257	132,580,913	53.7	114,293,421

10.3.3 Synopsis of Results

Our main theoretical results are summarized in Table 10.1; for more details, see our publications [13,14]. All of our methods use simple data structures such as a double-ended queues and are therefore easy to implement. The techniques used for many of these tiling problems in one dimension use a solution of an *Online Interval Maximum* (OLIM) problem via a windowing scheme reminiscent of that in [21]. However, the primary consideration in the applications in [21] was reduction of space because of the online nature of their problems, whereas we are more concerned with time-complexity issues since our tiling problems are off-line in nature (and hence space for storing the entire input is always used). Moreover, our windowing scheme is somewhat different

TABLE 10.3 [13,14] GTile Results for the 5 Model Eukaryotic Chromosomes. Maximal Coverage of the High Complexity DNA is Achieved with Minimal Repeat Nucleotide Inclusion, while the Number of Required Tiles Decreases. Sets of Nonoverlapping Tiles were Computed for the Size Range of 300 bp–1 Kb

Target Chromosome	# Tiles	High Complexity DNA (bp)	% Coverage	Repetitive DNA (bp)	% Repeats
		Initial sequence coverage			
C. elegans chrV	22,842	17,852,822	96.4		
A. thaliana chrI	30,075	25,972,994	98		
D. melanogaster chr3	57,568	47,366,173	98.3		
M. musculus chr1	142,165	90,988,520	85.5		
H. sapiens chr1	151,720	97,191,872	85		
		GTile, repeat penalty 6:1			
C. elegans chrV	19,034	18,299,667	99	237,772	1.28
A. thaliana chrI	25,349	26,376,577	99	196,222	0.74
D. melanogaster chr3	46,901	48,056,034	99	453,704	0.93
M. musculus chr1	128,472	96,280,008	90.5	2,314,565	2.34
H. sapiens chr1	137,403	101,866,284	89	2,026,782	1.95
		GTile, repeat penalty 5:1			
C. elegans chrV	18,975	18,329,464	99	290,152	1.55
A. thaliana chrI	25,344	26,391,095	99.5	213,917	0.8
D. melanogaster chr3	46,878	48,061,534	99.8	465,573	0.96
M. musculus chr1	127,146	97,953,586	92	4,304,560	4.2
H. sapiens chr1	136,457	103,434,234	90.4	3,788,374	3.53
		GTile, repeat penalty 4:1			
C. elegans chrV	18,891	18,345,048	99	348,086	1.86
A. thaliana chrI	25,342	26,396,637	99.5	226,559	0.85
D. melanogaster chr3	46,867	48,062,909	99.8	471,650	0.97
M. musculus chr1	125,787	98,617,314	92.7	5,765,790	5.52
H. sapiens chr1	135,305	104,138,841	91	5,247,600	4.79

from that in [21] since we need to maintain multiple windows of different sizes and data may not arrive at evenly spaced time intervals.

We also summarize the application of the GTile problem to the genomic sequences of 5 model eukaryotes. The single largest chromosome from each organism was considered as representative of the characteristics of that particular genome. Table 10.2 lists the target chromosomes and their sequence properties. The chromosomes vary in the degree of repeat density, where the first few examples contain relatively few repetitive elements in comparison to the two mammalian sequences. In the cases of *C. elegans*, *A. thaliana*, and *D. melanogaster*, the low repeat content allows us to tile the sequences fairly well simply by subdividing the remaining high complexity DNA into sequence fragments within the appropriate size range. However, as the repeat density increases in the genomes of higher eukaryotes, so does the fragmentation of the high complexity sequence containing genes and regulatory elements of biological significance. It soon becomes impossible to achieve maximal coverage of the high complexity sequence in the absence of further processing.

The results of applying the tiling algorithm to each chromosome appear in Table 10.3. GTile improves the sequence coverage in all cases, easily covering nearly 100% of the high complexity DNA in the smaller, less complex genomes with few incorporated repeats. In practice, the coverage will never reach 100% because there remains a population of small high complexity sequences whose sizes fall below the lower bound. In terms of experimental applications, these sequences are too small to be chemically amplified by PCR and are therefore excluded from consideration.

ACKNOWLEDGMENTS

Bhaskar DasGupta was supported in part by NSF grants IIS-0346973, IIS-0612044 and DBI-0543365. Ming-Yang Kao was supported in part by NSF grant EIA-0112934. The authors would also like to thank all their collaborators in these research topics. Figures 10.1–10.4 and the related text is included from [10] with kind permission of Springer Science and Business Media. Tables 10.1–10.3 and the related text is included from [13] with kind permission of Mary Ann Liebert, Inc.

REFERENCES

1. Akcoglu K, Aspnes J, DasGupta B, Kao M-Y. Opportunity Cost Algorithms for Combinatorial Auctions. In: Kontoghiorghes EJ, Rustem B, Siokos S, editors. *Applied Optimization: Computational Methods in Decision-Making, Economics and Finance*. Kluwer Academic Publishers; 2002. pp. 455–479.
2. Altschul SF, Gish W, Miller W, Myers EW, Lipman DJ. A basic local alignment search tool. *J Mol Biol* 1990;215:403–410.
3. Bafna V, Narayanan B, Ravi R. Nonoverlapping local alignments (Weighted independent sets of axis-parallel rectangles. *Discrete Appl Math* 1996;71:41–53.

4. Bafna V, Berman P, Fujito T. Constant ratio approximation of the weighted feedback vertex set problem for undirected graphs. *International Symporium on Algorithms and Computation, LNCS 1004*; 1995. pp. 142–151.
5. Bar-Noy A, Bar-Yehuda R, Freund A, Naor JS, Schieber B. A unified approach to approximating resource allocation and scheduling. *Proceedings of the 32nd Annual ACM Symposium on Theory of Computing*; 2000. pp. 735–744.
6. Bar-Yehuda R. One for the price of two: a unified approach for approximating covering problems. *Algorithmica*, 27 (2); 2000. pp. 131–144.
7. Bar-Yehuda R, Even S. A local-ratio theorem for approximating the weighted vertex cover problem. *Ann Discrete Math* 1985;25:27–46.
8. Bar-Yehuda R, Halldörsson MM, Naor J, Shachnai H, Shapira I. Scheduling split intervals. *14th ACM-SIAM Symposium on Discrete Algorithms*, 2002. pp. 732–741.
9. Berman P. A $d/2$ approximation for maximum weight independent set in d-claw free graphs. *Proceedings of the 7th Scandinavian Workshop on Algorithmic Theory, Lecture Notes in Computer Science, 1851*. Springer-Verlag; 2000. pp. 214–219.
10. Berman P, DasGupta B. A Simple Approximation Algorithm for Nonoverlapping Local Alignments (Weighted Independent Sets of Axis Parallel Rectangles). *In: Biocomputing, Vol. 1*. Pardalos PM, Principe J, editors. Kluwer Academic Publishers; 2002. pp. 129–138.
11. Berman P, DasGupta B. Improvements in Throughput Maximization for Real-Time Scheduling. *Proceedings of the 32nd Annual ACM Symposium on Theory of Computing*; 2000. pp. 680–687.
12. Berman P, DasGupta B. Multi-phase Algorithms for Throughput Maximization for Real-Time Scheduling. *J Comb Optim* 2000;4(3):307–323.
13. Berman P, Bertone P, DasGupta B, Gerstein M, Kao M-Y, Snyder M. Fast Optimal Genome Tiling with Applications to Microarray Design and Homology Search. J Comput Biol; 2004;11(4):766–785.
14. Berman P, Bertone P, DasGupta B, Gerstein M, Kao M-Y, Snyder M. Fast Optimal Genome Tiling with Applications to Microarray Design and Homology Search. *2nd International Workshop on Algorithms in Bioinformatics (WABI 2002), LNCS 2452*, Guigó R, Gusfield D, editors. Springer Verlag; 2002. 419–433.
15. Berman P, DasGupta B, Muthukrishnan S. Simple Approximation Algorithm for Nonoverlapping Local Alignments. *13th ACM-SIAM Symposium on Discrete Algorithms*; 2002. pp. 677–678.
16. Berman P, DasGupta B, Muthukrishnan S. Slice and dice: A simple, improved approximate tiling recipe. *Proceedings of the 13th Annual ACM-SIAM Symposium on Discrete Algorithms*; 2002. pp. 455–464.
17. Berman P, DasGupta B, Muthukrishnan S. On the exact size of the binary space partitioning of sets of isothetic rectangles with applications. *SIAM J Discrete Math* 2002;15(2):252–267.
18. Berman P, DasGupta B, Muthukrishnan S, Ramaswami S. Improved approximation algorithms for tiling and packing with rectangles. *Proceedings of the 12th Annual ACM-SIAM Symposium on Discrete Algorithms*; 2001;427–436.
19. Chlebík M, Chlebíková J. Approximation Hardness of Optimization Problems in Intersection Graphs of d-dimensional Boxes. *Proceedings of the 16th Annual ACM-SIAM Symposium on Discrete Algorithms*; 2005. pp. 267–276.

20. Cormen TH, Leiserson CE, Rivest RL, Stein C. *Introduction to Algorithms*. The MIT Press; 2001.
21. Datar M, Gionis A, Indyk P, Motwani R. Maintaining stream statistics over sliding windows. *Proceedings of the 13th Annual ACM-SIAM Symposium on Discrete Algorithms*; 2002. pp. 635–644.
22. Frenkel KA. The human genome project and informatics. *Commun ACM* 1991;34(11):41–51.
23. Garey MR, Johnson DS. *Computers and Intractability: A Guide to the Theory of NP-completeness*. W. H. Freeman, 1979.
24. Gusfield D. *Algorithms on Strings, Trees, and Sequences: Computer Science and Computational Biology.* Cambridge University Press; 1997.
25. Halldórsson MM. Approximating discrete collections via local improvements. *Proceedings of the 6th ACM-SIAM Symposium on Discrete Algorithms*; 1995. pp. 160–169.
26. Hochbaum D. *Approximation Algorithms for NP-hard Problems*, PWS publishers, 1996.
27. Joseph D, Meidanis J, Tiwari P. Determining DNA sequence similarity using maximum independent set algorithms for interval graphs. *3rd Scandinavian Workshop on Algorithm Theory, LNCS 621*. 1992. pp. 326–337.
28. Jurka J. Repbase Update: a database and an electronic journal of repetitive elements. *Trends Genet*. 2000;9:418–420.
29. Khanna S, Muthukrishnan S, Paterson M. On approximating rectangle tiling and packing. *Proceedings of the 9th Annual ACM-SIAM Symposium on Discrete Algorithms*; 1998. pp. 384–393.
30. Khanna S, Muthukrishnan S, Skiena S. Efficient array partitioning. In: Goos G, Hartmanis J, van Leeuwen J, editors. *Lecture Notes in Computer Science 1256: Proceedings of the 24th International Colloquium on Automata, Languages, and Programming*. Springer-Verlag, New York, NY; 1997. pp. 616–626.
31. Lander ES, Langridge R, Saccocio DM. Mapping and interpreting biological information. *Commun ACM* 1991;34(11):33–39.
32. Miller W, Scbwartz S, Hardison RC. A point of contact between computer science and molecular biology. *IEEE Comput Sci Eng*. 1994;1(1)69–78.
33. Mullis K, Faloona F, Scharf S, Saiki R, Horn G, Erlich H. Specific enzymatic amplification of DNA in vitro: the polymerase chain reaction. *Cold Spring Harb Sym*. 1986;51: 263–273.
34. Muthukrishnan S, Poosala V, Suel T. On rectangular partitions in two dimensions: Algorithms, complexity and applications. *Proceedings of the 7th International Conference on Database Theory*. 1999. pp. 236–256.
35. National Center for Biotechnology Information (NCBI). www.ncbi.nlm.nih.gov, 2002.
36. Papadimitriou CH. *Computational Complexity*, Addison-Wesley; reading, MA, 1994.
37. Rinn JL, Euskirchen G, Bertone P, Martone R, Luscombe NM, Hartman S, Harrison PM, Nelson K, Miller P, Gerstein M, Weissman S, Snyder M. The transcriptional activity of human chromosome 22. *Genes and Development*, Forthcoming.
38. Ruzzo WL, Tompa M. Linear time algorithm for finding all maximal scoring subsequences. *Proceedings of the 7th International Conference on Intelligent Systems for Molecular Biology*. 1999. pp. 234–241.
39. Smith AFA. Green P. RepeatMasker, repeatmasker.genome.washington.edu, 2002.

40. Smith A, Suri S. Rectangular tiling in multi-dimensional arrays. *Proceedings of the 10th Annual ACM-SIAM Symposium on Discrete Algorithms*. 1999. pp. 786–794.

41. Smith TF, Waterman MS. Identification of common molecular subsequences. *J Mol Biol* 1981;147:195–197.

42. Vazirani V. *Approximation Algorithms*. Springer-Verlag, 2001.

43. Venter JC, *et al.* The sequence of the human genome. *Science*. 2001; 291: pp. 1304–1351.

44. Waterman MS. Sequence alignments. In: Waterman MS, editor. *Mathematical Methods for DNA Sequences*. CRC, Boca Raton, FL; 1989. pp. 53–92.

45. Smith TF, Waterman MS. The identification of common molecular sequences. *J Mol Biol.* 1981;147:195–197.

46. Zhang Z, Berman P, Miller W. Alignments without low-scoring regions. *J Comput Biol* 1998;5(2):197–210.

11

ALGORITHMS FOR MULTIPLEX PCR PRIMER SET SELECTION WITH AMPLIFICATION LENGTH CONSTRAINTS

K. M. KONWAR, I. I. MĂNDOIU, A. C. RUSSELL, AND A. A. SHVARTSMAN

Department of Computer Science and Engineering, University of Connecticut, Storrs, CT, USA

11.1 INTRODUCTION

Numerous high throughput genomics assays require rapid and cost-effective amplification of a large number of genomic loci. Most significantly, Single Nucleotide Polymorphism (SNP) genotyping protocols often require the amplification of thousands of SNP loci of interest [13]. Effective amplification can be achieved using the polymerase chain reaction [17] (PCR), which cleverly exploits the DNA replication machinery in a cyclic reaction that creates an exponential number of copies of specific DNA fragments.

In its basic form, PCR requires a pair of short single-stranded DNA sequences called *primers* for each amplification target. More precisely, the two primers must be (perfect or near perfect) Watson–Crick complements of the $3'$ ends of the forward and reverse strands of the double-stranded amplification target (see Fig. 11.1). Typically, there is significant freedom in selecting the exact ends of an amplification target, that is, in selecting PCR primers. Consequently, primer selection can be optimized with respect to various criteria affecting reaction efficiency, such as primer length, melting temperature, secondary structure, and so on. Since

Bioinformatics Algorithms: Techniques and Applications, Edited by Ion I. Măndoiu and Alexander Zelikovsky

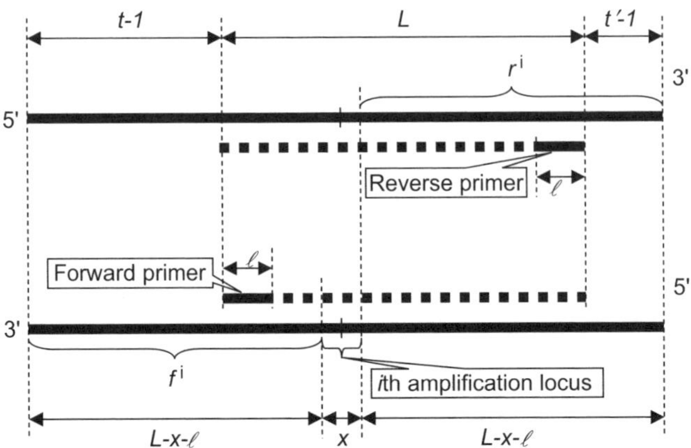

FIGURE 11.1 Strings f^i and r^i consist of the $L - x - \ell$ DNA bases immediately preceding in $3' - 5'$ order the ith amplification locus along the forward (respectively, reverse) DNA genomic sequence, where L is the given threshold on PCR amplification length, ℓ is the primer length, and x is the length of an amplification locus ($x = 1$ for SNP genotyping). If forward and reverse PCR primers cover f^i and r^i at positions t and t', respectively, then PCR amplification product length is equal to $[2(L - x - \ell) + x] - [(t - 1) + (t' - 1)]$. This is no larger than L if and only $t + t' \geq L' + 1$, where $L' = (L - x - \ell) - (\ell - 1)$.

the efficiency of PCR amplification falls off exponentially as the length of the amplification product increases, an important practical requirement is that the distance between the binding sites of the two primers should not exceed a certain threshold (typically around 1000 base pairs).

Multiplex PCR (MP-PCR) is a variant of PCR in which multiple DNA fragments are amplified simultaneously. While MP-PCR is still making use of two oligonucleotide primers to define the boundaries of each amplification fragment, a primer may now participate in the amplification of multiple targets. A primer set is feasible as long as it contains a pair of primers that amplify each target. Note that MP-PCR amplification products are available only as a mixture and may include unintended products. Nevertheless, this is not limiting the use of MP-PCR in applications such as SNP genotyping, since allelic discrimination methods (typically hybridization based) can be applied directly to complex mixtures of and are not significantly affected by the presence of a small number of undesired amplification products [13].

Much of the previous work on PCR primer selection has focused on single primer pair optimization with respect to the above biochemical criteria. This line of work has resulted in the release of several robust software tools for primer pair selection, the best known of which is the Primer3 package [21]. In the context of multiplex PCR, an important optimization objective is to minimize the total number of primers [4,18], since reducing the number of primers reduces assay cost, increases amplification efficiency by enabling higher effective concentration of the primers, and minimizes primer cross-hybridization and unintended amplification. Pearson et al. [19] were the first to consider minimizing the number of primers in their *optimal primer cover problem*: given a set of n DNA sequences and an integer ℓ, select a minimum number of ℓ-mers such that each sequence contains at least one selected ℓ-mer. Pearson et al. proved that the primer cover problem is as hard to approximate as set cover (i.e., not approximable within a factor better than $(1 - o(1))O(\log n)$ unless NP $\subseteq$ TIME($n^{O(\log \log n)}$) [5]), and that the classical greedy set cover algorithm achieves an approximation factor of $O(\log n)$.

The problem formulation in Pearson et al. [19] decouples the selection of forward and reverse primers, and in particular, cannot explicitly enforce bounds on PCR amplification length. A similar remark applies to problem formulations in recent works on *degenerate* PCR primer selection [15,23]. Such bounds can be enforced only by conservatively defining the allowable primer binding regions. For example, in order to guarantee a distance of L between the binding sites of the forward and reverse primers amplifying a SNP, one could confine the search to primers binding within $L/2$ nucleotides on each side of the SNP locus. However, since this approach reduces the number of feasible candidate primer pairs by a factor of almost 2,[1] it may lead to significant suboptimality in the total number of primers needed to amplify all given SNP loci.

Motivated by the requirement of unique PCR amplification in synthesis of spotted microarrays, Fernandes and Skiena [6] introduced an elegant *minimum multicolored subgraph* formulation for the primer selection problem, in which each candidate primer is represented as a graph node and each two primers that feasibly amplify a desired locus define an edge "colored" by the locus number. Minimizing the number of PCR primers reduces to finding a minimum subset of the nodes inducing edges of all possible colors. Unfortunately, approximating the minimum multicolored subgraph appears to be difficult — the best approximation factor derived via this reduction is currently $O(L \log n)$, where n is the number of amplification loci and L is the upper bound on the PCR amplification length [7].

In this chapter we make the following contributions.

- First, we introduce a new string covering formulation for the MP-PCR primer set selection problem with amplification length constraints that translates into integer programs that are much more compact than those resulting from the minimum multicolored subgraph formulation of Fernandes and Skiena [6]. Our compact integer programs enable computing exact solutions for moderate problem instances using general-purpose integer programming solvers such as CPLEX [3].
- Second, we show that a modification of the classical greedy algorithm for the set cover problem achieves an approximation factor of $1 + \ln(\Delta)$, where Δ is the maximum "coverage gain" of a primer. The value of Δ is never more than nL, and in practice it is up to orders of magnitude smaller. The approximation factor

[1]For example, assuming that all DNA ℓ-mers can be used as primers, out of the $(L - \ell + 1)(L - \ell + 2)/2$ pairs of forward and reverse ℓ-mers that can feasibly amplify a SNP locus, only $(L - \ell + 1)^2/4$ have both ℓ-mers within $L/2$ bases of this locus.

is established using a novel framework for analyzing greedy algorithms based on monotonic potential functions. Our potential function technique generalizes several results for the classical set cover problem and its variants [1,2,10,16,22], and is of interest in its own right.

- Finally, we give the results of a comprehensive experimental study comparing our integer programming and greedy algorithms with other heuristics proposed in the literature. Experiments on both synthetic and human genome test cases show that the new potential function greedy algorithm obtains significant reductions in the number of primers with highly scalable running time.

The rest of the chapter is organized as follows. In next section, we introduce notations and give a formal problem definition of MP-PCR primer selection with amplification length constraints. In Section 11.3, we introduce the string covering formulation of the problem and give a compact integer program formulation. In Section 11.4, we describe the greedy algorithm, give its performance analysis, and discuss practical implementation issues. Finally, we present experimental results in Section 11.5 and conclude in Section 11.6.

11.2 NOTATIONS AND PROBLEM FORMULATION

Let $\Sigma = \{A, C, G, T\}$ be the four nucleotide DNA alphabet. We denote by Σ^* the set of strings over Σ, and by $|s|$ the length of string $s \in \Sigma^*$. For a string s and an integer $1 \leq t \leq |s|$, we denote by $s[1, .., t]$ the prefix of length t of s. We use ℓ to denote the required primer length, L to denote the given threshold on PCR amplification length, and n to denote the number of amplification loci. We say that primer $p = p_1, p_2, \ldots, p_\ell$ *hybridizes* (or *covers*) string $s = s_1, s_2, \ldots, s_m$ at position $t \leq m - \ell + 1$ if $s_t, s_{t+1}, \ldots, s_{t+\ell-1}$ is the Watson–Crick complement of p, that is, if s_{t+j} is the Watson–Crick complementary base of $p_{\ell-j}$ for every $0 \leq j \leq \ell - 1$.

For each $i \in \{1, \ldots, n\}$, we denote by f^i (respectively, r^i) the string preceding the amplification locus in $3' - 5'$ order in the forward (respectively, reverse) DNA genomic sequence where potentially useful primer binding may occur. More precisely, if the length of the amplification locus is denoted by x ($x = 1$ for SNP genotyping), then f^i and r^i consist of the $L - x - \ell$ DNA bases immediately preceding in $3' - 5'$ order the ith amplification locus along the forward (respectively, reverse) DNA genomic sequence. Note that a primer can hybridize f^i (respectively, r^i) only at positions t between 1 and L', where $L' = (L - x - \ell) - (\ell - 1)$. Simple arithmetic shows that two primers that hybridize to f^i and r^i at positions t and t' lead to an amplification product of length at most L if and only if $t + t' \geq L' + 1$ (see Fig. 11.1, and note that f^i and r^i, and hence hybridization positions, are indexed in the respective $3' - 5'$ orders, that is, they increase when moving toward the amplification locus).

Primers p and p' (not necessarily distinct) are said to feasibly amplify SNP locus i if there exist integers $t, t' \in \{1, \ldots, L - \ell + 1\}$ such that the following conditions are simultaneously satisfied:

1. p hybridizes at position t of f^i,
2. p' hybridizes at position t' of r^i, and
3. $t + t' \geq L' + 1$.

A set of primers P is said to be an *L-restricted primer cover* for n SNPs defining sequences (f^i, r^i), if, for every $i = 1, \ldots, n$, there exist primers p, $p' \in P$ feasibly amplifying SNP locus i. The *minimum primer set selection problem with amplification length constraints* (MPSS-L) is defined as follows: Given primer length ℓ, amplification length upper bound L, and n pairs of sequences (f^i, r^i), $i = 1, \ldots, n$, find a minimum size L-restricted primer cover consisting of primers of length ℓ.

11.3 INTEGER PROGRAM FORMULATIONS FOR MPSS-L

Fernandes and Skiena [6] proposed an elegant *minimum multicolored subgraph* formulation for primer set selection. In this formulation, each candidate primer is viewed as a graph node, and each two primers that feasibly amplify a desired locus define an edge "colored" by the locus number. The objective is to find a minimum number of nodes inducing edges of all possible colors. The minimum multicolored subgraph formulation can be cast as an integer linear program by introducing a 0/1 variable x_p for every candidate primer p, and a 0/1 variable $y_{p,p'}$ for every two (not necessarily distinct) primers p and p' feasibly amplifying at least one of the SNP loci, as follows [7]:

$$\text{minimize} \quad \sum_{p \in \mathcal{P}} x_p, \tag{11.1}$$

subject to

$$\sum y_{p,p'} \geq 1, \quad i = 1, \ldots, n, \tag{11.2}$$

$$y_{p,p'} \leq x_p, \quad p \in \mathcal{P}, \tag{11.3}$$

$$x_p, \ y_{p,p'} \in \{0, 1\}, \tag{11.4}$$

where $\mathcal{P}$ is the set of $O(nL)$ candidate primers. The sum in Equation 11.2 is over all pairs (p, p') feasibly amplifying SNP locus i; this set of constraints ensures that each SNP locus is feasibly amplified by two of the selected primers. Constraints 11.3 ensure that only selected primers can be used to amplify SNP loci.

Unfortunately, the integer programs 11.1–11.4 cannot be used to solve practical MPSS-L problem instances due to its large size. In particular, the number of variables $y_{p,p'}$ can be as large as $\Theta(nL^2)$, which reaches into the millions for typical values of L.

Below we give a much more compact integer program formulation based on a novel string covering formulation of MPSS-L. The key idea is to view MPSS-L as a generalization of the partial set cover problem [22], in which the objective is to cover a certain fraction of the total number of elements of a ground set using the minimum number of given subsets. In the case of MPSS-L the elements to be covered are the nonempty prefixes in $\{f^i[1, .., j], r^i[1, .., j] \mid 1 \le i \le n,\ 1 \le j \le L'\}$, where, as in Section 11.2, $L' = (L - x - \ell) - (\ell - 1)$. Each primer p covers the set of prefixes $f^i[1, ..., j]$ and $r^i[1, .., j]$ for which p hybridizes to f^i, respectively, r^i, at a position $t \ge j$. The objective is to choose the minimum number of primers that cover at least $L' + 1$ of the $2L'$ elements of each set $\{f^i[1, .., j], r^i[1, .., j] \mid 1 \le j \le L'\}$ for $i \in \{1, \ldots, n\}$.

To formulate this as an integer program, we again introduce a 0/1 variable x_p for every candidate primer p, which is set to 1 if and only if primer p is selected. We also introduce 0/1 variables $z(f^i, j)$ (respectively, $z(r^i, j)$) for every $i = 1, \ldots, n$, $1 \le j \le L'$; such a variable is set to 1 if and only if the prefix $f^i[1, .., j]$ (respectively, $r^i[1, .., j]$) is covered by at least one of the selected primers. Using these variables, MPSS-L can be formulated as follows:

$$\text{minimize} \quad \sum_{p \in \mathcal{P}} x_p, \tag{11.5}$$

subject to

$$\sum_{j=1}^{L'} z(f^i, j) + \sum_{j=1}^{L'} z(r^i, j) \ge L' + 1 \quad i = 1, \ldots, n, \tag{11.6}$$

$$z(f^i, j) \le \sum_{\substack{p \text{ hybridizes} \\ \text{to } f^i \text{ at } t \ge j}} x_p, \quad i = 1, \ldots, n, 1 \le j \le L', \tag{11.7}$$

$$z(r^i, j) \le \sum_{\substack{p \text{ hybridizes} \\ \text{to } r^i \text{ at } t \ge j}} x_p, \quad i = 1, \ldots, n, 1 \le j \le L', \tag{11.8}$$

$$x_p,\ z(f^i, j),\ z(r^i, j) \in \{0, 1\}. \tag{11.9}$$

Integer programs 11.5–11.9 has $O(nL)$ variables and $O(nL)$ constraints. However, its solution via general-purpose solvers such as CPLEX still requires prohibitively long runtime, mostly due to the fact that each constraint has $O(L)$ variables, and therefore the underlying integer program matrix is relatively dense. An equivalent formulation leading to a much sparser matrix, and in practice, to greatly reduced runtime is obtained as follows. Let $p(f^i, j)$ (respectively, $p(r^i, j)$) be the unique primer hybridizing at position j of f^i (respectively, r^i). Constraints 11.7 ensure that $z(f^i, j)$ is set to 1 only when at least one of the primers hybridizing to f^i at a position $t \ge j$ is selected. This happens if either $p(f^i, j)$ or a primer hybridizing to f^i at a position $t > j$ is selected, and in the latter case $z(f^i, j + 1)$ will be set to 1 as well.

Thus, constraints 11.7 can be replaced by

$$z(f^i, L') \leq x_{p(f^i, L')}, \quad i = 1, \ldots, n, \tag{11.10}$$

$$z(f^i, j) \leq x_{p(f^i, j)} + z(f^i, j+1), \quad i = 1, \ldots, n, 1 \leq j < L', \tag{11.11}$$

and Equation 11.8 can be similarly replaced by the nL' constraints obtained from Equations 11.10 and 11.11 after substituting r^i for f^i.

11.4 A GREEDY ALGORITHM

In this section, we describe an efficient greedy algorithm for MPSS-L and then establish its approximation guarantee. The algorithm, which can be seen as a generalization of the greedy algorithm for the set cover problem, critically exploits the string covering formulation introduced in Section 11.3 . To enable future application of our techniques to other covering problems, we describe the algorithm and its analysis using an axiomatic framework based on monotonic potential functions.

For a set of primers P, let $\Phi_i(P)$ denote the minimum between $L' + 1$ and the number of prefixes of $\{f^i[1, .., j], r^i[1, .., j] \mid 1 \leq j \leq L'\}$ covered by at least one primer in P. Also, let $\Phi(P) = \sum_{i=1}^{n} \Phi_i(P)$. The following properties of the integer valued set function Φ are immediate

(A1) $\Phi(\emptyset) = 0$.

(A2) There exists a constant $\Phi_{\max}$ such that $\Phi(P) = \Phi_{\max}$ if and only if P is a feasible solution ($\Phi_{\max} = n(L' + 1)$ for MPSS-L).

(A3) Φ is a nondecreasing set function, that is, $\Phi(P) \geq \Phi(P')$ whenever $P \supseteq P'$, and furthermore, for every P such that $\Phi(P) < \Phi_{\max}$, there exists $p \notin P$ such that $\Phi(P \cup \{p\}) > \Phi(P)$.

Properties (A1)–(A3) suggest using $\Phi(\cdot)$ as a measure of progress toward feasibility, and employing the generic greedy algorithm in Fig. 11.2 to solve MPSS-L. The greedy algorithm starts with an empty set of primers and then iteratively adds the primer that gives the largest increase in Φ, until reaching feasibility. By (A1)–(A3),

```
(1) P ← ∅
(2) While Φ (P) < Φmax do
    (a) Find a primer p∉ P maximizing Δ(p,P) := Φ(P U {p})−Φ (P)
    (b) P ← P U {p}
(3) Return P
```

FIGURE 11.2 The generic greedy algorithm.

this algorithm will end in a finite number of steps and will return a feasible MPSS-L solution.

Let us denote by $\Delta(p, P)$ the increase in Φ (also referred to as the "gain") obtained by adding primer p to set P, that is, $\Delta(p, P) = \Phi(P \cup \{p\}) - \Phi(P)$. By (A3), it follows that the gain function Δ is nonnegative. It is easy to verify that Δ is also monotonically nonincreasing in the second argument, that is,

(A4) $\Delta(p, P) \geq \Delta(p, P')$ for every p and $P \subseteq P'$.

Theorem 11.1 *For every set function Φ satisfying (A1)–(A4), the greedy algorithm in Fig. 11.2 returns a feasible solution of size at most $1 + \ln \Delta$ times larger than the optimum, where $\Delta = \max_{p,P} \Delta(p, P)$.*

Proof. We begin with some additional notations. Let $P^* = \{p_1^*, p_2^*, \ldots, p_k^*\}$ be an optimum solution, that is, a feasible set of primers of minimum size. Let also $P = \{p_1, p_2, \ldots, p_g\}$ denote the solution returned by the greedy algorithm, with primers indexed in the order in which they are selected by the algorithm. Let $\Phi_i^j = \Phi(\{p_1^*, \ldots, p_i^*\} \cup \{p_1, \ldots, p_j\})$, $\Delta_i^j = \Phi_i^j - \Phi_i^{j-1}$, and $\delta_i^j = \Phi_i^j - \Phi_{i-1}^j$. Note that, by (A4) and (A2), $\Delta_0^j \geq \Delta_1^j \geq \cdots \geq \Delta_k^j = 0$ for every $0 \leq j \leq g$, and $\delta_i^0 \geq \delta_i^1 \geq \cdots \geq \delta_i^g = 0$ for every $0 \leq i \leq k$. Furthermore, note that $\Delta_0^j \geq \delta_i^{j-1}$ for every $1 \leq i \leq k$ and $1 \leq j \leq g$. Indeed, Δ_0^j is the gain achieved by the greedy algorithm when selecting primer p_j. This gain must be at least $\Delta(p_i^*, \{p_1, \ldots, p_{j-1}\})$ since the greedy algorithm selects the primer with maximum gain in each iteration. Finally, by (A4), $\Delta(p_i^*, \{p_1, \ldots, p_{j-1}\}) \geq \Delta(p_i^*, \{p_1, \ldots, p_{j-1}\} \cup \{p_1^*, \ldots, p_{i-1}^*\}) = \Phi_i^{j-1} - \Phi_{i-1}^{j-1} = \delta_i^{j-1}$.

To analyze the size of the solution produced by the greedy algorithm, we use a charging scheme in which a certain cost is assigned to each primer in the optimal solution for every greedy primer. More precisely, the cost charged to p_i^* by the greedy primer p_j is

$$c_i^j = \begin{cases} \ln(\delta_i^{j-1}) - \ln(\delta_i^j), & \text{if } \delta_i^{j-1} \geq \delta_i^j > 0 \\ \ln(\delta_i^{j-1}) + 1, & \text{if } \delta_i^{j-1} > \delta_i^j = 0 \\ 0, & \text{if } \delta_i^{j-1} = \delta_i^j = 0. \end{cases}$$

Notice that the total cost charged to primer p_i^*, $\sum_{j=1}^{g} c_i^j$, is a telescopic sum equal to $1 + \ln(\delta_i^0) \leq 1 + \ln \Delta$. Hence, the overall cost is at most $k(1 + \ln \Delta)$. To prove the approximation factor of $1 + \ln \Delta$, it suffices to prove that we charge at least one unit of cost for each greedy primer. Indeed, consider a fixed $j \in \{1, \ldots, g\}$. Since $\Delta_0^j \geq \delta_i^{j-1}$, it follows that

$$c_i^j \geq \frac{\delta_i^{j-1} - \delta_i^j}{\Delta_0^j}$$

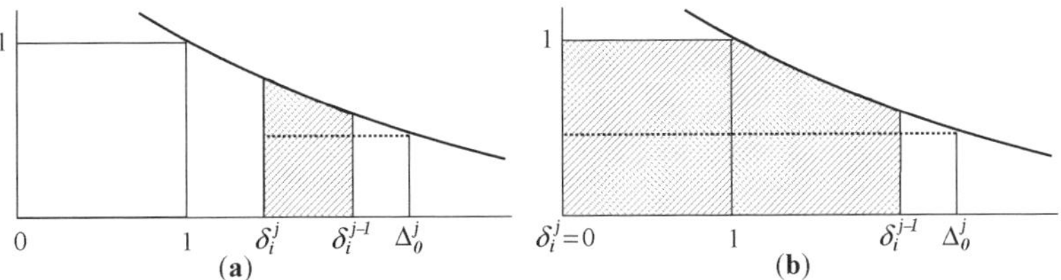

FIGURE 11.3 A graphical illustration of the cost lower bound used in the proof of Theorem 11.1 for $\delta_i^{j-1} \geq \delta_i^j > 0$ (**a**), and for $\delta_i^{j-1} > \delta_i^j = 0$ (**b**). In each case, c_i^j is equal to the area shaded under the curve $\min\{1, 1/x\}$. Since $\Delta_0^j \geq \delta_i^{j-1}$, the shaded area is larger than the area of a rectangle with width $\delta_i^{j-1} - \delta_i^j$ and height $1/\Delta_0^j$.

for every $1 \leq i \leq k$ (see Fig. 11.3). Using that $\delta_i^{j-1} - \delta_i^j = \Delta_j^{i-1} - \Delta_j^i$ and $\Delta_j^k = 0$ gives

$$\sum_{i=1}^{k} c_i^j \geq \sum_{i=1}^{k} \frac{\Delta_j^{i-1} - \Delta_j^i}{\Delta_0^j} = 1$$

which completes the proof. ■

Note that the maximum gain Δ is at most nL, and therefore Theorem 11.1 implies a worst case approximation factor of $1 + \ln(nL)$ for MPSS-L. For practical MPSS-L instances, Δ is much smaller than nL, implying a significantly better approximation factor on these instances.

11.4.1 Implementation Details

In this section, we discuss the details of an efficient implementation of the generic greedy algorithm in Fig. 11.2. First, we note that although there are 4^ℓ DNA sequences of length ℓ, no more than $2nL$ of these sequences (substrings of length ℓ of the input genomic sequences $S = \{f^i, r^i \mid 1 \leq i \leq n\}$) can be used as primers. Our implementation starts by creating a list with all feasible primers by removing substrings that do not meet user-specified constraints on GC content and melting temperature T_m (computed as in the Primer3 package [21]). Masking of repetitive elements and more stringent candidate filtering based, for example, on sophisticated statistical scoring models [24] can also be easily incorporated in this preprocessing step. For each surviving candidate primer, we precompute all hybridization positions within the strings of S, which allows to compute the coverage gain of a primer candidate p in time $O(n_p)$, where n_p is the number of hybridization positions for p. The primer with maximum gain is then found in step 2(a) of the algorithm by sequentially computing the gain of each remaining primer.

In order to speed up the implementation, we further use two optimizations. A feasible primer is called *unique* if it hybridizes only one of the sequences in S. The first optimization is to retain only the unique feasible primer closest to the amplification locus for each f^i and r^i. The exact number of eliminated unique candidate primers depends on primer length ℓ and number of amplification loci, but is often a significant fraction of the number of feasible candidate primers. Clearly, removing these primers does not worsen the quality of the returned solution.

The second optimization is to adopt a lazy strategy for recomputing primer gains in step 2(a). In first execution of step 2(a), we compute and store the gain for all feasible primers. In subsequent iterations, the gain of a primer is only recomputed if the saved gain is higher than the best gain seen in current iteration. Since gains are monotonically nonincreasing, this optimization is not affecting the set of primers returned by the algorithm.

11.5 EXPERIMENTAL RESULTS

We performed experiments on test cases extracted from the human genome databases as well as simulated test cases. The human genome test cases are regions surrounding known SNPs collected from National Center for Biotechnology Information's genomic databases. Random test cases were generated from the uniform distribution induced by assigning equal probabilities to each nucleotide. All experiments were run on a PowerEdge 2600 Linux server with 4 Gb of RAM and dual 2.8 GHz Intel Xeon CPUs—only one of which is used by our sequential implementations—using the same compiler optimization options. Integer programs were solved using the CPLEX solver version 9.1 with default parameters.

For all experiments we used a bound $L = 1000$ on the PCR amplification length, and a bound ℓ between 8 and 12 on primer length. Although it has been suggested that such short primers may not be specific enough [9], we note that hybridization outside the target region will not result in significant amplification unless *two* primers hybridize sufficiently closely to each other, a much less likely event [6]. Indeed, the feasibility of using primers with only 8–12 target specific nucleotides for simultaneous amplification of thousands of loci has been experimentally validated by Jordan et al. [11].[2] The potential function greedy algorithm in Fig. 11.2, referred to as G-POT, was implemented as described in Section 11.4.1, except that, in order to facilitate comparison with other algorithms we did not use any constraints on the GC content or melting temperature of candidate probes.

We ran experiments modeling two different scenarios. In the first scenario, the amplification target is a set of SNP loci where no two loci are within a distance of L of each other; under this scenario, the number of primers can only be reduced by primer reuse between different amplification reactions. In the second scenario, the amplification target is the set of all confirmed SNP loci within a gene, which results in much closer SNP loci. In this case, primer minimization is achieved by both primer reuse and inclusion of multiple SNP loci in a single amplification product.

[2] In addition to 8–12 specific nucleotides at the 3′ end, primers used in Jordan et al. contain a 5′ end sequence (CTCGAGNNNNNN) consisting of a fixed G/C rich 5′ anchor and 6 fully degenerate nucleotides.

11.5.1 Amplification of Sparse Sets of SNP Loci

In the first set of experiments, we compared G-POT with the following algorithms.

- The iterative beam-search heuristic of Souvenir et al. [23]. We used the primer-threshold version of this heuristic, MIPS-PT, with degeneracy bound set to 1 and the default values for the remaining parameters (in particular, beam size was set to 100).
- The greedy primer cover algorithm of Pearson et al. [19] (G-FIX). In this algorithm, the candidate primers are collected from the reverse and forward sequences within a distance of $L/2$ around the SNP. This ensures that the resulting set of primers meets the product length constraints. The algorithm repeatedly selects the candidate primer that covers the maximum number of not yet covered forward and reverse sequences.
- The optimum primer cover of the reverse and forward sequences within $L/2$ bases of each SNP (OPT-FIX), computed by running CPLEX on a natural integer program formulation of the problem.
- A naïve modification of G-FIX, referred to as G-VAR, in which the candidate primers are initially collected from the reverse and forward sequences within a distance of L around the SNP. The algorithm proceeds by greedily selecting primers like G-FIX, except that when a primer p covers for the first time one of the forward or reverse sequences corresponding to a SNP, say at position t, the algorithm truncates the opposite sequence to a length of $L - t$ to ensure that the final primer cover is L-restricted.
- The optimum MPSS-L solution (OPT) computed by running CPLEX on the compact integer linear program formulation described in Section 11.3.

Table 11.1 gives the number of primers selected and the running time (in CPU seconds) for the compared methods on instances consisting of up to 100 SNP loci extracted from the NCBI repository. The optimum primer cover of the reverse and forward sequences within $L/2$ bases of each SNP can be found by CPLEX for all instances, often in time comparable to that required by G-FIX. In contrast, the integer linear program in Section 11.3 can be solved to optimality only for instances with up to 20 SNP loci. For instances with 100 SNPs, even finding good feasible solutions to this ILP seems difficult for general-purpose solvers like CPLEX. Among greedy algorithms, G-POT has the best performance on all test cases, reducing the number of primers by up to 24% compared to G-FIX and up to 30% compared to G-VAR. In most cases, G-POT gives fewer primers than OPT-FIX, and always comes very close to the optimum MPSS-L solutions computed using CPLEX whenever the latter are available. The MIPS-PT heuristic has the poorest performance in both runtime and solution quality, possibly because it is fine-tuned to perform well with high degeneracy primers.

To further characterize the performance of the three greedy algorithms, in Fig. 11.4 we plot their average solution quality versus the number of target SNPs (on a

TABLE 11.1 Number of Primers (#P) and Runtime in Seconds (CPU) on NCBI Test Cases for Primer Length $\ell = 8, 10, 12$ and Amplification Length Constraint $L = 1000$. Entries Marked with a Dagger Represent the Best Feasible Solutions Found by CPLEX in 24 h

# SNPs	ℓ	MIPS-PT #P	MIPS-PT CPU	G-FIX #P	G-FIX CPU	OPT-FIX #P	OPT-FIX CPU	G-VAR #P	G-VAR CPU	G-POT #P	G-POT CPU	OPT #P	OPT CPU
	8	5	3	4	0.01	4	0.01	4	0.02	4	0.02	3	372
10	10	6	4	5	0.00	5	0.01	7	0.03	6	0.03	5	979
	12	10	6	8	0.00	8	0.01	9	0.03	7	0.03	6	518
	8	8	10	7	0.04	6	0.04	7	0.08	6	0.10	5	112,407
20	10	13	15	9	0.03	8	0.01	10	0.08	9	0.08	7	13,494
	12	18	26	14	0.04	14	0.01	13	0.08	13	0.11	11†	24h
	8	12	24	9	0.11	8	0.07	9	0.18	7	0.12	8†	24h
30	10	18	37	14	0.07	12	0.03	13	0.14	12	0.17	11†	24h
	12	26	84	20	0.12	19	0.03	19	0.19	21	0.15	15†	24h
	8	17	35	10	0.09	9	0.84	15	0.27	10	0.25	10†	24h
40	10	24	49	19	0.16	15	0.05	21	0.22	14	0.20	15†	24h
	12	32	183	24	0.10	24	0.03	25	0.23	22	0.28	21†	24h
	8	21	48	13	0.13	11	5.87	15	0.30	10	0.32	12†	24h
50	10	30	150	23	0.22	19	0.06	24	0.36	18	0.33	19†	24h
	12	41	246	31	0.14	29	0.03	32	0.30	29	0.28	25†	24h
	8	32	226	17	0.49	16	180.42	20	0.89	14	0.58	121†	24h
100	10	50	844	37	0.37	30	0.23	37	0.72	31	0.75	35†	24h
	12	75	2601	53	0.59	45	0.09	48	0.84	42	0.61	46†	24h

logarithmic scale) for randomly generated test cases. MIPS and the integer programming methods are not included in this comparison due to their nonscalable running time. In order to facilitate comparisons across instance sizes, the size of the primer cover is normalized by the double of the number of SNPs, which is the size of the trivial cover obtained by using two distinct primers to amplify each SNP. Although the improvement is highly dependent on primer length and number of SNPs, G-POT is still consistently outperforming the G-FIX algorithm and, with few exceptions, its G-VAR modification.

Fig. 11.5 gives a log–log plot of the average CPU running time (in seconds) versus the number of pairs of sequences for primers of size 10 and randomly generated pairs of sequences. The runtime of all three greedy algorithms grows linearly with the number of SNPs, with G-VAR and G-POT incurring only a small factor penalty in runtime compared to G-FIX. This suggests that a robust practical metaheuristic is to run all three algorithms and return the best of the three solutions found.

11.5.2 Amplification of Dense Sets of SNP Loci

In a second set of experiments, we used as amplification targets the SNP loci identified and verified within 14 genes at the Program for Genomic Applications

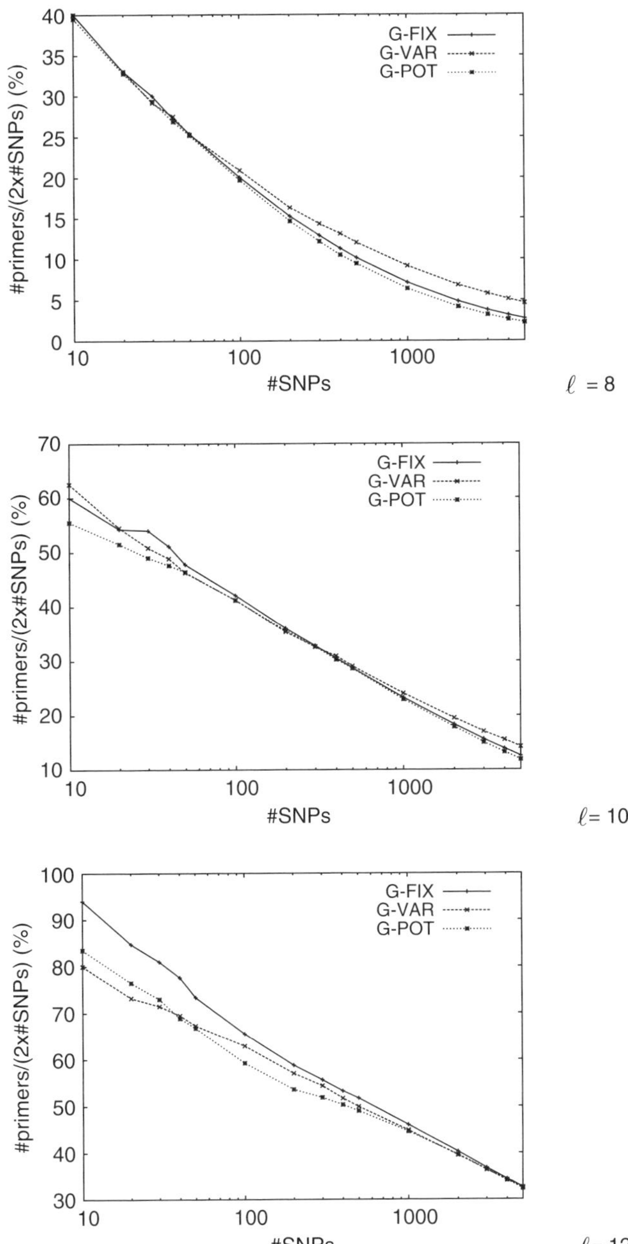

FIGURE 11.4 Performance of the compared algorithms, measured as relative improvement over the trivial solution of using two primers per SNP, for $\ell = 8, 10, 12$, $L = 1000$, and up to 5000 SNPs. Each number represents the average over 10 test cases of the respective size.

TABLE 11.2 Results for Dense Sets of SNPs, with Primer Length $\ell = 8, 10, 12$ and Amplification Length constraint $L = 1000$. The Minimum Number of Selected Primers for Each Testcase is Shown in Boldface. All Runtimes are Less Than 3 s.

HUGO Gene Name	# SNPs	Length (bp)	ℓ	Number of Selected Primers G-INT	G-FIX	G-VAR	G-POT
			8	30	13	12	**10**
AQP1	92	17649	10	30	27	**19**	**19**
			12	32	39	26	**24**
			8	16	9	9	**7**
CCR2	42	10073	10	16	16	14	**11**
			12	16	22	**13**	14
			8	34	18	19	**14**
CXCL12	122	18818	10	34	36	24	**23**
			12	**34**	56	38	35
			8	34	18	19	**14**
EPHB6	115	19655	10	34	37	30	**25**
			12	**34**	53	37	38
			8	40	16	18	**11**
F2R	114	24771	10	40	34	26	**21**
			12	42	46	30	**28**
			8	36	16	14	**11**
GATA3	131	22376	10	36	30	24	**18**
			12	36	45	31	**26**
			8	14	11	8	**7**
IFNG6	35	7665	10	14	15	**12**	**12**
			12	14	21	**15**	16
			8	10	7	7	**5**
IGF2	23	9013	10	10	9	11	**7**
			12	10	14	10	**9**
			8	12	10	8	**6**
IL8	37	7156	10	12	16	**10**	**10**
			12	**12**	20	16	14
			8	56	19	20	**12**
IRAK4	174	33033	10	56	42	36	**28**
			12	56	67	53	**44**
			8	42	15	14	**10**
NOS3	119	25106	10	42	31	25	**20**
			12	42	48	38	**35**
			8	28	14	13	**11**
STAT6	61	18891	10	28	24	23	**20**
			12	28	34	27	**25**
			8	40	18	18	**14**

TABLE 11.2 (*Continued*)

HUGO Gene Name	# SNPs	Length (bp)	ℓ	Number of Selected Primers: G-INT	G-FIX	G-VAR	G-POT
TGFB3	94	23990	10	40	32	24	**25**
			12	40	48	34	**35**
			8	54	16	16	**9**
TYK2	187	32167	10	54	27	25	**19**
			12	54	41	27	**23**

of the University of Washington [20]. For each gene, we consider SNP loci within all exons and introns, within the first 2000 bp upstream of first exon, and within the first 1500 bp downstream of the poly-A signal.

In addition to G-FIX, G-VAR, and G-POT, on these test cases we also ran a natural greedy primer selection algorithm, referred to as *greedy intervals* (G-INT), which works as follows. First, G-INT selects a forward primer immediately upstream of the leftmost SNP locus, and pairs it up with a reverse primer placed as far as possible downstream subject to the product length constraint. All SNP loci covered by the selected pair of primers are removed, and the above step is repeated until all loci are covered. It is easy to see that this algorithm minimizes the *number of amplification products* required to cover the given SNP loci. As shown in Table 11.2, G-POT continues to consistently outperform the other algorithms, with G-INT and G-VAR producing fewer primers for a few test cases.

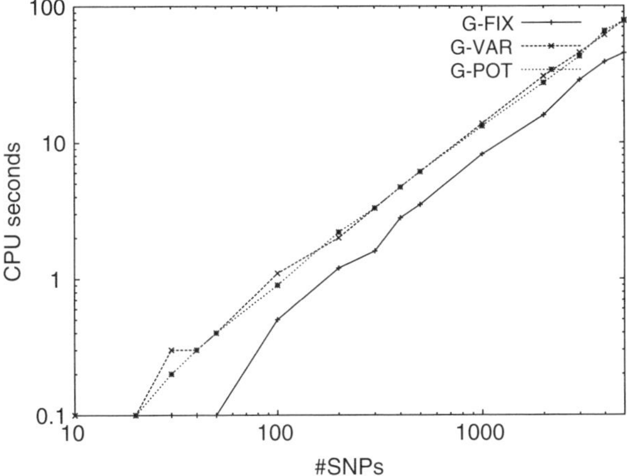

FIGURE 11.5 Average runtime of the compared algorithms for $\ell = 10$, $L = 1000$, and up to 5000 SNPs.

11.6 CONCLUSIONS

In this chapter, we have proposed exact algorithms based on integer programming and a more scalable potential function greedy approximation algorithm for MP-PCR primer set selection with amplification length constraints, and have presented experimental results showing that our methods lead to significant reductions in the number of primers compared to previous algorithms. Open source C implementations of both algorithms are available at http://dna.engr.uconn.edu/~software/G-POT/.

A promising approach to further increase the MP-PCR efficiency is the use of *degenerate PCR primers* [14,15,23], see also Section 5.3.3. A degenerate primer is essentially a mixture consisting of multiple nondegenerate primers sharing a common pattern. Remarkably, degenerate primer cost is nearly identical to that of a nondegenerate primer, since the synthesis requires the same number of steps (the only difference is that one must add multiple nucleotides in some of the synthesis steps). Since degenerate primers may lead to excessive unintended amplification, a bound on the degeneracy of a primer (i.e., the number of distinct nondegenerate primers in the mixture) is typically imposed [15,23].

Our greedy algorithm extends directly to the problem of selecting, for a given set of genomic loci, a minimum size L-restricted primer cover consisting of degenerate primers with bounded degeneracy. However, even for moderate degeneracy constraints, it becomes impractical to explicitly evaluate the gain function for all candidate primers. Indeed, as remarked by Linhart and Shamir [15], the number of candidate degenerate primers may be as large as $2nL\binom{k}{\delta}15^{\delta}$, where n is the number of loci, L is the PCR amplification length upper bound, and δ is the number of "degenerate nucleotides" allowed in a primer. To maintain a practical runtime, one may sacrifice optimality of the greedy choice in step 2(a) of the greedy algorithm, using instead approximation algorithms similar to those of Linhart and Shamir [15] for finding degenerate primers guaranteed to have near optimal gain. The analysis in Section 11.4 extends to this modification of the greedy algorithm as follows.

Theorem 11.2 *Assume that the greedy algorithm in Fig. 11.2 is modified to select in step 2(a) a primer whose gain is within a factor of α of the maximum possible gain, for some fixed $0 < \alpha \leq 1$. Then, the modified algorithm returns an L-restricted primer cover of size at most $(1 + \ln \Delta)\alpha$ times larger than the optimum, where $\Delta = \max_{p,P} \Delta(p, P)$.*

Another interesting direction for future research is extending primer selection algorithms to ensure that there is no cross hybridization between selected primers, which is one of the main causes of amplification failure in MP-PCR [8]. Cross hybridization constraints can be directly enforced in the integer program in Section 11.3 by the addition of inequalities of the form $x_p + x_{p'} \leq 1$ for every two primers p and p' predicted to cross hybridize. The potential function greedy algorithm can also ensure lack of primer cross hybridization via a simple modification: after selecting a primer

p, discard all candidates predicted to cross hybridize with p. Although this modification does no longer guarantee that the resulting set of primers is near minimal, preliminary experiments show that in practice it leads to only minor increases in the number of primers.

ACKNOWLEDGMENTS

The work of KMK and AAS was supported in part by NSF ITR grant 0121277. The work of IIM was supported in part by NSF CAREER award IIS-0546457, NSF DBI grant 0543365, and a Large Grant from the University of Connecticut's Research Foundation. A preliminary version of this work has appeared in [12].

REFERENCES

1. Berman P, DasGupta B, Kao M-Y. Tight approximability results for test set problems in bioinformatics. *Proceedings of the 9th Scandinavian Workshop on Algorithm Theory (SWAT)*; 2004. pp. 39–50.
2. Chvátal V. A greedy heuristic for the set covering problem. *Math Oper Res* 1979; 4:233–235.
3. ILOG Corp. Cplex optimization suite, http://www.ilog.com/products/cplex.
4. Doi K, Imai H. A greedy algorithm for minimizing the number of primers in multiple PCR experiments. *Genome Inform* 1999; 10:73–82.
5. Feige U. A threshold of $\ln n$ for approximating set cover. *J ACM* 1998; 45:634–652.
6. Fernandes RJ, Skiena SS. Microarray synthesis through multiple-use PCR primer design. *Bioinformatics* 2002; 18:S128–S135.
7. Hajiaghayi MT, Jain K, Lau LC, Măndoiu II, Russell AC, Vazirani VV. The minimum multicolored subgraph problem in haplotyping and PCR primer set selection. In Alexandrov VN, et al., editors. *Proceedings of the 6th International Conference on Computational Science (ICCS 2006), Part II*, Vol. 3992 of *Lecture Notes in Computer Science*, Berlin: Springer-Verlag; 2006. pp. 758–766.
8. Henegariu O, Heerema NA, Dlouhy SR, Vance GH, Vogt PH. Multiplex PCR: critical parameters and step-by-step protocol. *Biotechniques* 1997; 23:504–511.
9. Hsieh M-H, Hsu W-C, -Kay S, Tzeng CM. An efficient algorithm for minimal primer set selection. *Bioinformatics* 2003; 19:285–286.
10. Johnson DS. Approximation algorithms for combinatorial problems. *J Comput Syst Sci* 1974; 9:256–278.
11. Jordan B, Charest A, Dowd JF, Blumenstiel JP, Yeh Rf, Osman A, Housman DE, Landers JE. Genome complexity reduction for SNP genotyping analysis. *Proc Natl Acad Sci USA* 2002; 99:2942–2947.
12. Konwar KM, Măndoiu II, Russell AC, Shvartsman AA. Improved algorithms for multiplex PCR primer set selection with amplification length constraints. In Phoebe Chen Y-P, Wong L, editors. *Proceedings of the 3rd Asia-Pacific Bioinformatics Conference (APBC)*, London: Imperial College Press; 2005. pp. 41–50.

13. Kwok PY. Methods for genotyping single nucleotide polymorphisms. *Ann Rev Genomic Hum Genet* 2001; 2:235–258.

14. Kwok S, Chang SY, Sninsky JJ, Wong A. A guide to the design and use of mismatched and degenerate primers. *PCR Meth Appl* 1994; 3:S539–S547.

15. Linhart C, Shamir R. The degenerate primer design problem. *Bioinformatics* 2002; 18:S172–S181.

16. Lovász L. On the ratio of optimal integral and fractional covers. *Discrete Math* 1975; 13:383–390.

17. Mullis K. Process for amplifying nucleic acid sequences. U.S.Patent 4,683,202, 1987.

18. Nicodème P, Steyaert J-M. Selecting optimal oligonucleotide primers for multiplex PCR. *Proceedings of the 5th International Conference on Intelligent Systems for Molecular Biology*; 1997. pp. 210–213.

19. Pearson WR, Robins G, Wrege DE, Zhang T. On the primer selection problem for polymerase chain reaction experiments. *Discrete Appl Math* 1996; 71:231–246.

20. Program for Genomic Applications, University of Washington. Genes sequenced for snps, http://pga.gs.washington.edu/finished_genes.html

21. Rozen S, Skaletsky HJ. Primer3 on the WWW for general users and for biologist programmers. In Krawetz S, Misener S, editors. *Bioinformatics Methods and Protocols: Methods in Molecular Biology*. Totowa, NJ: Humana Press; 2000. pp. 365–386. Code available at http://www-genome.wi.mit.edu/genome_software/other/primer3.html

22. Slavik P. Improved performance of the greedy algorithm for partial cover. *Inform Process Lett* 1997; 64:251–254.

23. Souvenir R, Buhler J, Stormo G, Zhang W. Selecting degenerate multiplex PCR primers. *Proceedings of the 3rd International Workshop on Algorithms in Bioinformatics (WABI)*; 2003; pp.512–526.

24. Yuryev A, Huang J, Scott KE, Kuebler J, Donaldson M, Phillipes MS, Pohl M, Boyce-Jacino MT. Primer design and marker clustering for multiplex SNP-IT primer extension genotyping assay using statistical modeling. *Bioinformatics* 2004; 20(18):3526–3532.

12

RECENT DEVELOPMENTS IN ALIGNMENT AND MOTIF FINDING FOR SEQUENCES AND NETWORKS

SING-HOI SZE

Departments of Computer Science and of Biochemistry & Biophysics, Texas A&M University, College Station, Texas, USA

12.1 INTRODUCTION

Since Needleman and Wunsch [64] introduced the notion of sequence alignment in 1970, developing and improving sequence analysis algorithms has become one of the most important goals in computational biology. In 1981, Smith and Waterman [88] introduced a variant of pairwise alignment that can be used to analyze local similarities and showed that it can be solved efficiently in quadratic time using a dynamic programming technique that is similar to the one used in global alignment. On the contrary, the general problem of aligning multiple sequences has remained a very challenging problem, and it has been shown that the problem is NP-hard under many reasonable objective functions [38]. The best-known algorithm that always produces an optimal multiple alignment has time complexity $O(n^k)$ [16], where n is the maximum sequence length and k is the number of sequences, and thus is practical only when n and k are small.

Early heuristics to address the multiple alignment problem include a greedy strategy in [94] that constructs a multiple alignment from the results of conventional pairwise alignments. Most later approaches follow the progressive alignment strategy [25] that treats each input sequence as an alignment and iteratively chooses

Bioinformatics Algorithms: Techniques and Applications, Edited by Ion I. Măndoiu and Alexander Zelikovsky

and combines two smaller alignments into a larger one to obtain a final alignment. While CLUSTAL [96] is among one of the most well-known algorithms that employ this strategy, there are many recent ideas that lead to further improvement in biological accuracy of alignment algorithms, including a very effective consistency-based strategy that is employed in algorithms such as TCoffee [65]. In this chapter, we will investigate some of these developments that lead either to improved formulations of the multiple alignment problem or to more accurate multiple alignment algorithms.

While the alignment formulation is useful for finding similarities that span a large portion of the input sequences, it is not suitable for finding motifs when they do not occur at similar positions within each sequence or when most other nonmotif positions are random. In 1970, Kelly and Smith [47] developed one of the first motif finding algorithms to find restriction sites in a given sample. Later applications usually involve more complicated motifs, such as finding transcription factor binding sites in upstream regions given a set of potentially coregulated genes.

Early approaches usually assume that the motif is a string in the four-letter DNA alphabet and search over all 4^l candidate motifs of length l to look for their approximate occurrences [78,105]. Later approaches consider a more accurate representation of motifs as a collection of potentially different number of occurrences in some of the input sequences. Among one of the most popular approaches that employ this strategy is MEME [3], which uses statistical optimization techniques to ensure that high scoring motifs are identified. In 2000, Marsan and Sagot [59] and Pevzner and Sze [74] started a series of combinatorial approaches that lead to new ideas and many later improvements. We will describe many of these developments in this chapter.

To evaluate the effectiveness of alignment or motif finding algorithms, there have been many recent developments in the construction of benchmark datasets. These efforts have resulted in large-scale datasets that allow more accurate assessment of new algorithms. While it has been confirmed that the performance of multiple alignment algorithms is steadily increasing over the years, none of the motif finding algorithms are shown to have good performance when applied to finding transcription factor binding sites in higher organisms [100]. Thus, it is important to use these benchmark sets to understand the weaknesses of current algorithms and develop new strategies to improve them.

Although the alignment and motif finding problems were originally used for comparing sequences, as the amount of data that describe biological interactions increases rapidly at the genome scale, there is a need to consider generalized versions of these problems on biological networks. By defining a similarity measure for enzymes, Dandekar et al. [18] and Tohsato et al. [99] were among the few efforts that use pathway alignments to study the evolution of metabolic pathways. We will describe many recent approaches that further generalize the notion of alignments and motifs to nonlinear network alignments or network motifs in an attempt to find functional modules or other important substructures within one or more interaction networks. Since these problems are much more difficult than their linear counterparts, many new techniques have been proposed to address them.

12.2 MULTIPLE SEQUENCE ALIGNMENT

12.2.1 Recent Approaches

Although early datasets are small enough so that an exact dynamic programming algorithm such as MSA [16] can be used to produce optimal multiple alignments, it has been recognized that such an approach will not scale to larger datasets. By defining one of the input sequences as the center and aligning all the other sequences to it, Gusfield [34] developed approximation algorithms for multiple alignment that has a guaranteed performance bound of two under popular objective functions. However, this theoretical bound is too weak for practical purposes and such a star alignment strategy may not work well when large similarity variations among the sequences exist. Stoye [91] addressed this problem by proposing the DCA algorithm that uses a divide-and-conquer heuristic to cut the sequences into shorter segments until they become sufficiently short, at which time the exact algorithm MSA [16] is used to align the segments.

Since the above heuristic is still too slow for large-scale applications, most practical approaches follow a progressive alignment strategy that makes use of a guide tree [96] in which sequences that are more similar are grouped closer together on the tree to combine two smaller alignments along the tree. In many of these algorithms, an iterative refinement procedure [32] is also employed, usually by randomly breaking the alignment into two or more groups and realigning, or by estimating a new guide tree based on the current multiple alignment and repeating the process. Recently, Kececioglu and Starrett [43] showed that even the problem of aligning two alignments exactly is hard when the affine gap penalty scheme is used during the progressive step, although it can be solved in polynomial time when a constant gap penalty is used.

One of the most significant recent developments that leads to much improvement in alignment accuracy is the use of consistency-based approaches, in which the goal is to maximize the amount of consistently aligned pairs between the resulting multiple alignment and a given set of pairwise alignments [42]. TCoffee [65] is among the many successful approaches that utilize consistency-based pairwise alignments by aligning two sequences through each choice of a third sequence so that the initial pairwise alignments have better agreement with the final multiple alignment. Instead of finding the most probable alignment, ProbCons [21] significantly improved the accuracy of such approaches by finding an alignment with the maximum expected accuracy using a pair-HMM model. Probalign [82] further improved the accuracy by estimating posterior probabilities from the partition function of suboptimal alignments instead of using a pair-HMM model, while CONTRAlign [20] used a generalized conditional random field model to avoid making strong independence assumptions. MUMMALS [71] employed local structural information in addition to a pair-HMM model to improve alignment accuracy.

Since many of the above approaches are still computationally intensive, there were several attempts to seek appropriate trade-offs between computational time and accuracy for large-scale applications. MAFFT [41] constructed an alignment via fast Fourier transform by converting the sequences to an appropriate numerical format and using a simplified scoring function. MUSCLE [22] used k-mer counting to obtain quick distance estimates between two sequences, thus reducing the computational time of the pairwise alignment phase. Kalign [50] used a fast approximate string matching algorithm that allows for mismatches to similarly reduce the time for computing pairwise distance estimates. While most of the above approaches are designed to find global similarities, DIALIGN [63] used a different segment-to-segment approach to construct a multiple alignment from sets of locally aligned blocks, thus obtaining a better performance when there are extensive local similarities. Align-m [103] used a nonprogressive local heuristic approach while focusing on obtaining better performance for highly divergent sequences, whereas 3DCoffee [67] utilized structural pairwise alignments when they are available to improve alignment accuracy.

Since none of the above algorithms definitely outperform all the other algorithms in all situations, another line of research focuses on developing strategies to combine results of existing multiple alignment algorithms into a single improved alignment. ComAlign [13] extracted good quality subalignments from a given set of multiple alignments by investigating good subpaths via dynamic programming and showed that it is possible to obtain performance close to the exact algorithm MSA [16]. MCoffee [104] is an extension of TCoffee [65] that uses a consistency-based approach to construct such a combined alignment from multiple alignments given by a carefully selected set of algorithms.

While most algorithms view an alignment as placing sequences one on top of the other and adding gaps, POA [52] used a partial ordered graph to represent a multiple alignment that does not require that each letter be put into a definite column and showed that it is a better biological model in many situations. Sze et al. [93] developed an alternative formulation of multiple alignment by assuming that an additional tree that specifies a subset of pairwise alignments to be preserved is given and showed that the problem is solvable in polynomial time by constructing an alignment from a directed acyclic graph that is similar in structure to the graph produced by POA [52].

12.2.2 Using Additional Sequences from Database Search

Despite significant efforts, it remains very challenging to align highly divergent sequences. With the rapidly increasing size of biological databases, it is likely that some of the input sequences have similar hits in the databases. The use of these additional hits from database search can potentially help to improve alignment accuracy. This is especially useful when a hit from database search is intermediate between two input sequences, thus providing a missing link between them [31,69]. The effectiveness of such an approach is demonstrated by the inclusion of high scoring hits from database search in PREFAB [22], which, when used together with the original input sequences, produce more accurate alignments than using the input sequences alone. Similar ideas are also used in related areas such as finding distant homologies by utilizing multiple intermediate sequences from database search [55,83], clustering sequences via transitive homology [9], and using intermediate sequences to estimate reliable regions in alignments [58].

There are a few recent efforts that use this idea to improve multiple alignment accuracy. Heger et al. [35] used a graph-theoretic approach to link input sequences together along paths of neighboring intermediate sequences found from database search to identify sparse common motifs. Marti-Renom et al. [60], Simossis et al. [86], and Zhou and Zhou [111] constructed a profile from the hits produced by database search for each input sequence and showed that aligning these profiles instead of the original sequences gives much better performance. SPEM [111] also utilized structural alignments in the scoring of the newly constructed profiles to further improve alignment accuracy.

12.2.3 Benchmark Alignments

One very significant recent development in multiple alignment is the largely expanded availability of benchmark alignments on sets of protein sequences that can be used to evaluate algorithm performance. BAliBASE [97] is among one of the most popular benchmark datasets based on manually edited structural alignments that were originally subdivided into five categories, including alignments containing a small number of similar sequences that are further organized into four subclasses, that is, inclusion of orphan sequences, clusters of sequences from different families, sequences with large terminal extensions, and sequences with internal insertions, in which core blocks are defined to be regions that can be reliably aligned. The most recent version includes three more categories and a significant increase in the number of sequences and their lengths. Another popular benchmark database is HOMSTRAD [62], which is a collection of manually edited structure-based alignments with varying amount of sequence identity levels in different alignments.

In addition to the above databases, there are also two large benchmark sets that are based on pairwise alignments: PREFAB [22] contains automatically generated alignments, with each of them starting from a structural alignment of two sequences and then adding high scoring hits of the two sequences from database search to form the input sequence set. Accuracy assessment is based on the original two sequences with the datasets organized into many categories representing different levels of sequence identities. SABmark [103] contains an easier Superfamily set, a more difficult Twilight set, and variants of the two sets by adding false positive sequences, with each reference alignment represented by a collection of potentially conflicting pairwise alignments instead of a single alignment. Other recent benchmarks include OXBench [79] that contains automatically generated alignments constructed from clusters of structural domains, and IRMBASE [92] that contains alignments of sequences related by local instead of global similarities, which is designed to test the ability of an algorithm to align local motifs.

Usually, two score measures are used to evaluate the accuracy of a multiple alignment against a reference alignment [98]: the sum-of-pairs score (SPS) measures the percentage of letter pairs that are correctly aligned, while the column score (CS) measures the percentage of entire columns that are correctly aligned. To evaluate whether the overall accuracy of one algorithm is better than another algorithm, a statistical test such as the Wilcoxon matched-pairs signed-ranks test [106] is often used to check if there are significant performance differences. The use of the benchmark sets with these scoring measures confirms that the accuracy of multiple alignment algorithms has been improving steadily as new algorithms are introduced.

12.3 MOTIF FINDING

12.3.1 Recent Approaches

Although the assumption that a motif can be represented as a string in the four-letter DNA alphabet is inaccurate biologically, the corresponding motif finding problems are not extremely difficult to solve when the length of motifs l is short. By assuming that the number of substitutions between a motif and its occurrences is at most d, it is sufficient to consider only candidate motifs that are within d substitutions of a string that appears in the input sample [29,105], thus significantly improving the time complexity over early exhaustive approaches [78,105] when d is small compared to l. However, an important drawback of these approaches is that they cannot be used to find protein motifs, since the much larger alphabet size makes them impractical.

After these early efforts, the positional weight matrix (or profile) representation has become the most popular motif representation, in which a probability distribution over the DNA or the protein alphabet is used to model each motif position. This is a biologically more accurate representation, which facilities the development of many approaches that try to locate the motif occurrences directly within the input sample. CONSENSUS [90] used a greedy strategy to iteratively add occurrences to a growing motif while keeping only a certain amount of top motifs in each iteration and using an entropy score to evaluate motifs. Many later approaches use statistical optimization techniques to find high scoring motifs, although there is no guarantee that the motif with the highest score must be found.

Among the most popular algorithms that use this strategy is MEME [3], which uses the expectation-maximization technique to iteratively improve an initial motif by computing the probability of finding the current motif at each position within the input sample and using these probabilities to update the current motif. Another popular strategy is Gibbs sampling [51], which starts with a random motif and iteratively chooses an occurrence to delete and replace in order to improve the motif. Many variations of this technique have also been employed, including AlignACE [37], which uses Gibbs sampling and an iterative masking procedure to find multiple motifs, MotifSampler [95], which utilizes a higher order background model in an extended Gibbs sampling strategy, and ANN-Spec [107], which uses Gibbs sampling to train a perceptron network that is used to predict the locations of motif occurrences.

In 2000, Pevzner and Sze [74] proposed the (l, d)-motif model, which defines a motif of length l by implanting occurrences in the input sample that have at most d substitutions from the motif. The motif finding problem is then formulated as a graph-theoretic problem in which each vertex represents a string of length l that appears in the input sample and each edge connects two vertices that are at most $2d$ substitutions apart so that a motif is represented by a large clique in the graph. In another direction,

Marsan and Sagot [59] used a suffix tree coupled with tree-based pruning to develop an exact algorithm to find the motif pattern directly.

These efforts are followed by many later combinatorial approaches that further improve the computational and biological performance. Pavesi et al. [70] developed the WEEDER algorithm that reduces the search space in the suffix tree by imposing an additional condition that limits the percentage of mismatches that occur in every prefix of the motif. Eskin and Pevzner [24] developed the MITRA algorithm based on combining some of the advantages of the suffix tree in [59] and the WINNOWER algorithm in [74] to obtain a faster algorithm. Buhler and Tompa [15] proposed a random projection strategy that guesses a subset of positions in which the motif agrees on to pinpoint the motif. Keich and Pevzner [44] developed the MultiProfiler algorithm that uses a multipositional profile to eliminate improbable motif candidates. Price et al. [77] proposed a pattern branching strategy that starts with an arbitrary motif pattern and greedily changes the pattern one position at a time to improve the motif. Instead of addressing the NP-hard problem of finding large cliques, Matsuda [61] and Fratkin et al. [27] proposed to find a maximum density subgraph, which is defined to be the subgraph that has the highest ratio of the number of edges to the number of vertices so that the problem can be solved in polynomial time via a reduction to a series of maximum flow problems [30]. They showed that it is a reasonable model that can accurately represent biological motifs.

In addition to algorithms that make better use of the (l, d)-motif model, there is also much progress in the use of the profile representation for motifs. Price et al. [77] generalized their pattern branching strategy to give a profile branching technique that returns motifs represented as profiles. Kel et al. [45] employed a kernel-based method in which each local maximum of a probability density function corresponds to a motif profile so that a randomized iterative procedure can be used repeatedly to find them. Eskin [23] subdivided the profile space into many categories and used an upper bound on the scores to eliminate those categories that do not contain high scoring profiles. Leung and Chin [53] generalized the approach in [23] to guarantee that the highest scoring profile that corresponds to the optimal motif can always be found when the motif length is short. Since the profile representation ignores correlations among different motif positions, Barash et al. [4] used a more general model of Bayesian networks to represent dependencies between positions, while Zhou and Liu [110] extended the profile model to include pairs of correlated positions. Reddy et al. [80] developed a neighborhood profile search technique that avoids some of the problems associated with local maxima.

In addition to the above strategies, there are many other attempts to approach the motif finding problem from different directions. Rigoutsos and Floratos [81] developed the TEIRESIAS algorithm that uses a branch-and-bound technique to find all motifs that appear in at least a certain number of sequences while allowing don't care positions within motifs by starting with short motifs and iteratively combining them to produce longer ones. Sinha and Tompa [87] developed the YMF algorithm that exhaustively enumerates all motif patterns of a given length and evaluates them statistically using z-scores. Blanchette et al. [8] assumed that a phylogenetic tree is also given and used a dynamic programming technique to find strong motifs with respect to the tree. Apostolico and Parida [2] allowed don't care positions within motifs and imposed maximality and irredundancy constraints so that the problem can be solved in polynomial time when no mismatches are allowed. Leung et al. [54] proposed a biologically more accurate model by considering binding strengths of motifs to transcription factors. Kaplan et al. [39] used protein-DNA recognition preferences to predict binding sites for specific structural families by using the expectation-maximization technique. Zaslavsky and Singh [109] developed a general combinatorial optimization framework for motif finding by reducing to integer linear programming problems.

Since biological motifs usually do not occur in isolation, there are many attempts to discover motifs that work together in close proximity. Marsan and Sagot [59] generalized their suffix tree technique to handle multiple motifs that are separated by a range of distances. van Helden et al. [102] counted the number of occurrences of trinucleotide pairs separated by a fixed distance over a range of possible distances in an exhaustive manner while assessing their statistical significances. GuhaThakurta and Stormo [33] developed the Co-Bind algorithm that utilizes perceptrons coupled with profile-based probability estimates to find cooperative motifs that are close to each other. Liu et al. [56] developed the BioProspector algorithm that uses a modified Gibbs sampling strategy to identify multiple motifs within given distance constraints. Eskin and Pevzner [24] generalized their MITRA algorithm to handle sets of composite motifs.

12.3.2 Motif Finding by Alignment

Since the reliability of motif finding algorithms depends a lot on the quality of the input sample, it is often very difficult to obtain positive results when it is uncertain whether all the included genes are related or not. One important strategy to alleviate this problem is to consider sequences from orthologous genes in closely related species and align them so that highly conserved blocks within the alignment represent biological motifs that are separated by less conserved regions, a technique commonly known as phylogenetic footprinting. While these genes should be evolutionarily close enough to each other so that the order of the motifs is conserved, they should not be so close that the entire sequences become almost identical. Cliften et al. [17] used this strategy to align upstream regions of genes in several yeast species and showed that highly conserved blocks within the alignments correspond to functional elements.

An obvious way to perform phylogenetic footprinting is to use standard multiple alignment algorithms or algorithms that focus on aligning local similarities with multiple sequences [63,103]. Alternatively, a two-stage algorithm such as MUSCA [68] can be used to first search for motifs and then assemble compatible motifs together to form an alignment. Many other algorithms that are designed specifically for aligning DNA sequences can also be used, such as Multi-LAGAN [11], which is based on the progressive alignment strategy in which shorter local alignments are chained together to produce longer alignments during the pairwise stage, MAVID [10], which computes a maximum-likelihood ancestral sequence during progressive merging of two sequences to reduce computational time when aligning large genomic regions, and TBA [7], which produces a set of aligned blocks instead of conventional multiple alignments so that each position of the input sequences appears exactly once among the blocks.

12.3.3 Algorithm Assessment

To evaluate motif finding algorithms, it is important to develop benchmark datasets so that the relative performance of different algorithms can be compared. Tompa et al. [100] constructed a large-scale benchmark dataset for the identification of transcription factor binding sites that contain samples of upstream regions of genes from a few species, including yeast, drosophila, mouse, and human, with each sample containing sequences from one particular species. To allow fair comparisons of motif finding algorithms, three different types of background sequences are considered: real, which includes the original upstream sequences; generic, which includes random upstream sequences from the same species; and Markov, which includes sequences generated by a Markov process. Many statistics were also used in [100] for performance evaluations, both at the nucleotide and site levels, by computing overlaps between the predicted motifs and the reference motifs in each sample.

Tompa et al. [100] found that WEEDER [70] has the best overall performance and is much better than all the other assessed algorithms. Among the other top performing algorithms are AlignACE [37], ANN-Spec [107], MEME [3], MotifSampler [95], Oligo/Dyad [101,102], and YMF [87]. One very important observation in [100] is that the maximum overall correlation coefficient for all the algorithms is less than 0.2, and thus none of the algorithms perform sufficiently well to reliably identify motifs in these samples. This is especially true when higher organisms such as drosophila are involved, indicating that new strategies may be needed to find motifs in these organisms.

12.4 BIOLOGICAL NETWORK ANALYSIS

As the amount of data describing biological interactions increases, many algorithms have been proposed to analyze these interaction networks, which are often represented as graphs in which each vertex represents a gene, a protein, or an enzyme, and each edge represents interactions between them. One important problem is to find conserved linear paths given two graphs, which can be defined as the problem of finding high scoring alignments of two paths, one from each graph, so that vertex pairs with high enough similarity are considered to be matches, vertex pairs that are farther apart are mismatches, and vertices in one path that are not aligned to a vertex in the other path are indels.

A popular strategy to address this problem is to first construct a combined graph in which each vertex corresponds to a pair of matched vertices, one from each of the original graphs, and each edge represents that the corresponding vertices are in close proximity within the original graphs. The problem is then reduced to finding high scoring simple paths in the combined graph, in which the paths are required to be simple to avoid the dominance of highly repeating nonsimple paths. These high scoring paths can then be combined together to form a subnetwork structure that represents conserved pathways that are not necessarily linear. Note that a similar technique can be used to handle more than two graphs, and the above technique of combining high scoring simple paths can be applied to find functional modules within one or more networks by scoring edges within a path in terms of functional similarity.

Steffen et al. [89] used an exhaustive search strategy to find high scoring simple paths within one network over different lengths l but was only able to handle small l since the problem is NP-hard. They further combined these short simple paths to form functional modules within the network. Kelley et al. [46] found conserved pathways in two networks by randomly assigning a direction to each edge in the combined graph and deleting some of the conflicting edges to obtain a directed acyclic graph before finding the highest scoring path in polynomial time. By repeating the procedure an exponential number of times, they guaranteed that the probability of finding the highest scoring simple path of length l in the original graph is high. Scott et al. [84] used the color-coding technique [1] to randomly assign a color to each vertex. By finding a path in which each vertex has a distinct color and repeating the procedure a sufficient number of times, this technique increases the value of l that can be handled. They further showed that the technique can be extended to find more general substructures such as trees and series-parallel graphs in a network.

A common characteristic of the above approaches is that they first find high scoring paths before combining them into subnetworks or functional modules. Many approaches have also been proposed to obtain such subnetworks directly or to find functional modules that are not directly based on paths. Ogata et al. [66] formed clusters containing similar vertices in two graphs by starting from small vertex correspondences and iteratively combining them into larger clusters that represent functional modules. Berg and Lässig [6] defined the notion of graph alignment as a set of mutually disjoint subgraphs within a graph so that each vertex within a subgraph is associated with one vertex in each of the other subgraphs to form an alignment. They proposed a heuristic algorithm to extract such alignments and regard each subgraph as a network motif. Koyutürk et al. [48] used a depth-first enumeration to find small subgraphs that appear frequently in a large number of networks that act as important network motifs. Kashtan et al. [40] used a sampling technique to estimate the concentration of a given small subgraph within a large graph in an attempt to identify network motifs. Hu et al. [36] utilized a few graph reductions to extract potentially overlapping dense subgraphs that act as network modules. Sharan et al. [85] and Koyutürk et al. [49] developed greedy heuristics to find high scoring local network alignments that have a nonlinear structure from two or more networks.

In addition to finding functional modules directly, another strategy is to subdivide the given graph into clusters so that each cluster represents a functional module. Gagneur et al. [28] decomposed a given graph into modules so that each vertex within a module has the same set of neighbors as outside the module. Pereira-Leal et al. [73] constructed a line graph from the original graph, in which each vertex in the line graph represents an edge in the original graph and each edge represents an interaction pair with a shared protein, and used a clustering procedure to define functional modules. Luo and Scheuermann [57] generalized the notion of vertex indegree and outdegree to subgraphs and subdivided a given graph into modules so that the degree within a module is high while the degree between modules is small. Yamada et al. [108] grouped together enzymes that are close together on the graph and that have similar phylogenetic profiles [72], which are strings that indicate whether an enzyme has a homolog or not in a set of genomes, to form a hierarchical structure of modules.

12.5 DISCUSSION

Despite extensive efforts, more progress is needed to obtain reliable performance from multiple alignment and motif finding algorithms. When applied to analyze biological networks, the corresponding nonlinear problems become even harder to solve and it is important to develop better techniques to address them. In this concluding section, we will discuss a few directions that may lead to further advancements in these areas.

In multiple alignment, one obvious area of deficiency is the lack of statistical evaluation of alignments. Prakash and Tompa [76] addressed this problem by providing a significance score for local segments of a multiple alignment under the assumption that an additional phylogenetic tree is given that restricts how subsets of the input sequences can be related to each other. Similar statistics that can be used for evaluating global multiple alignments are high desirable. Another problematic area is the lack of algorithms that can produce local or incomplete multiple alignments directly, although a few existing methods [63,103] can already pinpoint subregions that are not aligned well by focusing on local similarities. In another direction, current approaches that take into account rearrangements during the computation of multiple alignments, such as SLAGAN [12], Mauve [19], and ProDA [75], usually employ a two-step approach that first identifies local collinear blocks before assembling them into a multiple alignment without requiring that the blocks are in linear order. A general formulation that allows such alignments to be defined directly in one step is desirable.

The successful incorporation of additional intermediate sequences in multiple alignment has led to the question of whether a similar strategy can be used in motif finding. Since motif finding performance is greatly affected by noise, much care has to be taken to develop a strategy to choose appropriate sequences from database search to exclude hits that are not related to any of the input sequences. Similarly, the successful use of a phylogenetic tree in motif finding in [8] has led to the question of whether such information can be better utilized in other areas. In progressive multiple alignment, it may be possible to incorporate such information directly rather than using a guide tree that is only loosely based on phylogenies. In a related direction, Buhler and Nordgren [14] have successfully developed an algorithm to find a local alignment between a query sequence and a multiple alignment by explicitly using a phylogenetic tree. In analyzing multiple biological networks, the use of a phylogenetic tree can be very helpful to restrict computations to pairwise comparisons within each internal node of the tree, while is much easier than performing simultaneous multiple comparisons [26]. This can also be helpful when developing algorithms for globally aligning multiple biological networks that are relatively small.

The rapid increase in the size of biological databases has created many opportunities to study less well-defined problems that can potentially lead to completely new types of information. Bejerano et al. [5] utilized large-scale data in noncoding regions by systematically clustering them and showed that this procedure can find unexpected clusters. In a different direction, it may be possible to develop formulations that allow study of evolutionary relationships among all known sequences in databases.

REFERENCES

1. Alon N, Yuster R, Zwick U. Color-coding. *J ACM* 1995;42:844–856.
2. Apostolico A, Parida L. Incremental paradigms of motif discovery. *J Comput Biol* 2004;11:15–25.
3. Bailey TL, Elkan CP. Fitting a mixture model by expectation maximization to discover motifs in biopolymers. *Proceedings of the 2nd International Conference on Intelligent Systems for Molecular Biology*. 1994. pp. 28–36.
4. Barash Y, Elidan G, Friedman N, Kaplan T. Modeling dependencies in protein-DNA binding sites. *Proceedings of the 7th Annual International Conference on Research in Computational Molecular Biology*. 2003. pp. 28–37.
5. Bejerano G, Haussler D, Blanchette M. Into the heart of darkness: large-scale clustering of human non-coding DNA. *Bioinformatics* 2004;20:SI40–SI48.
6. Berg J, Lässig M. Local graph alignment and motif search in biological networks. *Proc. Natl. Acad. Sci. USA* 2004;101:14689–14694.
7. Blanchette M, Kent WJ, Riemer C, Elnitski L, Smit AF, Roskin KM, Baertsch R, Rosenbloom K, Clawson H, Green ED, Haussler D, Miller W. Aligning multiple genomic sequences with the threaded blockset aligner. *Genome Res* 2004;14:708–715.
8. Blanchette M, Schwikowski B, Tompa M. Algorithms for phylogenetic footprinting. *J Comput Biol* 2002;9:211–223.
9. Bolten E, Schliep A, Schneckener S, Schomburg D, Schrader R. Clustering protein sequences — structure prediction by transitive homology. *Bioinformatics* 2001;17:935–941.
10. Bray N, Pachter L. MAVID: constrained ancestral alignment of multiple sequences. *Genome Res* 2004;14:693–699.
11. Brudno M, Do CB, Cooper GM, Kim MF, Davydov E, NISC Comparative Sequencing Program, Green ED, Sidow A, Batzoglou S. LAGAN and Multi-LAGAN: efficient tools for large-scale multiple alignment of genomic DNA. *Genome Res* 2003;13:721–731.
12. Brudno M, Malde S, Poliakov A, Do CB, Couronne O, Dubchak I Batzoglou S. Glocal alignment: finding rearrangements during alignment. *Bioinformatics* 2003;19:SI54–SI62.

13. Bucka-Lassen K, Caprani O, Hein J. Combining many multiple alignments in one improved alignment. *Bioinformatics* 1999;15:122–130.
14. Buhler J, Nordgren R. Toward a phylogenetically aware algorithm for fast DNA similarity search. *Lecture Notes in Bioinformatics, Vol. 3388*. 2005. pp. 15–29.
15. Buhler J, Tompa M. Finding motifs using random projections. *J Comput Biol* 2002;9:225–242.
16. Carillo H, Lipman D. The multiple sequence alignment problem in biology. *SIAM J Appl Math* 1988;48:1073–1082.
17. Cliften PF, Hillier LW, Fulton L, Graves T, Miner T, Gish WR, Waterston RH, Johnston M. Surveying *Saccharomyces* genomes to identify functional elements by comparative DNA sequence analysis. *Genome Res* 2001;11:1175–1186.
18. Dandekar T, Schuster S, Snel B, Huynen M, Bork P. Pathway alignment: application to the comparative analysis of glycolytic enzymes. *Biochem J* 1999;343:115–124.
19. Darling ACE, Mau B, Blattner FR, Perna NT. Mauve: multiple alignment of conserved genomic sequence with rearrangements. *Genome Res* 2004;14:1394–1403.
20. Do CB, Gross SS, Batzoglou S. CONTRAlign: discriminative training for protein sequence alignment. *Lecture Notes in Bioinformatics Vol. 3909.* 2006. pp. 160–174.
21. Do CB, Mahabhashyam MS, Brudno M, Batzoglou S. ProbCons: probabilistic consistency-based multiple sequence alignment. *Genome Res* 2005;15:330–340.
22. Edgar RC. MUSCLE: multiple sequence alignment with high accuracy and high throughput. *Nucleic Acids Res* 2004;32:1792–1797.
23. Eskin E. From profiles to patterns and back again: a branch and bound algorithm for finding near optimal motif profiles. *Proceedings of the 8th Annual International Conference on Research in Computational Molecular Biology.* 2004. pp. 115–124.
24. Eskin E, Pevzner PA. Finding composite regulatory patterns in DNA sequences. *Bioinformatics* 2002;18:S354–S363.
25. Feng D, Doolittle R. Progressive sequence alignment as a prerequisite to correct phylogenetic trees. *J Mol Evol* 1987;25:351–360.
26. Flannick J, Novak A, Srinivasan BS, McAdams HH, Batzoglou S. Græmlin: general and robust alignment of multiple large interaction networks. *Genome Res* 2006;16:1169–1181.
27. Fratkin E, Naughton BT, Brutlag DL, Batzoglou S. MotifCut: regulatory motifs finding with maximum density subgraphs. *Bioinformatics* 2006;22:E150–E157.
28. Gagneur J, Krause R, Bouwmeester T, Casari G. Modular decomposition of protein-protein interaction networks. *Genome Biol* 2004;5:R57.
29. Galas DJ, Eggert M, Waterman MS. Rigorous pattern-recognition methods for DNA sequences. Analysis of promoter sequences from *Escherichia coli. J Mol Biol* 1985;186:117–128.
30. Gallo G, Grigoriadis MD, Tarjan RE. A fast parametric maximum flow algorithm and applications. *SIAM J Comput* 1989;18:30–55.
31. Gerstein M. Measurement of the effectiveness of transitive sequence comparison, through a third 'intermediate' sequence. *Bioinformatics* 1998;14:707–714.
32. Gotoh O. Significant improvement in accuracy of multiple protein sequence alignments by iterative refinement as assessed by reference to structural alignments. *J Mol Biol* 1996;264:823–838.

33. GuhaThakurta D, Stormo GD. Identifying target sites for cooperatively binding factors. *Bioinformatics* 2001;17;608–621.
34. Gusfield D. Efficient methods for multiple sequence alignment with guaranteed error bounds. *Bull Math Biol* 1993;55:141–154.
35. Heger A, Lappe M, Holm L. Accurate detection of very sparse sequence motifs. *J Comput Biol* 2004;11:843–857.
36. Hu H, Yan X, Huang Y, Han J, Zhou XJ. Mining coherent dense subgraphs across massive biological networks for functional discovery. *Bioinformatics* 2005;21:SI213–SI221.
37. Hughes JD, Estep PW, Tavazoie S, Church GM. Computational identification of *cis*-regulatory elements associated with groups of functionally related genes in *Saccharomyces cerevisiae*. *J Mol Biol* 2000;296:1205–1214.
38. Just W. Computational complexity of multiple sequence alignment with SP-score. *J Comput Biol* 2001;8:615–623.
39. Kaplan T, Friedman N, Margalit H. *Ab initio* prediction of transcription factor binding sites using structural knowledge. *PLoS Comput Biol* 2005;1:E1.
40. Kashtan N, Itzkovitz S, Milo R, Alon U. Efficient sampling algorithm for estimating subgraph concentrations and detecting network motifs. *Bioinformatics* 2004;20:1746–1758.
41. Katoh K, Misawa K, Kuma K, Miyata T. MAFFT: a novel method for rapid multiple sequence alignment based on fast Fourier transform. *Nucleic Acids Res* 2002;30:3059–3066.
42. Kececioglu JD. The maximum weight trace problem in multiple sequence alignment. *Lecture Notes in Computer Science Vol. 684.* 1993. pp. 106–119.
43. Kececioglu J, Starrett D. Aligning alignments exactly. *Proceedings of the 8th Annual International Conference on Research in Computational Molecular Biology*. 2004. pp. 85–96.
44. Keich U, Pevzner PA. Finding motifs in the twilight zone. *Bioinformatics* 2002;18:1374–1381.
45. Kel A, Tikunov Y, Voss N, Wingender E. Recognition of multiple patterns in unaligned sets of sequences: comparison of kernel clustering method with other methods. *Bioinformatics* 2004;20:1512–1516.
46. Kelley BP, Sharan R, Karp RM, Sittler T, Root DE, Stockwell BR, Ideker T. Conserved pathways within bacteria and yeast as revealed by global protein network alignment. *Proc. Natl. Acad. Sci. USA* 2003;100:11394–11399.
47. Kelly TJ, Smith HO. A restriction enzyme from *Hemophilus influenzae*. II. *J Mol Biol* 1970;51:393–409.
48. Koyutürk M, Grama A, Szpankowski W. An efficient algorithm for detecting frequent subgraphs in biological networks. *Bioinformatics* 2004;20:SI200–SI207.
49. Koyutürk M, Kim Y, Topkara U, Subramaniam S, Szpankowski W, Grama A. Pairwise alignment of protein interaction networks. *J Comput Biol* 2006;13:182–199.
50. Lassmann T, Sonnhammer ELL. Kalign — an accurate and fast multiple sequence alignment algorithm. *BMC Bioinformatics* 2005;6:298.
51. Lawrence CE, Altschul SF, Boguski MS, Liu JS, Neuwald AF, Wootton JC. Detecting subtle sequence signals: a Gibbs sampling strategy for multiple alignment. *Science* 1993;262:208–214.

52. Lee C, Grasso C, Sharlow MF. Multiple sequence alignment using partial order graphs. *Bioinformatics* 2002;18:452–464.
53. Leung HC, Chin FY. Finding exact optimal motifs in matrix representation by partitioning. *Bioinformatics* 2005;21:SII86–SII92.
54. Leung HC, Chin FY, Yiu SM, Rosenfeld R, Tsang WW. Finding motifs with insufficient number of strong binding sites. *J Comput Biol* 2005;12:686–701.
55. Li W, Pio F, Pawlowski K, Godzik A. Saturated BLAST: an automated multiple intermediate sequence search used to detect distant homology. *Bioinformatics* 2000;16:1105–1110.
56. Liu X, Brutlag DL, Liu JS. BioProspector: discovering conserved DNA motifs in upstream regulatory regions of co-expressed genes. *Pac Sym Biocomput* 2001;127–138.
57. Luo F, Scheuermann RH. Detecting functional modules from protein interaction networks. *Proceedings of the 1st International Multi-Symposiums on Computer and Computational Sciences* 2006. pp. 123–130.
58. Margelevičius M, Venclovas Č. PSI-BLAST-ISS: an intermediate sequence search tool for estimation of the position-specific alignment reliability. *BMC Bioinformatics* 2005;6:185.
59. Marsan L, Sagot M-F. Algorithms for extracting structured motifs using a suffix tree with an application to promoter and regulatory site consensus identification. *J Comput Biol* 2000;7:345–362.
60. Marti-Renom MA, Madhusudhan MS, Sali A. Alignment of protein sequences by their profiles. *Protein Sci* 2004;13:1071–1087.
61. Matsuda H. Detection of conserved domains in protein sequences using a maximum-density subgraph algorithm. *IEICE Trans. Fund. Elec. Comm. Comp. Sci.* 2000;E83-A:713–721.
62. Mizuguchi K, Deane CM, Blundell TL, Overington JP. HOMSTRAD: a database of protein structure alignments for homologous families. *Protein Sci* 1998;7:2469–2471.
63. Morgenstern B, Dress A, Werner T. Multiple DNA and protein sequence alignment based on segment-to-segment comparison. *Proc. Natl. Acad. Sci. USA* 1996;93:12098–12103.
64. Needleman SB, Wunsch CD. A general method applicable to the search for similarities in the amino acid sequence of two proteins. *J Mol Biol* 1970;48:443–453.
65. Notredame C, Higgins DG, Heringa J. T-Coffee: a novel method for fast and accurate multiple sequence alignment. *J Mol Biol* 2000;302:205–217.
66. Ogata H, Fujibuchi W, Goto S, Kanehisa M. A heuristic graph comparison algorithm and its application to detect functionally related enzyme clusters. *Nucleic Acids Res* 2000;28:4021–4028.
67. O'Sullivan O, Suhre K, Abergel C, Higgins DG, Notredame C. 3DCoffee: combining protein sequences and structures within multiple sequence alignments. *J Mol Biol* 2004;340:385–395.
68. Parida L, Floratos A, Rigoutsos I. MUSCA: an algorithm for constrained alignment of multiple data sequences. *Proceedings of the 9th Workshop on Genome Informatics*. 1998. pp. 112–119.
69. Park J, Teichmann SA, Hubbard T, Chothia C. Intermediate sequences increase the detection of homology between sequences. *J Mol Biol* 1997;273:349–354.
70. Pavesi G, Mauri G, Pesole G. An algorithm for finding signals of unknown length in DNA sequences. *Bioinformatics* 2001;17:S207–S214.

71. Pei J, Grishin NV. MUMMALS: multiple sequence alignment improved by using hidden Markov models with local structural information. *Nucleic Acids Res* 2006;34:4364–4374.

72. Pellegrini M, Marcotte EM, Thompson MJ, Eisenberg D, Yeates TO. Assigning protein functions by comparative genome analysis: protein phylogenetic profiles. *Proc. Natl. Acad. Sci. USA* 1999;96:4285–4288.

73. Pereira-Leal JB, Enright AJ, Ouzounis CA. Detection of functional modules from protein interaction networks. *Proteins* 2004;54:49–57.

74. Pevzner PA, Sze S-H. Combinatorial approaches to finding subtle signals in DNA sequences. *Proceedings of the 8th International Conference on Intelligent Systems for Molecular Biology*. 2000. pp. 269–278.

75. Phuong TM, Do CB, Edgar RC, Batzoglou S. Multiple alignment of protein sequences with repeats and rearrangements. *Nucleic Acids Res* 2006;34:5932–5942.

76. Prakash A, Tompa M. Statistics of local multiple alignments. *Bioinformatics* 2005;21:SI344–SI350.

77. Price A, Ramabhadran S, Pevzner PA. Finding subtle motifs by branching from sample strings. *Bioinformatics* 2003;19:SII149–SII155.

78. Queen C, Wegman MN, Korn LJ. Improvements to a program for DNA analysis: a procedure to find homologies among many sequences. *Nucleic Acids Res* 1982;10:449–456.

79. Raghava GPS, Searle SMJ, Audley PC, Barber JD, Barton GJ. OXBench: a benchmark for evaluation of protein multiple sequence alignment accuracy. *BMC Bioinformatics* 2003;4:47.

80. Reddy CK, Weng Y-C, Chiang H-D. Refining motifs by improving information content scores using neighborhood profile search. *Algorithms Mol Biol* 2006;1:23.

81. Rigoutsos I, Floratos A. Combinatorial pattern discovery in biological sequences: the TEIRESIAS algorithm. *Bioinformatics* 1998;14:55–67.

82. Roshan U, Livesay DR. Probalign: multiple sequence alignment using partition function posterior probabilities. *Bioinformatics* 2006;22:2715–2721.

83. Salamov AA, Suwa M, Orengo CA, Swindells MB. Combining sensitive database searches with multiple intermediates to detect distant homologues. *Protein Eng* 1999;12:95–100.

84. Scott J, Ideker T, Karp RM, Sharan R. Efficient algorithms for detecting signaling pathways in protein interaction networks. *J Comput Biol* 2006;13:133–144.

85. Sharan R, Suthram S, Kelley RM, Kuhn T, McCuine S, Uetz P, Sittler T, Karp RM, Ideker T. Conserved patterns of protein interaction in multiple species. *Proc. Natl. Acad. Sci. USA* 2005;102:1974–1979.

86. Simossis VA, Kleinjung J, Heringa J. Homology-extended sequence alignment. *Nucleic Acids Res* 2005;33:816–824.

87. Sinha S, Tompa M. A statistical method for finding transcription factor binding sites. *Proceedings of the 8th International Conference on Intelligent Systems for Molecular Biology*. 2000. pp. 344–354.

88. Smith TF, Waterman MS. Identification of common molecular subsequences. *J Mol Biol* 1981;147:195–197.

89. Steffen M, Petti A, Aach J, D'haeseleer P, Church G. Automated modelling of signal transduction networks. *BMC Bioinformatics* 2002;3:34.

90. Stormo GD, Hartzell GW. Identifying protein-binding sites from unaligned DNA fragments. *Proc. Natl. Acad. Sci. USA* 1989;86:1183–1187.
91. Stoye J. Multiple sequence alignment with the divide-and-conquer method. *Gene* 1998;211:GC45–GC56.
92. Subramanian AR, Weyer-Menkhoff J, Kaufmann M, Morgenstern B. DIALIGN-T: an improved algorithm for segment-based multiple sequence alignment. *BMC Bioinformatics* 2005;6:66.
93. Sze S-H, Lu Y, Yang Q. A polynomial time solvable formulation of multiple sequence alignment. *J Comput Biol* 2006;13:309–319.
94. Taylor WR. Multiple sequence alignment by a pairwise algorithm. *Comput Appl Biosci* 1987;3:81–87.
95. Thijs G, Lescot M, Marchal K, Rombauts S, De Moor B, Rouzé P, Moreau Y. A higher-order background model improves the detection of promoter regulatory elements by Gibbs sampling. *Bioinformatics* 2001;17:1113–1122.
96. Thompson JD, Higgins DG, Gibson TJ. CLUSTAL W: improving the sensitivity of progressive multiple sequence alignment through sequence weighting, position specific gap penalties and weight matrix choice. *Nucleic Acids Res* 1994;22:4673–4680.
97. Thompson JD, Koehl P, Ripp R, Poch O. BAliBASE 3.0: latest developments of the multiple sequence alignment benchmark. *Proteins* 2005;61:127–136.
98. Thompson JD, Plewniak F, Poch O. A comprehensive comparison of multiple sequence alignment programs. *Nucleic Acids Res* 1999;27:2682–2690.
99. Tohsato Y, Matsuda H, Hashimoto A. A multiple alignment algorithm for metabolic pathway analysis using enzyme hierarchy. *Proceedings of the 8th International Conference on Intelligent Systems for Molecular Biology*. 2000. pp. 376–383.
100. Tompa M, Li N, Bailey TL, Church GM, De Moor B, Eskin E, Favorov AV, Frith MC, Fu Y, Kent WJ, Makeev VJ, Mironov AA, Noble WS, Pavesi G, Pesole G, Régnier M, Simonis N, Sinha S, Thijs G, van Helden J, Vandenbogaert M, Weng Z, Workman C, Ye C, Zhu Z. Assessing computational tools for the discovery of transcription factor binding sites. *Nature Biotechnol* 2005;23:137–144.
101. van Helden J, André B, Collado-Vides J. Extracting regulatory sites from the upstream region of yeast genes by computational analysis of oligonucleotide frequencies. *J Mol Biol* 1998;281:827–842.
102. van Helden J, Rios AF, Collado-Vides J. Discovering regulatory elements in non-coding sequences by analysis of spaced dyads. *Nucleic Acids Res* 2000;28:1808–1818.
103. Van Walle I, Lasters I, Wyns L. Align-m — a new algorithm for multiple alignment of highly divergent sequences. *Bioinformatics* 2004;20:1428–1435.
104. Wallace IM, O'Sullivan O, Higgins DG, Notredame C. M-Coffee: combining multiple sequence alignment methods with T-Coffee. *Nucleic Acids Res* 2006;34:1692–1699.
105. Waterman MS, Arratia R, Galas DJ. Pattern recognition in several sequences: consensus and alignment. *Bull Math Biol* 1984;46:515–527.
106. Wilcoxon F. Probability tables for individual comparisons by ranking methods. *Biometrics* 1947;3:119–122.
107. Workman CT, Stormo GD. ANN-Spec: a method for discovering transcription factor binding sites with improved specificity. *Pac Sym Biocomput* 2000;467–478.

108. Yamada T, Kanehisa M, Goto S. Extraction of phylogenetic network modules from the metabolic network. *BMC Bioinformatics* 2006;7:130.

109. Zaslavsky E, Singh M. A combinatorial optimization approach for diverse motif finding applications. *Algorithms Mol Biol* 2006;1:13.

110. Zhou Q, Liu JS. Modeling within-motif dependence for transcription factor binding site predictions. *Bioinformatics* 2004;20:909–916.

111. Zhou H, Zhou Y. SPEM: improving multiple sequence alignment with sequence profiles and predicted secondary structures. *Bioinformatics* 2005;21:3615–3621.

PART III

MICROARRAY DESIGN AND DATA ANALYSIS

13

ALGORITHMS FOR OLIGONUCLEOTIDE MICROARRAY LAYOUT

SÉRGIO A. DE CARVALHO JR.

Technische Fakultät, Bielefeld University, Bielefeld, Germany

SVEN RAHMANN

Bioinformatics for High-Throughput Technologies, Computer Science Department 11, Technical University of Dortmund, Germany

Microarrays are a ubiquitous tool in molecular biology with a wide range of applications on a whole-genome scale, including high-throughput gene expression analysis, genotyping, and resequencing. The advantage of oligonucleotide arrays is that their higher densities allow, for instance, the simultaneous measurement of the expression of several thousands of genes at once. High-density microarrays are usually produced by light-directed combinatorial chemistry that builds the probe sequences base-by-base. Because of the natural properties of light, the quality of a microarray can be improved by carefully designing the physical arrangement, or *layout*, of its probes. In this chapter, we review models for evaluating the layout of oligonucleotide microarrays and survey algorithmic approaches that can be used in their design.

Bioinformatics Algorithms: Techniques and Applications, Edited by Ion I. Măndoiu and Alexander Zelikovsky

13.1 INTRODUCTION

Oligonucleotide microarrays consist of short DNA fragments, called *probes*, affixed or synthesized at specific locations, called *features* or *spots*, on a solid surface. Microarrays are based on the principle of Watson–Crick base pairing. Each probe is a single-stranded DNA molecule of 10 to 70 nucleotides that perfectly matches with a specific part of a *target* molecule. The probes are used to verify whether (or in which quantity) the targets are present in a given biological sample.

The first step of a microarray experiment consists of collecting mRNAs or genomic DNA from the cells or tissue under investigation. The mixture to be analyzed is prepared with fluorescent tags and loaded on the array, allowing the targets to hybridize with the probes. Any unbound molecule is washed away, leaving on the array only those molecules that have found a complementary probe. Finally, the array is exposed to a light source that induces fluorescence, and an optical scanner reads the intensity of light emitted at each spot.

Under ideal conditions, each probe will hybridize only to its target. Thus, it is possible to infer whether a given molecule is present in the sample by checking whether there is light coming from the corresponding spot of the array. The expression level of a gene in a cell can also be inferred because each spot contains several million identical probes, and the strength of the fluorescent signal on a spot is expected to be proportional to the concentration of the target in the sample. In practice, each target is queried by several probes (its *probe set*), and complex statistical calculations are performed to infer the concentration from the observed signals.

High-density microarrays, also called DNA chips, can have more than a million spots, and are thus able to query tens of thousands of genes, covering the entire genome of an organism. The pioneering Affymetrix GeneChip® arrays, for instance, have up to 1.3 million spots on a coated quartz substrate, measuring a little over 1 cm^2. The spots are as narrow as 5 μm (0.005 mm), and are arranged in a regularly-spaced rectangular grid.

13.1.1 Microarray Production

GeneChip arrays are produced by combinatorial chemistry and techniques derived from microelectronics and integrated circuits fabrication. Probes are typically 25 bases long and are synthesized on the chip, in parallel, in a series of repetitive steps. Each step appends the same kind of nucleotide to the probes of selected regions of the chip. The selection of which probes receive the nucleotide is achieved by a process called *photolithography* [6].

Figure 13.1 illustrates this process: the quartz wafer of a GeneChip array is initially coated with a chemical compound topped with a light-sensitive protecting group that is removed when exposed to ultraviolet light, activating the compound for chemical coupling. A lithographic mask is used to direct light and remove the protecting groups of only those positions that should receive the nucleotide of a particular synthesis step. A solution containing adenine (A), thymine (T), cytosine (C) or guanine (G) is then flushed over the chip surface, but the chemical coupling occurs only in those positions

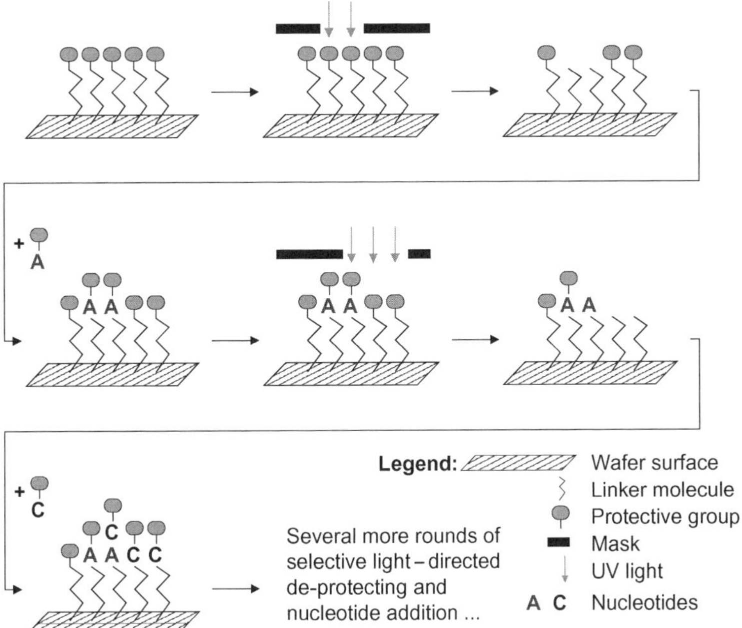

FIGURE 13.1 Affymetrix's probe synthesis via photolithographic masks. The chip is coated with a chemical compound and a light-sensitive protecting group; masks are used to direct light and activate selected probes for chemical coupling; nucleotides are appended to deprotected probes; the process is repeated until all probes have been fully synthesized.

that have been previously deprotected. Each coupled nucleotide also bears another protecting group so that the process can be repeated until all probes have been fully synthesized.

Photolithographic masks are notoriously expensive and cannot be changed once they have been manufactured. Thus, any change in the chip layout requires the production of a new set of masks. A similar method of *in situ* synthesis known as Maskless Array Synthesizer (MAS) was later developed to eliminate the need of such masks [13]. Probes are still built by repeating cycles of deprotection and chemical coupling of nucleotides. The illumination, however, relies on an array of miniature mirrors that can be independently controlled to direct or deflect the incidence of light on the chip.

NimbleGen Systems, Inc. uses its own Digital Micromirror Device (DMD) that can control up to 786,000 individual mirrors to produce microarrays with spots as small as 16 μm× 16 μm. The Geniom® system of febit biotech GmbH, a platform for customized microarray production, also uses a micromirror array to direct the synthesis process.

13.1.2 The Problem of Unintended Illumination

Regardless of the method used to direct light (masks or micromirror arrays), it is possible that some probes are accidentally activated for chemical coupling because of light diffraction, scattering, or internal reflection on the chip surface. This unwanted illumination of regions introduces unexpected nucleotides that change probe sequences, significantly reducing their chances of successful hybridization with their targets. Moreover, these faulty probes may also introduce cross-hybridizations, which can interfere in the experiments performed with the chip.

This problem is more likely to occur near the borders between a masked and an unmasked spot (in the case of maskless synthesis between a spot that is receiving light and a spot that is not). This observation has given rise to the term *border conflict*.

It turns out that by carefully designing the *arrangement* of the probes on the chip and their *embeddings* (the sequences of masked and unmasked steps used to synthesize each probe), it is possible to reduce the risk of unintended illumination. This issue becomes even more important as there is a need to accommodate more probes on a single chip, which requires the production of spots at higher densities and, consequently, with reduced distances between probes.

In this chapter, we address the problem of designing the layout of a microarray with the goal of reducing the chances of unintended illumination, which we call Microarray Layout Problem (MLP). We use the term *layout* to refer to where and how the probes are synthesized on the chip (their arrangement and their embeddings).

13.2 THE MICROARRAY LAYOUT PROBLEM

In this section, we give a more precise definition of the MLP and define criteria for evaluating a given layout. The description that follows assumes that synthesis is done by photolithographic masks, but the concepts apply to the maskless production as well. Two evaluation criteria are presented: *border length* and *conflict index*. As shown later, the conflict index model can be seen as a generalization of the border length model.

Formally, we have a set of probes $\mathcal{P} = \{p_1, p_2, \ldots, p_n\}$ (frequently, but not necessarily, all probes have the same length), where each $p_k \in \{A, C, G, T\}^*$ is produced by a series of T synthesis steps. Each step t uses a mask M_t to induce the addition of a particular nucleotide $N_t \in \{A, C, G, T\}$ to a subset of $\mathcal{P}$ (Fig. 13.2). The *nucleotide deposition sequence* $N = N_1, N_2, \ldots, N_T$ corresponding to the sequence of nucleotides added at each synthesis step is therefore a supersequence of all $p \in \mathcal{P}$.

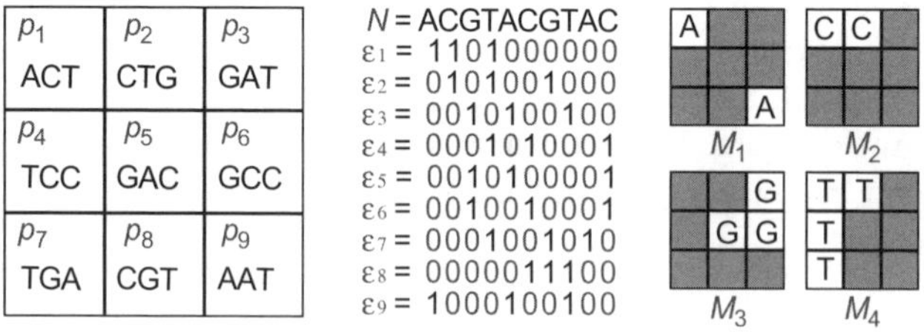

p_1 ACT	p_2 CTG	p_3 GAT
p_4 TCC	p_5 GAC	p_6 GCC
p_7 TGA	p_8 CGT	p_9 AAT

N = ACGTACGTAC
ε_1 = 1101000000
ε_2 = 0101001000
ε_3 = 0010100100
ε_4 = 0001010001
ε_5 = 0010100001
ε_6 = 0010010001
ε_7 = 0001001010
ε_8 = 0000011100
ε_9 = 1000100100

M_1 M_2 M_3 M_4

FIGURE 13.2 Synthesis of a hypothetical 3 × 3 chip with photolithographic masks. Left: chip layout and the 3-mer probe sequences. Center: deposition sequence and probe embeddings. Right: first four masks.

A microarray chip consists of a set of spots, or sites, $\mathcal{S} = \{s_1, s_2, \ldots, s_m\}$, where each spot s is specified by its coordinates on the chip surface and accommodates a unique probe $p_k \in \mathcal{P}$. Note that we usually refer to s as containing a single probe p_k although, in practice, it contains several million copies of it. Each probe is synthesized at a unique spot, hence there is a one-to-one assignment between probes and spots (provided we assume that there are as many spots as probes, i.e., $m = n$).

In general, a probe can be *embedded* within N in several ways. An embedding of p_k is a T-tuple $\varepsilon_k = (\varepsilon_{k,1}, \varepsilon_{k,2}, \ldots, \varepsilon_{k,T})$ in which $\varepsilon_{k,t} = 1$, if probe p_k receives nucleotide N_t (at step t), and 0 otherwise. In particular, a *left-most embedding* is an embedding in which the bases are added as early as possible (as in ε_1 in Fig. 13.2). We say that a spot or an embedding ε_k is *productive* (unmasked) at step t if $\varepsilon_{k,t} = 1$, or *unproductive* (masked) otherwise.

The deposition sequence is often a repeated permutation of the alphabet, mainly because of its regular structure and because such sequences maximize the number of distinct subsequences [2]. The deposition sequence shown in Fig. 13.2 is a 2.5-time repetition of ACGT, and we thus say that it has two and a half *cycles*.

For cyclic deposition sequences, it is possible to distinguish between two types of embeddings: *synchronous* and *asynchronous*. In the first case, each probe has exactly one nucleotide synthesized in every cycle of the deposition sequence; hence, 25 cycles or 100 steps are needed to synthesize probes of length 25. In the case of asynchronous embeddings, probes can have any number of nucleotides synthesized in any given cycle, allowing shorter deposition sequences. For this reason, asynchronous embeddings are usually the choice for commercial microarrays. For instance, all GeneChip arrays are asynchronously synthesized in 74 steps (18.5 cycles of TGCA), so only subsequences of this particular deposition sequence can be selected as probes on Affymetrix chips. [12] shows that this covers about 98.45% of all 25-mers.

Ideally, the deposition sequence should be as short as possible in order to reduce manufacturing time, cost, and probability of errors [11]. Finding the shortest deposition sequence to synthesize a set of probes is an instance of a classical computer science problem known as the Shortest Common Supersequence problem. Here, however, we assume that N is a fixed sequence given as input.

13.2.1 Problem Statement

Given a set of probes $\mathcal{P}$, a geometry of spots $\mathcal{S}$, and a deposition sequence N, as specified above, the MLP asks to specify a chip layout (k, ε) that consists of

1. a bijective assignment $k : \mathcal{S} \to \{1, \ldots, n\}$ that specifies a probe index $k(s)$ for each spot s (meaning that $p_{k(s)}$ will be synthesized at s),
2. an assignment $\varepsilon : \{1, \ldots, n\} \to \{0, 1\}^T$ specifying an embedding $\varepsilon_k = (\varepsilon_{k,1}, \ldots, \varepsilon_{k,T})$ for each probe index k, such that $N[\varepsilon_k] :\equiv (N_t)_{t:\varepsilon_{k,t}=1} = p_k$,

such that a given penalty function is minimized. We introduce two such penalty functions: total border length and total conflict index.

13.2.2 Border Length

A precursor of the MLP (that did not consider different embeddings) was formally stated by Hannenhalli and coworkers [7], who defined the *border length* $\mathcal{B}_t$ of a mask M_t as the number of borders separating masked and unmasked spots at synthesis step t, that is, the number of border conflicts in M_t. The total border length of a given layout is the sum of border lengths over all masks. For example, the four masks shown in Fig. 13.2 have $\mathcal{B}_1 = 4$, $\mathcal{B}_2 = 3$, $\mathcal{B}_3 = 5$, and $\mathcal{B}_4 = 4$. The total border length of that layout is 52 (masks 5 to 10 not shown).

The total border length is a possible penalty function to evaluate a proposed layout, and the *Border Length Minimization Problem* (BLP) is then defined as the problem of finding a layout minimizing total border length.

13.2.3 Conflict Index

The border length measures the quality of an individual mask or set of masks. With this model, however, it is not possible to know how the border conflicts are distributed among the probes. Ideally, all probes should have roughly the same risk of being damaged by unintended illumination, so that all signals are affected by the resulting imperfections in approximately the same way.

The *conflict index* is a quality measure defined with the aim of estimating the risk of damaging probes at a particular spot [4]—it is a per-spot or per-probe measure instead of a per-mask measure. Additionally, it takes into account two practical considerations observed in [8]:

(a) stray light might activate not only adjacent neighbors but also spots that lie as far as three cells away from the targeted spot;

(b) imperfections produced in the middle of a probe are more harmful than in its extremities.

For a proposed layout (k, ε), the conflict index $\mathcal{C}(s)$ of a spot s whose probe $p_{k(s)}$ is synthesized in T masking steps according to its embedding vector $\varepsilon_{k(s)}$ is

$$\mathcal{C}(s) := \sum_{t=1}^{T} \left(\mathbf{1}_{\{\varepsilon_{k(s),t}=0\}} \cdot \omega(\varepsilon_{k(s)}, t) \cdot \sum_{\substack{s': \text{ neighbor} \\ \text{of s}}} \mathbf{1}_{\{\varepsilon_{k(s'),t}=1\}} \cdot \gamma(s, s') \right), \tag{13.1}$$

where $\mathbf{1}_{\{cond\}}$ is the indicator function that equals 1 if condition *cond* is true, and 0 otherwise. The indicator functions ensure the following conflict condition: during step t, there is a conflict at spot s if and only if s is masked ($\varepsilon_{k(s),t} = 0$) and a close neighbor s' is unmasked ($\varepsilon_{k(s'),t} = 1$), since light directed at s' may somehow reach s. When s is productive, it does not matter if it accidentally receives light targeted at a neighbor; and when s' is unproductive, there is no risk that it damages probes of s. Function $\gamma(s, s')$ is a "closeness" measure between s and s' (to account for observation (a)). It is defined as

$$\gamma(s, s') := (d(s, s'))^{-2}, \tag{13.2}$$

where $d(s, s')$ is the Euclidean distance between the spots s and s'. Note that in Equation (13.1), s' ranges over all neighboring spots that are at most three cells away (horizontally and vertically) from s (see Fig. 13.3 left), which is in accordance with observation (a). The position-dependent weighting function $\omega(\varepsilon, t)$ accounts for the significance of the location inside the probe, where the undesired nucleotide is introduced in case of accidental illumination (observation (b)). It is defined as

$$\omega(\varepsilon, t) := c \cdot \exp\left(\theta \cdot \lambda(\varepsilon, t)\right), \tag{13.3}$$

where $c > 0$ and $\theta > 0$ are constants, and for $1 \leq t \leq T$,

$$\lambda(\varepsilon, t) := 1 + \min(b_{\varepsilon,t}, \ell_\varepsilon - b_{\varepsilon,t}), \tag{13.4}$$

$$b_{\varepsilon,t} := \sum_{t'=1}^{t} \varepsilon_{t'}, \qquad \ell_\varepsilon := \sum_{t=1}^{T} \varepsilon_t = b_{\varepsilon,T}. \tag{13.5}$$

In other words, ℓ_ε is the length of the final probe specified by ε (equal to the number of ones in the embedding), and $b_{\varepsilon,t}$ denotes the number of nucleotides synthesized up to and including step t.

Note that $\omega(\varepsilon, t)$ grows exponentially from the extremities of the probe to its center (see Fig. 13.3 right). The motivation behind this definition is that the probability of a successful stable hybridization of a probe with its target should increase exponentially with the absolute value of its Gibbs free energy, which increases linearly with the length of the longest perfect match between probe and target. The parameter θ controls

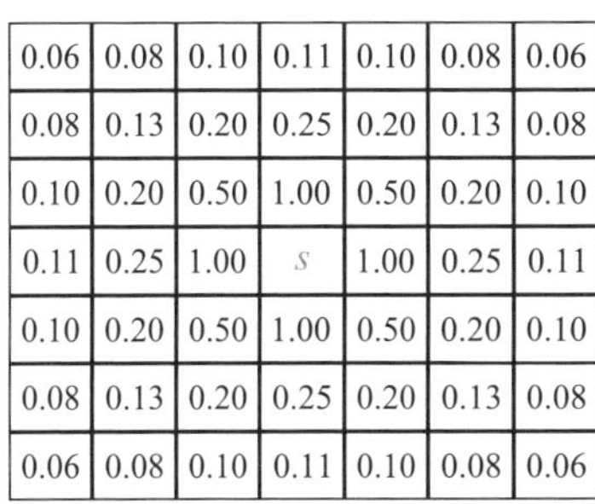

0.06	0.08	0.10	0.11	0.10	0.08	0.06
0.08	0.13	0.20	0.25	0.20	0.13	0.08
0.10	0.20	0.50	1.00	0.50	0.20	0.10
0.11	0.25	1.00	s	1.00	0.25	0.11
0.10	0.20	0.50	1.00	0.50	0.20	0.10
0.08	0.13	0.20	0.25	0.20	0.13	0.08
0.06	0.08	0.10	0.11	0.10	0.08	0.06

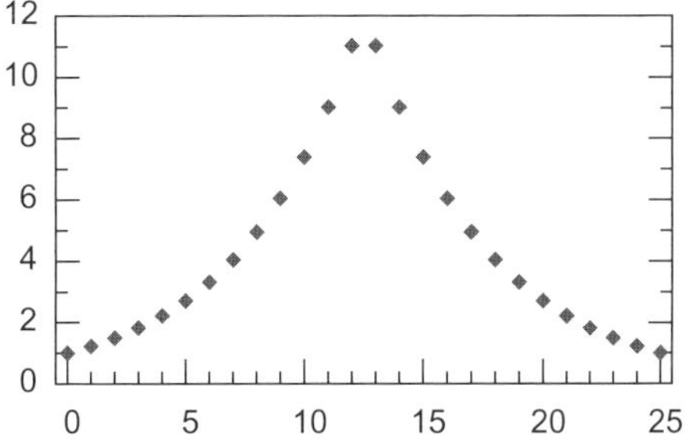

FIGURE 13.3 Ranges of values for both γ and ω on a typical Affymetrix chip where probes of length 25 are synthesized in 74 masking steps. Left: approximate values of the distance-dependent weighting function $\gamma(s, s')$ for a spot s in the center and close neighbors s'. Right: position-dependent weights $\omega(\varepsilon, t)$ on the y axis for each value of $b_{\varepsilon,t} \in \{0, \ldots, 25\}$ on the x axis, assuming $\ell_\varepsilon = 25$.

how steeply the exponential weighting function rises towards the middle of the probe. In Fig. 13.3 and our experiments, we use probes of length $\ell = 25$, and parameters $\theta = 5/\ell$ and $c = 1/\exp(\theta)$.

The conflict index $\mathcal{C}(s)$ can be interpreted as the fraction of probes in s damaged because of unwanted illumination.

13.2.4 Conflict Index and Border Length as Chip Quality Measures

The relation between conflict index and border length becomes clear if $\gamma(s, s')$ and $\omega(\varepsilon, t)$ are redefined as follows: Set $\gamma(s, s') := 1$ if s' is a direct neighbor of s, and $:= 0$ otherwise. Also, set $\omega(\varepsilon, t) := 1/2$, so that conflicts always have the same weight, independently of where they occur. Now $\sum_s \mathcal{C}(s) = \sum_{t=1}^{T} \mathcal{B}_t$, that is, total border length is equivalent to the sum of conflict indices for a particular choice of γ and ω. For the choices (13.2) and (13.3), they are not equivalent but still correlated, since a good layout has low border lengths as well as low conflict indices.

To better compare border lengths for chips of different sizes, we divide by the number of probes and call $1/|\mathcal{P}| \cdot \sum_{t=1}^{T} \mathcal{B}_t$ the *normalized border length*; this can be further divided by the number of synthesis steps to give the *normalized border length per mask* $1/(|\mathcal{P}| \cdot |\mathcal{T}|) \cdot \sum_{t=1}^{T} \mathcal{B}_t$. Reasonable values encountered in practice are between 30 and 40 per probe, or around 0.5 per probe and mask.

Similarly, we define the *average conflict index* as $1/|\mathcal{P}| \cdot \sum_s \mathcal{C}(s)$. The scale depends on our choice of γ and ω. In our experiments, reasonable values range from 300 to 600 per probe (or 4 to 8 per probe and mask).

13.2.5 How Hard is the Microarray Layout Problem?

The MLP appears to be hard because of the superexponential number of possible arrangements, although no NP-hardness proof is yet known. A formulation of the MLP as a Quadratic Assignment Problem (QAP) was given by [4]. The QAP is a classical combinatorial optimization problem that is, in general, NP-hard, and particularly hard to solve in practice [1]. Optimal solutions are thus unlikely to be found even for small chips and even if we assume that all probes have a single predefined embedding.

If we consider all possible embeddings (up to several million for a typical Affymetrix probe), the MLP is even harder. For this reason, the problem has been traditionally tackled in two phases. First, an initial embedding of the probes is fixed and an arrangement of these embeddings on the chip with minimum conflicts is sought. This is usually referred to as the *placement* phase. Second, a postplacement optimization phase *re-embeds* the probes considering their location on the chip, in such a way that the conflicts with neighboring spots are further reduced. Often, the chip is *partitioned* into smaller subregions before the placement phase in order to reduce running times, especially on larger chips.

The next section surveys the most important placement algorithms. Re-embedding algorithms are then discussed in Section 13.4, and partitioning algorithms are the focus of Section 13.5. Finally, we present recent developments that simultaneously place and embed probes (Section 13.6). A summary in Section 13.7 concludes the chapter.

13.3 PLACEMENT

The input for a placement algorithm consists of the deposition sequence N, a set of probes $\mathcal{P}$ (each probe is assumed to have at least one embedding in N), and a geometry of spots $\mathcal{S}$. In practice, microarrays may have complex physical structures, but we assume that the spots are arranged in a rectangular grid with n_r rows and n_c columns. We also assume that probes can be assigned to any spot.

The output of a placement algorithm is a one-to-one assignment of probes to spots. If there are more spots than probes to place, we can add enough "empty" probes that do not introduce any conflicts with the other probes (since light is never directed to such spots).

All algorithms discussed in this section assume that an initial embedding of the probes is given, which can be a left-most, right-most, synchronous, or otherwise pre-computed embedding—a placement algorithm typically does not change the given embeddings.

13.3.1 Early Approaches

Feldman and Pevzner [5] were the first to formally address the unintended illumination problem. They showed how an optimal placement can be constructed based on a two-dimensional Gray code. Their work, however, is restricted to *uniform arrays* (arrays containing all 4^ℓ probes of a given length ℓ) and synchronous embeddings, being thus of limited practical importance for current microarrays.

The border length problem on arrays of arbitrary probes was first discussed by [7]. The article reports that the first Affymetrix chips were designed using a heuristic for the traveling salesman problem (TSP). The idea is to build a weighted graph with nodes representing probes, and edges containing the Hamming distances between their embeddings, that is, the number of times their embeddings differ at a particular synthesis step. A TSP tour on this graph is heuristically constructed, resulting in consecutive probes in the tour being likely similar. The TSP tour is then *threaded* on the array in a row-by-row fashion (Fig. 13.4a).

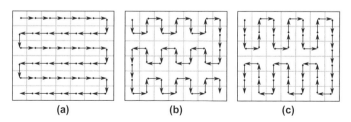

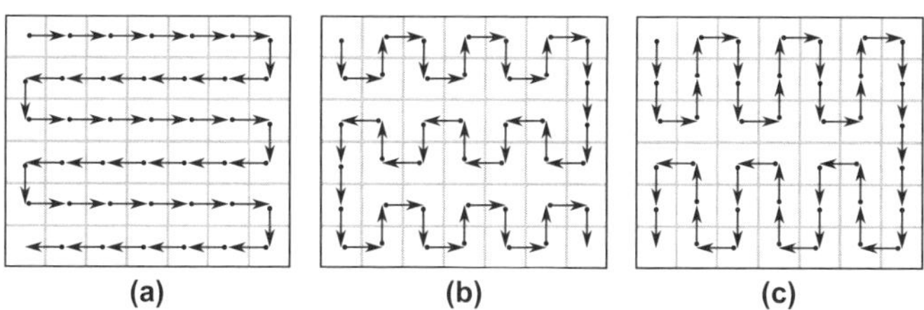

FIGURE 13.4 Different ways of *threading* probes on a chip. (**a**) Standard row-by-row (0-threading); (**b**) 1-threading; (**c**) 2-threading.

Hannenhalli and coworkers studied several threading alternatives, which they collectively called *k-threading* (Fig. 13.4b and c). A k-threading is a variation of the standard row-by-row threading, in which the right-to-left and left-to-right paths are interspaced with alternating upward and downward movements over k sites. (The row-by-row threading can be seen as a k-threading with $k = 0$.) Hannenhalli and coworkers experimentally observed that 1-threading may reduce border length in up to 20% for large chips when compared to row-by-row threading.

A different strategy, called Epitaxial placement, was proposed by [9]. It was originally designed for chips with synchronous embeddings, but it can be trivially implemented for asynchronous embeddings as well. The algorithm starts by placing a random probe in the center of the array and continues to insert probes in spots adjacent to already-filled spots. Priority is given to spots with four filled neighbors, in which case a probe with the minimum number of border conflicts with the neighbors is placed. Otherwise, all spots s with $i \geq 1$ filled neighbors are examined. For each spot, the algorithm finds an unassigned probe p whose number of conflicts with the filled neighbors, $c(s, p)$, is minimal, and assigns a cost $C(s, p) = k_i \cdot c(s, p)/i$ for this assignment, where $0 < k_i \leq 1$ are scaling coefficients (the authors propose $k_1 = 1$, $k_2 = 0.8$, and $k_3 = 0.6$). The assignment with minimum $C(s, p)$ is made and the procedure is repeated until all probes have been placed. With this algorithm, Kahng and coworkers claim a further 10% reduction in border conflicts over TSP + 1-threading.

Both the Epitaxial algorithm and the TSP approach have at least quadratic time complexity and hence do not scale well to large chips. This observation motivated the design of two new placement algorithms: Sliding-Window Matching (SWM) and Row-Epitaxial [8].

13.3.2 Sliding-Window Matching

The SWM algorithm is not exactly a placement algorithm as it iteratively improves an existing placement that can be constructed, for instance, by TSP + 1-threading, or much simpler, by lexicographically sorting the binary embedding vectors with a linear-time radix sort. The sorting is several times faster, but it is also likely to produce a worse initial placement than the TSP, with consecutive embeddings being similar only in their first synthesis steps. This, however, should be of little importance given that this placement is only used as a starting point for the SWM algorithm.

SWM works inside a window that starts at the top left of the chip and slides from left to right, top to bottom, while maintaining a certain amount of overlap between each iteration. When the window reaches the right-end of the chip, it is restarted at the left-end of the next set of rows, also retaining an overlap with the preceding rows. At each iteration, the algorithm attempts to reduce the total border length inside the window by relocating some probes (Fig. 13.5a). First, a random maximal independent set of spots is selected, and the probes assigned to these spots are removed. The term independent refers to the fact that selected spots can be reassigned to probes without affecting the border length of other selected spots. The algorithm creates a bipartite graph with nodes representing the removed probes and the now vacant spots (Fig. 13.5b). The edges of this graph are weighted with the number of border

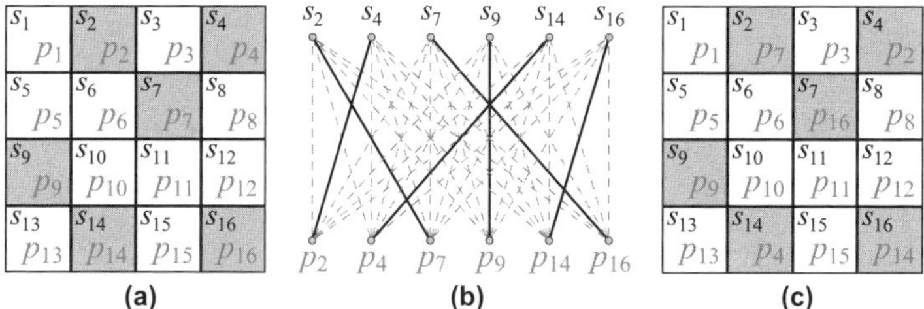

FIGURE 13.5 Sliding-Window Matching algorithm. (**a**) Initial arrangement of probes $p_1, \ldots, p_{16}$ inside a 4×4 window and the selected independent set of spots (shaded). (**b**) Bipartite graph and a minimum weight perfect matching (dark edges). (**c**) New arrangement inside the window.

conflicts that are generated by the corresponding assignment. Finally, a minimum weight perfect matching on this graph is computed, and the indicated assignments are made (Fig. 13.5c).

Selecting an independent set of spots ensures that the cost of each new assignment can be computed independently of the other assignments. SWM was designed for border length minimization and it takes advantage of the fact that, in this model, an independent set of spots can be constructed by selecting sites that are not immediate neighbors (spots that do not share a common border). SWM can be adapted for conflict index minimization (to our knowledge, this has not been implemented) by using larger windows containing relatively sparse independent sets. Therefore, several random independent sets should be constructed before moving the window.

13.3.3 Row-Epitaxial

The Row-Epitaxial algorithm is a variant of the Epitaxial algorithm with two main differences introduced to improve scalability: (i) spots are filled in a predefined order, namely, from top to bottom, left to right and (ii) only a limited number Q of probes are considered for filling each spot.

Like SWM, Row-Epitaxial improves an initial placement that is constructed by TSP + 1-threading or Radix-sort + 1-threading. For each spot s of the chip, it looks at the next Q probes that lie in close proximity (to the right or below s), and swaps the current probe of s with the probe that generates the minimum number of border conflicts with the top and left neighbors of s. Row-Epitaxial can be adapted to conflict index minimization by restricting the computation of the conflict index of s to those neighboring probes that are to the left or above s (those which have already found their final positions).

Figure 13.6 shows computational results for normalized border length and average conflict index for various chip dimensions and different values of Q. The running time of Row-Epitaxial is $O(Qn)$, that is, linear in the chip size, where Q is a user-defined constant. In this way, solution quality can be traded for running time: more candidates

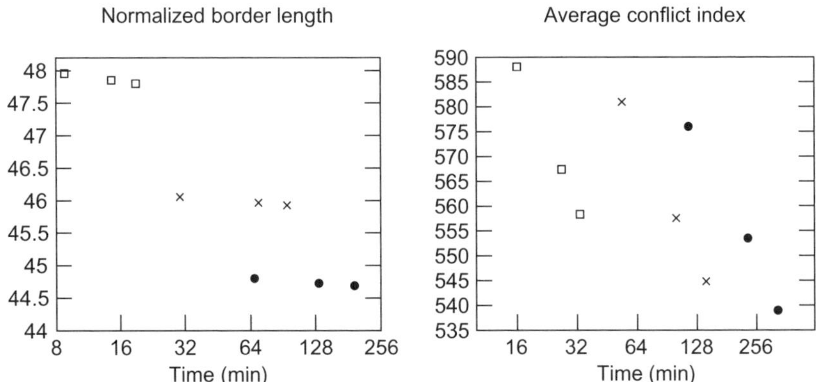

FIGURE 13.6 Trade-off between solution quality and running time with the Row-Epitaxial algorithm, on random chips of dimensions 200×200 (□), 300×300 (×) and 500×500 (·). The number Q of candidates per spot are 10 000; 20 000; and 30 000 from left to right. Layouts are measured by normalized border length (left) and average conflict index (right).

yield better layouts but also demand more time. For border length minimization, increasing Q above 10 000 has little positive effect.

According to experiments conducted by [8], Row-Epitaxial is the best known large-scale placement algorithm, achieving up to 9% reduction in border length over the TSP + 1-threading, whereas SWM achieves slightly worse results but requires significantly less time.

13.4 RE-EMBEDDING

Once the probes have been placed, conflicts can be further reduced by re-embedding the probes without changing their locations. All re-embedding algorithms presented in this section are based on the Optimum Single Probe Embedding (OSPE) algorithm introduced by [9]. OSPE is a dynamic programming for computing an optimum embedding of a single probe with respect to its neighbors, whose embeddings are considered as fixed. The algorithm was originally developed for border length minimization, but here we present a more general form designed for the conflict index model [3].

13.4.1 Optimum Single Probe Embedding

The OSPE algorithm can be seen as a special case of a global alignment between a probe sequence p of length ℓ and the deposition sequence N of length T, disallowing mismatches and gaps in N. We assume that p is placed at spot s, and that we know the embeddings of all probes placed at spots near s.

The optimal embedding of p into N is built by determining the minimum cost of embedding a prefix of p into a prefix of N: We use an $(\ell + 1) \times (T + 1)$ matrix

D, where $D[i, t]$ is defined as the minimum cost of an embedding of $p[1 \dots i]$ into $N[1 \dots t]$. The cost is the sum of conflicts induced by the embedding of $p[1 \dots i]$ on its neighbors, plus the conflicts suffered by $p[1 \dots i]$ because of the embeddings of its neighbors.

We can compute the value for $D[i, t]$ by looking at two previous entries in the matrix: $D[i, t-1]$ and $D[i-1, t-1]$. The reason is that $D[i, t]$ is the minimum cost of embedding $p[1, \dots, i]$ up to the t-th synthesis step, which can only be obtained from the previous step $(t-1)$ by either masking or unmasking spot s at step t.

If s is productive at step t, base N_t is appended to $p[1 \dots i-1]$; this is only possible if $p[i] = N[t]$. In this case a cost U_t is added for the risk of damaging probes at neighboring spots s'. We know that $p[1 \dots i-1]$ can be embedded in $N[1 \dots t-1]$ with optimal cost $D[i-1, t-1]$. Hence, the minimum cost at step t, if s is productive, is $D[i-1, t-1] + U_t$. According to the conflict index model,

$$U_t := \sum_{\substack{s':\text{ neighbor}\\ \text{of } s}} \mathbf{1}_{\{\varepsilon_{k(s'),t}=0\}} \cdot \omega(\varepsilon_{k(s')}, t) \cdot \gamma(s', s).$$

If s is masked at step t, no base is appended to $p[1 \dots i]$, but a cost $M_{i,t}$ must be added for the risk of damaging p (by light directed at neighboring spots s'). Since $D[i, t-1]$ is the minimum cost of embedding $p[1 \dots i]$ in $N[1 \dots t-1]$, the minimum cost up to step t, if s is unmasked, is $D[i, t-1] + M_{i,t}$.

Note that $M_{i,t}$ depends on the number of bases p already contains (that is, on i): each unmasked neighboring spot s' generates a conflict on p with cost $\gamma(s, s') \cdot c \cdot \exp[\theta \cdot (1 + \min\{i, \ell - i\})]$, in accordance with (13.3) – (13.5). Thus,

$$M_{i,t} := c \cdot \exp[\theta \cdot (1 + \min\{i, \ell - i\})] \cdot \sum_{\substack{s':\text{ neighbor}\\ \text{of } s}} \mathbf{1}_{\{\varepsilon_{k(s'),t}=1\}} \cdot \gamma(s, s').$$

Finally, $D[i, t]$ is computed as the minimum cost of the possible actions,

$$D[i, t] := \begin{cases} \min\{\, D[i, t-1] + M_{i,t},\ \ D[i-1, t-1] + U_t \,\}, & \text{if } p[i] = N[t] \\ D[i, t-1] + M_{i,t}, & \text{if } p[i] \neq N[t]. \end{cases}$$

The first column of D is initialized as follows: $D[0, 0] = 0$ and $D[i, 0] = \infty$ for $0 < i \leq \ell$, since no probe of length $\ell > 0$ can be embedded into an empty deposition sequence. The first row is initialized by setting $D[0, t] = D[0, t-1] + M_{0,t}$ for $0 < t \leq T$.

If we assume that costs U_t and $M_{i,t}$ can be computed in constant time, the time complexity of the OSPE algorithm is $O(\ell T)$ since there are $O(\ell T)$ entries in D to compute. The algorithm can be rather time-consuming in the general form presented here, since we have to look at the embeddings of up to 48 neighbors around s. Naturally, it runs much faster for border length minimization, since there are only four neighbors, and there are neither position-dependent (ω) nor distance-dependent (γ) weights to compute. In any case, a few optimizations significantly reduce the running time. For instance, in each row, only the columns between the left-most and the right-most embedding of p in N need to be computed.

Once D is computed, the minimum cost is $D[\ell, T]$, and an optimal embedding of p into N can be constructed by tracing a path from $D[\ell, T]$ back to $D[0, 0]$ similarly to the procedure used to build an optimal global alignment. This takes $O(T)$ time.

13.4.2 Re-embedding Algorithms

The OSPE algorithm is the basic operation of several postplacement optimization algorithms: Greedy, Batched Greedy, and Chessboard [9]; and Sequential [10]. Their main difference lies in the order in which the probes are re-embedded.

Since OSPE never increases the amount of conflicts in the region around the re-embedded probe, optimization algorithms can execute several re-embedding operations without risk of worsening the current solution. Moreover, probes can be re-embedded several times since new improvements may be possible once neighbors are changed. In fact, the following algorithms work in repeating cycles of optimization until no more improvements are possible (when a local optimal solution is found), or until improvements drop below a given threshold.

The Greedy algorithm uses OSPE to compute, for each spot of the chip, the maximum reduction of border conflicts achievable by optimally re-embedding its probe. It then selects a spot s with the highest gain (reduction of conflicts) and re-embeds its probe optimally, updating the gains of affected neighboring spots.

A faster version of this algorithm, called Batched Greedy, preselects several spots for re-embedding and thus sacrifices its greedy nature by postponing the update of gains.

The Chessboard optimization is based on the fact that a chip can be bicolored like a chessboard, in such a way that the embeddings of probes located on white spots are independent of those placed on black spots (with respect to border length), and vice versa. The Chessboard uses this coloring to alternate the optimal re-embedding of probes located on black and white spots.

The sequential optimization is the simplest algorithm among the four. It proceeds spot by spot, from top to bottom, from left to right, re-embedding each probe optimally. Once the end of the array is reached, it restarts at the top left for the next iteration.

Surprisingly, the Sequential algorithm achieves the greatest reduction of border conflicts with a running time comparable to Batched Greedy, the fastest among the four. All re-embedding algorithms mentioned here were initially developed for border length minimization, but they can all be applied to the conflict index model as well. For the Chessboard optimization, $4 \times 4 = 16$ colors must be used instead of 2.

13.5 PARTITIONING

We mentioned earlier that the MLP is usually approached in two phases: placement and re-embedding. The placement, however, is sometimes preceded by a *partitioning* phase, which breaks the problem into smaller subproblems that are easier to manage. This is especially helpful for placement algorithms with non-linear time or space complexities that are otherwise unable to handle very large chips.

A partitioning algorithm divides the set of probes $\mathcal{P}$ into smaller subsets, and assigns them to defined regions of the chip. Each region can then be treated as an independent chip (and processed by a placement algorithm) or recursively partitioned. Linear-time placement algorithms may also benefit from a partitioning since probes with similar embeddings are typically assigned to the same region (Row-Epitaxial, for instance, is more likely to find good candidates for filling a spot).

We describe four partitioning algorithms: one-dimensional partitioning (1D), two-dimensional partitioning, centroid-based quadrisection (CQ), and pivot partitioning (PP). Like placement algorithms, they assume that an initial (left-most, right-most, synchronous or otherwise precomputed) embedding of the probes is given. Pivot partitioning is the only algorithm that modifies these embeddings. As we shall see, 1D and 2D partitioning generate a few masks with extremely few conflicts, leaving the remaining masks with high levels of conflicts that are difficult to handle. CQ and PP offer a more uniform optimization over all masks. Results of [3] indicate that PP produces better layouts than CQ on large chips.

Partitioning is a compromise in solution quality, since it restricts the space of solutions and may lead to conflicts at partition borders. However, it can improve solution quality in practice when the placement algorithm cannot handle large regions well. It is not advisable to perform too many levels of partitioning because smaller subregions mean less freedom for optimization during placement. The right balance depends on both the placement algorithm and the partitioning algorithm.

13.5.1 One-Dimensional Partitioning

One-dimensional partitioning divides the set of probes based on the state of their embeddings at a particular synthesis step. It starts by creating two subsets of $\mathcal{P}$:

$$\mathcal{P}_0 = \{p_k \in \mathcal{P} | \varepsilon_{k,1} = 0\}, \qquad \mathcal{P}_1 = \{p_k \in \mathcal{P} | \varepsilon_{k,1} = 1\}.$$

In other words, $\mathcal{P}_0$ contains all probes whose embeddings are unproductive during the first synthesis step, whereas $\mathcal{P}_1$ contains the probes with productive embeddings. The chip is then divided into two horizontal bands, proportionally to the number of probes in $\mathcal{P}_0$ and $\mathcal{P}_1$, so that each band accommodates one subset of $\mathcal{P}$.

This procedure is recursively applied to each band, using the next synthesis steps to further divide each subset of probes. For instance, the following subsets of $\mathcal{P}_0$ and

$\mathcal{P}_1$ are created during step $t = 2$:

$$\mathcal{P}_{00} = \{p_k \in \mathcal{P}_0 | \varepsilon_{k,2} = 0\}, \qquad \mathcal{P}_{01} = \{p_k \in \mathcal{P}_0 | \varepsilon_{k,2} = 1\},$$

$$\mathcal{P}_{10} = \{p_k \in \mathcal{P}_1 | \varepsilon_{k,2} = 0\}, \qquad \mathcal{P}_{11} = \{p_k \in \mathcal{P}_1 | \varepsilon_{k,2} = 1\}.$$

The next assignments of subsets to the upper or lower band of their regions are made in such a way that regions with the same "state"—productive (unmasked) or unproductive (masked)—are joined as far as possible, resulting in masks that consist of alternating layers of masked and unmasked spots. This process is illustrated in Fig. 13.7, where at each step t, a band is labeled "0" when its embeddings are unproductive, and "1" when its embeddings are productive. The resulting binary numbers from top to bottom form a Gray code, that is, two successive numbers differ in only one bit.

The Gray code highlights an interesting property of 1D partitioning. After d levels of partitioning (based on steps 1 to d), the embeddings of any two immediate neighbors differ among the first d steps in at most one step. As a result, masks $M_1, \ldots, M_d$ exhibit a layered structure that effectively reduces border conflicts.

Unfortunately, the Gray code is disrupted as soon as a region cannot be divided (because all probes of that region are, for instance, masked at a particular step). This will certainly happen as several binary numbers are unlikely to be substrings of embeddings (think of, for example, a long run of zeros).

Moreover, 1D partitioning can optimize only a limited number of masks because the subregions soon become too narrow to be further divided. The maximum *partitioning depth* $d_{\max}$ is primarily limited by the number of rows in the chip. In practice, since regions are likely to be unevenly divided, $d_{\max}$ varies between regions. The algorithm can also be configured to stop partitioning a region, once its dimensions drop below a given threshold.

1D partitioning is easier to implement if the partitionings always produce rectangular regions (i.e., splitting a row between two regions is not allowed). In order to force an exact division of a region, however, it might be necessary to move a few probes from one subset of probes to the other.

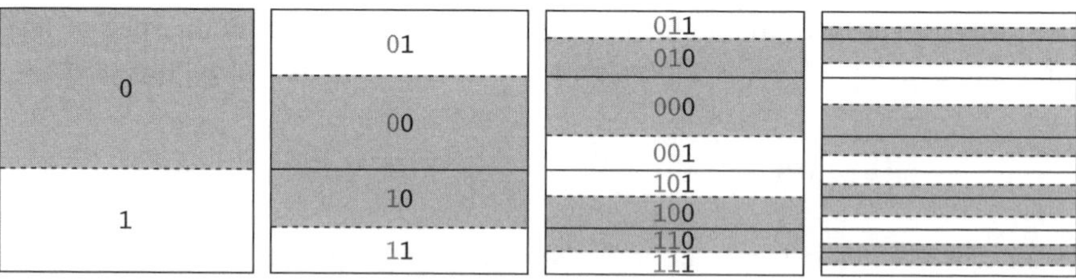

FIGURE 13.7 First four levels of one-dimensional partitioning. Dashed lines show the divisions performed in each step; solid lines indicate regions delimited in previous steps (there are no border conflicts between spots separated by solid lines). Masked (shaded) regions are labeled "0," unmasked (white) regions are labeled "1." This labeling forms a Gray code (shown in the first three steps only).

13.5.2 Two-Dimensional Partitioning

The 2D partitioning algorithm extends the idea of 1D partitioning to two dimensions, with the potential of optimizing twice as many masks. The algorithm is similar: $\mathcal{P}$ is divided into subsets based on the state of the embeddings at a particular synthesis step. The difference is that 2D partitioning alternates horizontal and vertical divisions of regions and that the assignments of probes to regions obey a two-dimensional Gray code (Fig. 13.8).

In a 2D Gray code, two neighboring numbers differ in at most one bit. Thus, regions whose embeddings are at the same state (productive or unproductive) are joined as far as possible.

If regions were always equally divided, 2D partitioning would have the same property as 1D partitioning: After d levels of partitionings (based on steps 1 to d), the embeddings of any two immediate neighbors would differ among the first d steps in at most one step. However, this is not always the case since 2D partitioning is likely to create regions with different dimensions, forcing some regions to share a border with more than its four natural neighbors (e.g., region "1100" in Fig. 13.8 borders with "0101" and "1111").

So far we have described both 1D and 2D partitionings using the state of the first d synthesis steps to divide the set of probes. The result of this approach is that, while the first masks are optimized, the remaining masks are left with high levels of border conflicts; we call this a *left-most mask optimization.*

However, a defect in the middle of the probe is more harmful than in its extremities, so it is more important to optimize the central masks, which synthesize the middle bases. Thus, we partition the chip based on the following sequence of synthesis steps, assuming that T is even and d is odd: $T/2$, $(T/2) \pm 1$, $(T/2) \pm 2, \ldots, (T/2) \pm \lfloor d/2 \rfloor$; we call this a *centered mask optimization.*

For left-most optimization, it makes sense to embed the probes in a left-most fashion in order to reduce conflicts in the last masks (which are not optimized by the partitioning); the left-most embeddings reduce the number of unmasked spots in the last steps, resulting in masks that largely consist of masked spots. Similarly, centered mask optimization produces better results with *centered embeddings.* A centered embedding is constructed by shifting a left-most embedding to the right, so that the

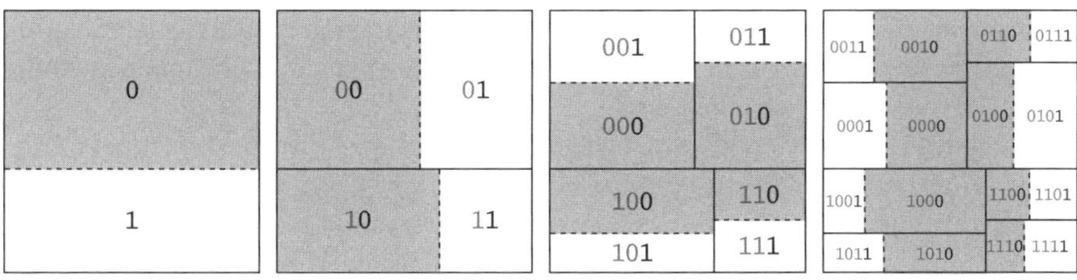

FIGURE 13.8 First four levels of two-dimensional partitioning. Dashed lines show the divisions performed in each step; solid lines indicate regions delimited in previous steps. Masked regions are labeled with "0," unmasked regions with "1;" this labeling forms an approximation to a two-dimensional Gray code.

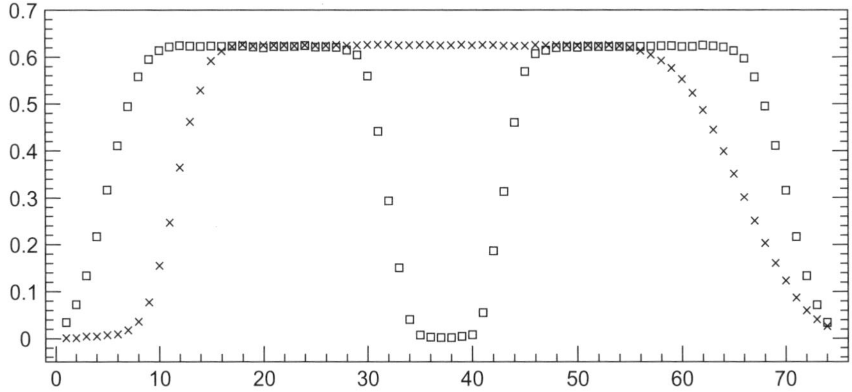

FIGURE 13.9 Normalized border length (on the y axis) per masking step (on the x axis) of a layout produced by 2D partitioning for a 1000×1000 chip with random probe sequences (embedded in the standard 74-step Affymetrix deposition sequence). Partitioning stops when a region becomes smaller than 64×64; Row-Epitaxial is used for the placement; (×) left-most mask optimization with left-most embeddings; (□) centered mask optimization with centered embeddings.

number of masked steps to the left of the first productive step approximately equals the number of masked steps to the right of the last productive step.

Figure 13.9 shows the results of 2D partitioning on a 1000×1000 chip with both optimizations. For left-most mask optimization, we obtain a normalized border length of 33.89 (up to approximately 0.6 per step). For centered mask optimization, the normalized border length improves slightly to 33.59. The average conflict index (not shown in the figure) for left-most mask optimization is 571.8; for centered mask optimization, it improves considerably to 383.5 because of the higher weight of the middle bases.

13.5.3 Centroid-based Quadrisection

Centroid-based quadrisection (CQ) [10] employs a different criterion for dividing the set of probes, and a different approach for partitioning. At each iteration, a region R is quadrisectioned into R_1, R_2, R_3, and R_4. Each subregion R_i is associated with a selected probe $p_{c_i} \in \mathcal{P}$, called *centroid*, that is used to guide the assignment of the remaining probes to the subregions.

A centroid is a representative of its region; it should symbolize the "average embedding" in that region. The remaining probes $p_k \in \mathcal{P} \setminus \{p_{c_1}, p_{c_2}, p_{c_3}, p_{c_4}\}$ are compared to each centroid and assigned to the subregion R_i whose centroid's embedding ε_{c_i} has minimum $H(k, c_i)$, where $H(k, k')$ is the Hamming distance between the embeddings ε_k of p_k and $\varepsilon_{k'}$ of $p_{k'}$ (i.e., the number of steps in which ε_k and $\varepsilon_{k'}$ differ).

In order to improve the clustering of similar probes, the four centroids should be very different from each other. The following heuristic is used: First, a probe index c_1 is randomly selected from $\{1, \ldots, |\mathcal{P}|\}$. Then, a probe index $c_2 \neq c_1$ maximizing

$H(c_2, c_1)$ is selected. Similarly, c_3 maximizing $H(c_3, c_1) + H(c_3, c_2)$, and c_4 maximizing $H(c_4, c_1) + H(c_4, c_2) + H(c_4, c_3)$ are selected. The assignment of centroids to the quadrisections of the chip is arbitrary.

In order to recover from a possibly bad choice of centroids, one can use a "multi-start heuristic," running the centroid selection procedure several times (using different "seeds" for c_1), and keeping those that lead to the best partitioning (partitioning quality is measured by the sum of Hamming distances of probe embeddings to their corresponding centroid embeddings).

The partitioning continues recursively until a predefined depth has been reached.

CQ was developed for border length minimization, but can be adapted for conflict index minimization by using the *conflict index distance* $C(k, k')$ instead of the Hamming distance $H(k, k')$ between the embeddings ε_k and $\varepsilon_{k'}$,

$$C(k, k') := \sum_{t=1}^{T} \Big(\mathbf{1}_{\{\varepsilon_{k,t}=0 \text{ and } \varepsilon_{k',t}=1\}} \cdot \omega(\varepsilon_k, t) + \mathbf{1}_{\{\varepsilon_{k',t}=0 \text{ and } \varepsilon_{k,t}=1\}} \cdot \omega(\varepsilon_{k'}, t) \Big). \tag{13.6}$$

It can be interpreted as the sum of the conflict indices resulting from placing probes p_k and $p_{k'}$ at hypothetical neighboring spots, ignoring the distance between these spots and the conflicts generated by other neighbors.

13.5.4 Pivot Partitioning: Merging Partitioning and Re-embedding

Pivot Partitioning (PP) [3] is, to a certain extent, similar to CQ: subregions are recursively associated with special probes p_{c_i}, here called *pivots* instead of centroids, that are used to guide the assignment of the other probes to the subregions. The main differences between PP and CQ are as follows.

Instead of quadrisectioning the chip, PP creates subregions by alternating horizontal and vertical divisions (like 2D partitioning). The advantage is that regions are divided proportionally to the size of each subset of probes, so they are not required to have the same size. Furthermore, for each partitioning level, only two pivots need to be selected.

Another distinction is motivated by the fact that different probes have different numbers of embeddings, ranging from a single one to several millions. Probes with more embeddings can more easily adapt to the other probes, that is, they are more likely to have an embedding with fewer conflicts to fill a particular spot than a probe that has only a limited number of embeddings. For this reason, PP uses probes with a single embedding (or few embeddings) as pivots, and chooses the other probes' embeddings and region assignments accordingly.

Indeed, the most important feature of PP is the simultaneous embedding and assignment of probes to subregions. Let $M(k, c_i)$ denote the minimum conflict index distance $C(k, c_i)$, as defined in Equation (13.6), over all embeddings of p_k; we call it the *minimum conflict index distance* between probes p_k and p_{c_i}. It can be efficiently computed with a variant of the OSPE algorithm that ignores the location of the probes and the distance-dependent weights γ. Now, a nonpivot probe p_k is assigned to the region R_i, whose pivot p_{c_i} has minimum $M(k, q_i)$ over $i = 1, 2$. Pivot partitioning continues recursively up to a predefined depth. Finally, each probe is embedded to minimize conflicts with its assigned pivot.

13.6 MERGING PLACEMENT AND RE-EMBEDDING

The problem with the traditional "place and re-embed" approach is that the arrangement of probes on the chip is decided on the basis of embeddings that are likely to change during the re-embedding phase. Intuitively, better results should be obtained when the placement and embedding phases are considered simultaneously, instead of separately. However, because of the generally high number of embeddings of each single probe, it is not easy to design algorithms that efficiently use the additional freedom and run reasonably fast in practice.

We describe Greedy$^+$, the first placement algorithm that simultaneously places and re-embeds the probes, and compare it with Row-Epitaxial, the best known large-scale placement algorithm.

13.6.1 Greedy$^+$

The goal is to design an algorithm that is similar to Row-Epitaxial, so that we can make a better assessment of the gains resulting from merging the placement and re-embedding phases.

Greedy$^+$ fills the spots row-by-row, from left to right, in a greedy fashion, similar to Row-Epitaxial. Also, for each spot s, it looks at Q probe candidates and chooses the one that can be placed at s with minimum cost. The difference is that we now consider all possible embeddings of a candidate p instead of only p's initial embedding. This is done by temporarily placing p at s and computing its optimal embedding with respect to the already-filled neighbors of s (using OSPE from Section 13.4).

Compared to Row-Epitaxial, Greedy$^+$ spends more time on evaluating each probe candidate p for a spot s. While Row-Epitaxial takes $O(T)$ time to compute the conflict index, or the border length resulting from placing p at s; Greedy$^+$ requires $O(\ell T)$ time, since it uses OSPE (recall that ℓ is the probe length and T is the length of the deposition sequence). To achieve a running time comparable to Row-Epitaxial, we must, therefore, consider lower candidate numbers Q.

There are a few optimizations that reduce the time spent with OSPE computations when several probe candidates are examined in succession for the same spot. First, we note that if two probe candidates p and p' share a common prefix of length l, the first $l + 1$ rows of the OSPE dynamic programming matrix D will be identical. In other words, if we have calculated the minimum cost of p, we can speed up the calculation of the minimum cost of p' by skipping the first $l + 1$ rows of D.

In order to fully exploit this fact, we examine the probes in lexicographical order, so that we can maximize the length of the common prefix between two consecutive candidates. We keep a doubly-linked list of probes and remove a probe p from the list when it is placed. For the next spot to be filled, we look at Q probes in the list around p's former position, for example, at $Q/2$ probes to the left and to the right of p.

Second, the U_t costs of OSPE need to be computed only once for a given spot s since U_t does not depend on the probe placed at s. Thus, in order to examine another candidate, we only need to recompute the $M_{i,t}$ costs.

Finally, once we know that a probe candidate p can be placed at s with minimum cost C, we can stop the OSPE computation for another candidate p' as soon as all values in a row of D are greater than or equal to C.

13.6.2 Results

We compare the results of Greedy$^+$ with Row-Epitaxial. To be fair, since Row-Epitaxial is a traditional placement algorithm that does not change the embeddings, we need to compare the layouts obtained by both algorithms after a re-embedding phase. For this task we use the Sequential algorithm (Section 13.4) with thresholds of $W = 0.1\%$ for border length minimization, and $W = 0.5\%$ for conflict index minimization, so that the algorithm stops as soon as the improvement in one iteration drops below W.

TABLE 13.1 Normalized Border Length (NBL) and Average Conflict Index (ACI) of Layouts Produced by Row-Epitaxial and Greedy$^+$ Placement (Pl), Followed by Sequential Re-embedding (Re-emb) with Thresholds $W= 0.1\%$ for Border Length Minimization, and W=0.5% for Conflict Index Minimization. Q is the Number of Probe Candidates Considered for Each Spot During Placement. Running Times are Given in Seconds

Border Length Min.	335 × 335 (*E.Coli*)		515 × 515 (*Maize*)	
Row-Epitaxial Q	10 K	20 K	10 K	20 K
Time (Pl. + Re-emb.)	629 + 9	1211 + 9	3333 + 38	6806 + 38
NBL (Pl.)	34.11	33.81	33.11	32.87
NBL (Pl. + Re-emb.)	33.93	33.66	32.95	32.73
Greedy$^+$ Q	350	700	350	700
Time (Pl. + Re-emb.)	596 + 12	1158 + 12	2633 + 53	4974 + 53
NBL (Pl.)	33.79	33.22	33.07	32.38
NBL (Pl. + Re-emb.)	33.53	32.98	32.82	32.16
Conflict index min.	335 × 335 (*E.Coli*)		515 × 515 (*Maize*)	
Row-Epitaxial Q	5 K	10 K	5 K	10 K
Time (Pl. + Re-emb.)	930 + 1169	1732 + 1167	4082 + 4424	7856 + 4415
ACI (Pl.)	584.92	544.93	604.04	574.68
ACI (Pl. + Re-emb.)	544.23	514.10	554.87	532.74
Greedy$^+$ Q	200	300	200	300
Time (Pl. + Re-emb.)	522 + 788	685 + 788	2131 + 2926	2757 + 2930
ACI (Pl.)	462.52	450.15	459.38	446.76
ACI (Pl. + Re-emb.)	458.02	445.98	454.84	442.55

Table 13.1 shows the total border length and the average conflict index of layouts, produced by both algorithms on two chips with dimensions 335×335 and 515×515, filled with probes randomly selected from existing GeneChip arrays (*E.Coli* Genome 2.0 and *Maize* Genome, respectively). Probes are initially left-most embedded into the standard 74-step Affymetrix deposition sequence $\{\text{TGCA}\}^{18}\text{TG}$. The parameter Q is chosen differently for both algorithms, so that the running time is approximately comparable (e.g., for border length minimization, $Q = 350$ for Greedy$^+$ corresponds to $Q = 10,000$ for Row-Epitaxial). We make the following observations.

First, increasing Q linearly increases placement time, while only marginally improving chip quality for border length minimization.

Second, re-embedding runs very quickly for border length minimization, even on the larger chip. For conflict index minimization, the time for the re-embedding phase exceeds the time for the placement phase for both algorithms.

Finally, Greedy$^+$ always produces better layouts in the same amount of time (or less) while looking at fewer probe candidates. In particular, for conflict index minimization on the 515×515 chip with $Q = 5000$ resp. 200, Greedy$^+$ and Sequential improve the average conflict index by 18% (from 554.87 to 454.84), and need only 60% of the time, compared to Row-Epitaxial and Sequential.

13.7 SUMMARY

We have surveyed algorithms for the microarray layout problem (MLP), divided into placement, (re-) embedding, and partitioning algorithms. Because of the super-exponential number of possible layouts and the relation to the quadratic assignment problem (QAP), we cannot expect to find optimal solutions. Indeed, the algorithms we present are heuristics with an emphasis on good scalability, and ideally a user-controllable trade-off between running time and solution quality, albeit without any known provable guarantees.

Among the presented approaches, two recent ones (pivot partitioning and Greedy$^+$) indicate that the traditional "place first and then re-embed" approach can be improved upon by merging the partitioning/placement and (re-) embedding phases. Ongoing work will show the full potential of such combined approaches.

REFERENCES

1. Çela E. *The Quadratic Assignment Problem: Theory and Algorithms*. Kluwer Academic Publishers; 1997.
2. Chase PJ. Subsequence numbers and logarithmic concavity. *Discrete Math* 1976; 16:123–140.

3. de Carvalho SA Jr., Rahmann S. Improving the layout of oligonucleotide microarrays: pivot partitioning. *Algorithms in Bioinformatics (Proceedings of WABI), Vol. 4175 of Lecture Notes in Computer Science*, Springer; 2006. pp. 321–332.
4. de Carvalho SA Jr., Rahmann S. Microarray layout as quadratic assignment problem. In: Huson D, Kohlbacher O, Lupas A, Nieselt K, Zell A, editors. *Proceedings of the German Conference on Bioinformatics, Vol. P-83 of Lecture Notes in Informatics (LNI).* Gesellschaft für Informatik; 2006. pp. 11–20.
5. Feldman W, Pevzner P. Gray code masks for sequencing by hybridization. *Genomics* 1994; 23(1):233–235.
6. Fodor SP, Read JL, Pirrung MC, Stryer L, Lu AT, Solas D. Light-directed, spatially addressable parallel chemical synthesis. *Science* 1991; 251(4995):767–773.
7. Hannenhalli S, Hubell E, Lipshutz R, Pevzner PA. Combinatorial algorithms for design of DNA arrays. *Adv Biochem Eng Biotechnol* 2002; 77:1–19.
8. Kahng AB, Mandoiu I, Pevzner P, Reda S, Zelikovsky A. Engineering a scalable placement heuristic for DNA probe arrays. *Proceedings of the Seventh Annual International Conference on Research in Computational Molecular Biology (RECOMB),* ACM Press; 2003. pp. 148–156.
9. Kahng AB, Mandoiu I, Pevzner PA, Reda S, Zelikovsky AZ. Border length minimization in DNA array design. Guigó R, Gusfield D, editors. *Algorithms in Bioinformatics (Proceedings of WABI), Vol. 2452 of Lecture Notes in Computer Science.* Springer; 2002. pp. 435–448.
10. Kahng AB, Mandoiu I, Reda S, Xu X, Zelikovsky AZ. Evaluation of placement techniques for DNA probe array layout. *Proceedings of the 2003 IEEE/ACM International Conference on Computer-aided Design (ICCAD).* IEEE Computer Society; 2003. pp. 262–269.
11. Rahmann S. The shortest common supersequence problem in a microarray production setting. *Bioinformatics* 2003; 19(Suppl 2):ii156–ii161.
12. Rahmann S. Subsequence combinatorics and applications to microarray production, DNA sequencing and chaining algorithms. In: Lewenstein M, Valiente G, editors. *Combinatorial Pattern Matching (CPM), Vol. 4009 of* LNCS. 2006; pp.153–164.
13. Singh-Gasson S, Green RD, Yue Y, Nelson C, Blattner F, Sussman MR, Cerrina F. Maskless fabrication of light-directed oligonucleotide microarrays using a digital micromirror array. *Nat Biotechnol* 1999; 17(10):974–978.

14

CLASSIFICATION ACCURACY BASED MICROARRAY MISSING VALUE IMPUTATION

YI SHI, ZHIPENG CAI, AND GUOHUI LIN†

Department of Computing Science, University of Alberta, Edmonton, Alberta, Canada

Gene expression microarray has been widely employed in biological and medical studies. In general, these studies involve the data analyses that require complete gene expression values, which, however, are not always possible due to various experimental factors. In the past several years, more than a dozen of missing value imputation methods have been proposed, and most of them adopt the (normalized) root mean squared errors to measure the imputation quality. Considering the fact that the purpose of missing value imputation is for downstream data analyses, and among which one of the most important applications is the genetic profiling, we propose to use the microarray sample classification accuracy based on the imputed expression values to measure the missing value imputation quality. Our extensive study on five imputation methods, from the most known ROWimpute and KNNimpute, to the most complexed BPCAimpute and SKNNimpute, to the most recent ILLSimpute, shows that BPCAimpute and ILLSimpute can fill in the missing values to achieve the sample classification accuracy as high as that can be achieved on the original complete expression data.

†Corresponding author.

Bioinformatics Algorithms: Techniques and Applications, Edited by Ion I. Măndoiu and Alexander Zelikovsky

14.1 INTRODUCTION

Microarrays, typically the high density oligonucleotide arrays such as Affymetrix GeneChip oligonucleotide (Affy) arrays, can monitor the expression levels of thousands to tens of thousands of genes simultaneously. Such a technology provides a unique tool for systems biology, and has become indispensable in numerous biological and medical studies. One of the most common and important applications of gene expression microarray is to compare the gene expression levels in tissues under different conditions, such as wild-type versus mutant, or healthy versus diseased, for genetic profiling. In general, a subset of a small number of biomarkers, which are discriminatory genes whose expression levels either increase or decrease under certain conditions, can be identified and used to build a classifier that predicts the microarray sample class membership, such as disease subtype and treatment effectiveness.

Genetic profiling, as well as many other applications, involves microarray data analysis that requires complete and accurate gene expression values. However, in practice, such a requirement is often not satisfied due to a number of defects in microarray experiments. These defects include systemic factors such as insufficient resolution and uneven distribution of fluids, and stochastic factors such as image corruption, dust and scratches on the slides, and glass flaws. All these could create the artifacts on the microarray chips that result in a certain percentage of expression data corruption [17,18]. Even with the high density oligonucleotide arrays such as Affymetrix GeneChip oligonucleotide (Affy) arrays, as high as 20% of expression spots on the arrays could be blemished that may cover hundreds of probes and affect the reading of a considerable percent of gene expression values [17]. Most microarray data analyses, such as gene clustering, biomarker identification, sample classification, and genetic and regulatory network prediction, which seek to address biological or medical issues, only accept complete expression values. Therefore, before the data analysis, the gene expression levels have to be preprocessed in order to impute the missing values, as well as correct some portion of the blemished data. In the past several years, more than a dozen of methods have been proposed for microarray missing value imputation including ZEROimpute, ROWimpute and COLimpute [1,18], KNNimpute and SVDimpute [18], BPCAimpute [13], GMCimpute [14], SKNNimpute [11], LSimpute [4], CMVE [16], LinCmb [8], LinImp [15], LLSimpute [10], and ILLSimpute [5].

When applying ZEROimpute, those logarithmic missing gene expression values are replaced by 0's [1,18]. By arranging the microarray samples in the way that a row represents a gene and a column represents a sample, a microarray dataset (which contains a number of samples, each of which contains a common set of genes) can be effectively represented as an expression matrix. In ROWimpute, a missing entry is filled with the average expression level of the corresponding gene across all samples; In COLimpute, a missing entry is filled with the average expression level of all the genes in the corresponding sample.

With the advance of the microarray technology and its increasing number of applications, missing value imputation attracts more attention and several more complexed imputation methods have been proposed, differing in pivotal ideas. Singular Value

Decomposition (SVDimpute) and the weighted K-Nearest Neighbor (KNNimpute) missing imputation methods are proposed by Troyanskaya et al. [18]. In SVDimpute, a set of mutually orthogonal expression patterns are obtained and linearly combined to approximate the expressions of all genes, through the singular value decomposition of the expression matrix. By selecting the K most significant eigengenes, a missing value in the target gene is estimated by first regressing the target gene against these K eigengenes and then using the coefficients of the regression to estimate the missing value from the linear combination of the K eigengenes. In KNNimpute method, for a target gene, its K nearest neighbor genes (or rows) which do not contain missing values in the same columns as the target gene, are selected. Then the missing values in the target gene are estimated by a weighted linear combination of the K nearest neighbor genes, where the weights are calculated as the inverse of the distances between the target gene expression vector and the neighbor gene expression vectors. Similar to KNNimpute, the Least Square imputation (LSimpute) method is proposed by Bø et al. [4]. It utilizes the least square principle to determine the weights in the linear combination of the K nearest neighbors, from which the missing values in the target gene are estimated. Different from LSimpute where nearest neighboring genes are used, the Local Least Square missing value imputation (LLSimpute), proposed by H. Kim et al. [10], estimates the missing values using the coherent genes under the Pearson correlation coefficients. Oba et al. [13] proposed a microarray missing value imputation method based on Bayesian Principal Component Analysis (BPCAimpute). BPCAimpute essentially employs three elementary processes, principal component regression, Bayesian estimation, and an expectation-maximization-like repetitive algorithm. It estimates the latent parameters for a probabilistic model under the framework of Bayesian inference and estimates the missing values using the model. Ouyang et al. [14] proposed GMCimpute method, which applies the idea of Gaussian Mixture Clustering and model averaging. CMVE, a Collateral Missing Value Estimation, is proposed by Sehgal et al. [16], in which for a missing value entry, it first calculates several missing value estimates according to different scoring functions and then the overall estimate is distilled from these estimates.

There are several extensions or variants to the above imputation methods. For example, SKNNimpute, or Sequential K-Nearest Neighbor imputation, is proposed by K.-Y. Kim et al. [11]. SKNNimpute sequentially imputes missing values from genes with the least number of missing entries to genes with the most number of missing entries. Within each iteration of SKNNimpute, the KNNimpute method is executed to impute the missing values in the target gene, where only those genes who have no missing value or whose missing values have already been imputed are the candidates of being neighbors. LinImp, which fits a gene expression value into a linear model concerning four factors, is proposed by Scheel et al. [15]. LinCmb, which is a convex combination of several imputation methods, is proposed by Jörnsten et al. [8]. Most recently, Cai et al. [5] proposed an iterated version of LLSimpute, the ILLSimpute method, for missing value imputation.

Among the above mentioned more than a dozen imputation methods, some have been compared with each other. In fact, most of the complexed methods have been compared with ROWimpute and KNNimpute. These comparative studies all adopt a measurement called the *Root Mean Square Error* (RMSE), or its normalized variant NRMSE. Let $E = \{E_1, E_2, \ldots, E_t\}$ denote the missing entries in the microarray expression matrix. For each missing entry E_i, $i = 1, 2, \ldots, t$, let e_i^* and e_i denote the corresponding true expression value and the imputed expression value, respectively. The root mean of the squared errors is calculated as

$$\mu = \sqrt{\frac{1}{t}\sum_{i=1}^{t}(e_i - e_i^*)^2}.$$

The mean of these t true expression values is

$$\bar{e} = \frac{1}{t}\sum_{i=1}^{t} e_i^*,$$

and the standard deviation is

$$\sigma = \sqrt{\frac{1}{t}\sum_{i=1}^{t}(e_i^* - \bar{e})^2}.$$

The NRMSE of the involved imputation method on this expression matrix is defined as the ratio of μ over σ, for example, NRMSE = μ/σ.

Note that when the expression matrix is given, σ is given as a constant. Therefore, according to the definition of NRMSE, it is obvious that a smaller NRMSE value indicates a better imputation quality. The existing comparison studies show that, under the RMSE or the NRMSE measurement, some of the above imputation methods consistently performed better than the others [4,5,8,10,11,13–16]. Typically, in the most recent study in [5], it is shown that BPCAimpute and ILLSimpute are both efficient and effective, regardless of the microarray dataset type (nontime series, time series dataset with low noise level, noisy time series) or missing value rate.

The NRMSE measurement presumes that all the observed gene expression levels accurately measure the hybridization intensities of the genes or probes on the microarray chips. Unfortunately, however, this is not always the case. Gene expression microarray is considered as a useful technology to provide expression profiles or patterns correlated to the conditions, but the expression levels of individual genes might not be all accurate. As we mentioned earlier, even on the high density oligonucleotide arrays such as Affymetrix GeneChip oligonucleotide (Affy) arrays, a significant percentage of probs could be blemished, and therefore in the gene expression values, a high percentage of them may be noisy or even should be treated as missing. Nevertheless, the boundary between noisy data or missing data is often difficult to determine, which red flags the use of only the RMSE or the NRMSE to measure the imputation quality. It has been suggested that, with known gene cluster information, one may use the percentage of misclustered genes as a measurement of imputation quality, in addition to NRMSE [14].

Note that in most of the existing missing value imputation methods, either implicitly or explicitly, the missing values in the target gene are estimated using the similarly expressed genes, the neighbors or the coherent genes. In this sense, it seems that using gene cluster information in final imputation quality measurement does not really tell much more than RMSE and NRMSE. Since one of the most important applications of gene expression microarray is for genetic profiling of the distinct experimental conditions, for example, for disease subtype recognition and disease treatment classification, we propose to adopt one downstream microarray data analysis, microarray sample classification, and to use the classification accuracy to measure the quality of imputed expression values. The main impact of using classification accuracy as a new measurement is that in general the imputed expression values themselves are not interesting, while whether or not the imputed expression matrix can be used in downstream applications is the major concern. To demonstrate that using classification accuracy is indeed a good measurement, we include two most known imputation methods ROWimpute and KNNimpute, two most complexed methods SKNNimpute and BPCAimpute, and the most recently proposed method ILLSimpute in our comparative study. The computational results on two real cancer microarray datasets with various simulated missing rates show that both BPCAimpute and ILLSimpute can impute the missing values such that the classification accuracy achieved on the imputed expression matrix is as high as that can be achieved on the original complete expression matrix, while the other methods do not seem to perform well. Some of these results are consistent with the previous experiments based solely on NRMSE measurement. One tentative conclusion we may draw from this study is that, for the purpose of microarray sample classification, both BPCAimpute and ILLSimpute have already achieved perfect performance and probably there is nothing left to do in terms of missing value imputation.

The rest of this chapter is organized as follows: In the next section, those five representative missing value imputation methods included in this study, ROWimpute, KNNimpute, SKNNimpute, BPCAimpute, and ILLSimpute, will be briefly introduced. The task of microarray sample classification, and its associated gene selection, is also introduced, where we present four representative gene selection methods, F-test, T-test, CGS-Ftest, and CGS-Ttest. We also briefly describe two classifiers built on the selected genes, the K Nearest Neighbor (KNN) classifier and the Support Vector Machine (SVM) classifier, along with the definition of classification accuracy. The descriptions of the two real cancer microarray datasets and all the computational results are presented in Section 3. We discuss our results in Section 4. Specifically, we examine the impacts of the adopted gene selection methods. Section 5 summarizes our conclusions.

14.2 METHODS

We assume there are p genes in the microarray dataset under investigation, and there are in total n samples/chips/arrays. Let a_{ij} denote the expression level of the ith gene in the jth sample, which takes U if it is a missing entry. The expression matrix representing this microarray dataset is

$$A_{p\times n} = (a_{ij})_{p\times n}.$$

Let $E = \{E_1, E_2, E_3, \ldots, E_t\}$ be the set of all missing value entries in the expression matrix, where t records the number of missing entries. The *missing rate* of the dataset is calculated as $r = t/p \times n$. In real microarray datasets, r ranges from 0% to as high as 20%.

14.2.1 The Imputation Methods

There are more than a dozen of microarray missing value imputation methods proposed in the past several years, adopting different mathematical models. For example, ZEROimpute, ROWimpute, and COLimpute are quite similar in the sense that they are simple and do not assume any correlations among the genes, neither the samples. The SVDimpute and KNNimpute are probably the first nontrivial ones, where SVDimpute looks for dependencies while KNNimpute seeks the help from neighbors. With various possible extensions, generalizations, or modifications, LSimpute, LLSimpute and LinImp are similar to KNNimpute in the essence; BPCAimpute, GMCimpute, and CMVE are similar to SVDimpute. SKNNimpute applies sequential imputation, trying to use the data in decreasing reliability, and ILLSimpute implements iterated imputation intending to improve the quality stepwise. For this reason, we only include ROWimpute, KNNimpute, SKNNimpute, BPCAimpute, and ILLSimpute as representatives in this study. Note that most of these imputation methods need the notion of expression similarity between two genes, which is defined in the following. Given a *target gene* that contains missing value entries to be estimated and a *candidate gene* (which should have known expression values corresponding to these missing value entries in the target gene), all of the missing value entries in the candidate gene are temporarily filled with the average expression value (row average). Then, by ignoring the same columns in both the target gene and the candidate gene, corresponding to the missing value entries in the target gene, we obtain two expression (sub-) vectors with no missing entries. The Euclidean distance between these two vectors is computed and it is taken as the distance between the target gene and the candidate gene. For example, if the target gene is (U, 1.5, U, 2.0, -1.2, U, 2.8) and the candidate gene is (1.6, U, U, -0.4, 2.2, 3.8, U), where U denotes a missing value, then the row average for the candidate gene is $\frac{1}{4}(1.6\text{-}0.4 + 2.2 + 3.8) = 1.8$; and the two vectors we obtain are (1.5, 2.0, -1.2, 2.8) and (1.8, -0.4, 2.2, 1.8); and the distance between these two genes is $\sqrt{18.41}$=4.29 [5]. In KNNimpute, the K closest candidate genes to the target gene are selected as the neighbors, or *coherent* genes, of the target gene, where K is prespecified and it is set at 10 in most of its implementations [11,18]. Suppose the target gene is i and its neighbors are $i_1, i_2, \ldots, i_K$. Let d_k denote the distance between gene i and gene i_k for $1 \le k \le K$. Then the missing value $a_{i,j}$ in the target gene i is estimated as

$$a_{i,j} = \sum_{k=1}^{K} \frac{1}{d_k} a_{i_k,j}.$$

Note that in the above version of KNNimpute, coherent genes are determined with respect to the target gene. Another version of KNNimpute is to determine coherent genes to the target gene with respect to one missing value entry. In this study, we examine the former version. In SKNNimpute, the missing value imputation is done sequentially and at every iteration, the gene containing the least number of missing value entries is chosen as the target gene, and KNNimpute is applied to estimate the missing values in this target gene where only those genes who have no missing values or whose missing values have already been imputed are considered as candidate genes. The K value in this internal KNNimpute is also set to 10 [11].

In LLSimpute [10], the coherent genes to a target genes are similarly determined but using the Pearson correlation coefficients rather than the Euclidean distance (in LSimpute), and its number is also prespecified. Afterwards, the target gene is also represented as a linear combination of its coherent genes, where the linear combination is done through a local least square. Essentially, coefficients in this linear combination are set in the way that the sum of the square differences between the known expression values in the target gene and the linear combination of coherent genes is minimized. Though LLSimpute has a process to learn what the best number of coherent genes would be, this number remains the same for all target genes. Cai et al. [5] realized that for distinct target genes, the distances between it and its coherent genes vary a lot, and consequently it is not wise to set a uniform number of coherent genes for all target genes. Instead, they proposed to learn a dataset dependent distance ratio threshold δ such that only candidate genes whose distances to the target genes within the threshold are considered as coherent genes. In addition, they proposed to iteratively reimpute the missing values using the imputation results from the last iteration, where LLSimpute is called, for a number of iterations or till the imputed values converge.

The missing value estimation method based on Bayesian Principle Component Analysis (BPCAimpute) consists of three primary progresses. They are (1) principle component regression, (2) Bayesian estimation, and (3) an expectation-maximization-like repetitive algorithm [13]. Given the gene expression matrix, the principle component regression seeks to represent every n-dimensional gene expression vector of gene i $a_i = \langle a_{i1}, a_{i2}, \ldots, a_{in} \rangle$ as a linear combination of K principal axis vectors a_{l_k}, $1 \leq k \leq K$:

$$a_i = \sum_{k=1}^{K} x_{l_k} a_{l_k} + \epsilon_i,$$

where K is a relatively small number ($K < n$), $x_{l_k} (1 \leq k \leq K)$ are the coefficients, or the so called *factor scores*, and ϵ_i denotes the *residual error* associated with gene i. By using a prespecified value of K, the principle component regression obtains x_{l_k}

and a_{l_k} such that the sum of squared error $\|\epsilon\|^2$ over the whole dataset is minimized [13]. In Bayesian estimation process, the residual errors $\epsilon_i (1 \le i \le p)$ and the factor scores $x_{l_k} (1 \le k \le K)$ are assumed to obey normal distributions at first. Then, the Bayesian estimation is used to obtain the posterior distribution parameters according to the Bayes theorem. In the last process, an expectation-maximization-like repetitive algorithm is applied to estimate or reestimate the missing values until the imputed results converge or the repetitive process attains the prespecified iteration numbers.

14.2.2 The Gene Selection Methods

For microarray sample classification purpose, normally an expression matrix is provided with every sample labeled by its class. Such a dataset is used as the training dataset to learn the genetic profiles associated with each class, and subsequently whenever a new sample comes, its class membership can be predicted. One can use all the genes to compose the genetic profiles, but as there are usually thousands of genes involved in the study while only tens of samples in a class, a process called *gene selection* is conducted to select a subset of discriminatory genes that are either over expressed or under expressed. Such a subset of genes are then fed to construct a classifier that can predict the class membership of a new sample.

There is a rich literature on general feature selection. Microarray gene selection only attracts attention since the technology becomes high throughput. Nevertheless, gene selection has its unique characteristics, which make itself distinct from the general feature selection. Many gene selection methods have been proposed in the past decade, though they all center at how to measure the class discrimination strength for a gene. F-test method [2,3] tries to identify those genes that have the greatest *inter class variances* and the smallest *intra class variances*. It scores a gene by the ratio of its inter class variance over its intra class variance — a greater score indicates a higher discrimination power the gene has. F-test method sorts all the genes in the nonincreasing score order and returns a prespecified number of top ranked genes. In T-test method [19], each gene has a score that is the classification accuracy of the classifier built on the single gene, and it returns also a prespecified number of top scored genes. Within our group, several gene selection methods have been proposed, among which one of the key ideas is to select only those genes that do not have overlapping class discrimination strength. The intention is that using genes having similar class discrimination strength in building classifiers would be redundant. To this purpose, we proposed to firstly cluster the genes under some measurements of class discrimination strength, and then limit the number of genes per cluster to be selected. Combining this gene clustering idea with F-test and T-test, we have CGS-Ftest and CGS-Ttest gene selection methods. We use these four gene selection methods, F-test, T-test, CGS-Ftest, and CGS-Ttest, in this study.

14.2.3 The Classifiers

Two classifiers are adopted in this study. One is the K-Nearest Neighbor (KNN) classifier [6] and the other is a linear kernel Support Vector Machine (SVM) classifier

[7]. The KNN-classifier predicts the class membership of a testing sample by using the expression values of (only) the selected genes. It identifies the K closest samples in the training dataset and then uses the class memberships of these K similar samples through a majority vote. In our experiments, we set the default value of K to be 5, after testing K from 1 to 10. The SVM-classifier, which contains multiple SVMs, finds decision planes to best separate (soft margin) the labeled samples based on the expression values of the selected genes. It uses this set of decision planes to predict the class membership of a testing sample. One may refer to Guyon et al. [7] for more details of how the decision planes are constructed based on the selected genes.

14.2.4 The Performance Measurements

At the end of experimental results, we will plot the NRMSE values for all imputation methods on the respective datasets. In this study, our main purpose is to demonstrate that microarray sample classification accuracy is another very effective measurement. Given a complete gene expression matrix with all samples being labeled with their classes, we adopt the *ℓ-fold cross validation* to avoid possible data overfitting. To this purpose, the complete dataset is randomly partitioned into ℓ equal parts, and $(\ell - 1)$ parts of them are used to form the *training dataset*, while the other part forms the *testing dataset* in which the class labels of the samples are removed. The predicted class memberships for the testing samples are then compared with the true ones to determine whether or not the prediction is correct. The process is repeated for each part. The percentage of the correctly predicted samples is the *classification accuracy* of the classifier. In this study, we report the experimental results on the 5-fold cross validation, where the partition process is repeated for 10 times. Consequently, the final classification accuracy is the average over 50 testing datasets. We remark that ℓ-fold cross validations for $\ell = 3, 7, 9, 11$ present similar results (data not shown).

14.2.5 The Complete Work Flow

To demonstrate that microarray sample classification accuracy is a very effective measurement for the imputation methods, we simulated missing values in the original complete gene expression matrix. On both the original and the imputed gene expression matrices, the sample classification was done by a classifier, whose classification accuracies were recorded and compared. In more details, given a complete microarray gene expression matrix containing p genes and n samples in L classes, we adopted 5-fold cross validation scheme to collect the sample classification accuracies for each of the four gene selection methods, F-test, T-test, CGS-Ftest, and CGS-Ttest, combined with the KNN-classifier and the SVM-classifier. The number of selected genes, x, ranges from 1 to 80. These accuracies are on the original dataset.

Next, for each of the missing rates $r = 1\%, 2\%, 3\%, 4\%, 5\%, 10\%, 15\%, 20\%$, we picked randomly $r \times p \times n$ entries from the original gene expression matrix and erased them to form a dataset containing missing values. The ROWimpute, KNNimpute, SKNNimpute, BPCAimpute, and ILLSimpute were called separately on the

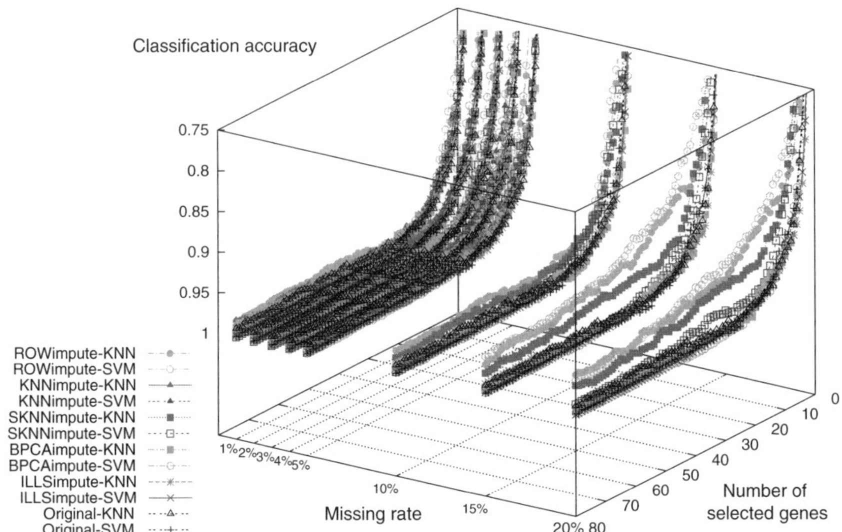

FIGURE 14.1 The 5-fold classification accuracies of the SVM-classifier and the KNN-classifier built on the genes selected by the F-test method, on the original and simulated SRBCT dataset. The x-axis labels the number of selected genes, the y-axis labels the missing rate, and the z-axis labels the 5-fold classification accuracy. The simulated datasets with missing values were imputed by each of the ROWimpute, KNNimpute, SKNNimpute, BPCAimpute, and ILLSimpute. The Original-SVM/KNN plot the classification accuracies of the classifiers on the original SRBCT dataset, for example, $r = 0\%$.

simulated dataset to estimate the missing values. After imputing the missing values in the simulated gene expression matrix, the subsequent procedure was the same as that for the original complete gene expression matrix in the above to collect the sample classification accuracies. For each missing rate, the missing value simulation was repeated for 10 times, and consequently the associated accuracies are the average over 500 entities.

To summarize, by regarding the original complete dataset as a dataset of 0% missing values, we have nine missing rates, each associated with 10 simulated datasets (except 0%), five imputation methods, four gene selection methods, and two classifiers, under the 5-fold cross validation scheme, which is repeated for 10 times.

14.3 EXPERIMENTAL RESULTS

Given a complete microarray gene expression dataset (regarded as a dataset of 0% missing values), we simulated 10 datasets for each of the missing rates $r = 1\%$, 2%, 3%, 4%, 5%, 10%, 15%, 20%. On each simulated dataset, all five missing data

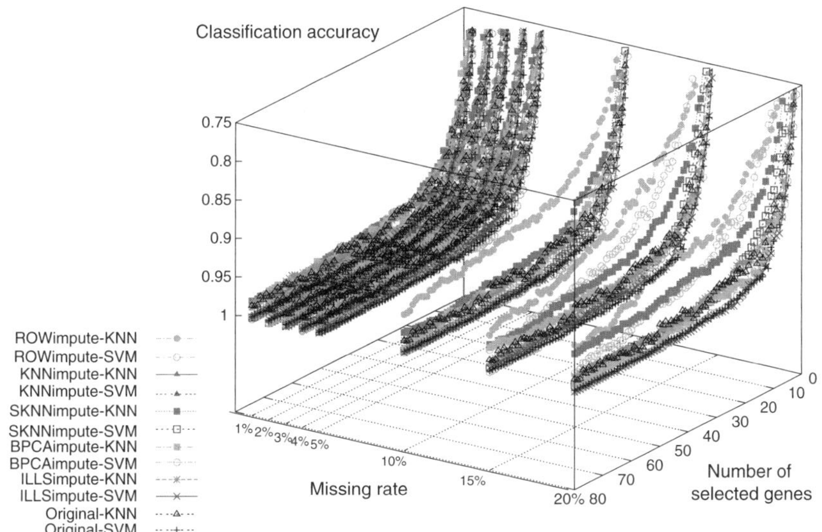

FIGURE 14.2 The 5-fold classification accuracies of the SVM-classifier and the KNN-classifier built on the genes selected by the T-test method, on the original and simulated SRBCT dataset. The x-axis labels the number of selected genes, the y-axis labels the missing rate, and the z-axis labels the 5-fold classification accuracy. The simulated datasets with missing values were imputed by each of the ROWimpute, KNNimpute, SKNNimpute, BPCAimpute, and ILLSimpute. The Original-SVM/KNN plot the classification accuracies of the classifiers on the original SRBCT dataset, for example, $r = 0\%$.

imputation methods, ROWimpute, KNNimpute, SKNNimpute, BPCAimpute, and ILLSimpute, were run separately to estimate the missing values. Afterwards, on either the original complete dataset or the imputed complete dataset, each gene selection method (F-test, T-test, CGS-Ftest, and CGS-Ttest) was called on randomly picked 80% samples to output x genes, for $x = 1, 2, \ldots, 80$. Each of the KNN-classifier and the SVM-classifier was then built on these x selected genes to predict the class memberships for the other 20% samples. The final classification accuracy was collected for further statistics.

We include two real cancer microarray gene expression datasets, SRBCT dataset [9] and GLIOMA dataset [12], in this study.

14.3.1 Dataset Descriptions

The SRBCT dataset [9] contains 83 samples in total, in four classes, *the Ewing family of tumors*, *Burkitt lymphoma*, *neuroblastoma*, and *rhabdomyosarcoma*.

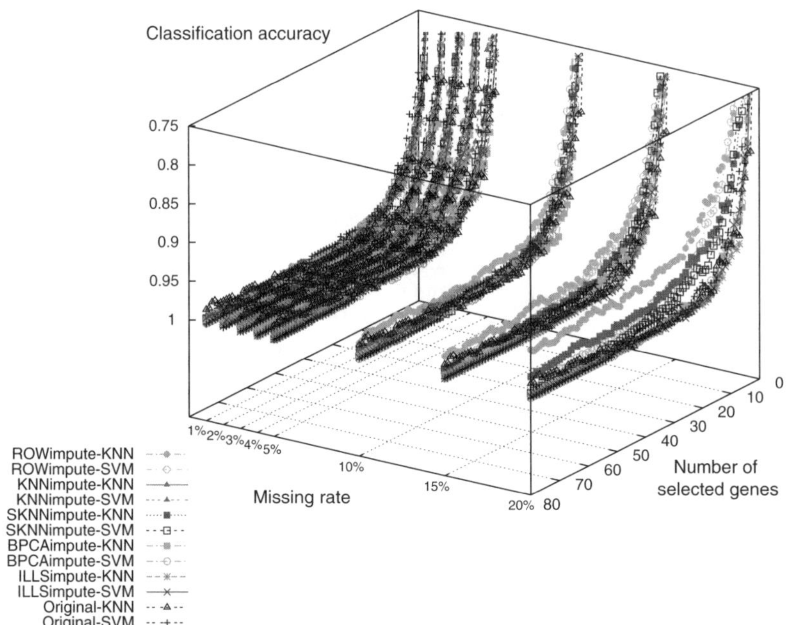

FIGURE 14.3 The 5-fold classification accuracies of the SVM-classifier and the KNN-classifier built on the genes selected by the CGS-Ftest method, on the original and simulated SRBCT dataset. The x-axis labels the number of selected genes, the y-axis labels the missing rate, and the z-axis labels the 5-fold classification accuracy. The simulated datasets with missing values were imputed by each of the ROWimpute, KNNimpute, SKNNimpute, BPCAimpute, and ILLSimpute. The Original-SVM/KNN plot the classification accuracies of the classifiers on the original SRBCT dataset, that is, $r = 0\%$.

Every sample in this dataset contains 2308 gene expression values after data preprocessing. Among the 83 samples, 29, 11, 18, and 25 samples belong to the four classes, respectively. The GLIOMA dataset [12] contains in total 50 samples in four classes, *cancer glioblastomas*, *noncancer glioblastomas*, *cancer oligodendrogliomas*, and *noncancer oligodendrogliomas*, which have 14, 14, 7, and 15 samples, respectively. This dataset is known to have a lower quality for sample classification [12,20]. In the preprocessing, for each gene, we calculated its expression standard deviation over all samples, and those genes with standard deviation lower than a threshold were filtered. Such a gene filtering is based on the intuition that if the expression standard deviation of a gene is too small, it may not have too much discrimination strength and thus is less likely to be selected by any gene selection method. After the preprocessing, we obtained a dataset with 4434 genes.

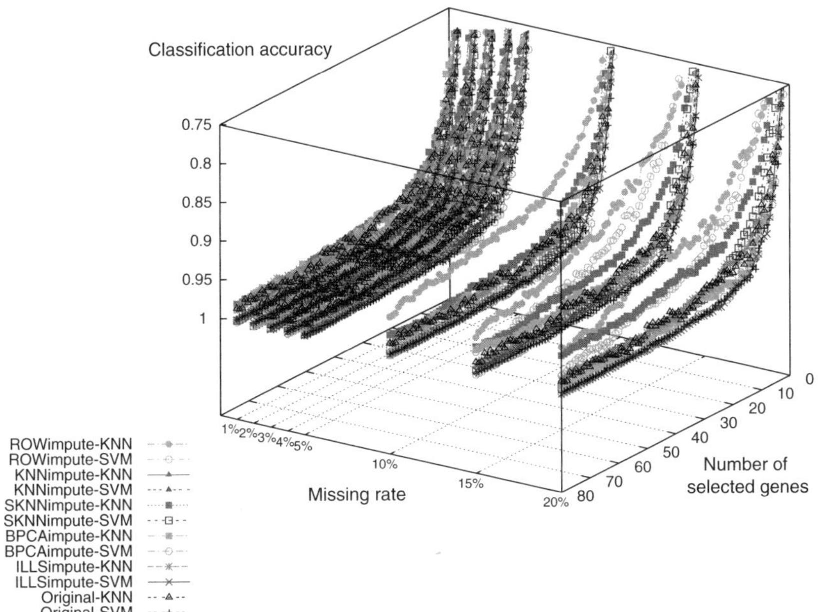

FIGURE 14.4 The 5-fold classification accuracies of the SVM-classifier and the KNN-classifier built on the genes selected by the CGS-Ttest method, on the original and simulated SRBCT dataset. The x-axis labels the number of selected genes, the y-axis labels the missing rate, and the z-axis labels the 5-fold classification accuracy. The simulated datasets with missing values were imputed by each of the ROWimpute, KNNimpute, SKNNimpute, BPCAimpute, and ILLSimpute. The original-SVM/KNN plot the classification accuracies of the classifiers on the original SRBCT dataset, that is, $r = 0\%$.

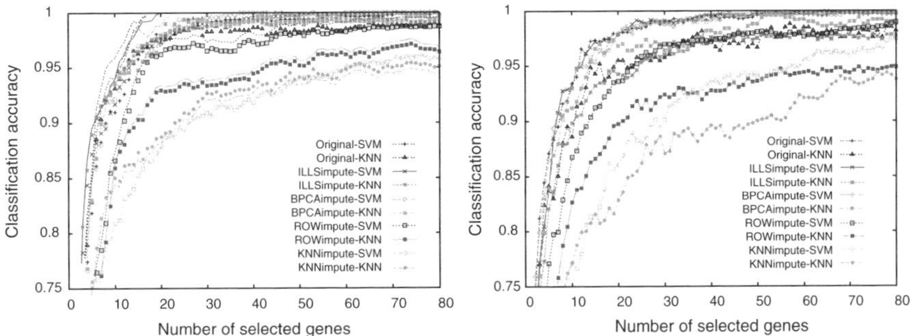

FIGURE 14.5 F-test (left) and T-test (right) performance on the SRBCT dataset simulated with missing rate $r = 20\%$.

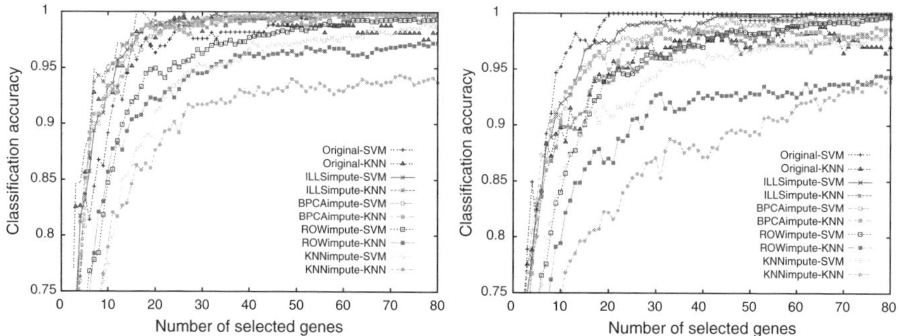

FIGURE 14.6 CGS-Ftest (left) and CGS-Ttest (right) performance on the SRBCT dataset simulated with missing rate $r = 20\%$.

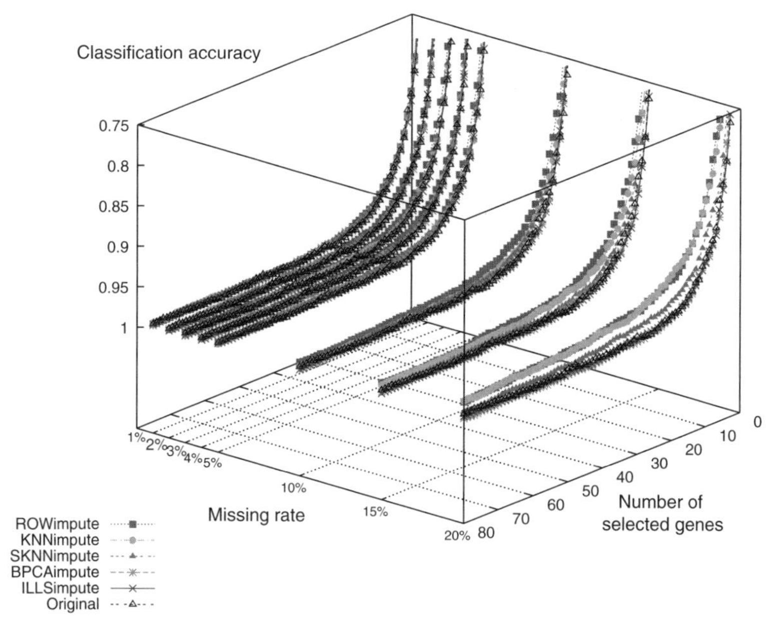

FIGURE 14.7 The 5-fold classification accuracies, averaged over eight combinations of a gene selection method and a classifier, on the SRBCT dataset. The x-axis labels the number of selected genes, the y-axis labels the missing rate, and the z-axis labels the average classification accuracy. The simulated datasets with missing values were imputed by each of the ROWimpute, KNNimpute, SKNNimpute, BPCAimpute, and ILLSimpute. The Original plots the average classification accuracies achieved on the original SRBCT dataset, that is, $r = 0\%$.

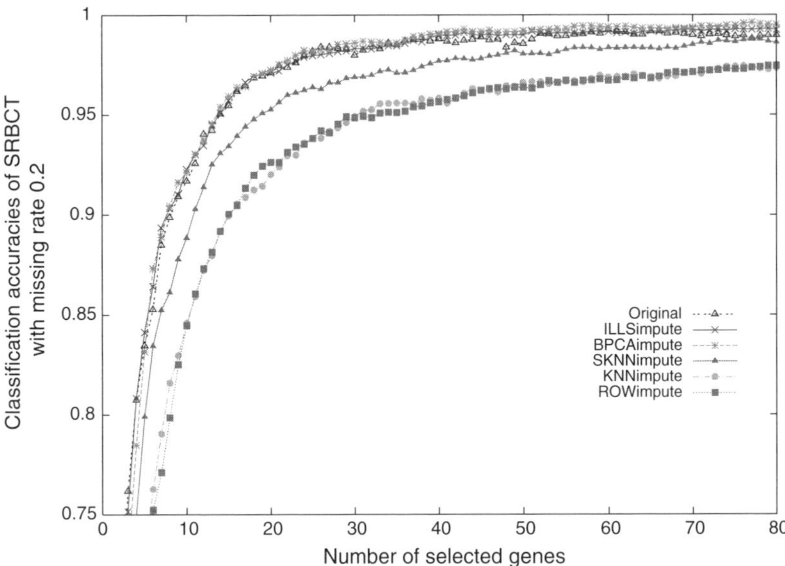

FIGURE 14.8 Average performances of ROWimpute, KNNimpute, BPCAimpute, and ILLSimpute methods, in terms of classification accuracies, on the SRBCT dataset with missing rate $r = 20\%$. The average classification accuracies on the original SRBCT dataset are also plotted for comparison purpose.

14.3.2 5-fold Cross Validation Classification Accuracies

For each combination of a gene selection method and a classifier, its sample classification accuracy is the average over 50 testing datasets on the original gene expression dataset, and over 500 testing datasets on each of the missing rates $r = 1\%, 2\%, 3\%, 4\%, 5\%, 10\%, 15\%, 20\%$, under the 5-fold cross validation scheme. For ease of presentation, we concatenate the sequentially applied method names to denote the associated 5-fold cross validation classification accuracy. For example, ILLSimpute-CGS-Ftest-SVM denotes the accuracy that is achieved by applying the ILLSimpute method, followed by the CGS-Ftest to select a certain number of genes for building an SVM-classifier for testing sample membership prediction. Our further statistics include the sample classification accuracies with respect to a missing value imputation method, a gene selection method, the gene clustering based gene selection or the other, and a classifier, to be detailed in the following. For example, ILLSimpute-SVM denotes the average accuracy over all four gene selection methods, that is achieved by applying the ILLSimpute method, followed by a gene selection method to select a certain number of genes for building an SVM-classifier for testing sample membership prediction.

14.3.2.1 The SRBCT Dataset For each of the four gene selection methods, F-test, T-test, CGS-Ftest, and CGS-Ttest, we plotted separately the 5-fold cross validation

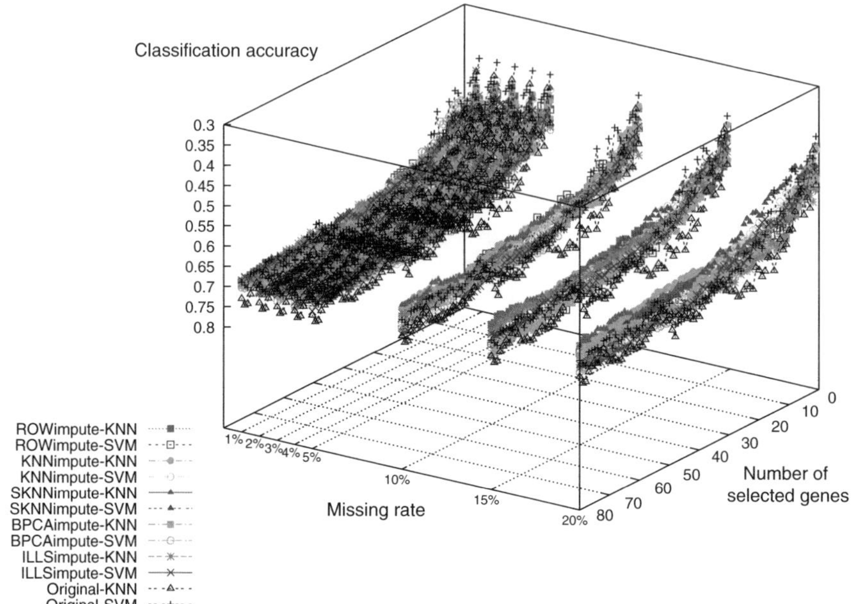

FIGURE 14.9 The 5-fold classification accuracies of the SVM-classifier and the KNN-classifier built on the genes selected by the F-test method, on the original and simulated GLIOMA dataset. The x axis labels the number of selected genes, the y axis labels the missing rate, and the z axis labels the 5-fold classification accuracy. The simulated datasets with missing values were imputed by each of the ROWimpute, KNNimpute, SKNNimpute, BPCAimpute, and ILLSimpute. The Original-SVM/KNN plot the classification accuracies of the classifiers on the original GLIOMA dataset, that is, $r = 0\%$.

classification accuracies for all combinations of a missing value imputation method and a classifier, on the original SRBCT dataset ($r = 0\%$, in which the missing value imputation methods were skipped) and simulated datasets with missing rates 1%, 2%, 3%, 4%, 5%, 10%, 15% and 20%, respectively. We chose to plot these classification accuracies in three dimensional where the x-axis is the number of selected genes, the y-axis is the missing rate, and the z-axis is the 5-fold cross validation classification accuracy. Figures 14.1–14.4 plot these classification accuracies for the F-test, T-test CGS-Ftest, and CGS-Ttest methods, respectively.

From Figs. 14.1–14.4, we can see that when the missing rate is less than or equal to 5% (the five groups of plots to the left), all five imputation methods worked almost equally well, combined with either of the two classifiers, compared to the baseline classification accuracies on the original SRBCT dataset. However, the plots started to diverge when the missing rate increases to 10%, 15% and 20%. For example, besides the observation that the classification accuracies of the SVM-classifier were a little higher than that of the KNN-classifier (this is more clear with the T-test method, in

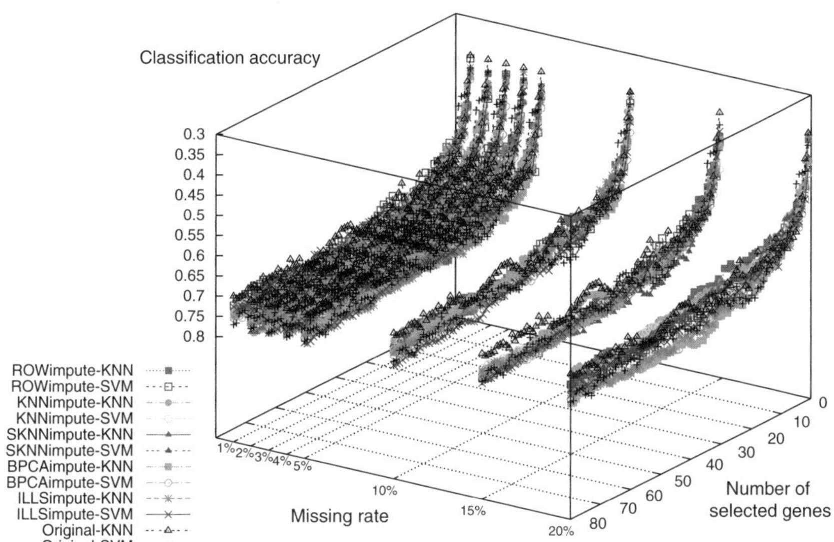

FIGURE 14.10 The 5-fold classification accuracies of the SVM-classifier and the KNN-classifier built on the genes selected by the T-test method, on the original and simulated GLIOMA dataset. The x-axis labels the number of selected genes, the y-axis labels the missing rate, and the z-axis labels the 5-fold classification accuracy. The simulated datasets with missing values were imputed by each of the ROWimpute, KNNimpute, SKNNimpute, BPCAimpute, and ILLSimpute. The Original-SVM/KNN plot the classification accuracies of the classifiers on the original GLIOMA dataset, that is, $r = 0\%$.

Fig. 14.2 and the right plot in Fig. 14.5), combined with the same imputation method. Overall, the general tendencies are that (1) ROWimpute and KNNimpute performed equally well, and worse than the other three, (2) ILLSimpute and BPCAimpute performed equally well, and the best among the five methods, (3) SKNNimpute performed in the middle, and (4) the gaps between the performances became larger with increased missing rate r. For missing rate $r = 20\%$, the classification accuracies are separately plotted in Fig. 14.5 and Fig. 14.6, in each of which the left plot is for the F-test/CGS-Ftest method and the right plot is for the T-test/CGS-Ttest method. It is clearly seen that, the BPCAimpute and ILLSimpute methods performed consistently the best, the ROWimpute and KNNimpute methods performed the worst, and the imputed datasets by BPCAimpute and ILLSimpute had almost the same quality as the original SRBCT dataset, in terms of the final sample classification accuracy. Furthermore, the last observation holds true across all missing rates, a strong demonstration that BPCAimpute and ILLSimpute are the methods of choices for microarray missing value imputation.

All of the above plots show that in general the KNN-classifier performed a little worse than the SVM-classifier on the SRBCT dataset. However, we remark that it

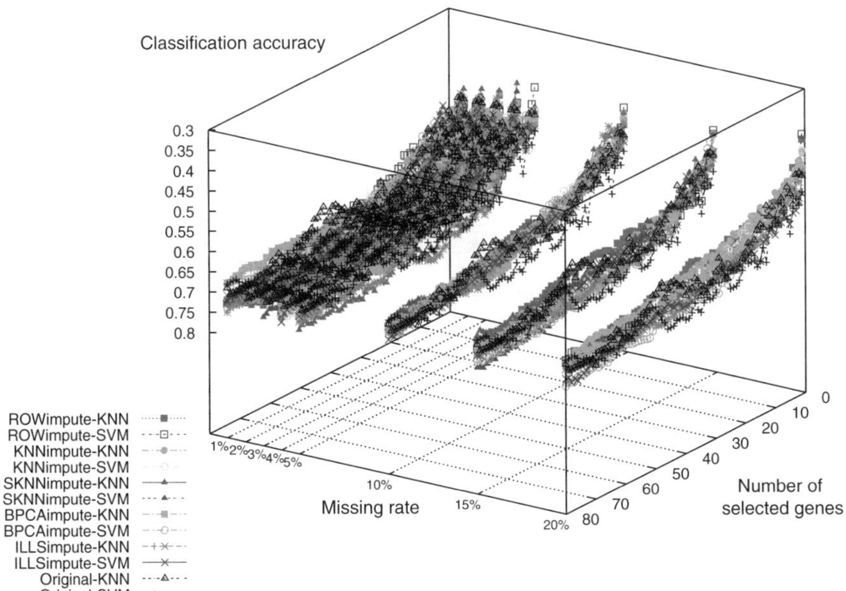

FIGURE 14.11 The 5-fold classification accuracies of the SVM-classifier and the KNN-classifier built on the genes selected by the CGS-Ftest method, on the original and simulated GLIOMA dataset. The x-axis labels the number of selected genes, the y-axis labels the missing rate, and the z-axis labels the 5-fold classification accuracy. The simulated datasets with missing values were imputed by each of the ROWimpute, KNNimpute, SKNNimpute, BPCAimpute, and ILLSimpute. The Original-SVM/KNN plot the classification accuracies of the classifiers on the original GLIOMA dataset, that is, $r = 0\%$.

is not necessarily the case that the KNN-classifier is always inferior (cf. [5]). By ignoring the detailed gene selection method and the classifier to calculate the classification accuracy of a missing value imputation method as the average over eight values, corresponding to in total eight combinations of a gene selection method and a classifier. We associated this classification accuracy with each of the five imputation methods. Fig. 14.7 plots these classification accuracies on the SRBCT dataset, with missing rate $r = 0\%$ (the original dataset), 1%, 2%, 3%, 4%, 5%, 10%, 15% and 20%, respectively. From this 3D plot, one can see again that essentially there was not much performance difference between the five missing value imputation methods when the missing rate r was less than or equal to 5% (the five groups of plots to the left); But their performances started to diverge when $r \geq 10\%$, and again the general tendencies are that (1) ROWimpute and KNNimpute performed equally well, and worse than the other three, (2) ILLSimpute and BPCAimpute performed equally well, and the best among the five methods, (3) SKNNimpute performed in the middle, and (4) the gaps between the performances became larger with increased missing

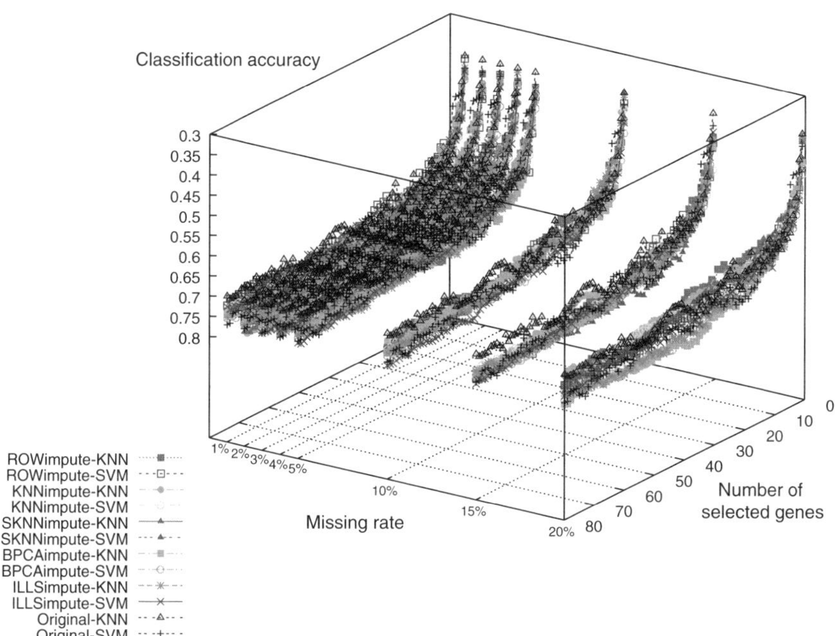

FIGURE 14.12 The 5-fold classification accuracies of the SVM-classifier and the KNN-classifier built on the genes selected by the CGS-Ttest method, on the original and simulated GLIOMA dataset. The x-axis labels the number of selected genes, the y-axis labels the missing rate, and the z-axis labels the 5-fold classification accuracy. The simulated datasets with missing values were imputed by each of the ROWimpute, KNNimpute, SKNNimpute, BPCAimpute, and ILLSimpute. The Original-SVM/KNN plot the classification accuracies of the classifiers on the original GLIOMA dataset, that is, $r = 0\%$.

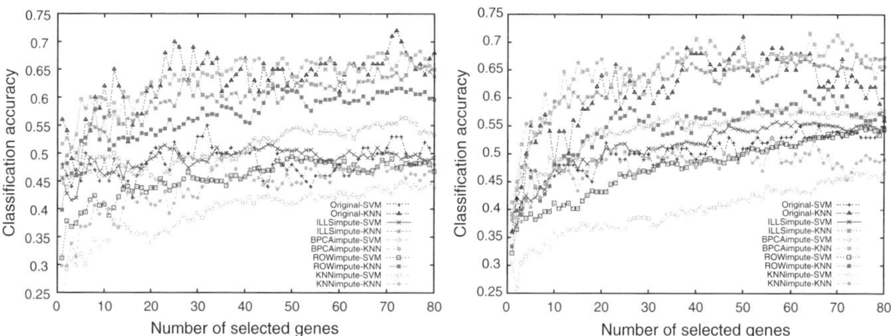

FIGURE 14.13 F-test (left) and T-test (right) performance on the GLIOMA dataset simulated with missing rate $r = 20\%$.

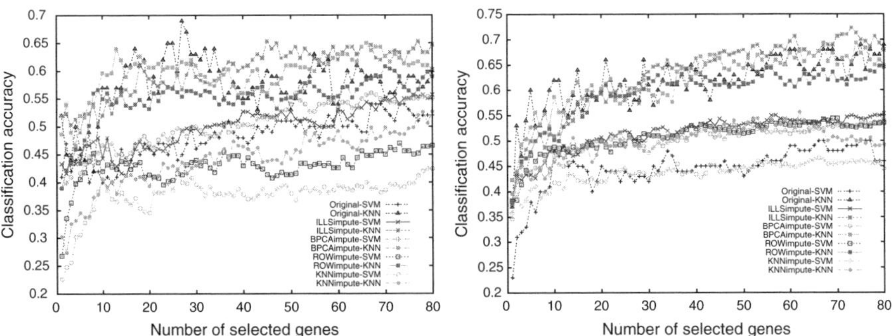

FIGURE 14.14 CGS-Ftest (left) and CGS-Ttest (right) performance on the GLIOMA dataset simulated with missing rate $r = 20\%$.

rate r. Similarly, for missing rate $r = 20\%$, the average classification accuracies are separately plotted in Fig. 14.8, where once again one can see that ROWimpute and KNNimpute performed the worst, and BPCAimpute and ILLSimpute performed the best. Furthermore, in terms of classification accuracy, the imputed expression matrices

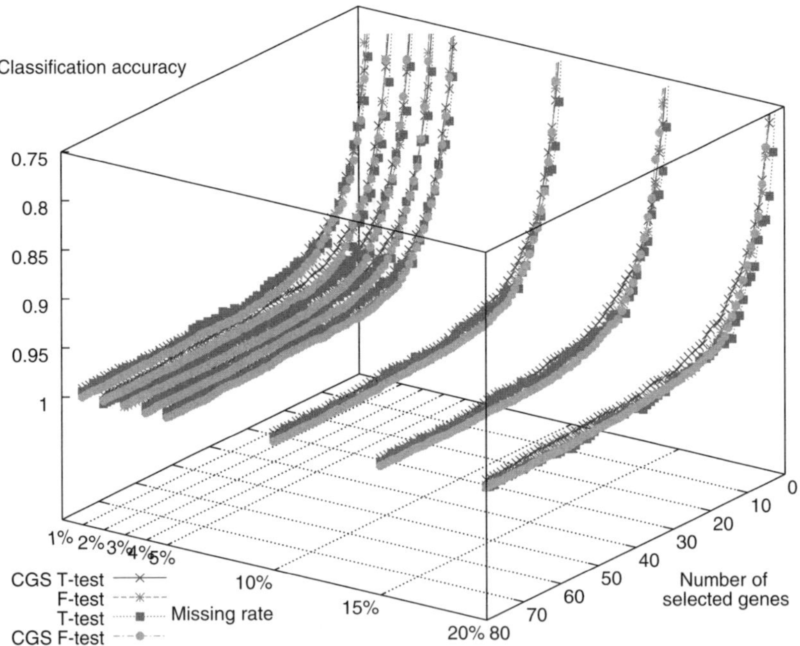

FIGURE 14.15 The 5-fold classification accuracies of four gene selection methods, F-test, T-test, CGS-Ftest, and CGS-Ttest, averaged over eight combinations of a missing value imputation method and a classifier, on the SRBCT dataset. The x-axis labels the number of selected genes, the y-axis labels the missing rate, and the z-axis labels the average classification accuracy.

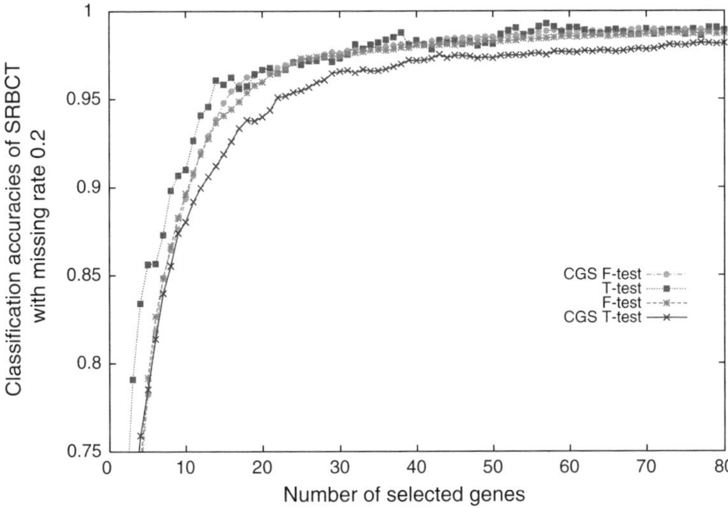

FIGURE 14.16 The 5-fold classification accuracies of four gene selection methods, F-test, T-test, CGS-Ftest, and CGS-Ttest, averaged over eight combinations of a missing value imputation method and a classifier, on the simulated SRBCT dataset with missing rate $r = 20\%$.

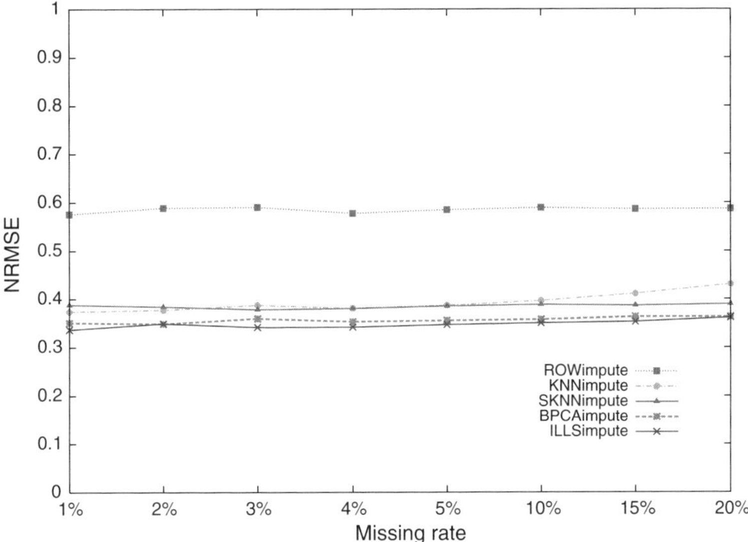

FIGURE 14.17 The NRMSE values of the five missing value imputation methods, ROWimpute, KNNimpute, SKNNimpute, BPCAimpute, and ILLSimpute, with respect to the missing rate.

by BPCAimpute and ILLSimpute had the same quality as the original expression matrix.

14.3.2.2 The GLIOMA Dataset It has been recognized that the quality of the GLIOMA dataset is lower than that of the SRBCT dataset [12,20]. Similarly, for each of the four gene selection methods, F-test, T-test, CGS-Ftest, and CGS-Ttest, we plotted separately the 5-fold cross validation classification accuracies for all combinations of a missing value imputation method and a classifier, on the original datasct ($r = 0\%$) and simulated datasets with missing rates $1\%, 2\%, 3\%, 4\%, 5\%, 10\%, 15\%$ and 20%, respectively. Figures 14.9–14.12 plot these classification accuracies for the F-test, T-test CGS-Ftest, and CGS-Ttest methods, respectively. From these plots, we can see that the performances of all the five imputation methods differed a bit more than those on the SRBCT dataset, at every missing rate, and more significantly with increasing missing rates. Nonetheless, overall, the general tendencies are still that (1) ROWimpute and KNNimpute performed equally well, and worse than the other three, (2) ILLSimpute and BPCAimpute performed equally well, and the best among the five methods, (3) SKNNimpute performed in the middle, and (4) the gaps between the performances became larger with increased missing rate r. Moreover, the imputed datasets by BPCAimpute and ILLSimpute have the same quality as the original one, in terms of the sample classification accuracy.

For missing rate $r = 20\%$, the classification accuracies are separately plotted in Figs. 14.13–14.14, in each of which the left plot is for the F-test/CGS-Ftest method and the right plot is for the T-test/CGS-Ttest method. It is clearly seen that, the BPCAimpute and ILLSimpute methods performed consistently the best, the ROWimpute and KNNimpute methods performed the worst, the SKNNimpute performed in the middle, and the imputed datasets by BPCAimpute and ILLSimpute had almost the same quality as the original GLIOMA dataset, in terms of the final sample classification accuracy. Furthermore, the last observation holds true across all missing rates, a strong demonstration that BPCAimpute and ILLSimpute are the methods of choices for microarray missing value imputation.

14.4 DISCUSSION

14.4.1 Gene Selection Methods

Clearly, the detailed gene selection method adopted in the study will result in different final sample classification accuracy. The collected average classification accuracies were taken over all the four gene selection methods, F-test, T-test, CGS-Ftest, and CGS-Ttest, and thus it is more convincing to conclude that BPCAimpute and ILLSimpute performed the best. We also compared the performances of the these four adopted gene selection methods by calculating their average classification accuracies over all the four missing value imputation methods ROWimpute, KNNimpute, SKNNimpute, BPCAimpute, and ILLSimpute. These classification accuracies and the classification accuracies obtained on the original SRBCT dataset are plotted in Figs. 14.15–14.16.

From these two plots, we can say that on the SRBCT dataset, all these four gene selection methods performed close to each other, though F-test/CGS-Ftest performed slightly better than T-test/CGS-Ttest.

14.4.2 NRMSE Values

We have also collected the NRMSE values for the five imputation methods on the simulated SRBCT datasets with all missing rates, which are plotted in Fig. 14.17 They again indicate that ILLSimpute and BPCAimpute performed the best among the five methods, and significantly better than the other three methods SKNNimpute, KNNimpute, and ROWimpute.

14.5 CONCLUSIONS

The performances of missing value imputation methods, BPCAimpute and ILLSimpute, have previously been shown to be better than most recent similar developments, using the NRMSE measurement [5]. The performance difference becomes significant when the missing rate is large. We realized that microarray gene expression data though is able to provide a global picture on the genetic profile, yet some portion of it is not reliable due to various experimental factors. Consequently, using solely the NRMSE measurement could sometimes be misleading. Considering the fact that missing value imputation is for the downstream data analysis, among which one of them is the sample classification, we proposed to adopt the classification accuracy as another measurement of imputation quality. Our simulation study on two real cancer microarray datasets, to include five imputation methods, four gene selection methods, and two classifiers, demonstrated that classification accuracy is a very effective measurement, and further confirmed that BPCAimpute and ILLSimpute are the best imputation methods. Furthermore, the imputed gene expression datasets by BPCAimpute and ILLSimpute can reach the same sample classification accuracy as that can be achieved on the original dataset.

ACKNOWLEDGMENTS

This research is supported in part by CFI, iCore, and NSERC.

REFERENCES

1. Alizadeh AA, Eisen MB, Davis RE, Ma C, Lossos IS, Rosenwald A, Boldrick JC, Sabet H, Tran T, Yu X, Powell JI, Yang L, Marti GE, Moore T, Hudson Jr J, Lu L, Lewis DB, Tibshirani R, Sherlock G, Chan WC, Greiner TC, Weisenburger DD, Armitage JO, Warnke R, Levy R, Wilson W, Grever MR, Byrd JC, Botstein D, Brown PO, and Staudt LM. Distinct types of diffuse large B-cell lymphoma identified by gene expression profiling. *Nature* 2000;403:503–511.

2. Baldi P, Long AD. A Bayesian framework for the analysis of microarray expression data: Regularized t-test and statistical inferences of gene changes. *Bioinformatics* 2001;17: 509–519.
3. Bhattacharjee A, Richards WG, Staunton J, Li C, Monti S, Vasa P, Ladd C, Beheshti J, Bueno R, Gillette M, Loda M, Weber G, Mark EJ, Lander ES, Wong W, Johnson BE, Golub TR, Sugarbaker DJ, Meyerso M. Classification of human lung carcinomas by mRNA expression profiling reveals distinct adenocarcinoma subclasses. *Proc Nat Acad Sci USA* 2001;98:13790–13795.
4. Bø TH, Dysvik B, Jonassen I. LSimpute: accurate estimation of missing values in microarray data with least squares methods. *Nucl Acid Res* 2004;32:e34.
5. Cai Z, Heydari M, Lin G-H. Iterated local least squares microarray missing value imputation. *J Bioinformatics Comput Biol* 2006;4(5):935–957.
6. Dudoit S, Fridlyand J, Speed TP. Comparison of discrimination methods for the classification of tumors using gene expression data. *J Am Stat Assoc* 2002;97:77–87.
7. Guyon I, Weston J, Barnhill S, Vapnik V. Gene selection for cancer classification using support vector machines. *Mach Learn* 2002;46:389–422.
8. Jörnsten R, Wang H-Y, Welsh WJ, Ouyang M. DNA microarray data imputation and significance analysis of differential expression. *Bioinformatics* 2005;21:4155–4161.
9. Khan J, Wei JS, Ringner M, Saal LH, Ladanyi M, Westermann F, Berthold F, Schwab M, Antonescu CR, Peterson C, Meltzer PS. Classification and diagnostic prediction of cancers using gene expression profiling and artificial neural networks. *Nat Med* 2001;7:673–679.
10. Kim H, Golub GH, Park H. Missing value estimation for DNA microarray gene expression data: Local least squares imputation. *Bioinformatics* 2005;21:187–198.
11. Kim K-Y, Kim B-J, Yi G-S. Reuse of imputed data in microarray analysis increases imputation efficiency. *BMC Bioinformatics* 2004;5:160.
12. Nutt CL, Mani DR, Betensky RA, Tamayo P, Cairncross JG, Ladd C, Pohl U, Hartmann C, McLaughlin ME, Batchelor TT, Black PM, Deimling AV, Pomeroy SL, Golub TR, Louis DN. Gene expression-based classification of malignant gliomas correlates better with survival than histological classification. *Cancer Res* 2003;63:1602–1607.
13. Oba S, Sato M, Takemasa I, Monden M, Matsubara K, Ishii S. A Bayesian missing value estimation method for gene expression profile data. *Bioinformatics* 2003;19:2088–2096.
14. Ouyang M, Welsh WJ, Georgopoulos P. Gaussian mixture clustering and imputation of microarray data. *Bioinformatics* 2004;20:917–923.
15. Scheel I, Aldrin M, Glad IK, Sørum R, Lyng H, Frigessi A. The influence of missing value imputation on detection of differentially expressed genes from microarray data. *Bioinformatics* 2005;21:4272–4279.
16. Sehgal MSB, Gondal L, Dooley LS. Collateral missing value imputation: a new robust missing value estimation algorithm for microarray data. *Bioinformatics* 2005;21:2417–2423.
17. Suárez-Fariñas M, Haider A, Wittkowski KM. "Harshlighting" small blemishes on microarrays. *BMC Bioinformatics* 2005;6:65.

18. Troyanskaya OG, Cantor M, Sherlock G, Brown P, Hastie T, Tibshirani R, Botstein D, Altman RB. Missing value estimation methods for DNA microarrays. *Bioinformatics* 2001;17:520–525.

19. Xiong M, Fang X, Zhao J. Biomarker identification by feature wrappers. *Genome Res* 2001;11:1878–1887.

20. Yang K, Cai Z, Li J, Lin G-H. A stable gene selection in microarray data analysis. *BMC Bioinformatics* 2006;7:228.

15

META-ANALYSIS OF MICROARRAY DATA

SAUMYADIPTA PYNE

The Broad Institute of MIT and Harvard, Cambridge, MA, USA

STEVE SKIENA

Department of Computer Science, Stony Brook University, Stony Brook, NY, USA

BRUCE FUTCHER

Department of Molecular Genetics and Microbiology, Stony Brook University, Stony Brook, NY, USA

15.1 INTRODUCTION

High throughput microarray technology has revolutionized the way gene expression studies are done and has greatly influenced fields such as genomics, medicine, and bioinformatics. Microarrays examine samples from two experimental conditions, for example, treatment and control, disease and normal, or wildtype and mutant, and compare the ratio of mRNA expression under each condition. As large number of genome-wide datasets from similar or related microarray experiments accumulate in the databases, integrative analysis of data becomes increasingly essential and useful for identifying features of potential biological interest [35].

A major concern in microarray meta-analysis is the lack of a single standard technological framework for data generation and analysis. It poses great challenge to comparison or combination of low level data across independent microarray studies. This is precisely where meta-analysis could prove to be immensely useful.

Bioinformatics Algorithms: Techniques and Applications, Edited by Ion I. Măndoiu and Alexander Zelikovsky

Meta-analysis is a classical statistical methodology for combining results in the form of high level data from different independent studies addressing similar scientific questions. Recently, meta-analysis has been successfully applied to various microarray datasets, in particular from cancer studies. Such application can help in identification of gene modules and pathways related to diseases like cancer, which might get ignored in individual studies. Meta-analysis identified candidate markers for prostate cancer by considering data from multiple labs despite the heterogeneity that existed with respect to their underlying platforms [44].

The present chapter shall focus on statistical combination of mRNA expression data in the form of effect sizes and probabilities from multiple comparable and independent microarray experiments. Often the number of such experiments addressing identical or related questions is small. Yet given the large number of tested features and the noise and heterogeneity in microarray data, it is worthwhile to combine multiple studies if available. We shall not discuss here various methods that *compare* but do not combine different datasets or platforms, for example, [8]. Also, we shall not cover the systems biology approaches to combine high throughput data across different omic measurements, for example, [60], nor the methods for pooling raw or low level data from different microarray experiments, for example, [62].

We proceed with a review of the small but steadily growing literature on integrative analysis of microarray studies. Then, the classical as well as new approaches of meta-analysis are described, in particular those that are well suited for microarray expression data. Methods to combine effect sizes and probabilities for a gene's expression estimates from multiple independent studies are covered in detail along with the new and promising approach of Bayesian meta-analysis. The scenario is complicated for microarray datasets because of multiple testing, which is briefly discussed as well. Integration-driven discovery rate, which is a measure of information gain due to integrative analysis, is also discussed. Finally, we take a tour of Oncomine, which is a compendium for cancer microarray data that can be used for meta-analysis.

- In the first microarray meta-analysis paper [45], results from four prostate cancer studies were integrated by combining the p-values for each gene from each study. The sum of logs method was used followed by permutation testing to compute the gene-specific combined p-value. Thus, a list of genes from the four studies was identified to be abnormally expressed in prostate cancer. Since each individual p-value provides a high level significance measure, the strategy can avoid the need to compare direct gene expression measurements that are tied to the underlying platforms and to issues such as cross-platform normalization and data transformation for the sake of compatibility.
- A large-scale meta-analysis was done in [46] to identify common transcriptional programs of neoplastic transformation and progression across diverse cancer types. The idea of vote counting was utilized to discover meta-signatures from genes that are differentially expressed in at least a particular number of selected studies. Later in the chapter, Oncomine, which is based on this work, is used to demonstrate the technique.

- Owing to intrinsic distinctions, combination of raw expression data can fail to yield useful integration. Overlap of gene expression measurements from Affymetrix and spotted cDNA data based on sixty cell lines was low enough in [30] to doubt that data from these platforms could be transformed into a common standardized index. Similarly, [27] found low agreement between microarray platforms by analyzing data from breast cancer cell lines. However, by comparing microarray data from 10 labs, it was shown by [25] that despite considerable differences, the studies agreed well for the best performing labs.
- Comparative analysis of data from multiple microarray platforms based on an integrative correlation technique was developed by [40] and was applied to lung cancer studies to identify genes with reproducible expression patterns across experiments. "Probability of expression" or *poe* was introduced in [41] as a platform-independent scale to measure expression, which can facilitate data integration across microarray experiments. Based on *poe*, [49] developed a two-stage mixture modeling of four breast cancer datasets to obtain meta-signature associated with breast cancer prognosis.
- Instead of *p*-values, [4] combined gene expression measures as effect sizes from the same cancer datasets as [45] into an average effect size. The effect sizes for each study was given by a standardized difference of the sample means between the two compared conditions. The standardization allowed the data to be integrated across platforms. Within-and cross-study errors were accounted for using the random-effects model. With effect sizes, small yet consistent expression changes were detected with increased sensitivity and reliability. A quality measure for weighted combination of effect sizes based on Affymetrix expression data were designed by [24] to model interstudy variation of gene expression profiles.
- Akin to the method in [4,61] combined effects based on the unstandardized difference of mean log of fold change in gene expression between chronic lymphocytic leukemia and normal B-cells across three studies from different platforms and identified genes that were consistently differentially expressed between the compared conditions. Both [5] and [19] combined effect sizes under random-effects model from four independent datasets each of liver and pancreatic cancer, respectively. Focussing on Affymetrix data, [54] combined signal log ratios for gene expression using the random-effects model and applied the method to mouse model data for multiple sclerosis from three labs.

The low comparability of independent datasets from diverse platforms can be attributed to various sources of uncertainty. Being capable of accounting for heterogeneity and uncertainty, Bayesian models for meta-analysis are particularly well suited to tackle the challenge. Also, prior distributions are useful for capturing information that is external to microarray experiments such as specific biological studies appearing in published literature (like PubMed) or annotated data (like GenBank). However, proper elicitation of prior distributions is often difficult. Complex modeling can help at the cost of tractability in evaluating the posterior estimates.

Bayesian meta-analysis for microarray has also been performed in [4]. In their Bayesian model, uninformative prior distributions were assigned to the overall mean effect and the cross-study variation parameters, whereas within-study gene effects were modeled as t distributions. The posterior estimate of the overall mean effect for each gene was produced by smoothing the effects across studies. In contrast, [6] used their hierarchical model to compute the posterior probability of differential expression based on two independent experiments with the bacterium *Bacillus subtilis*, and then used this probability to directly rank the differentially expressed genes.

Among other microarray meta-analysis approaches, [43] introduced a thresholded version of Fisher product to combine three budding yeast chIP-chip datasets. A certain minimum number of p-values for each gene that are less than or equal to experiment-specific false discovery restrictive thresholds formed the combined product, which ensured high power and controlled FDR. Using a distribution transformation method, [28] combined two lung cancer studies and used gene shaving to classify lung cancer patients from normal and reported differentially expressed genes. The classical sum of Zs method was employed by [37] to combine three genome-wide cell cycle experiments in fission yeast. A comparative analysis of 10 microarray studies of fission cell cycle by [34] revealed consistency in the phases of peak expression among the top periodically expressed genes.

In the following three sections, the general mechanisms of meta-analysis will be presented. The features studied by microarrays could be various such as genes, probes, loci, and so on; the commonly applied term "gene" shall be used here. Let the number of experiments to be combined be denoted by L. The words "study" and "experiment" have been used interchangeably in this chapter.

15.2 COMBINING EFFECT SIZES

Various effect sizes are used in meta-analysis: odds ratio, correlation, standardized mean difference, and so on [7]. They are combined across studies using either the fixed-effects model or the random-effects model [7]. The assumption in fixed-effect models that effect sizes are homogeneous is unrealistic for the massively high throughput and parallel microarray data. Indeed precisely, the capability to account for the heterogeneity that exists in the different assays done with microarrays makes the choice of random-effects modeling more natural than fixed-effects modeling. Not surprisingly, all published results on microarray meta-analysis with effect sizes are based on random-effect models. Therefore, below we shall devote more attention to random-effect modeling, and point the interested reader to detailed discussions on fixed-effect models in [21,22].

15.2.1 Fixed-Effects Modeling

For a particular gene, let Y_j for $j = 1, 2, \ldots, L$ be the observed effect size based on the gene's expression in experiment j and be modeled by normal distribution

$$Y_j \sim N(\mu, \sigma_j^2),$$

where σ_j^2 is the within-study variance for the gene. It is generally assumed that the variance σ_j^2 is known, and therefore the mean μ can be estimated as

$$\hat{\mu} = \frac{\sum_{j=1}^{L} w_j Y_j}{\sum_{j=1}^{L} w_j} \sim N(\mu, 1/\sum_{j=1}^{L} w_j),$$

where the weights $w_j = 1/\sigma_j^2$ are chosen to minimize the variance $(1/\sum_{j=1}^{L} w_j)$ of the estimate $\hat{\mu}$. This estimate of μ leads to a well-known test of homogeneity

$$Q = \sum_{j=1}^{L} \frac{(Y_j - \hat{\mu})^2}{\sigma_j^2} \sim \chi_{L-1}^2.$$

The null hypothesis ($Q = 0$) states that the L studies are homogeneous from the perspective of measuring a gene's expression and all the differences in their effects can be explained by sampling error alone. It may be noted that failure to reject the null hypothesis at a chosen level of significance does not imply that the hypothesis is true [14].

15.2.2 Random-Effects Modeling

In random-effects model, we discard the homogeneity assumption of the fixed-effects model by allowing a gene's true experimentwise effect to be random. The existing differences could be attributed to inexplicable and uncontrollable consequences of a variety of factors that are distinct across studies, for example, time, location, technicians, equipment, and so on. This is modeled using the normal distribution as follows:

$$Y_j \sim N(\theta_j, \sigma_j^2),$$

where Y_j is the observed gene expression effect and σ_j^2 is the within-study sampling error. The individual study effects are considered exchangeable, and these too follow normal distribution

$$\theta_j \sim N(\mu, \tau^2),$$

where μ represents the overall mean expression for the gene, and τ^2 the cross-study variation.

If a point estimate for τ^2 is known, then μ and its variance are estimated as follows:

$$\hat{\mu} = \frac{\sum_{j=1}^{L} w_j Y_j}{\sum_{j=1}^{L} w_j} \quad \text{and} \quad \mathrm{Var}(\hat{\mu}) = \frac{1}{\sum_{j=1}^{L} w_j},$$

where $w_j = 1/(\sigma_j^2 + \tau^2)$.

However, if τ^2 is unknown and the null hypothesis $\tau = 0$ is rejected, a method of moments estimator for τ^2 was developed by [10]

$$\hat{\tau}^2 = \max\left\{0, \frac{Q - (L-1)}{\sum_{j=1}^{L}(1/\sigma_j) - (\sum_{j=1}^{L}(1/\sigma_j^2)/\sum_{j=1}^{L}(1/\sigma_j))}\right\}.$$

To summarize, the random-effects model allows distinct underlying effects θ_j for each experiment j such that

$$\theta_j = \mu + \delta_j \ \text{ and thus } \ Y_j = \mu + \delta_j + \epsilon_j,$$

where $\epsilon_j \sim N(0, \sigma_j^2)$ and $\delta_j \sim N(0, \tau^2)$ are attributed, respectively, to within-study sampling error and cross-study variation for the particular gene in experiment j. By incorporating the uncertainties within the (random-effects) model, we can understand the expression effects for a gene as if these were random draws from a population of all possible effect sizes.

For a given gene, [4] combined effect sizes in the form of standardized mean difference using Cohen's d

$$d_j = \frac{\bar{X}_{T_j} - \bar{X}_{C_j}}{s_{P_j}},$$

where $\bar{X}_{T_j}$ and $\bar{X}_{C_j}$ are the sample means for the compared groups (say, treatment and control, respectively) in experiment j, while s_{P_j} is the pooled standard deviation given by

$$s_{P_j} = \sqrt{\frac{(n_{T_j} - 1)\sigma_{T_j}^2 + (n_{C_j} - 1)\sigma_{C_j}^2}{n_{T_j} + n_{C_j} - 2}},$$

where n_{T_j}, n_{C_j} and $\sigma_{T_j}, \sigma_{C_j}$ are the sizes and standard deviations of the samples from either group, respectively. However, d_j is a biased estimator of the population effect size and needs to be corrected. If $n = n_{T_j} + n_{C_j}$ is the number of samples in experiment j, an unbiased approximate estimator [22] is given by

$$\tilde{d}_j = \left(1 - \frac{3}{4n - 9}\right) d_j,$$

with the estimated variance [7]

$$\mathrm{Var}(\tilde{d}_j) = \frac{1}{n_{T_j}} + \frac{1}{n_{C_j}} + \frac{\tilde{d}_j^2}{2n}.$$

In meta-analysis of gene expression studies with Affymetrix data, the expression levels across two different conditions are compared and reported as a signal log ratio, which is the signed log base 2 of the signed fold change between the compared conditions. The Affymetrix estimate of $\tilde{d}_j$ as effect Y_j and its within-study variance $\mathrm{Var}(\tilde{d}_j)$ as σ_j^2 are used by [54] to combine effects for a given gene across experiments $j = 1, 2, \ldots, L$.

The estimated signal log ratio, when divided by variance, yields a t or Z score, which under the null hypothesis of no differential expression would lead to a p-value for every gene in every experiment. These p-values could be combined as such using techniques described in a later section. However, since the effect sizes for a gene's expression Y_j in each experiment j is directly available here, it is straightforward to combine the effects, and thus their magnitudes and directions, using the random-effects model described above. Thus, [54] tested the combined significance of gene expression with the help of a Z score ($Z = \hat{\mu}/\sqrt{\mathrm{Var}(\hat{\mu})}$) based on the above estimates. A similar combined Z based on unstandardized difference of sample means (i.e., $\bar{X}_{T_j} - \bar{X}_{C_j}$) of log fold change in a gene's expression in experiment j was used in [61].

For every gene in a given experiment using Affymetrix arrays, [24] observed the variability within the corresponding probe set to compute a quality-assessing measure that could be used for weighted combination of the gene's expression effects over multiple experiments. Under the assumption that negative log of the detection p-value[1] of a sample for a particular gene that belongs to group $g \in \{1, 2, \ldots, G\}$ (based on one of the G compared conditions, e.g., cancer, normal or treatment) follows a single parameter (λ_g) exponential distribution if the gene is not expressed, [24] suggests the following maximum likelihood estimate $\hat{\lambda}_g = 1/\bar{X}_j$, where $\bar{X}_j$ is the sample mean for group g. Then, the quality measure q for a particular gene in a given study j is computed as follows:

$$q_j = \max_{g \in \{1,2,\ldots,G\}} \exp(\hat{\lambda}_g \log s),$$

where s is a global cutoff chosen such that the p-values for those genes that yield poor measurements across different experimental conditions are greater than or equal to s. Then the quality measure q_j for each experiment j can be incorporated in the test of

[1] low p-value implies valid gene expression, Affymetrix Microarray Suite User Guide, version 5 (2001), http://www.affymetrix.com/support/technical/manuals.affx

homogeneity as follows:

$$Q = \sum_{j=1}^{L} q_j w_j (Y_j - \hat{\mu})^2,$$

and similarly in the other statistics described above

$$\hat{\mu} = \frac{\sum_{j=1}^{L} q_j w_j Y_j}{\sum_{j=1}^{L} q_j w_j} \quad \text{and} \quad Z = \frac{\hat{\mu}}{\text{Var}(\hat{\mu})}, \quad \text{where } \text{Var}(\hat{\mu}) = \sqrt{\frac{\sum_{j=1}^{L} q_j^2 w_j}{(\sum_{j=1}^{L} q_j^2 w_j)^2}},$$

such that $w_j = 1/\sigma_j^2$ for fixed-effect model and $w_j = 1/(\sigma_j^2 + \tau^2)$ for random-effect model where the cross-study variance τ^2 is estimated exactly as earlier but using the new weighted value of Q.

15.3 BAYESIAN META-ANALYSIS

The Bayesian paradigm is most naturally suited for meta-analysis. Both meta-analysis and Bayesian analysis try to include all available sources of information. They also try to account for the uncertainty associated with experimental results in order to yield meaningful integrative results. Moreover, the Bayesian hierarchical models resolve the fixed-effects versus random-effects modeling issue by offering a more flexible and robust framework for meta-analysis [13]. For its capability to modeling sources of uncertainty in a high throughput experiment, Bayesian approach is now extensively used for analysis of gene expression data [9]. Similarly, Bayesian meta-analysis has also found widespread use in several areas such as medicine [53]. Yet Bayesian meta-analysis of microarray data is still a new research area with only a couple of published papers, for example, [4,6].

In non-Bayesian meta-analysis, the combined results are validated by statistical comparisons, such as rank correlation or enrichment analysis, with published or annotated data. Such knowledge might be available to the researcher through published or unpublished results, from ontologies and annotations such as GO and MIPS, or simply by text mining the literature. In the Bayesian case, the meta-analyst has a choice of taking advantage of such existing information either for validation at the end of meta-analysis (as in the non-Bayesian case) or to use the information to specify informative prior distributions.

Of course, once the information is incorporated as prior probabilities, it can no longer be reused as validation criterion. The decision by the user about how to use the available information may be determined by a variety of factors such as how recently the information was generated, technological considerations, beliefs about reliability of the lab, the scale, relevance, and quality of the datasets, the precise hypotheses that are tested, the biological and epistemological relations between past and present evidence, and so on.

To illustrate such data diversity with an example, datasets that inform us about the protein–DNA binding in yeast (*S. cerevisiae*) could be in the form of a comparatively small 0/1 matrix of 185 intergenic regions $\times$ 70 transcription factors from TRANS-FAC database [33] or as genome-wide (approximately 5000 features) chIP-chip lists for more than hundred transcription factors that are reported as p-values [20,31]. However, if one wants to focus on yeast cell cycle regulation, then there exists further chIP-chip data about specific genes and transcription factors [26], similar data on all genes but for relevant transcription factors [51], and finally as cell cycle regulated mRNA expression data [52] both in the form of time courses for all 5000-odd transcripts as well as a subset of the most significant 800 genes. Likewise, the combination strategies could vary: whereas the lists due to [20,31,51] were meta-analyzed by [43] in a non-Bayesian manner and the combined list was validated by correlating with [26], Bayesian analysis by [39] was based only on the data of [51] and incorporating the information about the top 800 genes from [52] into the prior distribution.

Let the quantity of interest be θ and let prior beliefs about it be specified in the form of a probability density function $P(\theta)$. If data $\boldsymbol{Y}$ represent the values of θ observed in the experiments, then $P(\boldsymbol{Y}|\theta)$ is the likelihood function. In the light of the data $\boldsymbol{Y}$, Bayes' theorem helps us to update the prior beliefs about θ as follows:

$$P(\theta \mid \boldsymbol{Y}) \propto P(\boldsymbol{Y} \mid \theta) P(\theta).$$

By dividing by the constant of proportionality $\int P(\boldsymbol{Y} \mid \theta) P(\theta)\, d\theta$ (this is summation in the discrete case), we get the posterior density function $P(\theta \mid \boldsymbol{Y})$. The posterior distribution can then be used to estimate various statistics like mean and variance of the parameter of interest θ as well as to make probability statements about θ (based on experimental evidence $\boldsymbol{Y}$) in a direct way that a p-value cannot be. Indeed, the posterior distribution not only helps in updating the existing knowledge from the prior distribution, it can be used subsequently as prior information for the next round of analysis: $P(\theta|y_1, \ldots, y_k) \propto P(y_k|\theta) P(\theta|y_1, \ldots, y_{k-1})$. Such updating approach of Bayesian analysis may be interpreted as essentially meta-analytical. Thus, one can determine a predictive distribution for future observations or impute missing ones by averaging over the current parameters: $P(y_{k+1}|y_1, \ldots, y_k) = \int P(y_{k+1}|\theta) P(\theta|y_1, \ldots, y_k) d\theta$.

From the perspective of meta-analysis, the most important characteristic of the Bayesian approach is the explicit and formal inclusion of external information or experimental uncertainties within a hierarchical model. The underlying effects θ_j for a gene in experiment j are assumed to be randomly sampled from a common prior distribution which is, say, normal with mean μ and variance τ^2. Conditional on θ_j, the observed effect Y_j in experiment j is considered to be normal with mean θ_j and sampling error σ_j^2. This normal/normal assumption presents one of the best-studied models in the Bayesian meta-analysis

$$Y_j \mid \theta_j \sim N(\theta_j, \sigma_j^2),$$

$$\theta_j \mid \mu \sim N(\mu, \tau^2),$$

$$j = 1, 2, \ldots, L.$$

In meta-analysis, we are primarily interested to estimate the overall expression μ and the measure of heterogeneity τ. The modeling begins with elicitation of priors $\pi(\mu)$ and $\pi(\tau)$. Mixtures of distributions are also used. Many models use vague or noninformative priors such as constant or Jeffrey's priors to indicate lack of information but these assume all genes to be on equal footing, which is unrealistic in general. Empirical Bayes methods use prior distributions that are estimated from data. Finally, Bayesian methods extend the hierarchical models with an extra level in the hierarchy wherein the hyperparameters can capture either knowledge or ignorance of the analyst.

If the number of studies (L) to be combined is small, as is typical in microarray meta-analysis, the prior distributions can greatly influence the conclusions. For instance, the prior for τ can affect shrinkage (see below). If inclusion of external information is an advantage of Bayesian approach, then its proper specification in the form of prior distributions is a challenge. Sensitivity of the model's conclusions to a particular choice of prior should be analyzed, although this perhaps has not yet been attempted in microarray meta-analysis.

Depending on the complexity of the model, estimation of the parameters of interest could involve evaluation of complicated integrals. Until the recent advances in MCMC computational techniques like Gibbs sampling and the development of software packages like BUGS[2] and WinBUGS[3] or the open source software JAGS,[4] this was not feasible. Even in conjugate models, where the prior and posterior distributions belong to the same family, estimation is not always analytically tractable. Therefore, one had to do with basic models for which approximating the posterior quantities were easy, for instance, if all within-study variances were equal, that is, if every σ_j is σ, then direct estimates are obtained from sample mean and variance [32]

$$\hat{\mu} = \frac{1}{L}\sum_{j=1}^{L} Y_j \text{ and } \hat{\tau}^2 = \max\left\{0, \frac{1}{L-1}\sum_{j=1}^{L}(Y_j - \hat{\mu})^2 - \sigma^2\right\}.$$

In general, after obtaining the joint posterior density function of all unknown parameters, full conditional posterior distribution is derived for each. The integrals are evaluated by sampling the latter distributions (say, by Gibbs sampling with BUGS) and the posterior moments like mean and variance and the posterior marginal densities to compute probabilities are evaluated. With the classical normal/normal model, the posterior mean and variance are evaluated [14] as follows:

$$E(\mu|\boldsymbol{Y}, \tau) = \frac{\sum_{j=1}^{L} w_j Y_j}{\sum_{j=1}^{L} w_j} \text{ and } \mathrm{Var}(\mu|\boldsymbol{Y}, \tau) = \frac{1}{\sum_{j=1}^{L} w_j},$$

[2] http://www.mrc-bsu.cam.ac.uk/bugs/

[3] http://www.mrc-bsu.cam.ac.uk/bugs/winbugs/contents.shtml

[4] http://www-fi s.iarc.fr/~martyn/software/jags/

where $\boldsymbol{Y} = Y_1, Y_2, \ldots, Y_L$ and $w_j = 1/(\sigma_j^2 + \tau^2)$.

$$E(\theta_j|\boldsymbol{Y}, \tau) = B_j(\tau)E(\mu|\boldsymbol{Y}, \tau) + (1 - B_j(\tau))Y_j,$$

$$\text{Var}(\theta_j|\boldsymbol{Y}, \tau) = B_j(\tau)\tau^2 + B_j^2(\tau)\text{Var}(\mu|\boldsymbol{Y}, \tau),$$

where $B_j(\tau) = \sigma_j^2/(\sigma_j^2 + \tau^2)$ is the shrinkage factor that determines the "borrowing strength" among the studies, which is a major advantage of meta-analysis [13]. The shrinkage corresponds to the closeness of the posterior mean to the population mean relative to the data mean. For large τ, $B_j(\tau)$ is close to 0 and meta-analysis can be meaningless due to large cross-study variation. Conversely, $B_j(\tau)$ being close to 1, that is τ close to 0, would suggest the use of fixed-effects model for meta-analysis. Finally, the unconditional posterior mean, variance, and probability are evaluated as follows:

$$E(\mu|\boldsymbol{Y}) = \int E(\mu|\boldsymbol{Y}, \tau)\pi(\tau|\boldsymbol{Y})d\tau,$$

$$\text{Var}(\mu|\boldsymbol{Y}) = \int (\text{Var}(\mu|\boldsymbol{Y}, \tau) + (E(\mu|\boldsymbol{Y}, \tau) - E(\mu|\boldsymbol{Y}))^2)\pi(\tau|\boldsymbol{Y})d\tau,$$

$$P(\mu > 0|\boldsymbol{Y}) = \int \Phi(\frac{E(\mu|\boldsymbol{Y}, \tau)}{(\text{Var}(\mu|\boldsymbol{Y}, \tau))^{1/2}})\pi(\tau|\boldsymbol{Y})d\tau,$$

where Φ denotes the standard Normal cumulative distribution function. For the interested reader, a good example of meta-analysis using Bayesian hierarchical model is presented in [17].

15.4 COMBINING PROBABILITIES

In microarray literature, genewise significance is often reported as p-values. Sometimes, it is just the list of p-values that is available, for example [31,51]. This leaves the meta-analyst with no choice other than to combine p-values.Fortunately, the techniques for combining p-values, originally suggested by Fisher, are well established.

Moreover, combination of such high level significance measures as p-values allows the meta-analysis to avoid the platform-specific issues like normalization and data transformation.

If the p-values are not available, they can be generated by bootstrapping or permutation testing. For the sake of uniformity, the meta-analyst might try to recompute the p-values from raw data of all the experiments. This might be avoided only if the raw data are not available or if the studies are from the same laboratory and involves identical hypotheses and testing methods. However, if the measured phenomena are related but different (say, if ChIP-chip data [51] for cell-cycle regulation by transcription factors in yeast were to be combined with time course expression data for such regulation of its genes [52]) then it is necessary to understand that given the distinctions inherent in the p-value distribution of each study, careful validation, and multiple testing might be necessary upon meta-analysis.

Let the independent p-values be denoted as $\{p_j : j = 1, 2, \ldots, L\}$. The most popular technique for combining the ps is Fisher's inverse chi-square or sum of logs method [16]

$$\ln P = \sum_{j=1}^{L} (-2) \times \ln p_j \sim \chi^2_{2L}.$$

The above statistic P, often called the Fisher product, gives a simple yet elegant test of combined significance based on the fact that the sum of L independent χ^2_2 variates is a χ^2_{2L} variate. Thus, it has been extensively used in meta-analysis, and its behavior is well-understood [47]. For instance, the test performs well for combining a small number of experiments, which makes it well suited for microarray meta-analysis. Fisher product was found by [15] to be asymptotically optimal for combining independent tests among the standard meta-analysis methods. A randomized version of Fisher product was used by [45] to combine four microarray studies on prostrate cancer. A large population of products (P-s as defined above) was simulated by randomly picking p-values from each of experiment, and then the distribution was used to generate the combined probabilities.

Another classical method of combining significance is by addition of Z scores. Many experiments report Zs as, for example, the number of standard deviations between the present observation and the mean of the samples or their permutations, that is, as a standard normal deviate. Alternatively, one can generate Z scores from the p-values (say, due to t statistics) using the tails of the normal distribution. Under the assumption that each of the L experiments is represented by a standard normal variate, their sum is normal with mean 0 and standard deviation $\sqrt{L}$. Thus, the test statistic is as follows:

$$Z = \frac{\sum_{j=1}^{L} Z_j}{\sqrt{L}} \sim N(0, 1).$$

Unlike Fisher product, the performance of the above test, commonly known as the Stouffer's method [56], is not affected by the number of studies [47]. This makes it an ideal choice for extending a combination of p-values when the number of studies is initially small (less than 5), but is likely to increase later. For instance, while [37] used Stouffer's method to combine three microarray experiments for fission yeast cell cycle, seven more experiments from two different labs testing identical hypotheses were also published. Such scenario is even more likely for microarray studies of cancer.

Besides p-values, t scores can also be converted to Zs, even when the t distributions have large degrees of freedom [48]. However, if the number of experiments is 10 or more, then Winer's test that directly combines ts to produce a Z score is perhaps more readily applicable to microarray data than Stouffer's sum of Zs as well as it gives better performance than Fisher's sum of logs (which performs well when L is small). Given that the standard deviation of a t variate t_j in experiment j with d_j degrees of freedom is $\sqrt{d_j/(d_j-2)}$, the statistic for Winer's test is defined as

$$Z = \frac{\sum_{j=1}^{L} t_j}{\sqrt{\sum_{j=1}^{L} d_j/(d_j-2)}} \sim N(0,1).$$

Several methods for combining significance values, although not all of equal popularity, are listed in [1,47], and the user must select the one that best suits the characteristics of her data. For instance, if the significance values may be easy to transform to logits, one can use the Logit method due to [36]. It approximates the sum of logits with a t distribution as follows:

$$-\sum_{j=1}^{L} \ln \frac{p_j}{1-p_j} \sqrt{3(5L+4)/L\pi^2(5L+2)} \sim t_{5L+4}.$$

For a prespecified value τ^*, Tippett's Minimum p method [58] rejects the joint null hypothesis if the minimum of all ps, that is, $p_{[1]} < \tau = 1-(1-\tau^*)^{1/L}$. Along this direction, a more general testing scheme due to [11] uses Beta distribution to numerically compute the combined significance for the product of the k smallest of L p-values for a prespecified integer k between 1 and L. For $k = 1$, this test corresponds to Sidak's correction [50], whereas for $k = L$, it reduces to Fisher product.

In spite of widespread use, there could be disadvantages with the standard Fisher product, and different techniques have been suggested to avoid these. In case there are a substantial number of experiments, we have already discussed other methods of combining significance values. Discriminative meta-analysis using weighted Fisher product is difficult to handle, although approximations and computational techniques have been proposed [3,64]. A computationally much simpler (and perhaps better [63]) alternative is the weighted sum of Zs defined as follows:

$$Z = \frac{\sum_{j=1}^{L} w_j Z_j}{\sqrt{\sum_{j=1}^{L} w_j^2}} \sim N(0,1).$$

A major problem with microarray data is noise. In particular, randomly occurring spikes of noise are not rare. However, such random noise in unlikely to repeat for the same feature over multiple independent experiments and thus the effect can be neutralized by meta-analysis. Although the sum of logs method of Fisher product is generally recommended for its power [1], it has been observed by [47] that the test can lose power in cases where genuinely significant features have some poor scores. To fix this, [64] proposed the following thresholded version of Fisher product that helps to increase the power of the test by letting the poor p-values of a gene be ignored

$$W = \prod_{j=1}^{L} {p_j}^{\mathcal{I}(p_j \leq \tau)},$$

where τ is a prespecified p-value threshold and the function $\mathcal{I}(\text{True}) = 1$ and $\mathcal{I}(\text{False}) = 0$. Thus, only those p-values that are less than or equal to some specified cutoff value τ form the product. The combined significance of the statistic W is computed with the help of an analytical distribution in [64]. Further, in standard Fisher product, a combination of marginally significant probabilities could suggest unreasonably high significance. The statistic W guards against such false positives by requiring the presence of at least one p-value significant enough to be less than or equal to τ.

Large microarray datasets are often in need of cutoff values that allow control of FDR while being used as thresholds for reporting significant features [55]. However, a common cutoff τ is not useful to apply for a collection of independent and diverse experiments. Toward this, [43] suggested an experiment-specific cutoff $\tau_{j,\alpha}$ guided by the important additional objective of controlling the false discovery proportion (FDP) in experiment j at level α. The thresholded Fisher product was extended to combine only those p-values of a particular gene that are less or equal to their respective experiment-specific cutoffs $\tau_{j,\alpha}$ to form the generalized product

$$W_\alpha = \prod_{j=1}^{L} {p_j}^{\mathcal{I}(p_j \leq \tau_{j,\alpha})}.$$

Thus, the occasional poor p-values of otherwise truly significant genes are ignored, which increases the robustness and power of the product. Several approximations for the distribution of thresholded Fisher product are studied in [38]. Although the above threshold $\tau_{j,\alpha}$ has been defined for the purpose of restricting false positives, the general idea of experiment-specific thresholding can enable discriminative meta-analysis. Figure 15.1 illustrates this argument with fission yeast cell cycle studies. Moreover, thresholding can lead to binary (accept/reject) votes about a gene's significance in different experiments, which may be useful for a vote-counting strategy if the number of experiments L is large (see vote-counting methods in [7]).

Although experiments are conducted independently, dependence can still be present in the significance values and effect sizes for a variety of reasons. Owing to high degree of automation in microarray technology, subtle sources of dependence like replicated patterns of error may be present. Even nonexperimental factors may be responsible. For instance, the score used in [34] to identify a cell cycle regulated transcript in fission yeast combined the p-value of regulation with that of periodicity—both based on the same time course of a gene. Discussions about dependence and methods to tackle that appear in [42,57,64].

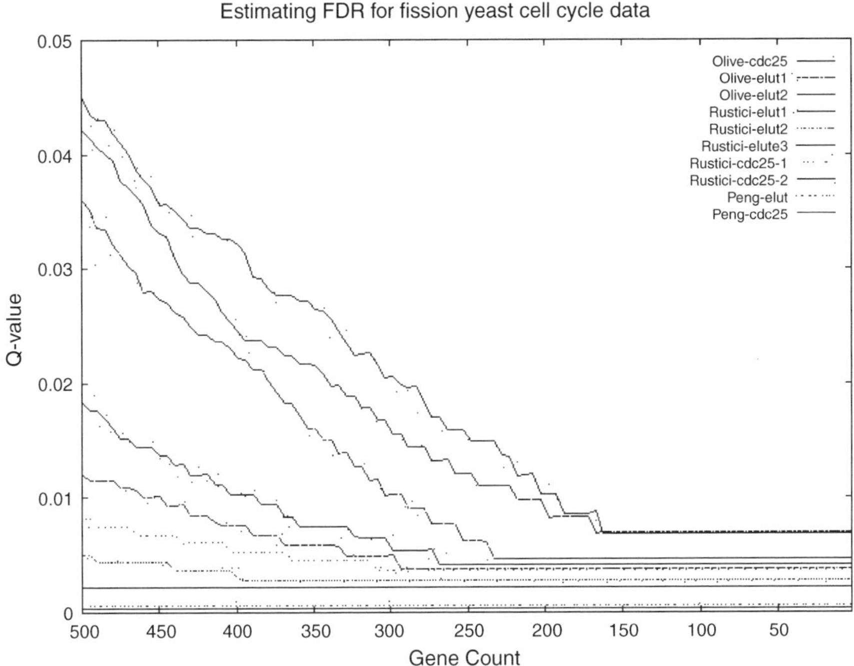

FIGURE 15.1 The q-value for a particular feature is defined [55] as the minimum expected proportion of false positives occurring up through that feature on the list. The divergence among q-values within the range of even the most significant 500 genes in the 10 datasets justifies the use of experiment-specific p-value cutoffs in thresholded Fisher product combination [43].

15.5 FDR AND IDR

Multiple hypotheses testing for thousands of genes are of special concern in the analysis of microarray data. Following [2], estimation of false discovery rate or FDR has become a standard practice in microarray studies. Naturally, most meta-analysis approaches adapt known methods of controlling FDR in a single study to assess the statistical significance of the combined results. Permutation tests derived from algorithms due to [59] and [55] were used upon meta-analysis of effect sizes and p-values by [4] and [44], respectively. For Bayesian meta-analysis, [6] employed the posterior expected FDR control of [18]. In a different approach, [43] pooled experiment-wise gene subsets each of which has controlled proportion (FDP) or count of false positives, as achieved by [29], to control the combined FDP. See [12] for a review of techniques for multiple hypotheses testing in microarray experiments.

Integration-driven discovery rate or IDR has been proposed in [4] to evaluate the number of genes that are identified as significant by meta-analysis but not by any of the individual studies. Therefore, it is a measure of information gain solely due to integrative analysis. Typically, such gain would be in terms of small effects, which are consistent (i.e., in the same direction) and hence add up during meta-analysis. Given a threshold, IDR is computed as the ratio of the counts of genes that are differentially expressed above the threshold in either direction (i.e., both up- and downregulated) in terms of the combined statistic but not at the corresponding level in any of the individual studies.

15.6 ONCOMINE: A RESOURCE FOR META-ANALYSIS

This section will describe Oncomine, a compendium for cancer microarray data, and demonstrate how one can perform meta-analysis using this resource. "Meta-analysis of microarrays" was originally developed and applied to four independent prostate cancer profiling studies [45] as well as to 40 cancer profiling datasets [46] using Oncomine. This cancer profiling platform currently includes 209 independent datasets, totaling more than 14,000 microarray experiments, which span 36 cancer types (www.oncomine.com).

Meta-analysis can be used to identify genes that share a common expression signature across multiple independent studies and thus, may have an inferred biological role. Many independent laboratories perform gene expression profiling on analogous tissue samples. An example might be seven datasets that include normal prostate samples and localized prostate carcinoma samples run in different laboratories on different array platforms. When defining candidate biomarkers and therapeutic targets, it is important to evaluate gene expression data across all available data, utilizing independent datasets to intervalidate each other.

Data are collected and stored in Oncomine by monitoring the literature and repositories such as GEO, SMD, and ArrayExpress. Cancer profiling studies are prioritized and available data is downloaded from repositories, author websites, and supplemental materials including sample facts from manuscripts. In addition, correspondence with authors is performed when data or sample facts are missing or incomplete. Standard normalization is performed (RMA for Affymetrix data, Lowess for cDNA arrays) when raw data files are provided. The data matrix and sample facts are standardized by expanding abbreviations, mapping to common synonyms, and NCI Thesaurus terms. An automated pipeline then maps reporters identified by Affymetrix Probeset IDs or Image Clone IDs to gene annotation.

Within Oncomine, a meta-analysis function allows a user to select any number of cancer profiles and identify genes that are commonly activated or repressed across the set. First, the user selects a set of cancer profiles and then sets the number of selected profiles in which a gene should be measured and significant. For example, one might select four lung andenocarcinoma profiles and require that a gene be present and overexpressed in three of four profiles. This setting is flexible so that users can explore various options ensuring that optimal markers and targets are not missed.

Meta-analysis begins from the point of selecting a cancer profile of interest. From the main Oncomine interface, the cancer profile of interest is entered as a search term (gene symbols, aliases, or keywords). The results for the search term "prostate" yield a list of studies that have been analyzed in Oncomine. These are ranked by the highest percentage of differentially expressed genes (Fig. 15.2). Each analysis

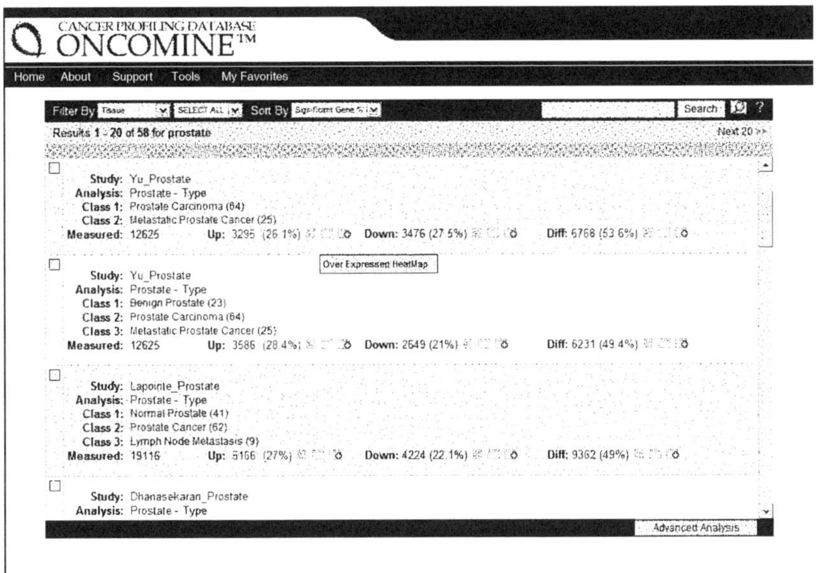

FIGURE 15.2 A profile search for "prostate" yields analyses ranked by the percentage of most significantly dysregulated genes. Each analysis listed contains direct links to heat maps and lists of genes that are up, down, or differentially regulated.

listed contains study information and the classes of samples that are being compared. In order to identify potential biomarkers specific for metastatic prostate cancer, we can filter our list to display cancer versus cancer comparisons. The question we pose is, which genes are activated in metastatic prostate carcinoma? The analysis begins with the selection of independent studies where the appropriate sample comparisons were made to identify genes significantly dysregulated in metastatic prostate cancer as compared to nonmetastatic prostate cancer.

Within individual profiles listed, the differentially expressed genes are represented in a heat map (Fig. 15.3). Here, higher level of expression can be noted in the 25 metastatic prostate carcinoma samples relative to the 64 prostate carcinoma samples in the Yu Study. The most significantly overexpressed gene EIF1X, a eukaryotic transcription factor, is listed at the top of the heat map reflecting specific over expression in metastatic prostate adenocarcinoma in this study. This finding alone often drives additional investigation of genes observed to be overexpressed based on a chosen significance level. The approach of meta-analysis within Oncomine, takes advantage of the large population of studies where genes are measured by multiple, heterogeneous reporters, and microarray platforms within different research organizations to provide robust validation and focus efforts on the most promising targets.

The next step in meta-analysis is to select the studies to include those genes where significant differential expression is observed. The top five analyses having the most differentially expressed genes are selected for inclusion in meta-analysis. Additional filters can be applied to limit the analysis to a particular functional category such as "cell cycle" (Fig. 15.4).

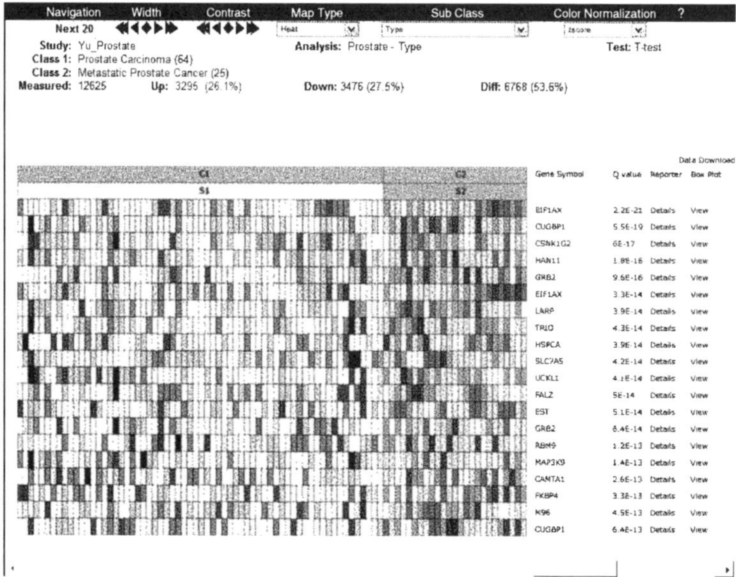

FIGURE 15.3 Genes that are significantly overexpressed in metastatic prostate carcinomas in the Yu study are represented in heat map as red cells in the website. Genes are ranked according to significance of over expression.

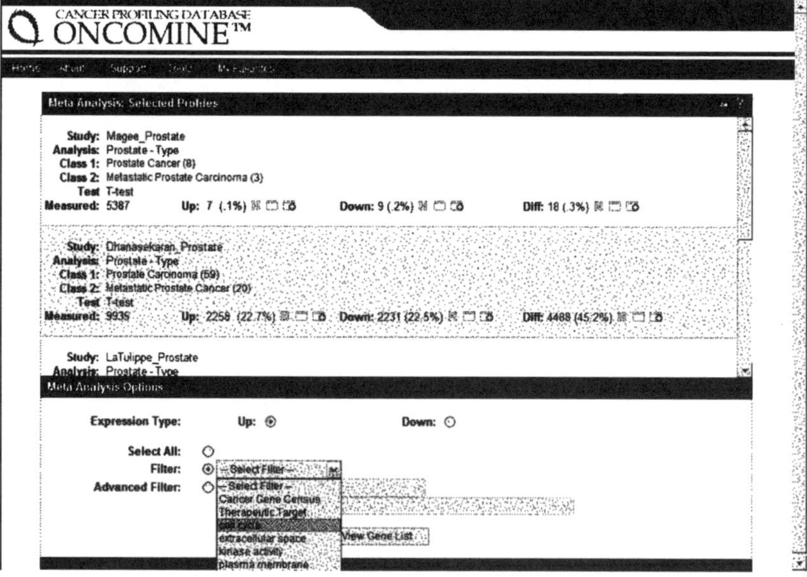

FIGURE 15.4 Meta-analysis parameters include selected profiles, over- or underexpressed genes, and can include the application of filters such as “cell cycle” to limit the genes that are returned in the metamap.

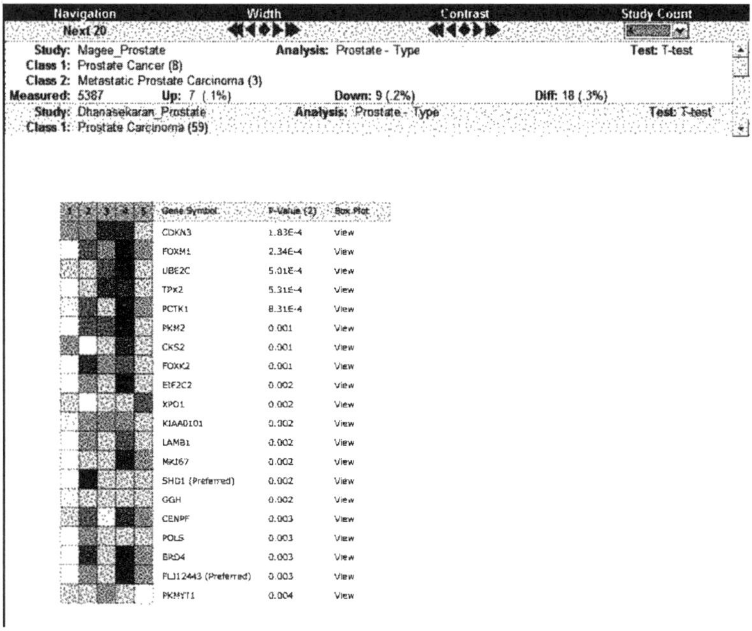

FIGURE 15.5 A metamap displays the most significantly overexpressed genes ranked and colored by p-value across five independent studies based on p-value for four out of the five studies. This option reduces the effect of genes that are not well measured or not present on the specific array used in the study such as the second gene, FOXM1, which was not measured in Study 1 as indicated by a white cell.

The resulting metamap displays each of the four profiles as columns and genes as rows. Cells are colored by significance of over expression (Fig. 15.5). Rows in the map correspond to the genes that are significantly overexpressed in four out of the five analyses. By default, one study is left out to remove bias from studies where the gene was not well measured or not present on the particular array used. Genes are ranked by the highest p-value of the studies included in the analysis. The number of studies included in the comparison can be adjusted to update the map and the resulting gene rank on the fly. Thus, we see different gene sets ranked by the most significant p-values, computed by Oncomine using the t-statistic, in four out of the five studies shown (Fig. 15.5) and in five out of five studies. Inclusion of all five studies in the meta-analysis generates a new gene ranking. CDKN3 remains the highest ranked while genes such as FOXM1 drop out of the list because it was not measured in study 1. This allows us to explore the genes that might be significantly overexpressed in metastatic prostate carcinoma but perhaps not represented or well measured on a particular array in one of the five studies chosen.

Including either four or five analysis across independent studies reveals CDKN3 as the consistently highest ranked, overexpressed gene in metastatic prostate carcinoma as compared to prostate carcinoma. Exploring further, this finding is confirmed by viewing the box plots for CDKN3 across all five studies and by noting over expression

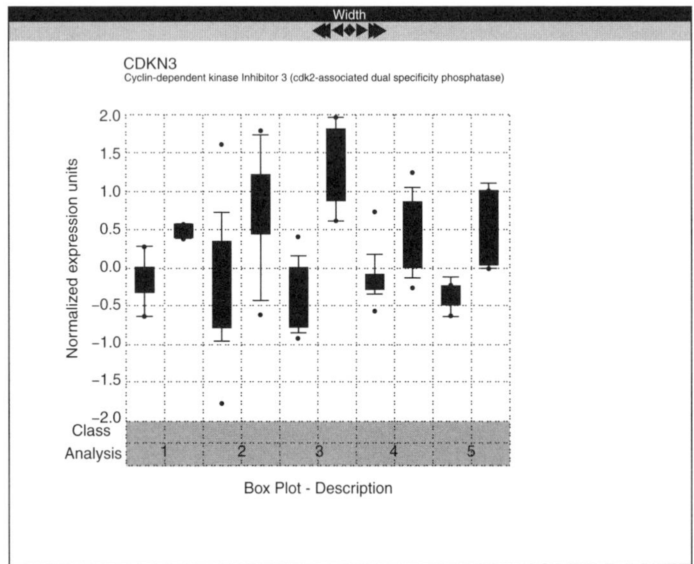

FIGURE 15.6 Distribution of gene expression of CDKN3 across five independent studies comparing prostate carcinoma (dark gray) and metastatic prostate carcinoma (light gray).

in metastatic prostate carcinoma shown in light gray versus prostate carcinoma in dark gray (Fig. 15.6). The box plot view provides a snapshot of the distribution of this biological change and the difference in array platforms between studies, while representing the consistent over expression of CDKN3.

15.6.1 Discussion

Thus, meta-analysis can be applied to a resource like Oncomine to identify common transcriptional programs. This was demonstrated in the identification of transcriptional profiles from a diverse collection of 40 published cancer datasets [46]. These profiles were found to be activated in most cancer types relative to corresponding normal tissue. It was expected that many of these universal cancer genes would be involved in cell proliferation and invasion. For example, TOP2A was found to be overexpressed in 18 of the cancer versus normal signatures that represented 10 cancer types. This gene encodes toposisomerase II that is involved in DNA replication and is the target of several cancer drugs.

Meta-analysis was also used to identify signatures characterizing cancer progression defined by classical histopathogical and clinical parameters. Analysis of undifferentiated versus differentiated cancer was used in meta-analysis to identify 69 genes present in at least four of seven signatures. Most of these genes were associated with proliferation and thus having overlapped with those found in cancers relative to normal tissue. Genes overexpressed in undifferentiated cancers were found to be broad transcription factors that play a role in maintaining undifferentiated state. Other genes found in this metasignature are known to be involved in embryogenesis and inhibition of apoptosis, thus contributing to the state of undifferentiation.

As an example of such an application, [23] used meta-analysis within Oncomine to investigate the expression of Metastasis-Associated Gene 1 (MTA1) in human neoplastic tissue. They found MTA1 was significantly dysregulated in 22 of 85 expression array studies representing a variety of tumors relative to healthy tissue. Furthermore, they were able to determine that MTA1 expression may be involved in tissue invasion but was not sufficient alone to drive metastasis.

Meta-analysis provides a powerful method for identification of a collection of genes that are differentially expressed in either a large panel of cancers or specific cancer subtypes and classifications. Using meta-analysis on collections of microarray data such as Oncomine, the underlying biological mechanisms can be explored and validated across a heterogeneous population of tissues and experiments providing broader and more robust validation while enabling new hypothesis generation in a variety of biological problems.

ACKNOWLEDGMENTS

The authors would like to thank Matt Anstett and Dan Rhodes of Compendia Bioscience (www.compendiabio.com) for their contribution on Oncomine.

REFERENCES

1. Becker BJ. Combining significance levels. In: Cooper H, Hedges LV, editors. *The Handbook of Research Synthesis*. New York: Russell Sage Foundation 1994.
2. Benjamini Y, Hochberg Y. Controlling the false discovery rate: a practical and powerful approach to multiple testing. *J Roy Stat Soc B* 1995;57:289–300.
3. Bhoj DS. On the distribution of the weighted combination of independent probabilities. *Stat Probab Let* 1992;15:37–40.
4. Choi JK, Yu U, Kim S, Yoo OJ. Combining multiple microarray studies and modeling interstudy variation. *Bioinformatics*19:Suppl. 1, i84–i90, 2003.
5. Choi JK, Choi JY. Integrative analysis of multiple gene expression profiles applied to liver cancer study. *FEBS Let* 2004;565:93–100.
6. Conlon EM, Song JJ, Liu JS. Bayesian models for pooling microarray studies with multiple sources of replications. *BMC Bioinformatics* 2006;7:247.
7. Cooper H, Hedges LV. *The Handbook of Research Synthesis*. New York: Russell Sage Foundation Publications; 1994.
8. Culhane AC, Perriere G, Higgins DG. Cross-platform comparison and visualisation of gene expression data using co-inertia analysis. *BMC Bioinformatics* 2003;4:59.
9. Do K-A, Müller P, Vannucci M. *Bayesian Inference for Gene Expression and Proteomics.* New York: Cambridge University Press; 2006.
10. DerSimonian R, Laird NM. Meta-analysis in clinical trials. *Controll Clini Trials.* 1986;7:177–188.

11. Dudbridge F, Koeleman BPC. Rank truncated product of P-values, with application to genomewide association scans. *Genet Epidemiol* 2003;25:360–366.

12. Dudoit S, Shaffer JP, Boldrick JC. Multiple hypothesis testing in microarray experiments. *Stat Sci* 2003;18:71–103.

13. DuMouchel WH, Harris JE. Bayes methods for combining the results of cancer studies in humans and other species. *J Am Stat Assoc* 1983;78:293–315.

14. DuMouchel W, Normand S-L. Computer-modeling and Graphical Strategies for Meta-analysis. In: *Meta-Analysis in Medicine and Health Policy*. Stangl D, Berry DA, editors. New York: Marcel Dekker; 2000.

15. Elston RC. On Fisher's method of combining p-values. *Biometrical J* 1991;33:339–345.

16. Fisher RA. *Statistical Methods For Research Workers*. London: Oliver and Boyd; 1932.

17. Gelman A, Carlin JB, Stern HS, Rubin DB. *Bayesian Data Analysis*. Boca Raton: Chapman & Hall/CRC; 2003. Chapter 5.

18. Genovese CR, Wasserman L. Operating characteristics and extensions of the false discovery rate procedure. *J Roy Stat Soc* B 2002;64:499–518.

19. Grützmann R, Boriss H, Ammerpohl O, Lüttges J, Kalthoff H, Schackert HK, Klöppel G, Saeger HD, Pilarsky C. Meta-analysis of microarray data on pancreatic cancer defines a set of commonly dysregulated genes. *Oncogene* 2005;24:5079–88.

20. Harbison CT, Gordon DB, Lee TI, Rinaldi NJ, Macisaac KD, Danford TW, Hannett NM, Tagne JB, Reynolds DB, Yoo J, Jennings EG, Zeitlinger J, Pokholok DK, Kellis M, Rolfe PA, Takusagawa KT, Lander ES, Gifford DK, Fraenkel E, Young RA. Transcriptional regulatory code of a eukaryotic genome. *Nature* 2004;431:99–104.

21. Hedges LV. Fixed Effects Models. In: Cooper H, Hedges LH, editors. *The Handbook of Research Synthesis*. New York: Russell Sage Foundation; 1994.

22. Hedges LV, Olkin I. *Statistical Methods for Meta-Analysis*. San Diego: Academic Press; 1985.

23. Hofer MD, Tapia C, Browne TJ, Mirlacher M, Sauter G, Rubin MA. Comprehensive analysis of the expression of the metastasis-associated gene 1 in human neoplastic tissue. *Arch Pathol Lab Med* 2006;130:989–996.

24. Hu P, Greenwood CMT, Beyene J. Integrative analysis of multiple gene expression profiles with quality-adjusted effect size models. *BMC Bioinformatics* 2005;6:128.

25. Irizarry RA, Warren D, Spencer F, Kim IF, Biswal S, Frank BC, Gabrielson E, Garcia JG, Geoghegan J, Germino G, Griffin C, Hilmer SC, Hoffman E, Jedlicka AE, Kawasaki E, Martínez-Murillo F, Morsberger L, Lee H, Petersen D, Quackenbush J, Scott A, Wilson M, Yang Y, Ye SQ, Yu W. Multiple-laboratory comparison of microarray platforms. *Nat Method* 2005;2:345–350.

26. Iyer VR, Horak CE, Scafe CS, Botstein D, Snyder M, Brown PO. Genomic binding sites of the yeast cell-cycle transcription factors sbf and mbf. *Nature* 2001;409:533–538.

27. Järvinen AK, Hautaniemi S, Edgren H, Auvinen P, Saarela J, Kallioniemi OP, Monni O. Are data from different gene expression microarray platforms comparable? *Genomics* 2004;83:1164–1168.

28. Jiang H, Deng Y, Chen HS, Tao L, Sha Q, Chen J, Tsai CJ, Zhang S. Joint analysis of two microarray gene-expression datasets to select lung adenocarcinoma marker genes. *BMC Bioinformatics* 2004;5:81.

29. Korn EL, Troendle JF, McShane LM, Simon R. Controlling the number of false discoveries: application to high dimensional genomic data. *J Stat Plann Infer* 2004;124:379–398.
30. Kuo WP, Jenssen TK, Butte AJ, Ohno-Machado L, Kohane IS. Analysis of matched mRNA measurements from two different microarray technologies. *Bioinformatics* 2002;18:405–412.
31. Lee TI, Rinaldi NJ, Robert F, Odom DT, Bar-Joseph Z, Gerber GK, Hannett NM, Harbison CT, Thompson CM, Simon I, Zeitlinger J, Jennings EG, Murray HL, Gordon DB, Ren B, Wyrick JJ, Tagne JB, Volkert TL, Fraenkel E, Gifford DK, Young RA. Transcriptional Regulatory Networks in Saccharomyces cerevisiae. *Science* 2002;298:799–804.
32. Louis TA, Zelterman D. Bayesian Approaches to Research Synthesis. In: Cooper H, Hedges LV, editors. *The Handbook of Research Synthesis*. New York: Russell Sage Foundation; 1994.
33. Manke T, Bringas R, Vingron M. Correlating protein-DNA and protein-protein interaction networks. *J Mol Biol* 2003;333:75–85.
34. Marguerat S, Jensen TS, de Lichtenberg U, Wilhelm BT, Jensen LJ, Bähler J. The more the merrier: comparative analysis of microarray studies on cell cycle regulated genes in fission yeast. *Yeast* 2006;23:261–277.
35. Moreau Y, Aerts S, De Moor B, De Strooper B, Dabrowski M. Comparison and meta-analysis of microarray data: from the bench to the computer desk. *Trend Genet* 2003;19:570–577.
36. Mudholkar GS, George EO. The logit statistic for combining probabilities - an overview. In: Rustagi JS, editor. *Optimizing Methods in Statistics*. New York: Academic Press; 1979.
37. Oliva A, Rosebrock A, Ferrezuelo F, Pyne S, Chen H, Skiena S, Futcher B, Leatherwood J. The cell cycle-regulated genes of *Schizosaccharomyces pombe*. *Pub Lib Sci Biol* 2005;3:123960.
38. Olkin I, Saner H. Approximations for trimmed Fisher procedures in research synthesis. *Stat Method Med Res* 2001;10:267–276.
39. Pan W. Incorporating biological information as a prior in an empirical bayes approach to analyzing microarray data. *Stat Appl Genet Mol Biol* 2005;4:12.
40. Parmigiani G, Garrett ES, Anbazhagan R, Gabrielson E. A cross-study comparison of gene expression studies for the molecular classification of lung cancer. *Clin Cancer Res* 2004;10:2922–2927.
41. Parmigiani G, Garrett ES, Anbazhagan R, Gabrielson E. A statistical framework for expressionbased molecular classification in cancer. *J Roy Stat Soc B* 2002;64:717–736.
42. Pesarin F. *Multivariate Permutation Tests: With Applications in Biostatistics*. Chichester: John Wiley & Sons, 2001.
43. Pyne S, Futcher B, Skiena S. Meta-analysis based on control of false discovery rate: combining yeast ChIP-chip datasets. *Bioinformatics*. 2006;22(20):2516–22.
44. Rhodes DR, Barrette TR, Rubin MA, Ghosh D, Chinnaiyan AM. Integrative analysis of the cancer transcriptome. *Nat Genet* 2005;37:S31–S37.
45. Rhodes DR, Barrette TR, Rubin MA, Ghosh D, Chinnaiyan AM. Meta-analysis of microarrays: interstudy validation of gene expression profiles reveals pathway dysregulation in prostate cancer. *Cancer Res* 2002;62:4427–4433.

46. Rhodes DR, Yu J, Shanker K, Deshpande N, Varambally R, Ghosh D, Barrette T, Pandey A, Chinnaiyan AM. Large-scale meta-analysis of cancer microarray data identifies common transcriptional profiles of neoplastic transformation and progression. *PNAS USA* 2004;101:9309–9314.
47. Rosenthal R. *Meta-Analytic Procedures for Social Research.* Newbury Park: SAGE Publications; 1991.
48. Rosenthal R, Rubin DB. Comparing significance levels of independent studies. *Psychol Bull* 1979;86:1165–1168.
49. Shen R, Ghosh D, Chinnaiyan AM. Prognostic meta-signature of breast cancer developed by two-stage mixture modeling of microarray data. *BMC Genomics* 2004;5:94.
50. Sidak Z. Rectangular confidence regions for the means of the multivariate normal distributions. *J Am Stat Ass* 1967;62:626–33.
51. Simon I, Barnett J, Hannett N, Harbison CT, Rinaldi NJ, Volkert TL, Wyrick JJ, Zeitlinger J, Gifford DK, Jaakkola TS, Young RA. Serial regulation of transcriptional regulators in the yeast cell cycle. *Cell* 2001;106:697–708.
52. Spellman PT, Sherlock G, Zhang MQ, Iyer VR, Anders K, Eisen MB, Brown PO, Botstein D, Futcher B. Comprehensive identification of cell cycle-regulated genes of the yeast saccharomyces cerevisiae by microarray hybridization. *Mol Biol Cell* 1998;9:3273–3297.
53. Stangl D, Berry DA. *Meta-Analysis in Medicine and Health Policy.* New York: Marcel Dekker; 2000.
54. Stevens JR, Doerge RW. Combining Affymetrix microarray results. *BMC Bioinformatics* 2005;6:57.
55. Storey JD, Tibshirani R. Statistical significance for genome-wide studies. *PNAS USA* 2003;100:9440–9445.
56. Stouffer SA, Suchman EA, Devinney LC, Star SA, Williams Jr. RM. *The American Soldier: Adjustments during army life, Vol. 1.* Princeton: Princeton University Press; 1949.
57. Strube MJ. Combining and comparing significance levels from nonindependent hypothesis tests. *Psychol Bull* 1985;97:334–341.
58. LHC Tippett. *The Methods of Statistics*. London: Williams and Norgate; 1931.
59. Tusher VG, Tibshirani R, Chu G. Significance analysis of microarrays applied to the ionizing radiation response. *PNAS USA* 2001;98:5116–5121.
60. Varambally S, Yu J, Laxman B, Rhodes DR, Mehra R, Tomlins SA, Shah RB, Chandran U, Monzon FA, Becich MJ, Wei JT, Pienta KJ, Ghosh D, Rubin MA, Chinnaiyan AM. Integrative genomic and proteomic analysis of prostate cancer reveals signatures of metastatic progression. *Cancer Cell* 2005;8:393–406.
61. Wang J, Coombes KR, Highsmith WE, Keating MJ, Abruzzo LV. Differences in gene expression between B-cell chronic lymphocytic leukemia and normal B cells: a meta-analysis of three microarray studies. *Bioinformatics* 2004;20:3166–3178.
62. Warnat P, Eils R, Brors B. Cross-platform analysis of cancer microarray data improves gene expression based classification of phenotypes. *BMC Bioinformatics* 2005;6:265.
63. Whitlock MC. Combining probability from independent tests: the weighted Z-method is superior to Fisher's approach *J Evol Biol* 2005;18:1368.
64. Zaykin DV, Zhivotovsky LA, Westfall PH, Weir BS. Truncated product method for combining *P*-values. *Genet Epidemiol* 2002;22:170–185.

PART IV

GENETIC VARIATION ANALYSIS

16

PHASING GENOTYPES USING A HIDDEN MARKOV MODEL

P. Rastas, M. Koivisto, H. Mannila, and E. Ukkonen

Department of Computer Science and HIIT Basic Research Unit, University of Helsinki, Finland

16.1 INTRODUCTION

Much of the genetic variation between individuals of the same species is due to *single nucleotide polymorphisms (SNPs)*, sites of the DNA where two or more of the four nucleotides A, C, G, T, called *alleles*, occur in the population. In the human genome, common SNPs (minor allele frequency at least 1%) occur relatively frequently (every 100 to 300 bases) and make up about 90% of all genetic variations (see, e.g., [28] and references therein). Thus, SNPs are of unique importance for studying genomic variations, especially in association analysis that aims at the location of causal variants responsible for complex genetic traits. To enhance the understanding of genetic variability in human populations, large genotyping efforts have recently been conducted to collect high quality, genome-wise SNP data from diverse ethnic groups [11,12].

Although lab techniques for measuring (typing) SNPs have evolved rapidly, they still produce incomplete data. First, it is not feasible to type all existing SNPs, but only a small fraction of them. This implies that causal variants will rarely be typed. Fortunately, an unobserved causal variant is typically strongly correlated with its neighboring SNPs. This is because a *haplotype*, a sequence of alleles over multiple SNPs in a single chromosome, is inherited as it is, as long as no recombination occurs in the region spanned by the SNPs. In this light, it is another major shortcoming of the current SNP typing methods that they do not provide the two haplotypes of a

Bioinformatics Algorithms: Techniques and Applications, Edited by Ion I. Măndoiu and Alexander Zelikovsky

diploid organism, but only an unordered allele pair for each SNP, called the *unphased genotypes*. For example, suppose the measured genotype of an individual is $\{A, C\}$ at one SNP and $\{G, T\}$ at another SNP. Then the underlying haplotype pair is either $\{AG, CT\}$ or $\{AT, CG\}$. The haplotyping problem arises due to *heterozygous* sites in the genotypes; a site of a genotype is called heterozygous if the two alleles at the site are different; otherwise, the site is called *homozygous*. If a genotype contains s heterozygous sites, then it is compatible with 2^{s-1} distinct haplotype pairs.

The *phasing problem*, also called the *haplotyping problem*, is about reconstructing the unobserved haplotypes for a given set of unphased genotypes. Existing haplotyping methods can be classified into (a) those that make use of the physical order of the SNPs and (b) those that ignore this information. The latter methods include early combinatorial approaches, which aim at resolving the genotypes with as few distinct haplotypes as possible [2,9]. Related probabilistic approaches shared the same idea of parsimony but were able to tolerate "noise" (genotyping errors and recent mutations), while showing that maximum likelihood inference automatically yields a small number of haplotypes [5,18,20]. However, improved reconstruction accuracy is often achieved when likelihood is combined with a biologically motivated prior, namely a phylogenetic model of the evolution of the haplotypes [8,27].

Methods of type (a) take advantage of the physical location of the SNPs, and are necessary when larger genomic regions are considered. First attempts to extend methods of type (b) to larger regions were based on the *partition ligation (PL)* technique introduced by Niu et al. [20]. PL first infers haplotypes at disjoint short blocks of consecutive SNPs, then at blocks of doubled size, and so on until the haplotypes for the entire region of interest have been inferred. The usefulness (as well as potential weakness) of this approach relies on the greedy construction of candidate haplotypes when merging blocks: the candidate haplotypes for a block are obtained as the crossproduct of the haplotypes inferred at its two subblocks. Remarkably, the most accurate haplotyping method currently available, PHASE, uses the PL scheme for handling large genomic regions [26,27]. Another approach to haplotyping makes use of the so called haplotype block structure. Haplotype blocks are regions of the genome where the haplotype diversity is relatively low compared to the physical length of the region; the relatively short gaps between low diversity blocks are called recombination hot spots. Haplotyping methods by Greenspan and Geiger [6] and by Kimmel and Shamir [14] are based on partitioning the region of interest into several haplotype blocks and modeling the haplotypes over successive blocks with a first-order Markov chain, that is, a haplotype depends only on the haplotype in the preceding block.

Recently, block-free hidden Markov models (HMMs) of haplotypes have been proposed in three independent works, by us [23], Kimmel and Shamir [15], and Scheet and Stephens [24]. Under these models, the haplotypes in the present population are viewed as a result of iterated recombinations applied on a few founder haplotypes (i.e., ancestral sequences). Compared to other proposed approaches, HMMs provide a flexible model for historical recombination structure, at the expense of paying less attention to phylogenetic, treelike relationships. Given that biologically more faithful models, the ancestral recombination graph [7] in particular, are computationally just impractical, the HMM approach seems to provide a good trade off between performance quality and computational feasibility. A major advantage of HMMs compared to Markovian haplotype models [4] is that HMMs can more easily handle missing values, recent mutations, and genotyping errors.

In this paper we describe our HMM technique for the phasing problem, slightly extending our earlier method [23]. The methods are implemented in the program HIT (Haplotype Inference Technique) that is now publicly available.[1] We compare the haplotyping accuracy of HIT to that of state-of-the-art methods, PHASE [26,27], fastPHASE [24], HAP [10], and GERBIL [14], using several real datasets. Our results suggest that HMM based methods, HIT and fastPHASE, are the current best methods for large scale haplotype reconstruction.

The rest of this paper is structured as follows. In Section 16.2 we describe our HMM for recombinant haplotypes. In Section 16.3 we present an EM algorithm for estimating the HMM from a set of unphased genotypes. In Section 16.4 we describe our method for reconstructing haplotypes given an estimated HMM; some alternative approaches are also discussed. In Section 16.5 we report experimental results on several real genotype datasets, mostly obtained from the HapMap data [12]. In Section 16.6 we provide a summary and discuss potential directions for future research.

With kind permission of Springer Science and Business media we, in Sections 16.2 and 16.3, reproduce textual material that only slightly deviates from the original text in [23] (Section 2, 3.1–3.3 on pp. 142–146).

16.2 A HIDDEN MARKOV MODEL FOR RECOMBINANT HAPLOTYPES

We consider m SNPs, indexed by the numbers $1, 2, \ldots, m$ in their physical order along the chromosome (in arbitrary direction). We assume that each SNP has two alleles; we label the most frequent allele by 1 and the other allele by 2. A haplotype over the m SNPs is a sequence $h = h_1, h_2, \ldots, h_m$ with $h_j \in \{1, 2\}$, while a genotype over the m SNPs is a sequence $g = g_1, g_2, \ldots, g_m$ with $g_j \in \{1, 2\} \times \{1, 2\}$. A genotype g with $g_j = (x, y)$ is heterozygous at j if $x \neq y$, and homozygous otherwise. In the observed data the genotypes are unphased: the order of the alleles x and y in the pair (x, y) is arbitrary and does not fix the haplotype memberships of the alleles.

Our hidden Markov model (HMM) for SNP haplotypes is a pair $M = (S, \theta)$, where S is the set of states and $\theta = (\tau, \varepsilon)$ consists of the state transition probabilities τ, and the allele emission probabilities ε. The set of states $S = S_0 \cup S_1 \cup \ldots \cup S_m$ consists of disjoint state sets S_j for each SNP j, and a special initial state in $S_0 = \{s_0\}$. The transition probabilities $\tau(s_{j-1}, s_j)$ are defined for all $s_{j-1} \in S_{j-1}$ and $s_j \in S_j$, that is, only transitions from states in S_{j-1} to states in S_j are allowed, for all $j = 1, 2, \ldots, m$. The transition probabilities from each fixed state s_j form a probability distribution, that is, their sum equals 1. Each state $s_j \in S_j$ is assigned an emission probability distribution, that is, the probabilities $\varepsilon(s_j, a)$ of emitting $a \in \{1, 2\}$. We restrict our consideration to the case where each S_j contain a fixed number K of states. The parameter K, called the *number of founders* in M, and the number of SNPs m determine

[1] HIT is available at http://www.cs.helsinki.fi/u/prastas/hit/.

the topology of the HMM. The *initial state* s_0 is a dummy state from which the HMM does not emit any allele. Any path from the dummy state to a state in S_m generates a haplotype over the m SNPs, with a probability determined as the product of the transition and emission probabilities along the path.

The model embodies the idea of founder haplotypes as follows. Haplotypes in the present population are viewed as recombinants of a few ancestral haplotypes. A large transition probability $\tau(s_{j-1}, s_j)$ suggests that states s_{j-1} and s_j belong to the same founder haplotype and only rarely have recombinations broken the corresponding haplotypes in between the SNPs $j-1$ and j. Likewise, a small transition probability suggests recombinations have rarely combined the corresponding fragments of ancestral haplotypes. An illustration of the model is shown in Fig. 16.1. We note that related combinatorial and probabilistic models have been proposed earlier by Ukkonen [29], Schwartz et al. [25], and Jojic et al. [13].

We extend the haplotype model to unphased genotypes as follows. We assume that the two haplotypes that form a genotype are independent given the haplotype model (i.e., random mating). We also assume that the two haplotypes are perfectly compatible with the genotype, that is, there is no additional noise beyond what is modeled by the emission probabilities in the haplotype model.

Our HMM can also handle missing data in a principled manner. If a datum is missing, the corresponding emission probability is considered to be 1 (any other constant could be used as well). This corresponds to the assumption that the data are missing at random.

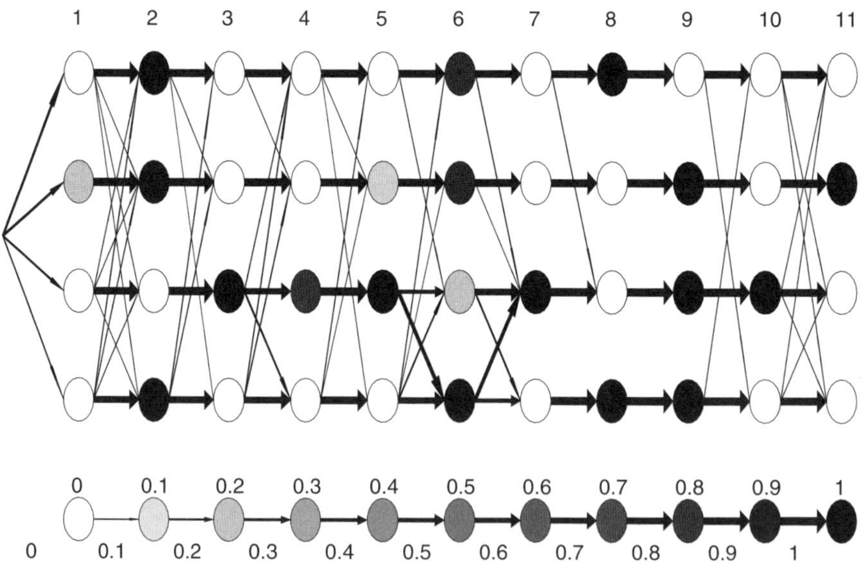

FIGURE 16.1 An example HMM for $m = 11$ markers and $K = 4$ founders. The states are represented as circles, the jth column of four states corresponding to the jth marker. A gray scale is used to indicate the emission probability of the allele "1," black corresponding to the probability 1. The thickness of each transition line indicates the corresponding transition probability.

16.3 LEARNING THE HMM FROM UNPHASED GENOTYPE DATA

We use the maximum likelihood principle to fit our hidden Markov model to the observed genotype data G we want to phase. That is, for a fixed number of founders, we search for the parameters $\theta = (\tau, \varepsilon)$ so as to maximize the likelihood $P(G|\theta)$. This estimation problem is known to be hard in general HMMs, and this seems to be the case also in our application. Therefore we resort to the commonly adopted family of expectation-maximization (EM) algorithms, which are guaranteed to converge to a *local* optimum [19].

The generic EM algorithm approaches an intractable optimization problem by completing the original data with auxiliary hidden data. Then the expected log-likelihood of the complete data—where the expectation is with respect to the distribution of the hidden data given the current parameter values—is maximized in an iterative fashion. Usually the choice of the hidden data is natural and direct from the problem. For the standard HMMs the hidden data contains the unobserved hidden states.

In our case it is natural to treat the hidden state sequences, two per genotype, as the hidden data. This is, in essence, the choice that has been made in a number of related applications of EM to the haplotype reconstruction problem; for example, [6,14]. While this approach works nicely when a state is deterministically related to an allele, computational problems will arise as soon as emission parameters are included in the model [14]. In such a case, Kimmel and Shamir [14,15] use a (multivariate) numerical maximization routine within each EM iteration.

We propose an alternative instantiation of the EM algorithm that yields efficient closed-form expressions for maximizing parameter values within each EM iteration. The idea is simple; in the hidden data we include not only the hidden states but also indicators that for any pair of states and the corresponding observed pair of alleles determine which one of the two states emitted the first allele in the pair, the second allele being emitted by the other state. We next provide some technical details.

16.3.1 Our EM Algorithm

Let $G = \{g_1, g_2, \ldots, g_n\}$ be a set of n genotypes over m markers. We suppose the topology (the state space S) of our HMM $M = (S, \theta)$ is fixed and we wish to find parameter values $\theta = (\tau, \epsilon)$ that maximize the probability of the genotype data, $P(G|\theta)$.

In this setting, the EM algorithm is as follows. Starting from some initial values $\theta^{(0)}$ the algorithm iteratively improves the current values $\theta^{(r)}$ by setting

$$\theta^{(r+1)} := \arg\max_{\theta} \sum_{Z} P(Z|G, \theta^{(r)}) \ln P(G, Z|\theta)\,, \tag{16.1}$$

where Z runs through a chosen set of additional (hidden) data. In words, the new parameter values are obtained by maximizing the expected log-likelihood of the complete data. For a large enough r the increment in the likelihood becomes negligible and the algorithm terminates.

We choose the hidden data Z such that the complete likelihood $P(G, Z|\theta)$ factorizes into a product of individual transition and emission probabilities, as described below. This is the key to obtain a computationally efficient evaluation of Equation 16.1. Recall that our HMM $M = (S, \theta)$ defines a probability distribution over singleton haplotypes. A genotype is obtained as a pair of two independent haplotypes, each generated by M along a path through some m states of M. From this generative model we extract the hidden data Z as the the combination of (a) the two state sequences per observed genotype and (b) the alleles emitted from the states.

The paths are given by an $n \times m \times 2$ matrix $T = (t_{ijk})$ of states of M. The entry $t_{ijk} \in S_j$ gives the state from which the jth allele for the first ($k = 1$) or the second ($k = 2$) haplotype for building g_i is to be emitted. The emitted allele from the possible alternatives that are consistent with g_i is indicated by an $n \times m \times 2$ matrix $U = (u_{ijk})$. The entries of U are selector variables that take values in $\{1, 2\}$. Recall that g_i consists of observed genotypes $g_{i1}, \ldots, g_{im}$ over the m markers, each genotype being a pair $g_{ij} = (g_{ij1}, g_{ij2})$ of alleles; note that we do not know which of the two alleles comes from which of the two underlying haplotypes. Here we only have arbitrarily fixed the order of the two observations. Element u_{ijk} of U specifies the jth allele of the first ($k = 1$) or of the second ($k = 2$) haplotype for building g_i: if $u_{ijk} = 1$ then the allele is g_{ij1} and if $u_{ijk} = 2$ then the allele is g_{ij2}. Both alleles must always be used, so we require that $\{u_{ij1}, u_{ij2}\} = \{1, 2\}$.

The point in introducing the hidden data $Z = (T, U)$ is that the complete likelihood factorizes into

$$P(G, T, U|\theta) = \left(\frac{1}{2}\right)^n \prod_{i=1}^{n} \prod_{j=1}^{m} \prod_{k=1,2} \tau(t_{i(j-1)k}, t_{ijk}) \varepsilon(t_{ijk}, g_{iju_{ijk}}) \,.$$

Here the coefficient $(1/2)^n$ appears, since all the 2^n values for U are a priori equally likely (independently of θ). Thus, the expected log-likelihood is

$$\sum_{T,U} P(T, U|G, \theta^{(r)}) \ln P(G, T, U|\theta) = \sum_{j=1}^{m} A_j(\tau) + \sum_{j=1}^{m} B_j(\varepsilon) - n \ln 2 \,,$$

where

$$A_j(\tau) = \sum_{i=1}^{n} \sum_{k=1,2} \sum_{T,U} P(T, U|G, \theta^{(r)}) \ln \tau(t_{i(j-1)k}, t_{ijk}) \,,$$

$$B_j(\varepsilon) = \sum_{i=1}^{n} \sum_{k=1,2} \sum_{T,U} P(T, U|G, \theta^{(r)}) \ln \varepsilon(t_{ij}, g_{iju_{ijk}}) \,.$$

Furthermore, each A_j only depends on the transition probability parameters for transitions from a state in S_{j-1} to a state in S_j. Similarly B_j only depends on the emission probability parameters for states in S_j. Thus, the maximizing parameter values can be found separately for each A_j and B_j.

Standard techniques of constrained optimization (e.g., the general Lagrange multiplier method [1] or the more special Kullback—Leibler divergence minimization approach [19]) now apply. For the transition probabilities $\tau(a, b)$, with $a \in S_{j-1}$, $b \in S_j$, we obtain the update equation

$$\tau^{(r+1)}(a, b) = c \sum_{i=1}^{n} \sum_{k=1,2} P(t_{i(j-1)k} = a, t_{ijk} = b|G, \theta^{(r)}), \tag{16.2}$$

where c is the normalization constant of the distribution $\tau^{(r+1)}(a, \cdot)$. That is, $\tau^{(r+1)}(a, b)$ is proportional to the expected number of transitions from a to b. Note that the hidden data U plays no role in this expression. Similarly, for the emission probabilities $\varepsilon(b, y)$, with $b \in S_j$, $y \in A_j$, we obtain

$$\varepsilon^{(r+1)}(b, y) = c \sum_{i=1}^{n} \sum_{k=1,2} P(t_{ijk} = b, g_{iju_{ijk}} = y|G, \theta^{(r)}), \tag{16.3}$$

where c is the normalization constant of the distribution $\varepsilon^{(r+1)}(b, \cdot)$. That is, $\varepsilon^{(r+1)}(b, y)$ is proportional to the expected number of emissions from b to y. Note that the variable u_{ijk} is free meaning that the expectation is over both its possible values.

16.3.2 Computation of the Maximization Step

We next show how the well-known forward–backward algorithm of hidden Markov Models [22] can be adapted to evaluation of the update formulas (16.2) and (16.3).

Let a_j and b_j be states in S_j. For a genotype $g_i \in G$, let $L(a_j, b_j)$ denote the (left or backward) probability of emitting the initial segment $g_{i1}, g_{i2}, \ldots, g_{i(j-1)}$ and ending at (a_j, b_j) along the pairs of paths of M that start from s_0. It can be shown that

$$L(a_0, b_0) = 1$$

and

$$L(a_{j+1}, b_{j+1}) = \sum_{a_j, b_j} P(g_{ij}|a_j, b_j, \varepsilon) L(a_j, b_j) \tau(a_j, a_{j+1}) \tau(b_j, b_{j+1}), \tag{16.4}$$

where

$$P(g_{ij}|a_j, b_j, \varepsilon) = \frac{1}{2}\varepsilon(a_j, g_{ij1})\varepsilon(b_j, g_{ij2}) + \frac{1}{2}\varepsilon(a_j, g_{ij2})\varepsilon(b_j, g_{ij1}).$$

(Recall that here we treat g_i as an ordered pair, though the ordering of the alleles is arbitrary.) Then the probability of the genotype g_i is obtained as

$$P(g_i|\theta) = \sum_{a_m, b_m} L(a_m, b_m) P(g_{im}|a_m, b_m, \varepsilon), \tag{16.5}$$

and the probability of the entire dataset is $P(G|\theta) = \prod_{g_i \in G} P(g_i|\theta)$. Note that for each g_i we have its own $L(\cdot, \cdot)$.

Direct evaluation of Equation 16.4 would use $O(|G| \sum_j |S_j|^4) = O(nmK^4)$ time in total. By noting that

$$L(a_{j+1}, b_{j+1}) = \sum_{a_j} \tau(a_j, a_{j+1}) \sum_{b_j} L(a_j, b_j) P(g_{ij}|a_j, b_j, \varepsilon) \tau(b_j, b_{j+1})$$

and by storing the sum $\sum_{b_j} L(a_j, b_j) P(g_{ij}|a_j, b_j, \varepsilon) \tau(b_j, b_{j+1})$ for each a_j and b_{j+1} the running time reduces to $O(nmK^3)$. The space requirement is $O(mK^2)$.

We call $L(\cdot, \cdot)$ the forward (or left) table. Similarly, we define the backward (or right) table $R(\cdot, \cdot)$. For a genotype $g_i \in G$, let $L(a_j, b_j)$ denote the probability of emitting the end segment $g_{i(j+1)}, g_{i(j+2)}, \ldots, g_{im}$ along the pairs of paths of M that visit (a_j, b_j).

We are now ready to show how formulas (16.2) and (16.3) can be evaluated. We consider the latter formula; the former is handled similarly. First notice that it is sufficient to consider the evaluation of the conditional probabilities

$$P(t_{ijk} = b, g_{iju_{ijk}} = y|G, \theta^{(r)}) = P(t_{ijk} = b, g_{iju_{ijk}} = y, g_i|\theta^{(r)}) \Big/ P(g_i \mid \theta^{(r)}).$$

We already described a way to compute the denominator, in Equation 16.5. The numerator can be written as

$$\sum_{a_j} \sum_{u_{ijk}=1,2} I(g_{iju_{ijk}} = y) \frac{1}{2} L(a_j, b) \varepsilon(a_j, g_{iju_{ijk}}) \varepsilon(b, g_{ij(3-u_{ijk})}) R(a_j, b),$$

where $I(\cdot)$ is the indicator function that evaluates to 1 when its argument is true, and to 0 otherwise. Note that both u_{ijk} and $3 - u_{ijk}$ take values in $\{1, 2\}$. For update (Eq. 16.3), a similar forward–backward expression is found. Thus, the total time complexity of an EM iteration is the above given $O(nmK^3)$.

16.3.3 Initialization and Model Training

As the EM algorithm is guaranteed to find only a local optimum, it is important to find a good initial configuration of the model parameters. Our initialization routine greedily finds a promising region in the parameter space. It consists of three steps.

First, we fix the transition probabilities and emission probabilities without looking at the data, as follows. Let ρ and ν be small constants specified by the user (in our experiments reported in Section 16.5 we used the values $\rho = 0.1$ and $\nu = 0.01$). Let $s_{j1}, s_{j2}, \ldots, s_{jK}$ be the states in S_j. For the first transition we set $\tau(s_0, s_{1l}) = 1/K$ for $l = 1, 2, \ldots, K$. Then for each SNP $j = 1, 2, \ldots, m$, we set the transition probability $\tau(s_{(j-1)l}, s_{jl'})$ to $1 - \rho$, if $l = l'$ (along the same founder), and to $\rho/(K-1)$ otherwise (jump from one founder to another). The emission probabilities for the states $s_j \in S_j$ are initialized by setting $\varepsilon(s_j, b) = 1 - \nu$ for a selected major allele b that is specific to the state s_j, and $\varepsilon(s_j, a) = \nu$ for the other allele a.

Second, we select the major alleles in a greedy manner based on the observed data. We traverse the sets S_j from left to right and assign to the states in S_j the major alleles that locally maximize the likelihood of the initial segments of the genotype data G up to SNP j. This is done by simply trying all 2^K possible choices for the K founder states of the SNP. Using dynamic programming in a manner described in Section 16.3.2, the running time would be $O(nmK^3 2^K)$. However, we can improve the running time by a factor of K by exploiting the special structure in the transition distributions; this speedup is very useful, as the initialization procedure dominates the running time of the method. The key idea is to express the recursive step (16.4) for computing the forward probabilities $L(a_{j+1}, b_{j+1})$ in terms of four simpler summations; we omit the details here.

In the third step, we make another pass from left to right and again choose the locally optimal major alleles but now in the context of the current solution on both sides of S_j. This second pass takes also $O(nmK^2 2^K)$ time.

We use the above initialization procedure only for small numbers K. When K is greater than 10 we use a faster algorithm that does not exhaustively try all 2^K possible choices for the major alleles of the founder states at each SNP. Instead, we start from a random configuration of the major alleles (at a SNP) and improve the configuration by local search (changing one major allele at time) until a local optimum is found. During the second pass of the initialization procedure, we improve emission probabilities in a similar manner, but starting from the current configuration instead of a random one. This algorithm runs in $O(nmK^4)$ time.

After initialization, we apply the EM algorithm to find a maximum likelihood HMM for the genotype data G. We run EM algorithm until the difference in consecutive log likelihoods is less than a tolerance t. In most cases we used $t = 0.1$, but in cross-validation step we used $t = 0.5$.

16.3.4 Selecting the Number of Founders by Maximizing Data Reconstruction Accuracy

Selecting a good number of founders, K, is a puzzling issue. We have experimentally found that, as long as K is sufficiently large, the phasing accuracy has a fairly robust behavior. Specifically, it seems that overfitting is not a serious problem in this application. However, it seems to depend on the dataset whether, say, 5, 7, or 9 is a sufficient number of founders. Also, as described above, the running time of the method depends crucially on the number of founders. It would be therefore be useful to have an automatic method for selecting the number of founders.

We have observed that the traditional model selection criteria, AIC, MDL, and BIC favor consistently too small numbers of founders; Scheet and Stephens [24] make the same observation concerning their related model that, however, has much fewer parameters. To find a reasonable number of founders, Scheet and Stephens [24] evaluate the genotype prediction accuracy of different number of founders in a cross-validation fashion. The insight is that a model that accurately predicts missing data, should also perform well in haplotype reconstruction. We have implemented a modified version of this technique.

Instead of selecting a single number of founders for the entire dataset, we let the number of founders depend on the genotype to be phased. More precisely, we generate N (we used $N = 20$ in our experiments) incomplete copies of the original dataset by hiding a fraction (10% in our experiments) of heterozygous single-SNP genotypes selected at random. For each multilocus input genotype g we select a number of founders K_g such that the average prediction accuracy of the hidden data of g over the N incomplete datasets is maximized. Finally, for each value of K_g we estimate a final K_g-founder HMM using the original genotype dataset. Each input genotype g is then phased using the corresponding K_g-founder HMM.

16.4 HAPLOTYPE RECONSTRUCTION

Given a trained HMM $M = (S, \theta)$ we reconstruct a haplotype pair (h, h'), called here the *Viterbi haplotypes*, for each input genotype g as follows. First we find a pair (p, p') of paths through the model M such that the probability of (p, p') given g is maximized. This can be done efficiently by a Viterbi algorithm that is a variant of the algorithm described in Section 16.3.2. Then we generate from p a haplotype h and from p' a haplotype h' such that (h, h') is compatible with g and the joint probability of the haplotype pair, $P(h, h'|g, p, p', \theta)$, is maximized. This can be done efficiently, since the allele pairs at different SNPs are independent, given the paths and the model parameters. The total running time of this algorithm is $O(nmK^3)$.

We note that this two-stage algorithm does not necessarily yield a haplotype pair that has the highest possible probability, given the genotype g and the model M. This is because the reconstruction relies on a single optimal pair of paths through the HMM, instead of averaging over all pairs of paths. Unfortunately, it seems that optimal haplotype reconstruction, with averaging over all pairs of paths, is not possible in polynomial time. Here we extend the method described above (see also [23]) as follows. First we generate a random sample of pairs of paths (p, p') from the conditional distribution $P(p, p|g, \theta)$. This can be done efficiently using a forward–backward algorithm. Then, from each sampled pair (p, p') we generate a corresponding haplotype pair (h, h') as described earlier. Next we compute the probability $P(h, h'|g, \theta)$ of each (h, h') in the sample, now averaging over all pairs of paths through the HMM. Finally, we pick a haplotype pair that has the highest possible probability among the pairs included in the sample. (We also include the Viterbi haplotypes in the sample.) Scheet and Stephens [24] use essentially the same method, so we omit the details here.

It is also worth noting that maximizing the probability of the reconstructed haplotype pair is not always the most reasonable goal. Maximizing the probability makes sense if one wants to minimize the 0–1 error (i.e., whether the two haplotypes are correct or not) but less so when one wants to minimize some other error measure, for example, the commonly used switch distance (the proportion of heterozygous sites that are phased incorrectly relative to the previous heterozygous site). In general, it makes sense to minimize the expected error. The sampling approach applies also in this more general case. The idea is then to find the center-of-weight haplotype pair in the generated sample, that is, a pair that minimizes the expected error. In our preliminary experiments, this technique did not yield significant improvement for the switch distance; this is possibly because the weights, that is, the haplotype probabilities, are not always "well calibrated" due to the relatively large number of model parameters fitted to a limited dataset. Scheet and Stephens [24], however, report promising results using this technique.

16.5 EXPERIMENTAL RESULTS

16.5.1 Datasets

We report phasing results for 136 real datasets. Of these datasets, 132 were obtained from the HapMap data [12], which consist of over one million SNPs typed in samples from four ethnic groups. We selected data from two groups: Yoruba in Ibadan, Nigeria (abbreviation: YRI) and CEPH (Utah residents with ancestry from northern and western Europe) (abbreviation: CEU). For both these groups unphased genotypes are available for 30 trios (of mother, father, and child), resulting in the total of 120 known haplotypes. From each of the 22 chromosomes, we chose one data fragment covering the first 200 SNPs (datasets referred to as CEU-200 and YRI-200) and another fragment covering 1000 consecutive SNPs starting from the 5001th SNP (datasets referred to as CEU-1000 and YRI-1000). From the 1000-SNP datasets, we also analyzed sparser variants obtained by keeping every 10th SNP and discarding the rest (CEU-100 and YRI-100).

The dataset studied by Daly et al. [3] (referred to as Daly et al.) is a sample from a European-derived population and spans a 500-kb region on human chromosome 5q31 that contains a genetic risk factor for Crohn disease. From that area there are genotypes for 103 SNP markers, collected from 129 trios. The trios were used to infer the true haplotypes for the 129 genotypes of the children.

The three other datasets are genotype samples over 68 SNPs from three datasets from Finland [16,21]. We call these datasets Population1 (32 haplotypes), Population2 (108 haplotypes), and Population3 (108 haplotypes).

16.5.2 Switch Distance

We measure the accuracy of haplotype reconstruction using the commonly adopted switch distance (1 minus the switch accuracy of Lin et al. [17]). The switch distance is the proportion of heterozygous sites that are phased incorrectly relative to the previous heterozygous site. For example, the number of phase switches needed to turn the haplotype pair {111111, 222222} into {111222, 222111} is 1, whereas the maximum number of 5 switches is needed between the pairs {111111, 222222} and {121212, 212121}. Thus, the switch distance is $\frac{1}{5}$ in the former case and $\frac{5}{5} = 1$ in the latter case. When multiple haplotype reconstructions are compared, we define the switch distance as the total number of needed phase switches divided by the corresponding maximum. For example, if the two reconstruction errors given above are made, then the corresponding combined (total) switch distance is $(1 + 5)/(5 + 5) = 6/10$. Note that this is generally *not* the same as the average of the individual switch distances.

16.5.3 Tested Methods

We tested two versions of the phasing technique described in this paper. In the basic variant the number of founders, K, is fixed by the user; we report results for the values $K = 5, 6, \ldots, 11$, and refer to the corresponding methods as HIT5, HIT6, ..., HIT11, respectively. The other variant, here denoted as HIT*, automatically selects the number of founders as described in Section 16.3.4. For comparison, we have also run the publicly available versions of the programs PHASE [26,27] (version 2.1.1), fastPHASE [24], GERBIL [14], and HAP [10].

Unfortunately, we were able to run only HIT (all variants) and fastPHASE for all the 136 datasets. PHASE cannot handle dataset with 200 or more SNPs in reasonable time, and GERBIL is prohibitely slow for 1000-SNP datasets. While HAP is very fast, using the server implementation (as we did) requires some amount of human interaction for each dataset—therefore, we did not run HAP for the 132 HapMap datasets.

16.5.4 Comparison of Haplotyping Accuracy

Table 16.1 summarizes the phasing accuracy results for different variants of HIT. We observe that the switch distance behaves fairly robustly across different number of founders. For the HapMap datasets HIT5 is consistently the least accurate, while the best performance is achieved by HIT10 and HIT11. This trend is less clear for the four other datasets. HIT* achieves almost the same accuracy as the best of HIT5, HIT6, ..., HIT11.

From Table 16.2 we see that PHASE and fastPHASE are the most accurate of the methods compared. The performance of HIT* is only slightly behind, and in many cases it is clearly better than of GERBIL and HAP. We also see how the number of SNPs affects the average phasing accuracy: First, the results are more accurate with 1000 SNPs than with 200 SNPs. Second, as expected, the results with a dense set of 1000 SNPs are substantially better than with its 100-SNP subset—yet less than ten times more accurate.

A pairwise comparison of HIT* against fastPHASE and GERBIL on the 132 HapMap datasets is shown in Figs. 16.2 and 16.3, respectively. We see

TABLE 16.1 Phasing Accuracy of HIT Measured by the Switch Distance[a]

Dataset	HIT5	HIT6	HIT7	HIT8	HIT9	HIT10	HIT11	HIT*
CEU-100	**0.21**	**0.21**	**0.21**	0.22	**0.21**	**0.21**	**0.21**	**0.21**
YRI-100	0.29	**0.28**	**0.28**	**0.28**	**0.28**	0.29	0.29	**0.28**
CEU-200	0.078	0.076	0.073	0.072	0.072	**0.071**	**0.071**	0.072
YRI-200	0.13	0.12	0.12	**0.11**	**0.11**	**0.11**	**0.11**	**0.11**
CEU-1000	0.042	0.038	0.037	0.036	**0.035**	**0.035**	**0.035**	0.035
YRI-1000	0.076	0.069	0.063	0.060	0.057	**0.055**	**0.055**	0.057
Pop1	0.21	0.23	0.24	**0.19**	0.22	0.21	0.23	0.21
Pop2	0.17	0.17	0.17	0.17	0.17	**0.16**	**0.16**	0.18
Pop3	0.20	0.21	**0.17**	0.20	0.21	0.20	**0.17**	0.19
Daly et al.	0.029	**0.028**	0.034	0.030	0.031	0.034	0.034	0.030

[a] For CEU-200, YRI-200, CEU-1000, and YRI-1000 the switch distance is averaged over the 22 included datasets.

TABLE 16.2 Phasing Accuracy of Some Methods Measured by the Switch Distance[a]

Dataset	HIT*	fastPHASE	GERBIL	PHASE	HAP
CEU-100	0.21	**0.20**	0.22	**0.20**	—
YRI-100	0.28	0.27	0.30	**0.26**	—
CEU-200	0.072	**0.068**	0.085	—	—
YRI-200	**0.11**	**0.11**	0.14	—	—
CEU-1000	0.035	**0.033**	—	—	—
YRI-1000	0.057	**0.051**	—	—	—
Pop1	**0.21**	**0.21**	0.25	**0.21**	0.26
Pop2	0.18	0.16	0.19	**0.15**	0.18
Pop3	0.19	0.19	0.21	**0.17**	0.19
Daly et al.	0.030	**0.027**	0.031	0.037	0.039

[a] For CEU-200, YRI-200, CEU-1000, and YRI-1000 the switch distance is averaged over the 22 included datasets.

that the performance differences of the methods are consistent across different datasets:GERBIL is seldom more accurate than HIT*, and HIT*, in turn, is just occasionally more accurate than fastPHASE.

Figure 16.3 also shows a comparison of HIT* against PHASE on the 100-SNP datasets. On the CEU-100 datasets HIT* is consistently slightly behind PHASE. Interestingly, on the YRI-100 datasets HIT* is more accurate than PHASE on the hard cases, whereas PHASE is more accurate on the easier cases.

16.6 DISCUSSION

We have described a hidden Markov model for SNP haplotypes. In the HMM each haplotype in the present generation is viewed as a mosaic of a limited number of common "founder" haplotypes. The founder haplotypes should be understood as a sort of minimal haplotype "basis" or "effective ancestral material" rather than any

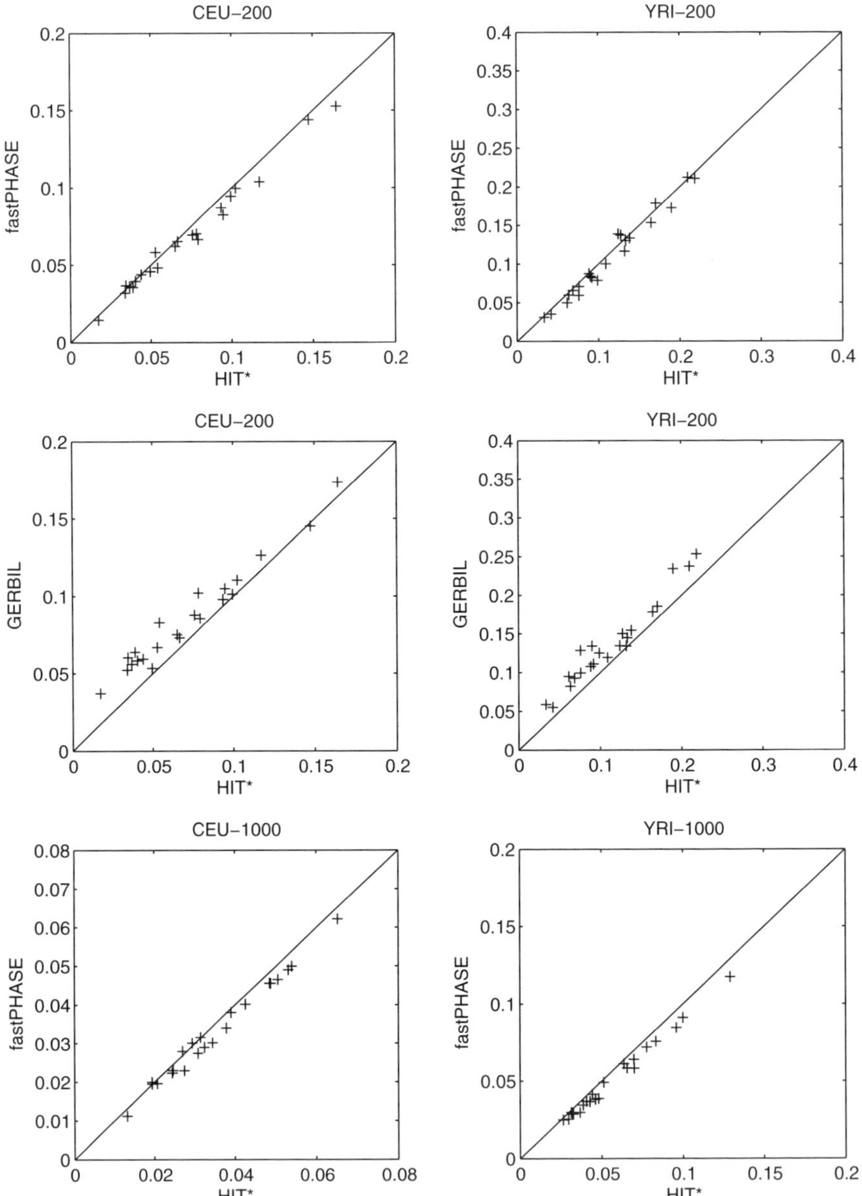

FIGURE 16.2 Comparison of phasing accuracy on 200-SNP and 1000-SNP HapMap datasets. For each dataset (from chromosomes 1, 2, ..., 22) and method (HIT*, fastPHASE, and GERBIL) the switch distance between the true and the reconstructed haplotype pairs is shown.

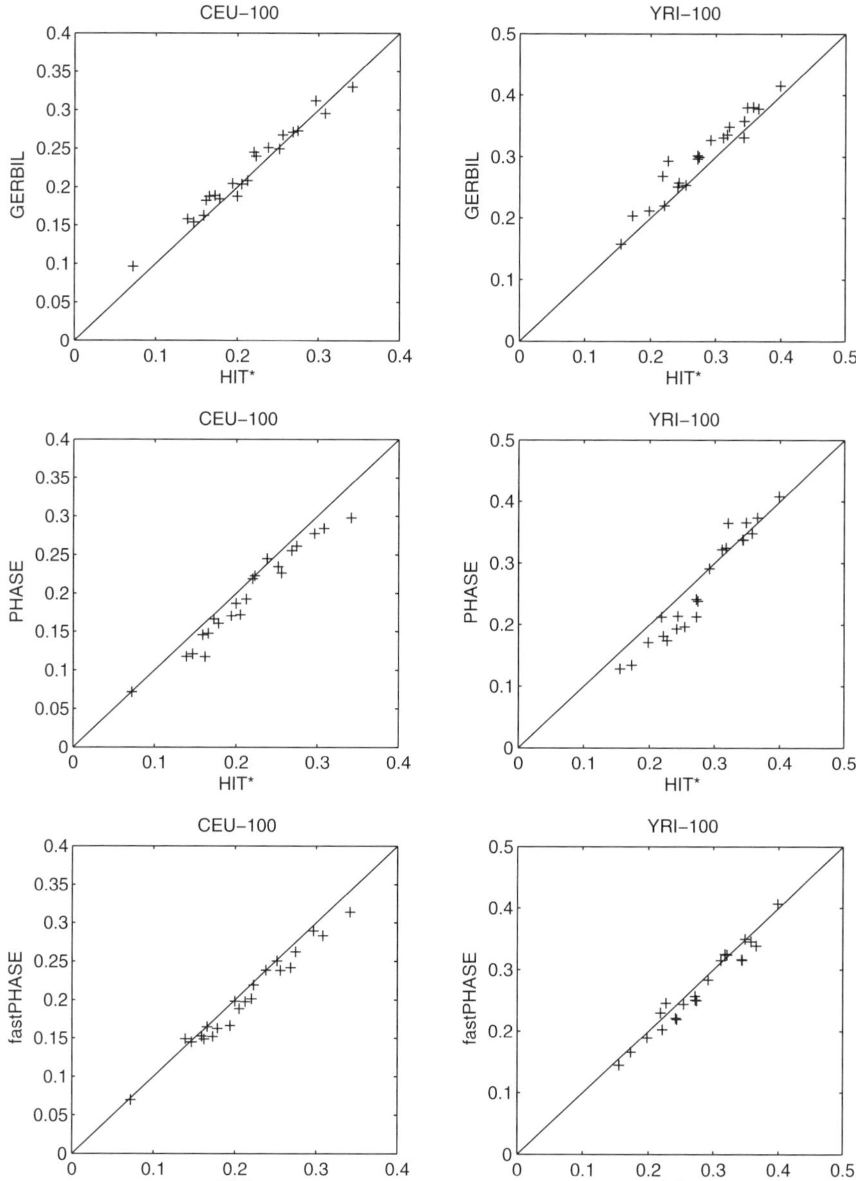

FIGURE 16.3 Comparison of phasing accuracy on 100-SNP HapMap datasets. For each dataset (from chromosomes 1, 2, ..., 22) and method (HIT*, fastPHASE, GERBIL, and PHASE) the switch distance between the true and the reconstructed haplotype pairs is shown.

real ancestral haplotypes. That said, we think that the number of founders should, in general, grow with the size of the data sample. The model is not new. Schwartz et al. [25] and Ukkonen [29] proposed essentially the same model but applied it to phase-known haplotype data. After a series of other models and methods developed for haplotype analysis [6,9,14,26], especially for the phasing problem, the HMM approach has attracted a renowned interest very recently by Scheet and Stephens [24], Kimmel and Shamir [15], and us [23].

There are some differences in these three methods. First, our EM algorithm is designed to yield an efficient maximization step, whereas the EM algorithm of Kimmel and Shamir [15] relies on numeric optimization routines. Second, our HMM is different from that of Scheet and Stephens [24] in that we use fully parameterized transition distributions between adjacent SNPs, whereas Scheet and Stephens [24] use fewer parameters, letting the transition probabilities at each SNP be independent of the founder state at the previous SNP. Furthermore, we (like Kimmel and Shamir) estimate a single maximum likelihood HMM, whereas Scheet and Stephens use an ensemble of high likelihood HMMs.

Our experimental results on the haplotype reconstruction problem suggest that the HMM-based methods represent the current state-of-the-art for phasing large-scale genotype datasets. Namely, the programs HIT and fastPHASE are as accurate as the popular PHASE program (a sophisticated MCMC method), but much faster. Scheet and Stephens [24], based on another set of experiments, have arrived at the same conclusion. Of the two HMM-based methods, fastPHASE seems to be slightly more accurate than HIT. Indeed, there are only a few datasets where HIT achieves a smaller switch distance. We do not know why this is the case. We believe that the advantage of fastPHASE can be attributed to the way it exploits multiple HMMs estimated by quick EM runs from random initial models. This explanation is supported by our observation [23], agreeing with Scheet and Stephens [24], that the phasing accuracy only loosely depends on the likelihood. A natural direction for future research is to investigate whether the performance of HIT can be significantly enhanced by using an ensemble approach. This would also shed light to the question whether the full parameterized transitions implemented in HIT have any advantages over the simple model of fastPHASE.

Can we find still better phasing methods? We do not know if the accuracy of the current best methods—PHASE, fastPHASE, and HIT—can be improved. These methods are about equally accurate, which might suggest that the optimum has been practically achieved. Knowing reasonable upper bounds for phasing accuracy (lower bounds for phasing error) would be very useful. Unfortunately, deriving tight and general upper bounds seems difficult, if not impossible. However, it might be possible to obtain useful bounds relative to some specific data generating models; the HMM studied in this paper is a good candidate for such analyses.

But haplotype reconstruction is just one application of haplotype models. In fact, while haplotype reconstruction is often executed as an intermediate step of many association analysis methods, direct analysis of unphased genotype data may become more popular in the future. In principle, direct analysis has the advantage of taking the uncertainty in the haplotype reconstruction into account. It is important to note, however, that direct genotype analysis also needs good haplotype models. That said, the phasing problem, although not necessarily of direct interest, serves as an interesting and well-defined benchmark problem on which new haplotype models can be tested.

ACKNOWLEDGMENTS

This research was supported in part by the Academy of Finland, grant 211496 (From Data to Knowledge).

REFERENCES

1. Bertsekas DP. *Constrained Optimization and Lagrange Multiplier Methods*. New York: Academic Press; 1982.
2. Clark AG. Inference of haplotypes from PCR-amplified samples of diploid populations. *Mol Biol Evol* 1990;7:111–122.
3. Daly MJ, Rioux JD, Schaffner SF, Hudson TJ, Lander ES. High-resolution haplotype structure in the human genome. *Nat Genet* 2001;29:229–232.
4. Eronen L, Geerts F, Toivonen HTT. A Markov chain approach to reconstruction of long haplotypes. *Pacific Symposium on Biocomputing (PSB '04)*. World Scientific; 2004. pp. 104–115.
5. Excoffier L, Slatkin M. Maximum-likelihood estimation of molecular haplotype frequencies in a diploid population. *Mol Biol Evolut* 1995;12:921–927.
6. Greenspan G, Geiger D. Model-based inference of haplotype block variation. *Research in Computational Molecular Biology (RECOMB '03)*. ACM Press; 2003. pp. 131–137.
7. Griffiths RC, Marjoram P. Ancestral inference from samples of DNA sequences with recombination. *J Comput Biol* 1996;3:479–502.
8. Gusfield D. Haplotyping as perfect phylogeny: conceptual framework and efficient solutions. *Research in Computational Molecular Biology (RECOMB '02)*. ACM Press; 2002. pp. 166-175.
9. Gusfield D. Haplotype inference by pure parsimony. Technical Report CSE-2003-2, Department of Computer Science, University of California, 2003.
10. Halperin E, Eskin E. Haplotype reconstruction from genotype data using imperfect phylogeny. *Bioinformatics* 2004;20:1842–1849.
11. Hinds DA, Stuve LL, Nilsen GB, et al. Whole-genome patterns of common DNA variation in three human populations. *Science* 2005;307:1072–1079.
12. The International HapMap Consortium. A haplotype map of the human genome. *Nature* 2005;437:1299–1320.
13. Jojic N, Jojic V, Heckerman D. Joint discovery of haplotype blocks and complex trait associations from SNP sequences. *Proceedings of the 20th conference on Uncertainty in Artificial Intelligence (UAI '04)*. AUAI Press; 2004. pp. 286–292.
14. Kimmel G, Shamir R. GERBIL: Genotype resolution and block identification using likelihood. *P Nat Acad Sci USA (PNAS)* 2005;102:158–162.

15. Kimmel G, Shamir R. A block-free hidden Markov model for genotypes and its application to disease association. *J Comput Biol* 2005;12:1243–1260.
16. Koivisto M, Perola M, Varilo T, Hennah W, Ekelund J, Lukk M, Peltonen L, Ukkonen E, Mannila H. An MDL method for finding haplotype blocks and for estimating the strength of haplotype block boundaries. *Pacific Symposium on Biocomputing (PSB '03)* . World Scientific; 2002. pp. 502–513.
17. Lin S, Cutler DJ, Zwick ME, Chakravarti A. Haplotype inference in random population samples. *Am J Hum Genet* 2002;71:1129–1137.
18. Long JC, Williams RC, Urbanek M. An E-M algorithm and testing strategy for multiple-locus haplotypes. *Am J Hum genet* 1995;56:799–810.
19. McLachlan GJ, Krishnan T. *The EM Algorithm and Extensions*. John Wiley and Sons; 1996.
20. Niu T, Qin ZS, Xu X, Liu JS. Bayesian haplotype inference for multiple linked single nucleotide polymorphisms. *Am J Hum Genet* 2002;70:157–169.
21. Paunio T, Ekelund J, Varilo T, Parker A, Hovatta I, Turunen J, Rinard K, Foti A, Terwilliger J, Juvonen H, Suvisaari J, Arajarvi R, Suokas J, Partonen I, Lönnqvist J, Meyer J, Peltonen L. Genome-wide scan in a nationwide study sample of schizophrenia families in Finland reveals susceptibility loci on chromosomes 2q and 5q. *Hum Mol Genet* 2001;10:3037–3048.
22. Rabiner LR. A tutorial on hidden Markov models and selected applications in speech recognition. *P IEEE* 1989;77:257–285.
23. Rastas P, Koivisto M, Mannila H, Ukkonen E. A hidden Markov technique for haplotype reconstruction. *Algorithms in Bioinformatics (WABI '05), Lecture Notes in Computer Science 3692*. Berlin, Heidelberg: Springer Verlag; 2005. pp. 140–151.
24. Scheet P, Stephens M. A fast and flexible statistical model for large-scale population genotype data: Applications to inferring missing genotypes and haplotype phase. *Am J Hum Genet* 2006;78:629–644.
25. Schwartz R, Clark AG, Istrail S. Methods for inferring block-wise ancestral history from haploid sequences. *Workshop on Algorithms in Bioinformatics (WABI '02), Lecture Notes in Computer Science 2452*. Springer; 2002. pp. 44–59.
26. Stephens M, Scheet P. Accounting for decay of linkage disequilibrium in haplotype inference and missing-data imputation. *Am J Hum Genet* 2005;76:449–462.
27. Stephens M, Smith NJ, Donnelly P. A new statistical method for haplotype reconstruction from population data. *Am J Hum Genet* 2001;68:978–989.
28. Thorisson GA, Stein LD. The SNP Consortium website: past, present and future. *Nucl Acid Res* 2003;31:124–127.
29. Ukkonen E. Finding founder sequences from a set of recombinants. *Algorithms in Bioinformatics (WABI '02), Lecture Notes in Computer Science 2452*. Springer; 2002. pp. 277–286.

17

ANALYTICAL AND ALGORITHMIC METHODS FOR HAPLOTYPE FREQUENCY INFERENCE: WHAT DO THEY TELL US?

STEVEN HECHT ORZACK
Fresh Pond Research Institute, Cambridge, MA, USA

DANIEL GUSFIELD
Department of Computer Science, University of California, Davis, CA, USA

LAKSHMAN SUBRAHMANYAN
University of Massachusetts Medical School, Worcester, MA, USA

LAURENT ESSIOUX
Hoffmann-La Roche Ltd, Basel, Switzerland

SEBASTIEN LISSARRAGUE
Genset SA, Paris, France

In this chapter, we compare an analytical likelihood method and various algorithmic methods for inferring haplotype frequency from phase-unknown two-site genotypic data. We show that the analytical method is preferable to the EM algorithm when estimating haplotype frequency via maximum likelihood since it allows one to readily detect multiple likelihood maxima, it is quicker (especially when many pairs of sites are analyzed), and it is easy to implement. We also show that substantial differences exist

Bioinformatics Algorithms: Techniques and Applications, Edited by Ion I. Măndoiu and Alexander Zelikovsky

among the algorithms with respect to the frequency estimate they generate. In addition, the frequency estimate derived from stochastic methods can differ among sample paths even when there is a single maximum of the likelihood function. We conclude that an investigator should compare the results of several inference algorithms before deciding upon an estimate of haplotype frequency and that multiple sample paths should be assessed for any stochastic algorithm. If different sample paths result in different frequency estimates, one possibility for generating a single estimate is the use of a consensus method; further research is needed to assess the usefulness of this approach.

17.1 INTRODUCTION

Most empirical studies of genetic polymorphism lack information on the association between variants segregating at different sites, as the scoring of polymorphism at any given site is usually independent of the scoring at other sites. In such a circumstance, the identities of the two haplotypes in any diploid individual heterozygous at two or more autosomal sites are unknown and such an individual is said to have an "ambiguous" genotype. If a sample contains such individuals, even the standard measure of association for variants at two sites, the coefficient of linkage disequilibrium, cannot be directly calculated (see [18] for further discussion).

Both molecular and algorithmic methods have been developed for inferring haplotypes from samples of unrelated individuals. The algorithms include expectation-maximization (EM) ([6,7,15,20,38]), partial ligation using the Gibbs sampler [24] or EM [30], the coalescent-based approach [36] (see also [19,35]), the rule-based approach ([3,9,25]), and the perfect phylogeny-based approach ([5,10]). These algorithms generate estimates of haplotype frequencies as well as infer pairs of haplotypes for each ambiguous genotype.

These algorithms and others reflect significant progress in the development of tools for analyzing the veritable flood of data on genetic variation, especially data on DNA sequence variation. However, there are gaps in the assessment of the performance of these tools.

One gap is the scarcity of comparisons involving datasets containing "real" haplotype pairs (those inferred from molecular analyses, e.g., cloning, strand-specific PCR, or somatic cell hybridization; their error rate is likely very low as compared to the error rate for algorithmic inference.) Instead of using such data, most studies of inference accuracy have used either simulated data (generated by a neutral model) or randomly paired real haplotypes (e.g., [1,7,21,23,24,45–47]; several of these studies contain other kinds of comparisons as well). These important studies generally have favorable assessments of the performance of inference algorithms. However, such samples are affected by some processes (e.g., random mating or random pairing of haplotypes) that may not influence real populations (even if they are in Hardy–Weinberg equilibrium) and they are not affected by other processes that may influence real populations (natural selection). To this extent, these studies do not by themselves allow us to conclude that these algorithms generally provide accurate results—that is, that they generally infer correctly a high proportion of haplotype pairs.

The use of real haplotype pairs is essential if we are to adequately assess the accuracy of haplotyping algorithms. A few studies have used such pairs (or those inferred from pedigrees) to assess the accuracy of haplotype-frequency inference [33,39]. A few other studies have assessed the accuracy of haplotype-pair inference by using real haplotype pairs. Two involve datasets with only two sites [44] or small numbers of individuals [37] and two of the others do not completely implement one of the algorithms being analyzed (see [25] for further details). Only a few studies involve many sites (in one locus or several), a reasonably large sample size, and completely implement the algorithms being studied. Of these studies, [25,29,31] assessed algorithmic and experimental inferences and [12] compared algorithmic and pedigree inferences. While these studies are encouraging in that high proportions of haplotype pairs are shown to be inferred by some algorithms, the paucity of such studies speaks to the fact that it is premature to conclude that present algorithms generally provide accurate results when applied to datasets containing real haplotype pairs. This is the canonical type of application many investigators have in mind, especially those whose research focus is on a relatively short DNA sequence such as a single locus.

The second gap in our assessment of inference methods is the lack of comparisons between analytical and algorithmic results, a likely reason being the lack of analytical results for genotypes with an arbitrary number of sites. Such comparisons are essential given the complexity of the inference problem and the fact that many of the algorithms are stochastic, which implies that the results may be sample-path-dependent.

Here, we present a comparison of analytical and algorithmic results for the two-site case when each site has two variants. This case is of particular importance given its connection with the estimation of linkage disequilibrium and also because many analyses assess association between two sites, one being, say, a possible disease-causing mutation and the other being a molecular marker (see [28] for a review).

When each of the two sites has two variants, all four haplotype frequencies are completely determined by an estimate of any one haplotype frequency and the (unambiguous) estimates of the frequency of variants at each of the sites. Given the observed allele frequencies and the assumption that the population is at Hardy–Weinberg equilibrium, Hill [16] derived a cubic equation that can be solved to provide a maximum likelihood estimate of the unknown haplotype frequency. He suggested finding solutions of this equation by using what is now known as the EM algorithm. Weir and Cockerham [40] noted problems with this approach for finding solutions and suggested noniterative numerical solution; they also provided analytical solutions for degenerate cases in which one or more of the four haplotypes is missing. As discussed below, one can use standard formulae to generate analytical solutions of the cubic equation and then compare their likelihoods in order to find the maximum likelihood estimate of the haplotype frequency. We denote this sequence of two steps as the "analytical method." Given the maximum likelihood estimate, one can also generate the most probable haplotype pair for each ambiguous genotype. Here, we focus only on the estimation of haplotype frequency.

Despite the existence of these results, we know of only two uses of this analytical approach [4,43]; both stem from our unpublished analyses. Instead, most analyses of the two-site case employ the EM algorithm (e.g., [34]) While this algorithm is an important inference tool, its use can be problematic. It can converge to a local maximum of the likelihood surface, but convergence to the maximum can be time consuming as compared to the analytical method, and two maxima can have identical likelihoods. We provide below illustrations of some of these problems. In addition, as noted by Weir and Cockerham [40], there can be nonconvergence of the algorithm for certain initial haplotype frequencies. All of these problems are avoided with the analytical method. More generally, this approach along with visualization of the likelihood surface allows one to gain a much more complete picture of the inference problem than that provided by the EM algorithm.

The algorithms whose results we compare with those of the analytical method are EM and those described in [1,2,12,24–26,30,36]. We chose these as being representative of the present variety of algorithms. Choice or omission does not denote any judgment on our part in regard to algorithmic importance and performance.

17.2 METHODS

We first describe the analytical method. Although we discovered it independently of Hill [16], he has priority in regard to the discovery that the two-site case can be solved analytically; Weir and Cockerham [40] provided further development of Hill's approach.

17.2.1 Notation

In what follows, "site" can refer to a genetic locus as classically defined or to a particular site within such a locus, while "variant" can refer to an allele as classically defined or to, say, a nucleotide segregating at a particular site within a locus.

We assume that the first site has variants A and a with frequencies p and $1 - p$ and that the second site has variants B and b with frequencies q and $1 - q$. N_{ij} denotes the observed number of genotype ij (as shown in Table 17.1), f_{11}, f_{12}, f_{21}, and f_{22} denote the frequencies of haplotypes AB, Ab, aB, and ab, respectively, and X_{11}, X_{12}, X_{21}, and X_{22} denote the counts of haplotypes from unambiguous genotypes as

TABLE 17.1 Notation for Observed Genotype Numbers. N_{ij} Denotes the Number of Individuals of Genotype ij

		Site 2		
		BB	Bb	bb
	AA	N_{11}	N_{12}	N_{13}
Site 1	Aa	N_{21}	N_{22}	N_{23}
	aa	N_{31}	N_{32}	N_{33}

follows:

$$
\begin{aligned}
X_{11} &= 2N_{11} + N_{12} + N_{21} \\
X_{21} &= 2N_{31} + N_{21} + N_{32} \\
X_{12} &= 2N_{13} + N_{12} + N_{23} \\
X_{22} &= 2N_{33} + N_{23} + N_{32}.
\end{aligned}
$$

By definition, the observed number of double heterozygotes N_{22} does not contribute to the counts of haplotypes from unambiguous genotypes.

If the population is in Hardy–Weinberg equilibrium, it is straightforward to show [16] that the maximum likelihood estimate of the unknown haplotype frequency, say, $\hat{f}_{11}$, is a real root of

$$
\begin{aligned}
&4N\hat{f}_{11}^{3} + (2N(1 - 2\hat{p} - 2\hat{q}) - 2X_{11} - N_{22})\hat{f}_{11}^{2} \\
&+ (2N\hat{p}\hat{q} + X_{11}(2\hat{p} + 2\hat{q} - 1) - N_{22}(1 - \hat{p} - \hat{q}))\hat{f}_{11} - X_{11}\hat{p}\hat{q} = 0.
\end{aligned}
\tag{17.1}
$$

Here, N is the total number of individuals in the sample, and $\hat{p}$ and $\hat{q}$ are the maximum likelihood estimates of the population frequencies of variants A and B, respectively. These estimates are given by

$$
\begin{aligned}
\hat{p} &= \frac{X_{11} + X_{12} + N_{22}}{2N} \\
\hat{q} &= \frac{X_{11} + X_{21} + N_{22}}{2N}.
\end{aligned}
$$

One can show that the cubic equation (17.1) can have (1) one real root and a pair of complex roots, (2) two real roots (one real and a pair of roots having identical real parts and zero imaginary parts), or (3) three distinct real roots. This variety makes it imperative that special care be taken when calculating these roots. We recommend an algorithm designed for use on a digital computer (e.g., [27], pp. 179–180); an algorithm not so designed can readily give incorrect results. If there is more than one real root, one must compare their likelihoods in order to find the maximum likelihood estimate of the haplotype frequency.

17.2.2 Model Genotypic Cases

In order to compare analytical and algorithmic results, we used the genotypic configurations shown in Table 17.2. Several of the cases are based upon real data sets. For each case we show the haplotype numbers and Ln(likelihood) values associated with valid solutions of Equation 17.1.

Case 1 has two maxima with identical likelihoods that are end points of a U-shaped likelihood surface (see Fig. 17.1). This case is particularly interesting

TABLE 17.2 The Genotype Numbers for Cases 1–5 and Haplotype Numbers Associated with Valid Solutions of Equation 17.1. Haplotype Numbers are Rounded to the Nearest Integer. GM and LM Denote the Global and Local Maximum Likelihood Estimates. I is the Inflection Point Between the Two Maxima. Likelihood Values are Calculated Without the Constant

Case	Genotypes				Haplotypes					
		BB	Bb	bb	AB	Ab	aB	ab	AB Frequency	Ln(Likelihood)
	AA	7	13	7	27	29	2	0	0.46551725 GM	−47.480226
1	Aa	0	2	0	28	28	1	1	0.48275861 I	−47.515948
	aa	0	0	0	29	27	0	2	0.50000000 GM	−47.480226
	AA	31	1	0	101	63	227	39	0.23544239 GM	−464.800460
2	Aa	21	79	0	141	23	186	80	0.32807544 I	−467.402927
	aa	72	0	11	158	6	170	96	0.36787754 LM	−466.885080
	AA	20	5	61	105	215	116	166	0.17484833 LM	−714.089840
3	Aa	2	141	5	115	205	106	176	0.19149581 I	−714.095945
	aa	15	1	51	137	183	84	198	0.22750969 GM	−714.046978
	AA	2	2	2	62	21	386	151	0.09993113 GM	−601.073664
4	Aa	49	13	9						
	aa	106	119	8						
	AA	10	0	30	38	128	80	70	0.11870803 LM	−369.716729
5	Aa	1	82	3	62	104	56	94	0.19580439 I	−370.588124
	aa	7	0	25	89	77	29	121	0.28042430 GM	−369.431641

because the known haplotype numbers provide equal support for two haplotype frequency estimates; these result from the two ways of assigning the same haplotype pair to the two ambiguous genotypes. In addition, assigning each of the two genotypes a different haplotype pair results in a frequency estimate with a lower likelihood than assigning the same pair to both.

Case 2 has two maxima; this case reveals whether an algorithm finds the global maximum if there is also a local maximum. We note that it is often suggested that one obtain results from multiple sample paths of, say, the EM algorithm, each starting with a different initial estimate of the unknown haplotype frequency so that one might detect multiple maxima. While straightforward in conception, this approach can be cumbersome and one can miss a maximum unless the choice of initial estimates is exhaustive.

Case 3 has a very flat likelihood surface across a broad range of haplotype frequencies; it also has two maxima that have very similar likelihood values. Such a surface indicates a slow convergence of the EM algorithm to the maximum likelihood haplotype frequency estimate. In addition, the single point estimate it generates does not reveal the substantial uncertainty as to the best haplotype frequency estimate.

Case 4 has only one maximum on the likelihood surface (see Fig. 17.2). This case is a positive control for the EM-based methods. One expects that each should

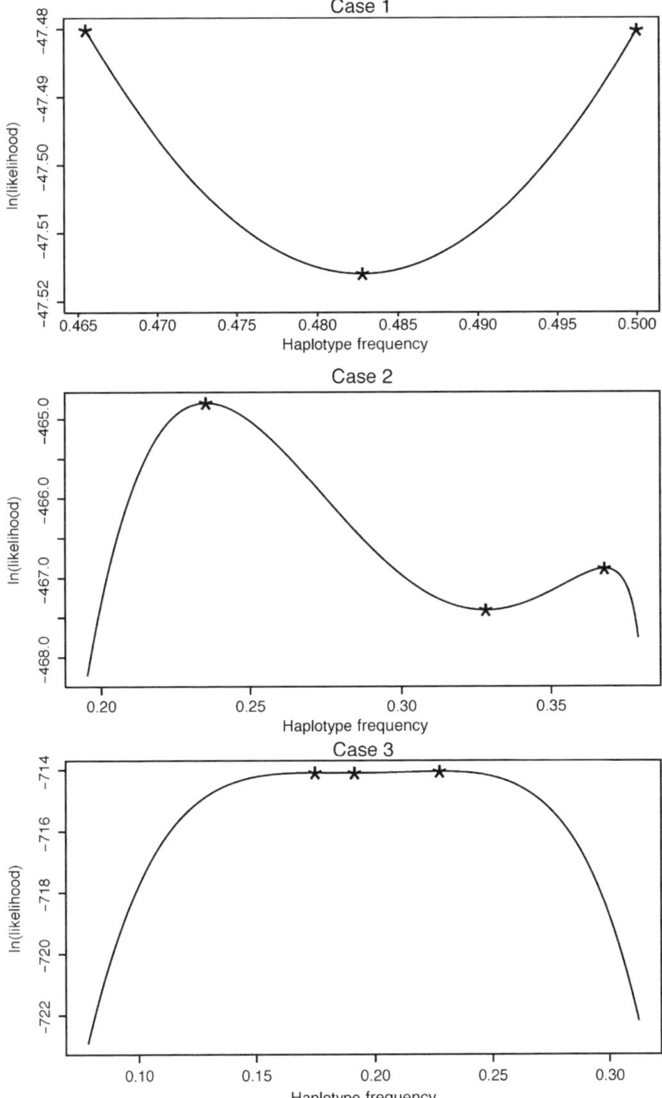

FIGURE 17.1 The likelihood surfaces for cases 1–3. "*" denotes the maxima and the inflection point on each surface. These values are solutions to Equation 17.1. Each likelihood surface is plotted from the minimum to the maximum possible frequency of haplotype AB.

find this maximum, either via a single sample path or via an ensemble of paths. For non-EM-based methods, this case provides a way of judging how distinct their results are from those of the likelihood approach.

Case 5 has two maxima that have very similar likelihood values, but the intervening haplotype frequencies have distinctly lower likelihood values in contrast to the surface for Case 3.

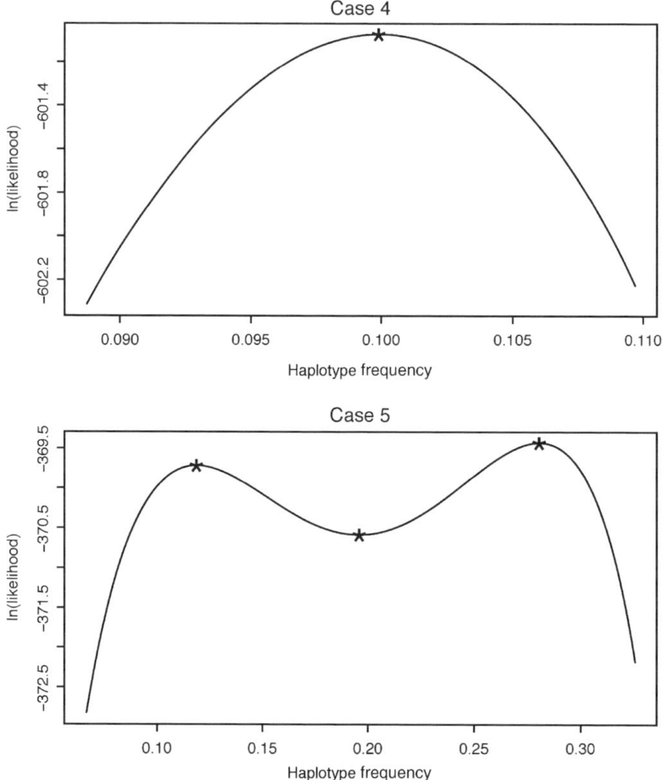

FIGURE 17.2 The likelihood surfaces for cases 4 and 5. "*" denotes the maxima and the inflection point on each surface. These values are solutions to Equation 17.1. Each likelihood surface is plotted from the minimum to the maximum possible frequency of haplotype AB.

For all five cases, the genotype frequencies at each of the two sites are statistically consistent with Hardy–Weinberg genotype frequencies (see Table 17.3). This is especially important to note, given that all of the algorithms we used, except RB, have the assumption that the individuals analyzed are a random sample from a population in Hardy-Weinberg equilibrium and also given the focus of Weir and Cockerham [40] on cases in which one or both of the sites are not in Hardy–Weinberg equilibrium. Their focus along with their statement (page 107) that "problems with multiple roots, and convergence to the wrong root, seem to arise when [single-locus genotype frequencies] depart from [Hardy-Weinberg] frequencies," might lead one to mistakenly believe that such problems are found only when such departures occur. Our results show that such problems can occur when both sites are in Hardy–Weinberg equilibrium.

17.2.3 Algorithms and Programs Used

It is important in this context to distinguish between an algorithm and instantiations of an algorithm (i.e., "program"). We regard the results concerning the performance

TABLE 17.3 Tests for Hardy–Weinberg Proportions for Cases 1–5. χ^2 Tests have 1 Degree of Freedom

Case	Site	χ^2 test value	χ^2 p value	Exact test p-value
1	1	0.047	0.828	0.806
	2	1.895	0.169	0.203
2	1	0.044	0.834	0.885
	2	0.171	0.679	0.850
3	1	0.048	0.826	0.817
	2	0.782	0.376	0.456
4	1	0.037	0.847	1.0
	2	0.034	0.853	1.0
5	1	1.320	0.251	0.338
	2	1.879	0.170	0.233

of any given program implementing a particular algorithm as having no necessary implication as to the performance of other programs implementing the same algorithm. The term "sample path" refers to a single run of an algorithm as initiated by a random number either to generate an initial frequency estimate or to shuffle the list of input genotypes. As described in what follows, we used six stochastic algorithms, which involve the use of such a random number, and four deterministic algorithms, which do not.

We first implemented the EM algorithm using a program that we wrote. This program started the algorithm from a random initial haplotype frequency chosen from a uniform distribution having lower and upper bounds corresponding to the minimum and maximum possible frequency estimates, respectively. We used a "minimal standard" multiplicative congruential random number generator with shuffled output to create the initial frequency estimate (see [27], pp. 269–271 for further details.)

The output of each sample path of our program is a "direct" estimate of the four haplotype frequencies and an "indirect" estimate found by counting haplotypes among the inferred pairs. When applied to the results of an EM algorithm, the latter kind of estimate will tend to overestimate frequencies of common haplotypes and underestimate rare ones since the inferred pair is taken to be the most probable pair among the possible pairs.

The second stochastic algorithm we used combines the Gibbs sampler along with a "divide, conquer, and combine" technique known as partial ligation so as to allow one to make haplotype inferences for datasets involving more sites than can be accomodated by the standard EM algorithm. The program that implements this algorithm is Haplotyper version 2 [24]. In this Bayesian approach, the prior distribution of haplotype frequencies is sampled from a uniform Dirichlet distribution. The random number generator used to create the initial frequency estimate is "Unran" from the Ranlib package (Qin, personal communication); this routine sums several random numbers generated by a multiplicative congruential generator in order to produce each random uniform number. Haplotyper provides only an indirect estimate of the haplotype frequencies found by counting the haplotypes in the most probable haplotype pair for each individual.

The third stochastic algorithm we used combines EM with partial ligation (see above). The program that does this is PL–EM [30]. This program starts the algorithm from a random initial haplotype frequency chosen from a uniform distribution having lower and upper bounds of 0.0 and 1.0, respectively. The random number generator used to create the initial frequency estimate is the Unran routine (Qin, personal communication). This program provides a direct estimate of haplotype frequency and an indirect estimate found by counting haplotypes in the most probable haplotype pair.

The fourth stochastic algorithm we used is variation 1, as described by [25] and implemented by a program that we wrote. This rule-based (RB) algorithm uses the unambiguous haplotypes in a sample as the initial basis for resolving ambiguous genotypes. Each such genotype receives a single inference. To this extent, a given sample path provides identical direct and indirect estimates of haplotype frequencies. At the start of any given sample path, the list of genotypes is randomized. Before attempting to solve each ambiguous genotype, the order of the "reference" list of real and inferred haplotypes is randomized. If there is more than one haplotype that could resolve a given genotype, one is randomly chosen. The random number generator used to shuffle the genotype and haplotype lists is a multiplicative congruential generator as implemented in a standard C library function (details available upon request). As shown by [25], variation 1 may produce different results for a given dataset than does the rule-based method described by [3].

The fifth stochastic algorithm we used is a Bayesian method in which the prior distribution of initial haplotype frequencies is approximately the neutral coalescent distribution; it also uses partial ligation. The program we used is version 2.0.2 of Phase [35,36]. This program calculates the posterior mean in order to provide a direct estimate of haplotype frequencies; this mean is proportional to the sum (over all individuals) of the probability that a haplotype occurs in a given individual. This program also provides an indirect estimate based on the most probable haplotype pair. We note in this regard that previous versions of Phase produced only this kind of indirect estimate of haplotype frequency, although the estimates published by Stephens et al. were direct and were based on the posterior mean (Stephens, personal communication). To this extent, one could have used previous versions of Phase with the mistaken expectation that they produced direct estimates, while, in fact, they produced indirect estimates, which will generally be less accurate. We ran simulations that assumed there was no recombination (MS). We used the default settings for each sample path (100 iterations, 100 steps in the burn-in, and a thinning interval of 1.) The random number generator we used to create the initial frequency estimate is the Wichmann–Hill algorithm as implemented in Python (see [41,42]); this algorithm generates a random integer seed for the random number generator contained in Phase.

The sixth stochastic algorithm we used is a method based on an entropy minimization principle put forth by [13]. In essence, this approach is a generalization of the parsimony approach in that haplotype frequencies and haplotype number contribute to the objective function that is minimized. The program we used is ENT, as described in [26]. This program provides only an indirect estimate of the haplotype frequencies. The random number generator we used is the Python generator (see above).

For each stochastic algorithm, we analyzed the results of two different simulations for each case. For the EM, Haplotyper, PL-EM, RB, and ENT programs, each simulation consisted of 10,000 independent sample paths (each providing a set of inferences); for Phase, each simulation consisted of 2000 sample paths. Further details of our implementation of the programs are available upon request.

The first deterministic algorithm we used determines whether a given set of genotypes is consistent with a perfect phylogeny (that is, whether it is consistent with the infinite-sites model without recombination) and outputs the haplotype pairs inferred by this phylogeny. The program we used is DPPH (see [2,11] for further details). This program produces inferences for all perfect phylogenies for a given dataset. It always produces the same results for a given dataset.

The second deterministic algorithm we used combines inference from a perfect phylogeny, likelihood analysis, and dynamic programming so as to make haplotype inferences for a dataset that may not fit a perfect phylogeny because of recombination between sites or multiple mutations at a given site. The program we used is HAP [12]. This always produces the same inferences for a given order of data input, but if a dataset is consistent with two or more perfect phylogenies with identical likelihoods, the inferred haplotypes can be dependent upon the order of input (Eskin, personal communication). To this extent, HAP should be used as a stochastic algorithm (requiring multiple sample paths). However, since Halperin and Eskin presented their method as requiring one sample path, we have implemented it as such.

The third deterministic algorithm we used is based on a graph-theoretic method for inferring haplotype pairs consistent with a infinite-sites model with recombination. The program we used is 2SNP [1]. It always produces the same results for a given dataset.

The fourth deterministic algorithm we used is based upon an analysis in which the likelihood function (e.g., as described above for the two-site case) is "relaxed," that is, each haplotype frequency is treated as an n-dimensional vector instead of as a single real number. This assumption along with the assumption of Hardy–Weinberg equilibrium (and that there are no missing data) is sufficient to guarantee that the maximum of the relaxed likelihood function converges to the maximum of the standard likelihood function as the sample size increases. The use of the relaxed likelihood function allows the solution to be attained in polynomial time. The program we used is HaploFreq [14]. It always produces the same results for a given dataset.

DPPH, HAP, 2SNP each generates only an indirect estimate of haplotype frequencies, whereas HaploFreq generates only a direct estimate.

17.3 RESULTS

The estimates of haplotype frequency are shown in Tables 17.4–17.6. For Cases 2–5, many of the distributions produced by RB and Phase have been consolidated for ease of presentation. Full distributions are available upon request. For any given method, we used a two-tailed exact test to compare the distributions resulting from the two simulations. Each such test involved a $2 \times n$ contingency table, where n is the number of outcomes. For example, the Haplotyper analyses of Case 4 produced two different indirect estimates of haplotype number (see Table 17.6), 55 and 68, thereby producing a 2×2 table. The exact test p-value was calculated using the network algorithm of [22] as implemented in SAS. Statistical significance was assessed at the 0.05 level.

17.3.1 Direct Estimates

As shown in Table 17.4, the EM program produced distributions of direct estimates in the two simulations that were not significantly different (case 1: $p = 0.072$; case 2: $p = 0.071$; case 3: $p = 0.368$; case 5: $p = 0.095$). For all cases, the simulation results are consistent with those predicted by the likelihood surface; for example, the results reveal that the global maximum for case 2 has a larger domain of attraction than the local maximum does. However, the virtue of the analytical approach we describe is made clear by the fact that for cases 1 and 5, random sampling of initial haplotype frequencies resulted in the two simulations having different majority outcomes. For any one simulation with more than one outcome, one might be tempted to choose the majority (plurality) outcome as the best estimate of haplotype frequency. The difficulty of this naive approach is underscored by the fact that depending on which simulation was in hand, one might make a different conclusion about the best estimate of haplotype frequency. Of course, with all of these results in hand, an investigator would know not to take the results of any simulation as definitive. However, the extensive computation this entails underscores the usefulness of the analytical method we describe.

The PL-EM program produces direct estimates of haplotype frequencies that are generally similar to those produced by our EM program. However, for three cases, the distributions produced in the two simulations were significantly different (case 1: $p = 0.084$; case 2: $p < 10^{-7}$; case 3: $p < 10^{-7}$; case 5: $p < 10^{-11}$). For cases 1 and 3, there are unexpectedly large numbers of sample paths that resulted in the solution to Equation 17.1 that is the inflection point between the maxima. The reason for these large numbers is unknown.

The RB program produced distributions of direct estimates that are generally distinct from those we've just discussed. For example, for case 4, there were estimates from 55 to 65 AB haplotypes, whereas the analytical method and the EM algorithm produced only an estimate of 62 haplotypes. The reason for the distinctiveness of the RB results is straightforward. The presence of the randomized haplotype reference list in the inference process has the consequence that the probability of assigning either of the two haplotype pairs is binomially distributed, with the underlying probabilities being determined by the possibly changing frequencies of the different haplotypes

TABLE 17.4 The Distribution of Direct Estimates of Haplotype Numbers for Cases 1–5 (Number of Sample Paths). Estimates for EM, PL-EM, and Phase are Rounded to the Nearest Integer. GM and LM Denote the Global and Local Maximum Likelihood Estimates. I is the Inflection Point Between the Two Maxima. These Values are the Solutions to Equation 17.1. For Each Case, the Lower and Upper Bounds of AB Haplotypes are the Lowest and the Highest Possible Number, Respectively. Bold Numbers Denote $p < 0.05$; Each p Value is the Result of an Exact Test Comparing the Distributions of the Outcomes from the Two Simulations (see text for the Exact Value)

		Method							
		EM		PL-EM		RB		Phase MS	
	Number of AB	Simulation							
Case	Haplotypes	1	2	1	2	1	2	1	2
	27 GM	4917	5044	4358	4474	2474	2550	0	0
1	28 I	0	1	589	530	4971	4835	2000	2000
	29 GM	5083	4955	5053	4996	2555	2615	0	0
	84 – 100	0	0	0	0	16	10	0	0
	101 GM	7197	7312	**7180**	**7528**	15	18	0	0
	102 – 140	0	0	0	0	9969	9972	1991	1988
2	141 I	0	0	0	0	0	0	1	7
	142 – 157	0	0	0	0	0	0	8	5
	158 LM	2803	2688	**2820**	**2472**	0	0	0	0
	159 – 163	0	0	0	0	0	0	0	0
	47 – 104	0	0	0	0	624	633	0	0
	105 LM	4791	4892	**4834**	**5053**	189	204	0	0
	106 – 114	0	0	0	0	3722	3708	195	181
3	115 I	2	1	**168**	**86**	540	529	61	63
	116 – 136	0	0	0	0	4909	4908	1744	1756
	137 GM	5207	5107	**4998**	**4861**	7	7	0	0
	138 – 188	0	0	0	0	9	11	0	0
	55	0	0	0	0	49	62	0	0
	56 – 61	0	0	0	0	8855	8899	875	878
4	62 GM	10000	10000	10000	10000	709	668	1125	1122
	63 – 67	0	0	0	0	387	371	0	0
	68	0	0	0	0	0	0	0	0
	21	0	0	0	0	0	0	0	0
	22 – 37	0	0	0	0	0	0	0	0
	38 LM	4906	5025	**5276**	**4783**	0	0	0	0
	39 – 61	0	0	0	0	5414	5417	439	420
5	62 I	0	0	0	0	708	690	96	109
	63 – 88	0	0	0	0	3878	3893	1465	1471
	89 GM	5094	4975	**4724**	**5217**	0	0	0	0
	90 – 102	0	0	0	0	0	0	0	0
	103	0	0	0	0	0	0	0	0

TABLE 17.5 The Haplotype Numbers for Cases 1–5 Produced by Deterministic Algorithms. Haplotype Numbers are Rounded to the Nearest Integer for HaploFreq. GM and LM Denote the Global and Local Maximum Likelihood Estimates. NA Denotes not Applicable Because Cases 2–5 Do Not Have an Associated Perfect Phylogeny, as Required for DPPH

Case		Haplotype				Found by			
		AB	Ab	aB	ab	DPPH	HAP	2SNP	HaploFreq
1	GM	27	29	2	0	Yes	No	Yes	Yes
	GM	29	27	0	2	Yes	Yes	No	No
		84	80	244	22	NA	Yes	No	No
2	GM	101	63	227	39	NA	No	No	Yes
	LM	158	6	170	96	NA	No	No	No
		163	1	165	101	NA	No	Yes	No
		47	273	174	108	NA	Yes	No	No
3	LM	105	215	116	166	NA	No	No	Yes
	GM	137	183	84	198	NA	No	No	No
		188	132	33	249	NA	No	Yes	No
		55	28	393	144	NA	Yes	No	No
4	GM	62	21	386	151	NA	No	No	Yes
		68	15	380	157	NA	No	Yes	No
		21	145	97	53	NA	Yes	No	No
5	LM	38	128	80	70	NA	No	No	Yes
	GM	89	77	29	121	NA	No	No	No
		103	15	63	135	NA	No	Yes	No

on the current reference list. Thus, for example, one can see that the approximately 1:2:1 distribution of haplotype numbers for case 1 occurred because the underlying probability of assigning either haplotype pair to the first ambiguous genotype is 0.5 (= 27/54), and consequently the probability of assigning the same haplotype pair to the second genotype was either 0.482 (= 27/56) or 0.518 (= 29/56). The two RB simulations produced distributions of direct estimates that were not significantly different (case 1: P = 0.155; case 2: P = 0.424; case 3: P = 1.0; case 4: P = 0.364; case 5: P = 0.876).

Phase produced distributions of direct estimates that share some features with all of the results discussed previously. For example, for case 4 Phase MS produced estimates of 61 and 62 AB haplotypes. In contrast, the other Phase MS results were similar to the RB results in having relatively wide distributions of frequency estimates. For example, for case 3, there were 195 haplotype number estimates ranging from 106 to 114 in the first simulation and 181 in the second simulation. The Phase output revealed that the posterior probability of either haplotype pair for each ambiguous genotype was very close to 0.5. This reflects the more or less flat likelihood surface across most of the range of valid haplotype frequencies. The two Phase MS simulations produced distributions of direct estimates that were not significantly different (case 2: P = 0.080; case 3: P = 0.742; case 4: P = 0.949; case 5: P = 0.529).

TABLE 17.6 The Distribution of Indirect Estimates of Haplotype Numbers for Cases 1–5 (Number of Sample Paths). For Each Case, the Lower and Upper Bounds of AB Haplotypes are the Lowest and the Highest Possible Number, Respectively. Indirect Estimates Generated by RB are Identical to the Direct Estimates Shown in Table 17.4. Bold Numbers Denote P < 0.05; Each P Value is the Result of an Exact Test Comparing the Distributions of Outcomes from the two Simulations (see text for the Exact Value)

		Method									
		EM		PL-EM		Haplotyper		Phase MS		ENT	
	Number of AB	Simulation									
Case	Haplotypes	1	2	1	2	1	2	1	2	1	2
1	27	4917	5044	**4458**	**4739**	**5065**	**4832**	904	894	4958	5050
	28	0	1	0	0	0	0	176	173	0	0
	29	5083	4955	**5542**	**5261**	**4935**	**5168**	920	933	5042	4950
2	84	7197	7312	**7180**	**7528**	7729	7783	1663	1638	6785	6829
	85 – 162	0	0	0	0	0	0	12	17	0	0
	163	2803	2688	**2820**	**2472**	2271	2217	325	345	3215	3171
3	47	4793	4893	5002	5139	**4432**	**4599**	459	427	5235	5139
	48 – 187	0	0	0	0	0	0	101	92	0	0
	188	5207	5107	4998	4861	**5568**	**5401**	1440	1481	4765	4861
4	55	0	0	0	0	**1666**	**1846**	0	0	1370	1398
	56 – 67	0	0	0	0	0	0	0	0	0	0
	68	10000	10000	10000	10000	**8334**	**8154**	2000	2000	8630	8602
5	21	4906	5025	**5276**	**4783**	**4333**	**4501**	455	438	4552	4514
	22 – 102	0	0	0	0	0	0	29	38	0	0
	103	5094	4975	**4724**	**5217**	**5667**	**5499**	1516	1524	5448	5486

The direct estimates generated by HaploFreq are shown in Table 17.5. HaploFreq found one of the global maxima for case 1. It found the local maximum for cases 3 and 5 and the global maximum for cases 2 and 4.

17.3.2 Indirect Estimates

The indirect estimates shown in Table 17.6 were generally quite different from direct estimates. The reason is that in any given sample path of the EM-based methods, all individuals with an ambiguous genotype are assigned the same most probable haplotype pair. However, the identity of this pair may differ across sample paths if there is more than one maximum on the likelihood surface. The result is the binary outcome of indirect frequency estimates observed for the cases that have two maxima (1, 2, 3, and 5). In contrast, case 4 has a single outcome because there is only one maximum. The EM algorithm produced distributions of indirect estimates that were not significantly different (case 1: $p = 0.072$; case 2: $p = 0.071$; case 3: $p = 0.161$; case 5: $p = 0.095$).

The PL–EM algorithm produced indirect estimates that were generally similar to those produced by our EM algorithm. However, for three of five cases, the distributions produced by the two simulations were significantly different (case 1: $p < 10^{-4}$; case 2: $p < 10^{-7}$; case 3: $p = 0.054$; case 5: $p < 10^{-11}$).

Haplotyper also produced indirect estimates that are generally similar to those produced by the EM algorithm. The exception is case 4, which has a mix of the two extreme haplotype numbers (55: all Ab/aB and 68: all AB/ab). The reason for this binary outcome is unknown. For four of the five cases, the distributions produced by the two simulations were significantly different (case 1: $p = 0.001$; case 2: $p = 0.369$; case 3: $p = 0.018$; case 4: $p < 10^{-3}$; case 5: $p = 0.017$).

Phase produced indirect estimates that were generally quite different from all of the results discussed previously. The reason for this was that individuals with ambiguous genotypes can differ in which of the two possible haplotype pairs is most probable, even though in the cases studied all such individuals have identical genotypes. So, for example, the three outcomes for case 1 are AB frequencies of 27 (two ambiguous genotypes resolved as Ab/aB), 28 (one as Ab/aB and one as AB/ab), and 29 (two as AB/ab). This occurs despite the fact that all sample paths in the first simulation and almost all paths in the second simulation produced a direct estimate of 28; this difference reflects the distinction between the direct estimate, which is based on the posterior mean and the indirect estimate, which is based on the posterior probability.

We note that the reason that identical ambiguous genotypes may be inferred differently in a given sample path is that the posterior probability for an individual is based upon an ensemble of inferences, one for each step in the sample path. These ensembles differ due to random sampling, and consequently the most probable haplotype pair may differ for individuals with identical genotypes. The probability of this happening should decrease as the number of iterations increases. So, for example, as shown in Table 17.6, there were 101 "mixed" sample paths (those with identical ambiguous individuals inferred differently) in the first simulation for case 3; each inference was based upon a sample path with 100 iterations. Additional simulations with 2000 sample paths (not shown) resulted in 92 mixed sample paths when there were 1000 iterations for each inference and 28 sample paths when there were 5000 iterations for each inference. The two Phase MS simulations produced distributions of indirect estimates that did not differ significantly (case 1: $p = 0.919$; case 2: $p = 0.468$; case 3: $p = 0.342$; case 5: $p = 0.461$).

The indirect estimates generated by DPPH, HAP, and 2SNP are shown in Table 17.5. DPPH produced results only for case 1, since the other four cases are not consistent with a perfect phylogeny (each has four unambiguous haplotypes present). The program found the two solutions that have identical likelihoods as shown in Table 17.2. HAP produced results for all five cases. The solution for case 1 was AB = 29, Ab = 27, aB = 0, and ab = 2; the two ambiguous genotypes were phased as AB/ab. The other solution for this case, which is consistent with a different perfect phylogeny and has the same likelihood as the observed solution, was not found. For the other cases, the observed solution is that generated by phasing all ambiguous genotypes as Ab/aB.

2SNP also produced results in which all of the ambiguous genotypes were identically resolved. However, the solution produced for case 1 was AB = 27, Ab = 29, aB = 2, and ab = 0; the two ambiguous genotypes were phased as Ab/aB. For the other cases, the observed solution is that generated by phasing all ambiguous genotypes as AB/ab. As a result, all of the resolutions produced by 2SNP were opposite to those produced by HAP. The reason for this difference between the two programs is unknown.

17.4 DISCUSSION

There are four issues that we would like to discuss: (1) how to relate the analytical likelihood approach to the EM approach, (2) how to understand the similarities and the differences among the approaches, (3) the heterogeneity of results within some approaches, and (4) the relevance of our results to the general problem of haplotype inference. We discuss these issues in turn.

Our results indicate that the analytical approach is clearly preferable as compared to the EM algorithm if one is using the likelihood approach to analyze two-site data. Results are obtained quickly and one can readily determine whether there is a complexity to the inference problem that a partial or even comprehensive implementation of the EM algorithm might not reveal. For example, as noted above, if the EM algorithm is used as a "black box," that is, it is used just to generate a point estimate of the haplotype frequency, one can miss the fact that many frequencies have very similar likelihoods or the fact that there are multiple maxima, possibly with equal likelihoods. Visual inspection of the surface and analytical calculations of the maxima provides much more complete information about the meaning of the inferences based on likelihood.

We next discuss the similarities and the differences among the approaches. The likelihood approach and most of the others share some assumptions, for example, that the population is in Hardy–Weinberg equilibrium. However, most of their differences are substantive; for example, some of the approaches are Bayesian and some are not. But even when comparing, say, Bayesian, approaches with one another, we believe it is essential to remember the possible model dependency of the results (see also [35]). The Phase program incorporates population-genetic assumptions that clearly apply to some loci and possibly to many. However, it is easy to identify loci whose biology is not consistent with these assumptions. Of course, since the assumptions underlying any inference approach will rarely be met exactly, what we need are tests of the accuracy of inference that use real haplotype pairs. At present, there are still few such tests (as described above) and we caution against regarding present evidence as implying that any one program is to be preferred. We note in this context that our five cases were not generated by a simulation of a neutral coalescent process.

Our third issue is the heterogeneity of results within each approach. We do not know why there are differences between simulations for PL–EM and also for Haplotyper. We suggest that Haplotyper program be used with caution when estimating haplotype frequencies. One reason is that it generates only indirect frequency estimates. Second, it is capable of generating results like those observed for case 4, in which a substantial fraction of sample paths result in an indirect frequency estimate that appears to be highly deviant (see Table 17.6).

We also suggest that the HAP and 2SNP programs be used with caution (at least for two-site data) as they are also capable of producing a frequency estimate that appears to be highly deviant (see Table 17.5).

The results generated by HaploFreq suggest that this program does not necessarily produce maximum likelihood estimates for sample sizes that are typically found in many real applications. The comparison of the results for cases 3 and 4 are revealing in this regard (see Table 17.5). Their sample sizes are approximately equal but HaploFreq finds the global maximum only for case 4. This suggests that genotypic configuration influences the attainment of global maxima by the program. This dependency is not just a matter of there being two maxima since HaploFreq finds the global maximum for case 2, which has two maxima (and a smaller sample size). Of course, such a dependency does not rule out an influence of sample size; a smaller sample size may explain why HaploFreq does not find the global maximum for case 5. We regard this program as important and hope that it can be elaborated so as to perform better. We believe that the present version of HaploFreq should be used with caution; we recommend the analytical approach for two-site data.

Finally, we address the relevance of our results to the larger problem of haplotype inference. A central issue in this regard is whether the reduced dimensionality that allows one to make analytical predictions (two sites) introduces an artificial simplicity that reduces the relevance of our findings to the problem of inferring haplotypes for many sites. In fact, it is possible to argue that it is more difficult to infer haplotype frequencies or haplotype pairs in the two-site case than in the multisite (>2) case. In the former case, each ambiguous individual is heterozygous at every site, while in the latter case, this is possible but unlikely. To this extent, there is no partial information in the two-site case about the haplotypes in ambiguous individuals. In contrast, in the multisite case, one ambiguous individual may be, say, homozygous for several sites that are multiply heterozygous in other ambiguous individuals; in such an instance, one gains some partial information about the possible haplotypes in the latter individuals. However, the fact that all ambiguous individuals in the two-variant, two-site case have identical genotypes would seem to simplify the inference problem. At present, we are unaware of a satisfactory means of reconciling these conflicting inferences about the general relevance of our two-site analyses. Of course, multiple simulations involving many different multisite (>2) datasets would provide some insight into how likely it is that, say, the EM algorithm results in different frequency estimates for a given set of genotypes. Such a general investigation is a daunting task, at least in lieu of some meaningful constraints on the number of individuals, genotype frequencies, and number of sites involved. At the very least, we believe that our results should generate caution in users' minds about the algorithmic inference of haplotype frequencies for multisite data.

A related issue concerns the context of application of haplotype inference algorithms. One current (but not universal) piece of "folk wisdom" in the biological community is that common haplotypes are reliably inferred by present algorithms (if such haplotypes need algorithmic inference at all); this is said to contrast with the situation for rare haplotypes, for which inference is regarded as more error prone at best. To this extent, one could believe that much of the recent work concerning the testing and refinement of haplotyping algorithms as unnecessary or of secondary importance at most, especially if traits of, say, clinical importance are most often associated with common haplotypes (see [17] for a discussion of this and related issues). Our results clearly show that such a belief would be mistaken. For almost all of the cases we analyzed, all four haplotypes are common in the set of unambiguous genotypes (the only exception is the Ab haplotype in case 2), and there are more unambiguous genotypes than ambiguous ones (the only exception is case 5). Nonetheless, a single algorithmic inference of haplotype frequencies for these datasets is obviously not reliable since most programs do not generate a "fixed" answer. The only arguable exception is case 4. Our overall conclusion is that meaningful algorithmic inference of even common haplotype frequencies requires careful interpretation of the results generated by multiple sample paths. It is also important to compare the results generated by several programs. It is blind faith to think there are meaningful alternatives at present, save for experimental inference. Of course, particular knowledge of the evolutionary processes underlying the evolution of the sequences being analyzed might allow one to prefer one algorithm and rule out others; such knowledge is invaluable for guiding the investigator.

In lieu of such knowledge, the investigator potentially faces the challenge of reconciling sets of inferences (even if just one program is used). In such a circumstance, one possibility is some kind of consensus method, as suggested by [25] (see also [8]), in which, say, the most common set of inferences is used. As discussed in [25], additional genetic criteria can be used to determine the inference sets queried in order to determine the consensus inferences. This general approach is promising, especially in as much as it provides a clear way to determine an answer and they show that it performs well for the locus studied. Nonetheless, additional research is needed to assess how generally useful it will be (see [32]).

We end with a general point about our simulations. They involved particular programs run on a particular platform in a way that was not necessarily expected by the creators of each program (all of whom deserve substantial thanks for their work). We have tried to make our analyses as unbiased as possible. Nonetheless, it is always possible that results would differ if the simulations were designed differently and/or run on a different platform. We welcome such simulations although we regard a qualitatively different outcome to be unlikely. No matter what their outcome is, such simulations would provide much needed further investigation of the present state of the art of haplotype inference.

ACKNOWLEDGMENTS

This work has been partially supported by NSF awards SES-9906997, EIA-0220154, SEI 0513910, NIH R01 DA015789-01A2, NIA P01-AG0225000-01, and Variagenics, Inc. We thank S. Qin and M. Stephens for technical assistance, K. Norberg for statistical computations, R. Hudson, D. Posada, M. Stephens, M. Uyenoyama, C. Wiuf for comments, and I. Măndoiu and A. Zelikovsky for the opportunity to contribute this chapter. Source code to implement the analytical method is available upon request.

REFERENCES

1. Brinza D, Zelikovsky A. 2SNP: scalable phasing based on 2-SNP haplotypes. *Bioinformatics* 2006; 22:371–374.
2. Chung RA, Gusfield D. Perfect phylogeny haplotyper: haplotype inferral using a tree model. *Bioinformatics* 2003; 19:780–781.
3. Clark AG. Inference of haplotypes from PCR-amplified samples of diploid populations. *Mol Biol Evol* 1990; 7:111–122.
4. De Vivo I, Huggins GS, Hankinson SE, Lescault PJ, Boezen M, Colditz GA, Hunter DJ. A functional polymorphism in the promoter of the progesterone receptor gene associated with endometrial cancer risk. *Proc Nat Acad Sci USA* 2002; 99:12263–12268.
5. Eskin E, Halperin E, Karp RM. Efficient reconstruction of haplotype structure via perfect phylogeny. *J Bioinform Comput Biol* 2003; 1:1–20.
6. Excoffier L, Slatkin M. Maximum-Likelihood estimation of molecular haplotype frequencies in a diploid population. *Mol Biol Evol* 1995; 12:921–927.
7. Fallin D, Schork NJ. Accuracy of haplotype frequency estimation for biallelic loci, via the expectation-maximization algorithm for unphased diploid genotype data. *Am J Hum Genet* 2000; 67:947–959.
8. Fullerton SM, Buchanan AV, Sonpar VA, Taylor SL, Smith JD, Carlson CS, Salomaa V, Stengard JH, Boerwinkle E, Clark AG, Nickerson DA, Weiss KM. The effects of scale: variation in the APOA1/C3/A4/A5 gene cluster. *Human Genetics* 2004; 115:36–56.
9. Gusfield D. Inference of haplotypes from samples of diploid populations: complexity and algorithms. *J Comput Biol* 2001; 8:305–323.
10. Gusfield D. Haplotyping as perfect phylogeny: conceptual framework and efficient solutions. In Myers G, Hannenhalli S, Istrail S, Pevzner P, Waterman M. editors. *Proceedings of RECOMB 2002: The Sixth annual International Conference on Computational Biology*. ACM Press; 2002. pp. 166–175.
11. Gusfield D, Orzack SH. Haplotype inference. In Aluru S, editor. *Handbook of Computational Molecular Biology*, Chapman & Hall/CRC, Computer and Information Science Series. 2005. pp. 18-1 – 18-28.
12. Halperin E, Eskin E. Haplotype reconstruction from genotype data using imperfect phylogeny. *Bioinformatics* 2004; 20:1842–1849.
13. Halperin E, Karp RM. The minimum-entropy set cover problem. In Díaz J, Karhumäki J, Lepistö A, Sannella D, editors. *Proceedings of the 31st International Colloquium on Automata, Languages and Programming*. Lecture Notes in Computer Science. Springer; 2004. pp. 733–744.
14. Halperin E, Hazan E. HAPLOFREQ—Estimating Haplotype Frequencies Efficiently. *J Comput Biol* 2006; 13:481–500.
15. Hawley ME, Kidd KK. HAPLO: a program using the EM algorithm to estimate the frequencies of multi-site haplotypes. *J Hered* 1995, 86:409–411.

16. Hill WG. Estimation of linkage disequilibrium in randomly mating populations. *Heredity* 1974; 33:229–239.

17. Hoehe MR. Haplotypes and the systematic analysis of genetic variation in genes and genomes. *Pharmacogenomics* 2003; 4:547–570.

18. Hudson RR. Linkage disequilibrium and recombination. In Balding DJ, Bishop M, Canning C, editors. *Handbook of Statistical Genetics* 2nd ed. Wiley, 2003. pp. 662–678.

19. Lin S, Cutler DJ, Zwick ME, Chakravarti A. Haplotype inference in random population samples. *Am J Hum Genet* 2002; 71:1129–1137.

20. Long JC, William RC, Urbanek M. An E-M algorithm and testing strategy for multiple-locus haplotypes. *Am J Hum Genet* 1995; 56:799–810.

21. Marchini J, Cutler D, Patterson N, Stephens M, Eskin E, Halperin E, Lin S, Qin ZS, Munro HM, Abecasis GR, Donnelly P. A Comparison of Phasing Algorithms for Trios and Unrelated Individuals. *Am J Hum Genet* 2006; 78:437–450.

22. Mehta CR, Patel NR. A network algorithm for performing Fisher's exact test in $r \times c$ contingency tables. *J Am Stat Assoc* 1983; 78:427–434.

23. Niu T. Algorithms for inferring haplotypes. *Genet Epidemiol* 2004; 27:334–337.

24. Niu T, Qin ZS , Xu X, Liu JS. Bayesian haplotype inference for multiple linked single-nucleotide polymorphisms. *Am J Hum Genet* 2002; 70:157–169.

25. Orzack SH, Gusfield D, Olson J, Nesbitt S, Subrahmanyan L, Stanton VP, Jr. Analysis and exploration of the use of rule-based algorithms and consensus methods for the inferral of haplotypes. *Genetics* 2003; 165:915–928.

26. Pasaniuc B, Mandoiu II. Highly Scalable Genotype Phasing by Entropy Minimization. *Proceedings of the 28th Annual International Conference of the IEEE Engineering in Medicine and Biology Society*. IEEE Press; 2006; pp. 3482–3486.

27. Press WP, Flannery BP, Teukolsky SA, Vetterling WT. *Numerical Recipes in Fortran 77: The Art of Scientific Computing*. Cambridge: Cambridge University Press; 1992.

28. Pritchard JK, Przeworski M. Linkage disequilibrium in humans: models and data. *Am J Hum Genet* 2001; 69:1–14.

29. Proudnikov D, LaForge KS, Hofflich H, Levenstien M, Gordon D, Barral S, Ott J, Kreek MJ. Association analysis of polymorphisms in serotonin 1B receptor (HTR1B) gene with heroin addiction: a comparison of molecular and statistically estimated haplotypes. *Pharmacogenetics and Genomics* 2006; 16:25–36.

30. Qin ZS, Niu T, Liu JS. Partition-ligation–expectation-maximization algorithm for haplotype inference with single-nucleotide polymorphisms. *Am J Hum Genet* 2002; 71:1242–1247.

31. Sabbagh A, Darlu P. Inferring haplotypes at the *NAT2* locus: the computational approach. *BMC Genetics* 2005; 6:30 doi:10.1186/1471-2156-6-30.

32. Saeed Q. An efficient parallel algorithm for haplotype inference based on rule-based approach and consensus methods. Masters Thesis. University of Windsor. Windsor, Ontario, Canada, 2007.

33. Schipper RF, D'Amaro J, de Lange P, Th.Schreuder GM, van Rood JJ, Oudshoorn M. Validation of haplotype frequency estimation methods. *Hum Immunol* 1998; 59:518–523.

34. Slatkin M, Excoffier L. Testing for linkage disequilibrium in genotypic data using the Expectation-Maximization algorithm. *Heredity* 1996; 76:377–383.

35. Stephens M, Donnelly P. A comparison of Bayesian methods for haplotype reconstruction from population genotype data. *Am J Hum Genet* 2003; 73:1162–1169.

36. Stephens M, Smith NJ, Donnelly P. A new statistical method for haplotype reconstruction from population data. *Am J Hum Genet* 2001; 68:978–989.

37. Stephens M, Smith NJ, Donnelly P. Reply to Zhang *et al*. *Am J Hum Genet* 2001; 69:912–914.

38. Templeton AR, Sing CF, Kessling A, Humphries S. A cladistic-analysis of phenotype associations with haplotypes inferred from restriction endonuclease mapping. 2. The analysis of natural-populations. *Genetics* 1988; 120:1145-1154.

39. Tishkoff SA, Pakstis AJ, Ruano G, Kidd KK. The accuracy of statistical methods for estimation of haplotype frequencies: an example from the CD4 locus. *Am J Hum Genet* 2000; 67:518-522.

40. Weir BS, Cockerham CC. Estimation of linkage disequilibrium in randomly mating populations. *Heredity* 1979; 42:105-111.

41. Wichmann BA, Hill ID. Algorithm AS 183: An efficient and portable pseudo-random number generator. *Appl Statist* 1982; 31:188-190.

42. Wichmann BA, Hill ID. Correction: Algorithm AS 183: An efficient and portable pseudo-random number generator. *Appl Statist* 1984; 33:123.

43. Zee RYL, Hegener HH, Cook NR, Ridker PM. C-reactive protein gene polymorphisms and the risk of venous thromboembolism: a haplotype-based analysis. *J Thromb Haemost* 2004; 2:1240-1243.

44. Zhang S, Pakstis AJ, Kidd KK, Zhao H. Comparisons of two methods for haplotype reconstruction and haplotype frequency estimation from population data. *Am J Hum Genet* 2001; 69:906-912.

45. Zhang J, Vingron M, Hoehe MR, 2005 Haplotype reconstruction for diploid populations. *Hum Hered* 2005; 59:144–156.

46. Zhang Y, Niu T, Liu JS. A coalescence-guided hierarchical bayesian method for haplotype inference. *Am J Hum Genet* 2006; 79:313–322.

47. Zhang K, Zhao H. A comparison of several methods for haplotype frequency estimation and haplotype reconstruction for tightly linked markers from general pedigrees. *Genet Epidemiol* 2006; 30:423–437.

18

OPTIMIZATION METHODS FOR GENOTYPE DATA ANALYSIS IN EPIDEMIOLOGICAL STUDIES

Dumitru Brinza, Jingwu He, and Alexander Zelikovsky

Department of Computer Science, Georgia State University, Atlanta, GA, USA

18.1 INTRODUCTION

Recent improvement in accessibility of high throughput DNA sequencing brought a great deal of attention to disease association and susceptibility studies. Successful genome-wide searches for disease-associated gene variations have been recently reported [18,26]. However, complex diseases can be caused by combinations of several unlinked gene variations. This chapter addresses computational challenges of genotype data analysis in epidemiological studies including selecting of informative SNPs, searching for diseases associated SNPs, and predicting of genotype susceptibility.

Disease association studies analyze genetic variation across exposed to a disease (diseased) and healthy (non diseased) individuals. The difference between individual DNA sequences occurs at a single base sites, in which more than one allele is observed across population. Such variations are called single nucleotide polymorphisms (SNPs). The number of simultaneously typed SNPs for association and linkage studies is reaching 10^6 for SNP Mapping Arrays [1]. High density maps of SNPs as well as massive DNA data with large number of individuals and number of SNPs become publicly available [12]. Diploid organisms, like human, have two near identical copies of each chromosome. Most genotyping techniques (e.g., SNP Mapping Arrays [1]) do not provide separate SNP sequences (*haplotypes*) for each of the two

Bioinformatics Algorithms: Techniques and Applications, Edited by Ion I. Măndoiu and Alexander Zelikovsky

chromosomes. Instead, they provide SNP sequences (*genotypes*) representing mixtures of two haplotypes—each site is defined by an unordered pair of allele readings, one from each haplotype—while haplotypes are computationally inferred from genotypes [5]. To genotype data we refer as unphased data and to haplotype data we refer as phased data. The disease association study analyze data given as genotypes or haplotypes with disease status.

Several challenges in genome-wide association studies of complex diseases have not yet been adequately addressed [10]: interaction between nonlinked genes, multiple independent causes, multiple testing adjustment, and so on. Since complex common diseases can be caused by multiloci interactions, two-loci analysis can be more powerful than traditional one-by-one SNP association analysis [24]. Multiloci analysis is expected to find even deeper disease-associated interactions. The computational challenge (as pointed in [10]) is caused by the dimension catastrophe. Indeed, two-SNP interaction analysis (which can be more powerful than traditional one-by-one SNP association analysis [24]) for a genome-wide scan with 1 million SNPs (3 kb coverage) will afford 10^{12} possible pairwise tests. Multi-SNP interaction analysis reveals even deeper disease-associated interactions but is usually computationally infeasible and its statistical significance drastically decreases after multiple testing adjustment [25,29].

Disease-association analysis searches for a SNP with frequency among diseased individuals (cases) considerably higher than among nondiseased individuals (controls). Only statistically significant SNPs (whose frequency distribution has p-value less than 0.05) are reported. Successful as well as unsuccessful searches for SNPs with statistically significant association have been recently reported for different diseases and different suspected human genome regions (see e.g., [9]). Unfortunately, reported findings are frequently not reproducible on different populations. It is believed that this happens because the p-values are unadjusted to multiple testing—indeed, if the reported SNP is found among 100 SNPs then the probability that the SNP is associated with a disease by mere chance becomes roughly 100 times larger.

This chapter discusses optimization approach to resolve these issues instead of traditionally used statistical and computational intelligence methods. In order to handle data with huge number of SNPs, one can extract informative (indexing) SNPs that can be used for (almost) lossless reconstructing of all other SNPs [34]. To avoid information loss, index SNPs are chosen based on how well the other nonindex SNPs can be reconstructed. The corresponding informative SNP selection problem (ISSP) can be formulated as follows (See Fig. 18.1). Given a sample S of a population P of *individuals* (either haplotypes or genotypes) on m SNPs, select positions of k $(k < m)$ SNPs such that for any individual, one can predict non selected SNPs from these k selected SNPs. The em Multiple Linear Regression based MLR-tagging algorithm [16] solves the optimization version of ISSP that asks for k informative SNPs *minimizing the prediction error* measured by the number of incorrectly predicted SNPs. The number of tags (informative SNPs) k depends on the desirable data size. More tags will keep more genotype information while less tags allows deeper analysis and search.

In the reduced set of SNPs one can search for deeper disease association. In this chapter, we discuss the optimization problem of finding the most disease-associated

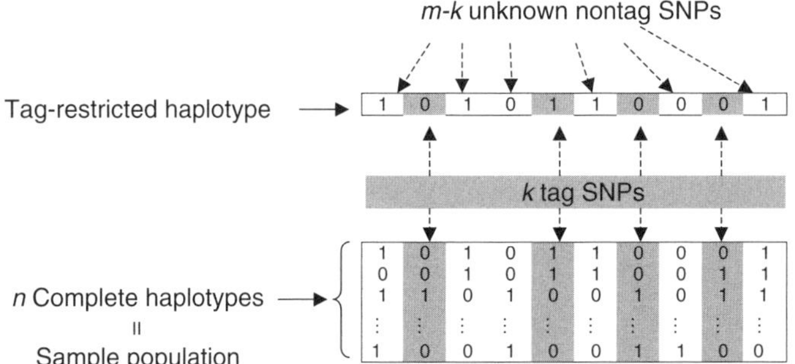

FIGURE 18.1 Informative SNP selection problem (ISSP). The shaded columns correspond to k tag SNPs and the clear columns correspond to nontag SNPs. The unknown m-k nontag SNP values in tag-restricted individual (top) are predicted based on the known k tag values and complete sample population.

multi-SNP combination for given case-control data. Since it is plausible that common diseases can have also genetic resistance factors, one can also search for *the most disease-resistant multi-SNP combination.* Association of risk or resistance factors with the disease can be measured in terms of p-value of the skew in case and control frequencies, risk rates or odds rates. Here we concentrate on two association measurements: p-value of the skew in case and control frequencies and *positive predictive value* (PPV), which is the frequency of case individuals among all individuals with a given multi-SNP combination. This optimization problem is NP-hard and can be viewed as a generalization of the maximum independent set problem. A fast *complimentary greedy search* proposed in [6] is compared with the *exhaustive search* and *combinatorial search* that has been discussed in [7]. Although complimentary greedy search cannot guarantee finding of close to optimum MSCs, in the experiments with real data, it finds MSCs with nontrivially high PPV. For example, for Crohn's disease data [11], complimentary greedy search finds in less than second a case-free MSC containing 24 controls, while exhaustive and combinatorial searches need more than 1 day to find case-free MSCs with at most 17 controls.

We next address the disease susceptibility prediction problem (see [19,21,23,30,32]) exploiting the developed methods for searching associated risk and resistance factors. A novel optimum clustering problem formulation has been proposed in [6]. There has also been suggested a model-fitting method transforming a clustering algorithm into the corresponding model-fitting susceptibility prediction algorithm. Since common diseases can be caused by multiple independent and coexisting factors, an association-based clustering of case/control population has been proposed in [6]. The resulted association-based combinatorial prediction algorithm significantly outperforms existing prediction methods. For all three real datasets that were available to us (Crohn's disease [11], autoimmune disorder [31], and tick-borne encephalitis [4]) the accuracy of the prediction based on combinatorial search is respectively, 76%, 74%, and 80%, which is higher by 7% compared to the accuracy of all previously known methods implemented in [22,23]. The accuracy of the prediction based on complimentary greedy search almost matches the best accuracy but is much more scalable.

The next section formulates the Informative SNP Selection Problem and discusses MLR-tagging method for informative SNPs extraction. In Section 18.3 the disease association search problem is formulated, the searching algorithms and their quality measures are described, the optimization version of disease association search is reformulated as an independent set problem and the fast complimentary greedy search algorithm is given. Section 18.4 is devoted to the disease susceptibility prediction problem. The prediction and relevant clustering optimization problem formulations are given, the model-fitting approach of transforming clustering into prediction and corresponding two prediction algorithms are described. Section 18.5 compares the MLR tag selection [16] with STAMPA [15] and discusses the application of association search and susceptibility prediction methods [6] to three real datasets.

18.2 INFORMATIVE SNP SELECTION

In this section we first briefly overview several tagging algorithms and then give detailed overview of the MLR-tagging algorithm [16].

Originally, haplotype tags have been selected based on the squared correlation R^2 between true and predicted SNPs in [8] and true and predicted halotype dosage in [28]. Since linkage disequilibrium is usually higher for closer SNPs, the entire SNP sequence is partitioned into blocks ([2,33]) based on limited haplotype variability and then select tags in each block separately thus ensuring high correlation between tags and predicted SNPs.

Reconstructing an individual from its typed tag SNPs has received much less attention. Zhang et al. [33] presents a method for selecting tag SNPs based on haplotype data, then reconstructing haplotypes with the partition-ligation-expectation-maximization algorithm. Halldorsson et al. [14] describes a block-free approach for tag selection. Their method considers a graph with vertices representing SNPs and edges if one SNP can be used to predict the other. The vertices (SNPs) with high degree are chosen as tags. To predict a nontag SNP, that SNP's neighbor's values are inspected and a majority vote is taken. The method is tested with leave-one-out cross validation and can recover 90% of the haplotype data using only 20% of SNPs as tags.

Halperin et al. [15] describes a new method STAMPA for SNP prediction and tag selection. A SNP is predicted by inspecting the two closest tag SNPs from both sides; the value of the unknown SNP is given by a majority vote over the two tag SNPs. They use dynamic programming to select tags to reach best prediction score. Their methods are compared with ldSelect and HapBlock on a variety of datasets, and could predict with 80% accuracy the SNPs in the Daly dataset [11] using only 2 SNPs as tags.

Lee et al. [20] introduce BNTagger, a new method for tagging SNP selection, based on conditional independence among SNPs. Using the formalism of Bayesian networks (BNs), their system aims to select a subset of independent and highly predictive SNPs. For example, BNTagger uses 10% tags to reach 90% prediction accuracy. However, BNTagger comes at the cost of compromised running time. Its running time varies from several minutes (when the number of SNPs is 52) to 2–4 h (when the number is 103).

18.2.1 MLR-Tagging Algorithm

The MLR-tagging algorithm [16] for solving the ISSP on genotypes is based on multiple linear regression analysis. This method directly predicts genotypes without the explicit requirement of haplotypes.

Usually, a genotype is represented by a vector with coordinates 0, 1, or 2, where 0 represents the homozygous site with major allele, 1 represents the homozygous site with minor allele, and 2 represents the heterozygous site. Respectively, each haplotype's coordinate is 0 or 1, where 0 represents the major allele and 1 represents the minor allele. The sample population S together with the tag-restricted individual x are represented as a matrix M. The matrix M has $n + 1$ rows corresponding to n sample individuals and the individual x and $k + 1$ columns corresponding to k tag SNPs and a single nontag SNP s. All values in M are known except the value of s in x. In case of haplotypes, there are only two possible resolutions of s, namely, s_0 and s_1 with the unknown SNP value equal to 0 or 1, respectively. For genotypes, there are 3 possible resolutions s_0, s_1, and s_2 corresponding to SNP values 0, 1, or 2, respectively. The SNP prediction method should chose correct resolution of s.

Given the values of k tags of an unknown individual x and the known full sample S, a SNP prediction algorithm A_k predicts the value of a single nontag SNP s in x (if there is more than one nontag SNP to predict, then each one is handled separately). Therefore, without loss of generality, each individual is assumed to have exactly $k + 1$ SNPs.

18.2.1.1 Multiple Linear Regression Method The general purpose of multiple linear regression is to learn the relationship between several independent variables and a response variable. The multiple linear regression model is given by

$$\boldsymbol{y} = \beta_0 + \beta_1 \boldsymbol{x}_1 + \beta_2 \boldsymbol{x}_2 + \cdots + \beta_k \boldsymbol{x}_k + \epsilon = \boldsymbol{X}\beta + \epsilon, \tag{18.1}$$

where $\boldsymbol{y}$ is the response variable (represented by a column with n coordinates $(k \leq n - 1)$), $\boldsymbol{x}_i$, $i = 1, \ldots, k$ are independent variables (columns), β_i, $i = 1, \ldots, k$ are regression coefficients, and ϵ (a column) is the model error. The regression coefficient β_i represents the independent contribution of the independent variable x_i to the prediction of $\boldsymbol{y}$. The MLR method computes b_i, $i = 1, \ldots, k$ to estimate unknown *true coefficients* β_i, $i = 1, \ldots, k$ to minimize the error $||\epsilon||$ using the least squares method. Geometrically speaking, in the *estimation space span*(X), which is the linear closure of vectors x_i, $i = 1, \ldots, k$, we find the vector $\hat{y} = b_0 + b_1 x_1 + b_2 x_2 + \cdots + b_k x_k = Xb$ estimating y. The vector $\hat{y}$ minimizing distance (error) $||\epsilon|| = ||\hat{y} - y||$ is the projection of y on span(X) and equals $\hat{y} = X(X^t X)^{-1} X^t y$. Given the values of independent variables $x^* = (x_1^*, \ldots, x_k^*)$, the MLR method can predict (estimate) the corresponding response variable y^* with $\hat{y}^* = x^*(X^t X)^{-1} X^t y$.

18.2.1.2 SNP Prediction In SNP prediction, y is a nontag SNP and x_i, $i = 1, \ldots, k$ are tags. Given the known tag values x^* in an individual, the nontag SNP value y^* should be predicted. There are three possible values for each SNP (-1, 0, 1) corresponding to homozygous major allele, heterozygous allele, and homozygous minor allele. Note that rather than encode SNP with more common notations (0, 2, 1), we use $(-1, 0, 1)$-notation, called sigma-encoding. An obvious way to predict y^* is to round expression (3) for $\hat{y}^*$. Instead MLR SNP prediction algorithm finds the value of $(-1, 0$, or $1)$ that better fits the MLR model (1), that is, minimizes the error $||\epsilon||$. The MLR SNP prediction method proposed in [16] considers all possible resolutions of s together with the set of tag SNPs T as the vectors in $(n+1)$-dimensional Euclidean space. It assumes that the most probable resolution of s should be the "closest" to T. The distance between resolution of s and T is measured between s and its projection on the vector space span(T), the span of the set of tag SNPs T (see Fig. 18.2).

Formally, let T be the $(n+1) \times k$ matrix consisting of $n+1$ rows corresponding to a tag-restricted genotype $x = (x_1^*, \ldots, x_k^*)$ and n sample genotypes x_i, $i = \overline{1, n}$, from X, $g_i = \{x_{i,1}, \ldots, x_{i,k}\}$, whose k coordinates correspond to k tag SNPs. The SNP s, a nontag SNP, is represented by a $(n+1)$-column with known values y_i, $i = \overline{1, n}$, for genotypes from X and the unknown value y^* for the genotype g which should be predicted.

$$T = \begin{bmatrix} x_1^* & \ldots & x_k^* \\ x_{1,1} & \ldots & x_{1,k} \\ \vdots & \ddots & \vdots \\ x_{n,1} & \ldots & x_{n,k} \end{bmatrix} \qquad s = \begin{bmatrix} y^* \\ y_{1,k+1} \\ \vdots \\ y_{n,k+1} \end{bmatrix}$$

Let $d = ||\epsilon||$ be the least square distance between s and T, that is, $d = |T \cdot (T^t \cdot T)^{-1} \cdot T^t \cdot s - s|$. The algorithm finds the value $(-1, 0$ or $1)$ for y^* and selects one minimizing d.

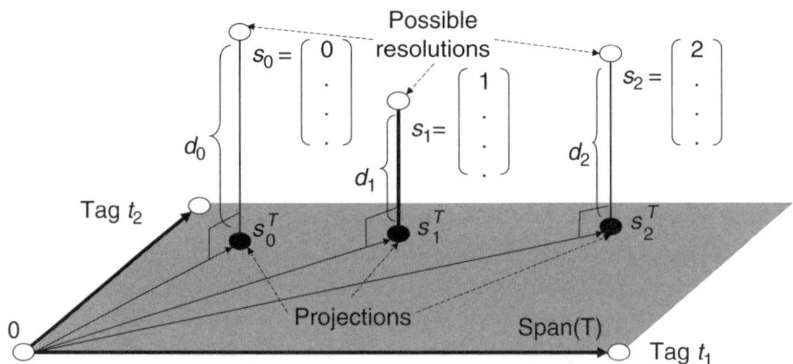

FIGURE 18.2 MLR SNP Prediction algorithm. Three possible resolutions s_0,s_1, and s_2 of s are projected on the span of tag SNPs (a dark plane). The unknown SNP value is predicted 1 since the distance between s_1 and its projection s_1^T is the shorter than for s_0 and s_2.

18.2.1.3 Tag Selection Algorithm starts with the best tag t_0, that is, the SNP minimizing the error when predicting all other SNPs. Then it finds tag t_1 which minimizes the prediction error of the tag set (t_0, t_1) as follows. Each nontag SNP is added to the original tag set, then other SNPs are predicted from the extended set using MLR SNP prediction. The SNP that achieves the highest prediction accuracy will be t_1. Best tags are added until reaching the specified size k.

18.2.1.4 Running Time Computing of $T^t \cdot T$ is $O(nk^2)$ since T is a $n \times k$ matrix and T^t is a $k \times n$ matrix. For inverting the $k \times k$ matrix $T^t \cdot T$, $O(k^3)$ steps are needed. Let $k < n$, then the running time for computing $T' = T \cdot (T^t \cdot T)^{-1} \cdot T^t$ is $O(n^2k)$. The matrix of T' is the same for all these (m-k) nontag SNPs, thus, the total running time for predicting a complete individual is $O(kn^2 + n^2(m - k)) = O(n^2m)$. If $k \geq n$, then only $(n - 1)/2$ closest tags to the right and to the left of the predicted SNP are used. There are only $k - n + 1$ different matrices T' to compute and the total running time is $O(n^3m)$. The MLR SNP prediction need knm steps for prediction, thus, the total runtime of MLR-tagging is $O(knmT) = O(kn^3m^2)$ when $k < n$ and $O(kn^4m^2)$ when $k \geq n$.

18.3 DISEASE ASSOCIATION SEARCH

In this section, the search of statistically significant disease-associated multi-SNP combinations is formally described. Then the corresponding optimization problem is formulated and its complexity is discussed. The combinatorial search introduced in [7] and the fast complementary greedy search introduced in [6] are described.

The typical case/control or cohort study results in a sample population S consisting of n individuals represented by values of m SNPs and the disease status. Since it is expensive to obtain individual chromosomes, each SNP value attains one of three values 0, 1, or 2, where 0s and 1s denote homozygous sites with major allele and minor allele, respectively, and 2s stand for heterozygous sites. SNPs with more than 2 alleles are rare and can be conventionally represented as biallelic. Thus the sample S is an $(0, 1, 2)$-valued $n \times (m + 1)$-matrix, where each row corresponds to an individual, each column corresponds to a SNP except last column corresponding to the disease status (0 stands for disease and 1 stands for nondisease). Let S_0 and S_1 be the subsets of rows with nondisease and disease status, respectively. For simplicity, it is assumed that there are no two rows identical in all SNP columns.

Risk and resistance factors representing gene variation interaction can be defined in terms of SNPs as follows. A *multi-SNP combination* (MSC) C is a subset of SNP-columns of S (denoted snp(C)) and the values of these SNPs, 0, 1, or 2[1]. The subset of individuals-rows of S whose restriction on columns of snp(C) coincide with values of C is denoted cluster(C). A subset of individuals is called a *cluster* if it coincides with cluster(C) for a certain MSC C. For example, if S is represented by an identity

[1] In this chapter we restrict ourselves to 0,1, or 2, while in general, the values of MSC can also be negations $\bar{0}$, $\bar{1}$ or $\bar{2}$, where $\bar{i}$ means that MSC is required to have value unequal to i.

matrix I_5, then rows 3, 4, and 5 form a cluster for MSC C with $snp(C) = \{1, 2\}$ and both values equal to 0. Obviously, a subset X of rows of S may not form a cluster, but it always can be represented as a union of clusters, for example, as a union of trivial clusters containing its individual rows. Let $h(C) = \text{cluster}(C) \cap S_0$ be the set of control individuals and $d(C) = \text{cluster}(C) \cap S_1$ be the set of diseased individuals in cluster(C).

The association of an MSC C with the disease status can be measured with the following parameters ($h = |h(C)|, d = |d(C)|, H = |S_0|, D = |S_1|$):

- odds ratio $OR = \frac{d\cdot(H-h)}{h\cdot(D-d)}$ (for case-control studies)
- relative risk $RR = \frac{d\cdot(H+D-h-d)}{(D-d)(h+d)}$ (for cohort studies)
- positive predictive value $PPV = \frac{d}{h+d}$ (for susceptibility prediction)
- p-value of the partition of the cluster into cases and controls:

$$p = \sum_{k=0}^{d} \binom{h+d}{k} \left(\frac{D}{H+D}\right)^k \left(\frac{H}{H+D}\right)^{h+d-k}.$$

Since MSCs are searched among all SNPs, the computed p-value requires adjustment for multiple testing which can be done with simple but overly pessimistic Bonferroni correction or computationally extensive but more accurate randomization method.

18.3.1 Accurate Searches for Associated MSCs

General disease association searches for all MSCs with one of the parameters above (or below) a certain threshold. The common formulation is to find all MSCs with adjusted p-value below 0.05.

18.3.1.1 Exhaustive Search (ES) The search for disease-associated MSCs among all possible combinations can be done by the following *exhaustive search*. In order to find a MSC with the p-value of the frequency distribution below 0.05, one should check all one-SNP, two-SNP, ..., m-SNP combinations. The checking procedure takes $O(n\sum_{k=1}^{m}\binom{m}{k}3^k)$ runtime for unphased combinations since there are three possible SNP values $\{0, 1, 2\}$. Similarly, for phased combination, the runtime is $O(n\sum_{k=1}^{m}\binom{m}{k}2^k)$ since there only two possible SNP values. The exhaustive search is infeasible even for small number of SNPs, therefore the search is limited to the small number of SNPs, that is, instead of searching all MSCs, one can search only containing at most $k = 1, 2, 3$ SNPs. We refer to k as *search level* of exhaustive search. Also one can reduce the depth (number of simultaneously interacting SNPs) or reduce m by extracting informative SNPs from which one can reconstruct all other SNPs. The MLR-tagging is used to choose maximum number of index SNPs that can be handled by ES in a reasonable computational time.

18.3.1.2 Combinatorial Search (CS) Here we discuss as suggested in [7] search method for disease-associated MSCs that avoids insignificant MSCs or clusters without loosing significant ones. CS searches only for closed MSCs, where closure is defined as follows. The *closure* $\bar{C}$ of MSC C is an MSC with minimum control elements $h(\bar{C})$ and the same case elements $d(\bar{C}) = d(C)$. $\bar{C}$ can be easily found by incorporating into snp(C) all SNP with common values among all case individuals in C.

The combinatorial search proposed [7] finds the best p-value of frequency distribution of the closure of each single SNP, after that it searches for the best frequency distribution p-value among closure of all 2-SNP combinations and so on. The procedure stops after all closure of all k-SNP combinations ($k < m$) are checked. The corresponding *search level* is the number of SNPs selected for closuring, for example, on the level 2 of searching combinatorial search will test closure of all 2-SNP combinations for association with a disease. Because of the closure, for the same level of searching combinatorial search finds better association than exhaustive search. However, the above combinatorial search is as slow as exhaustive search.

A faster implementation of this method avoids checking MSCs, which are not (and cannot lead to) statistically significant ones. Formally, a MSC C is called an *intersection* of MSC C_1 and C_2 if $d(C) = d(C_1) \cap d(C_2)$ and $|h(C)|$ is minimized. A MSC C is called *trivial* if its unadjusted p-value is larger than 0.05 even if the set $h(C)$ would be empty. Note that intersection of a trivial MSC with another is trivial.

A faster implementation of the combinatorial search is as follows:

1. Compute a set G_1 of all 1-SNP closed MSCs, exclude trivial combinations.
2. Compute sets G_k of all pairwise intersections of the MSCs from G_{k-1}, exclude trivial combinations and already existing in $G_1 \cup G_2 \cup \ldots \cup G_{k-1}$, $k = 2 \ldots N$.
3. For each G_k output MSCs whose unadjusted $p < 0.05$.

Still, in order to find all MSCs associated with a disease one has to check all possible SNP combinations with all possible SNP values. This searching approach is also computationally intensive and step 2 from the algorithm can generate an exponential number of MSCs. However, closure avoids generation and checking of nonsignificant MSCs. Additionally, removing of trivial MSCs at each iteration of step 2 considerably reduces the number of newly generated MSCs. CS has been shown much faster than ES and capable of finding more significant MSCs than ES for equivalent search level.

18.3.2 Approximate Search for Maximum Control-Free Cluster

Following [6], we next consider another optimization formulation corresponding to the general association search problem, for example, find MSC with the minimum adjusted p-value. In particular, we focus on maximization of PPV. Obviously, the MSC with maximum PPV should not contain control individuals in its cluster and the problem can be formulated as follows.

Maximum Control-Free Cluster Problem (MCFCP) Find a cluster C which does not contain control individuals and has the maximum number of case individuals.

It is not difficult to see that this problem includes the maximum independent set problem. Indeed, given a graph $G = (V, E)$, for each vertex v we put into correspondence a case individual v' and for each edge $e = (u, v)$ we put into correspondence a control individual e' such that any cluster containing u' and v' should also contain e' (e.g., u', v', and e' are identical except one SNP where they have three different values 0,1, and 2). Obviously, the maximum independent set of G corresponds to the maximum control-free cluster and vice versa. Thus, one cannot reasonably approximate MCFCP in polynomial time for an arbitrary sample S.

On the contrary, the sample S is not "arbitrary"—it comes from a certain disease association study. Therefore, one may have hope that simple heuristics (particularly greedy algorithms) can perform much better than in the worst arbitrary case.

18.3.2.1 Complimentary Greedy Search (CGS) In graphs, instead of the maximum independent set one can search for its complement, the minimum vertex cover-repeat picking, and removing vertices of maximum degree until no edges left. In this case one can minimize the relative cost of covering (or removal) of control individuals, which is the number of removed case individuals. The corresponding heuristic for MCFCP is the following.

Complimentary Greedy Search
  $C \leftarrow S$
  Repeat until $h(C) > 0$
    For each 1-SNP combination $X = (s, i)$, where s is a SNP and $i \in \{0, 1, 2\}$
      find $\bar{d} = d(C) - d(C \cap X))$ and $\bar{h} = h(C) - h(C \cap X)$
    Find 1-SNP combination X minimizing $\bar{d}/\bar{h}$
    $C \leftarrow C \cap X$

Similarly to the maximum control-free cluster corresponding to the most expressed risk factor, one can also search for the maximum diseased-free cluster corresponding to the most expressed resistance factor.

The experiments with three real datasets (see Section 18.6) show that the complimentary greedy search can find nontrivially large control-free and case-free clusters.

18.4 DISEASE SUSCEPTIBILITY PREDICTION

This section shows how to apply association search methods to disease susceptibility prediction following [6]. First the problem and cross-validation schemes are discussed. Then the relevant formulation of the optimum clustering problem is given and the general method how any clustering algorithm can be transformed into a prediction algorithm is described. We conclude with description of two association search-based prediction algorithms.

Below is the formal description of the problem from [6].

Disease Susceptibility Prediction Problem Given a sample population S (a training set) and one more individual $t \notin S$ with the known SNPs but unknown disease status (testing individual), find (predict) the unknown disease status.

The main drawback of such problem formulation that it cannot be considered as a standard optimization formulation. One cannot directly measure the quality of a prediction algorithm from the given input since it does not contain the predicted status.

A standard way to measure the quality of prediction algorithms is to apply a cross-validation scheme. In the leave-one-out cross validation, the disease status of each genotype in the population sample is predicted while the rest of the data is regarded as the training set. There are many types of leave-many-out cross validations where the testing set contains much larger subset of the original sample. Any cross-validation scheme produces a confusion table (see Table 18.1). The main objective is to maximize prediction accuracy, while all other parameters also reflect the quality of the algorithm.

18.4.1 Optimization Formulation

Paper [6] proposes to avoid cross validation and instead suggests a different objective by restricting the ways how prediction can be made. It is reasonable to require that every prediction algorithm should be able to predict the status inside the sample.

Therefore, such algorithms is supposed to be able to partition the sample into subsets based only on the values of SNPs, that is, partition of S into clusters defined by MSCs. Of course, a trivial clustering where each individual forms its own cluster can always perfectly distinguish between case and control individuals. On the contrary such clustering carries minimum information. Ideally, there should be two clusters perfectly distinguishing diseased from control individuals. There is a trade-off between number of clusters and the information carried by clustering which results in trade-off between number of errors (i.e., incorrectly clustered individuals) and informativeness which was proposed to measure by information entropy instead of number of clusters [6].

TABLE 18.1 Confusion Table

	True Disease Status		
	Cases	Controls	
Predicted case	True positive TP	False positive FP	Positive prediction value PPV= TP/(TP+FP)
Predicted control	False negative FN	True negative TN	Negative prediction value NPV= TN/(FN+TN)
	Sensitivity TP/(TP+FN)	Specificity TN/(FP+ TN)	Accuracy (TP+TN)/(TP+FP+FN+TN)

Optimum Disease Clustering Problem Given a population sample S, find a partition $\mathcal{P}$ of S into clusters $S = S_1 \cup \cdots \cup S_k$, with disease status 0 or 1 assigned to each cluster S_i, minimizing

$$\text{entropy}(\mathcal{P}) = -\sum_{i=1}^{k} \frac{|S_i|}{|S|} \ln \frac{|S_i|}{|S|}$$

for a given bound on the number of individuals who are assigned incorrect status in clusters of the partition $\mathcal{P}$, $\text{error}(\mathcal{P}) < \alpha \cdot |\mathcal{P}|$.

The above optimization formulation is obviously NP-hard but has a huge advantage over the prediction formulation that it does not rely on cross-validation and can be studied with combinatorial optimization techniques. Still, in order to make the resulted clustering algorithm useful, one needs to find a way how to apply it to the original prediction problem.

18.4.2 Model-Fitting Prediction

The following general approach has been proposed in [6]. Assuming that the clustering algorithm indeed distinguishes *real* causes of the disease, one may expect that the major reason for erroneous status assignment is in biases and lack of sampling. Then a plausible assumption is that a larger sample would lead to a lesser proportion of clustering errors. This implies the following transformation of clustering algorithm into prediction algorithm:

Clustering-based Model-Fitting Prediction Algorithm

Set disease status 0 for the testing individual t and
  Find the optimum (or approximate) clustering $\mathcal{P}_0$ of $S \cup \{t\}$
Set disease status 1 for the testing individual t and
  Find the optimum (or approximate) clustering $\mathcal{P}_1$ of $S \cup \{t\}$
Find which of two clusterings $\mathcal{P}_0$ or $\mathcal{P}_1$ better fits model, and
  accordingly predict status of t,

$$\text{status}(t) = \arg\min_{i=0,1} \text{error}(\mathcal{P}_i).$$

Two clustering algorithms based on combinatorial and complementary greedy association searches has been proposed in [6]. These clustering methods find for each individual an MSC or its cluster that contains it and is the most associated according to a certain characteristic (e.g., RR, PPV, or lowest p-value) with disease susceptibility and disease resistance. Then to each individual is attributed the ratio between these two characteristic values—maximum disease susceptibility and disease resistance. Although the resulted partition of the training set S is easy to find, it is still necessary to decide which threshold between case and control clusters should be used. The threshold can be chosen to minimize the clustering error.

The *combinatorial search-based prediction algorithm* (CSP) exploits combinatorial search to find the most-associated cluster for each individual. Empirically, the best association characteristic is found to be the relative risk rate RR. The *complimentary greedy search-based prediction algorithm* (CGSP) exploits complimentary greedy search to find the most-associated cluster for each individual. Empirically, the best association characteristic is found to be the positive predictive value PPV. The leave-one-out cross validation (see Section 18.5) shows significant advantage of CSP and GCSP over previously known prediction algorithms for all considered real datasets.

18.5 RESULTS AND DISCUSSION

In this section, we discuss the results of methods for searching disease associated multi-SNP combinations and susceptibility prediction on real datasets. We first describe four real datasets, then overview search and prediction methods and conclude with description and discussion of their performance. All experiments were ran on Processor Pentium 4 3.2Ghz, RAM 2Gb, OS Linux.

18.5.1 Datasets

Crohn's disease ($5q31$): The dataset Daly et al.[11] is derived from the 616 kilobase region of human Chromosome $5q31$ that may contain a genetic variant responsible for Crohn's disease by genotyping 103 SNPs for 129 trios. All offspring belong to the case population, while almost all parents belong to the control population. In the entire data, there are 144 case and 243 control individuals.
Autoimmune disorder: The dataset of Ueda et al.[31] are sequenced from 330 kb of human DNA containing gene CD28, CTLA4, and ICONS that are proved related to autoimmune disorder. A total of 108 SNPs were genotyped in 384 cases of autoimmune disorder and 652 controls.
Tick-borne encephalitis: The tick-borne encephalitis virus-induced dataset of Barkash et al. [4] consists of 41 SNPs genotyped from DNA of 21 patients with severe tick-borne encephalitis virus-induced disease and 54 patients with mild disease.
HapMap datasets: Regions ENr123 and ENm010 from two population: 45 Han Chinese from Beijing (HCB) and 44 Japanese from Tokyo (JPT) for three regions (ENm013, ENr112, ENr113) from 30 CEPH family trios obtained from HapMap ENCODE Project [12]. Two gene regions STEAP and TRPM8 from 30 CEPH family trios were obtained from HapMap.

The datasets have been phased using 2SNP software [5]. The missing data (16% in [11] and 10% in [31]) have been imputed in genotypes from the resulted haplotypes. We have also created corresponding haplotype datasets in which each individual is represented by a haplotype with the disease status inherited from the corresponding individual genotype.

TABLE 18.2 Number of Tags Used by MLR-Tagging, STAMPA and LR to Achieve 80% and 90% Prediction Accuracy in Leave-One-Out Tests

Acc.	Algorithm	ENm013 (360)	Enr112 (411)	ENr113 (514)	STEAP (22)	TRPM8 (101)	5q31 (103)
80%	MLR	2	6	4	1	1	1
	STAMPA	5	9	11	2	3	2
90%	MLR	6	14	10	1	4	5
	STAMPA	12	17	18	2	6	6

18.5.2 Informative SNP Selection

Two datasets from above have been used to measure the quality of the SNP prediction and informative SNP selection algorithms as well as comparison with the results of [15]. We use 2SNP algorithms [5] for resolving missing data. The SNPs with only one allele are removed from the original data.

We have applied leave-one-out cross validation to evaluate the quality of the MLR-tagging solution for the Genotype Tagging Problem as follows: (1) one by one, each genotype vector is removed from the sample, (2) tag SNPs are selected using only the remaining genotypes, and (3) the "left out" genotype is reconstructed based on its tag SNPs and the values of tag and nontag SNPs in the remaining genotypes. In Table 18.2, we compare MLR with STAMPA. Note that if one predicts each SNP as 0 (i.e., homozygous with major allele), then the prediction accuracy on STEAP, TRPM8, and 5q31 data will be 79.36%, 72.53%, and 63.57%, respectively. MLR first predicts each SNP as 0 and then gets even higher prediction accuracy when it uses a single tag while STAMPA requires at least two tags for prediction. STAMPA is asymptotically faster but MLR is more accurate compared on four HapMap datasets.

18.5.3 Search for Disease-Associated MSCs

Here we discuss the results of four methods for searching disease associated MSCs on real phased and unphased datasets. The p-values of the frequency distribution of the found MSCs are used as a quality measurement.

18.5.3.1 Search Methods We have compared the following five methods for search disease-associated MSCs.

- Exhaustive search (ES).
- Indexed exhaustive search (IES(30)): exhaustive search on the indexed datasets obtained by extracting 30 indexed SNPs with MLR based tagging method [17].
- Combinatorial search (CS).
- Indexed combinatorial search (ICS(30)): combinatorial search on the indexed datasets obtained by extracting 30 indexed SNPs with MLR based tagging method [17].

- Complimentary greedy search (CGS): approximate search for the maximum control-free cluster.

Significant MSCs have been found only on levels 1 and 2 because adjusted p-value grows with the level. The size of the datasets is large enough to make exhaustive search impossible even for a combination of 6 SNPs.

18.5.3.2 Comparison of Accurate Searches The quality of searching methods is compared by the number of found statistically significant MSCs (see the seventh column) in genotypes (see Table 18.3) and haplotypes (see Table 18.4). Since statistical significance should be adjusted to multiple testing, we report for each method and dataset the 0.05 threshold adjusted for multiple testing (this threshold is computed by randomization and given in the third column of Tables 18.3 and 18.4). In the third, fourth, and fifth columns, we give the frequencies of the best MSC among case and control population and the unadjusted p-value, respectively.

TABLE 18.3 Comparison of Four Methods for Searching Disease-Associated Multi-SNPs Combinations for Unphased Genotype Datasets

		SNP Combination with Minimum p-value			p-value	# of MSCs	
Search Level	Search Method	Case Frequency	Control Frequency	Unadjusted p-value	Corresp. to MT-Adjusted p=0.05	with MT-Adjusted p<0.05	Runtime s
Crohn's disease [11]							
1	ES	0.31	0.16	1.8×10^{-3}	1.6×10^{-3}	0	0.9
	IES(30)	0.30	0.16	4.7×10^{-3}	3.9×10^{-3}	0	0.5
	CS	0.30	0.11	2.0×10^{-5}	5.1×10^{-5}	2	1.0
	ICS(30)	0.30	0.14	4.6×10^{-3}	2.2×10^{-4}	1	0.6
2	ES	0.30	0.13	3.1×10^{-4}	1.9×10^{-5}	0	15.0
	IES(30)	0.31	0.14	4.4×10^{-4}	1.0×10^{-4}	0	1.0
	CS	0.17	0.02	6.5×10^{-7}	1.5×10^{-6}	2	7.0
	ICS(30)	0.17	0.04	3.7×10^{-5}	5.0×10^{-5}	1	0.4
Autoimmune disorder[31]							
1	ES	0.43	0.28	1.1×10^{-4}	1.3×10^{-3}	2	1.0
	IES(30)	0.43	0.28	1.1×10^{-4}	3.1×10^{-3}	4	0.6
	CS	0.43	0.28	9.2×10^{-5}	1.8×10^{-4}	2	1.1
	ICS(30)	0.43	0.28	1.1×10^{-4}	1.6×10^{-3}	4	0.6
2	ES	0.25	0.12	1.5×10^{-6}	2.7×10^{-6}	2	30.0
	IES(30)	0.25	0.12	1.5×10^{-6}	8.0×10^{-5}	9	3.0
	CS	0.16	0.06	8.5×10^{-7}	1.1×10^{-6}	3	20.0
	ICS(30)	0.25	0.12	1.1×10^{-6}	4.7×10^{-5}	10	1.0
Tick-borne encephalitis virus-induced disease [4]							
1	ES	0.33	0.07	1.5×10^{-2}	6.1×10^{-3}	0	0.08
	IES(30)	0.33	0.07	1.5×10^{-2}	9.4×10^{-3}	0	0.03
	CS	0.33	0.00	1.3×10^{-4}	4.8×10^{-4}	1	0.08
	ICS(30)	0.33	0.02	8.1×10^{-4}	8.1×10^{-4}	1	0.03
2	ES	0.29	0.00	4.8×10^{-4}	2.5×10^{-4}	0	0.82
	IES(30)	0.29	0.00	4.8×10^{-4}	1.3×10^{-4}	0	0.10
	CS	0.33	0.00	1.3×10^{-4}	4.3×10^{-5}	0	0.60
	ICS(30)	0.29	0.00	4.8×10^{-4}	1.3×10^{-4}	0	0.08

TABLE 18.4 Comparison of Four Methods for Searching Disease-Associated Multi-SNPs Combinations for Phased Genotype Datasets

Search Level	Search Method	SNP Combination with Minimum p-value: Case Frequency	Control Frequency	Unadjusted p-value	p-value corresp. to MT-Adjusted p=0.05	# of MSCs with MT-Adjusted p<0.05	Runtime s
Crohn's disease [11]							
1	ES	0.52	0.40	9.7×10^{-3}	2.4×10^{-3}	0	1.0
	IES(30)	0.52	0.41	1.6×10^{-2}	7.2×10^{-3}	0	0.6
	CS	0.52	0.36	4.3×10^{-4}	1.3×10^{-4}	0	1.1
	ICS(30)	0.52	0.40	1.0×10^{-2}	1.6×10^{-2}	1	0.7
2	ES	0.05	0.01	1.4×10^{-3}	3.0×10^{-5}	0	23.0
	IES(30)	0.55	0.42	5.5×10^{-3}	1.7×10^{-4}	0	3.0
	CS	0.48	0.30	5.9×10^{-5}	7.0×10^{-7}	0	17.0
	ICS(30)	0.48	0.35	3.1×10^{-3}	5.8×10^{-5}	0	1.0
Autoimmune disorder [31]							
1	ES	0.65	0.53	3.2×10^{-4}	9.2×10^{-4}	2	6.0
	IES(30)	0.66	0.55	1.4×10^{-3}	5.3×10^{-3}	2	2.0
	CS	0.37	0.28	2.9×10^{-4}	8.3×10^{-4}	5	6.2
	ICS(30)	0.66	0.55	1.4×10^{-3}	7.4×10^{-2}	10	2.1
2	ES	0.17	0.09	6.8×10^{-7}	2.1×10^{-6}	2	173.0
	IES(30)	0.19	0.12	3.7×10^{-5}	1.7×10^{-4}	2	16.0
	CS	0.02	0.00	1.6×10^{-8}	5.0×10^{-7}	8	75.0
	ICS(30)	0.19	0.12	3.0×10^{-5}	9.5×10^{-5}	2	5.7
Tick-borne encephalitis virus-induced disease [4]							
1	ES	0.33	0.16	4.1×10^{-2}	2.3×10^{-3}	0	0.13
	IES(30)	0.33	0.16	4.1×10^{-2}	4.1×10^{-3}	0	0.06
	CS	0.24	0.05	4.1×10^{-3}	1.3×10^{-4}	0	0.14
	ICS(30)	0.24	0.05	4.1×10^{-3}	2.7×10^{-4}	0	0.06
2	ES	0.24	0.05	4.1×10^{-3}	1.7×10^{-4}	0	2.40
	IES(30)	0.29	0.00	4.8×10^{-4}	2.8×10^{-4}	0	1.10
	CS	0.30	0.06	6.2×10^{-4}	1.5×10^{-4}	0	2.03
	ICS(30)	0.29	0.00	4.8×10^{-4}	1.7×10^{-4}	0	0.80

18.5.3.3 Comparison of Approximate and Accurate Searches We have compared IES(30) and ICS(30) with CGS (see Section 18.3) for search disease associated multi-SNP combinations with the largest PPV.

The quality of searching methods is compared by the PPV of found clusters as well as their statistical significance Table 18.5.

18.5.4 Disease Susceptibility Prediction Methods

We compare the prediction algorithms based on combinatorial and complimentary greedy searches (see Section 18.4) proposed [6] with the following three prediction methods. We have chosen these three methods out of six compared in [23] and two other methods from [22] since they have best prediction results for two real datasets [11] and [31].

TABLE 18.5 Comparison of Three Methods for Searching the Disease-Associated and Disease-Resistant Multi-SNPs Combinations with the Largest PPV. The Starred Values Refer to Results of the Runtime-Constrained Exhaustive Search

		Max PPV Risk Factor				Max PPV Resistance Factor			
Dataset of	Search Method	Case Freq.	Control Freq.	Unadjusted p-value	Run time s	Case Freq.	Control Freq.	Unadjusted p-value	Run time s
Crohn's	IES(30)	0.09*	0.00	8.7×10^{-7}	21530	0.00	0.07*	3.7×10^{-4}	869
disease	ICS(30)	0.11	0.00	3.1×10^{-9}	7360	0.00	0.09	5.7×10^{-5}	708
[11]	CGS	0.06	0.00	1.4×10^{-4}	0.1	0.00	0.10	2.2×10^{-5}	0.1
Autoimmune	IES(30)	0.04*	0.00	2.5×10^{-8}	7633	0.00	0.04*	4.0×10^{-6}	39
disorder	ICS(30)	0.04	0.00	2.5×10^{-8}	5422	0.00	0.04	4.0×10^{-6}	36
[31]	CGS	0.02	0.00	3.4×10^{-4}	0.1	0.00	0.04	2.5×10^{-5}	0.1
Tick-borne	ES	0.29*	0.00	4.8×10^{-4}	820	0.00	0.39	1.0×10^{-3}	567
encephalitis	CS	0.33	0.00	1.3×10^{-4}	780	0.00	0.39	1.0×10^{-3}	1
[4]	CGS	0.19	0.00	6.1×10^{-3}	0.1	0.00	0.32	3.8×10^{-3}	0.1

Support Vector Machine (SVM) SVM is a generation learning system based on recent advances in statistical learning theory. SVMs deliver state-of-the-art performance in real world applications and have been used in case/control studies [21,32]. We use SVM-light [13] with the radial basis function with $\gamma = 0.5$.

Random Forest (RF) A random forest is a collection of CART-like trees following specific rules for tree growing, tree combination, self-testing, and postprocessing. We use Leo Breiman and Adele Cutler's original implementation of RF version 5.1 [3]. RF tries to perform regression to generate the suitable model and using bootstrapping produces random trees.

LP-based Prediction Algorithm (LP) This method is based on a graph $X = \{H, G\}$, where the vertices H correspond to distinct haplotypes and the edges G correspond to genotypes connecting its two haplotypes. The density of X is increased by dropping SNPs which do not collapse edges with opposite status. Solving a linear program it assigns weights to haplotypes such that for any control genotype the sum of weights of its haploptypes is less than 0.5 and greater than 0.5 otherwise. We maximize the sum of absolute values of weights over all genotypes. The status of testing genotype is predicted as sum of its end points [22].

Table 18.6 reports comparison of all considered prediction methods. Their quality is measured by sensitivity, specificity, accuracy, and runtime. Since prediction accuracy is the most important quality measure, it is given in bold.[2] Figure 18.3 shows the receiver operating characteristics (ROC) representing the trade off between specificity and sensitivity. ROC is computed for all five prediction methods applied to the tick-borne encephalitis data [4].

[2]The prediction accuracy of methods CGSP and CSP has been erroneously reported [6], in this chapter, we report corrected values in Table 18.6.

TABLE 18.6 Leave-One-Out Cross Validation Results of Four Prediction Methods for Three Real Datasets. Results of Combinatorial Search-Based Prediction (CSP) and Complimentary Greedy Search-Based Prediction (CGSP) are Given When 20, 30, or all SNPs are Chosen as Informative SNPs

		Prediction Methods								
	Quality				CGSP			CSP		
Dataset	Measure	SVM	LP	RF	20	30	all	20	30	all
Crohn's	Sensitivity	20.8	37.5	34.0	28.5	72.1	53.1	63.9	72.0	—
disease	Specificity	88.8	88.5	85.2	90.9	69.1	90.0	74.2	81.7	—
[11]	**Accuracy**	**63.6**	**69.5**	**66.1**	**68.2**	**70.5**	**76.3**	**70.2**	**76.1**	**—**
	Runtime (h)	3.0	4.0	0.08	0.01	0.17	9.0	611	1189	∞
Autoimmune	Sensitivity	14.3	7.1	18.0	29.4	32.3	46.3	60.9	71.0	—
disorder	Specificity	88.2	91.2	92.8	90.7	84.0	85.7	75.0	80.1	—
[31]	**Accuracy**	**60.9**	**61.3**	**65.1**	**68.0**	**68.2**	**73.5**	**69.3**	**74.2**	**—**
	Runtime (h)	7.0	10.0	0.20	0.01	0.32	25.6	9175	17400	∞
Tick-borne	Sensitivity	11.4	16.8	12.7	51.9	42.4	56.7	77.5	70.2	67.2
encephalitis	Specificity	93.2	92.0	95.0	90.2	93.1	89.4	86.2	87.4	89.4
[4]	**Accuracy**	**72.2**	**75.5**	**74.2**	**75.3**	**75.7**	**76.0**	**79.1**	**79.5**	**80.3**
	Runtime (h)	0.2	0.08	0.01	0.01	0.01	0.02	1.8	6.3	8.5

18.5.5 Discussion

Comparing indexed counterparts with exhaustive and combinatorial searches shows that indexing is quite successful. Indeed, indexed search finds the same MSCs as

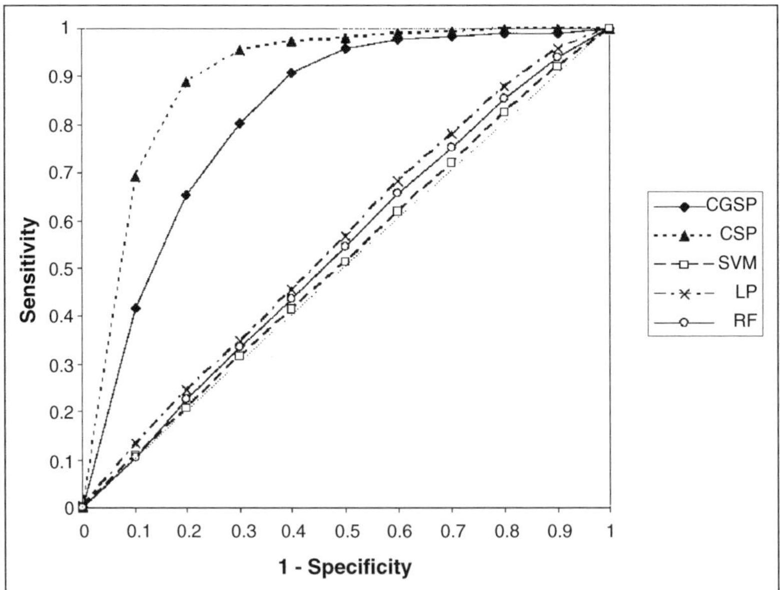

FIGURE 18.3 The receiver operating characteristics (ROC) for the five prediction methods applied to the tick-borne encephalitis data [4]. All SNPs are considered tags for CGSP and CSP.

nonindexed search but it is much faster and its multiple testing adjusted 0.05-threshold is higher and easier to meet.

Comparing combinatorial searches with the exhaustive counterparts is advantageous to the former. Indeed, for unphased data [11] the exhaustive search on the first and second search levels is unsuccessful while the combinatorial search finds several statistically significant MSCs for the same searching level. Similarly, for unphased and phased data of [31], the combinatorial search found much more statistically significant MSCs than the exhaustive search for the same searching level.

Results show (see Tables 18.3 and 18.4) that the indexing approach and the combinatorial search method are very promising techniques for searching statistically significant diseases-associated MSCs that can lead to discovery disease causes. The next step is biological validation of statistically significant MSCs discovered by proposed searching methods.

The comparison of three association searches (see Table 18.5) shows that combinatorial search always finds the same or larger cluster than exhaustive search and is significantly faster. The usage of search method runtime is critical in deciding whether it can be used in the clustering and susceptibility prediction. Note that both the exhaustive and combinatorial searches are prohibitively slow on the first two datasets and, therefore, we reduce these datasets to 30 index SNPs while complementary greedy search is fast enough to handle the complete datasets. This resulted in improvement of the complementary greedy over combinatorial search for the first dataset when search for the largest case-free cluster—after compression to 30 tags the best cluster simply disappears.

The comparison of the proposed association search-based and previously known susceptibility prediction algorithms (see Table 18.6) shows a considerable advantage of new methods. Indeed, for the first dataset the best proposed method (CGSP) beats the previously best method (LP) in prediction accuracy 76.3–69.5%. For the second dataset, the respective numbers are 74.2% (CSP(30)) to 65.1% (RF), and for the third dataset that are 80.3% (CSP) to 75.5% (LP). It is important that this lead is the result of much higher sensitivity of new methods—the specificity is almost always very high since all prediction methods tend to be biased toward nondiseased status. The ROC curve also illustrates advantage of CSP and GCSP over previous methods. Indeed the area under ROC curve for CSP is 0.81, for SVM is 0.52 compared with random guessing area of 0.5. Another important issue is how proposed prediction algorithms tolerate data compression. The prediction accuracy (especially sensitivity) increases for CGSP when more SNPs are made available, for example, for the second dataset, the sensitivity grows from 29.4% (20 SNPs) to 32.3% (30 SNPs) to 46.3% (all 108 SNPs).

We conclude that the indexing approach, the combinatorial and complementary greedy search methods, and association search-based susceptibility prediction algorithms are very promising techniques that can possibly help (i) to discover gene interactions causing common diseases and (ii) to create diagnostic tools for genetic epidemiology of common diseases.

REFERENCES

1. Affymetrix (2005). *http://www.affymetrix.com/products/arrays/*
2. Avi-Itzhak HI, Su X, de la Vega FM. Selection of minimum subsets of single nucleotide polymorphism to capture haplotype block diversity. *Proc Pac Symp Biocomput* 2003; 8:466–477.
3. Breiman L, Cutler A. http://www.stat.berkeley.edu/users/breiman/RF
4. Brinza D, Perelygin A, Brinton M, Zelikovsky A. Search for multi-SNP disease association. *Proceedings of the Fifth International Conference on Bioinformatics of Genome Regulation and Structure (BGRS'06)* 2006; pp. 122–125.
5. Brinza D, Zelikovsky A. 2SNP: Scalable phasing based on 2-SNP haplotypes. *Bioinformatics* 2006;22(3):371–373.
6. Brinza D, Zelikovsky A. Combinatorial Methods for Disease Association Search and Susceptibility Prediction. *Proceedings of the Sixth Workshop on Algorithms in BioInformatics (WABI 2006)* 2006; pp. 286–297.
7. Brinza D, He J, Zelikovsky A. Combinatorial search methods for multi-SNP disease association. *Proceedings of International Conference of the IEEE Engineering in Medicine and Biology (EMBC'06)* 2006; pp. 5802–5805.
8. Chapman JM, Cooper JD, Todd JA, Clayton DG. Detecting disease associations due to linkage disequilibrium using haplotype tags: a class of tests and the determinants of statistical power. *Hum Hered* 2003;56:18–31.
9. Clark AG. Finding genes underlying risk of complex disease by linkage disequilibrium mapping. *Curr Opin Genet Dev.* 2003;13(3):296–302.
10. Clark AG, Boerwinkle E, Hixson J, Sing CF. Determinants of the success of whole-genome association testing. *Genome Res* 2005;15:1463–1467.
11. Daly M, Rioux J, Schaffner S, Hudson T, Lander E. High resolution haplotype structure in the human genome. *Nat Genet* 2001;29:229–232.
12. International HapMap Consortium. The international HapMap project. *Nature* 2003;426:789–796. *http://www.hapmap.org*
13. Joachims T. http://svmlight.joachims.org/
14. Halldorsson BV, Bafna V, Lippert R, Schwartz R, de la Vega, FM, Clark AG, Istrail S. Optimal haplotype block-free selection of tagging SNPs for genome-wide association studies. *Genome Res* 2004;14:1633–1640.
15. Halperin E, Kimmel G, Shamir R. 'Tag SNP Selection in Genotype Data for Maximizing SNP Prediciton Accuracy.' *Bioinformatics* 2005;21:195–203.
16. He J, Zelikovsky A. MLR-Tagging: Informative SNP selection for unphased genotypes based on multiple linear regression. *Bioinformatics* 2006;22(20):2558–2561.
17. He J, Zelikovsky A. Tag SNP selection based on multivariate linear regression, *Proceedings of International Conference on Computational Science (ICCS 2006). LNCS 3992* 2006; pp. 750–757.
18. Herbert A, Gerry NP, McQueen MB. A common genetic variant is associated with adult and childhood obesity. *Science* 2006;312:279–284.
19. Kimmel G, Shamir R. A block-free hidden markov model for genotypes and its application to disease association. *J Comput Biol* 2005;12(10):1243–1260.

20. Lee PH, Shatkay H. BNTagger: Improved tagging SNP selection using Bayesian Networks. *Proceedingss of ISMB2006* in 2006. Preparation.

21. Listgarten J, Damaraju S, Poulin B, Cook L, Dufour J, Driga A, Mackey J, Wishart D, Greiner R, Zanke B. Predictive models for breast cancer susceptibility from multiple single nucleotide polymorphisms *Clin Cancer Res* 2004;10:2725–2737.

22. Mao W, He J, Brinza D, Zelikovsky A. A combinatorial method for predicting genetic susceptibility to complex diseases. *Proceedings International Conference of the IEEE Engineering in Medicine and Biology Society (EMBC'05)* 2005; pp. 224–227.

23. Mao W, Brinza D, Hundewale N, Gremalschi S, Zelikovsky A. Genotype susceptibility and integrated risk factors for complex diseases. *Proceedingss IEEE International Conference on Granular Computing (GRC 2006)* 2006; pp. 754–757.

24. Marchini J, Donnelley P, Cardon LR. Genome-wide strategies for detecting multiple loci that influence complex diseases. *Nat Genet* 2005;37:413–417.

25. Nelson MR, Kardia SL, Ferrell RE, Sing CF. A combinatorial partitioning method to identify multilocus genotypic partitions that predict quantitative trait variation. *Genome Res* 2001;11:458–470.

26. Spinola M, Meyer P, Kammerer S, Falvella F, Stefania, Boettger MB, Hoyal CR, Pignatiello C, Fischer R, Roth RB, Pastorino U, Haeussinger K, Nelson MR, Dierkesmann R, Dragani TA, Braun A. Association of the PDCD5 locus with lung cancer risk and prognosis in smokers. *Am J Clin Oncol* 2006;24:11.

27. Stephens M, Smith NJ, Donnelly P. A new statistical method for haplotype reconstruction from population data. *Am J Hum Genet* 2001;68:978–998.

28. Stram D, Haiman C, Hirschhorn J, Altshuler D, Kolonel L, Henderson B, Pike M. Choosing haplotype-tagging SNPs based on unphased genotype data using as preliminary sample of unrelated subjects with an example from the multiethnic cohort study, *Hum Hered* 2003;55:27–36.

29. Tahri-Daizadeh N, Tregouet DA, Nicaud V, Manuel N, Cambien F, Tiret L. Automated detection of informative combined effects in genetic association studies of complex traits. *Genome Res* 2003;13:1952–1960.

30. Tomita Y, Yokota M, Honda H. Classification method for prediction of multifactorial disease development using interaction between genetic and environmental factors. *IEEE CS Bioinformatics Conference*, 2005. abstract.

31. Ueda H, Howson JMM, Esposito L, Heward J, Snook H, Chamberlain G, Rainbow DB, Hunter KMD, Smith AN, Di Genova G. Association of the T cell regulatory gene CTLA4 with susceptibility to autoimmune disease. *Nature* 2003;423:506–511.

32. Waddell M, Page D, Zhan F, Barlogie B, Shaughnessy J. Predicting cancer susceptibility from single nucleotide polymorphism data: A case study in multiple myeloma,*Proceedingss of BIOKDD 2005*.

33. Zhang K, Qin Z, Liu J, Chen T, Waterman M, Sun F. Haplotype block partitioning and tag SNP selection using genotype data and their applications to association studies. *Genome Res* 2004;14:908–916.

34. Zhang P, Sheng H, Uehara R. A double classification tree search algorithm for index SNP selection. *BMC Bioinformatics* 2004;5:89–95.

PART V

STRUCTURAL AND SYSTEMS BIOLOGY

19

TOPOLOGICAL INDICES IN COMBINATORIAL CHEMISTRY

Sergey Bereg

Department of Computer Science, University of Texas at Dallas, Dallas, TX, USA

19.1 INTRODUCTION

There are several approaches to making correlations between chemical structure and some desired property or bioactivity (either of which is here spoken of simply as the "activity"). Quantitative-structure-activity-relationships (QSAR) have achieved widespread use, perhaps most especially in evaluating bioactivities, for example, in drug development. A general approach is to correlate a desired activity with various *topological indices*, which are usually referred to as *graph invariants* in graph theory.

This paper outlines some topological indices and recent results in the study of combinatorial properties of topological indices. We also address computational problems involving topological indices. Apart from the mathematical properties of topological indices, the main question is the correlation of descriptors and physical, chemical and biological properties of molecular compounds. Modern QSARs use not only topological features. They incorporate local vertex invariants with real numbers and geometric features.

19.2 TOPOLOGICAL INDICES

Molecules and molecular compounds are often modeled by *molecular graphs*. Topological indices of molecular graphs are one of the oldest and most widely used

Bioinformatics Algorithms: Techniques and Applications, Edited by Ion I. Măndoiu and Alexander Zelikovsky

descriptors in quantitative structure activity relationships. Quantitative structure activity relationships (QSAR) is a popular computational biology paradigm in modern drug design [9,42].

Graphs are finite, undirected, connected, without loops and multiple edges. Let $G = (V, E)$ be a graph. The *distance* $d_G(u, v)$ between vertices u and v in a graph G is the number of edges in a shortest path from u to v in G [3]. The *distance of a vertex* $v \in V$, denoted by $d_G(v)$ is the sum of distances between v and all other vertices of G. One of the most widely known topological descriptor [22,31] is the *Wiener index* named after chemist Harold Wiener [55] who devised it and studied it in 1947.

Definition 19.1 *The Wiener index of a graph $G(V, E)$ is defined as the sum of the distances between all pairs of vertices in G*

$$W(G) = \sum_{\{u,v\} \in V} d_G(u, v) = \frac{1}{2} \sum_{v \in V} d_G(v). \tag{19.1}$$

Wiener [55] studied acyclic graphs representing paraffins and defined $W(G)$ as the *path number*. "The path number w is defined as the sum of the distances between any two carbon atoms in the molecule."

In the mathematical literature, the Wiener index studied under different names such as *distance* of a graph [18]. A related graph invariant is the *average distance* of a graph [10], defined as $W(G)/\binom{n}{2}$.

For acyclic molecular graphs Wiener [55] discovered a remarkably simple method for the calculation of the Wiener index. Let $T = (V, E)$ be a tree and let e be an edge of T. Let $n_1(e)$ and $n_2(e)$ be the number of vertices of two trees of $T - e$. Then,

$$W(T) = \sum_{e \in E} n_1(e) n_2(e). \tag{19.2}$$

The proof follows from the fact that there are exactly $n_1(e)n_2(e)$ shortest paths containing an edge e, see Fig. 19.1 for an example.

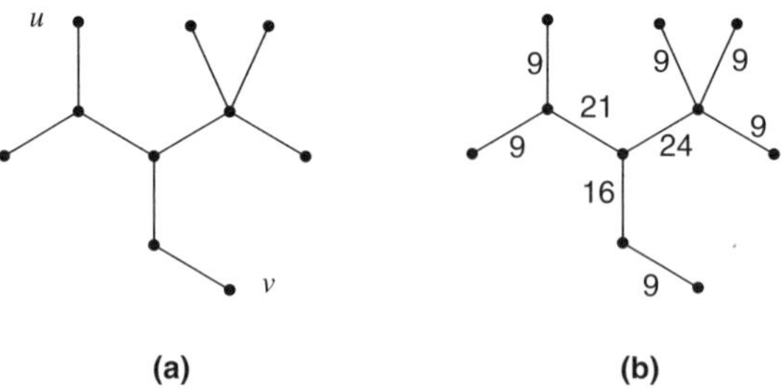

FIGURE 19.1 Carbon skeleton of 3-ethyl-2,2,4-trimethylpentane. Its Wiener index is equal to 115, which is (*a*) the sum of the distances $d()$ (e.g., $d(u, v) = 4$) and (*b*) the sum of the edge costs by Equation 19.2.

The quantities $n_1(e)$ and $n_2(e)$ can be defined for general graphs as follows. Let $e = (x, y)$ be an edge of a graph $G = (V, E)$. Let $n_1(e)$ be the number of vertices of G closer to x than to y and let $n_2(e)$ be the number of vertices of G closer to y than to x. This allows to define the *Szeged index*.

Definition 19.2 *The* Szeged index *of a graph* $G = (V, E)$ is *defined as the sum of the distances between all pairs of vertices in G*

$$Sz(G) = \sum_{e \in E} n_1(e) n_2(e). \tag{19.3}$$

A generalization of the Wiener index has been studied recently [28].

Definition 19.3 *The* multiplicative *Wiener index of a graph* $G = (V, E)$ *is defined as the sum of the distances between all pairs of vertices in G*

$$W_\lambda(G) = \sum_{\{u,v\} \subseteq V} (d_G(u, v))^\lambda. \tag{19.4}$$

Definition 19.4 *The* σ*-index* $\sigma(G)$ *of a graph G is the number of independent vertex subsets of G (including the empty set), where a set of vertices is said to be independent if there is no pair of connected vertices in it.*

Definition 19.5 *The c-index* $c(G)$ *of a graph G is the number of cliques of G (including the empty clique), that is, the number of complete subgraphs.*

Definition 19.6 *The Z-index* $Z(G)$ *of a graph G is the number of independent edge subsets of G (including the empty set), where a set of edges is said to be independent if there is no pair of edges sharing a common vertex in it.*

We denote the degree of a vertex v of a graph G by δ_v. Schultz [51] considered a graph invariant whose essential part is the *Schultz index*,

$$S(G) = \sum_{\{u,v\} \in V} (\delta_u + \delta_v) d_G(u, v). \tag{19.5}$$

Gutman [23] examined the *modified Schultz index*,

$$S^*(G) = \sum_{\{u,v\} \in V} \delta_u \delta_v d_G(u, v). \tag{19.6}$$

19.3 WIENER INDICES OF TREES

A vertex of degree one is called a *pendent vertex*. Let P_n be the *path*, the n-vertex tree with two pendent vertices. Let S_n be the *star*, the n-vertex tree with $n-1$ pendent vertices. Their Wiener indices [18] are

$$W(P_n) = \binom{n+1}{3} \quad \text{and} \quad W(S_n) = (n-1)^2. \tag{19.7}$$

If T is an n-vertex graph different from P_n and S_n, then [27]

$$W(S_n) < W(T) < W(P_n). \tag{19.8}$$

The expected value of $W(T)$ over all ordered/rooted, labeled/rooted binary trees if size n is asymptotic to $cn^{5/2}$, where the constant c depends on the class of trees [19].

19.4 COMPUTING THE WIENER INDEX

Most of the algorithms for computing the Wiener index of a graph use its definition and compute all pairwise distances [49]. Let $G = (V, E)$ be a connected graph with n vertices and m edges. The total running time is dominated by computing all pairs shortest paths. They can be computed in $O(n^3)$ time by Dijkstra algorithm. For sparse graphs, the running time can be reduced to $O(n^2 \log n + mn)$ using Fibonacci heaps [20]. Alternatively, Johnson's algorithm [33] can be used. The main open problem is to design an efficient algorithm for computing the Wiener index avoiding computation of all pairwise distances [49].

Several algorithms are known for computing the Wiener index of a tree [13]. Equation 19.9 can be used for computing the Wiener index of a tree T. The values $n_1(e)$ and $n_2(e)$ for all edges e can be computed in total linear time as follows. First, make a rooted tree from T by assigning a vertex of T as the root. Then, compute the size of the subtree rooted at v, for all vertices v in bottom-to-top fashion. Note that $n_1(e) + n_2(e) = n$ for every edge e in T.

Equation 19.1 provides another way of computing the Wiener index using the distances $d_T(v)$. The values of $d_T(v)$ can be computed in $O(n)$ time by the following theorem (which holds for graphs with cycles as well!).

Theorem 19.1 [18] *For any edge $e = (x, y)$ of a connected graph G,*

$$d_G(x) - d_G(y) = n_2(e) - n_1(e). \tag{19.9}$$

Equation 19.1 is not a unique expression of the Wiener index through the distances $d_T(v)$. The following formula shows how irregularity of the distances of adjacent vertices influences the Wiener index [14].

Theorem 19.2 *Let $T = (V, E)$ be a tree with n vertices. Then*

$$W(T) = \frac{1}{4}\Big[n^2(n-1) - \sum_{(u,v)\in E} \big(d_T(v) - d_T(v)\big)^2\Big]. \tag{19.10}$$

Equation 19.1 expresses the Wiener index as a linear combination of the distances $d_T(v)$ with coefficients equal to 1/2. The next formula demonstrates another linear combination with coefficients equal to the vertex degrees.

Theorem 19.3 *Let $T = (V, E)$ be a tree with n vertices. Then*

$$W(T) = \frac{1}{4}\Big[n(n-1) + \sum_{v\in V} deg_T(v) d_T(v)\Big], \tag{19.11}$$

where $deg_T(v)$ is the degree of a vertex v of T.

Three different proofs of Equation 19.11 are known [14,23,38].
Canfield et al. [6] applied a recursive approach for calculating the Wiener index of a tree. For a rooted tree T, we denote by $l(T)$ the sum of the distances from the root v_{root} of T to all its vertices, $l(T) = \sum_{v\in T} d(v_{root}, v)$. Note that $l(T) = d_T(v_{root})$.

Theorem 19.4 *Canfield* et al. *[6] Let T be a tree of size n with the root v_{root} and let v_i, $1 \le i \le k$ be the vertices adjacent to v_{root}. Let T_i, $1 \le i \le k$ be the subtree of T rooted at v_i. Let n_i be the size of T_i, $1 \le i \le k$, see Fig. 19.2. Then*

$$W(T) = n(n-1) + \sum_{i=1}^{k} [W(T_i) + (n - n_i)\, l(T_i) - n_i^2], \tag{19.12}$$

$$l(T) = n - 1 + \sum_{i=1}^{k} l(T_i). \tag{19.13}$$

The computation of $W(T)$ and $l(T)$ by Equations 19.12 and 19.13 takes $O(k)$ time. The total running time is $O(n)$.

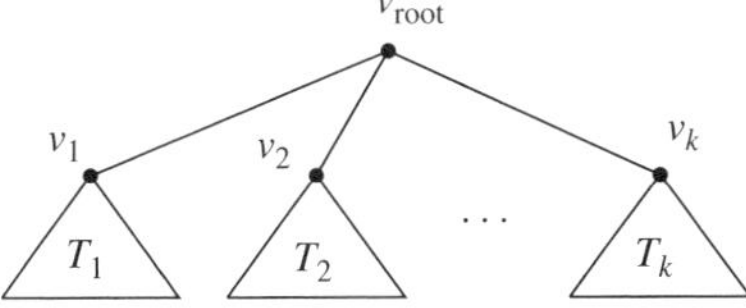

FIGURE 19.2 Recursive computation of the Wiener index.

19.5 COMPUTING THE WIENER INDEX USING BRANCHINGS

A *branching* vertex of a tree is a vertex of degree at least three. A *segment* of a tree T is a path such that its vertex has degree two in T if and only if it is an internal vertex of the path. The edges of T are partitioned into segments. If T has no vertices of degree two then all segments of T are single edges. The length of a segment S (the number of edges in S) is denoted by l_S.

Doyle and Graver [17] discovered a formula for the calculation of the Wiener index of trees with few branching vertices. Consider a tree T whose structure is described in connection with Theorem 19.4 (see Fig. 19.2).

Theorem 19.2 [17] *Let T be a tree of size n. Then*

$$W(T) = \binom{n+1}{3} - \sum_{u} \sum_{1 \le i < j < k \le deg_T(u)} n_i n_j n_k, \tag{19.14}$$

where the first summation goes over branching vertices $u \in T$ and $n_i, 1 \le i \le deg_T(u)$ is the size of ith tree in $T - u$ (as in Theorem 19.1).

Note that $\sum_{i=1}^{\deg_T(u)} n_i = n - 1$ in Equation 19.14.

Dobrynin [12] discovered a formula similar to Wiener's Equation 19.2. Let S be a segment of a tree T and let T_1 and T_2 be two trees obtained by removing edges of S and internal vertices of S from T. Let $n_i(S), i = 1, 2$ be the size of the tree T_i.

Theorem 19.3 [12] *Let T be a tree of size n. Then*

$$W(T) = \sum_{S} n_1(S) n_2(S) l_S + \frac{1}{6} \sum_{S} l_S(l_S - 1)(3n - 2l_S + 1), \tag{19.15}$$

where the summations go over all segments S of T.

19.6 LAPLACIAN EIGENVALUES AND THE WIENER INDEX

Let $G = (V, E)$ be a graph with n vertices $v_1, v_2, \ldots, v_n$. The diagonal matrix Δ is defined as

$$\Delta_{ij} = \begin{cases} \deg_G(v_i), & \text{if } i = j \\ 0, & \text{otherwise.} \end{cases} \tag{19.16}$$

The adjacency matrix A is defined as

$$A_{ij} = \begin{cases} 1, & \text{if } (v_i, v_j) \in E \\ 0, & \text{otherwise.} \end{cases} \tag{19.17}$$

The Laplacian matrix of G is defined as $L = \Delta - A$. The Laplacian graph spectrum is the set of eigenvalues of L, denoted by $\lambda_1, \lambda_2, \ldots, \lambda_n$. It is known that the smallest eigenvalue of L is zero and the other eigenvalues are positive. The theory of Laplacian spectra of graphs has been extensively studied (for a review see [46,48]).
The following result was communicated independently in [44,45,47,48].

Theorem 19.4 *Let T be a tree of size n. If $\lambda_1 \geq \lambda_2 \geq \ldots \geq \lambda_n$ are the Laplacian eigenvalues of T, then*

$$W(T) = n \sum_{i=1}^{n-1} \frac{1}{\lambda_i}. \tag{19.18}$$

Theorem 19.4 is an unexpected result since it connects the Wiener index (a quantity defined on the basis of graph distances) and matrix eigenvalues. Hopefully, powerful tools of linear algebra will be used for more interesting results in the theory of the Wiener index.

19.7 HOSOYA POLYNOMIAL

Hosoya [30] introduced a distance-based polynomial whose first derivative gives the Wiener index. Due to this property, Hosoya called it the Wiener polynomial. Recently, the polynomial is also called the Hosoya polynomial [26,53]. Let $G = (V, E)$ be a graph with n vertices and m edges. Let $d(G, k)$ be the number of pairs of vertices of the graph G at distance k. In particular, $d(G, 0) = n$, $d(G, 1) = m$, and $\sum_{k \geq 0} d(G, k) = \binom{n}{2} + n = n(n+1)/2$. The *Hosoya polynomial* is defined as

$$H(G, x) = \sum_{k \geq 0} d(G, k)\, x^k. \tag{19.19}$$

Using distances $d(G, k)$, the Wiener index can be written as

$$W(G) = \sum_{k \geq 0} k\, d(G, k). \tag{19.20}$$

Equations 19.19 and 19.20 imply that the first derivative of the Hosoya polynomial at $x = 1$ is equal to the Wiener index. Equivalently, the Hosoya polynomial can be written as

$$H(G, x) = \sum_{\{u,v\} \subseteq V} x^{d(u,v)}. \tag{19.21}$$

Similar to the distance of a vertex $d_G(v)$, we define the *vertex Hosoya polynomial* for a vertex v:

$$H_v(G, x) = \sum_{u \in V} x^{d(u,v)}.$$

Then,

$$H(G, x) = \frac{1}{2} \sum_{v \in V} H_v(G, x).$$

Stevancović [53] found formulas for calculating the Hosoya polynomial of a graph composed from two graphs using the graph operations: the sum, join, composition, corona, and cluster. Ivanciuc and Klein [32] provided a formula for the Hosoya polynomial of a graph with a cut edge. Let (a, b) be a cut edge between two subgraphs A and B of a graph G, that is, $V(G) = V(A) \cup V(B)$, $V(A) \cap V(B) = \emptyset$ and $E(G) = E(A) \cup E(B) \cup \{(a, b)\}$, $a \in V(A)$, $b \in V(B)$ as in Fig. 19.3. Then the Hosoya polynomial of G is

$$\begin{aligned} H(G, x) &= \sum_{\{u,v\} \subseteq V(A)} x^{d(u,v)} + \sum_{u \in V(A)} \sum_{v \in V(B)} x^{d(u,v)} + \sum_{\{u,v\} \subseteq V(B)} x^{d(u,v)} \\ &= H(A, x) + \sum_{u \in V(A)} \sum_{v \in V(B)} x^{d(u,a)+1+d(b,v)} + H(B, x) \\ &= H(A, x) + x\, H_a(A, x)\, H_b(B, x) + H(B, x). \end{aligned}$$

The Schultz index related to the Wiener index as

$$S(G) = 4W(G) - n(n-1). \tag{19.22}$$

This relation follows from Equation 19.11.

Recently, Gutman [24] studied graph polynomials related to the Schultz and modified Schultz indices (19.5,19.6). These polynomials are

$$H_1(G, x) = \sum_{\{u,v\} \subseteq V} (\delta_u + \delta_v) x^{d(u,v)},$$

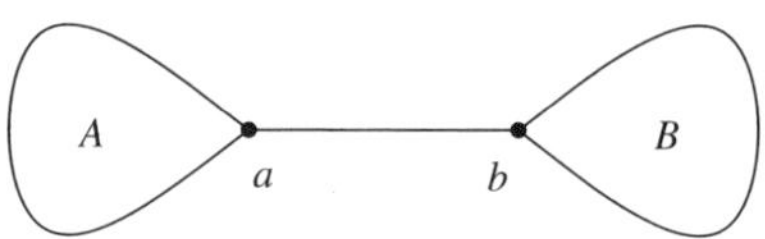

FIGURE 19.3 The graph G is composed of two graphs A and B and an edge (a, b).

$$H_2(G,x) = \sum_{\{u,v\}\subseteq V} (\delta_u \delta_v) x^{d(u,v)}.$$

If G is a tree on n vertices then the polynomials $H_1(G,x)$ and $H_2(G,x)$ are related to the Hosoya polynomial as

$$H_1(G,x) = 2\left(1+\frac{1}{x}\right) H(G,x) - 2\left(1+\frac{n}{x}\right),$$

$$H_2(G,x) = \left(1+\frac{1}{x}\right)^2 H(G,x) - \left(1+\frac{1}{x}\right)\left(2+\frac{1}{x}\right) n$$
$$+ \left(1+\frac{1}{x}\right) + \frac{1}{2}\sum_{v\in V} (\delta_v)^2.$$

19.8 INVERSE WIENER PROBLEM

The natural question arising in the study of topological indices is: What integers can be Wiener indices of graphs?

Bytautas and Klein [4] used combinatorial techniques to enumerate isomers for up to 40 carbons. Later, they [5] found average Wiener numbers for alkanes with at most 90 carbons. Dobrynin and Gutman [15] found the average value of the Wiener index of hexagonal chains (unbranched catacondensed benzenoid systems) with a fixed number of hexagons.

For the class of all graphs, the question about integers that are Wiener indices has been solved [21,29]. Specifically, for any positive integer $w \neq 2, 5$, there exists a graph G such that $W(G) = w$. Gutman and Yeh [29] proved that every positive integer different from 2, 3, 5, 6, 7, 11, 12, 13, 15, 17, 19, 33, 37, and 39 is the Wiener index of a bipartite graph. They also conjectured the following.

Conjecture 19.1 *There is only a finite number of positive integers that are not Wiener indices of some trees.*

Lepović and Gutman [40] presented an exhaustive search algorithm that verifies Conjecture 19.1 up to 1206. They enumerated all unlabeled nonisomorphic trees of up to 20 vertices and found 49 positive integers that are not Wiener indices of trees: 2, 3, 5, 6, 7, 8, 11, 12, 13, 14, 15, 17, 19, 21, 22, 23, 24, 26, 27, 30, 33, 34, 37, 38, 39, 41, 43, 45, 47, 51, 53, 55, 60, 61, 69, 73, 77, 78, 83, 85, 87, 89, 91, 99, 101, 106, 113, 147 and 159. This result justifies a somewhat stronger hypothesis [40].

Conjecture 19.2 *There are exactly 49 positive integers that are not Wiener indices of some trees. These are just the above listed numbers.*

The enumeration of trees requires an exponential time. Goldman et al. [21] applied a dynamic programming approach based on Theorem 19.1 avoiding the enumeration

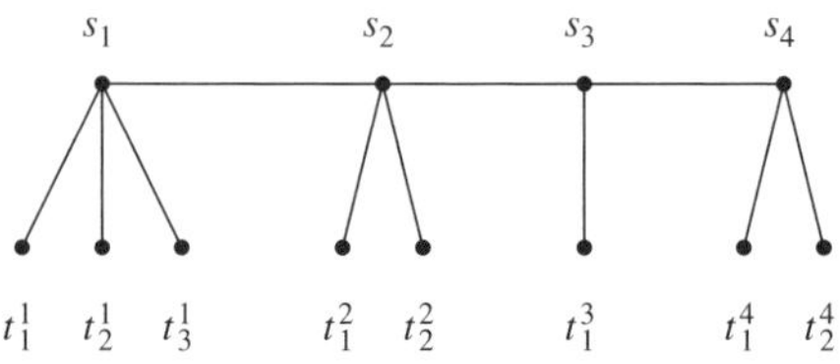

FIGURE 19.4 The tree $T(3, 2, 1, 2)$.

of trees. Their algorithm stores only triples (n, l, w) for rooted trees. The algorithm is more efficient and verified that all numbers between 159 (exclusively) and 10 ,000 are the Wiener indices of trees.

Ban et al. [2] found an interesting class of trees that is promising for solving the conjecture. Let $(r_1, r_2, \ldots, r_k)$ be a sequence of integers such that $r_i \geq 1, i = 1, \ldots, k$. A tree $T(r_1, r_2, \ldots, r_k)$ is defined using the set of vertices

$$V = \{s_1, \ldots, s_k\} \cup \{t_1^1, \ldots, t_{r_1}^1, \ldots, t_1^k, \ldots, t_{r_k}^k\}$$

and the set of edges

$$E = \{(s_i, s_{i+1}),\ 1 \leq i \leq (k-1)\} \cup \{(t_l^j, s_j),\ 1 \leq j \leq k,\ 1 \leq l \leq r_j\},$$

see Fig. 19.4 for an example. If k is fixed, then the set of trees is denoted by T_k. They designed a fast algorithm for enumerating the Wiener indices of these trees. They found 56 positive integers smaller than 10^8 that are not Wiener indices of these trees: 2, 3, 5, 6, 7, 8, 11, 12, 13, 14, 15, 17, 19, 21, 22, 23, 24, 26, 27, 30, 33, 34, 37, 38, 39, 41, 43, 45, 47, 51, 53, 55, 60, 61, 69, 72, 73, 77, 78, 83, 85, 87, 89, 91, 99, 101, 106, 113, 117, 129, 133, 147, 157, 159, 173, and 193. This leads to a new conjecture [2].

Conjecture 19.3 *Except the above 56 numbers, all positive integers are the Wiener indices of trees in* T_k, $k \geq 1$.

Ban et al. [2] explored the question whether all sets T_k are needed to solve Conjecture 19.1. It turns out that the set T_5 produces many Wiener indices. Specifically, the Wiener indices of T_k, $k \leq 5$ cover all integers in the range $557 < W \leq 10^8$. Actually, this range is covered using just the set of trees T_5 and they [2] conjectured:

Conjecture 19.4 *Except a set of 102 numbers (the largest number is 557), all positive integers are the Wiener indices of trees in* T_5.

19.9 HEXAGONAL SYSTEMS

There are many molecules of interest in chemistry whose graphs are cyclic. One class of cyclic molecules is the *benzenoid hydrocarbons*. The carbon-atom skeleton of these hydrocarbons consists of mutually fused hexagons. They can be modeled by *hexagonal systems* [16], see Fig. 19.5 for an example. A vertex v of a graph G is said to be a *cut-vertex* if the subgraph obtained by deleting v from G has more connected components than G.

Definition 19.7 *A* hexagonal system *is a connected plane graph without cut-vertices in which all inner faces are hexagons (and all hexagons are faces), such that two hexagons are either disjoint or have exactly one common edge, and no three hexagons share a common edge.*

19.9.1 Hexagonal Systems with Extreme Wiener Indices

Definition 19.8 *A hexagonal system is said to be* simple *if it can be embedded into the regular hexagonal lattice in the plane without overlapping of its vertices. Hexagonal systems that are not simple are called* jammed*, see Fig. 19.6 for an example.*

Definition 19.9 *A vertex of a hexagonal system is* internal *if it is shared by three hexagons. The number of internal vertices is denoted by n_i. A hexagonal system is said to be* catacondensed *if it does not have internal vertices ($n_i = 0$). A hexagonal system is said to be* pericondensed *if it has at least one internal vertex ($n_i > 0$).*

Hexagons sharing a common edge are said to be *adjacent*. The *characteristic graph* (or *dual graph*) of a hexagonal system consists of vertices corresponding to hexagons of the system; two vertices are adjacent if and only if the corresponding hexagons are adjacent. A hexagonal system is catacondensed if and only if its characteristic graph is a tree, see Fig. 19.6.

Simple Hexagonal Chains. Dobrynin [11] determined hexagonal chains minimizing and maximizing the Wiener index. The maximum and minimum Wiener index is realized on the *serpent* and the *linear chain*, see Fig. 19.7. The minimum Wiener

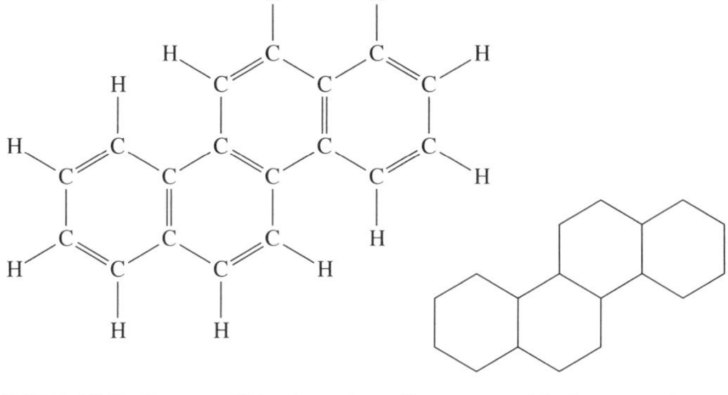

FIGURE 19.5 Benzenoid hydrocarbon Chrysene and its hexagonal system.

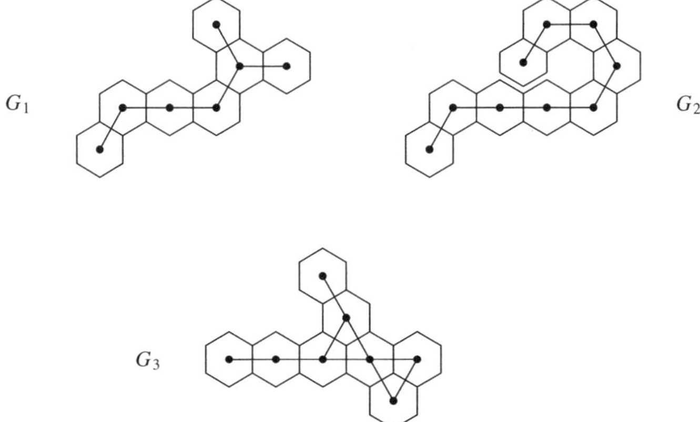

FIGURE 19.6 Simple hexagonal system G_1, jammed hexagonal system G_2, pericondensed hexagonal system G_3, and their characteristic graphs.

index is equal to

$$W(G_1) = \frac{1}{9}(32h^3 + 168h^2 + \phi(h)),$$

where h is the number of hexagons and

$$\phi(h) = \begin{cases} -6\text{h} + 81, & \text{if } h = 3m \\ -6\text{h} + 49, & \text{if } h = 3m + 1 \\ -6\text{h} + 161, & \text{if } h = 3m + 2. \end{cases} \tag{19.23}$$

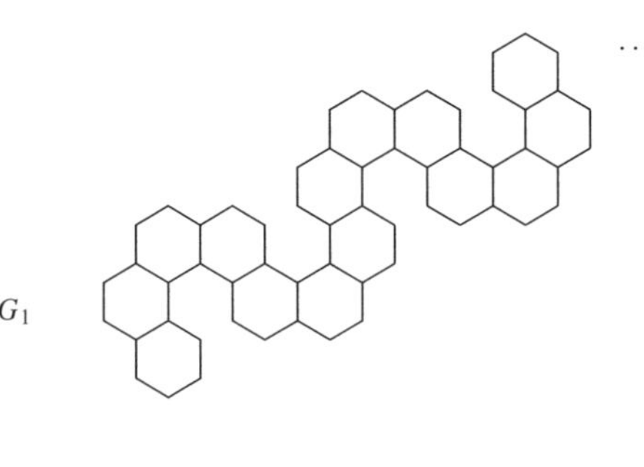

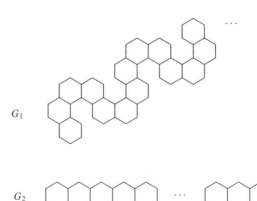

FIGURE 19.7 The serpent G_1. The linear chain G_2.

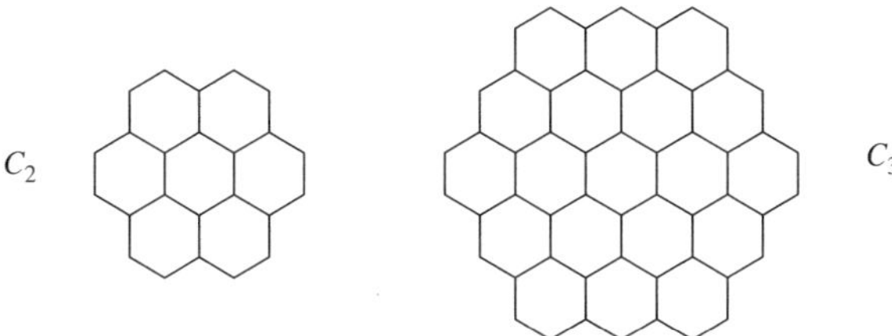

FIGURE 19.8 The coronene C_2 and the circumcoronene C_3.

The maximum Wiener index is equal to

$$W(G_2) = \frac{1}{3}(16h^3 + 36h^2 + 26h + 3).$$

Pericondensed Hexagonal Systems. The hexagonal system C_2 shown in Fig. 19.8 is called the *coronene* (the name borrowed from chemistry). The *circumcoronene* C_k, $k \geq 3$ is constructed by circumscribing C_{k-1} with hexagons, see C_3 in Fig. 19.8. The basic properties of circumcoronenes see [52].

Pericondensed hexagonal systems minimizing the Wiener index are similar to the circumcoronenes. These systems can be obtained from circumcoronenes by deleting their peripheral hexagons. The number of hexagons of C_k is $h = 3k^2 - 3k + 1$ and its Wiener index [25,52] is equal to

$$W(C_k) = \frac{1}{5}(164k^5 - 30k^3 + k).$$

The Wiener index $W(C_k)$ depends on h as $\Theta(h^{2.5})$.

19.9.2 Isometric Embeddings of Hexagonal Systems

Let $G = (V, E)$ be a connected graph. Its subgraph H is said to be *isometric*, if for any pair of vertices u, v of H, we have $d_G(u, v) = d_H(u, v)$. For instance, any hexagon of a hexagonal system is its isometric subgraph.

The *hypercube graph* Q_n is a special regular graph with 2^n vertices, which correspond to the subsets of a set with n elements. Two vertices labeled by subsets S_1 and S_2 are joined by an edge if and only if S_1 can be obtained from S_2 by adding or removing a single element. Each vertex of Q_n is incident to exactly n edges. Klavžar et al. [37] proved the following theorem.

Theorem 19.4 *Any hexagonal system is an isometric subgraph of a hypercube.*

Every hexagon has three pairs of opposite edges. Using these pairs we can partition the edges into three sets $E = E_1 \cup E_2 \cup E_3$. Let $G_i = (V, E - E_i)$, $i = 1, 2, 3$ and let T_i be the graph whose vertices are connected components of G_i, two vertices of T_i being adjacent if there is an edge in G between the corresponding components of G_i. It turns out that T_i, $i = 1, 2, 3$ is a tree. This construction is illustrated in Fig. 19.9.

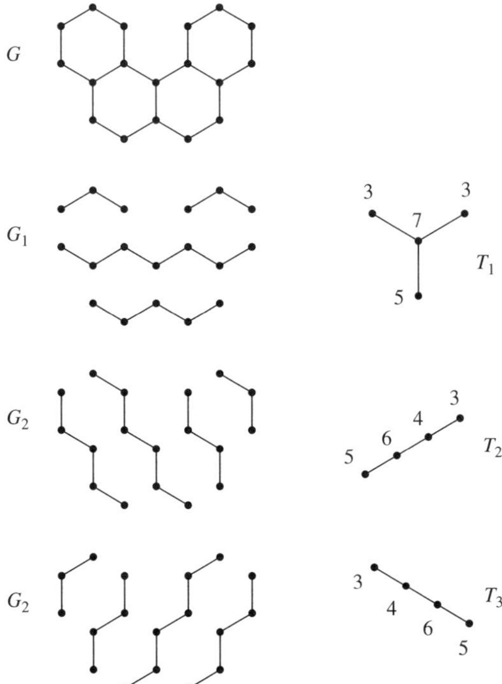

FIGURE 19.9 Benzenoid hydrocarbon chrysene and its hexagonal system.

Define a mapping $\alpha : G \to T_1 \square T_2 \square T_3$ as follows. For a vertex v of G, set $\alpha(v) = (v_1, v_2, v_3)$, where v_i is the vertex of T_i corresponding to v. Chepoi [7] proved an isometric property of the mapping α.

Theorem 19.5 *Let G be a hexagonal system. Then $\alpha(G)$ is an isometric subgraph of $T_1 \square T_2 \square T_3$.*

Theorem 19.5 is the starting point for a fast method of computing the Winer index of a hexagonal system. A *weighted graph* (G, w) is a graph $G = (V, E)$ together with a *weight function* $w : V \to N^+$. The Wiener index of a weighted graph (G, w) is defined as [36]

$$W(G, w) = \sum_{\{u,v\} \subseteq V} w(u)w(v)d_G(u, v).$$

Note that if all the weights are 1, then $W(G, w) = W(G)$.

Let G be a hexagonal system, and T_1, T_2, T_3 be the trees as in Theorem 19.5. For a vertex u of a tree T_i, let the weight $w_i(u)$ be the number of vertices x of G, whose ith position in the label $\alpha(x)$ is equal to u, see Fig. 19.9 for an example. Chepoi and Klavžar [8] found a formula for the Wiener index of G.

Theorem 19.6 *Let G be a hexagonal system, and* (T_1, w_1), (T_2, w_2), *and* (T_3, w_3) *be the corresponding weighted trees. Then*

$$W(G) = W(T_1, w_1) + W(T_2, w_2) + W(T_3, w_3).$$

The Wiener index of a hexagonal system on n vertices can be computed in $O(n)$ *time.*

19.10 THE WIENER INDEX OF PEPTOIDS

In drug design, new compounds are constructed using compounds from a combinatorial library. The central problem is the construction of a molecular graph with given chemical or physical properties. A chemical or physical property can be quantitatively represented by some topological index. Goldman et al. [21] studied the Wiener indices of *peptoids*, graphs constructed from given molecular graphs by joining them in a linear scaffold way.

Definition 19.10 ([21]) *A* (chemical) fragment *is a graph G with a special vertex v denoted as its* anchor, *or* hooking point. *A* peptoid *is a graph obtained by joining in a linear fashion from left to right, k fragments* $G_1, G_2, \ldots, G_k$ *via a path through their hooking points, see Fig. 19.10 for an example. Note that, when* $k = 1$, *a fragment is a special case of a peptoid. For a peptoid* $D = (V, E)$, *by* $l(D) = \sum_{v \in V} d_G(v, v_k)$ *we denote the total distance of all vertices from the rightmost hooking point* v_k. *If* $k = 1$, $l()$ *is the total distance from all nodes of a fragment to its anchor.*

A *flower-compressed peptoid*, or *flower* is constructed from fragments by identifying their anchors. For example, in Fig. 19.10 the flower can be constructed by compress the vertices v_1, v_2 and v_3 to one vertex.

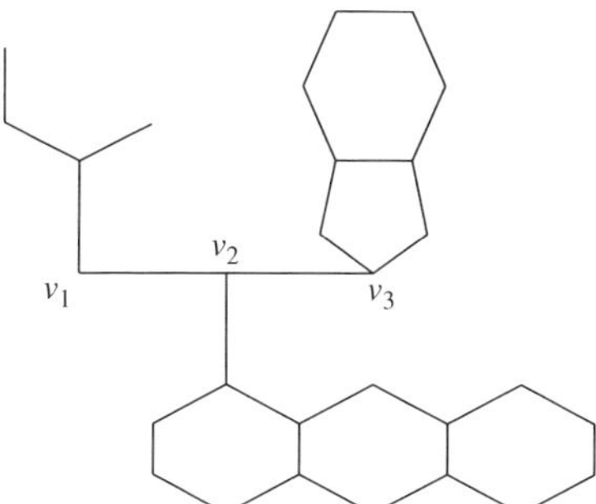

FIGURE 19.10 A 3-peptoid. The three fragments are anchored on a linear scaffold at positions v_1, v_2, and v_3.

Theorem 19.7 ([21]) *The Wiener index of a linear scaffold peptoid constructed from k fragments* $f_1, f_2, \ldots, f_k$ *is*

$$W(G) = \sum_{i=1}^{k} \sum_{j=i+1}^{k} [n_i l_j + (j-i) n_i n_j + n_j l_i] + \sum_{i=1}^{k} w_i, \tag{19.24}$$

where n_i *is the number of nodes in the fragment* f_i, w_i *is the Wiener index of the fragment* f_i *and* $l_i = l(f_i)$.

Let F be the flower *constructed from the k fragments* $f_1, f_2, \ldots, f_k$. *The Wiener index of F is*

$$W(F) = \sum_{i=1}^{k} \sum_{j=i+1}^{k} [n_i l_j + n_j l_i] + \sum_{i=1}^{k} w_i. \tag{19.25}$$

The difference of the Wiener indices of two peptoids is

$$D = W(G) - W(F) = \sum_{i=1}^{k} \sum_{j=i+1}^{k} (j-i) n_i n_j.$$

If we use a permutation π of the fragments in the linear scaffold peptoid, then the difference is

$$D(\pi) = \sum_{i=1}^{k} \sum_{j=i+1}^{k} (j-i) n_{\pi(i)} n_{\pi(j)}.$$

Goldman et al. [21] studied the minimum and maximum Wiener indices of peptoids and conjectured the following.

Conjecture 19.5 *(Minimum Wiener index peptoid [21]) Given* $n_1 \leq n_2 \leq \ldots \leq n_k$, *the permutation* π *minimizing* $D(\pi)$ is

$$\pi(i) = \begin{cases} \text{2i}-1, & \text{if } i \leq k/2 \\ 2(\text{k}-\text{i}+1), & \text{if } i > k/2. \end{cases}$$

Conjecture 19.6 *(Maximum Wiener index peptoid [21]) Given* $n_1 \leq n_2 \leq \ldots \leq n_k$, *the permutation* π *maximizing* $D(\pi)$ *can be computed as follows:*

$L_p = 0$; $L = 0$;
$R_p = 0$; $R = 0$;
for $i = k$ down to 1 do

if $R \geq L$, then
  $\pi(L_p) = i;\ L_p = L_p + 1;\ L = L + n_i;$

else
  $\pi(R_p) = i;\ R_p = R_p + 1;\ R = R + n_i;$

Both conjectured have been extensively tested [21]. Recently, Conjecture 19.5 has been proved by Li and Wang [41] using Hardy, Littlewood, and Polya's inequality. They found counterexamples to Conjecture 19.6 and posed an open problem of finding a polynomial-time algorithm for computing a permutation π maximizing $D(\pi)$ for given k fragments of size $n_1 \leq n_2 \leq \ldots \leq n_k$.

19.11 THE σ-INDEX AND RELATED INDICES

The σ-index is also known as the Merrifield–Simmons index due to the original work by Merrifield and Simmons [43] where they showed the correlation between this index and boiling points.

In mathematics, the σ-index has been introduced in 1982 as the Fibonacci number of a graph by Prodinger and Tichy [50]. In this and two subsequent papers [34,35], the σ-index for trees, especially t-ary trees, was investigated. They proved that (i) the tree of maximal σ-index is the star S_n, and (ii) the tree of minimal σ-index is the path P_n. If G is a graph G with n vertices then

$$F_{n+2} = \sigma(P_n) \leq \sigma(G) \leq \sigma(S_n) = 2^{n-1} + 1,$$

where $F_0 = 0$, $F_1 = 1$, and $F_{k+1} = F_k + F_{k-1}$ is the sequence of Fibonacci numbers.

Alameddine [1] proved bounds for the σ-index of a maximal outerplanar graph. Knopfmacher et al. [39] studied trees with large σ-index and determined all trees T with n vertices satisfying

$$2^{n-2} + 5 < \sigma(T) \leq \sigma(S_n) = 2^{n-1} + 1.$$

The c-index can be viewed as the complement of the σ-index since $c(G) = \sigma(\overline{G})$, where $\overline{G}$ is the complement graph. This follows from the fact that an independent subset in $\overline{G}$ is a clique in G and vice versa. Graphs with extreme c-index are studied in [54].

The Z-index is related to the σ-index in the following way: for a graph G, define the line graph G' to be the graph that results from replacing the edges by vertices and connecting vertices whose corresponding edges in G have a common vertex. Then, it is easy to verify that $\sigma(G') = Z(G)$.

The removal of an edge increases the σ-index and decreases the Z-index. The complete graph K_n has the largest Z-index among all graphs with n vertices. Unlike the σ-index, it is a nontrivial problem to determine the exact value for the Z-index of the complete graph K_n. It can be calculated using the following sum:

$$Z(K_n) = \sum_{k=0}^{\lfloor n/2 \rfloor} \frac{n!}{2^k k!(n-2k)!}.$$

For small n, the exact values are 1, 1, 2, 4, 10, 26, 76, 232, 764, 2620, 9496.

REFERENCES

1. Alameddine AF Bounds on the Fibonacci number of a maximal outerplanar graph. *Fibonacci Quart* 1998; 36:206–210.
2. Ban A, Bereg S, Mustafa N. On a conjecture of Wiener indices in computational chemistry. *Algorithmica* 2004; 40(2):99–118.
3. Buckley F, Harary F. *Distance in Graphs*. Addison-Wesley, Erdwood, 1990.
4. Bytautas L, Klein DJ. Chemical combinatorics for alkane-isomer enumeration and more. *J Chem Inf Comput Sci* 1998; 38:1063–1078.
5. Bytautas L, Klein DJ. Mean Wiener numbers and other mean extensions for alkane trees. *J Chem Inf Comput Sci* 2000; 40:471–481.
6. Canfield ER, Robinson RW, Rouvray DH. Determination of the Wiener molecular branching index for the general tree. *J. Comput Chem* 1985; 6:598–609.
7. Chepoi V. On distances in benzenoid systems. *J Chem Inf Comput Sci* 1996; 36:1169–1172.
8. Chepoi V, Klavžar S. The Wiener index and the Szeged index of benzenoid systems in linear time. *J Chem Inf Comput Sci* 1997; 37:752–755.
9. Corwin H, Kurup A, Garg R, Gao H. Chem-bioinfomatics and QSAR: a review of QSAR lacking positive hydrophobic terms. *Chem Rev* 2001; 101:619–672.
10. Dankelmann P. Average distance and independence numbers. *Discrete Appl Math* 1994; 51:75–83.
11. Dobrynin AA. Graph distance numbers of nonbranched hexagonal systems. *Siberian Adv Math* 1992; 2:121–134.
12. Dobrynin AA. Branchings in trees and the calculation of the Wiener index of a tree. *Comm Math Chem (MATCH)* 2000; 41:119–134.
13. Dobrynin AA, Entringer R, Gutman I. Wiener index of trees: Theory and applications. *Acta Appl Math* 2001; 66:211–249.
14. Dobrynin AA, Gutman I. On a graph invariant related to the sum of all distances in a graph. *Publ Inst (Beograd)* 1994; 56:18–22.
15. Dobrynin AA, Gutman I. The average Wiener index of trees and chemical trees. *J Chem Inf Comput Sci* 1999; 39:679–683.
16. Dobrynin AA, Gutman I, Klavžar S, Žigert P. Wiener index of hexagonal systems. *Acta Appl Math* 2002; 72:247–294.
17. Doyle JK, Graver JE Mean distance in a graph. *Discrete Math* 1977; 7:147–154.
18. Entringer RC, Jackson DE, Snyder DA. Distance in graphs. *Czech Math J* 1976; 26:283–296.

19. Entringer RC, Meir A, Moon JW, Székely LA. On the Wiener index of trees from some families. *Australa J Combin* 1994; 10:211–224.

20. Fredman ML, Tarjan RE. Fibonacci heaps and their uses in improved network optimization algorithms. *J ACM* 1987; 34:596–615

21. Goldman D, Istrail S, Lancia G, Piccolboni A, Walenz B. Algorithmic strategies in combinatorial chemistry. *Proceedings of 11th ACM-SIAM Symposium. Discrete Algorithms* 2000; pp. 275–284.

22. Gozalbes R, Doucet J, Derouin F. Application of topological descriptors in QSAR and drug design: history and new trends. *Curr Drug Target Infect Disord* 2002; 2:93–102.

23. Gutman I. Selected properties of the Schultz molecular topological index. *J Chem Inf Comput Sci* 1994; 34:1087–1089.

24. Gutman I. Some relations between distance–based polynomials of trees. *Bulletin de l'Académie Serbe des Sciences et des Arts (Cl Math Natur)* 2005; 131:1–7.

25. Gutman I, Klavžar S. A method for calculating Wiener numbers of benzenoid hydrocarbons. *ACH Models Chem* 1996; 133:389–399.

26. Gutman I, Klavžar S, Petkovšek M, Žigert P. On Hosoya polynomials of benzenoid graphs. *Commun Math Chem (MATCH)* 2001; 43:49–66.

27. Gutman I, Linert W, Lukovits I, Dobrynin AA. Trees with extremal hyper-Wiener index: Mathematical basis and chemical applications. *J Chem Inf Comput Sci* 1997; 37:349–354.

28. Gutman I, Linert W, Lukovits I, Tomović Ž. The multiplicative version of the Wiener index. *J Chem Inf Comput Sci* 2000; 40:113–116.

29. Gutman I, Yeh YN. The sum of all distances in bipartite graphs. *Math Slovaca* 1995; 45:327–334.

30. Hosoya H. On some counting polynomials in chemistry. *Discrete Appl Math* 1988; 19:239–257.

31. Ivanciuc O. QSAR comparative study of Wiener descriptor for weighted molecular graphs. *J Chem Inf Comput Sci* 2000; 40:1412–1422.

32. Ivanciuc O, Klein D. Building-block computation of Wiener-type indices for the virtual screening of combinatorial libraries. *Croat Chem Acta* 2002; 75(2):577–601.

33. Johnson DB. Efficient algorithms for shortest path in sparse networks. *J ACM* 1977; 24:1–13.

34. Kirschenhofer P, Prodinger H, Tichy RF. Fibonacci numbers of graphs. II. *Fibonacci Quart* 1983; 21:219–229.

35. Kirschenhofer P, Prodinger H, Tichy RF. Fibonacci numbers of graphs. III. Planted plane trees. *Fibonacci Numbers and Their Applications* Vol. 28, Reidel, Dordrecht; 1986. pp. 105–120.

36. Klavžar S, Gutman I. Wiener number of vertex-weighted graphs and a chemical application. *Discrete Appl Math* 1997; 80:73–81.

37. Klavžar S, Gutman I, Mohar B. Labeling of benzenoid systems which reflects the vertex distance relations. *J Chem Inf Comput Sci* 1995; 35:590–593.

38. Klein DJ, Mihalić Z, Plavšić D, Trinajstić N. Molecular topological index: a relation with the Wiener index. *J Chem Inf Comput Sci* 1992; 32:304–305.

39. Knopfmacher A, Tichy RF, Wagner S, Ziegler V. Graphs, partitions and Fibonacci numbers. *Discrete Appl Math* 2004. Forthcoming.

40. Lepović M, Gutman I. A collective property of trees and chemical trees. *J Chem Inf Comput Sci* 1998; 38:823–826.
41. Li X, Wang L. Solutions for two conjectures on the inverse problem of the Wiener index of peptoids. *SIAM J Discrete Math* 2003; 17(2):210–218.
42. Martin YC. 3D QSAR. Current state, scope, and limitations. *Perspect Drug Discov* 1998 12:3–32.
43. Merrifield RE, Simmons HE. *Topological Methods in Chemistry*. Wiley, New York, 1989.
44. Merris R. An edge version of the matrix-tree theorem and the Wiener index. *Linear and Multilinear Algebra* 1989; 25:291–296.
45. Merris R. The distance spectrum of a tree. *J Graph Theory* 1990; 14:365–369.
46. Merris R. Laplacian matrices of graphs: a survey. *Linear Algebr Appl* 1994; 197/198:143–176.
47. Mohar B. Eigenvalues, diameter, and mean distance in graphs. *Graphs Combin* 1991; 7:53–64.
48. Mohar B. The laplacian spectrum of graphs. In: Alavi Y, Chartrand G, Ollermann OR, Schwenk AJ, editors. *Graph Theory, Combinatorics, and Applications* Wiley, New York; 1991. pp. 871–898.
49. Mohar B, Pisanski T. How to compute the Wiener index of graph. *J Math Chem* 1988; 2:267–277.
50. Prodinger H, Tichy RF. Fibonacci numbers of graphs. *Fibonacci Quart* 1982; 20:16–21.
51. Schultz HP. Topological organic chemistry. 1. graph theory and topological indices of alkanes. *J Chem Inf Comput Sci* 1989; 29:227–228.
52. Shiu WC, Lam PCB. The Wiener number of the hexagonal net. *Discrete Appl Math* 1997; 73:101–111.
53. Stevanović D. Hosoya polynomial of composite graphs. *Discrete Math* 2001; 235(1):237–244.
54. Tichy RF, Wagner S. Extremal problems for topological indices in combinatorial chemistry. *J Comput Biol* 2005; 12(7):1004–1013.
55. Wiener H. Structural determination of paraffin boiling points. *J Amer Chem Soc* 1947; 69:17–20.

20

EFFICIENT ALGORITHMS FOR STRUCTURAL RECALL IN DATABASES

HAO WANG

Department of Computer Science, Georgia State University, Atlanta, GA, USA

PATRA VOLARATH

Department of Chemistry, Georgia State University, Atlanta, GA, USA

ROBERT W. HARRISON*

Department of Computer Science, Georgia State University, Atlanta, GA, USA

20.1 INTRODUCTION

Chemoinformatics is the study of the use of databases in handling chemical knowledge. Chemoinformatics, unlike bioinformatics focuses more on small molecules and a wider range of molecules rather than genes and gene products. It serves a critical role in the development of new materials and new pharmaceuticals, by aiding in the selection of starting points for experimental development. As in bioinformatics many new structures along with their chemical properties are published annually resulting in a huge mass of data that have to be organized into a database for efficient search and recall. Traditional relational database engines like Oracle are required for performance because of the volume of data. However, the properties of the data do

*Dr. Harrison is Georgia Cancer Coalition Distinguished Scholar.

Bioinformatics Algorithms: Techniques and Applications, Edited by Ion I. Măndoiu and Alexander Zelikovsky

not map in an immediate sense into the purely numerical and string-based data types the relational database engines are designed to handle. Therefore, one important problem in chemoinformatics is the development of efficient representations of the chemical and physical properties as well as the structures of molecules. Intimately related to the development of the representation of molecular properties is the ability to compare molecules and extract which ones are most similar in some sense. The ideal representation of chemical and structural data would allow for the rapid and highly specific recall of molecules that are similar in structure and properties. Current approaches tend to be either rapid and imprecise or precise and relatively slow. Therefore, the more accurately the chemical information can be represented in the native representation for the database engine, the more the overall system meets this ideal.

Typically, there are three kinds of queries that are applied in chemoinformatics: shared substructure, similar subset, and molecular property. In a shared substructure query, molecules are selected that share a chemical group or structural framework but differ in other features. For example, aspirin and benzoic acid share a benzene ring and carboxylic acid group but do not share the phenol oxygen and acetyl group of aspirin. In a similar subset query, features that are in common among a set of molecules are extracted and then used to find similar molecules. Superimposing HIV protease inhibitors, for example, would reveal that they share many structural features that would not be readily apparent on casual inspection [1–3]. Finally, with molecular property queries, molecules are selected based on a desired chemical feature or property. An example of this would be the selection of hydrophobic monomers for the design of a novel water-repelling polymer.

20.2 COMPOUND REPRESENTATION

In most databases, molecules are represented in one of two representations: (1) graphs or trees, and (2) strings or line notation. While these representations may seem disjoint, they are intimately related in the sense that the graph or tree could be generated from the string notation by a parsing process.

Molecular graphs/trees represent the chemical bonds and covalent structure of the molecule. For example, benzoic acid is shown in Fig. 20.1. The two-dimensional graphical representation (Fig. 20.1) is useful because it is familiar to the chemists. However, this form of representation is incomplete and highly simplified. For example, the lines show single chemical bonds between carbon atoms, the double lines for double bonds, and only relatively heavy atoms like oxygen are shown explicitly. Most of the hydrogen atoms are omitted. Additionally, the pattern of double and single bonds in the ring structure is defined by convention and does not represent the true electronic structure of the molecule.

The three-dimensional representation of the molecule, also shown for benzoic acid in Fig. 20.1**b** and **c**, is more complete and in many senses more useful than the two-dimensional representation. Many molecular properties including size, charge distribution, heats of formation, vibrational spectra, and relative solubility can be estimated directly from the three-dimensional representation [3–9]. Additionally,

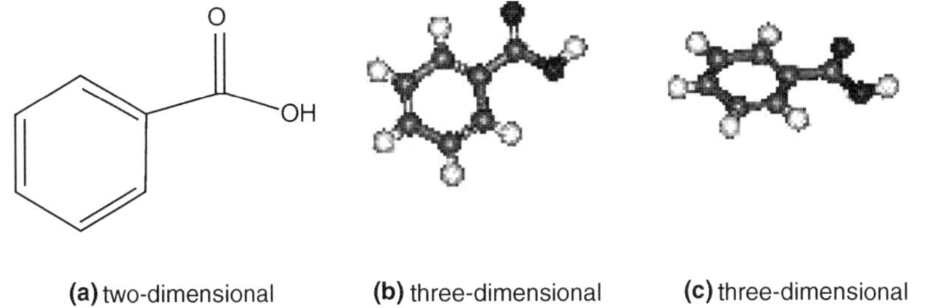

FIGURE 20.1 Two-dimensional (**a**) and three-dimensional (**b** and **c**) representations of benzoic acid.

steric factors that affect molecular stability and ease of synthesis are often more readily visible in the three-dimensional representation in the two-dimensional representation. Finally, it is necessary to have a three-dimensional model of a molecule in applications like pharmaceutical development where the small molecule will be docked into a large molecule that is a drug target such as HIV protease [10–20]. Therefore, parsing the two-dimensional representation and generating a three-dimensional structure is an important task.

One common and effective approach to convert a two-dimensional chemical representation to its three-dimensional structure is to use a molecular mechanics program. Molecular mechanics programs numerically find a minimum in a model of the molecular internal energy defined by a potential or "force field" as a function of the atomic coordinates. The first step in setting up this model of the energy is to first arrange the atoms and bonds in a form of a graph or a tree representation. This allows the covalent atomic geometry of each of the atoms to be determined. It is important that the atomic geometry (or atomtypes) is determined accurately because if they are missassigned then the three-dimensional model will be incorrect. Molecular modeling programs use a force field method [21–31], which relies solely on the parameters that are specifically designed for each of the atomtypes, for the structural simulation. In most cases, the process of determining the atomtypes is straightforward. For instance, AMMP (Advanced Molecular Modeling Program) [32–34] defines a carbonyl functional group as a combination of a sp^2 carbon (or a C3 atomtype) and a sp^2 oxygen (or an O2 atom type), and an alkene as a combination of two C3 atomtypes. However, when an atom participates in a larger system (such as in a chemical ring), assigning an atomtype to the atom may be complicated. One of the reasons is due to the ambiguous representation of aromatic ring, the number, and the types of atoms that are involved in the ring, and the presence of fused rings. Algorithmic approaches have been developed for interpretation and analyze of ring representations [35–38]. These approaches can be highly effective, for example, as a test with AMMP, the entire NCI-Openmol database was converted from two-dimensional to three-dimensional form with no detected errors.

20.2.1 Molecular Graphs and Trees

Molecules can be expressed in a form of a graph or a tree, which consists of a series of nodes (representing the atoms) that are connected by edges (representing the bonds).

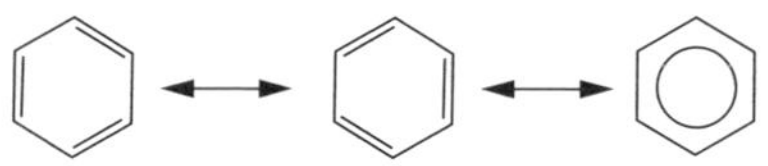

FIGURE 20.2 Common representations of chemical rings.

This is one of the preferred methods of representing the molecules because, first of all, it mimics the way atoms are bond in the real molecules, and second of all, the structural information and properties can be derived using operations of graph theory [39,40].

Graph representation is the most preferred representation of molecules. In practice, several issues must be considered when converting the molecule into a graph. An example is the representations of the ring system. Aspirin, for instance, can have three different graphs that are chemically equivalent. One way of representing an aromaticity within a ring is to define the bond value of aromatic system to be a specially fixed value. AMMP defined this value as 1.5. This rule is enforced in all the inputs and data in the chemical database to ensure structural compatibility during structure comparison.

The difference between the graph and the tree representations is that cyclic structures are not allowed in the tree, Fig. 20.2. Instead, a cyclic structure is indicated by a duplication of a joined atom (Fig. 20.3). The advantage of using the tree representation is that the tree comparison can be completed within polynomial time; this makes the tree more favorable than the graph, whose problems are usually NP-problems. The

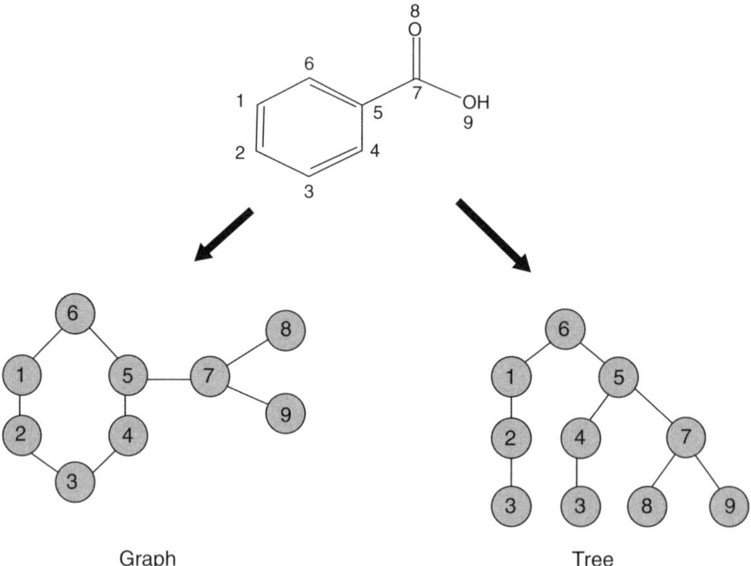

FIGURE 20.3 A graph and a tree representation of benzoic acid. In the tree, the cyclic structure is indicated by the duplication of the atom number 3.

breakage of the cyclic structure in the tree is determined by a set of subjective rules. The mapping of a molecule to tree is not unique. In substructure comparison, the tree representation may need to be rebuilt to compensate for the possible loss of the connectivity information caused by the cycle breakage. However, the tree representation greatly reduces the computation complexity imposed on the graph problems. The choice of which of the representations to use depends on the program users.

20.2.2 Matrix Representation

Molecular graphs can also be represented as matrices, Fig. 20.4. An advantage is that the calculation of paths and cycles (for ring structures) can be performed quickly by matrix operations. A typical molecular matrix consists of n rows and n columns ($n \times n$ matrix) for a molecule with n atoms. The matrix elements can be any data (a bond order, a physical distance, etc.) that represents a relationship between a given pair of atoms [36]. This depends on the type of information that is being emphasized. Some of the matrices that have been used in chemoinformatics are adjacency, distance, incidence, bond, and bond-electron matrices [41].

20.2.3 Connection Table

A connection table for a molecule consists of two sections: a list of atoms that are in a molecule, and a list of their bond connectivity [42,43]. In the first section, the atoms of a compound are listed, according to the order they were entered into a molecule drawing program, in a tabular form (Fig. 20.5).

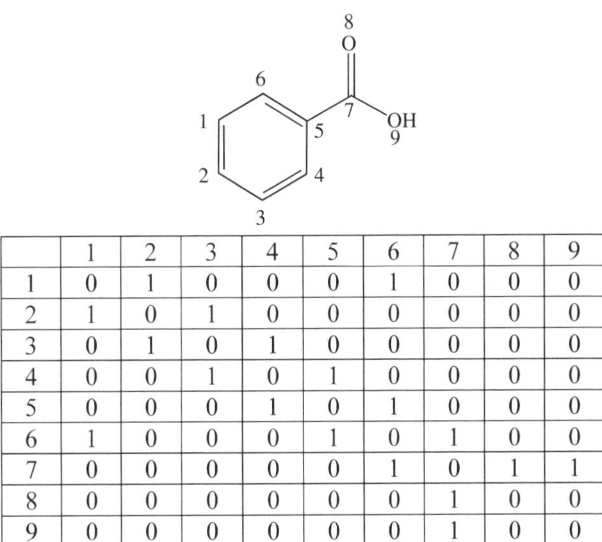

	1	2	3	4	5	6	7	8	9
1	0	1	0	0	0	1	0	0	0
2	1	0	1	0	0	0	0	0	0
3	0	1	0	1	0	0	0	0	0
4	0	0	1	0	1	0	0	0	0
5	0	0	0	1	0	1	0	0	0
6	1	0	0	0	1	0	1	0	0
7	0	0	0	0	0	1	0	1	1
8	0	0	0	0	0	0	1	0	0
9	0	0	0	0	0	0	1	0	0

FIGURE 20.4 A matrix representation of benzoic acid. The numbers 1–9 in the first column and the first row represent the atoms in the molecule. Inside each of the cells, 1 indicates bonding between the atom pair, and 0 indicates otherwise.

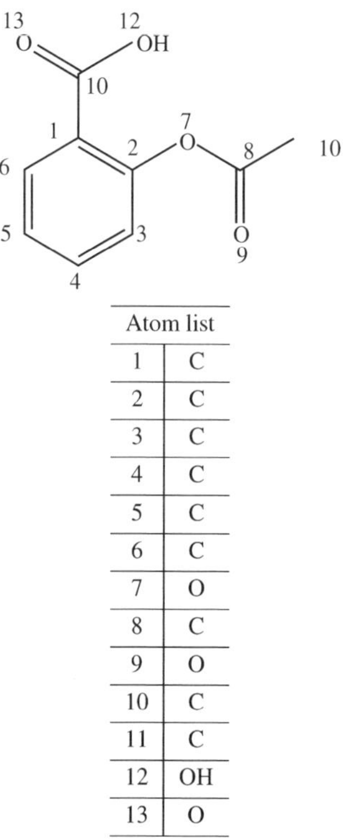

Atom list	
1	C
2	C
3	C
4	C
5	C
6	C
7	O
8	C
9	O
10	C
11	C
12	OH
13	O

FIGURE 20.5 Atom list of aspirin.

Similarly, a connection between a pair of atoms (represented by their indices) in the bond connectivity list is indicated by a numerical value corresponding to the bond order (1 = single bond, 2 = double bond, etc.), Table 20.1.

A MDL.mol file is a well-known file format that uses the connection table to represent the molecules, and a typical MDL.mol file is shown in Fig. 20.6. The first section contains description of the atoms, and these include the Cartesian coordinates, the atomic symbol, followed by columns of property descriptions (e.g., atomic charges, hybridization state). The chemistry of molecule is more completed in the connectivity table than in the graph/tree form because the properties (usually represented via numerical values) can be expressed in the columns. In MDL.mol file, hydrogen atoms are usually omitted in the 2D.mol file, but are included in the 3D version.

20.2.4 Bond Partition

Another way of representing a molecule, which is being currently developed in our lab, through a method called bond partition (Fig. 20.7). In this method, instead of representing atoms via their atomic symbols, the atoms are represented by their atomic numbers. The goal here is to classify the chemical bonds in a molecule into different bond types. The significance of this design is that these atomic values can be further

TABLE 20.1 Bond List of Aspirin

Bond List		
1st Atom	2nd Atom	Bond Order
1	2	2
1	6	1
1	11	1
2	3	1
2	7	1
3	4	2
4	5	1
5	6	2
7	8	1
8	9	2
8	10	1
11	12	1
12	13	2

```
aspirin.mol
  ChemDraw08140618222D

 13 13  0  0  0  0  0  0  0  0999 V2000
   -1.1953    0.2062    0.0000 C   0  0  0  0  0  0  0  0  0
   -0.4809   -0.2062    0.0000 C   0  0  0  0  0  0  0  0  0
   -0.4809   -1.0313    0.0000 C   0  0  0  0  0  0  0  0  0
   -1.1953   -1.4438    0.0000 C   0  0  0  0  0  0  0  0  0
   -1.9098   -1.0313    0.0000 C   0  0  0  0  0  0  0  0  0
   -1.9098   -0.2062    0.0000 C   0  0  0  0  0  0  0  0  0
    0.3160    0.0073    0.0000 O   0  0  0  0  0  0  0  0  0
    1.1129   -0.2062    0.0000 C   0  0  0  0  0  0  0  0  0
    1.1129   -1.0313    0.0000 O   0  0  0  0  0  0  0  0  0
    1.9098    0.0073    0.0000 C   0  0  0  0  0  0  0  0  0
   -1.1953    1.0313    0.0000 C   0  0  0  0  0  0  0  0  0
   -0.4809    1.4438    0.0000 O   0  0  0  0  0  0  0  0  0
   -1.9098    1.4438    0.0000 O   0  0  0  0  0  0  0  0  0
  1  2  2  0
  2  3  1  0
  3  4  2  0
  4  5  1  0
  5  6  2  0
  6  1  1  0
  2  7  1  0
  7  8  1  0
  8  9  2  0
  8 10  1  0
  1 11  1  0
 11 12  1  0
 11 13  2  0
M  END
```

FIGURE 20.6 Connectivity table of aspirin (see Fig. 20.5) generated by ChemDraw Ultra 6.0.

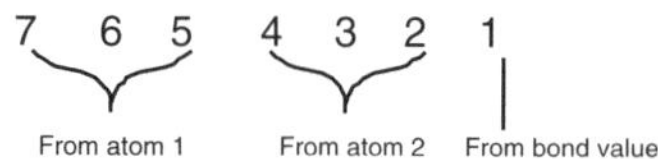

FIGURE 20.7 Numeric representation of bond type.

used in calculations that are specific for each atom. In this design, a pair of atoms and its bond order (collectively referred to as a bond type) is represented by seven digits (figure reffig:numeric). The first and the second three digits are determined based on the atomic numbers of the first and the second atoms, respectively. The last digit represents the bond order between the two atoms.

This design is based on the fact that each of the atoms has a unique atomic number. The largest atom in the periodic table is 118; thus, it is more than enough to have a 3-digit to present that numeric value. In this descriptor, two atoms are arranged in an ascend order of their atom numbers. For example, a bond type of a double bond between a carbon and an oxygen can be defined as 0060082. In this representation, the numerical value 6 is the atomic number of the carbon, 7 is the atomic number of the oxygen, and the last digit 2 represents the double bond between the atoms. In a given molecule, a bond type is determined for each of the bonds in the molecule. The bond types are then collected into a bond group, based on the identities of the atoms that are involved in the bonding and the bond order. Each bond group,therefore, consists of bonds with identical pairwise atoms and connection value. The atoms in the group are represented by their positions (x, y). x represents the position of the atom with a lower atom number, and y represents the position of the atom with a higher atomic number. A bond partition of the aspirin graph is shown in Fig. 20.8.

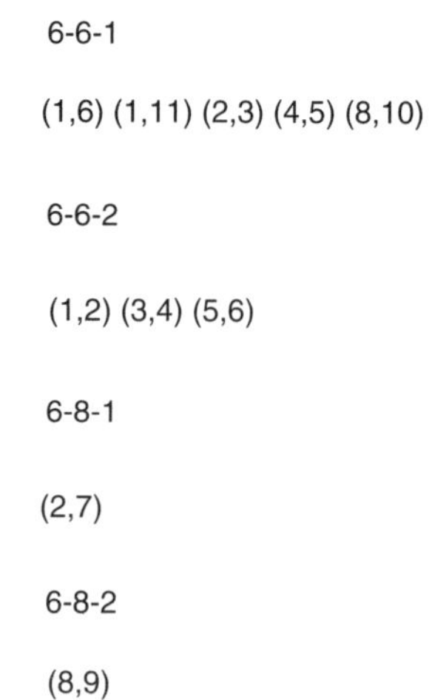

FIGURE 20.8 Revised graph representation of aspirin.

20.2.5 Line Notations

Another way of expressing molecules is through the use of a linear or string notation. A linear notation uses characters and digits to encode the molecular structure. Linear notations are more compact than the graph/tree and the connection table forms. Therefore, linear notations are very useful for storing and transmitting large numbers of molecules, particularly, when used in conjunction with relational databases that support only characters and digits. Linear notations can be rapidly searched for approximate similarities using string search algorithms similar to those used for sequence alignment such as BLAST [44–46], but the results can be relatively inaccurate.

An early line notation that became widely used was the Wiswesser Line Notation (WLN) [47]. WLN uses a complex set of rules to represent different functional groups and their connectivity in molecules. A more recent linear notation that has been developed and became widely accepted is the SMILES notation [48,49].

In SMILES, the atoms are represented by the atomic symbols. The elements with the number of attached hydrogens conform to the lowest normal valence consistent with explicit bonds can be written without brackets [50]. For example, water molecule can be expressed as O, while hydronium cation is express as [OH3+]. No information on three-dimensional arrangement of atoms is represented, and hydrogen atoms can be omitted or included. Single, double, triple, and aromatic bonds are represented by the symbols, respectively, and branches are specified by parentheses. Atoms in aromatic rings are represented by lower case letters, and the aromatic bonds are usually omitted. Cyclic structures are represented by breaking one single (or aromatic) bond in each ring. The bonds are numbered in any order, designating ring-opening (or ring-closure) bonds by a digit immediately following the atomic symbol at each ring closure. Pyridine, for instance, can be expressed in SMILES as n1ccccc1. Table 20.2 shows SMILES for some of the organic compounds.

Since the publication of its original version, SMILES has been improved and made into different versions. Canonical SMILES is a version of the SMILES that was designed to ensure a single unique SMILES representation for a chemical compound. Another version of SMILES called Isomeric SMILES extends the string representation to support the chemical properties such as isotopes, chirality, and configuration about double bonds [50]. Other descendents of SMILES include SMARTS [51] that

TABLE 20.2 SMILES Notations for Nine Compounds [50]

Compound Names	SMILES Notations
Butane	CCCC
Isobutene	C(C)(CCl)C
Anthracene	C(c(ccc1)ccc2)(c1)c2
Benzene	c1ccccc1
Naphthalene	c1ccc2ccccc2c1
Methylcyclohexane	CC1CCCCC1
Trichloromethane	C(CL)(CL)CL
Nitromethane	CN(=O)=O
1,3-cyclohexadiene	C1=CC=CCC1

describes molecular patterns, which is useful for structure comparison, and SMIRKS [52] that contains rules for molecular transformations, which is useful for chemical reactions.

20.2.6 Canonical Representation and Canonical Structure Determination Algorithms

A major task that is performed on chemical databases is a search for compounds whose structures or characteristics fit the target molecules. When a search for particular compounds is performed, it is important that each of the returned results represents specifically one structure. Otherwise, redundant results, lengthy computational time, and unpredictable computational behaviors may occur. The compound representations mentioned thus far represent only the topology of compounds. This means, in the table form, the atoms can be numbered in different orders that represent the same molecule. Likewise, the atoms in SMILES can be combined in a number of ways that yield the same molecule. The term canonical representation refers to methods of ordering atoms such that the resulting order is a unique representation for a given compound. Morgan algorithm [53,54] and CANGEN [49] method are two of the well-known approaches that have been used to determine a canonical order of the atoms in the connectivity table and in SMILES, respectively.

The basic operation of the Morgan algorithm is a calculation of "connectivity values." In the initial step, each of the atoms is assigned a numerical value (a class value) equivalent to the sum of its immediate neighbors (a node degree). In the second and the subsequent steps, the algorithm readjusts the class value of each of the atoms by summing the class values of its adjacent neighbors. The readjusted value is referred to as an extended connectivity (EC) value. One way to understand the assignment of EC value is to imagine an atom and its immediate neighbors within a sphere (Fig. 20.9). Each of the EC values (3, 4, and 5) represents the total number of bonds covered in a sphere. After each iteration, the sphere expands outward one level at a time. During this step, the algorithm calculates the number of equivalent classes based on the EC values, and this number is used to determine when to terminate the iteration.

The Morgan algorithm involves two steps. The first step is to assign EC values for the atoms, and the algorithm operates as follows:

1. In the initial step (the formation of the first sphere), the EC value for each atom is calculated based on its node degree.The number of equivalent class for each of the atoms is then calculated.
2. For the second and subsequence steps (higher sphere levels), the EC value for each atom is recalculated by summing the EC values, which were assigned from the previous step, of the immediate neighboring atoms. A new equivalent class number is calculated.
3. If the new equivalent class number is greater than that of the previous iteration, continue iteration as described previously.
4. The last iteration with the highest equivalent class number is taken for the next step.

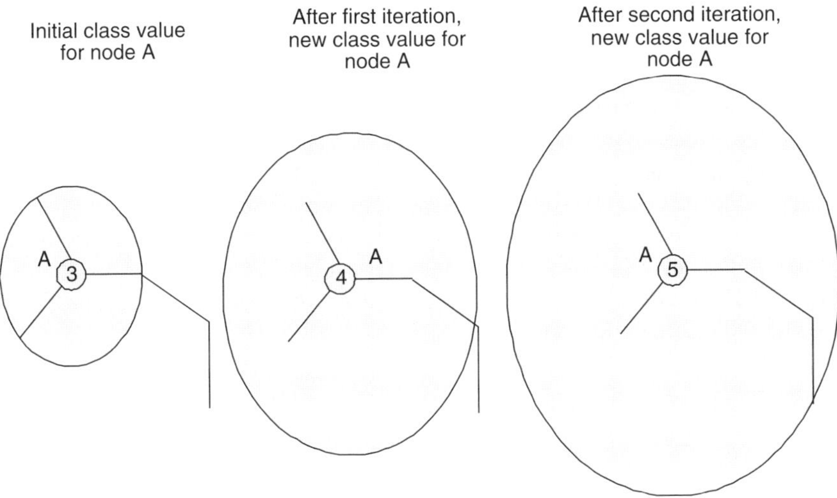

FIGURE 20.9 Sphere coverage and EC value.

The second step in the Morgan algorithm involves an assignment of a unique sequence number to the atoms. The algorithm of this step is as follows:

1. The atom with the highest EC value assigned by the first part of the algorithm is chosen as the first atom (a current target) in the connection table. Its direct neighbors are listed in a descending order of their EC values. If there is a tie in the EC values, additional rules (such as atomic identity, bond, charges) are introduced.
2. Next, the EC values of all the assigned sequence-number atoms, except the current target, are compared. The highest EC numbered atom becomes a new current target. All unassigned sequence-number atoms attached to the current target are numbered as in the previous step. This process continues until all the atoms are enumerated.

The Stereochemically Extended Morgan Algorithm (SEMA) is an extended version of the Morgan algorithm to include the stereochemistry information into the selection process [55].

An algorithm called CANGEN has also been developed based on a similar principal to the Morgan algorithm, to generate a unique SMILES string for each compound. CANGEN combines the molecular labeling of CANON algorithm and the string generation method of GENES algorithm [49].

20.3 CHEMICAL COMPOUND DATABASE

Chemical databases store chemical structures and their information. The sizes of the structures stored in databases can range from those of small molecules, as in the Cambridge Structural Database and Inorganic Crystal Structure Database, to those of macromolecules such as proteins and nucleic acids stored in the Protein Data Bank (PDB) database, Table 20.3. Other databases, such as Quantum Chemical Literature Database, store information from the literature regarding chemical properties that can be used in the analysis. Other useful chemical databases include PubChem, KEGG LIGAND Database, ChemIDplus, Indiana University Molecular Structure Center, NCI-3D Database, and Chmoogle.

20.3.1 Indexing of Database

Relational databases are the prevailing type of databases used to store chemical information. They are powerful tools for organizing information; however, they are designed to handle numeric and string data rather than chemical structures. Therefore, the characteristics of the chemical structure must first be converted into a representation using strings and digits that is, in turn, stored inside the database. Clearly, the choice of this transformation will affect the flexibility and accuracy of the recall process. The characteristics can be any of the properties and features of the molecule. This method of labeling, or indexing, of the characteristics allows the information to be stored efficiently in the relational database. Another purpose of indexing the database is to predetermine the solutions to some of the expected queries to shorten the response time. For instance, the result returned by popular search engines (such as Google, Yahoo, and MSN) is an indexed portion of presearch pages. This allows the viewers to access the pages without having to wait for tedious calculations.

TABLE 20.3 A List of Some of the Common Chemical Databases Used in Chemoinformatics

Data Source	Web Sites
Cambridge Structural Database	http://www.ccdc.cam.ac.uk
Databases on STN International	http://www.stn-international.de/stndatabases/c_datab.html
Protein Database	http://www.rcsb.org
NCBI PubChem	http://pubchem.ncbi.nlm.nih.gov
KEGG LIGAND Database	http://www.genome.jp/ligand
National Library Medicine Specialized Information Service	http://chem.sis.nlm.nih.gov/chemidplus/
Indiana University Molecular Structure Center	http://www.iumsc.indiana.edu/database/index.html
TOXNET(Toxicology Data Network)	http://toxnet.nlm.nih.gov/cgi-bin/sis/htmlgen?Multi
eMolecules Chemcial Searching	http://www.chmoogle.com/

In chemical databases, indexing can be used to label chemical features. Two methods that have been used to index the chemical databases are a fragment code and a fingerprint.

The fragment code method [56,57] is sometimes referred to as a structural key method. In this method, the molecule is broken down into fragments with predefined patterns. Each of the patterns represents a characteristic (such as atomic content, functional groups, ring systems) of a molecule. Depending on the molecules, different types of fragment codes can be defined. String representations, like SMILES, are well suited to this decomposition. Unlike the canonical structures, fragment codes can be ambiguous, and different structures could possess identical fragment codes. This is because the code does not specify the connection orientation. The key in designing a fragment code dictionary is to first determine the type of search that will be performed on the databases. This is to optimize the search performance by eliminating the irrelevant molecules, which, in turn, reduces the searching time. It is also necessary to design the dictionary according to the compounds stored in the database and the queries that might be submitted. Although any type of chemical features and queries maybe used, there are certain types that are frequently encountered.

A fingerprint method [54,57] describes properties and characteristics of a molecule using a string of binary digits 1 and 0: 1 represents a positive response and 0 represents a negative response. The string can be of any size, which allows as many chemical features and properties of a molecule to be expressed. A fingerprint of a benzoic acid, for example, can be 111 for the presence of a benzene ring, a carbonyl, and a hydroxyl group, respectively. If a second molecule with a fingerprint of 011 is compared with the acid's fingerprint, the difference between the two fingerprints indicates that the second molecule contains a carbonyl and a hydroxyl, but no benzene ring. Because of its flexibility, the fingerprint method is often used as a similarity measurement tool between structures and/or in a substructure searching routine during the screening of the molecule databases.

20.3.2 Database Searching Algorithm

The search routine that is often performed on the chemical database can be divided into two categories: structure searching and similarity searching.

20.3.2.1 Structure Search Structure searching [58–61] depends on the target structure of whether it is partially (substructure searching) or fully known (exact-structure searching). Analyzing molecular structure using a computer is a challenge because the computer is not designed to understand structures. An approach to deal with this challenge is to encode this capability into the computer. Two algorithmic methods that have been developed for this purpose are a *hash key* and a *backtracking* mechanism.

A hash key method is an extension of the fragment code [62–64]. The input structure, regardless of its representation, is first translated to an input source consisting of alphabetical and numerical codes. These codes are then transformed by the hash algorithm into a preset and fixed number of characters. These characters are hash codes, or "keys," which represent the storage, where the corresponded data are stored in the hash table. This technique allows information to be retrieved instantaneously by a direct access to the location specified by the key, instead of performing a one-by-one comparison. Theoretically, each canonical structure is expected to produce a different hash key. This makes the method suitable for the exact-structure searching. However, in practice, there is no guarantee that a clash between the keys (address collision) will not occur [65]. There are algorithms for hash key generation with an emphasis on avoiding potential key clashes led by two different structures. However, it is still necessary to integrate a mechanism that can resolve the problem if it happens. The hash key method has been used in a generation of SMILES string, as well as in a design of the Augmented Connectivity Molecular Formula (ACMF) to describe chemical structures in the Chemical Abstracts Service Registry System [65].

Another method that has been used to compare two structures during the searching routine is a backtracking mechanism [66]. This method uses an atom mapping approach in which the nodes (or atoms) of the target molecular graph/tree are superimposed onto the nodes of the graph/tree of the molecules in the databases (database molecules). The mapping is performed atom by atom until it is impossible to find a match. When this occurs, the algorithm returns (backtrack) to the last successful match and attempts another route for mapping. This process continues until all the nodes in both the target molecule and the database molecule have been successfully matched (for an exact-structure matching), or all the nodes in the target molecule are matched (for a substructure matching). When all possible mappings of the initial node have been attempted, the algorithm terminates. Ullmann algorithm, one of the well-known algorithms for substructure searches, efficiently uses the backtracking mechanism for generalized isomorphism. Ullman algorithm has been applied to both substructure and maximum substructure problems. It has been demonstrated that the average running time of this algorithm falls into an acceptable polynomial time complexity range. For this reason, although it has been developed in the 70s, the Ullman algorithm remains one of the best graph isomorphism algorithms.

The Ullmann algorithm involves three matrices: two adjacency matrices that represent the desired substructure and the database structure, and one matching matrix that represents the mapping result [67]. Each of the adjacency matrices is a square matrix, whose size is determined by the contained atoms. The numerical number 1 in each of the matrix cells indicates a bonding between atomsij, while 0 indicates a bond absence between the two. For the matching matrix, the number of rows is equal to number of atoms in the substructure, and the number of the columns is equal to the number of atoms in the database structure. As the elements in the two adjacency matrices are compared, the matching results are initially recorded in the matching matrix. A value 1 in each of the matching matrix elements indicates an atom matching possibility between the substructure and the database structure, and the values 0s indicate otherwise.

The goal is to refine the matching matrix such that in the final matching matrix, each row contains just one element equal to 1 and each column contains no more than one element equal to 1. This final matching matrix represents a unique mapping for every atom of the substructure. The initial mapping matrix can be constructed by taking neighboring connectivity into consideration. The Ullmann algorithm allows the atoms to match only if their neighboring atoms also match. The backtracking mechanism is repeated until either a complete match for the substructure is discovered on until all options have been attempted.

Another popular method for substructure searching is to use fragment coding. This method is based on a rationale that a substructure mapping of two molecules is possible if and only if all the fragments in the smaller molecule have a match in the larger molecule. Most of the current chemical databases have a fragment dictionary. Each molecule is fragment coded, and the resulting codes are saved in the database. With a sensitive choice of fragment dictionary, substructure searching can be carried out by matching the fragment codes of the molecules. This process can be performed quickly because fragment codes are in a binary format. However, the method may generate a false positive result, in which the returning structures, although meet all the fragment requirements in the query structure, do not contain query structure as a whole. The reason for this is that the connectivity among the fragments is usually not indicated along with the fragments. Another challenge for this method is the effectiveness of the fragment dictionary used, which may yield varied results depending on their definitions and application cases.

20.3.2.2 Similarity Search It is not always possible to have a complete structure, or even substructure, of the target molecule available prior to the search. During a drug screening process, for example, it is often that only some desirable properties of the target molecule are known. In such cases, it is more sensible to be able to search the chemical databases for structures that have similar properties to the desired structures. Similarity searching is operated based on the rational that molecules that are similar in structures are likely to have similar behaviors under the same condition [68–76]. The effectiveness of the search, therefore, relies on the similarity measure that is used to perform the comparison. An example of this similarity measure problem is a maximum common subgraph (MCS). The result returned by MCS indicates a largest subgraph that is common to a pair of graphs. In the chemical context, this is equivalent to the largest common substructure existed in a pair of molecules. Although the conceptual approach used in MCS similarity measurement is straightforward, the calculations can become complicated when the sizes of the comparing molecules become large. It has been shown that the complexity in the MCS calculation can reach the NP-complete level, as in the Maximum clique problem. Thus, using the MCS method as a similarity measure may not be feasible when dealing with large compounds.

A method that has been used extensively in structure similarity search is similarity coefficients. The coefficients are often used in a similarity metric [77–82] that determines similarity based on the similarity "distance" between two fingerprints. An example of such coefficient is the *Tanimoto Coefficient*, TC, which is defined as

$$TC = \left(\frac{B_C}{B_1 + B_2 - B_C} \right). \quad (20.1)$$

In this equation, BC is the number of 1s common to both fingerprints, B1 is the number of 1s in the first fingerprint, and B2 is the number of 1s in the second fingerprint. If two structures are identical, their Tanamoto Coefficient will be 1.0, and it will decrease to 0.0 as they become more dissimilar [83]. A number of similarity coefficients are available [84,85]. A challenge in working with the coefficients is an assigning appropriate threshold values. This is significant because the effectiveness of these values depend on the chosen fingerprints and also on the studied compound classes.

Candidate Ligand Identification Program (CLIP) is an example virtual screen program that utilizes the coefficients for structure comparison [86]. The two coefficients that are used in this program are the Tanimoto and a modified form of Simpson's coefficients. The Simpson's coefficient is an association coefficient that has been used in information retrieval. In this program, a structure is represented by a set of pharmacophore points that corresponds to the geometric arrangement. The similarity comparison between two given structures is performed by comparing the results of the two coefficients calculated from MSC. The Simpson's coefficient is defined as

$$\frac{a}{\min(b, c)}, \tag{20.2}$$

where a is the number of the pharmacophore points in the MCS; while, b and c are the numbers of the points in the target and the database structures. These terms are also used to construct the formula for Tanimoto coefficient as in Equation 20.1,

$$\frac{a}{b + c - a}. \tag{20.3}$$

CLIP uses the Bron–Kerbosch clique detection algorithm to identify structures in a given file that have large substructures in common with a target structure. The coefficients incorporate the distance tolerance factor to ensure that the interatomic distances are appropriate for the clique-construction stage of the matching algorithm.

Each of the coefficients has been designed specifically for different characteristics of molecules. Some of these coefficients can be combined to optimize the similarity search performance [87]. For instances, it has been shown that a combination that contains Forbes and Simple Match coefficients seems to have an increased performance when dealing with small molecules. On the contrary, for larger compounds, the combinations that contain Russell–Rao coefficient seem to have a better coefficient combination performance than others. A similar study has also been conducted on the coefficients for searching of the natural product molecules in the *Dictionary of Natural Products* (DNP) database [88]. Here, it has also been shown that *Russell–Rao coefficient* has a better performance in retrieving large molecules, and *Forbes coefficient* results in a better retrieving of small molecules from the database. However, there has been no computational evidence showing any one combination demonstrating a consistently high performance across all types of activity. The *Tanimoto coefficient* remains a good single measure as no other combinations gave consistent improvement over its use.

Other approaches have also been developed to improve the similarity measure of two structures. One of these approaches is a reduced graph method [43]. In a typical molecular graph, the nodes represent the atoms and the edges represent the bonds. However, in a reduced graph, the nodes represent groups of atoms and the edges represent the physical bonds between the groups. In the reduced graph approach, groups of atoms are clustered into a node. This can be done based on definitions in a dictionary of fragments or by sending the atoms through a node labeling scheme. The labeling of a group of atoms based on the fragment dictionary can be performed straightforwardly. However, with the node labeling scheme, the atoms must go, in a descending order, through layers of differentiation until the final result is achieved. This results in a hierarchy of reduced graphs, whose top layer being the least discriminated and the last bottom layer being the most discriminated. The resulting reduced graph is then converted to a pseudo-SMILES representation, where the comparison between structures can be performed by node and edge mappings. The results show that the reduced graph method not only has a potential to improve the similarity search, but also is capable of retrieving more diverse active compounds than those found using Daylight fingerprints.

Machine learning has also been recently used to improve the similarity search. A method called a *turbo similarity searching*(TSS) has been developed to improve the performance of a similarity searching engine by using the reference structure's *nearest neighbors*(NNs) [89]. NNs are those structures that have been determined to be the most similar to the reference structure. *Substructure analysis*(SSA) [90,91] and *binary kernel discrimination*(BKD) [92] are two machine learning procedures that have been applied to TSS. SSA is a weight-assigning scheme that assigns a weight to each bit (or substructure) in a fingerprint. This weight represents the bit's differential occurrence in the active and inactive molecules that are used in a training set. BKD is a training-set ranking procedure that is based on the calculated score for each of the members in the training set. The results have indicated that an application of an appropriate machine learning approach enhances the performance of the similarity search.

20.3.3 Screening

Although efficient algorithms for identifying subgraph isomorphism [67,93] are well established, they are usually too slow to be used with large chemical databases. For this reason, most chemical database systems use a two-stage mechanism to perform substructure search [94]. The first step is to perform a rapid screening on the data to eliminate the compounds that do not match the query. This step is to reduce the sample size, which, in turn, decreases the processing time. The remaining structures are to be further determined if they truly match the query substructure.

Most of the screening methods use the fragment code and/or the fingerprint representations for the chemical features. The features are expressed in a bitstring that consists of a sequence of 0 and 1, where 1 indicates a presence of a particular feature, and 0 indicates an absence of the feature. For example, two bitstrings A and B are compared. String A represent the target substructure, and string B represent a database structure. A positive result would be returned only if all the bits in A have a match in B. This logic operation can be performed quickly in the computers; therefore, the screening process can be completed within a short time. A number of the screening methods have been developed for the searching of the chemical and biological databases [95–103].

Some of the screening methods require the data in the database to be constructed correspondingly to chemical features. An example is the compound data that are stored in different tables based on the contained atom number. In the substructure searching routine, a minimum atom number required by the query structure is first calculated. This allows those compound data with an atom number lower than the calculated value to be eliminated immediately. This screening process is, in other words, boosted by the internal data model organization in the database. In practice, data model can be constructed to allow complicated logic. In the hierarchical tree substructure search (HTSS) system [104], the entire database is stored in a treelike structure based on the encoded atoms. A substructure search on the entire database is then reduced to a set of simple tree searches. One potential drawback of these systems is that it can be difficult to update the database with new structures. This may not be a problem for database that does not need to be updated very often. Another problem is that, data models with highly complicated logic may not be constructed easily in the relational database.

20.4 PRACTICAL CONCERNS FOR COMPOUND DATABASES

There are two challenges in working with the chemical databases: keeping the data up to date, and controlling the data size. New data is continually being deposited in the data repositories, and it is important for a local source to keep an accurate mirror of this data. It is preferred that information enriched chemical databases are available to public. However, many of the information are private and only available to those with licenses. For those open-to-public databases, the formats of their compound representations are often different; it makes the exporting and merging of the data challenging. Hence, establishing a standard data format for compounds may alleviate this problem. However, this work is not a straightforward task, mainly due to different research focuses and interests.

Similarly, the data size is already large and continually growing. Though many efficient algorithms have been developed, their accuracy and speed are often impaired by the large amount of data that need to be processed. The use of the fragment code and the fingerprint methods, for example, simplifies the computational process. However, they can impair the accuracy of routines like similarity search. In these cases, the effectiveness of the search depends on the similarity measurement used, whose effectiveness varies from case to case. If the database contains millions of chemical compounds, even with efficient screening methods that can discard over 99cannot afford to apply a one-to-one isomorphism operation on the remaining structures. There is often a trade-off between processing speed and accuracy. However, it must be remembered that the experimental use of these compounds in a real chemistry lab may take months or even years so it is important not to be overly aggressive at trimming processing speed at the cost of missing critical leads. It is more important to find good lead compounds than it is to reduce the time of the query from a month to a second.

Methods dealing with pairwise calculations may provide a solution to these problems because they are independent of each other. Methods like parallel computing and database arrangement can, therefore, be fully explored in the comparison applications. Cluster analysis methods, for example, can be applied to obtain structural clusters for organization in the chemical database. The clustered data can be organized in the database in a distributed cluster way, a function which is provided by most of the-state-of-art database systems. A cluster data arrangement can organize the size of each of the participating databases in a manageable manner. For example, all clusters can be logically connected, in a tree-structure fashion, based on their structure features. This, in turn, allows the search routine to be performed quickly via comparing the features. In a case of compound database searching, the features of the query structure are first extracted. These features are then used as criteria for searching through the cluster tree to find the cluster nodes that match the features. Only those cluster data that meet the requirements are chosen for next step processing.

ACKNOWLEDGMENTS

This work was partially supported by NIH P20 GM065762-01A1, the Georgia Research Alliance, and the Georgia Cancer Coalition. Dr. Harrison is Georgia Cancer Coalition Distinguished Scholar.

REFERENCES

1. Jenwitheesuk E, Samudrala R. Virtual screening of HIV-1 protease inhibitors against human cytomegalovirus protease using docking and molecular dynamics. *Aids* 2005;19(5):529–531.
2. Zhu Z, Schuster, Samudrala, Tuckerman ME. Molecular dynamics study of the connection between flap closing and binding of fullerene-based inhibitors of the HIV-1 protease. *Biochemistry* 2003;42(5):1326–1333.
3. Reddy MR, Viswanadhan VN, Weinstein, V. Relative differences in the binding free energies of human immunodeficiency virus 1 protease inhibitors: a thermodynamic cycle-perturbation approach. *Proc Natl Acad Sci USA* 1991;88(22):10287–10291.
4. Hu H, Elstner M, Hermans J. Comparison of a QM/MM force field and molecular mechanics force fields in simulations of alanine and glycine "dipeptides" (Ace-Ala-Nme and Ace-Gly-Nme) in water in relation to the problem of modeling the unfolded peptide backbone in solution. *Proteins* 2003;451–463.
5. Zheng L, Thompson DL. VOn the accuracy of force fields for predicting the physical properties of dimethylnitramine. *J Phys Chem B Condens Matter Mater. Surf Interface Biophys* 2006;110(32):16082–16088.

6. Fernandez LE, Varetti EL. Vibrational spectra of the trifluoromethylsulfinate anion and scaled quantum mechanical force fields for CF(3)SO(2)(-) and CF(3)SeO(2)(-). *Spectrochim Acta A Mol Biomol Spectrosc* 2006.
7. McKean DC, Craig NC, Panchenko YN. s-trans-1,3-butadiene and isotopomers: vibrational spectra, scaled quantum-chemical force fields, fermi resonances, and C-H bond properties. *J Phys Chem A Mol Spectrosc Kinet Environ Gen Theory* 2006;110(26): 8044–8059.
8. Tu Y, Laaksonen A. Atomic charges in molecular mechanical force fields: a theoretical insight. *Phys Rev E Stat Nonlin Soft Matter Phys* 2001;64(2 Pt 2):26703.
9. Zhan L, Chen JZ, Liu WK. Conformational study of Met-enkephalin based on the ECEPP force fields. *Biophys J* 2006.
10. Jenwitheesuk E, Samudrala R. Prediction of HIV-1 protease inhibitor resistance using a protein-inhibitor flexible docking approach. *Antivir Ther* 2005;10(1):157–166.
11. Vieth M, Cummins DJ. DoMCoSAR: a novel approach for establishing the docking mode that is consistent with the structure-activity relationship. Application to HIV-1 protease inhibitors and VEGF receptor tyrosine kinase inhibitors *J Med Chem* 2000;43(16): 3020–3032.
12. Schaffer L, Verkhivker GM. Predicting structural effects in HIV-1 protease mutant complexes with flexible ligand docking and protein side-chain optimization. *Proteins* 1998;33(2): 295–310.
13. Olson AJ, Goodsell DS. Automated docking and the search for HIV protease inhibitors. *SAR QSAR Environ Res* 1998;8(3-4):273–285.
14. Verkhivker GM, Rejto PA, Gehlhaar DK, Freer ST. Exploring the energy landscapes of molecular recognition by a genetic algorithm: analysis of the requirements for robust docking of HIV-1 protease and FKBP-12 complexes. *Proteins* 1996;25(3): 342–353.
15. King BL, Vajda S, DeLisi C. Empirical free energy as a target function in docking and design: application to HIV-1 protease inhibitors *FEBS Lett* 1996;384(1): 87–91.
16. DesJarlais RL, Dixon JS. A shape- and chemistry-based docking method and its use in the design of HIV-1 protease inhibitors *J Comput Aided Mol Des* 1994;8(3)231–242.
17. Liu F, Boross PI, Wang YF, Tozser J, Louis JM, Harrison RW, Weber IT. Kinetic, stability, and structural changes in high-resolution crystal structures of HIV-1 protease with drug-resistant mutations L24I, I50V, and G73S, *J Mol Biol* 2005;354(4):789–800.
18. Tie Y, Boross PI, Wang YF, Gaddis L, Liu F, Chen X, Tozser J, Harrison RW, Weber IT. Molecular basis for substrate recognition and drug resistance from 1.1 to 1.6 angstroms resolution crystal structures of HIV-1 protease mutants with substrate analogs. *FEBS* 2005;272(20):5265–5277.
19. Chen X, Weber IT, Harrison RW. Molecular dynamics simulations of 14 HIV protease mutants in complexes with indinavir. *J Mol Model (online)* 2004;10:373–381.
20. Mahalingam B, Wang YF, Boross PI, Tozser J, Louis JM, Harrison RW, Weber IT. Crystal structures of HIV protease V82A and L90M mutants reveal changes in the indinavir-binding site. *Eur J Biochem* 2004;271(8):1516–1524.
21. Kini RM, Evans HJ. Molecular modeling of proteins: a strategy for energy minimization by molecular mechanics in the AMBER force field *J Biomol Struct Dyn* 1991; 9(3):475–488.

22. Curco D, Rodriguez-Ropero F, Aleman C. Force-field parametrization of retro-inverso modified residues: development of torsional and electrostatic parameters. *J Comput Aided Mol Des* 2006;20(1):13–25.

23. Arnautova YA, Jagielska A, Scheraga HA. A new force field (ECEPP-05) for peptides, proteins, and organic molecules. *J Phys Chem B Condens Matter Mater Surf Interfaces Biophys* 2006;110(10):5025–5044.

24. Oda A, Yamaotsu N, Hirono S. New AMBER force field parameters of heme iron for cytochrome P450s determined by quantum chemical calculations of simplified models. *J Comput Chem* 2005;26(8):818–826.

25. Kosinsky YA, Volynsky PE, Lagant P, Vergoten G, Suzuki E, Arseniev AS, Efremov RG. Development of the force field parameters for phosphoimidazole and phosphohistidine. *J Comput Chem* 2004;25(11):1313–1321.

26. Chessari, G, Hunter CA, Low CM, Packer MJ, Vinter JG, Zonta C. An evaluation of force-field treatments of aromatic interactions. *Chemistry* 2002;8(13):2860–2867.

27. Hancock RD, Reichert DE, Welch MJ. Molecular mechanics force field for modeling technetium(V) complexes. *Inorg Chem* 1996;35(8):2165–2166.

28. Brooks BR, Bruccoleri RE, Olafson BD, States DJ, Swaminathan S, Karplus M. CHARMM: A program for macromolecular energy, minmimization, and dynamics calculations. *J Comp Chem* 1983;4:187–217.

29. Allinger NL. Conformational Analysis 130. MM2. A hydrocarbon force field utilizing V1 and V2 torsional terms. *J Am Chem Soc* 1977;99:8127–8134.

30. Allinger NL, Yuh YH, Lii J-H. Molecular Mechanics. The MM3 force field for hydrocarbons. *J Am Chem Soc* 1989;111:8551–8565.

31. Rappe AK, Casewit CJ, Colwell KS, Goddard. UFF a full periodic table force field for molecular mechanics and molecular dynamics simulations. *J Am Chem Soc* 1992;114:10024–10035.

32. Weber IT, Harrison RW. Molecular mechanics analysis of drug-resistant mutants of HIV protease. *Protein Eng* 1999;12(6):469–474.

33. Weber IT, Harrison RW. Molecular mechanics calculations on Rous sarcoma virus protease with peptide substrates. *Protein Sci* 1997;6(11):2365–2374.

34. Weber IT, Harrison RW. Molecular mechanics calculations on HIV-1 protease with peptide substrates correlate with experimental data. *Protein Eng* 1996;9(8): 679–690.

35. Cyranski M, Krygowski TM. Separation of the energetic and geometric contributions to aromaticity. 3. Analysis of the aromatic character of benzene rings in their various topological and chemical environments in the substituted benzene derivatives. *J Chem Inf Comput Sci* 1996;36:1142–1145.

36. Volarath P, Wang H, Fu H, Harrison RW. Knowledge-Based algorithms for chemical structure and property analysis. *EMBS 26th IEEE EMBS Annual International Conference*, California, USA; 2004.

37. Krygowski TM, Szatylowicz H, Zachara JE. How H-Bonding affects aromaticity of the ring in variously substituted phenol complexes with bases. 4. Molecular geometry as a source of chemical information. *J Chem Inf Comput Sci* 2004;44:2077–2082.

38. Lipkus AH. Exploring chemical rings in a simple topological-descriptor space. *J Chem Inf Comput Sci* 2001;41:430–438.

39. Trinajstic N, editor. Chemical Graph Theory. Boca Raton: CRC Press; 1983.
40. Beck A, Bleicher M, Crowe D. *Excursion into Mathematics*. Wroth; 1969.
41. Engel T. *Chemoinformatics, A Textbook*. Germany: John Wiley & Sons; 2003.
42. Dalby A, Nourse JG, Hounshell WD, Gushurst AKI, Grier DL, Leland BA, Laufer J. Description of several chemical structure file formats used by computer programs developed at Molecular Design Limited. *J Chem Inf Comput Sci* 1992;32:244–255.
43. Leach AR, Gillet VJ. *An Introduction to Chemoinformatics*. Netherlands; Springer: 2003.
44. Ganesan N, Bennett NF, Velauthapillai M, Pattabiraman N, Squier R, Kalyanasundaram, B. Web-based interface facilitating sequence-to-structure analysis of BLAST alignment reports. *Biotechniques* 2005;39(2):186–188.
45. Margelevicius M, Venclovas C. PSI-BLAST-ISS: an intermediate sequence search tool for estimation of the position-specific alignment reliability. *BMC Bioinformatics* 2005;6:185.
46. Labesse G. MulBlast 1.0: a multiple alignment of BLAST output to boost protein sequence similarity analysis. *Comput Appl Biosci* 1996;12(6):463–467.
47. Wiswesser WJ. *A Chemical Line-Formula Notation*. New York: Crowell Co; 1954.
48. Weininger D. SMILES, a chemical language and information system. 1. Introduction to methodology and encoding rules. *J Chem Inf Comput Sci* 1988;28:31–36.
49. http://www.daylight.com/dayhtml/doc/theory/theory.smiles.html
50. http://www.daylight.com/dayhtml/doc/theory/theory.smarts.html
51. http://www.daylight.com/meetings/summerschool01/course/basics/smirks.html
52. Morgan HL. The Generation of a unique machine description for chemical structures, a technique developed at chemical abstracts service. *J Chem Doc* 1965;5:107–113.
53. Xu Y, Johnson M. Algorithm for naming molecular equivalence classes represented by labeled pseudographs. *J Chem Inf Comput Sci* 2001;41:181–185.
54. Weininger D, Weininger A, Weininger JL. SMILES. 2. Algorithm for generation of unique SMILES notation. *J Chem Inf Comput Sci* 1989;29: pp. 97–101.
55. Wipke WT, Dyott TM. Stereochemically unique naming algorithm. *J Am Chem Soc* 1974;96:4834–4842.
56. Bayada DM, Hamersma H, van Geerestein VJ. Molecular diversity and representativity in chemical databases. *J Chem Inf Comput Sci* 1999;39:1–10.
57. Wild DJ, Blankley CJ. Comparison of 2D fingerprint types and hierarchy level selection methods for structural grouping using ward's clustering. *J Chem Inf Comput Sci* 2000;40:155–162.
58. Xue L, Godden JW, Stahura FL, Bajorath J. Design and evaluation of a molecular fingerprint involving the transformation of property descriptor values into a binary classification scheme. *J Chem Inf Comput Sci* 2003;43:1151–1157.
59. Yang JM, Tung CH. Protein structure database search and evolutionary classification. *Nucleic Acids Res* 2006;34(13):3646–3659.
60. Iwata Y, Arisawa M, Hamada R, Kita Y, Mizutani MY, Tomioka N, Itai A, Miyamoto S. Discovery of novel aldose reductase inhibitors using a protein structure-based approach3D-database search followed by design and synthesis. *J Med Chem* 2001;44(11):1718–1728.

61. An J, Nakama T, Kubota Y, Sarai A. 3DinSightan integrated relational database and search tool for the structure, function and properties of biomolecules. *Bioinformatics* 1998;14(2):188–195.

62. Fidelis K, Stern PS, Bacon D, Moult J. Comparison of systematic search and database methods for constructing segments of protein structure. *Protein Eng* 1994;7(8):953–960.

63. Willett P, Winterman V, Bawden D. Implementation of nearest-neighbor searching in an online chemical structure search system. *J Chem Inf Comput Sci* 1986;26:36–41.

64. Wipke WT, Krishnan S, Ouchi GI. Hash Functions for Rapid Storage and Retrieval of Chemical Structures *J Chem Inf Comput Sci* 1978;18:32–37.

65. Zupan J. *Algorithms for chemists*. New York: John Wiley & Sons; 1989.

66. Freeland RG, Funk SA, O'Korn LJ, Wilson GA. The chemical abstracts service chemical registry system. II. Augmented connectivity molecular formula *J Chem Inf Comput Sci* 1979;19:94–98.

67. Ray LC, Kirsch RA. Finding chemical records by digital computers. *Science* 1957;126:814–819.

68. Ullman JR. An algorithm for subgraph isomorphism. *J Asso Comput Mach* 1976;23: 31–42.

69. Karakoc E, Cherkasov A, Sahinalp SC. Distance based algorithms for small biomolecule classification and structural similarity search. *Bioinformatics* 2006;22(14):e243–e251.

70. Merkeev IV, Mironov AA. PHOG-BLAST–a new generation tool for fast similarity search of protein families. *BMC Evol Biol* 2006;6:51.

71. Seno S, Takenaka Y, Kai C, Kawai J, Carninci P, Hayashizaki Y, Matsuda H. A method for similarity search of genomic positional expression using CAGE. *PLoS Genet* 2006;2(4):e44.

72. Camoglu O, Kahveci T, Singh AK. Towards index-based similarity search for protein structure databases. *Proc IEEE Comput Soc Bioinform Conf* 2003;2:148–158.

73. Park SH, Ryu KH, Gilbert D. Fast similarity search for protein 3D structures using topological pattern matching based on spatial relations. *Int J Neural Syst* 2005;15(4): 287–296.

74. Sun Y, Buhler J. Designing multiple simultaneous seeds for DNA similarity search. *J Comput Biol* 2005;12(6):847–861.

75. Cantalloube H, Chomilier J, Chiusa S, Lonquety M, Spadoni JL, Zagury JF. Filtering redundancies for sequence similarity search programs. *J Biomol Struct Dyn* 2005;22(4):487–492.

76. Can T, Wang YF. Protein structure alignment and fast similarity search using local shape signatures. *J Bioinform Comput Biol* 2004;2(1):215–239.

77. Weskamp N, Kuhn D, Hullermeier E, Klebe G. Efficient similarity search in protein structure databases by k-clique hashing. *Bioinformatics* 2004;20(10):1522–1526.

78. Krasnogor N, Pelta DA. Measuring the similarity of protein structures by means of the universal similarity metric. *Bioinformatics* 2004;20(7):1015–1021.

79. Ming Li XC, Xin Li, Bin Ma, Paul MBV. The Similarity Metric. *IEEE Trans Inform Theor* 2004;50(12):3250–3264.

80. Schuffenhauer A, Floersheim P, Acklin P, Jacoby E. Similarity metrics for ligands reflecting the similarity of the target proteins *J Chem Inf Comput Sci* 2003;43:391–405.

81. Chagoyen M, Carmona-Saez P, Gil C, Carazo JM, Pascual-Montano A. A literature-based similarity metric for biological processes. *BMC Bioinformatics* 2006;7(1):363.
82. Cherepinsky V, Feng J, Rejali M, Mishra B. Shrinkage-based similarity metric for cluster analysis of microarray data. *Proc Natl Acad Sci USA* 2003;100(17):9668–9673.
83. Hunter L, Taylor RC, Leach SM, Simon R. GESTa gene expression search tool based on a novel Bayesian similarity metric. *Bioinformatics* 2001;17 Suppl 1:S115–S122.
84. Everitt B. *Cluster Analysis*, London; Halsted-Heinemann: 1980.
85. Monev V. Introduction to Similarity Searching in Chemistry. *Match-Communi Math Co* 2004;51:7–38.
86. Corruccini RS. Size and shape in similarity coefficients based on metric characters. *Am J Phys Anthropol* 1973;38(3):743–753.
87. Rhodes N, Willet P, Calvet A, Dunbar JB. CLIPSimilarity searching of 3D databases using clique detection. *J Chem Inf Comput Sci* 2003;43:443–448.
88. Salim N, Holliday J, Willett P. Combination of fingerprint-based similarity coefficients using data fusion. *J Chem Inf Comput Sci* 2003;43:435–442.
89. Whittle M, Willet P, Klaffke W, van Noort P. Evaluation of similarity measures for searching the dictionary of natural products database. *J Chem Inf Comput Sci* 2003;43: 449–457.
90. Hert J, Willet P, Wilton DJ, Acklin P, Azzaoui K, Jacoby E, Schuffenhauer A. New methods for ligand-based virtual screeninguse of data fusion and machine learning to enhance the effectiveness of similarity searching. *J Chem Inf Model* 2006;46:462–470.
91. Cramer RD, Redl G, Berkoff CE. Substructural analysis. Novel approach to the problem of drug design. *J Med Chem* 1974;17:533–535.
92. Wilton D, Willett P, Lawson K, Mullier G. Comparison of ranking methods for virtual screening in lead-discovery programs. *J Chem Inf Comput Sci* 2003;43:469–474.
93. Harper G, Bradshaw J, Gittins JC, Green DVS. Prediction of biological activity for high-throughput screening using binary kernel discrimination. *J Chem Inf Comput Sci* 2001;41:1295–1300.
94. Read RC, Coreneil DG. The Graph isomorphism disease. *J Graph Theor* 1977;1: 339–363.
95. Barnard JM. Substructure searching methods: Old and new. *J Chem Inf Comput Sci* 1993;33:532–538.
96. Barreca ML, Rao A, De Luca L, Zappala M, Gurnari C, Monforte P, DeClercq E, Van Maele B, Debyser Z, Witvrouw M, Briggs JM, Chimirri A. Efficient 3D database screening for novel HIV-1 IN inhibitors. *J Chem Inf Comput Sci* 2004;44:1450–1455.
97. Schnecke V, Swanson CA, Getzoff ED, Tainer JA, Kuhn LA. Screening a peptidyl database for potential ligands to proteins with side-chain flexibility. *Proteins* 1998;33(1): 74–87.
98. Wildner G, Thurau SR. Database screening for molecular mimicry. *Immunol. Today* 1997;18(5):252.
99. Faranda S, Frattini A, Zucchi I, Patrosso C, Milanesi L, Montagna C, Vezzoni P. Characterization and fine localization of two new genes in Xq28 using the genomic sequence/EST database screening approach. *Genomics* 1996;34(3):323–327.
100. Good AC, Ewing TJ, Gschwend DA, Kuntz ID. New molecular shape descriptorsapplication in database screening. *J Comput Aided Mol Des* 1995;9(1):1–12.

101. Shen J. HAD An automated database tool for analyzing screening hits in drug discovery. *J Chem Inf Comput Sci* 2003;43:1668–1672.
102. Dury L, Latour T, Leherte L, Barberis F, Vercauteren DP. A new graph descriptor for molecules containing cycles. Application as screening criterion for searching molecular structures within large databases of organic compounds. *J Chem Inf Comput Sci* 2001;41:1437–1445.
103. Halgren TA, Murphy RB, Friesner RA, Beard HS, Frye LL, Pollard WT, Banks JL. GlideA new approach for rapid, accurate docking and scoring. 2. Enrichment factors in database screening. *J Med Chem* 2004;47:1750–1759.
104. Jorissen RN, Gilson MK. Virtual screening of molecular databases using a support vector machine. *J Chem Inf Model* 2005;45:549–561.
105. Nagy M, Kozics S, Veszpremi T, Bruck P. Substructure search on very large files using tree-structured databases. In: Warr WA, editor. Chemical Structures: The International Language of Chemistry. Berlin: Springer-Verlag; 1988. pp. 127–130.

21

COMPUTATIONAL APPROACHES TO PREDICT PROTEIN–PROTEIN AND DOMAIN–DOMAIN INTERACTIONS

RAJA JOTHI AND TERESA M. PRZYTYCKA

National Center for Biotechnology Information, National Library of Medicine, National Institutes of Health, Bethesda, MD, USA

21.1 INTRODUCTION

Knowledge of protein and domain interactions provides crucial insights into their functions within a cell. Various high-throughput experimental techniques such as mass spectrometry, yeast two hybrid, and tandem affinity purification have generated a considerable amount of large-scale high-throughput protein interaction data [9,19,21,28,29,35,36,58]. Advances in experimental techniques are paralleled by a rapid development of computational approaches designed to detect protein–protein interactions [11,15,24,37,45,46,48,50]. These approaches complement experimental techniques and, if proven to be successful in predicting interactions, provide insights into principles governing protein interactions.

A variety of biological information (such as amino acid sequences, coding DNA sequences, three-dimensional structures, gene expression, codon usage, etc.) is used by computational methods to arrive at interaction predictions. Most methods rely on statistically significant biological properties observed among interacting proteins/domains. Some of the widely used properties include co-occurence, coevolution, co-expression, and co-localization of interacting proteins/domains.

Bioinformatics Algorithms: Techniques and Applications, Edited by Ion I. Măndoiu and Alexander Zelikovsky

This chapter is, by no account, a complete survey of all available computational approaches for predicting protein and domain interactions but rather a presentation of a bird's-eye view of the landscape of a large spectrum of available methods. For detailed descriptions, performances, and technical aspects of the methods, we refer the reader to the respective articles.

21.2 PROTEIN–PROTEIN INTERACTIONS

21.2.1 Phylogenetic Profiles

The patterns of presence or absence of proteins across multiple genomes (phylogenetic or phyletic profiles) can be used to infer interactions between proteins [18,50]. A phylogenetic profile for each protein i is a vector of length n that contains the presence or absence information of that protein in a reference set of n organisms. The presence or absence of protein i in organism j is recorded as $P_{ij} = 1$ or $P_{ij} = 0$, respectively, which is usually determined by performing a BLAST search [4] with an E-value threshold t. If the BLAST search results in a hit with E-value $< t$, then it is construed as an evidence for the presence of protein p in G. Otherwise, it is assumed that p is absent in G.

Proteins with identical or similar profiles are inferred to be functionally interacting under the assumption that proteins involved in the same pathway or functional system are likely to have been co-inherited during evolution [18,50] (Fig. 21.1a). Similarities between profiles can be measured using matrics such as Hamming distance, Jaccard coefficient, or mutual information. It has been shown that measuring profile similarity using mutual information rather than matrics such as Hamming distance results in a better prediction accuracy [22]. By clustering proteins based on their profile similarity scores, one can construct functional pathways and interaction network modules [12,22]. One of the main limitations of the profile comparison approach is the lineage-specific gains and losses of genes, thought to be more pervasive in microbial evolution [39], which could artificially decrease the similarity between functionally interacting genes.

Instead of using an ad hoc E-value threshold and binary values as originally proposed [50], recent studies have been using $P_{ij} = -1/\log E_{ij}$ to record the presence/absence information, where E_{ij} is the BLAST E-value of the top-scoring sequence alignment of protein i in organism j. To avoid algorithm-induced artifacts, $P_{ij} > 1$ are truncated to 1. Notice that a zero (or a one) entry in the profile now indicates the presence (absence, respectively) of a protein. It is being argued that using real values for P_{ij}, instead of binary values, captures varying degrees of sequence divergence, providing more information than the simple presence or absence of genes [12,33,37]. For a more comprehensive assessment of the phylogenetic profile comparison approach, we refer the reader to [33].

21.2.2 Gene Fusion Events

There are instances where a pair of interacting proteins in one genome is fused together into a single protein (referred to as the Rosetta Stone protein [37]) in another genome.

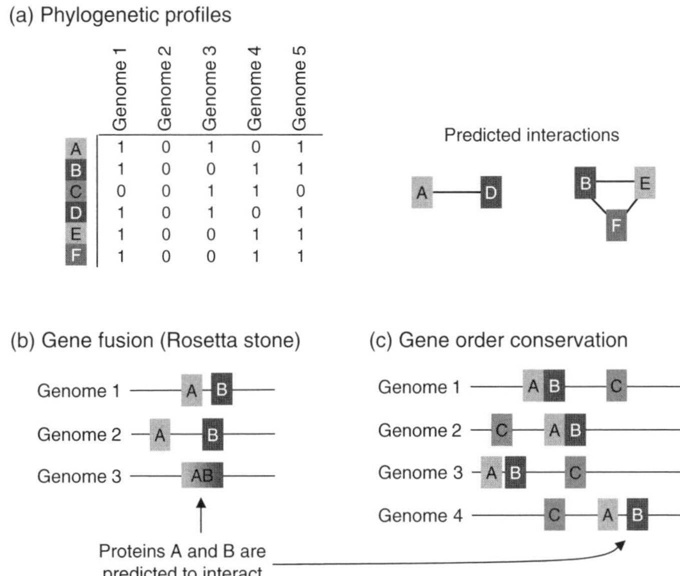

FIGURE 21.1 Computational approaches for predicting protein–protein interactions from genomic information. (**a**) Phylogenetic profiles [18,50]. A profile for a protein is a vector of 1s and 0s recording presence or absence, respectively, of that protein in a set of genomes. Two proteins are predicted to interact if their phylogenetic profiles are identical (or similar). (**b**) Gene fusion (Rosetta stone) [15,37]. Proteins *A* and *B* in a genome are predicted to interact if they are fused together into a single protein (Rosetta protein) in another genome. (**c**) Gene order conservation [11,45]. If the genes encoding proteins *A* and *B* occupy close chromosomal positions in various genomes, then they are inferred to interact. Figure adapted from [59].

For example, interacting proteins Gyr A and Gyr B in *Escherichia coli* are fused together into a single protein (topoisomerase II) in *Saccharomyces cerevisiae* [7]. Amino acid sequences of Gyr A and Gyr B align to different segments of the topoisomerase II. On the basis of such observations, methods have been developed [15,37] to predict interaction between two proteins in an organism based on the evidence that they form a part of a single protein in other organisms. A schematic illustration of this approach is shown in Fig. 21.1b.

21.2.3 Gene Order Conservation

Interactions between proteins can be predicted based on the observation that proteins encoded by conserved neighboring gene pairs interact (Fig. 21.1c). This idea is based on the notion that physical interaction between encoded proteins could be one of the reasons for evolutionary conservation of gene order [11]. Gene order conservation between proteins in bacterial genomes has been used to predict functional interactions [11,45]. This approach's applicability only to bacterial genomes, in which the genome order is a relevant property, is one of its main limitations [59]. Even within the bacteria, caution must be exercised while interpreting conservation of gene order between evolutionarily closely related organisms (for example, *Mycoplasma genitalium* and *Mycoplasma pneumoniae*), as lack of time for genome rearrangements after divergence of the two organisms from their last common ancestor could be a reason for the observed gene order conservation. Hence, only organisms with relatively long evolutionary distances should be considered for such type of analysis. However, the evolutionary distances should be small enough in order to ensure that a significant number of orthologous genes are still shared by the organisms [11].

21.2.4 Similarity of Phylogenetic Trees

It is postulated that the sequence changes accumulated during the evolution of one of the interacting proteins must be compensated by changes in its interaction partner. Such correlated mutations have been subject of several studies [3,23,41,55]. Pazos et al. [46] demonstrated that the information about correlated sequence changes can distinguish right interdocking sites from incorrect alternatives. In recent years, a new method has emerged, which, rather than looking at coevolution of individual residues in protein sequences, measures the degree of coevolution of entire protein sequences by assessing the similarity between the corresponding phylogenetic trees [24,25,31,32,34,46–48,51,54]. Under the assumption that interacting protein sequences and their partners must coevolve (so that any divergent changes in one partner's binding surface are complemented at the interface by their interaction partner) [6,30,40,46], pairs of protein sequences exhibiting high degree of coevolution are inferred to be interacting.

In this section, we first describe the basic "mirror-tree" approach for predicting interaction between proteins by measuring the degree of coevolution between the corresponding amino acid sequences. Next, we describe an important modification to the basic mirror-tree approach that helps in improving its prediction accuracy. Finally, we discuss a related problem of predicting interaction specificity between two families of proteins (say, ligands and receptors) that are known to interact.

21.2.4.1 The Basic Mirror-Tree Approach This approach is based on the assumption that phylogenetic trees of interacting proteins are highly likely to be similar due to the inherent need for coordinated evolution [24,49]. The degree of similarity between two phylogenetic trees is measured by computing the correlation between the corresponding distance matrices that implicitly contain the evolutionary histories of the two proteins.

A schematic illustration of the mirror-tree method is shown in Fig. 21.2. The multiple sequence alignments (MSA) of the two proteins, from a common set of species, are constructed using one of the many available MSA algorithms such as ClustalW [57], MUSCLE [14], or T-Coffee [43]. The set of orthologous proteins for a MSA is usually obtained by one of the two following ways: (i) a stringent BLAST search with a certain E-value threshold, sequence identity threshold, alignment overlap percentage threshold or a combination thereof, or (ii) reciprocal (bidirectional) BLAST best-hits. In both approaches, orthologous sequences of a query protein q in organism Q is searched by performing a BLAST search of q against sequences in other organisms.

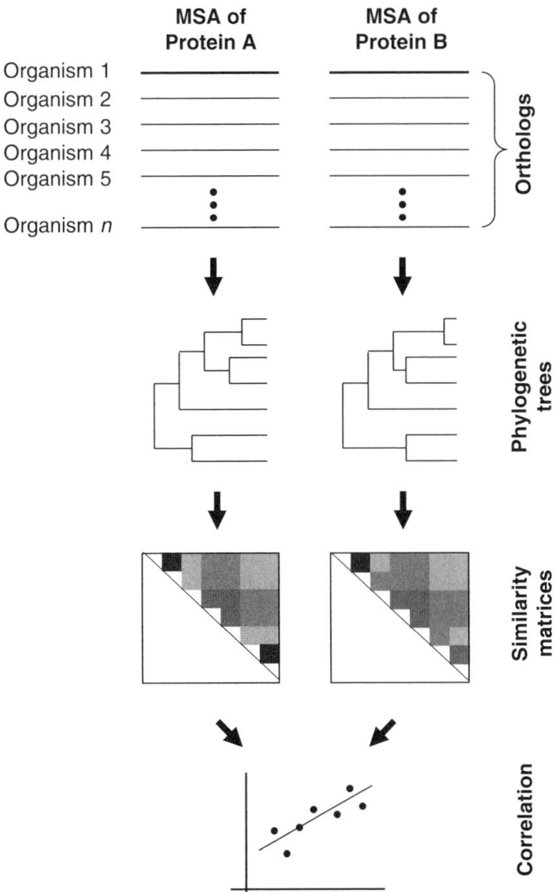

FIGURE 21.2 Schema of the mirror-tree method. Multiple sequence alignments of proteins A and B, constructed from orthologs of A and B, respectively, from a common set of species, are used to generate the corresponding phylogenetic trees and distance matrices. The degree of coevolution between A and B is assessed by comparing the corresponding distance matrices using a linear correlation criteria. Proteins A and B are predicted to interact if the degree of coevolution, measured by the correlation score, is high (or above a certain threshold).

In the former, q's best-hit h in organism H, with E-value $< t$, is considered to be orthologous to Q. In the latter, q's best-hit h in organism H (with no specific E-value threshold) is considered to be orthologous to q if and only if h's best-hit in organism Q is q. Using reciprocal best-hits approach to search for orthologous sequences is considered to be much more stringent than just using unidirectional BLAST searches with an E-value threshold t.

In order to be able to compare the evolutionary histories to two proteins, it is required that the two proteins have orthologs in at least a common set of n organisms. It is advised that n be large enough for the trees and the corresponding distance matrices contain sufficient evolutionary information. It is suggested that $n \geq 10$ [31,47,48]. Phylogenetic trees from MSA are constructed using standard tree construction algorithms (such as neighbor joining [53]), which are then used to construct the distance matrices (algorithms to construct trees and matrices from MSAs are available in the ClustalW suite).

The extent of agreement between the evolutionary histories of two proteins is assessed by computing the degree of similarity between the two corresponding distance matrices. The extent of agreement between matrices A and B can be measured using Pearson's correlation coefficient, given by

$$r_{AB} = \frac{\sum_{i=1}^{n-1}\sum_{j=i+1}^{n}(A_{ij} - \overline{A})(B_{ij} - \overline{B})}{\sqrt{\sum_{i=1}^{n-1}\sum_{j=i+1}^{n}(A_{ij} - \overline{A})^2 \sum_{i=1}^{n-1}\sum_{j=i+1}^{n}(B_{ij} - \overline{B})^2}}, \qquad (21.1)$$

where n is the number of organisms (number of rows or columns) in the matrices, A_{ij} and B_{ij} are the evolutionary distances between organisms i and j in the tree of proteins A and B, respectively, and $\overline{A}$ and $\overline{B}$ are the mean values of all A_{ij} and B_{ij}, respectively. The value of r_{AB} ranges from -1 to +1. The higher the value of r, the higher the agreement between the two matrices and thus the higher the degree of coevolution between A and B.

Pairs of proteins with correlation scores above a certain threshold are predicted to interact. A correlation score of 0.8 is considered to be a good threshold for predicting protein interactions [24,49]. Pazos et al. [49] estimated that about one third of the predictions by the mirror-tree method are false positives. A false positive in this context refers to a non-interacting pair that was predicted to interact due to their high correlation score. It is quite possible that the evolutionary histories of two non-interacting proteins are highly correlated due to their common speciation history. Thus, in order to truly assess the correlation of evolutionary histories of two proteins, one should first subtract the background correlation due to their common speciation history. Recently, it has been observed that subtracting the underlying speciation component greatly improves the predictive power of the mirror-tree approach by reducing the number of false positives. Refined mirror-tree methods that subtract the underlying speciation signal are discussed in the following subsection.

21.2.4.2 Accounting for Background Speciation As pointed at the end of the previous section, to improve the performance of the mirror-tree approach, the coevolution due to common speciation events should be subtracted from the overall coevolution signal. Recently, two approaches, very similar in technique, have been proposed to address this problem [47,54].

For an easier understanding of the speciation subtraction process, let us think of the distance matrices used in the mirror-tree method as vectors (i.e., the upper right triangle of the distance matrices is linearized and represented as a vector), which will be referred to as *evolutionary vectors* hereafter. Let $\overrightarrow{V_A}$ and $\overrightarrow{V_B}$ denote the evolutionary vector computed from a multiple sequence alignment of orthologs of proteins A and B, respectively, for a common set of species. Let $\overrightarrow{S}$ denote the canonical evolutionary vector, also referred to as the *speciation vector*, computed in the same way but based on a multiple sequence alignment of 16S rRNA sequences for the same set of species. Speciation vector $\vec{S}$ approximates the interspecies evolutionary distance based on the set of species under consideration. The differences in the scale of protein and RNA distance matrices are overcome by rescaling the speciation vector values by a factor computed based on "molecular clock" proteins [47].

A pictorial illustration of the speciation subtraction procedure is shown in Fig. 21.3. The main idea is to decompose evolutionary vectors $\vec{V_A}$ and $\vec{V_B}$ into two components: one representing the contribution due to speciation, and the other representing the contribution due to evolutionary pressure related to preserving the protein function (denoted by $\vec{C_A}$ and $\vec{C_B}$, respectively). To obtain $\vec{C_A}$ and $\vec{C_B}$, the speciation component $\vec{S}$ is subtracted from $\vec{V_A}$ and $\vec{V_B}$, respectively. Vectors $\vec{C_A}$ and $\vec{C_B}$ are expected to contain only the distances between orthologs that are not due to speciation but to other reasons related to function [47]. The degree of coevolution between A and B is then measured by computing the correlation between $\vec{C_A}$ and $\vec{C_B}$, rather than between $\vec{V_A}$ and $\vec{V_B}$ as in the basic mirror-tree approach.

The two speciation subtraction methods, by Pazos et al. [47] and Sato et al. [54], differ in how speciation subtraction is performed (see Fig. 21.3). An in-depth analysis of the pros and cons of two methods is provided in [34]. In a nutshell, Sato et al. attribute all changes in the direction of the speciation vector to the speciation process and thus assume that vector $\vec{C_A}$ is perpendicular to the speciation vector $\vec{S}$, whereas Pazos et al. assume that the speciation component in $\vec{V_A}$ is constant and independent on the protein family. As a result, Pazos et al. compute $\vec{C_A}$ to be the difference between $\vec{V_A}$ and $\vec{S}$, which explains the need to rescale RNA distances to protein distances in the vector $\vec{S}$. Interestingly, despite this difference, both speciation correction methods produce similar results [34]. In particular, Pazos et al. report that the speciation subtraction step reduces the number of false positives by about 8.5%.

The above-mentioned methods for subtracting the background speciation have recently been complemented by the work of Kann et al. [34]. Under the assumption that in conserved regions of the sequence alignment functional coevolution may be less concealed by speciation divergence, they demonstrated that the performance of the mirror-tree method can be improved further by restricting the coevolution analysis to the relatively highly conserved regions in the protein sequence [34].

21.2.4.3 Predicting Protein Interaction Specificity In this section, we address the problem of predicting interaction partners between members of two proteins families that are known to interact [20,32,51]. Given two families of proteins that are known to interact, the objective is to establish a mapping between the members of one family with the members of the other family.

To better understand the protein interaction specificity (PRINS) problem, let us consider an analogous problem, which we shall refer to as the *matching* problem. Imagine a social gathering attended by n married couples. Let $H = \{h_1, h_2, \ldots, h_n\}$ and $W = \{w_1, w_2, \ldots, w_n\}$ be the sets of husbands and wives attending the gathering. Given that husbands in set H are married to the wives in set W and that the marital

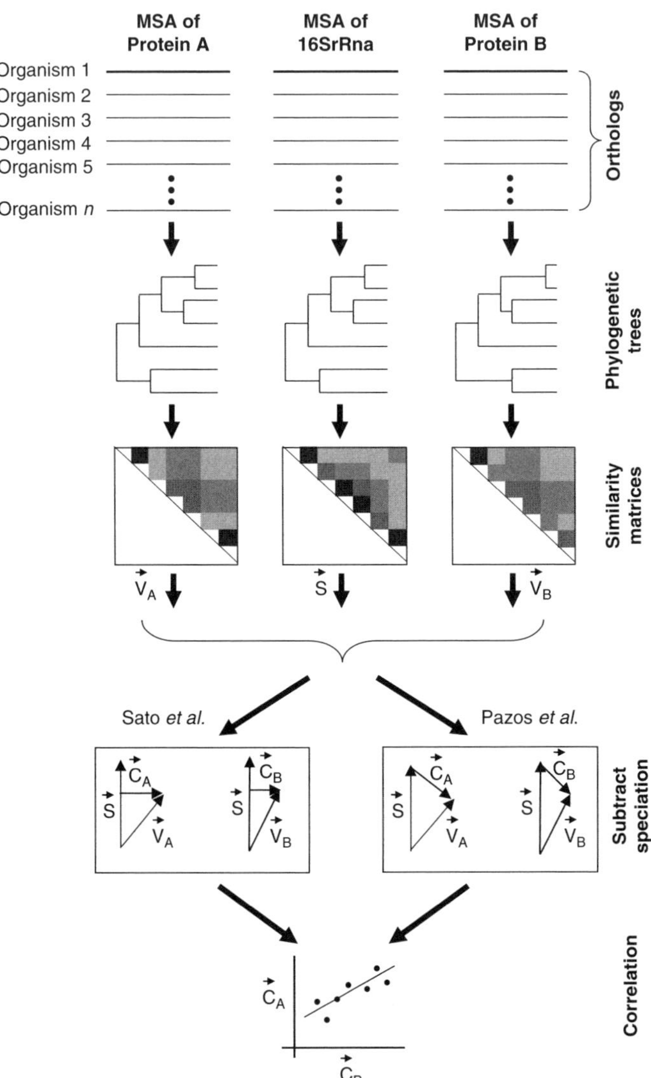

FIGURE 21.3 Schema of the mirror-tree method with a correction for the background speciation. Correlation between the evolutionary histories of two proteins could be due to (i) a need to coevolve in order to preserve the interaction and/or (ii) common speciation events. To estimate the coevolution due to the common speciation, a canonical tree-of-life is constructed by aligning the 16 S rRNA sequences. The rRNA alignment is used to compute the distance matrix representing the species tree. $\overrightarrow{V_A}$, $\overrightarrow{V_B}$, and $\overrightarrow{S}$ are the vector notations for the corresponding distance matrices. Vector $\overrightarrow{C_X}$ is obtained from $\overrightarrow{V_X}$ by subtracting it by the speciation component $\overrightarrow{S}$. The speciation component $\overrightarrow{S}$ is calculated differently based on the method being used. The degree of coevolution between A and B is then assessed by computing the linear correlation between $\overrightarrow{C_A}$ with $\overrightarrow{C_B}$. Proteins A and B are predicted to interact if the correlation between $\overrightarrow{C_A}$ and $\overrightarrow{C_B}$ is sufficiently high.

relationship is monogamous, the matching problem asks for a one-to-one mapping of the members in H to those in W such that each mapping (h_i, w_j) holds the meaning "h_i is married to w_j." In other words, the objective is to pair husbands and wives such that all n pairings are correct. The matching problem has a total of $n!$ possible mappings out of which only one is correct. The matching problem becomes much more complex if one were to remove the constraint that requires that the marital relationship is monogamous. Such a relaxation would allow the sizes of sets H and W to be different. Without knowing the number of wives (or husbands) each husband (wife, respectively) has, the problem becomes intractable.

The PRINS problem is essentially the same as the matching problem with the two sets containing proteins instead of husbands and wives. Let A and B be the two sets of proteins. Given that the proteins in A interact with those in B, the objective is to map proteins in A to their interaction partners in B. To fully appreciate the complexity of this problem, let us first consider a simpler version of the problem that assumes that the number of proteins in A is the same as that in B and the interaction between the members of A and B is one to one.

Protein interaction specificity (a protein binding to a specific partner) is vital to cell function. To maintain the interaction specificity, it is required that it persists through the course of strong evolutionary events, such as gene duplication and gene divergence. As genes are duplicated, the binding specificities of duplicated genes (paralogs) often diverge, resulting in new binding specificities. Existence of numerous paralogs for both interaction partners can make the problem of predicting interaction specificity difficult as the number of potential interactions grow combinatorially [51].

Discovering interaction specificity between the two interacting families of proteins, such as matching ligands to specific receptors, is an important problem in molecular biology, which remains largely unsolved. A naive approach to solve this problem would be to try out all possible mappings (assuming that there is an oracle to verify whether a given mapping is correct). If A and B contain n proteins each, then there are a total of $n!$ possible mappings between matrices A and B. For a fairly large n, it is computationally unrealistic to try out all possible mappings.

Under the assumption that interacting proteins undergo coevolution, Ramani and Marcotte [51] and Gertz et al. [20], in independent and parallel works, proposed the "column-swapping" method for the PRINS problem. A schematic illustration of the column-swapping approach is shown in Fig. 21.4. Matrices A and B in Fig. 21.4 correspond to distance matrices of families A and B, respectively. In this approach, a Monte Carlo algorithm [38] with simulated annealing is used to navigate through the search space in an effort to maximize the correlation between the two matrices. The Monte Carlo search process, instead of searching through the entire landscape of all possible mappings, allows for a random sampling of the search space in a hope to find the optimal mapping. Each iteration of the Monte Carlo search process, referred to as a "move," constitutes the following two steps.

1. Choose two columns uniformly at random and swap their positions (the corresponding rows are also swapped).

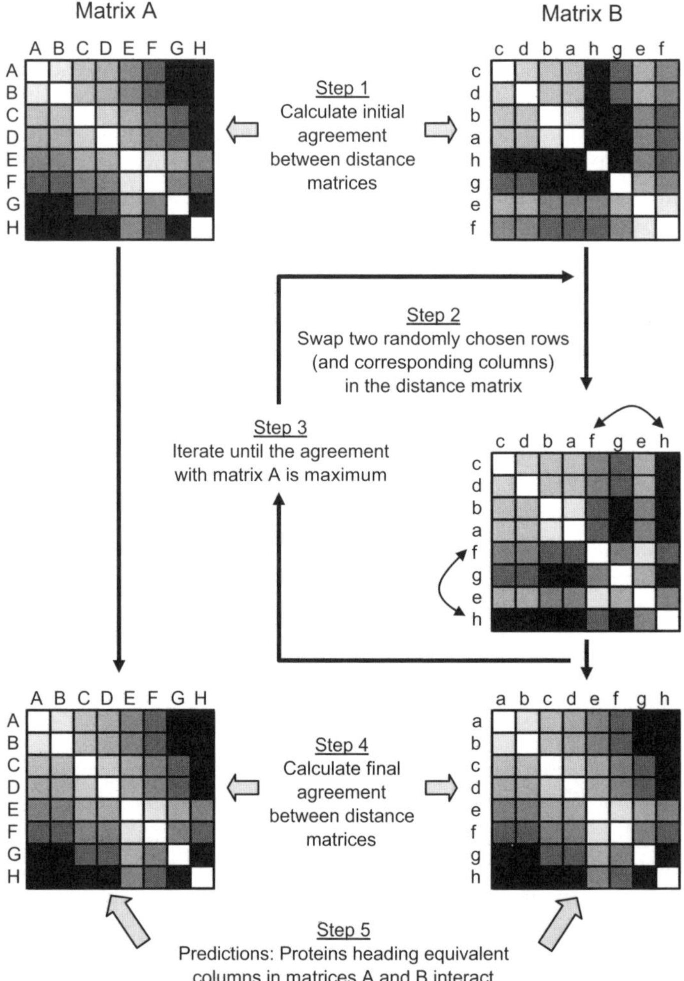

FIGURE 21.4 Schema of the column-swapping algorithm. Image reproduced from [51] with permission.

2. If, after the swap, the correlation between the two matrices has improved, the swap is kept. Else, the swap is kept with the probability $p = \exp(-\delta/T)$, where δ is the decrease in the correlation due to the swap, and T is the temperature control variable governing the simulation process.

Initially, T is set to a value such that $p = 0.8$ to begin with, and after each iteration the value of T is decreased by 5%. After the search process converges to a particular mapping, proteins heading equivalent columns in the two matrices are predicted to interact. As with any local search algorithm, it is difficult to say whether the final mapping is an optimal mapping or a local optima.

The main downside of the column-swapping algorithm is the size of search space ($n!$), which it has to navigate in order to find the optimal mapping. Since the size of the search space is directly proportional to search (computational) time, column-swapping algorithm becomes impractical even for families of size 30.

In 2005, Jothi et al. [32] introduced a new algorithm, called MORPH, to solve the PRINS problem. The main motivation behind MORPH is to reduce the search space of the column-swapping algorithm. In addition to using the evolutionary distance information, MORPH uses topological information encoded in the evolutionary trees of the protein families. A schematic illustration of the MORPH algorithm is shown in Fig. 21.5. While MORPH is similar to the column-swapping algorithm at the top level, the major (and important) difference is the use of phylogenetic tree topology to guide the search process. Each move in the column-swapping algorithm involves swapping two random columns (and the corresponding rows), whereas each move in MORPH involves swapping two isomorphic[1] subtrees rooted at a common node (and the corresponding sets of rows and columns in the distance matrix).

Under the assumption that the phylogenetic trees of protein families A and B are topologically identical, MORPH essentially performs a topology-preserving embedding (superimposition) of one tree onto the other. The complexity of the topology of the trees plays a key role in the number of possible ways that one could superimpose one tree onto another. Figure 21.6 shows three sets of trees, each of which has different number of possible mappings based on the tree complexity. For the set of trees in Fig. 21.6a, the search space (number of mappings) for the column-swapping algorithm is $4! = 24$, whereas it is only eight for MOPRH.

To apply MORPH, the phylogenetic trees corresponding to the two families of proteins must be isomorphic. To ensure that the trees are isomorphic, MORPH starts by contracting/shrinking those internal tree edges in both trees with bootstrap score less than a certain threshold. It is made sure that equal number of edges are contracted on both trees. If, after the initial edge contraction procedure, the two trees are not isomorophic, additional internal edges are contracted on both trees (in increasing order of the edge bootstrap scores) until the trees are isomorphic. The benefits of edge contraction procedure is twofold: (i) ensure that the two trees are isomorphic to begin with and (ii) decrease the chances of less reliable edges (with low bootstrap scores) wrongly influencing the algorithm. Since MORPH relies heavily on the topology of the trees, it is essential that the tree edges are trustworthy. In the worst case, contracting all the internal edges on both trees will leave two star-topology trees (like those in Fig. 21.6c), in which case the number of possible mappings considered by MORPH will be the same as that considered by the column-swapping algorithm. Thus, in the worst case, MORPH's search space will be as big as that of the column-swapping algorithm.

After the edge contraction procedure, a Monte Carlo search process similar to that used in the column-swapping algorithm is used to find the best possible

[1]Two trees T_1 and T_2 are isomorphic if there is a one-to-one mapping between their vertices (nodes) such that there is an edge between two vertices in T_1 if and only if there is an edge between the two corresponding vertices in T_2.

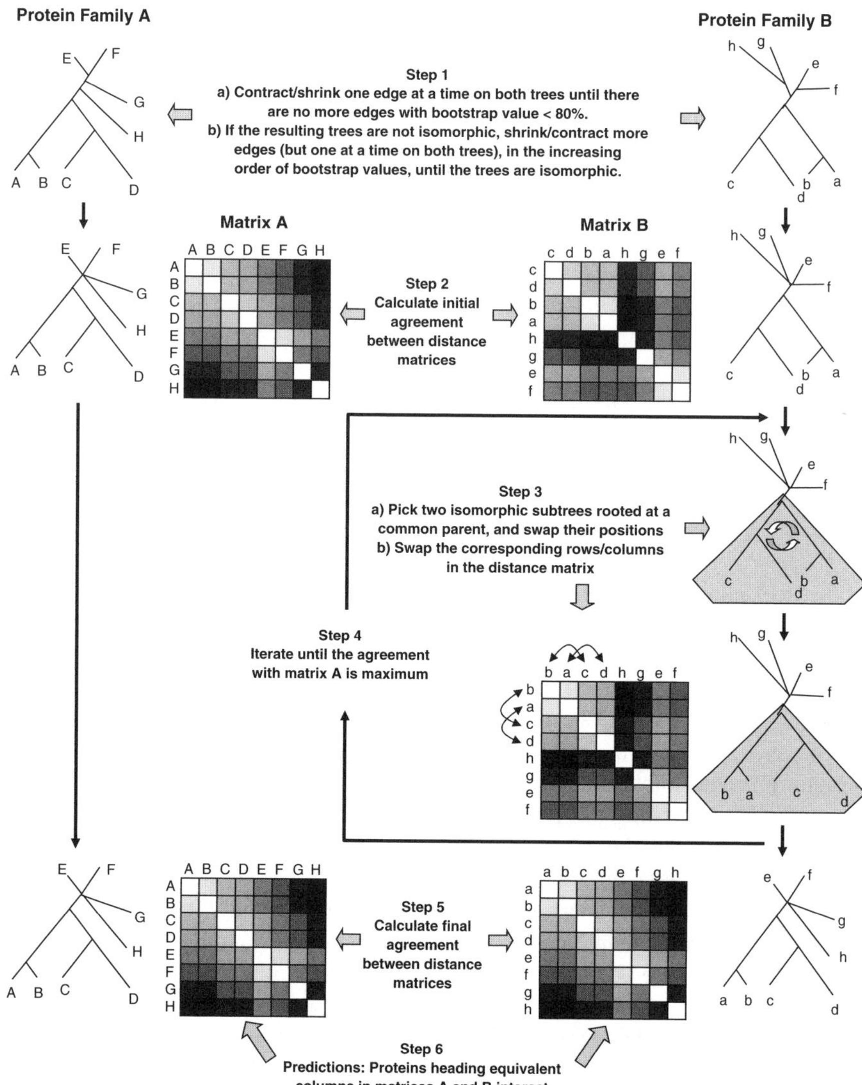

FIGURE 21.5 Schema of the MORPH algorithm. Image reprinted from [32] with permission.

superimposition of the two trees. As in the column-swapping algorithm, the distance matrix and the tree corresponding to one of the two families are fixed, and transformations are made to the tree and the matrix corresponding to the second family. Each iteration of the Monte Carlo search process constitutes the following two steps:

1. Choose two isomorphic subtrees, rooted at a common node, uniformly at random and swap their positions (and the corresponding sets of rows/columns)

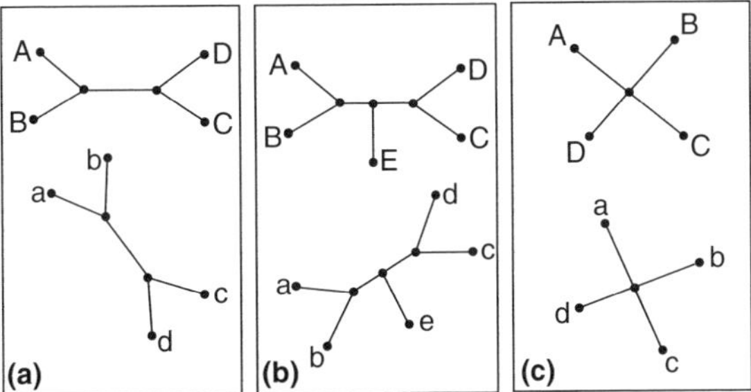

FIGURE 21.6 Three sets of topologically identical (isomorphic) trees. The number of topology preserving mappings of one tree onto another is (**a**) 8, (**b**) 8, and (**c**) 24. Despite the same number of leaves in (**a**) and (**c**), the number of possible mappings is different. This difference is due to the increased complexity of the tree topology in (**a**) when compared to that in (**c**). Image reprinted from [32] with permission.

2. If, after the swap, the correlation between the two matrices has improved, the swap is kept. Else, the swap is kept with the probability $p = \exp(-\delta/T)$.

Parameters δ and T are the same as those in the column-swapping algorithm. After the search process converges to a certain mapping, proteins heading equivalent columns in the two matrices are predicted to interact.

The sophisticated search process used in MORPH reduces the search space by multiple orders of magnitude in comparison to the column-swapping algorithm. As a result, MORPH can help solve larger instances of the PRINS problem. For more details on the column-swapping algorithm and MORPH, we refer the reader to [20,51] and [32], respectively.

21.3 DOMAIN–DOMAIN INTERACTIONS

Recent advances in molecular biology combined with large-scale high-throughput experiments have generated huge volumes of protein interaction data. The knowledge gained from protein interaction networks has definitely helped to gain a better understanding of protein functionalities and inner workings of the cell. However, protein interaction networks by themselves do not provide insights into interaction specificity at the domain level. Most of the proteins are composed of multiple domains. It has been estimated that about two thirds of proteins in prokaryotes and about four fifths of proteins in eukaryotes are multidomain proteins [5,10]. Most often, the interaction between two proteins involves binding of a pair(s) of domains. Thus, understanding the interaction at the domain level is a critical step toward a thorough understanding of the protein–protein interaction networks and their evolution. In this section, we will discuss computational approaches for predicting protein domain interactions. We restrict our discussion to sequence- and network-based approaches.

21.3.1 Relative Coevolution of Domain Pairs Approach

Given a protein–protein interaction, predicting the domain pair(s) that is most likely mediating the interaction is of great interest. Formally, let protein P contain domains $\{P_1, P_2, \ldots, P_m\}$ and protein Q contain domains $\{Q_1, Q_2, \ldots, Q_n\}$. Given that P and Q interact, the objective is to find the domain pair $P_i Q_j$ that is most likely to mediate the interaction between P and Q. Recall that under the coevolution hypothesis, interacting proteins exhibit higher level of coevolution. On the basis of this hypothesis, it is only natural and logical to assume that interacting domain pairs for a given protein–protein interaction exhibit higher degree of coevolution than the non-interacting domain pairs. Jothi et al. [31] showed that this is indeed the case and, based on this, proposed the *relative coevolution of domain pairs* (RCDP) method to predict domain pair(s) that is most likely mediating a given protein–protein interaction.

Predicting domain interactions using RCDP involves two major steps: (i) make domain assignment to proteins and (ii) use mirror-tree approach to assess the degree of coevolution of all possible domain pairs. A schematic illustration of the RCDP method is shown in Fig. 21.7. Interacting proteins P and Q are first assigned with domains (HMM profiles) using HMMer [1], RPS-BLAST [2], or other similar tools. Next, MSAs for the two proteins are constructed using orthologous proteins from a common set of organisms (as described in Section 21.2.4.1). The MSA of domain P_i in protein P is constructed by extracting those regions in P's alignment that correspond

(a) Domain architecture

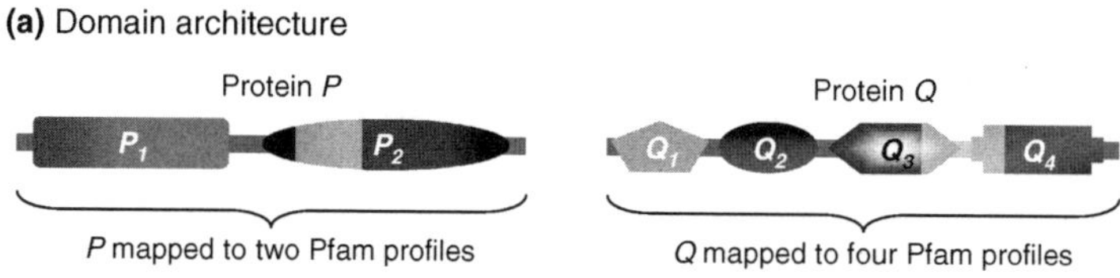

(b) Extent of coevolution of domain pairs

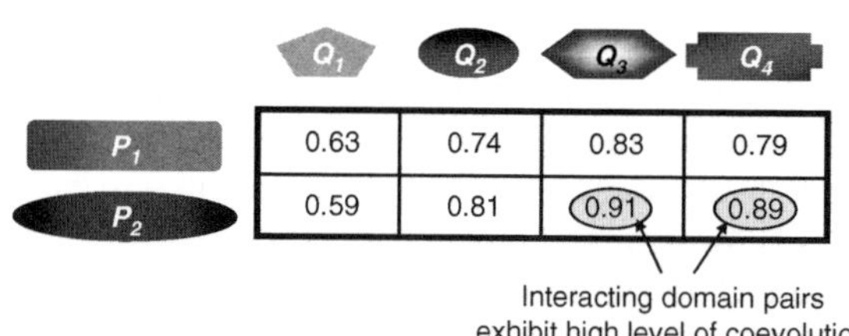

	Q_1	Q_2	Q_3	Q_4
P_1	0.63	0.74	0.83	0.79
P_2	0.59	0.81	0.91	0.89

FIGURE 21.7 Relative coevolution of domain pairs in interacting proteins. (**a**) Domain assignments for interacting proteins P and Q. Interaction sites in P and Q are indicated by thick light-colored bands. (**b**) Correlation scores for all possible domain pairs between interacting proteins P and Q are computed using the mirror-tree method. The domain pair with the highest correlation score is predicted to be the one that is most likely to mediate the interaction between proteins P and Q. Figure adapted from [31].

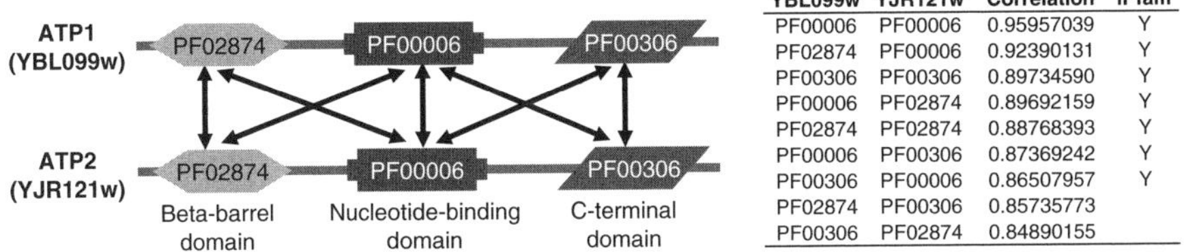

YBL099w	YJR121w	Correlation	iPfam
PF00006	PF00006	0.95957039	Y
PF02874	PF00006	0.92390131	Y
PF00306	PF00306	0.89734590	Y
PF00006	PF02874	0.89692159	Y
PF02874	PF02874	0.88768393	Y
PF00006	PF00306	0.87369242	Y
PF00306	PF00006	0.86507957	Y
PF02874	PF00306	0.85735773	
PF00306	PF02874	0.84890155	

FIGURE 21.8 Protein–protein interaction between alpha (ATP1) and beta (ATP2) chains of F1-ATPase in *Saccharomyces cerevisiae.* Protein sequences YBL099w and YJR121w (encoded by genes ATP1 and ATP2, respectively) are annotated with three Pfam [17] domains each: beta-barrel domain (PF02874), nucleotide-binding domain (PF00006), and C-terminal domain (PF00306). The correlation scores of all possible domain pairs between the two proteins are listed (table on the right) in decreasing order. Interchain domain–domain interactions that are known to be true from PDB [8] crystal structures (as inferred in iPfam [16]) are shown using double arrows in the diagram and "Y" in the table. Interacting domain pairs between the two proteins have higher correlation than the non-interacting domain pairs. RCDP will correctly predict the top-scoring domain pair to be interacting. Figure adapted from [31].

to domain P_i. Then, using the mirror-tree method, the correlation (similarity) scores of all possible domain pairs between the two proteins are computed. Finally, the domain pair $P_i Q_j$ with the highest correlation score (or domain pairs, in case of a tie for the highest correlation score), exhibiting the highest degree of coevolution, is inferred to be the one that is most likely to mediate the interaction between proteins P and Q.

Figure 21.8 shows the domain-level interactions between alpha (YBL099w) and beta (YJR121w) chains of F1-ATPase in *Saccharomyces cerevisiae*. RCDP will correctly predict the top-scoring domain pair (PF00006 in YBL099w and PF00006 in YJR121w) to be interacting. In this case, there is more than one domain pair mediating a given protein–protein interaction. Since RCDP is designed to find only the domain pair(s) that exhibits highest degree of coevolution, it may not be able to identify all the domain level interactions between the two interacting proteins. It is possible that the highest scoring domain pair may not necessarily be an interacting domain pair. This could be due to what Jothi et al. refer to as the "uncorrelated set of correlated mutations" phenomenon, which may disrupt coevolution of proteins/domains. Since the underlying similarity of phylogenetic trees approach solely relies on coevolution principle, such disruptions can cause false predictions. RCDP's prediction accuracy was estimated to be about 64%. A naive random method that picks an arbitrary domain pair out of all possible domain pairs between the two interacting proteins is expected to have a prediction accuracy of 55% [31,44]. RCDP's prediction accuracy of 64% is significant considering the fact that Nye et al. [44] showed, using a different dataset, that the naive random method performs as well as Sprinzak and Margalit's association method [56], Deng et al.'s maximum likelihood estimation approach [13], and their own lowest p-value method, all of which are discussed in the following section. For a detailed analysis of RCDP and its limitations, we refer the reader to [31].

21.3.2 Predicting Domain Interactions from Protein–Protein Interaction Network

In this section, we describe computational methods to predict interacting domain pairs from an underlying protein–protein interaction network. To begin with, all proteins in the protein–protein interaction network are first assigned with domains using HMM profiles. Interaction between two proteins typically (albeit not always) involves binding of pair(s) of domains. Recently, several computational methods have been proposed that, based on the assumption that each protein–protein interaction is mediated by one or more domain–domain interactions, attempt to recover interacting domains.

We start by introducing the notations that will be used in this section. Let $\{P_1, \ldots, P_N\}$ be the set of proteins in the protein–protein interaction network and $\{D_1, \ldots, D_M\}$ be the set of all domains that are present in these interacting proteins. Let $\mathcal{I} = \{(P_{mn})|m, n = 1, \ldots, N\}$ be the set of protein pairs observed experimentally to interact. We say that the domain pair D_{ij} belongs to protein pair P_{mn} (denoted by $D_{ij} \in P_{mn}$) if D_i belongs to P_m and D_j belongs to P_n or vice versa. Throughout this section, we will assume that all domain pairs and protein pairs are unordered, that is, X_{ab} is the same as X_{ba}. Let N_{ij} denote the number of occurrences of domain pair D_{ij} in all possible protein pairs and let $\hat{N}_{ij}$ be the number of occurrences of D_{ij} in interacting protein pairs only.[2]

*21.3.2.1 **Association Method*** Sprinzak and Margalit [56] made the first attempt to predict domain–domain interactions from a protein–protein interaction network. They proposed a simple statistical approach, referred to as the *Association Method* (AM), to identify those domain pairs that are observed to occur in interacting protein pairs more frequently than expected by chance. Statistical significance of the observed domain pair is usually measured by the standard log-odds value A or probability α, given by

$$A_{ij} = \log_2 \frac{\hat{N}_{ij}}{N_{ij} - \hat{N}_{ij}}; \qquad \alpha_{ij} = \frac{\hat{N}_{ij}}{N_{ij}}. \tag{21.2}$$

The AM method is illustrated using a toy protein–protein interaction network in Fig. 21.9. It was shown that among high scoring pairs are pairs of domains that are know to interact, and a high α value can be used as a predictor of domain–domain interaction.

*21.3.2.2 **Maximum Likelihood Estimation Approach*** Following the work of Sprinzak and Margalit, several related methods have been proposed [13,42]. In particular, Deng et al. [13] extended the idea behind the association method and

[2]Not all methods described in this section use unordered pairings. Some of them use ordered pairings, that is, X_{ab} is not the same as X_{ba}. Depending on whether one uses ordered or unordered pairing, the number of occurrences of a domain pair in a given protein pair is different. For example, let protein P_m contain domains D_x and D_y and let protein P_n contain domains D_x, D_y, and D_z. The number of occurrences of domain pair D_{xy} in protein pair P_{mn} is four if ordered pairing is used and two if unordered pairing is used.

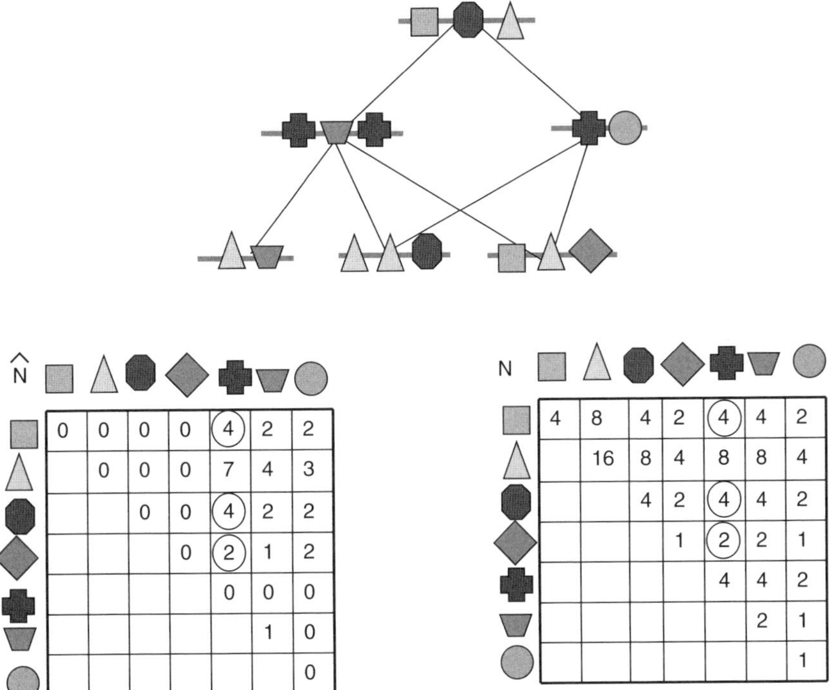

FIGURE 21.9 Schematic illustration of the association method. The toy protein–protein interaction network is given in the upper panel. The constituent domains of all the proteins in the network are represented using polygons of varying shapes. The lower panel shows domain pair occurrence tables $\hat{N}$ and N. Each entry $\hat{N}_{i,j}$ represents the number of times the domain pair (i, j) occurs in interacting protein pairs, and each entry $N_{i,j}$ represents the number of times (i, j) occurs in all protein pairs. A domain pair is counted only once even if it occurs more than once between a protein pair. Three domain pairs with maximum scores are encircled.

proposed a maximum likelihood approach to estimate the probability of domain–domain interactions. Their expectation maximization algorithm (EM) computes domain interaction probabilities that maximize the expectation of observing a given protein–protein interaction network $\mathcal{N}et$. An important feature of this approach is that it allows for an explicit treatment of missing and incorrect information (in this case, false negatives and false positives in the protein–protein interaction network).

In the EM method, protein–protein and domain–domain interactions are treated as random variables denoted by P_{mn} and D_{ij}, respectively. In particular, we let $P_{mn} = 1$ if proteins P_m and P_n interact with each other, and $P_{mn} = 0$ otherwise. Similarly, $D_{ij} = 1$ if domains D_i and D_j interact with each other, and $D_{ij} = 0$ otherwise. The probability that domains D_i and D_j interact is denoted by $\mathcal{P}r(D_{ij}) = \mathcal{P}r(D_{ij} = 1)$.

The probability that proteins P_m and P_n interact is given by

$$\mathcal{P}r(P_{mn} = 1) = 1 - \prod_{D_{ij} \in P_{mn}} (1 - \mathcal{P}r(D_{ij})). \tag{21.3}$$

Random variable $\mathcal{O}_{mn}$ is used to describe the experimental observation of protein–protein interaction network. Here, $\mathcal{O}_{mn} = 1$ if proteins P_m and P_n were observed to interact (that is $P_{mn} \in \mathcal{I}$), and $\mathcal{O}_{mn} = 0$ otherwise. False negative rate is given by $f_n = \mathcal{P}r(\mathcal{O}_{mn} = 0 \mid P_{mn} = 1)$, and false positive rate is given by $f_p = \mathcal{P}r(\mathcal{O}_{mn} = 1 \mid P_{mn} = 0)$. Estimations of false positive rate and false negative rate vary significantly from paper to paper. Deng et al. estimated f_n and f_p to be 0.8 and $2.5E - 4$, respectively.

Recall that the goal is to estimate $\mathcal{P}r(D_{ij}), \forall_{ij}$ such that the probability of the observed network $\mathcal{N}et$ is maximum. The probability of observing $\mathcal{N}et$ is given by

$$\mathcal{P}r(\mathcal{N}et) = \prod_{P_{mn} \mid \mathcal{O}_{mn}=1} \mathcal{P}r(\mathcal{O}_{mn} = 1) \prod_{P_{mn} \mid \mathcal{O}_{mn}=0} \mathcal{P}r(\mathcal{O}_{mn} = 0), \tag{21.4}$$

where

$$\mathcal{P}r(\mathcal{O}_{mn} = 1) = \mathcal{P}r(P_{mn} = 1)(1 - f_n) + (1 - \mathcal{P}r(P_{mn} = 1))f_p \tag{21.5}$$

$$\mathcal{P}r(\mathcal{O}_{mn} = 0) = 1 - \mathcal{P}r(\mathcal{O}_{mn} = 1). \tag{21.6}$$

The estimates of $\mathcal{P}r(D_{ij})$ are computed iteratively in an effort to maximize $\mathcal{P}r(\mathcal{N}et)$. Let $\mathcal{P}r(D^t_{ij})$ be the estimation of $\mathcal{P}r(D_{ij})$ in the tth iteration and let D^t denote the vector of $\mathcal{P}r(D^t_{ij}), \forall_{ij}$ estimated in the tth iteration. Initially, values in D^0 can all be set the same, or to the estimated values obtained using the AM method. Note that each estimation of D^{t-1} defines $\mathcal{P}r(P_{mn} = 1)$ and $\mathcal{P}r(\mathcal{O}_{mn} = 1)$ using Equations 21.3 and 21.4. These values are, in turn, used to compute D^t in the current iteration as follows. First, for each domain pair D_{ij} and each protein pair P_{mn} the expectation that domain pair D_{ij} physically interacts in protein pair P_{mn} is estimated as

$$E(D_{ij}\text{interacts in } P_{mn}) = \begin{cases} \frac{\mathcal{P}r(D^{t-1}_{ij})(1-f_n)}{\mathcal{P}r(\mathcal{O}_{mn}=1)} & \text{if } P_{mn} \in \mathcal{I} \\ \frac{\mathcal{P}r(D^{t-1}_{ij})f_n}{\mathcal{P}r(\mathcal{O}_{mn}=0)} & \text{otherwise.} \end{cases} \tag{21.7}$$

The values of $\mathcal{P}r(D^t_{ij})$ for the next iteration are then computed as

$$\mathcal{P}r(D^t_{ij}) = \frac{1}{N_{ij}} \sum_{P_{mn} \mid D_{ij} \in P_{mn}} E(D_{ij}\text{interacts in} P_{mn}). \tag{21.8}$$

Thus, similar to the AM method, the EM method provides a scoring scheme that measures the likelihood of interaction of a given domain pair.

Since our knowledge of interacting domain pairs is limited (only a small fraction of interacting domains pairs have been inferred from crystal structures), it is not clear as to how any two methods predicting domain interactions can be compared. Deng et al. [13] compared the performance of their EM method to that of Sprinzak and Margalit's AM method [56] by assessing how well the domain–domain interaction predictions by the two methods can, in turn, be used to predict protein–protein interactions. For the AM method, $\mathcal{P}r(D_{ij})$ in Equation 21.3 is replaced by α_{ij}. Thus, rather than performing a direct comparison of predicted interacting domain pairs, they tested the method that leads to a more accurate prediction of protein–protein interactions. It was shown that the EM method outperforms the AM method significantly [13]. This result is not surprising considering the fact that the values of $\mathcal{P}r(D_{ij})$ in the EM method are computed so as to maximize the probability of observed interactions. Comparison of domain interaction prediction methods based on how well they predict protein–protein interaction is, however, not very satisfying. The correct prediction of protein interactions does not imply that the interacting domains have been correctly identified.

21.3.2.3 Domain Pair Exclusion Analysis (DPEA) An important problem in inferring domain interactions from protein interaction data using the AM and EM methods is that the highest scoring domain interactions tend to be nonspecific. The difference between specific and nonspecific interactions is illustrated in Fig. 21.10. Each of the interacting domains can have several paralogs within a given organism—several instances of the same domain. In a highly specific (nonpromiscuous) interaction, each such instance of domain D_i interacts with a unique instance of domain D_j (see Fig. 21.10a). Such specific interactions are likely to receive a low score by methods (AM and EM) that detect domain interactions by measuring the probability of interaction of corresponding domains. To deal with this issue, Riley et al. [52] introduced a new method called *domain pair exclusion analysis* (DPEA). The idea behind this method is to measure, for each domain pair, the reduction in the likelihood of the protein–protein interaction network if the interaction between this domain pair were to be disallowed. This is assessed by comparing the results of executing an expectation maximization protocol under the assumption that all pairs of domains can interact and that a given pair of domains cannot interact. The E-value is defined to be the ratio of the corresponding likelihood estimators. Figure 21.10b and c shows real-life examples with low θ scores and a high E-values.

The expectation maximization protocol used in DPEA is similar to that used in the EM method but performed under the assumption that the network is reliable (no false positives). The DPEA method has been compared to the EM and AM methods by measuring the frequency of retrieved (predicted) domain pairs that are known to interact (based on crystal structure evidence as inferred in iPFAM [16]). Riley et al. [52] showed that the DPEA method outperforms the AM and EM methods by a significant margin.

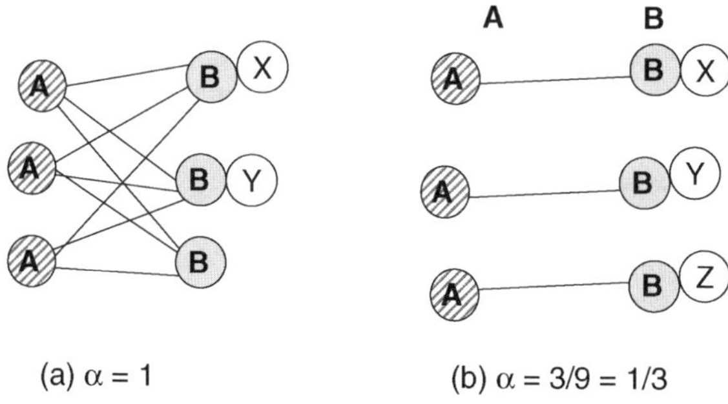

FIGURE 21.10 (**a**) Promiscuous and (**b**) specific.

21.3.2.4 Lowest p-Value Method The lowest p-value method, proposed by Nye et al. [44], is an alternate statistical approach to predict domain–domain interactions. The idea behind this approach is to test, for every domain pair $D_{ij} \in P_{mn}$, the null hypothesis $\mathcal{H}_{ij}$ that the interaction between proteins P_m and P_n is independent of the presence of domain pair D_{ij}. They also consider a global null hypothesis $\mathcal{H}_{\infty}$ that the interaction between proteins P_m and P_n is entirely unrelated to the domain architectures of proteins. There are two specific assumptions made by this method, which were not made by other network-based approaches. First, every protein interaction is assumed to be mediated by exactly one domain–domain interaction. Second, each occurrence of a domain in a protein sequence is counted separately.

To test the hypothesis $\mathcal{H}_{ij}$, for each domain pair D_{ij}, consider the following two-by-two matrix X_{ij}:

	D_{ij}	Domain Pairs Other Than D_{ij}
Interacting domain pairs	$X_{ij}(1, 1)$	$X_{ij}(1, 2)$
Noninteracting domain pairs	$X_{ij}(2, 1)$	$X_{ij}(2, 2)$

In particular, $X_{ij}(1, 1)$ denotes the number of times domain pair D_{ij} is in physical interaction, and $X_{ij}(1, 2)$ denotes the number of times domain pairs other than D_{ij} interact. The method for estimating the values of table X_{ij} is given later in this subsection. Given the matrix X_{ij}, the log-odds score s_{ij} for domain D_{ij} is defined as

$$s_{ij} = \log \frac{X_{ij}(1, 1)/X_{ij}(2, 1)}{X_{ij}(1, 2)/X_{ij}(2, 2)} \tag{21.9}$$

The score s_{ij} is then converted into a p-value measuring the probability that hypothesis $\mathcal{H}_{ij}$ is true. This is done by estimating how likely a score at least this high can be obtained by chance (under hypothesis $\mathcal{H}_{\infty}$). To compute the p-value, the domain composition within the proteins is randomized. During the randomization procedure, the degree of each node in the protein–protein interaction network remains the same. The details of the randomization procedure exceeds the scope of this chapter and for the complete description we refer the reader to [44].

Finally, we show how to estimate the values in table X_{ij}. Value $X_{ij}(1, 1)$ is computed as the expected number of times domain pair D_{ij} mediates a protein–protein interaction under the null hypothesis $\mathcal{H}_\infty$ given the experimental data $\mathcal{O}$:

$$E(D_{ij}) = \sum_{P_{mn}} \mathcal{P}r(P_{mn} = 1|\mathcal{O})\mathcal{P}r(D_{ij} = 1|P_{mn} = 1), \tag{21.10}$$

where $\mathcal{P}r(P_{mn} = 1|\mathcal{O})$ is computed from the approximations of false positive and false negative rates in a way similar to that described in the previous subsection. The computation of $\mathcal{P}r(D_{ij} = 1|P_{mn} = 1)$ takes into account multiple occurrences of the same domain in a protein chain. Namely, let N_{ij}^{mn} be the number of possible interactions between domains D_i and D_j in protein pair P_{nm}. Then

$$\mathcal{P}r(D_{ij} = 1|P_{mn} = 1) = \frac{N_{ij}^{mn}}{\sum_{D_{kt}} N_{kt}^{mn}}, \tag{21.11}$$

and the value N_{ij} is, in this case, computed as

$$N_{ij} = \sum_{P_{kt}} N_{ij}^{kt}.$$

Consequently, the values of the table are estimated as follows:

$$\begin{aligned}
X_{ij}(1, 1) &= E(D_{ij}) \\
X_{ij}(2, 1) &= N_{ij} - E(D_{ij}) \\
X_{ij}(1, 2) &= \sum_{D_{kt} \neq D_{ij}} E(D_{kt}) \\
X_{ij}(2, 2) &= \sum_{D_{kt} \neq D_{ij}} (N_{kt} - E(D_{kt})).
\end{aligned}$$

Nye et al. [44] evaluated their method using a general approach introduced by them, which is described in Section 21.3.1. Namely, they predict that within the set of domain pairs belonging to a given interacting protein pair, the domain pair with the lowest p-value is likely to form a contact. To confirm this, they used protein complexes in the PQS database [27] (a database of quaternary states for structures contained in the Brookhaven Protein Data Bank (PDB) that were determined by X-ray crystallography) restricted to protein pairs that are meaningful in this context (e.g., at least one protein must be multidomain, both proteins contain only domain present in the yeast protein–protein interaction network used in their study, etc.). It is striking from this comparison that the improvement these methods achieve over a random

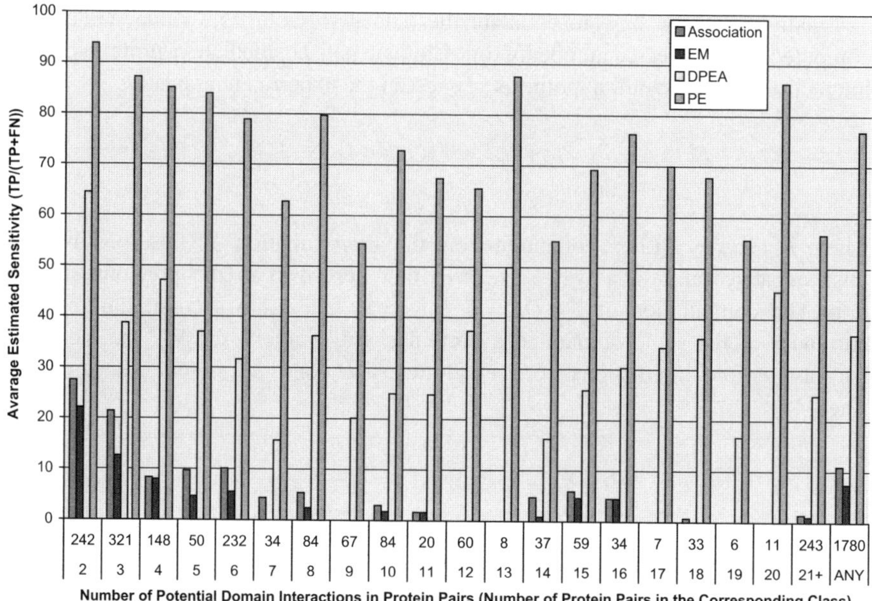

FIGURE 21.11 Domain–domain contact prediction results. The results are broken down according to the potential number of domain–domain contacts between protein pairs in the given interacting pair of proteins. Pairs of interacting proteins are selected so that each pair contains an iPFAM domain pair which is assumed to be in contant. Figure adapted from [26].

selection is small, although the improvement increases with the number of possible domain pair contacts.

21.3.2.5 Most Parsimonious Explanation (PE) Recently, Guimaraes et al. [26] introduced a new domain interaction prediction method called the most parsimonious explanation [26]. Their method relies on the hypothesis that interactions between proteins evolved in a parsimonious way and that the set of correct domain–domain interactions is well approximated by the minimal set of domain interactions necessary to justify a given protein–protein interaction network. The EM problem is formulated as a linear programming optimization problem, where each potential domain–domain contact is a variable that can receive a value ranging between 0 and 1 (called the *LP-score*), and each edge of the protein–protein interaction network corresponds to one linear constraint. That is, for each (unordered) domain pair D_{ij} that belongs to some interacting protein pair, there is a variable x_{ij}. The values of x_{ij} are computed using the linear program (LP):

$$\text{minimize} \sum_{D_{ij}} x_{ij} \tag{21.12}$$

$$\text{subject to} \sum_{D_{ij} \in P_{mn}} x_{ij} \geq 1, \text{ where } P_{mn} \in \mathcal{I}.$$

To account for the noise in the experimental data, a set of linear programs is constructed in a probabilistic fashion, where the probability of including an LP constraint in Equation 21.12 equals the probability with which the corresponding protein–protein interaction is assumed to be correct. The LP-score for a domain pair D_{ij} is then averaged over all LP programs. An additional randomization experiment is used to compute p-values and prevent overprediction of interactions between frequently occurring domain pairs. Guimaraes at al. [26] demonstrated that the PE method outperforms the EM and DPEA methods (Fig. 21.11).

GLOSSARY

Coevolution Coordinated evolution. It is generally agreed that proteins that interact with each other or have similar function undergo coordinated evolution.

Gene fusion A pair of genes in one genome is fused together into a single gene in another genome.

HMMer HMMer is a freely distributable implementation of profile HMM (hidden Markov model) software for protein sequence analysis. It uses profile HMMs to do sensitive database searching using statistical descriptions of a sequence family's consensus.

iPfam iPfam is a resource that describes domain–domain interactions that are observed in PDB crystal structures.

Ortholog Two genes from two different species are said to be orthologs if they evolved directly from a single gene in the last common ancestor.

PDB The protein data bank (PDB) is a central repository for 3D structural data of proteins and nucleic acids. The data, typically obtained by X-ray crystallography or NMR spectroscopy, are submitted by biologists and biochemists from around the world, released into the public domain, and can be accessed for free.

Pfam Pfam is a large collection of multiple sequence alignments and hidden Markov models covering many common protein domains and families.

Phylogenetic profile A phylogenetic profile for a protein is a vector of 1s and 0s representing the presence or absence of that protein in a reference set organisms.

Distance matrix A matrix containing the evolutionary distances of organisms or proteins in a family.

ACKNOWLEDGMENTS

This work was funded by the intramural research program of the National Library of Medicine, National Institutes of Health.

REFERENCES

1. HMMer. http://hmmer.wustl.edu
2. RPS-BLAST. http://www.ncbi.nlm.nih.gov/Structure/cdd/wrpsb.cgi
3. Altschuh D, Lesk AM, Bloomer AC, Klug A. Correlation of coordinated amino acid substitutions with function in viruses related to tobacco mosaic virus. *J Mol Biol* 1987;193(4):683–707.
4. Altschul SF, Gish W, Miller W, Myers EW, Lipman DJ. Basic local alignment search tool. *J Mol Biol* 1990;215(3):403–410.
5. Apic G, Gough J, Teichmann SA. Domain combinations in archaeal, eubacterial and eukaryotic proteomes. *J Mol Biol* 2001;310(2):311–325.
6. Atwell S, Ultsch M, De Vos AM, Wells JA. Structural plasticity in a remodeled protein–protein interface. *Science* 1997;278(5340):1125–1128.
7. Berger JM, Gamblin SJ, Harrison SC, Wang JC. Structure and mechanism of DNA topoisomerase II. *Nature* 1996;379(6562):225–232.
8. Berman HM, Westbrook J, Feng Z, Gilliland G, Bhat TN, Weissig H, Shindyalov IN, Bourne PE. The Protein Data Bank. *Nucl Acid Res* 2000;28(1):235–242.
9. Butland G, Peregrin-Alvarez JM, Li J, Yang W, Yang X, Canadien V, Starostine A, Richards D, Beattie B, Krogan N, Davey M, Parkinson J, Greenblatt J, Emili A. Interaction network containing conserved and essential protein complexes in escherichia coli. *Nature* 2005;433(7025):531–537.
10. Chothia C, Gough J, Vogel C, Teichmann SA. Evolution of the protein repertoire. *Science* 2003;300(5626):1701–1703.
11. Dandekar T, Snel B, Huynen M, Bork P. Conservation of gene order: a fingerprint of proteins that physically interact. *Trends Biochem Sci* 1998;23(9):324–328.
12. Date SV, Marcotte EM. Discovery of uncharacterized cellular systems by genome-wide analysis of functional linkages. *Nat Biotechnol* 2003;21(9):1055–1062.
13. Deng M, Mehta S, Sun F, Chen T. Inferring domain–domain interactions from protein–protein interactions. *Genome Res* 2002;12(10):1540–1548.
14. Edgar RC. MUSCLE: multiple sequence alignment with high accuracy and high throughput. *Nucl Acid Res* 2004;32(5):1792–1797.
15. Enright AJ, Iliopoulos I, Kyrpides NC, Ouzounis CA. Protein interaction maps for complete genomes based on gene fusion events. *Nature* 1999;402(6757):86–90.
16. Finn RD, Marshall M, Bateman A. iPfam: visualization of protein–protein interactions in PDB at domain and amino acid resolutions. *Bioinformatics* 2005;21(3): 410–412.
17. Finn RD, Mistry J, Schuster-Bockler B, Griffiths-Jones S, Hallich V, Lassmann T, Moxon S, Marshal M, Khanna A, Durbin R, Eddy SR, Sonnhammer EL, Bateman A. Pfam: clans, web tools and services. *Nucleic Acids Res* 2006,34(Database issue):D247–D251.
18. Gaasterland T, Ragan MA. Microbial genescapes: phyletic and functional patterns of ORF distribution among prokaryotes. *Microb Comp Genomics* 1998;3(4):199–217.
19. Gavin AC, Bosche M, Krause R, Grandi P, Marzioch M, Bauer A, Schultz J, Rick JM, Michon AM, Cruciat CM, Remor M, Hofert C, Schelder M, Brajenovic M, Ruffner H, Merino A, Klein K, Hudak M, Dickson D, Rudi T, Gnau V, Bauch A, Bastuck S,

Huhse B, Leutwein C, Heurtier MA, Copley RR, Edelmann A, Querfurth E, Rybin V, Drewes G, Raida M, Bouwmeester T, Bork P, Seraphin B, Kuster B, Neubauer G, Superti-Furga G. Functional organization of the yeast proteome by systematic analysis of protein complexes. *Nature* 2002;415(6868):141–147.

20. Gertz J, Elfond G, Shustrova A, Weisinger M, Pellegrini M, Cokus S, Rothschild B. Inferring protein interactions from phylogenetic distance matrices. *Bioinformatics* 2003;19(16):2039–2045.

21. Giot L, Bader JS, Brouwer C, Chaudhuri A, Kuang B, Li Y, Hao YL, Ooi CE, Godwin B, Vitals E, Vijayadamodar G, Pochart P, Machineni H, Welsch M, Kong Y, Zerhusen B, Malcalm R, Varrone Z, Callis A, Minto M, Burgess S, McDaniel L, Stimpson E, Spriggs E, Williams J, Neurath K, Ioime N, Agee M, Voss E, Furtak K, Renzulli R, Aanensen N, Carrolla S, Bickelhaupt E, Lazovatsky Y, DaSilva A, Zhong J, Stanyon CA, Knight Jr J, Shimkets RA, McKenna MP, Chant J, Rothberg JM. A protein interaction map of drosophila melanogaster. *Science* 2003;302(5651):1727–1736.

22. Glazko GV, Mushegian AR. Detection of evolutionarily stable fragments of cellular pathways by hierarchical clustering of phyletic patterns. *Genome Biol* 2004;5(5):R32.

23. Gobel U, Sander C, Schneider R, Valencia A. Correlated mutations and residue contacts in proteins. *Proteins* 1994;18(4):309–317.

24. Goh CS, Bogan AA, Joachimiak M, Walther D, Cohen FE. Co-evolution of proteins with their interaction partners. *J Mol Biol* 2000;299(2):283–293.

25. Goh CS, Cohen FE. Co-evolutionary analysis reveals insights into protein–protein interactions. *J Mol Biol* 2002;324(1):177–192.

26. Guimaraes K, Jothi R, Zotenko E, Przytycka TM. Predicting domain–domain interactions using a parsimony approach. *Genome Biol* 2006;7(11):R104.

27. Henrick K, Thornton JM. PQS: a protein quarternary structure file server. *Trends Biochem Sci* 1998;23(9):358–361.

28. Ho Y, Gruhler A, Heilbut A, Bader GD, Moore L, Adams SL, Millar A, Taylor P, Bennett K, Boutilier K, Yang L, Walting C, Donaldson I, Schandorff S, Shewnarane J, Vo M, Taggart J, Goudreault M, Muskat B, Alfarano C, Dewar D, Lin Z, Michalickova, Willims AR, Sassi H, Nielson PA, Rasmussen KJ, Andersen JR, Johansen LE, Hansen LH, Jespersen H, Podtelejnikov A, Nielsep E, Crawford J, Poulsen V, Sorensen BD, Mathhiesen J, Hendrickson RC, Gleeson F, Pawson T, Moran MF, Durocher D, Mann M, Hogue CW, Figeys D, Tyers M. Systematic identification of protein complexes in saccharomyces cerevisiae by mass spectrometry. *Nature* 2002;415(6868):180–183.

29. Ito T, Chiba T, Ozawa R, Yoshida M, Hattori M, Sakaki Y. A comprehensive two-hybrid analysis to explore the yeast protein interactome. *Proc Natl Acad Sci USA* 2001;98(8):4569–4574.

30. Jespers L, Lijnen HR, Vanwetswinkel S, Van Hoef B, Brepoels K, Collen D, De Maeyer M. Guiding a docking mode by phage display: selection of correlated mutations at the staphylokinase-plasmin interface. *J Mol Biol* 1999;290(2):471–479.

31. Jothi R, Cherukuri PF, Tasneem A, Przytycka TM. Co-evolutionary analysis of domains in interacting proteins reveals insights into domain–domain interactions mediating protein–protein interactions. *J Mol Biol* 2006;362(4):861–875.

32. Jothi R, Kann MG, Przytycka TM. Predicting protein–protein interaction by searching evolutionary tree automorphism space. *Bioinformatics* 2005;21(Suppl 1):i241–i250.

33. Jothi R, Przytycka TM, Aravind L. Discovering functional linkages and cellular pathways using phylogenetic profile comparisons: a comprehensive assessment. *BMC Bioinformatics* 2007;8:173.

34. Kann MG, Jothi R, Cherukuri PF, Przytycka TM. Predicting protein domain interactions from co-evolution of conserved regions. *Proteins* 2007;67(4)811–820.

35. Krogan NJ, Cagney G, Yu H, Zhong G, Guo X, Ignatchenko A, Li J, Pu S, Datta N, Tikuisis P, Punna T, Peregrin-Alvaraz JM, Shales M, Zhang X, Davey M, Robinson MD, Paccanaro A, Bray JE, Sheung A, Beattie B, Richards DP, Canadien V, Lalev A, Mena F, Wong P, Starostine A, Canete MM, Vlasblom J, Wu S, Orsi C, Collins SR, Chandran S, Haw R, Rilstone JJ, Gandi K, Thompson NJ, Musso G, St-Onge P, Ghanny S, Lam MH, Butland G, Altaf-Ul AM, Kanaya S, Shilatifard A, O'Shea E, Weissman JS, Ingles CJ, Hughes TR, Parkinson J, Gerstein M, Wodak SJ, Emili A, Greenblatt JF. Global landscape of protein complexes in the yeast saccharomyces cerevisiae. *Nature* 2006;440(7084):637–643.

36. Li S, Armstrong CM, Bertin N, Ge H, Milstein S, Boxem M, Vidalain PO, Han JD, Chesneau A, Hao T, Goldberg DS, Li N, Martinez M, Rual JF, Lamesch P, Xu L, Tewari M, Wong SL, Zhang LV, Berriz GF, Jacotot L, Vaglio P, Reboul J, Hirozane-Kishikawa T, Li Q, Gabel HW, Elewa A, Baumgartner B, Rose DJ, Yu H, Bosak S, Sequerra R, Fraser A, Mango SE, Saxton WM, Strome S, Van Den Heuvel S, Piano F, Vandenhaute J, Sardet C, Gerstein M, Doucette-Stamm L, Gunsalus KC, Harper JW, Cusick ME, Roth FP, Hill DE, Vidal M. A map of the interactome network of the metazoan c. elegans. *Science* 2004;303(5657):540–543.

37. Marcotte EM, Pellegrini M, Ng HL, Rice DW, Yeates TO, Eisenberg D. Detecting protein function and protein–protein interactions from genome sequences. *Science* 1999;285(5428):751–753.

38. Metropolis N, Rosenbluth AW, Teller A, Teller EJ. Simulated annealing. *J Chem Phys* 1955;21:1087–1092.

39. Mirkin BG, Fenner TI, Galperin MY, Koonin EV. Algorithms for computing parsimonious evolutionary scenarios for genome evolution, the last universal common ancestor and dominance of horizontal gene transfer in the evolution of prokaryotes. *BMC Evol Biol* 2003;3:2.

40. Moyle WR, Campbell RK, Myers RV, Bernard MP, Han Y, Wang X. Co-evolution of ligand-receptor pairs. *Nature* 1994;368(6468):251–255.

41. Neher E. How frequent are correlated changes in families of protein sequences? *Proc Natl Acad Sci USA* 1994;91(1):98–102.

42. Ng SK, Zhang Z, Tan SH. Integrative approach for computationally inferring protein domain interactions. *Bioinformatics* 2003;19(8):923–929.

43. Notredame C, Higgins DG, Heringa J. T-Coffee: A novel method for fast and accurate multiple sequence alignment. *J Mol Biol* 2000;302(1):205–217.

44. Nye TM, Berzuini C, Gilks WR, Babu MM, Teichmann SA. Statistical analysis of domains in interacting protein pairs. *Bioinformatics* 2005;21(7):993–1001.

45. Overbeek R, Fonstein M, D'Souza M, Pusch GD, Maltsev N. Use of contiguity on the chromosome to predict functional coupling. *In Silico Biol* 1999;1(2):93–108.

46. Pazos F, Helmer-Citterich M, Ausiello G, Valencia A. Correlated mutations contain information about protein–protein interaction. *J Mol Biol* 1997;271(4):511–523.

47. Pazos F, Ranea JA, Juan D, Sternberg MJ. Assessing protein co-evolution in the context of the tree of life assists in the prediction of the interactome. *J Mol Biol* 2005;352(4): 1002–1015.

48. Pazos F, Valencia A. Similarity of phylogenetic trees as indicator of protein–protein interaction. *Protein Eng* 2001;14(9):609–614.

49. Pazos F, Valencia A. In silico two-hybrid system for the selection of physically interacting protein pairs. *Proteins* 2002;47(2):219–227.

50. Pellegrini M, Marcotte EM, Thompson MJ, Eisenberg D, Yeates TO. Assigning protein functions by comparative genome analysis: protein phylogenetic profiles. *Proc Natl Acad Sci USA* 1999;96(8):4285–4288.

51. Ramani AK, Marcotte EM. Exploiting the co-evolution of interacting proteins to discover interaction specificity. *J Mol Biol* 2003;327(1):273–284.

52. Riley R, Lee C, Sabatti C, Eisenberg D. Inferring protein domain interactions from databases of interacting proteins. *Genome Biol* 2005;6(10):R89.

53. Saitou N, Nei M. The neighbor-joining method: a new method for reconstructing phylogenetic trees. *Mol Biol Evol* 1987;4(4):406–425.

54. Sato T, Yamanishi Y, Kanehisa M, Toh H. The inference of protein–protein interactions by co-evolutionary analysis is improved by excluding the information about the phylogenetic relationships. *Bioinformatics* 2005;21(17):3482–3489.

55. Shindyalov IN, Kolchanov NA, Sander C. Can three-dimensional contacts in protein structures be predicted by analysis of correlated mutations? *Protein Eng* 1994;7(3): 349–358.

56. Sprinzak E, Margalit H. Correlated sequence-signatures as markers of protein–protein interaction. *J Mol Biol* 2001;311(4):681–692.

57. Thompson JD, Higgins DG, Gibson TJ. CLUSTAL W: improving the sensitivity of progressive multiple sequence alignment through sequence weighting, position-specific gap penalties and weight matrix choice. *Nucl Acid Res* 1994;22(22):4673–4680.

58. Uetz P, Giot L, Cagney G, Mansfield TA, Judson RS, Knight JR, Lockshon D, Narayan V, Srinivasan M, Pochart P, Qureshi-Emili A, Li Y, Godwin B, Conover D, Kalbfleisch T, Vijayadamodar G, Yang M, Johnston M, Fields S, Rothberg JM. A comprehensive analysis of protein–protein interactions in saccharomyces cerevisiae. *Nature* 2000;403(6770):623–627.

59. Valencia A, Pazos F. Computational methods for the prediction of protein interactions. *Curr Opin Struct Biol* 2002;12(3):368–373.

INDEX

Bioinformatics Algorithms: Techniques and Applications, Edited by Ion I. Măndoiu and Alexander Zelikovsky